Regulating Railroad Innovation

Efforts to create and mold new technologies have been a central, recurrent feature of the American experience since at least the time of the Revolution. Many of the most tumultuous events in the nation's history have, at their core, involved disputes over the appropriateness and desirability of particular technologies. In *Regulating Railroad Innovation*, historian Steven Usselman brings this neglected aspect of American history to light. For nearly a century, railroad technology persistently posed novel challenges for Americans, prompting them to reexamine their most cherished institutions and beliefs. Business managers, inventors, consumers, and politicians all strained to contain the forces of innovation and to channel technical change toward the ends they desired. Usselman traces their myriad struggles in rich detail. Moving through time from the first experimental lines through the polished but troubled railroad machines of the early twentieth century, he examines diverse forums ranging from legislatures, courts, and evolving corporate bureaucracies to laboratories, engineering societies, and world's fairs. In the process, he develops a novel synthesis, one that at once situates technology within the dynamic history of an emergent industrial nation and elucidates its enduring place in American society.

Steven W. Usselman is Associate Professor of History in the School of History, Technology, and Society at the Georgia Institute of Technology. His study "IBM and Its Imitators" received the Newcomen Award for Excellence in Business History from the Business History Conference.

Regulating Railroad Innovation

Business, Technology, and Politics in America, 1840–1920

STEVEN W. USSELMAN
Georgia Institute of Technology

CAMBRIDGE
UNIVERSITY PRESS

PUBLISHED BY THE PRESS SYNDICATE OF THE UNIVERSITY OF CAMBRIDGE
The Pitt Building, Trumpington Street, Cambridge, United Kingdom

CAMBRIDGE UNIVERSITY PRESS
The Edinburgh Building, Cambridge CB2 2RU, UK
40 West 20th Street, New York, NY 10011-4211, USA
477 Williamstown Road, Port Melbourne, VIC 3207, Australia
Ruiz de Alarcón 13, 28014 Madrid, Spain
Dock House, The Waterfront, Cape Town 8001, South Africa

http://www.cambridge.org

First published 2002

Printed in the United States of America

Typeface Sabon 10/12 pt.   *System* LATEX 2$_\varepsilon$ [TB]

A catalog record for this book is available from the British Library.

Library of Congress Cataloging in Publication Data
Usselman, Steven W.
Regulating railroad innovation : business, technology, and politics in America,
1840–1920 / Steven W. Usselman.
p. cm.
Includes bibliographical references and index.
ISBN 0-521-80636-4 – ISBN 0-521-00106-4 (pb.)
1. Railroads – United States – History.   2. Railroads – Technological
innovations.   I. Title.
TF23 .U58   2002
385′.0973′09034–dc21   2001043216

ISBN 0 521 80636 4 hardback
ISBN 0 521 00106 4 paperback

To Marion,
who sustains me,
and in memory of Lillian Walters Usselman,
who got me started

Contents

Illustrations

Preface and Acknowledgments

Some two decades ago, when I was first tilling the soil that would ultimately yield this book, a group of graduate students at the University of Delaware met to welcome a new member of the faculty. In the fashion of academia, each of us by way of introduction offered a brief synopsis of our research. When my turn came, I eagerly discussed my imminent departure for Chicago and the Newberry Library. There, in the archives of the Chicago, Burlington and Quincy Railroad, I hoped to discover precisely how late-nineteenth-century executives had "managed" technological change. "Oh," replied the bemused new arrival with devilish feigned innocence, "*did* they manage it?" As heart plunged toward rapidly tightening gut and mind sifted feverishly for a suitable response, I sensed for the first time the slippery indeterminancy of my subject. "Well," I shrugged at last, "they certainly tried."

This brief exchange has haunted me ever since. It did not, in fact, prove difficult to confirm that railroad executives sought in a variety of ways to make technological innovation more predictable and routine. My doctoral dissertation readily documented many of their efforts. It described how executives at the Burlington and several other lines developed managerial structures that helped them evaluate new technology and monitor its diffusion. It traced the increasing prominence of college-trained engineers and of engineering societies in the technical affairs of the industry. It evaluated the changing relationships between railroads and their suppliers, as suggested by the diminishing role for inventors of patented devices and the growing emphasis on negotiated specifications. Together, these measures marked a pioneering effort to reshape the process of technical change, one which anticipated similar attempts by managers in other industries during the twentieth century. Documenting that effort, which I have come to think of as "the engineering epoch" of American railroading, remains a primary goal of this study.

Yet as my gentle cross-examiner sensed, considerable doubt necessarily persisted about precisely how those efforts influenced the pace or character of railroad innovation. In attempting to contain innovation within a regular, predictable routine, railroad executives were in a sense trying to manage the unmanageable. Pressures to innovate came relentlessly, often from unexpected quarters. Railroad management could not possibly anticipate every demand or stem the flow of novel technologies opening new possibilities. Whatever success railroads enjoyed in keeping such disruptive forces in check during the late nineteenth century, moreover, took on a much different cast when considered in light of the subsequent difficulties railroading encountered in the early twentieth century and beyond. All of this suggested that the efforts to manage railroad technology needed to be set in a much broader context. They should be situated within a longer temporal framework, so that we might appreciate why techniques for managing technology flourished at particular times and not at others. And they should be linked more explicitly to broad forces in politics and economics that operated on the railroad industry across that longer span of time.

As I set about trying to comprehend the ties between technology, economics, and politics in a leading industry across nearly a century of American history, scholars from a variety of disciplines generated an impressive body of studies aimed at deciphering the mysteries of technical change. Much of this work emphasized the ways in which technologies are "socially constructed" by networks of actors, interests, and institutions. Such ideas resonated to considerable degree with my own focus on efforts to manage innovation. Like my early studies, however, this work frequently stopped short of connecting those people immediately involved with the technologies to a larger social and economic context. Too often, studies of social construction probed deeply into the inner workings of bureaucracies but shied away from the messy realms of popular politics and the marketplace. For this reason, I found myself drawn increasingly toward interpretative concepts advanced in recent years by political historians and economists. The former have greatly enriched our understanding of the complex interplay among political ideals, political parties, administrative structures, and government policy. The latter have examined the utility of market-based theories for explaining technical change, identifying their limitations and introducing important modifying concepts such as path dependency, technological trajectories, and asymmetrical information flows. I have tried in these pages to wear such theory lightly, taking care at every turn to ground my narrative firmly in the course of historical events. Still, this book can in some respects be read as an attempt to integrate insights from these various disciplines in order to develop a comprehensive set of tools for understanding the framework in which technical change occurs in the American context.

Yet in the end it is that context itself, not some set of case studies or abstractions regarding the elusive subject of technical change, that has ultimately come most to concern me. Somewhere in the course of my endeavors, this project evolved from a study aimed at documenting the dynamics of technology into a more general inquiry intended to shed light on fundamental elements of American history and culture. As I set about trying to situate my actors and events within a larger context, I came to appreciate how efforts to manage or regulate significant technical innovations such as railroading are not peripheral matters involving a few specialists or experts. Rather, such efforts are an absolutely central element of the American experience. Perhaps never has this been more obvious than in our own times, as the phenomenal pace of change in electronic communications and computing garners so much attention and occupies such a large share of our energies in seemingly every realm. But it was true as well two centuries ago, when citizens of the new nation first attempted to reconcile dynamic changes in technology with their revolutionary political inheritance, and it has remained true ever since. In examining how several generations of Americans attempted to come to grips with one transforming technical innovation, I have thus come to learn not merely about technology but about Americans and the institutions and values that bind them.

No writer can trace such an odyssey without ringing up enormous debts along the way. Among the many professional colleagues who have aided and inspired me over the years, one stands out above all others. David Hounshell, now of Carnegie Mellon University, arrived at the University of Delaware as a young assistant professor the same year I began my graduate studies. From those first encounters onward, he has remained the most loyal, patient, and supportive of mentors. I am proud to count myself among his pupils and grateful for his friendship. Our years at Delaware were enlivened by what I have come to appreciate was a very special community of faculty and students. Among faculty, I benefited especially from the teaching and counsel of Glenn Porter, who to my good fortune has remained steadfast in his support ever since. Eugene Ferguson, George Basalla, Richard Bushman, and the late Reed Geiger were also outstanding teachers who opened new worlds to me in their own distinctive fashions. Each profoundly shaped my thinking in ways that continue to inform my scholarship and teaching. My fellow students included such old hands as Stuart Leslie and Bruce Seely, as well as my contemporaries Bill Sisson, Mark Wilde, Kim Carrell, and my dear friend John Kenly Smith. The mix of fun, friendship, and intellectual passion we shared will always serve as my ideal of graduate study at its best.

On either side of my experience at Delaware, I had the good fortune to come under the influence of an individual whose ideas and support inspired me to tackle problems I otherwise would not have. The first was Harry Scheiber, my undergraduate honors advisor, who drew me away from a career in engineering and gave me the confidence to pursue my interests in history and the railroads. The issues addressed in this book are the direct legacy of ideas raised in his classes in American economic and legal history some quarter-century ago. The other was Jim Livingston, now of

Rutgers University. During two marvelous years we overlapped as colleagues at UNC–Charlotte, Jim opened a challenging yet constructive dialogue that to this day stimulates and informs my thinking about business history and political economy. My decade at Charlotte was further enlivened and enriched by colleagues and friends Julia Blackwelder, John Diemer, Dan Dupre, David Goldfield, and Carole Haber. Each patiently guided me through unfamiliar terrain, historical and professional. Through years of treasured conversation, my Latin Americanist colleague Lyman Johnson taught me as much about the United States (among other subjects) as anyone ever has. John Smail, with whom I have spent many fruitful times discussing the business of innovation, remains for me a model of how to live an academic life. An unusually fine group of graduate students, including Craig Brashear, Jon De Klerk, Jennifer Galan, Fred Gates, Shep McKinley, and Craig Pascoe, helped me work through many ideas pertaining to American political economy. The UNC–Charlotte Foundation provided financial assistance for several summers of research.

At Georgia Tech's School of History, Technology, and Society, I have had the good fortune to join a community of colleagues and students who make studying the history of technology a rich and pleasurable experience. I appreciate the opportunity to discuss issues pertaining to the contents and production of this book with Mike Allen, Gus Giebelhaus, Ken Knoespel, Daniel Kleinman, Bob McMath, Greg Nobles, Helen Rozwadowski, Phil Scranton, Bruce Sinclair, Andrea Tone, and Steve Vallas. At an especially critical juncture, Doug Flamming gave the manuscript the sort of careful, sympathetic reading every author craves. I am forever grateful to him for that kindness and for his gracious, sustaining fellowship during the final stages of the birthing process.

So many professional colleagues at other institutions have taken time to comment on portions of this manuscript over the years I cannot possibly recall them all. At minimum, the list includes Jeremy Atack, Jack Brown, Alfred Chandler, Sally Clarke, Carolyn Cooper, Colin Divall, Colleen Dunlavy, Will Hausman, Thomas Hughes, Richard John, Walter Licht, Ken Lipartito, Steve Lubar, John Majewski, Tom Misa, Bob Post, Joe Pratt, Steven Salsbury, Ken Sokoloff, Jane Summerton, Richard Tedlow, Peter Temin, John Wilson, Gavin Wright, Mary Yeager, and especially Naomi Lamoreaux, who read the entire manuscript and has done so much to open the world of economic history to me. These colleagues had something to read only because many librarians took care to identify critical resources and to make them available to me. I would in particular like to thank the staffs of the Maryland Historical Society, the Newberry Library, the Hagley Museum and Library, and the prints and photographs department of the Library of Congress. Michael Nash and Christopher Baer at the Hagley have assisted me in so many ways that I cannot imagine this book existing in anything like its current form without them. Financial assistance from the Hagley and the

Newberry enabled me to make much greater use of their collections than I otherwise could have.

Some of the material these dedicated professionals helped me unearth has appeared previously in various other guises. I thank Westview Press, the National Bureau of Economic Research, the University of Chicago Press, and the editors and publishers of *Business and Economic History*, *Business History Review*, *Technology and Culture*, and the *Journal of Industrial History* for permission to make use of this material here.

Authors, especially slow ones, place extraordinary burdens on their families. Three treasured members of mine – Karen, Laura, and Nathan – have spent their entire lives sharing their father's time and attention with this most demanding of rival siblings. Not only have they shown exemplary tolerance; their hopeful encouragement and abiding optimism have sustained and inspired me as only the wonder of youth can. My sisters Leann Drummond and Louise Maier and their families carried me through the long, trying ordeal of our mother's death, graciously indulging their kid brother his frequent withdrawals into work. I appreciate also the continuing interest and support of my father, Leo Usselman. In what must be some sort of authorial record, four households of in-laws quite literally lived with this project for extended periods. I thank Anne and John, Phil and Pam, Myron and Marilou, and Phil and Dot for their generous hospitality and all members of the extended Curtis clan for showing such concern for me and my work. Anne deserves special mention for her unique matchmaking talents, which somehow helped secure me both her dissertation advisor as an undergraduate thesis supervisor and her sister as a spouse. For the latter, no words can capture my depths of gratitude. Marion is the rock of my life, an unwavering source of reason, encouragement, and love. She has stayed with this project from beginning to end, ever the ideal companion, in this as in all life's adventures.

Introduction

innovation (*n*): 1. the introduction of something new; 2. a new idea, method, or device: NOVELTY.

regulate (*vt*): 1. to govern or direct according to rule; 2. to bring order, method, or uniformity to; 3. to fix or adjust the time, amount, degree, or rate of.

– Webster's New Collegiate Dictionary

The subject of this book is, quite literally, a contradiction in terms. Genuine novelty knows no rules. We cannot reduce to routine what we do not yet know. Yet of course we cannot resist trying. For like death and taxes, technical innovation has proven to be an irresistible force in modern affairs. Its pervasive influence, its startling ability to transform lives and upset social norms, ineluctably draws our attention. For most of humanity, the encounter comes as a pragmatic response to concrete realities. For those historians, economists, and others who enjoy the luxury of observing technical change from a distance, the desire to tame innovation assumes a more abstract guise. Like theologians pondering the afterlife, they seek to decipher its mysteries, to identify patterns and governing principles, and thus to impose a measure of order and regularity upon this most beguiling of phenomena.

This book contributes to that effort by evaluating the prolonged attempt by Americans of a century ago to seize control over the most profound technological innovation of their lives: the railroad. The marriage of steam power and iron rail, conceived in Europe during the first quarter of the nineteenth century and mimicked across the Atlantic soon after, presented Americans with challenges and opportunities as profound as those posed by any new technology in their history. Capable of reshaping the contours of nature and dramatically compressing time and space, the railroad possessed enormous

I

potential to restructure social and economic affairs.[1] Nowhere was this so true as in the United States, with its abundance of land and expansive frontier. In this environment, railroads would not merely alter established patterns of trade and travel and draw people into larger orbits of commerce and culture; they would also give shape to an expanding nation whose course of development remained a matter of intense controversy. This prospect, at once exhilarating and unsettling, was all the more challenging because the new technology taxed the technical and economic capabilities of the young nation like virtually no other. If Americans wished to seize the potential inherent in the railroad innovation, they would have to acquire a broad array of new skills, and they would need to devise new methods of marshaling the economic resources necessary to support the railroad enterprise.

This initial encounter with the basic railroad innovation was no one-time event. In the rapidly expanding and politically decentralized United States, it occurred afresh in different locales under various political jurisdictions across the span of several decades during the mid-nineteenth century. Like a series of explosive charges detonating across the landscape, railroads spurted to life in fits and starts, each jolt shaking the immediate surroundings to their foundations while also sending tremors back through the established network to those places that had previously felt the transforming power of the railroad innovation. Only with the tumult of the Civil War would the rail network emerge on a continental scale and begin to assume the orderly form that Charles E. Perkins, president of the giant Chicago, Burlington and Quincy, aptly likened to a complex machine.[2]

Even after that network took shape, moreover, railroads remained in constant flux. Each component in the railroad ensemble – locomotives, cars, rails, and elements of the physical infrastructure such as bridges and stations – underwent virtually perpetual refinement. Much of this innovative effort, we see below, went toward bulking up the basic system. Cars, locomotives, and rails all increased dramatically in heft. Despite basic constraints on height and width imposed by initial choices of gauge and overpass clearances, the typical freight boxcar grew in capacity from around 30,000 pounds at mid-century to 100,000 by century's end. Rails grew proportionally, as did motive power. This rapid scaling up was no simple matter. Increasing the size of locomotives and rolling stock raised an array of complex

---

[1] For perceptive treatments of the transforming power of railroads, see Wolfgang Schivelbusch, *The Railway Journey: The Industrialization of Time and Space in the 19th Century* (Berkeley: University of California Press, 1986), and Daniel J. Boorstin, *The Americans: The National Experience* (New York: Random House, 1965) and *The Americans: The Democratic Experience* (New York: Random House, 1973). For a succinct statement regarding their economic significance, see Stanley Lebergott, *The Americans: An Economic Record* (New York: Norton, 1984), pp. 107–112.

[2] C. E. Perkins, "Organization of Railroads," ca. 1885, Papers of the Chicago, Burlington, and Quincy Railroad, Newberry Library, Chicago (hereafter, CBQ Papers), 3P6.36.

technical problems involving matters such as suspension, braking, and heat transfer. Mechanics continually redesigned parts or devised entirely new ones, often making use of new materials such as steel, alloys, and chemical lubricants. Even changing the size of the rail, seemingly the simplest of technologies, proved far from straightforward. For in altering the shape of the rail, railroads sparked a succession of changes in areas such as wheel design and track maintenance procedures. Perhaps more important, they disrupted established procedures among rail manufacturers. Scaling up the basic components of railroading thus involved a broad-based effort among numerous parties whose efforts needed to be integrated and coordinated in novel ways.

Besides steadily pursuing changes in scale, railroads also responded to pressures from various quarters encouraging them to alter the character of their services. Passengers sought to travel at faster speeds in luxurious cars outfitted with the latest amenities and equipped with novel devices promising to protect them from the dangers of transit. Though railroads often balked at introducing such complex novelties into their operations, enterprising innovators such as George Pullman and George Westinghouse forced their hands. Buttressed by strong patent protection and ultimately by legislation pertaining to railroad safety, these men compelled railroads to adopt popular technical novelties derived from unfamiliar technologies. Shippers of commodities such as livestock, dressed meat, fresh fruit, and a growing variety of expensive manufactured goods likewise demanded special services such as fast stock trains, refrigerated transit, and express delivery. Here, too, railroads often resisted. But over time, railroad services grew steadily more diverse and the array of railroad technologies more plentiful.

In addition to pressures generated by shifts in demand for railroad services, impetus for technical innovation came from changes in the supply of key factor inputs into the railroad industry. Born in a world of abundant land and wood and scarce capital, railroading matured in a far different environment. Once the first lines took shape and attracted commercial development, civil engineers and operating personnel faced continual challenges in trying to squeeze more traffic through increasingly congested locales. They accomplished a great deal by altering operating procedures. But in at least some cases, railroads resorted to using novel technologies such as automatic electric signals or electric traction. In choosing such radical alternatives, railroad executives confronted perhaps the most critically important factor input of all: their employees. Mobilized through strikes, unions, and an increasingly effective political movement, and aided by a labor market that rewarded the sorts of skilled personnel who worked in railroading, these employees exerted a steadily stronger influence that swayed thinking about new technology in complex ways.

At no point in its history, then, did American railroading reach some steady state in which pressures to innovate abated and technology stagnated. Though certainly constrained as they went along by previous choices and commitments, railroads innovated continually. Change was always the order of the day. And though other technologies such as electric light and power and the telephone came along and captured the limelight, railroading remained on the frontiers of technical change well through the turn into the twentieth century. For even after the sheen of novelty faded and railroads acquired the patina of age, the task of sustaining technical innovation posed fresh challenges not previously encountered by any other industry. As railroading matured, it gave rise to a stream of novel techniques and methods of analysis aimed at managing technology and innovation in an orderly fashion. These efforts to render technical change more predictable and routine – in effect, to regulate innovation – themselves constituted one of the most significant technological developments of their day.

The dual challenge of regulating the basic railroad innovation while also regulating subsequent innovation in railroading was no mere matter of a few businessmen responding in logical fashion to a changing set of factor endowments. No simple calculus governed the choices of technologies and dictated their form; no inner logic inexorably gave shape to the system. Rather, railroading emerged and evolved under intensely combative circumstances through processes whose outcomes were highly contingent.[3] Commanding a vast share of the nation's resources and operating at the vanguard of change for nearly a century, railroading and railroad technology persistently posed novel challenges of such profound importance and apparently far-reaching implications they transcended the concerns of owners, operators, and customers. Time and again, these matters spilled into the domain of politics and government, ultimately engaging Congresses, courts, Presidents, public administrators, and the electorate at large. Decisions regarding railroad technology consequently occurred within a complex framework of public and private institutions encompassing a broad array of Americans in many capacities, and the course of technical change in railroading at once reflected and influenced issues residing at the very core of American politics and political ideology.

Far from taking us to a complacent and unchanging domain, railroading thus actually opens a uniquely revealing window into the dynamics not just

---

[3] For an interpretation of railroad history emphasizing the single-minded pursuit of efficient throughput, see the pioneering studies of Alfred D. Chandler, Jr., especially his *The Visible Hand: The Managerial Revolution in American Business* (Cambridge, Mass.: Belknap Press, 1977), pp. 81–205. While Professor Chandler's work brought a welcome corrective to portrayals depicting railroading strictly as a product of political and economic manipulation by powerful individuals, his treatment overlooks important elements of choice and contingency that shaped the course of railroading and railroad technology. For an explicit critique of Chandler, see Gerald Berk, *Alternative Tracks: The Constitution of American Industrial Order, 1865–1917* (Baltimore: Johns Hopkins University Press, 1994). Though I am not fully persuaded about the viability of the particular alternative Berk posits, I share his sense that railroading might have assumed a different form than it did.

of technical change but of American history. For while perhaps no technology of the nineteenth century generated more controversy than railroading, the complex interplay among business, technology, and politics that shaped railroad innovation was by no means confined to that industry. Efforts to create and to mold new technologies have been a central, recurrent feature of the American experience since at least the time of the Revolution, when individuals such as Thomas Jefferson grappled with the implications of steam engines and patent systems for the infant republic.[4] Many of the most tumultuous events in the nation's history have, at their core, involved disputes over the appropriateness and desirability of particular technologies. No significant transforming technology, including those of more recent times, has emerged untouched by such controversies. In unpacking and examining the choices made regarding railroad technology, this book seeks above all to bring this underappreciated dimension of American life to light and to develop some insight into the distinctive ways in which Americans have confronted the persistent challenges posed by new technology. For what, besides the past, do we have to guide us as we attempt to manage the unmanageable, to regulate the new?

How, then, did Americans go about trying to regulate railroad innovation? One thing seems apparent from the start. Unlike their counterparts in many other nations, Americans generally left responsibility for the immediate choices regarding technology in the hands of private individuals who had a direct personal stake in the matter. Though some informed parties embraced the idea of establishing a government board for railroad technology or even nationalizing the industry entirely, such proposals ultimately failed to take hold. Except for a brief experiment with legislation mandating the use of certain safety appliances, the specifics of railroad technology remained the province of individuals operating in the private sphere. At no point, however, did those individuals function entirely outside the influence of politics and public policy. Far from it. At virtually every turn, those directly responsible for railroad technology felt pressure from forces in the public arena. Rather than intervening directly in decisions pertaining to technology, those forces typically worked more circumspectly, serving instead to alter the incentives operating upon those immediately involved with railroad technology. In

---

4 Hugo A. Meier, "Technology and Democracy," *Mississippi Valley Historical Review* 43 (1957): 618–640; Leo Marx, *The Machine in the Garden: Technology and the Pastoral Ideal in America* (New York: Oxford University Press, 1964); John F. Kasson, *Civilizing the Machine: Technology and Republican Values in America* (New York: Grossman, 1976), pp. 1–51; Merritt Roe Smith, *Harpers Ferry Armory and the New Technology: The Challenge of Change* (Ithaca: Cornell University Press, 1977), pp. 24–32; Eugene S. Ferguson, *Oliver Evans: Inventive Genius of the American Industrial Revolution* (Greenville, Del.: Hagley Museum, 1980); and John R. Nelson, Jr., *Liberty and Property: Political Economy and Policymaking in the New Nation, 1789–1812* (Baltimore: Johns Hopkins University Press, 1987).

some cases, as when the federal government embarked on controversial ventures to open Western lands rapidly for railroad construction or to set the rates railroads could charge for their services, this entailed actively shaping demand for railroad services in ways that ultimately influenced the course of technical change. In many others, as when Congress and the courts addressed the role of patents in railroading or shifted the liabilities for accidents from employees to the lines themselves, it involved manipulating the structures through which the incentives to innovate flowed.

These attempts to adjust the incentives to innovate, in large part by altering the structures through which those incentives operated, constitute the primary means through which Americans sought to regulate railroad innovation. Time and again in the history of American railroading, business managers and government officials alike attempted to gain a measure of control over the course of technical change in these ways. On many occasions this process involved negotiation or even open conflict between railroads and government. But the efforts to restructure incentives also occurred among railroads themselves, without direct involvement from government. At individual lines and through various interfirm arrangements such as engineering societies, trade associations, and inside agreements with suppliers and contractors, railroad management intervened to restructure the pathways of technical change. Frequently, government became involved only when these measures initiated by railroads sparked protests from some segment of the populace or appeared to conflict with established laws or ideals.

Regardless of who took the lead, the ongoing attempts to alter incentive structures worked to channel technical change toward certain areas and away from others at different moments in time. Often this channeling occurred as managers weighed the merits of known alternatives, as when they persisted in using hand brakes and manual semaphores rather than adopting automatic air brakes and electric signals. But more was involved than railroads acting as informed consumers, methodically selecting their preferences from an array of existing technical choices. The channeling of innovation also operated upon the realm of possibilities. Railroads chose at various moments in their history to pursue certain opportunities while neglecting or bypassing others. Lines attacked some problems vigorously while sidestepping or overlooking other matters that might justifiably have garnered their attention. In the process, railroads inevitably drew the creative efforts of their employees and of the broader technical community toward a few areas while diverting them away from other possible paths of technical change. In effect, railroads created pipelines of innovation, whose very effectiveness in focusing inventive efforts upon certain tasks served to impede or even to foreclose alternative developments of potentially far-reaching impact.[5] The frequent

---

[5] These ideas about the channeling of innovative activity along particular pathways or through certain pipelines draw upon the pioneering studies of Nathan Rosenberg.

public controversies regarding railroads often at root involved disputes over the suitability of these pipelines and the desirability of the innovations they would likely foster.

Efforts to channel technical change and reshape railroad innovation, while influenced always by various economic incentives, seldom boiled down simply to making rational choices grounded strictly in hard economic data. By its very nature, innovation involves uncertainty. Neither railroads nor their critics and overseers could escape that fundamental truth. Try as they might, they could not anticipate every eventuality and comprehend in advance the full effects of their choices regarding technologies. No one could say with absolute certainty that the selection of one technology over another or the decision to pursue some lines of innovation while neglecting others led to optimal or even preferred outcomes. This was especially true in railroading because the various components of the technical ensemble interacted to form an immensely complex system, one that included not only many coupled artifacts, but also numerous routines and bodies of acquired expertise. Changes in one area could easily wreak havoc in unanticipated places.[6]

In choosing to emphasize certain lines of innovation, railroads in effect sought out those paths that appeared least likely to cause disruptions. To some degree, of course, this search involved assessing anticipated costs and benefits and reading economic signals sent by the market. But the process also hinged upon key judgments exercised in the form of simplifying assumptions about how best to manage the system. Those axioms, essential for conducting business in a complex environment, on occasion ultimately acquired something approaching the authority of truth. For the very act of setting clear priorities and establishing broadly understood ground rules, whatever their merits, fostered a measure of consensus and bred a familiarity that enhanced the chances of implementing certain types of change without significant disruption. In this sense, the channeling of innovation was to a degree both arbitrary and self-reinforcing. Those approaches deemed best in advance generated the best results in practice, thus legitimizing the reasoning that privileged them in the first place.[7]

See especially his "The Direction of Technological Change: Inducement Mechanisms and Focusing Devices," in his *Perspectives on Technology* (Cambridge: Cambridge University Press, 1976), pp. 108–125.

[6] On technical innovation in system-based industries, see Thomas P. Hughes, *Networks of Power: Electrification in Western Society* (Baltimore: Johns Hopkins University Press, 1983) and "The Evolution of Large Technological Systems," in Wiebe E. Bijker, Thomas P. Hughes, and Trevor J. Pinch, eds., *The Social Construction of Technological Systems: New Directions in the Sociology and History of Technology* (Cambridge, Mass.: MIT Press, 1987), pp. 51–82.

[7] This phenomenon bears a strong resemblance to notions such as technological paradigms and trajectories. See Giovanni Dosi, "Technological Paradigms and Technological Trajectories," *Research Policy* 11 (1982): 147–162, and Edward W. Constant II, *The Origins of the Turbojet Revolution* (Baltimore: Johns Hopkins

In addition to remaining cognizant of these underlying assumptions and judgments, those wishing to comprehend technical change in railroading must also account for the deep emotions felt by many Americans who encountered the railroad and its many technical accouterments. Railroads had the power, as Lewis Mumford noted of electric light and many other technical novelties of the day, to "stir the minds and spark the senses."[8] Long after they had become common features on the American scene, railroads remained technological marvels. Trains equipped with an array of technical novelties moved across the landscape at startling speeds, along routes shaped by stunning feats of civil engineering, governed in orderly fashion by sophisticated methods and, in some cases, automatic devices that appeared to promise fail-safe protection. Such technical virtuosity was alluring. It could dazzle even the staunchest of critics, and for many Americans, it held out the promise of seemingly endless possibilities. Even the act of subjecting the complex railroad system to engineering study and rendering innovation more routine could generate enormous enthusiasm among the public. At the 1904 World's Fair in St. Louis, visitors flocked to see a team of engineering professionals operate a plant built by the Pennsylvania Railroad for testing locomotives.

This ability to evoke such intense emotion, together with the obvious significance railroads held for social and economic relations and the uncertainties inherent to innovation, insured that the disputes through which railroading took shape went well beyond the matter of how best to provide efficient transport. Railroad technology, like so many other innovations, emerged and evolved amidst great hype, in a climate where hope and imagination could matter more than cold economic calculus. This was obviously true at the start, when promoters competed avidly to attract investors and political favors in support of their proposed lines. But even long after this initial frenzy of oft-fanciful enthusiasm had subsided, Americans still saw enormous potential and possibilities in railroads and railroad technology. Though sometimes troubled by changes railroads had wrought, they looked optimistically toward further triumphs of inventiveness and engineering in railroading. The recurrent concern with restructuring the incentives to innovate betrayed this persistent feature of the public psyche. New marvels, Americans seemed convinced, were always just around the corner. They need only find ways to unleash them.

University Press, 1980). It might also be seen as a variant of path dependency. See Paul David, "Clio and the Economics of QWERTY," *American Economic Review* 75 (1985): 332–336; W. B. Arthur, "Competing Technologies, Increasing Returns, and Lock-In by Historical Events," *Economic Journal* 99 (1989): 116–131; and Michael L. Katz and Carl Shapiro, "Systems Competition and Network Effects," *Journal of Economic Perspectives* 8 (1994): 93–115.

[8] Lewis Mumford, *The Brown Decades: A Study of the Arts in America, 1865–1895* (New York: Harcourt, Brace, 1931), p. 35.

The maturing railroad industry of the late nineteenth century put this persistent optimism to the test. As the system took hold and railroads grew seemingly ever more effective at channeling innovation down particular paths, Americans grappled with a dilemma they would encounter time and again as they embraced the transforming technologies of the twentieth century. How, they wondered, might they encourage pursuit of cost-reducing refinement and routine without stifling the flow of technical novelties? How could they reap the benefits of order and system while leaving the door open for continued inventiveness that might take them to new possibilities? How, in regulating the railroad innovation, might they keep from regulating innovation out of railroading?

In tracing the experiences through which Americans arrived at this essential tension between efficiency and innovation, this book follows the lead of Charles Perkins, the railroad president who in a lengthy memorandum written to his corporate staff sometime around 1880 likened the sprawling railroad they supervised to a complex machine.[9] In running this machine, Perkins noted, he and other managers turned increasingly toward an array of technical experts trained in the "exact sciences" of engineering. Able to identify opportunities for increased economy and efficiency that would yield significant savings when applied throughout the entire system, this engineering force conducted a sustained effort at refinement. The seasoned executive contrasted this advanced stage of railroad development with the more chaotic conditions prevailing during his managerial apprenticeship, when he supervised construction of the Burlington's lines across the sparsely settled territory of Nebraska. Under those circumstances the railroad operated with considerably less exactitude. Managers paid more attention to tasks such as recruiting customers and acquiring the basic equipment, rather than to making sure trains ran at peak efficiency or rails provided longer service for less cost.

Part I of this book examines railroading during its long adolescence, before the machine paradigm took hold. This extended stage of development began during the 1820s and 1830s, when the pioneering synthesis of a self-propelled engine linked to a train of carriages mounted on a fixed track of low resistance first appeared. This stage persisted for nearly five decades, as Americans repeatedly sought to exploit the spectacular potential inherent in the marriage of railroad technology and virgin land. As entrepreneurs embarked on a set of modest concurrent experiments organized at the state or local level, debate swirled through American politics over how government might encourage such activities and direct them toward serving particular purposes. Some parties desired to build extensive, integrated facilities aimed at promoting through shipments of commodities to be sold in an international market.

[9] Perkins, "Organization of Railroads."

Others looked upon the railroad primarily as a tool for promoting diverse local economic activity. Disputes between these groups occupied a central place in American politics from the Age of Jackson through the Civil War, as various parties struggled to devise inducements that would serve their interests. By the conclusion of the war, the new technology had become the indispensable tool of an emerging empire built on continental proportions.

Throughout this tumultuous formative period, application of the basic technical assembly to new locales remained the paramount objective. Managers sought above all to bring the technology of railroading to new areas and to foster economic development in the process. Choices of technologies often reflected particular local circumstances, including investment opportunities of managers who in many cases had received charters from government based on their ability to promote growth. Efforts to innovate often exuded an idiosyncratic and speculative character, with great wealth flowing to those who turned inside knowledge to their advantage. Managers often obtained key technologies from firms in which they themselves had invested. Patent rights and personal relations loomed large during this period, as insiders looked to capitalize upon the opportunities opened by massive public subsidies of enterprises based on the most complex technical assemblies of the day. At the same time, railroads often flaunted the rights of patent holders who stood outside the inner circles. This cavalier approach left them exposed to significant liabilities, as they belatedly discovered during a well-publicized series of costly lawsuits after midcentury.

Troubles such as these helped usher in the second stage of American railroading. As the expansive building boom at last subsided during the 1870s, managers such as Perkins turned to the daunting task of evaluating and routinizing the sprawling networks they had created. Like parents belatedly discovering a precocious but troubled child, they threw themselves with abandon into what Perkins termed "running the machine." Curtailing the rampant experiment and insider dealing of an earlier day, managers placed responsibility for technology in the hands of technicians and administrators who imposed rigorous technical standards and channeled innovative energies toward particular objectives. To facilitate these efforts, railroads turned increasingly to the ranks of college-trained engineers who had mastered the methodical, systematic techniques of scientific analysis. They founded pioneering laboratories grounded in a common methodology of testing and materials analysis. Knowledge of railroad technology came increasingly to reside in published studies readily accessible to a community of expert professionals.

This shift toward professional engineering brought fundamental changes in the organizational arrangements structuring technological change. Believing the market-based patent system actually interfered with the flow of those technical improvements they most desired, railroads pressed Congress and the courts to revise the patent laws or at least alter fundamental doctrines pertaining to them. Ultimately, railroads would circumvent the patent system by entering into trade associations and by devising other cooperative arrangements that created alternative pathways of innovation. Working through a growing network of trade associations and engineering societies, experts from the railroads and from their suppliers developed procedures for setting technical standards that effectively provided a basis for negotiating the course of technical change. In this way railroads effectively substituted industry-wide agreements for the more chaotic and uncertain exchanges of the open market. Their efforts prompted Americans to assess how the rise of a corporate economy changed the ways in which incentives to innovate worked their way through the economy and fundamentally altered the pathways of technical change.

Imposing a degree of routine and order virtually unprecedented in any other industry, managers tamed the basic railroad innovation while sustaining a more predictable flow of less radical innovations that helped railroads substantially enhance their productivity. This impressive performance, documented in Part II, persuaded virtually everyone connected with the industry to adopt the machine analogy. By the turn into the twentieth century, politicians and the public as well as executives and investors had come to see railroading as a well-honed conveyor belt for transporting goods and people in highly routinized fashion. Many influential figures now approached the industry as something like a grand engineering problem susceptible to the analytical methods and quantitative measures of technical experts. Engineering standards became the accepted language of the day, providing a source of hope and even enthusiasm not just among the business community but among the mounting ranks of reformers and the broader public as well. Governments asserted a new role as potential stewards of the industry, in which they might draw upon engineering methods to dictate operating procedures and to set appropriate rates.

Yet just as the engineering approach became enshrined in railroad finance and in public policy, American railroads reached a juncture that revealed the inherent limitations of the engineering methods Perkins espoused. Faced with mounting demand from increasingly diverse customers, railroads discovered that continued pursuit of improvements along the established trajectories of greater bulk and increased power no longer yielded the productivity gains they desired. Newly purchased cars and locomotives sat idle in congested yards. Steel rails of unprecedented heft broke with alarming frequency. The situation, as discussed in Part III, called for a shift to a new paradigm built upon a new set of underlying assumptions that Perkins and most others connected with the industry had not anticipated. Searching for remedies to the pressing problems and responding to renewed pressure from government for improved safety, lines reluctantly found themselves considering radical new departures in technology such as automatic brakes and signals and electric traction. These techniques posed challenges and concerns of a sort railroads had successfully evaded for much of the late nineteenth century. Lines needed to develop competence in electrical technology and in other technical domains outside the narrow expertise of their established engineering forces. In an effort to meet the specialized needs of particular customers, railroads experimented with new operating procedures intended to build greater flexibility into train movements, disrupting established measures of performance in the process. At virtually every turn, moreover, managers found themselves confronting an increasingly powerful labor force. For while the technological trajectories of the late nineteenth century had largely served to help railroads sidestep labor conflict, the innovations of the early twentieth brought managers and workers face-to-face over problems they could not easily resolve.

The mounting friction in the railroad machine reached the breaking point with the arguments over rate increases and federal control that occupied the industry from 1906 through the end of World War I. While railroads found their faith in engineering methods waning, the public and the regulatory community grew increasingly enamored with the potential of engineering expertise to provide ordered stewardship of the vast railroad enterprise. During the famous Eastern Rate Case of 1911, railroads stood immobilized as Louis Brandeis, evoking the virtues of Frederick Winslow Taylor and his methods of scientific management, defeated their attempt to win a rate increase. Trapped by the rhetoric and methods they had done so much to promote, railroads could not during the subsequent decade turn their industry down a more innovative path. Wartime demands distorted traffic patterns, creating circumstances that resembled those of the late nineteenth century while masking the trends toward specialized service that had seemed to herald the future of railroading. At war's end, government and the railroads ultimately settled into an uneasy regulatory arrangement that would prove more of an impediment than an inducement to innovation. Railroading slipped into a long, steady decline during which it acquired the trappings of a technical backwater.

Such a fate could only have astounded an observer from a century before, when the nascent technology of railroading opened the door to an uncertain future brimming with challenges and opportunities. In tracing the shifting paradigms of railroad innovation, we turn first to this world of expectancy and anxiety and examine how Americans of the mid-nineteenth century struggled over the course of many decades to assemble railroad machines in forms that would serve their diverse aspirations and objectives.

PART I

Assembling the Machine, 1840–1876

American railroading began as a series of localized experiments with an unproven technology of revolutionary potential. In cities up and down the Atlantic Coast, groups of enthusiasts sought to acquire sufficient expertise and capital to patch together lines that would penetrate the hinterland. Promoters of these pioneering ventures never perceived the railroad as merely a means of transportation. From the start, they embraced it as an engine of change that would alter the character of economic activity. This desire to spark economic diversification and stimulate growth infused railroading with a sense of public purpose. Though most lines were funded primarily by private capital, virtually all received substantial legal privileges from local and state governments. Employing various mixes of public incentives and private initiatives, cities and regions engaged in a developmental rivalry, with the railroad as the lever of growth. The goal was not so much to race westward to a common destination and compete for the same pool of traffic, but to build an infrastructure and foster a healthy regional commerce that would lure capital and human resources away from other locales.

The abundance of sparsely settled land sustained this developmental phase far longer in the United States than in most other places that adopted the railroad. Long after railroading in many European nations had attained a measure of maturity in which a few well-established routes were used ever more intensively, westward expansion continued to open new opportunities for Americans looking to exploit the revolutionary developmental potential of railroading. New lines emerged in succession across the steadily receding Western frontier, replicating what had occurred to the east, while a few established railroads pursued their existing developmental strategies on a far grander scale. The choice between creating new local lines and extending existing ones sparked intense controversy, for all understood that it would significantly shape the distribution of wealth and power. But in either scenario, new construction would continue to garner the lion's share of attention from investors, managers, and the populace. Though older lines of course came to carry more traffic and their operations grew accordingly more complex, expansive development remained the paramount consideration for nearly half a century.

Throughout this extended adolescence, American railroading teemed with the excitement and uncertainty of invention and discovery. Far and away the most important innovation remained the railroad itself: the pioneering combination of a steam locomotive pulling a train of cars over fixed rails of minimal resistance. As different groups of entrepreneurs brought that basic innovation to each new locale, they experienced afresh the exhilaration and frustration associated with technical novelty. Individual projects frequently encountered unprecedented conditions that forced their builders to adapt the basic form to particular circumstances. Some of the improvisations proved so versatile that they became virtually universal features on American railroads. Many others remained known only to their creators. Most railroads entrusted their technical affairs to a master mechanic and an engineer in charge of construction, who used their latitude and authority to impart a distinctive style to the track and equipment of each line. Skilled enginemen generally assumed exclusive charge of particular locomotives, which they could customize as they saw fit. Some of the most significant innovations of all, such as steel rails and air brakes, were bound up closely with investment opportunities associated with the emergent railroad equipment industry located along the routes of major lines. Often railroad managers entered into lucrative reciprocal relationships with suppliers and inventors.

In all of these respects, innovation in American railroading retained a highly individualistic and personal quality. Something of a sense of shared ordeal prevailed among the various mechanics and engineers, and because railroads seldom engaged in direct competition, they showed little inclination to protect ideas and innovations from one another. But because most lines operated entirely independently from one another, with cars as well as locomotives dedicated exclusively to a given line, such cooperation did not yet involve formal industry standards. The situation, as railroads discovered to their chagrin around the time of the Civil War, left companies exposed to vast liabilities from the patent system. Their troubles only mounted when an emergent state regulatory apparatus, buoyed by growing public resentment toward railroads, threatened to compel lines to adopt particular technological devices such as air brakes. The resulting legal and political troubles spelled the end of adolescence for railroading, as the industry began rapidly to impart ordered managerial discipline over its affairs.

1

Engines of Expansion and Extraction: The Politics of Development

When a dying Ulysses S. Grant sat down to pen his memoirs, he had no doubts about where to begin. The great epic of disunion and reunion that Grant saw as the centerpiece both of his own life and that of the young nation he had served could be traced back to 1846 and the decision to wage war against Mexico. Grant understood that the Mexican War had unleashed transforming forces no one had fully anticipated and no institution could fully contain. By opening broad untrammeled vistas, both real and imagined, the war at once presented Americans with startling new economic opportunities and compelled them to rethink the very nature of their society and nation. The bloody sectional conflict that eventually drew Grant from obscurity and thrust him into the public limelight was but one momentous result; the path to the Civil War involved far more than the end of slavery. It entailed a fundamental restructuring of American economic life around dynamic new nodes of activity: mining and ranching in the Mountain West; wheat, corn, and hogs across the upper Midwest; timber along the northern reaches of the Great Lakes; coal, iron, and oil back to the settled East and old Northwest. In every section of the country, Americans combed the land, dug into its surface, and plucked from it spectacular returns.[1]

To reap this bonanza, Americans needed only to apply the tools made available by heavy industry: reapers, oil derricks, steam shovels, coal chutes and breakers, and, above all, railroads. So bound up was railroading with the extractive epic that attempts to isolate and measure its contribution are

---

[1] Stuart Bruchey, *Enterprise: The Dynamic Economy of a Free People* (Cambridge, Mass.: Harvard University Press, 1990), emphasizes these features of the American economy during the mid-nineteenth century. For an interesting note on the significance of the Mexican War for the American political economy, see Stanley Lebergott, "The Hinge of Fate," ch. 19 of his *The Americans: An Economic Record* (New York: Norton, 1984), pp. 226–229.

fraught with difficulty.[2] Railroads resided at the center of two intersecting dynamic economic processes, each subject to its own powerful feedback mechanisms. They occupied a central place in the emergent coal and iron complex, the developmental engine that had transformed much of Britain and in the 1840s had belatedly begun to do the same for the northeastern United States.[3] Railroads not only provided the essential means of transporting the bulky ore and coal from isolated locations to central processing plants; they put up much of the capital for the steel industry and generated enormous demand for its finished products. It is not much of an exaggeration to say that Americans developed their capacity to work and machine metal in lockstep with the railroads.[4]

This vital coal and iron complex benefited as well from the second economic dynamic unleashed by the railroads. By dramatically lowering the cost of transportation, the network of tracks bound the various nodes of the extractive economy together, enabling each to attain a degree of specialization unprecedented in the United States outside the plantation South. As Adam Smith well understood when he wrote his famous dicta that "the degree of specialization is limited by the extent of the market," such specialization could yield large benefits. Americans had glimpsed the potential effect following the opening of the Erie Canal in 1825, when New Yorkers located in the rich valleys along the canal dedicated themselves to commercial wheat production while farmers in the Bay State turned to textile production and other manufactures. By concentrating their energies and organizing themselves into slightly larger units, both groups had achieved significant improvements in productivity and earned higher returns on their labors, without necessarily making substantial investments in new technology.[5] The

[2] Moses Abramovitz, "The Search for the Sources of Growth: Areas of Ignorance, Old and New," *Journal of Economic History* 53 (1993): 217–243, and Moses Abramovitz and Paul A. David, "Reinterpreting American Economic Growth: Parables and Realities," *American Economic Review* 63 (1972): 428–437.

[3] Alfred D. Chandler, Jr., "Anthracite Coal and the Beginnings of the Industrial Revolution in the United States," *Business History Review* 46 (1972): 141–181.

[4] The connections between railroads and the iron and steel industries are discussed more fully in Chapter 2. On the importance of railroad machine shops, see Albert Fishlow, *American Railroads and the Transformation of the Ante-Bellum Economy* (Cambridge, Mass.: Harvard University Press, 1965), and Nathan Rosenberg, "Technological Change in the Machine Tool Industry, 1840–1910," *Journal of Economic History* 23 (1963): 414–443.

[5] Claudia Goldin and Kenneth Sokoloff, "Women, Children, and Industrialization in the Early Republic: Evidence from the Manufacturing Censuses," *Journal of Economic History* 42 (1982): 741–747; Claudia Goldin and Kenneth Sokoloff, "The Relative Productivity Hypothesis of Industrialization: The American Case, 1820 to 1850," *Quarterly Journal of Economics* 99 (1984): 461–488; Kenneth L. Sokoloff, "Was the Transition from the Artisanal Shop to the Non-Mechanized Factory Associated with Gains in Efficiency," *Explorations in Economic History* 21 (1984): 351–382; and Kenneth L. Sokoloff, "Productivity Growth in Manufacturing during Early Industrialization: Evidence from the American Northeast, 1820–1860," in Stanley Engerman

massive investment in railroads that followed promised still larger economies and even greater freedom from geographic constraints, thus enabling Americans to pursue specialization on a continental scale.

With railroads providing the linchpin, the American economy of the mid-nineteenth century thus merged two fundamental types of economic change. It reaped the fruits of market integration anticipated by Smith and other classical market economists, and it experienced a transforming shift in the basis of production of the sort associated with developmental economists such as Karl Marx and Joseph Schumpeter. The effect was explosive. In early February 1846, when President James K. Polk dispatched the young West Point graduate Ulysses S. Grant and the rest of the American forces to Mexico, the United States was still an overwhelmingly agrarian society. With the exception of the recently emergent manufacturing belt across Massachusetts and some pockets of more diverse economic activity clustered around Eastern Seaboard cities, in most areas the vast majority of residents provided for much of their own subsistence. Most traded on only a very limited basis, generally with small-scale artisans and shopkeepers who often enjoyed something approaching a local monopoly. Though for some decades that society had been busily replicating itself by rolling back its near frontier, only a small percentage of Americans had yet crossed the Mississippi. Weeks before the declaration of war against Mexico, a group of enterprising citizens had only just laid plans for the first railroad in Illinois, a modest line linking Grant's hometown of Galena with Chicago. Few could have imagined that by the time Grant ignominiously departed from the presidency thirty years later, the marriage of railroad and soil would have transformed the United States into an economic empire, with farms and steel mills of unprecedented scale and productive efficiency competing in world markets.[6]

Viewed from a distance through the opaque lens of aggregate data, this American variant on what E. J. Hobsbawm aptly called "the Age of Capital" can appear as an undifferentiated and seemingly preordained passage into modernity.[7] But those who lived through the transformation perceived it far differently. For Americans of Grant's generation, the continental extractive economy arose as the startling outcome of an intense and violent political struggle. War, the most extreme of political acts, permeated the entire era. From the time of Polk's election through Custer's annihilation at Little Bighorn, the United States passed through a period of virtually uninterrupted

and Robert Gallman, eds., *Long-Term Factors in American Economic Growth*, National Bureau of Economic Research, Studies in Income and Wealth, vol. 51 (Chicago: University of Chicago Press, 1986), pp. 679–736.

6 These generalizations about the character of the American economy are derived from Jeremy Atack and Peter Passell, *A New Economic View of American History: From Colonial Times to 1940*, 2nd ed. (New York: Norton, 1994). On the Galena and Chicago Union Railroad, see William Cronon, *Nature's Metropolis: Chicago and the Great West* (New York: Norton, 1991), pp. 65–68.

7 E. J. Hobsbawm, *The Age of Capital, 1848–1875* (New York: Scribner's, 1975).

state-sanctioned violence. Those thirty years at the middle of the nineteenth century, punctuated by an extraordinarily bloody civil war, constitute one of the most sweeping and sustained periods of militarization in American history. The military conflicts occurred, moreover, within a political system already fomenting with the energies of democracy and expansive capitalism. More people held the right to vote in the United States of 1846 than in any other country, and few voters had more opportunities to exercise their franchise. With representative bodies and elected officials operating at local, state, and federal levels, public life in the United States involved virtually perpetual electioneering.

Nothing enlivened those politics more than the challenges and opportunities posed by new technology. The basic structure of American politics – its two-party system, incessant electioneering, multiple legislative bodies, and minimal administrative apparatus – had evolved largely in response to the need to distribute incentives and subsidies to groups that might pursue ventures based upon technical innovations.[8] Courts and legislatures at every level of governance ladled their attentions upon the matter of internal improvements in transportation and communication. Two other burning issues of the day, banking and the tariff, were well understood by participants in the political system to be intimately connected with efforts to foster technical development. The largest and most ornate building in Washington, other than the Capitol itself, was the elaborate edifice built to house the U.S. Patent Office (Fig. 1.1) and its collection of models submitted by inventors. Both houses of Congress maintained permanent committees to oversee the patent system, and many members grew deeply involved with particular patent disputes either in their official capacities or through their private legal practices. Their ranks included the former U.S. Representative and occasional counsel to the Illinois Central Railroad Abraham Lincoln. When Lincoln set out on the speaking circuit in February 1859, during the critical interim between his senatorial debates with Stephen Douglas and his successful campaign for the presidency that would trigger secession and war, he chose for his subject the topic "On Discoveries and Inventions."[9]

Considered altogether, the tumultuous politics of mid-nineteenth-century America amounted to little more than an ongoing struggle to seize control of the twin dynamic forces of geographic expansion and technical innovation. Various groups attempted to contain those forces and to direct them in ways they hoped would advance their particular notion of what constituted a

[8]   This is a major theme in the seminal essays of Richard L. McCormick, *The Party Period and Public Policy: American Politics from the Age of Jackson to the Progressive Era* (New York: Oxford University Press, 1986).

[9]   Abraham Lincoln, "Lecture on Discoveries and Inventions," Jacksonville, Decatur, and Springfield, February 11, 1859, in Roy P. Basler, ed., *The Collected Works of Abraham Lincoln*, 9 vols. (New Brunswick: Rutgers University Press, 1953–55), vol. 3, pp. 358–360.

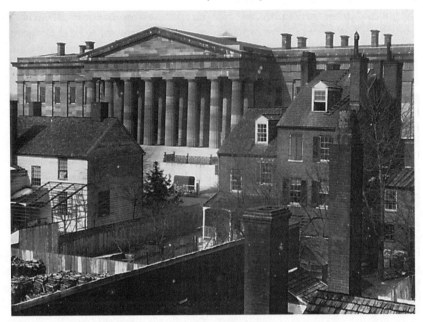

Figure 1.1. United States Patent Office, Washington, D.C., c. 1840. *Courtesy*: Library of Congress.

just and good society. As Lincoln's choice of lecture topics on the eve of the sectional conflict suggests, even the Civil War and the divisive issue of slavery cannot be understood apart from that larger struggle. The war attained such atrocious ferocity in large part because the combatants came to see it as a conflict between visions of political economy that were not only starkly divergent, but also each still evolving rapidly, with diverse interests in each region contesting for the right to determine the outcome.

No technology figured more prominently in those politics, or mattered more to the lives of most Americans, than railroading. Offering enormous advantages in cost and reliability over alternative forms of transport, railroads held a potential to restructure the contours of trade and to reshape the nature of economic activity in ways so profound that virtually no one could ignore them.[10] Inescapably, they drew forth deep reserves of entrepreneurial

---

[10] For careful estimates of the costs and economic significance of rail transport, see George Rogers Taylor, *The Transportation Revolution, 1815–1860* (New York: Holt, Rinehart, and Winston, 1951); Fishlow, *American Railroads*; and Lebergott, *The Americans: An Economic Record*, pp. 107–113. Robert Fogel, *Railroads and American Economic Growth: Essays in Econometric History* (Baltimore: Johns Hopkins University Press, 1964), cautioned against asserting the indispensability of railroads, noting that Americans might have substituted canals with little apparent effect on economic growth. This finding sparked intense controversy, summarized in Atack

energy and fomented unprecedented interest and concern at all levels of government. Precisely how railroads might alter the social and economic landscape, however, remained very much open to question. Eventually, railroading assumed forms, apparent in maps and organizational charts, that betrayed an underlying coherence and reason. But such documents mask more than they reveal. They express ideals as much as they record actual accomplishments, and as a result they obscure the virulent controversies that perpetually whirled about the railroad industry, infusing it with an unsettling mix of urgency and uncertainty, promise and trepidation.

In reality, railroading took shape in fits and starts, compelled forward by the unrelenting logic of expansive capitalism but buffeted continually by the capricious winds of a decentralized and volatile politics. The great through lines of the 1870s emerged in piecemeal fashion, stitched together by ongoing conglomeration of numerous state-chartered companies and municipal corporations that at birth had embodied the hopes and conflicts of countless local communities. Even the handful of federally sponsored transcontinental initiatives exhibited a fragmented, contested character. Coupled to land grants intended to foster local development and built and operated under contract by private firms, the projects retained essential elements of more localized ventures. Despite their federal origins, moreover, the issue of who would maintain authority over these lines remained very much open to dispute. From the time of the Mexican adventure, when expansionists first hatched plans for them, until years after a northern-dominated Congress authorized them in the midst of the most extreme political tumult in American history, the transcontinentals remained lightning rods in state and national politics and subjects of intense judicial scrutiny.

To comprehend the essence of American railroading during the extractive epic, we must then first gain some appreciation for this intensely combative and highly contingent political climate in which the industry emerged. What follows in this chapter is a primer on the subject. It offers a synthesis of railroad politics from the decade preceding the Mexican War until the economic crisis of the mid-1870s. Because railroading informed so many aspects of politics during this period, this synopsis runs some risk of attempting to reduce the whole of American political history to a single chapter. In an effort to make the task more manageable while, it is hoped, lending greater depth to the analysis, I use as a touchstone the career of the man who would

and Passell, *New Economic View*, pp. 427–456. Though skeptical about the indispensability of railroads, Fogel did not deny the enormous impact of transport innovation upon American economy and society. In suggesting railroads were merely one viable alternative and that investment in them may have resulted in part from irrational enthusiasm, his study in some respects complements my own view that railroads emerged not simply as an economically logical choice but through a contentious and highly emotional political process.

eventually summon Grant to lead the Union armies. Abraham Lincoln was in many respects the quintessential political figure of his age, a career politician distinguished from his colleagues only because he happened to be elected to the presidency. Like hundreds of others in public life during this period, Lincoln found himself wrestling time and again with the potential implications of transport innovation for American society. With remarkable consistency, he sought ways to articulate a vision of society that embraced railroads as engines of development while resisting their tendency to promote commercial empire. His sustained attempts at persuasion, which met with mixed success at best, provide unusually rich insights into the politics of the period.

JACKSONIAN PARTY POLITICS: INTERNAL IMPROVEMENT OR EXTERNAL EMPIRE?

Along with many others who achieved public prominence in the middle decades of the nineteenth century, Abraham Lincoln grew up in the expansive border regions of southern Illinois, northern Kentucky, and western Tennessee, where slave state intersected with free and both pressed against the Western boundary of the nation. Lincoln came of age during the presidency of Andrew Jackson, the first Westerner to attain the nation's highest office, and like most young men of his generation he defined himself politically primarily by dint of his response to Old Hickory. Lincoln unabashedly sided with Jackson's opposition. He developed an intense admiration for Henry Clay, the Kentuckian whom the incumbent Jackson handily defeated in the election of 1832. In a move characteristic of middle-class professionals and town dwellers, the young lawyer from Springfield joined the new Whig Party that coalesced in reaction against the Jacksonian Democrats. Elected to the state legislature and then to Congress during the 1840s, Lincoln pursued the standard items on the Whig agenda. He backed programs to encourage internal improvements, pressed for higher tariffs to help pay for them, and argued vigorously in favor of rechartering the national bank that Jackson had destroyed.[11]

In all of this, Lincoln was entirely typical of politicians operating in the second American party system. Virtually all of the contestants in that system believed in material progress, and each party pursued policies intended to foster it. In the course of the ordinary fracas of turning out the vote and fighting for legislative plums, the two parties often appeared almost indistinguishable

---

[11] These and other details in this chapter pertaining to Lincoln come primarily from David Herbert Donald, *Lincoln* (New York: Simon and Schuster, 1995). My interpretation of Lincoln differs substantially from that offered by Donald, who emphasizes political expediency and downplays ideological matters other than Lincoln's opposition to slavery.

from one another.[12] But Whigs and Democrats in fact held quite different visions of prosperity. Jacksonians typically derived their core beliefs from the agrarian ideals commonly associated with Thomas Jefferson.[13] They envisioned a nation of rural landholders bound together by their common condition as independent proprietors. This bucolic image could encompass a broad cross-section of American society, from wealthy slaveholders who exported staples via an international marketing network to small farmers living in virtual isolation from even local commerce. Democrats often celebrated the prospects of an expanding agrarian empire, in which farmers of all ilks spread westward across the continent and perhaps eventually southward into the Caribbean and Latin America as well. The only thing necessary to secure such a society was continued ready access to land and capital. The principal obstacles in its path were entrenched privilege and oppressive government, which in the view of Jackson and his followers had joined in alliance to erect such barriers to unfettered freedom as the national bank and the customs office.

While Jacksonians tended to associate progress with mere quantitative expansion, Whigs were committed to qualitative development.[14] They were far more likely than Democrats to settle down and live in town, and like town dwellers throughout history, they looked toward steady investment, brisk local commerce, and rising property values. As self-conscious elites, Whigs spoke often of personal character and in politics tended to focus on candidates rather than platforms. But in most walks of life they were thoroughgoing modernizers – institution builders who embraced functional specialization and professionalization as the best means to cope with a society of growing complexity.[15] Whigs turned enthusiastically toward evangelical religion, which spoke to their sense that individuals could seize control of their own destinies, but they rejected the fatalism of Methodists and Baptists, who preached a doctrine of hopelessness in the face of earthly oppression followed by redemption before God. Whigs refused to see themselves as being swept up in forces beyond their control, whether those forces were

---

[12] Parties were ideal instruments for getting out the vote and distributing favors; they thrived in a climate where people voted in large numbers but desired little in the way of sustained administration from government. See McCormick, *The Party Period*, and Joel H. Silbey, *The American Political Nation, 1838–1893* (Palo Alto: Stanford University Press, 1991).

[13] John Ashworth, *Slavery, Capitalism, and Politics in the Antebellum Republic* (New York: Cambridge University Press, 1995).

[14] My discussion of Whig party ideology owes much to the fine collective biography of Daniel Walker Howe, *The Political Culture of the American Whigs* (Chicago: University of Chicago Press, 1979).

[15] The ultimate modernizer of this ilk was William Seward, who saw himself living through a revolution in which "political freedom, public education, and technological progress were all synthesized into a comprehensive vision of modernization." Howe, *Political Culture*, p. 199.

held to be divine in nature or the product of the "natural" workings of the free market.

These sensibilities led Whigs to embrace government as a positive instrument that could be used to shape the pace and character of economic change. A few sustained public initiatives, such as those advocated by Lincoln, would encourage ordered internal development rather than reckless expansion. This conviction as much as anything is what distinguished Whigs from Democrats in public life.[16] Jacksonians were "a let-alone party," declared Democratic partisan Horatio Seymour, while their Whig and Republican opponents "were a meddling party."[17] Jacksonians stood above all for limited government. They attacked banks and the customs office as bastions of privilege, susceptible to corruption. The few activist policies Democrats advocated called for sweeping exercises of executive authority that would leave little need for sustained management in their wake. They sought blanket reductions of tariffs, wholesale removal of Indians, and rapid expansion through annexation and wars of imperialism.

Whigs criticized such executive actions as heavy-handed escapades that played to the basest emotions of the electorate. They rejected claims that a strong President such as Jackson could most effectively exercise the people's will and instead celebrated the daily workings of representative legislatures as the truest expressions of democratic government.[18] Few things stirred them to greater heights of passion than the memory of Jackson's veto of the proposed Maysville Road across Kentucky. In an instant, Jackson had pulled the plug on a project that had been conceived by the people's representatives through months of painstaking compromise. The veto symbolized the essential fact of political life that cast a shadow over everything Lincoln and his fellow

[16] "Despite the local character of much of American politics in the nineteenth century," writes Joel H. Silbey, "national issues dominated political debate.... The debate over national issues was the glue that bonded all levels of the American political nation in the 1830s and 1840s. The national debates resonated with, and focused, local divisions, gave them texture, and, given the pluralism of the United States, strongly suggested a reassuring level of national unity in political discourse." Silbey, *American Political Nation*, pp. 86–87.

[17] Quoted in Jean H. Baker, *Affairs of Party: The Political Culture of Northern Democrats in the Mid-Nineteenth Century* (Ithaca: Cornell University Press, 1983), p. 143.

[18] Supporting Zachary Taylor in 1848, Lincoln painted a picture of the Democrats wielding the veto and embedding particular issues in a comprehensive platform, thus undermining the authority of the legislature. "That the constitution gives the President a negative on legislation, all know; but that this negative should be so combined with platforms, and other appliances, as to enable him, and, in fact, almost compel him, to take the whole of the legislation into his own hands, is what we object to, is what Gen. Taylor objects to, and is what constitutes the broad distinction between you and us. To thus transfer legislation, is clearly to take it from those who understand, with minuteness, the interests of the people, and give it to one who does not, and can not so well understand it." Abraham Lincoln, Speech to the U.S. House of Representatives, July 27, 1848.

Whigs attempted. At any moment, Democrats might scuttle their careful labors simply by raising the banner of liberty and crying out for freedom from government oppression. Lincoln's rich legacy of letters and speeches reveals a politician whose lifelong challenge was to find ways to persuade voters that liberty did not flow from the complete abdication of government authority but from its judicious use.

The election of James K. Polk and subsequent military expedition toward the Southwest taxed the patience and the persuasive powers of Lincoln and his Whig colleagues to their limits. In the immediate aftermath of the 1844 election, Lincoln bitterly denounced the abolitionist Liberty Men for having mounted a third-party ticket. Merely for the pleasure of having registered their protest that Henry Clay owned slaves, Lincoln complained, these men had swung the election to the expansionist Polk. In December 1845, with the annexation of Texas pending and war still two months away, Lincoln wrote to a friend that the United States had no right to acquire a territory whose citizens had already established themselves as an independent republic. Polk was pursuing the matter, Lincoln thought, solely to provoke and justify an imperial war.[19]

Political prudence kept the frontier congressman from voicing such sentiments publicly until three years later, when during the course of the 1848 presidential campaign Congress held hearings to investigate the suspicious origins of the war. Whigs sought to brand the Democrats as a party that used executive authority to run roughshod over the legislature while portraying their own candidate, the victorious general Zachary Taylor, as a man who would ever act as humble servant to the people's will. Lincoln supported the strategy even though it meant bypassing his hero, Henry Clay. When his friend and law partner William Herndon wrote to express his opinion that Lincoln had committed political suicide, the young and now lame-duck congressman responded pithily. "The provision of the Constitution giving the war-making powers to Congress, was dictated, as I understand it, by the following reasons," Lincoln wrote. "Kings had always been involving and impoverishing their nation's peoples in wars, pretending generally, if not always, that the good of the people was the object. This, our convention understood to be the most oppressive of all Kingly oppressions; and they resolved to frame the Constitution so that *no one man* should hold the power of bringing this oppression upon us."[20]

This impassioned outburst, expressed in private to his closest friend, betrayed not only the depth of Lincoln's disgust for the imperial politics practiced by Jackson and Polk, but also his enormous frustration with the turn of events during the previous four years. The Polk administration had cast a deep shadow over a Whig cause that had once looked very bright. Following

---

[19] Abraham Lincoln to Williamson Durley, December 3, 1845.
[20] Abraham Lincoln to William H. Herndon, December 15, 1848.

Jackson's departure from the presidency in 1836, Whigs had made steady gains at virtually every level of politics. With the incumbent Democrats shouldering blame for the financial woes associated with the Panic of 1837, the party had even claimed the presidency in 1840. That victory did not lead to immediate restoration of a national bank or passage of a coherent program of federal internal improvements along lines once envisioned by Clay and other supporters of the American System. But a Whig-dominated Congress did succeed in pushing through lenient new bankruptcy legislation and several other policies intended to foster economic development.

By the early 1840s, when Lincoln joined that Congress, the Whig Party seemed on the brink of forging a new national coalition built around a commitment to government encouragement of diverse enterprise. During the 1830s the party had managed to recast its appeal in ways that enabled it to break free from its moorings in the mercantile community and to reach out successfully to the growing numbers of small proprietors. Most significantly, it had begun to embrace the emergent manufacturing sector. Shedding the Jeffersonian ambivalence toward industry and manufacturing that had once characterized the party, many Whigs now praised such activities for combining moral and economic purposes into an ordered whole. Success in manufacturing seemed to bear a close connection to personal qualities such as skill and energy. The fortunes of those engaged in mercantile activities, by contrast, often seemed linked to such chance occurrences as a shipwreck or a sudden rise in prices. The change in attitude was reflected in the arguments Whigs used to defend high tariffs. Rather than stress the importance of generating revenue, Whigs increasingly argued that high duties would promote the growth of infant industries.[21]

Not surprisingly, such sentiments found many of their strongest proponents among the iron manufacturers of Pennsylvania, who badly desired tariff protection for their industry and knew they faced stiff opposition from merchants engaged in foreign trade. Protectionist feelings ran so strong in the Keystone State that in 1844 Democrats there broke with the national platform and joined Whigs in support of higher tariffs.[22] But the Whig program encouraging domestic manufacturing also held appeal among those with less obvious self-interest. Contrasts between the virtues of industry and the corrupting influence of trade resonated broadly in a society that consisted overwhelmingly of small producers who had limited contact with the world of international commerce. Seaboard merchants, who generated much of their income by providing services to an international clientele, seemed insulated from most Americans. Their one significant staple export, cotton, came overwhelmingly from the comparatively few Americans who owned significant numbers of slaves. Because large plantations generally produced sufficient foodstuffs to feed their owners and their work forces,

---

[21] Howe, *Political Culture*, pp. 97–110.   [22] Silbey, *American Political Nation*, p. 91.

these planters, too, remained economically detached from the vast majority of white Americans. Whigs thus had good reason to believe that a program emphasizing the nurture of domestic manufacturing might meet with widespread acceptance and perhaps form the basis of a powerful new political alliance. Even John Quincy Adams, who had grown up among the merchant elites of New England and as President had held to their internationalist agenda, now supported higher tariffs and opposed the annexation of Texas and the Mexican War.[23]

Local Promotionalism and the Equalization of Benefits

This subtle refashioning of the Whig appeal in national politics was paralleled by developments at the state and local level, which if anything gained heightened significance in the wake of Jackson's successful attack upon federal economic initiatives. Ohio presents a good example.[24] The same Jacksonian sentiments that brought down the national bank also undermined such bastions of state government authority as the Ohio Canal Board. For nearly two decades before that state's Jacksonian revolution of 1836, this board had constructed and operated the most comprehensive system of state-financed transport in the nation. Under the sustained management of two Whig administrators, the board had kept Ohio's debt to a modest level of $2 million. It had done so in large part by funneling most of those limited resources into a few major arteries such as the Ohio and Erie Canal, which bisected the state from north to south, linking the Ohio River with Lake Erie. Such conservative policies earned the board the admiration of Eastern financiers but made it an irresistible target for the ascendant Jacksonians, who demanded that membership rotate with elections and be broadened to include representatives from all areas of the state.

This attack on the board did not, however, reflect a broader desire to curb all internal improvements. Quite the contrary. The Jacksonian appeals to egalitarianism and fairness sparked a proliferation of new, smaller-scale projects of more local orientation. By 1845, public indebtedness in Ohio had soared to nearly $15 million, most of it in the form of loans by local governments to transport enterprises of limited scope. These mixed public–private ventures included many railroads, which small investors embraced as a less expensive alternative to canals. Start-up costs stayed especially low if the proposed rail line received the privileges of eminent domain and limited liability. Most of the seventy-seven corporate charters granted to railroads by the Ohio legislature before 1840 provided these benefits. Unlike earlier

[23]   Howe, *Political Culture*, p. 121.
[24]   This and the following two paragraphs are based on Harry N. Scheiber, *Ohio Canal Era: A Case Study of Government and the Economy, 1820–1861* (Athens: Ohio University Press, 1968).

corporate charters, moreover, those granted during the Jacksonian heyday (all but nineteen of the 1840 total) did not carry significant constraints on private enterprise. Though the state ostensibly retained some power to regulate rates and to determine routes, in practice government exerted little influence over the railroads. The stipulated rate levels were so generous that they seldom came into play, while Jacksonian suspicion of state authority prevented the legislature from establishing a meaningful mechanism for monitoring details such as specific routes. Lacking both a regulatory agency and the leverage of a bondholder, the state could do little to direct the entrepreneurial energies it had helped release. Passage of a general railroad incorporation act in 1848 did little to reverse the trend toward unregulated enterprise. The law made only slight gestures toward curbing the freedom of corporate activity, and by making chartering routine it effectively foreclosed efforts to reimpose government authority through special restrictive provisions.

Many Ohio Whigs no doubt felt some unease over the relaxation of government authority that accompanied the burst of local internal improvement occurring in the late thirties and early forties. Only the astute financial juggling of Whigs and conservative Democrats, together with income from the canal tax, enabled the state to avoid defaulting on its obligations during the depression of 1839–45. Yet Whigs could also find much to celebrate in the new ventures. Coming in the midst of economic depression at a time when criticism of government enterprise ran high, the surge of new projects lent powerful impetus to the emerging Whig vision of a society bound together by diverse local commerce. Even before the Jacksonian assault, the Canal Board had itself begun to encourage economic diversification through rate structures that favored local manufactures over imports. Now railroads seemingly gave proponents of manufacturing and economic diversity another tool toward the same end. For as historian Harry Scheiber has noted, Ohio railroads in these early years had an overwhelmingly local orientation. "Some local railroad organizers advertised their projects as potential links in a transcontinental system that would carry the trade with the Far West and Asia through their towns," writes Scheiber. "Others, less pretentious, merely sought to assure their communities of a place on one of the new lines. But however they boosted their schemes, railroad organizers made local needs and local objectives their main point of reference. Few men spoke in terms of a state program of railroad construction. Instead railroads were planned, and presented to the public, as a means of fulfilling parochial, localistic ambitions."[25]

Much the same drift away from centralized, state-sponsored commercialism and toward localized, state-promoted diversity occurred among Whigs in New York State. When Whigs there coalesced in opposition to Martin

Van Buren and the Democrats, they attempted first to buttress the Federalist legacy of large-scale internal improvements. Governor William Seward pressed in 1838 for an improvements bill that would have increased the state debt in order to fund a substantial enlargement of the Erie Canal. Samuel Ruggles, a prominent Whig legislator who reported on the bill in his capacity as chairman of the committee on ways and means, stressed that the enlargement would generate revenue from commerce with the West. "The consequence then of perfecting these systems of intercommunication will inevitably be a distribution of labor, on a grand scale, through the whole northern part of the continent: the maritime portions engrossing the active pursuits of navigation, commerce, and manufactures, while this central group of agricultural states will become the common granary of the Union, and discharge the important duty of supplying subsistence to all the surrounding communities."[26] Ruggles dismissed the revenue generated from local, intrastate commerce as "inconsequential" when compared with the tariffs on through trade.

Ruggles's assessment, though remarkably prophetic of long-term developments, met with a tepid response in the political climate of the late 1830s and early 1840s. The radical Barnburner element of the Democrats, anchored by Van Buren, had built a strong coalition through its sustained attacks on government authority. In 1842, the Barnburners launched the "Stop and Tax" campaign, which called for a moratorium on state-sponsored internal improvements and repayment of the state debt. Any subsequent improvements would have to be funded through taxation of those who used the transport or otherwise benefited directly from it. Four years later the Barnburners, in alliance with some influential Whigs, led the movement for a new state constitution designed to further undercut the administrative power of government. The new document greatly broadened representation while placing severe restrictions on state indebtedness. It also eliminated inspection laws, which had long provided a basis for regulating exports and marketplaces, and substituted general incorporation laws for the specific legislative charters that had usually included some regulatory provisions. Some supporters of the new constitution even pressed, without success, for the curtailment of limited liability.

As in Ohio, however, the intense partisanship of the Jacksonian era did not so much curtail the drive for internal improvements as to redirect it toward smaller-scale ventures of local orientation. While state subsidies of internal improvements during the half-century following completion of the

[26] Quoted in L. Ray Gunn, *The Decline of Authority: Public Economic Policy and Political Development in New York State, 1800–1860* (Ithaca: Cornell University Press, 1988), pp. 41–42. This and the following two paragraphs are based primarily on Gunn.

Erie Canal totaled just $1 million, New York municipalities pumped some $37 million into transport projects and other improvements. Much of that investment flowed into schemes conceived during the thirties and forties. Whigs such as Seward, though still dreaming of economic diversity occurring across a grand east–west axis of continental proportions, toned down their rhetoric of empire and instead emphasized the mutuality of interests linking countryside and city within New York State. In an attempt to preserve at least some support for an activist legislature, Seward articulated the doctrine of "equalization of benefits," which celebrated the proliferation of local projects as a means of ensuring that no group or area went unrewarded. In a similar vein, the Whig editor Horace Greeley fought to preserve limited liability by arguing that it provided a tool that could support a wide variety of small enterprises.

Abraham Lincoln, observing the trends toward deregulation and local promotionalism from his posts in Springfield and Washington, likewise found refuge in the notion of equalization of benefits. Lincoln had witnessed the mounting enthusiasm for internal improvements first-hand in Illinois, where in the early 1840s even Democrats joined in support of a program of state-financed canals.[27] In January of 1846, a month before Polk declared war, some 300 delegates gathered at Rockford passed a series of resolutions supporting construction of the railroad between Chicago and Galena. Promising that land values would double with commencement of operations, they called on farmers to "come forward and subscribe to the stock of the proposed railroad to the extent of their ability."[28] Chicagoans invested heavily in the project as well and assumed an active role in its management. In a classic illustration of Whiggery, these men "expected to profit personally from their efforts, and in a variety of ways," notes William Cronon in his history of the Windy City. For some, "the road's expected effect on real estate investments may have been as attractive as the profits it would produce in moving freight and passengers."[29]

In one of his final addresses to Congress, Representative Lincoln rose to defend government-sponsored internal improvements. To those who complained that people located nearest the roads and railways would benefit at the expense of others, Lincoln responded that anything worth attempting could be criticized on such grounds. The benefits of internal improvements, in his view, clearly outweighed the injustices. By vigorously pursuing improvements at both state and federal levels, moreover, Lincoln thought that any inequities would be smoothed out so that "the sum of the whole might not be very unequal."[30] Like others within his party, Lincoln could celebrate

[27] Baker, *Affairs of Party*, p. 145.
[28] Quoted in Cronon, *Nature's Metropolis*, p. 65.   [29] Ibid., p. 66.
[30] Abraham Lincoln, "Speech to the U.S. House of Representatives," June 30, 1848.

a political system in which elected representatives routinely doled out favors, employing instruments that offered the great convenience of being infinitely divisible. He took comfort in the fact that just because one legislature granted a series of charters, nothing precluded its successors from issuing strings of their own.[31] Meanwhile, Democrats stood ready to brand the whole business as corrupt, while committing the nation to grand endeavors that could not easily be duplicated, such as Polk's imperialist march to the Halls of Montezuma.

Nationalism and Project-Based Populism

The war with Mexico imparted a fervor for empire into American politics that worked steadily to undermine the Whig vision of government fostering diverse commerce and industry on a largely local basis. The first blow came in 1846, when Democrats in Congress, aided by the critical assistance of votes from the recently admitted delegation from Texas, pushed through a comprehensive reduction in tariff schedules.[32] These cuts not only opened American manufacturers to foreign competition; they also deprived government of funds it might have spent on internal improvements at the very moment the war had begun to place additional strains on the budget. The decisive American victory only made things worse. With the territory of the United States suddenly enlarged by over a third and extended westward to the Pacific, the limited funds available for internal improvements would be spread much thinner. Military zealotry, moreover, had unleashed pressure to concentrate the available monies upon grand projects of continental reach. Like war itself, such ventures could capture the popular imagination while quietly but dramatically altering the economic landscape. If subcontracted to private firms, projects such as a transcontinental railroad or a canal linking the Mississippi with the Gulf of California would place no burden of permanent administration upon government, much as the army after its military campaign could be disbanded.

Whigs got a taste of this project-oriented populism through their brief experience with the telegraph. In 1842, after years of debate, Congress agreed to contribute a modest sum of $44,000 toward helping a group of private investors build a pilot line between Washington and Baltimore. This project, like most subsequent telegraph lines, would primarily serve the interests of financial intermediaries who desired to receive information about prices as quickly as possible. Several members of Congress stood to benefit directly from the service. Supporters of the project carried the day, however, only by coupling such commercial considerations to questions of national

---

[31]   McCormick, *Party Period*, p. 208, citing Harry N. Scheiber, "Federalism and the American Economic Order, 1789–1910," *Law and Society Review* 10 (1975): 57–118.

[32]   Howe, *Political Culture*, on Giddings.

defense. The line would establish instantaneous communications between the commander-and-chief and the naval forces in Baltimore harbor, its advocates asserted, and prevent any repeat of the confusion that had imperiled the nation during the War of 1812. Thus swathed in the cloak of patriotism, an experimental venture with profound commercial and technological implications went forward. The first message sent over the wire, on the first of May in 1844, relayed news the Whigs had nominated Henry Clay as their candidate for the presidency.[33]

Clay's defeat that fall at the hands of the expansionist Polk proved momentus for the emergent technology of telegraphy. Propelled forward by the immediate military necessities of the war with Mexico and by the obvious advantages it offered financiers and merchants, overland telegraphy rapidly grew commonplace. A line stretching southwest from Washington had reached New Orleans by 1851. Even more astounding, wires connected East Coast cities with Chicago as early as 1848. Virtually overnight, Eastern and Western commodity markets began to function almost as one, as news of changes in New York grain prices circulated almost instantaneously on the floor of the newly created Chicago Board of Trade.[34] Before long, influential Manhattanites such as Cyrus Field talked of laying a cable beneath the Atlantic, thus placing themselves at the center of a commercial axis stretching from the Midwest to London.[35]

Competition between large-scale projects promoting military and commercial empire and more modest ones fostering local development only intensified when Congress turned its attention to railroads. Though railroading was a less experimental technology than telegraphy had been in 1842, it was far more costly. Construction of a line to California and the Pacific – the dream of military expansionists and China traders – would put an enormous strain on the budget. Government might use military personnel to conduct surveys or perhaps even to build the lines, and postal contracts might provide some incentives for private operators while ultimately pumping revenue back into the federal coffers. But anyone who gave much thought to the matter knew that Congress could not seriously hope to fund such an ambitious venture without cashing in some of its land reserves. The land grants would have to be especially large, moreover, because so much of the prospective railroad would pass through desolate territory that would generate no operating revenue or land sales for its proprietors. In effect, Congress would have to trade a vast chunk of the lands immediately west of the Mississippi in order to obtain passage to the distant Pacific. Such a policy would likely drive down property values in more settled areas, as private capital leapfrogged over

---

[33] Robert L. Thompson, *Wiring a Continent: The History of the Telegraph Industry in the United States, 1832–1866* (Princeton: Princeton University Press, 1947).

[34] Cronon, *Nature's Metropolis*, pp. 102–121.

[35] Bernard S. Finn, *Submarine Telegraphy: The Grand Victorian Technology* (London: Science Museum, 1973).

them to take advantage of the opportunities made possible by government subsidy in the West.

As Lincoln and Polk each retreated from Washington in early 1849 and prepared to resume lives outside of elected office in their respective Western communities, they thus left behind a political world charged with unprecedented energy and brimming with potential conflict. By removing constraints that had earlier circumscribed government promotional activities while leaving the instruments of promotion largely intact, Jacksonians had in effect turned every forum of government, from local councils to state legislatures to Congress, into a free-for-all in which groups scrambled to obtain favors for their pet projects. Meanwhile, the fervent expansionist policies carried out by Jackson and Polk had broadened the projected scale of such improvements and dramatically upped the stakes of the contest. Disputes over internal improvements, though still occurring largely in state and local forums, would now necessarily involve pressing issues of national purpose and empire, both military and commercial. Such matters, moreover, could not help but exacerbate the persistent tensions over slavery and sectionalism that lay just beneath the surface of antebellum politics.

RAILROADS, SLAVERY, AND SECTIONAL CONFLICT

The Jacksonian brand of politics that so offended Lincoln had always in the eyes of many of its critics been closely associated with slavery. As early as 1838, in his first major public address, Lincoln had contrasted "the pleasure hunting masters of the slaves, and the order loving citizens of the land of steady habits."[36] This glib distinction did not correlate with party divisions so neatly as Lincoln might have preferred, and he soon learned to temper such sentiments when catering to the slaveholding elites and other Southerners with ties to towns who formed an important contingent of the Whig Party.[37] Still, the comment captured Lincoln's guiding belief that slaveholding ultimately posed the most fundamental threat to his vision of a properly ordered society. Slavery, like monarchy, drove people to extremes, causing them to indulge in behaviors that undermined the rules and guiding principles necessary to achieve an ordered, balanced society in which all individuals might flourish. It gave rise to abolitionist mobs, which Lincoln decried in his speech of 1838, and it unleashed the crass, aggrandizing politics practiced by

[36] Abraham Lincoln, "Speech before the Lyceum," Springfield, January 27, 1838.
[37] The Whig Party had attracted many slaveholding Southerners, including luminaries such as Henry Clay and, for a time, John Calhoun, the South Carolinian who had unsuccessfully stood down Andrew Jackson during the nullification crisis of the early 1830s. As in the North, the Whigs drew especially from the ranks of wealthy town-dwellers who desired to see their investments in real estate enhanced by prudent public investment.

Jackson, Polk, and their Texas cronies. Such men belonged to that class of restless entrepreneurs, familiar to Lincoln from his youth in western Kentucky and Tennessee, who had discovered that quick fortunes could be made by transplanting the slave system from the exhausted Southeastern tidewater regions to the rich river valleys of the vast southern Mississippi basin. Devoted to nothing so much as their own self-interest, these men had in Lincoln's view learned to manipulate the instruments of democratic government and to exploit the rhetoric of liberty and democracy in ways that served their selfish ends.[38] Having eroded the constraints once imposed by sober representative leadership, the slaveholders with their bold move westward and their proposals for rapid construction of railroads now appeared poised to secure their way of life for the indefinite future. For once slavery took hold among even a small segment of the population in any place, Lincoln believed, it would remain forever entrenched there, its poison seeping steadily into the body politic.

Young America and National Empire

In the years that elapsed between Lincoln's withdrawal from Congress until his shocking ascendance to the presidency in 1860, this dark vision grew seemingly ever closer to reality. Spurred on by vigorous expansion in the highly profitable agricultural export sectors of cotton and wheat, the United States experienced an unprecedented boom that drew the country ever deeper into the orbit of international trade. The share of population living in the mercantile cities located along its coasts and inland waterways increased more rapidly than at any comparable period in the nation's history before or since. As commercial fortunes mounted and new horizons opened, interest in railroads and other internal improvements reached new heights. Legislatures in virtually every state dramatically accelerated the rates at which they chartered corporations and funded transport projects, while in Washington

---

[38] Lincoln elaborated upon these themes most forcefully in his "Speech on the Kansas–Nebraska Act," Peoria, October 16, 1854. In departing from sixty years of tradition in which American law addressed slavery pragmatically as a regrettable fact of history, the act in Lincoln's view had created a situation in which slaveowners proclaimed "the liberty of making slaves of other people" as the highest form of liberty. The argument angered Lincoln not just because he deplored "the monstrous injustice of slavery," but "because it deprives our republican example of its just influence in the world – enables the enemies of free institutions, with plausibility, to taunt us as hypocrites – causes the real friends of freedom to doubt our sincerity, and especially because it forces so many really good men amongst ourselves into an open war with the very fundamental principles of civil liberty – criticizing the Declaration of Independence, and insisting that there is no right principle of action but *self-interest*." For a perceptive analysis of Lincoln's critique of propertied self-interest as the basic guiding principle of civil society, see J. David Greenstone, *The Lincoln Persuasion: Remaking American Liberalism* (Princeton: Princeton University Press, 1993).

Congress implemented a program that granted federal lands in aid to state-sponsored improvements. As the number of projects proliferated, moreover, overburdened governments generally further relaxed their enforcement of regulations such as maximum rate provisions and stopped collecting railroad taxes that had been designed to protect earlier state investments in canals.

Not surprisingly, given this favorable climate, private capital flowed into railroads at unprecedented rates. In 1850, railroads already accounted for 6.8 percent of the capital stock of the United States; a decade later their share had nearly doubled, to 12.7 percent. Railroads in Prussia, by comparison, accounted for just 3.0 percent and 5.4 percent of the national capital stock in the same two years. Railroad investment per capita in the United States, already double the Prussian level in 1850, grew to two and a half times that of the German state over the course of the next decade. American railroads, moreover, stretched the available funds much further than their Prussian counterparts. In 1850, the United States had over three times as much railroad mileage per capita as the Prussians. A decade later, despite the fairly modest increase in the difference of investment per capita, the American advantage in mileage per capita had grown to an astonishing five times the Prussian figure. All told, the United States in 1860 had eight times as many miles as the Prussians with only four times the capital.[39]

In the Prairie State capital of Springfield, Lincoln had ample opportunity to observe the rapidly changing character of American political economy. Construction of the first thirty-one miles of the Galena and Chicago Union Railroad began during March of 1848, at virtually the same moment that the Chicago Board of Trade opened with telegraphic connections to New York City. By 1852, over half of Chicago's wheat was arriving via its tracks. Managers and investors of this and other upstart railroads pressed eagerly to extend their lines westward across the prairie into Iowa, where in the wake of the Mexican War the federal government had rewarded tens of thousands of veterans with free plots of land. The new prairie railroads proved powerful magnets for capital, which flowed into the Midwest from New England merchants fleeing the depressed China trade and from Europeans who saw their local markets flood with imported American grain.[40] When the Crimean War deprived the British of Russian grain during 1853–54, the volume of American wheat exports doubled and their value tripled, driving the domestic price of wheat to twice its prewar levels. Chicago and its hinterland benefited disproportionately from this bonanza, as the amount of grain shipped from the city tripled between 1853 and 1856. The surge pushed Chicago past

---

[39] Colleen A. Dunlavy, *Politics and Industrialization: Early Railroads in the United States and Prussia* (Princeton: Princeton University Press, 1994), pp. 28–31.

[40] Arthur M. Johnson and Barry E. Supple, *Boston Capitalists and Western Railroads* (Cambridge, Mass.: Harvard University Press, 1967), and John Lauritz Larsen, *Bonds of Enterprise: John Murray Forbes and Western Development in America's Railway Age* (Cambridge: Harvard University Press, 1984).

St. Louis, which in 1850 had handled twice as much grain as the Windy City, and made it the largest shipper of grain in the Midwest.[41]

Much of the credit for this stunning rise to international prominence went to, or at least was claimed by, Illinois Democratic Senator Stephen Douglas. An Easterner who had married the daughter of a wealthy Alabama plantation owner before relocating to Chicago, Douglas worked steadily to transform his new home into a trading metropolis with direct links to international markets. With the aid of Eastern allies in Congress, he secured a federal land grant that helped the Illinois Central Railroad build a branch into the Windy City. In addition to creating a small fortune for Douglas, who purchased large tracts of land on bluffs overlooking Lake Michigan where the tracks entered the city, the new extension effectively reoriented what had been intended by Whigs as an engine of localized internal development and turned it into a key link in a prospective transcontinental empire. The branch, which soon carried more traffic than any other stretch of railroad in Illinois, would serve as the vital common element of a vast two-pronged fork stretching westward to the Pacific and southward to the Gulf Coast.[42]

Not all residents of Illinois embraced this ambitious plan with unfettered enthusiasm or celebrated the prosperity of the Illinois Central so wholeheartedly. The naysayers included Lincoln. Now cultivating a vigorous legal practice, Lincoln was by no means an opponent of prosperity and enterprise. Indeed, he had ridden the boom to an ever more secure position among the increasingly affluent middle class. Lincoln even did some work on behalf of the Illinois Central. In perhaps his most famous legal triumph, he absolved the railroad from responsibility when the operator of the steamboat *Effie Afton* collided with its bridge over the Mississippi River. Unlike Douglas, however, the downstate lawyer was not closely affiliated with the Chicago interests who increasingly dominated the railroad's board. His political ties lay with the group of old Whigs centered in the Illinois midsection, many of whom had sought to keep the railroad from gaining access to the riverfront at Cairo and the lakefront in Chicago.[43] Some measure of Lincoln's

[41] Cronon, *Nature's Metropolis*, pp. 110 and 115.

[42] Ibid., p. 70. On Douglas, see Robert W. Johannsen, *Stephen A. Douglas* (New York: Oxford University Press, 1973). On a similar turn toward the coastal entrepot of Philadelphia, see John Majewski, *A House Dividing: Economic Development in Pennsylvania and Virginia before the Civil War* (Cambridge: Cambridge University Press, 2000). See, also, James A. Ward, "Promotional Wizardry: Rhetoric and Railroad Origins, 1820–1860," *Journal of the Early Republic* 11 (1991): 69–88.

[43] Johannsen, *Douglas*, pp. 306–317. Whigs in Galena similarly ran afoul of Douglas in 1853 when they refused to support improvements to the riverfront rail docks of the Galena and Chicago Union, which now served as the western branch of the Illinois Central. The Illinois Central promptly relocated its western terminus to Dubuque, Iowa, where Douglas had negotiated a more favorable agreement with local authorities. See Kenneth N. Owens, *Galena, Grant, and the Fortunes of War* (Dekalb: Northern Illinois University Press, 1963), p. 14.

own alienation from the railroad can be gleaned from the fact he found it necessary on at least one occasion to sue its board for payment of his legal fees.[44]

For Douglas to carry the day in building his railroad empire, he needed to overcome not just the likes of Lincoln, but also the considerable resistance from those within his own party who looked with suspicion on such government-sponsored ventures. Early during the administration of Franklin Pierce, the Democratic devotee of laissez-faire who won the presidency in 1852, Douglas rose to lead the Illinois congressional delegation in vigorous objection after Pierce vetoed river and harbor improvement bills that would have benefited Chicago.[45] Douglas faced an even tougher challenge in persuading the mass of Democratic voters, many of whom lived on the fringes of commercial activity and had built their allegiance to the party around its opposition to government initiatives. Small farmers in northern Alabama, as loyal a group of Jacksonian Democrats as one could find, once tore down the telegraph line to New Orleans when they became convinced that it had caused a drought in their region.[46] In attempting to rally such insulated voters in support of his technologically progressive expansionist agenda, Douglas conjured up the image of Young America, in which he portrayed the United States as a brimming adolescent male poised on the brink of a brilliant future made possible by technology and commerce. Only the timid whining of Old Fogy, the stodgy naysayer who refused to make way for progress, could prevent this healthy youth from entering adulthood and seizing his rightful place at the forefront of the world's nations (see Fig. 1.2). The imagery played to the manliness of voters and cleverly turned longstanding Whig complaints about Democratic obstructionism back on themselves, leaving Lincoln and other advocates of more modest internal improvements to explain why they now opposed what they had long trumpeted so loudly. First formulated during the unsuccessful run for the Democratic presidential nomination that propelled Douglas to national prominence in 1852, the theme of Young America would remain his primary rallying cry for the remainder of the decade, right through his famous campaigns against Lincoln for the Senate and the presidency.[47]

In tirelessly preaching the rhetoric of Young America, Douglas sought also to divert criticism from those who believed his plans served to advance the cause of expansionist slaveholders. This concern grew especially urgent after 1854, when in his eagerness to realize his grand vision Douglas orchestrated the Kansas–Nebraska Act, which exempted the Kansas Territory from the strict prohibition on slavery contained in the Missouri Compromise. In the

---

[44] Donald, *Lincoln*, pp. 156–157. [45] Baker, *Affais of Party*, p. 145.

[46] J. Mills Thornton, *Politics and Power in a Slave Society: Alabama, 1800–1860* (Baton Rouge: Louisiana State University Press, 1978), p. 316.

[47] In addition to Johannsen, *Douglas*, see Greenstone, *The Lincoln Persuasion*, pp. 140–153 and 223–225.

LOCO FOCO CANDIDATES TRAVELLING,
ON THE CANAL SYSTEM.

Figure 1.2. Diminutive Senator Stephen Douglas of Illinois brands his challengers for the 1852 Democratic nomination "Old Fogies," out of step with "Young America." *Courtesy*: Library of Congress.

eyes of critics such as Lincoln, this measure marked the boldest move yet in the sustained efforts of certain slaveholders to extend their empire. Since his departure from Washington, Lincoln had seen proponents of this course secure one victory after another in national affairs. President Taylor's strategy of pressing rapidly for California annexation, endorsed reluctantly by Lincoln, had failed to slam the door closed on the Mexican adventure and refocus political attention on the Whig developmental agenda. The proposed Compromise of 1850 had actually torn the party apart. Among the northern leadership of the Whig party, unambiguous support for the Compromise came only from Daniel Webster of Massachusetts and Millard Fillmore of New York, men with strong ties to urban commercial interests. In the assessment of historian Daniel Walker Howe, the willingness of Whigs such as Webster and Fillmore to join urban elite Democrats and slaveholding Whigs in support of the compromise lent credence to those who detected "a disposition among certain northeastern businessmen, particularly bankers and textile manufacturers, to seek accommodation with slave-owners who were their customers and suppliers." In the end, Congress passed the compromise measures only because Northern Democrats joined in alliance with Southern

Whigs. When the deaths of Webster, Clay, and Taylor left the presidency and the party in Fillmore's hands, the Whigs soon lay in ruins. Though the nascent Republican Party was rapidly rising from its ashes, this political upstart did not yet pose a clear alternative to the expansionist Democratic agenda. Its most prominent figure was Senator William Seward, a New Yorker who dreamed of seeing his native city displace London at the center of international commerce.[48]

As the Whigs disintegrated, the ascendent Democrats found common ground in the free-trade policies long associated with Southern slaveholders. In 1852, Democrats attacked tariffs so vehemently that Whig Party literature hammered almost exclusively upon the supposed alliance between "the Locofoco party in the United States and England to BREAK DOWN American Manufactures and thus secure the Market for England."[49] Sidestepping such attacks, Democrats soft-pedaled their internationalist ties and played up their militant nationalism. Nathaniel Hawthorne, enlisted to write a campaign biography of Pierce, crafted his narrative around the candidate's service in the Mexican War, limited though it was. In the years following Pierce's victory, notes Jean Baker in her comprehensive study of the party, Democratic appeals for "geographical inclusiveness" increasingly gave way to slogans that more overtly advocated "expansive nationalism."[50] Democratic leaders celebrated when Admiral Peery sailed into the Sea of Japan in 1853 and drummed up enthusiasm for similar ventures into the Caribbean and Latin America. Senator George Pugh of Ohio, a close confidante of Douglas's, led a group pressing for annexation of Cuba and construction of an interoceanic canal. Many Southern Democrats, fearful that the booming Northern and Western economies might lure enough immigrants to swing the balance of power and facilitate a constitutional assault on the rights of slaveholders, embraced expansion into Latin America as both a means of securing access to markets and a way of adding more slave states to the Union. A few vociferous Southerners even called for removing the British from Central and South America.[51]

The unchecked expansionist crusade deeply troubled Lincoln. In his rare public appearances during the early 1850s, he often groped for language that would draw out the connections between northern merchants, Southern planters, and the British free traders. When the Hungarian freedom fighter

---

[48] Howe, *Political Culture*; quote from p. 224.
[49] Quoted in Silbey, *American Political Nation*, p. 105.
[50] Baker, *Affairs of Party*, p. 322.
[51] On Southern expansionism during the 1850s, see William L. Barney, *The Road to Secession: A New Perspective on the Old South* (New York, 1972), and Richard Slotkin, *The Fatal Environment: The Myth of the Frontier in the Age of Industrialization, 1800–1890* (New York: Atheneum, 1985), pp. 227–278. On expansionism in general, see Thomas R. Hietala, *Manifest Design: Anxious Aggrandizement in Late Jacksonian America* (Ithaca: Cornell University Press, 1985).

Lajos Kossuth visited Springfield in 1852, for instance, Lincoln used the occasion to register his disgust with Britain. "There is nothing in the past history of the British government, or in its present expressed policy, to encourage the belief that she will aid, in any manner, in the delivery of continental Europe from the yoke of despotism," Lincoln declared in his testimonial. "Her treatment of Ireland," he continued, "forces the conclusion that she will join her efforts to the despots of Europe in suppressing every effort of the people to establish free governments, based upon the principles of true religious and civil liberty."[52] Such comments betrayed Lincoln's emergent sense that the world stood on the brink of a disaster. The winds of economic and political change, propelled by a powerful minority speaking in the name of liberty for the masses, threatened to sweep aside the ideals he most valued.

His sense of impending doom reached a crescendo when James Buchanan succeeded Pierce in the White House in 1857. Now the libertarian Democratic rout appeared complete. Upon taking office, Buchanan promptly negotiated a tariff reduction, much to the ire of Representative Henry Carey and other iron manufacturers who had thrown their support to their fellow Pennsylvanian.[53] In 1857 and again the following year, Buchanan authorized military expeditions up the Colorado River from the Gulf of Mexico in hopes of finding a navigable waterway connecting the Southwestern interior with the Pacific.[54] And in a dramatic gesture that seemed to encapsulate the entire Democratic agenda and capture the full flavor of the party's political style, Buchanan lent the assistance of the U.S. Navy to a privately funded scheme to lay a telegraph cable beneath the Atlantic to Britain. Upon transmission of the first garbled message – a paean to science, trade, and the glories of Anglo-American culture dispatched by Queen Victoria to Buchanan – working-class New Yorkers would spill into the streets to enjoy a raucous celebration, replete with fireworks provided by the city's Democratic leadership.[55]

Lincoln's concern with this course of events spilled over when he at last rose to challenge Douglas in the famed Illinois senate race of 1858. Angered that Douglas had embraced the notorious Dred Scott decision, which in the view of Lincoln and many others effectively prevented Americans from banning slavery in the territories, the former congressman burst forth with a speech so impassioned that it has been cited as often by his critics as by his admirers. In it Lincoln spun a tale of conspiracy involving Senator Douglas, President Buchanan, and Chief Justice Taney, the slaveholding Southerner

---

[52] Abraham Lincoln, "Testimonial to Lajos Kossuth," January 9, 1852.

[53] Howe, *Political Culture*, p. 120. By the 1850s, even some loyal Democrats in iron-rich areas such as Pennsylvania had begun to support higher tariffs. See Baker, *Affairs of Party*, p. 145.

[54] Wallace Stegner, *Beyond the Hundredth Meridian: John Wesley Powell and the Second Opening of the West* (Boston: Houghton Mifflin, 1954), p. 69.

[55] Finn, *Submarine Telegraphy*, pp. 21–22.

who had authored the decision.[56] Tracing the various actions of this unholy Democratic triumvirate, Lincoln identified what in his view had been its calculated but carefully guarded intent: to pave the way for the unlimited expansion of slavery not only across the continent but into the Caribbean as well. By agreeing to delay announcement of the Supreme Court's decision until after Buchanan was safely elected, Lincoln charged, Taney and the new President had violated the separation of powers. Likening their machinations to "king-craft," Lincoln reminded his audience that the Revolutionary inheritance empowered Americans to overcome the oppressions wreaked by such corrupt alliances. The people would appeal the decision, he assured the crowd, and even amend the Constitution if necessary. Lincoln ridiculed Douglas for urging people instead to maintain strict obedience to the Constitution and the courts. Such thinking implied that the Founding Fathers had merely intended the Declaration of Independence to establish legal separation from Britain, that it had said nothing more than Americans would no longer be British. In fact, Lincoln insisted on this and other occasions, the Declaration had expressed the desire of Americans to no longer live as the British did, and it had held that desire up as an ideal to strive for constantly.[57]

Lincoln pursued these themes with more polished subtlety in his debates with Douglas the following summer and fall. Rather than harp on conspiracy, he pointed out the contradiction Douglas exhibited in advancing the notion of "popular sovereignty," which celebrated the right of settlers in the territories to decide whether slavery should be legal, while defending a Supreme Court decision that compelled them to decide in its favor. In many of his addresses Lincoln elaborated upon his notion of a "living" Declaration, often embellishing it in ways designed to cultivate new allegiances. Playing to a largely immigrant audience in Chicago, he pointed out that Douglas's legalistic interpretation of the Declaration and steadfast defense of constitutional principles created a static image of America that would exclude "you Germans." Later in the same speech he deftly appeased abolitionists by employing similar rhetoric to ridicule the idea that one could help blacks by

[56]   Commonly known as the "House Divided" speech, Lincoln delivered it in Springfield, June 16, 1858. The speech echoed themes Lincoln had expressed for at least a year, since his initial response to the Dred Scott decision, delivered in Springfield on June 26, 1857. As many historians have pointed out, politicians of the day routinely spoke of conspiracies, by which they generally meant that their opponents had failed to disclose their true motives. See Karen Halttunen, *Confidence Men and Painted Women: A Study of Middle-Class Culture in America, 1830–1870* (New Haven: Yale University Press, 1982).

[57]   Abraham Lincoln, "Speech in Response to the Dred Scott Decision," Springfield, June 26, 1857. If Douglas were right, Lincoln asked, why will we read the Declaration on the Fourth? For similar rhetoric, see speeches in reply to Senator Douglas given in Chicago, July 10, 1858, and in Springfield, July 17, 1858. On Lincoln and the Declaration, see Garry Wills, *Lincoln at Gettysburg: The Words That Remade America* (New York: Simon and Schuster, 1992).

enslaving them. Such arguments "are the arguments that kings have made for enslaving the people in all ages of the world. You will find that all the arguments in favor of king-craft were of this class; they always bestrode the necks of the people, not that they wanted to do it, but because the people were better off for being ridden. That is their argument, and this argument of the Judge is the same old serpent that says you work and I eat, you toil and I will enjoy the fruits of it." [58] A year later, after he had narrowly lost the Senate race and as he contemplated a run for the presidency, Lincoln found simpler terms with which to draw the connection. "*Equality*, in society, alike beats *inequality*," he scribbled to himself while preparing a speech in Ohio, "whether the latter be of the British aristocratic sort, or of the domestic slavery sort." [59]

In confronting Douglas in these terms, Lincoln was doing far more than proclaiming his moral opposition to slavery; he was also attacking the brand of political economy that slavery exemplified. His antagonism for slave-based societies, which stretched back to his youth, had only deepened during the booming 1850s. For the spectacular economic growth during that decade had drawn out in still sharper relief the features of those societies Lincoln found most objectionable. This was true not just in the jingoistic expansionism that increasingly characterized Southern political economy at the national level, but also in the political disputes over transport occurring within the Southern states themselves.

Southern Railroad Politics and Secession

On the surface, the economic boom of the 1850s seemed to draw Southern society toward the Whig ideal of diverse local commerce. In upstate South Carolina, where the arrival of the first railroads helped stimulate a decade-long surge in commercial activity, residents frequently described the changes taking place in their region as having "Yankee" overtones. Such comments referred not to the sources of capital and management of the new enterprises but to the character of the emerging society they fostered. [60] But the boom in the South actually differed in profound ways from that occurring in the Northeast. Rather than spark economic diversification, the new rail lines intensified the South's commitment to slave-based cotton monoculture. Cotton output in the South Carolina upcountry, for instance, more than doubled during the 1850s, as the worldwide surge in prices enticed large numbers of small farmers to convert from subsistence farming to staple production.

[58] Abraham Lincoln, "Speech in Response to Douglas," Chicago, July 10, 1858.
[59] Abraham Lincoln, "Fragment on Free Labor," September 17, 1859 (?).
[60] Lacy K. Ford, *Origins of Southern Radicalism: The South Carolina Upcountry, 1800–1860* (New York: Oxford University Press, 1988), p. 277. My discussion of events in South Carolina is based on this fine study. For a parallel treatment of Virginia railroad politics with particular relevance for this chapter, see Majewski, *A House Dividing*.

Railroads and new merchant enterprises, which were funded almost exclusively with capital from large planters, facilitated this transition by providing farmers with a much cheaper means of obtaining foodstuffs and tools from sources outside their immediate area. For upcountry residents who remained outside cotton's expanding orbit, however, opportunities shrank with the coming of the railroad. Ambitious ventures into textile manufacturing and iron production, launched with modest success during the prolonged slump of the 1840s, languished in the boomtimes of the 1850s as investors funneled capital into land, railroads, and slaves. As land prices more than doubled, the white population and the number of farms in the upcountry actually fell, with the greatest attrition occurring in the lower counties served by the railroads. White residents of the more mountainous areas did grow slightly more numerous during the forties and fifties. But these farmers and grazers remained largely insulated from the market, indifferent to private campaigns for internal improvements and hostile to government programs that might encourage them. Far from the engines of social cohesion that Lincoln imagined they could be, railroads in the slaveholding cotton regions of South Carolina thus imparted a new divisiveness into society and politics.[61]

Those tensions, moreover, involved more than mounting resentment among small farmers on the fringes of the cotton economy. Boosters of internal improvements also differed among themselves over the proper way to spend the limited funds available. Much of the squabbling amounted to little more than the customary bickering over routes that accompanied internal improvement programs everywhere. But in addition to these intramural disputes, advocates of internal improvements within the upcountry also faced competition from wealthy coastal merchants who entertained much grander visions.[62] Residents of Charleston massed their resources behind the proposed Blue Ridge Railroad, which promised ultimately to connect their Atlantic port with the Ohio River. To achieve this lofty objective the line would have to pass through the rugged mountains to the northwest, most of which lay outside the state. Construction plans called for a long tunnel within South Carolina and other extravagant feats of engineering that would drive per mile costs well above those of other proposed railroads. Though the Blue Ridge would traverse through the upcountry, planters there saw little reason to invest in such a risky interstate venture. Rivers already provided them with adequate transport to the Atlantic. Better to spend the money on

---

[61]   This course of events characterized the entire slave South during the 1850s. See Gavin Wright, *The Political Economy of the Cotton South* (New York: Norton, 1978) and *Old South, New South: Revolutions in the Southern Economy since the Civil War* (New York: Basic, 1986), esp. pp. 17–26.

[62]   On the links between coastal merchants and the plantation districts, see Eugene Genovese and Elizabeth Fox-Genovese, *Fruits of Merchant Capital* (New York: Oxford University Press, 1983).

a few modest east–west rail lines and spurs that would interconnect those natural waterways and create a web of transport in the upcountry.

Competition between these two visions of trade inevitably spilled into the realm of state politics, for with private capital so scarce, virtually anyone wishing to build a railroad must try to tap South Carolina's revolving trust for internal improvements. Upcountry areas, with their comparatively large white populations, might seem to have possessed an inherent advantage in the contest for state funds. But in actuality the reverse was true. Under an agreement dating from 1808, coastal parishes maintained a majority of votes in the state senate. Much of the upcountry population, moreover, saw little to gain from the railroads proposed for their region. Indeed, many poor whites may actually have harbored greater resentment toward supporters of those lines than they did toward advocates of a through route to distant Charleston. Upcountry boosters faced the additional difficulty of having to advance separate bills for each of their small projects, rather than a single comprehensive measure such as that which would subsidize the Blue Ridge Railroad. Their repeated petitions and continual efforts to forge alliances left upcountry legislators especially vulnerable to charges of corruption and cronyism, themes that always played well among an electorate quick to embrace Jefferson's dicta that the best government was that which governed least. Meanwhile coastal legislators, having secured well over $2 million in state aid for the Blue Ridge, could retreat to the comfort and protection of their populist rights–based philosophy of negative government. With the aid of another million from the city of Charleston, these apostles of laissez-faire managed to pour over $2.5 million of public funds into their aborted project while contributing only $53,000 of their own private capital. Boosters of the more numerous upcountry roads obtained less than a third of their $6 million in capital from public sources but were left shouldering the brunt of criticism for pursuing activist policies.[63]

Much the same situation prevailed to the southwest, in the frontier black belt state of Alabama, which had entered the Union as the slave-state companion to Lincoln's Illinois. The cotton boom pumped new vigor into Alabama's two most vibrant areas of staple cultivation, the Black Belt stretching across its midsection and the Tennessee River counties strung along its northern border. Ambitious proposals for banks and internal improvements surfaced, with planter capital and initiative taking the lead. Charles T. Pollard, a former Whig living in the Black Belt center of Montgomery, put in motion a complex set of ventures that would eventually have placed his town at the center of a radial network of rail lines. Residents of the Tennessee River valley pursued railroads that would supplement their existing water route. A third major proposal called for construction of a railroad cutting across the Black Belt along a southwest to northeast diagonal between the Alabama

[63] Ibid., pp. 228–230.

and Tennessee rivers. All three ventures emphasized internal development of an existing cotton district. Though the Pollard interests openly sought to construct a line to Pensacola on the Florida Gulf Coast in order to free Montgomery from its dependence upon Mobile, the major thrust of their radial plan was to transform their city into the focal point of a vast region of internal commerce. The first tracks laid linked Montgomery with the interior town of Columbus, Georgia. The developmental emphasis was still more apparent in the case of the Alabama and Tennessee rivers line. Its route lay entirely within Alabama's borders, with no connections to the outside except by transhipment to river vessels. Like many of the lines proposed for the South Carolina upcountry, it would cut across the natural flow of waterborne trade and create a transport web in the Black Belt.

Supporters of such ambitious schemes necessarily turned to government for assistance, and during the mid-fifties they achieved considerable success. In addition to receiving state funds, the Pollard group obtained a land grant of 400,000 acres from the federal government. To the chagrin of the Montgomeryites but in keeping with the Whig philosophy that more projects were the best protection against privilege, Congress authorized distribution of another 300,000 acres to a competitive railroad that would have run directly from Columbus to Mobile. Promoters of the Alabama and Tennessee rivers line fared even better. After an exhaustive lobbying effort, they received $200,000 from the state legislature and 640,000 acres from Congress. As the cotton boom flourished, Whiggish policies thus seemed to grow ever more prevalent, even though Alabama's Whig Party itself had nearly collapsed following the secession crisis of 1851.[64]

As in the case of South Carolina, however, the developmental agenda soon foundered in the face of popular resentment mobilized by urban merchant interests. The catalyst of this counterrevolution was John A. Winston, a planter-merchant who had struck it rich in the newly opened western part of the state during the 1840s before relocating to Mobile, where he operated a thriving brokerage business and regularly served as a representative to the state assembly. Winston exemplified the new breed of so-called Young Democrats. He combined a vigorous commercial outlook with an intense ideological commitment to the laissez-faire doctrines then popular in England. Such men tended to congregate in trading centers such as Mobile, and their enterprises often focused outward to the world of international commerce. During the early 1850s, a group of them invested heavily in the Mobile and Ohio Railroad. This line would stretch northward to the Ohio River, where it would connect with the tracks of the Illinois Central descending from Chicago (Fig. 1.3). Aside from the transcontinental railroad itself, virtually no proposed rail venture of the 1850s surpassed its ambitious

[64] This discussion of events in Alabama is based on Thornton, *Politics and Power,* esp. pp. 268–280.

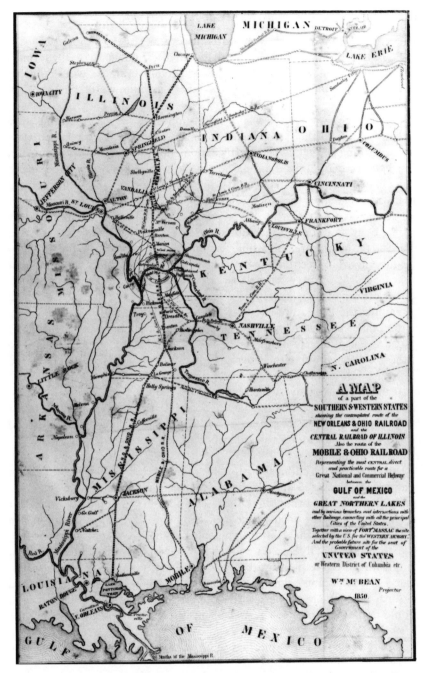

Figure 1.3. An 1850 promotional map projects the Mobile and Ohio Railroad linking with the Illinois Central, which branches into Chicago. The
caption identifies Fort Massac, where the railroad crosses the Ohio River, as
"the probable future site for the seat of Government of the United States."
Courtesy: Library of Congress.

reach. Yet when compared with more modest lines such as those proposed by Pollard, the road would have virtually no direct influence on the farmers and planters of Alabama. After departing Mobile its tracks would quickly swing westward into Mississippi; only sixty of its miles would pass through Alabama.

Like their counterparts in Charleston, supporters of this grand line from the Gulf Coast to the Great Lakes managed to suspend their laissez-faire principles long enough to secure substantial aid from the state government. The legislature authorized $400,000 for the sixty miles of the Mobile and Ohio. Having obtained what would prove to be by far the largest sum granted to any railroad enterprise by the state, the Mobile interests then used their political influence to frustrate the efforts of others who hoped to obtain state aid for their more developmental ventures. Dissatisfied with the course of affairs in the legislature, the Mobilites took their case directly to the people in the gubernatorial election of 1853. The flamboyant Winston, who had first gained public notoriety when he was exonerated in court after admitting to the murder of his wife's lover, conducted a raucous campaign in which he painted the legislature as a bastion of corruption and held himself up as the valiant protector of liberty. Upon assuming office, Winston promptly vetoed the legislatively approved subsidies to other routes and refused to authorize distribution of the federal land grants, while leaving the $400,000 for the Mobile and Ohio intact. These stances drew the ire of many planters but earned Winston overwhelming support among poor whites living on the fringes of the cotton regions. Other candidates quickly seized upon this latest variant of the Jacksonian political calculus. Young Democrats and others preaching hostility toward public support of internal improvements swept into office.

This fervently rejectionist version of politics, firmly rooted in Jacksonian traditions and directed initially toward the perennial issue of state aid, eventually proved itself a catalyst of radical secessionism.[65] The masses, with their negativist sentiments aroused, groped about for an enemy toward which they might channel their disillusionment. Lacking a coherent target within Alabama, they readily seized upon the message of the radical fireeaters who had identified the Republican Party as the supreme threat to liberty.[66] The 1860 election became a virtual referendum on whether Alabamians should perform the ultimate act of negative politics and withdraw from the Union should that enemy prove victorious. Winston himself headed the statewide

---

[65] Mills Thornton is surely correct when he calls the Civil War "the catastrophe of Jacksonian America, the denouement of the Jacksonian drama." Thornton, *Politics and Power*, p. xxi.

[66] The collapse of the Whig Party had created a void within Alabama politics, as it had throughout much of the country. On the importance of party breakdown to the coming of the Civil War, see Michael F. Holt, *The Political Crisis of the 1850s* (New York: Oxford University Press, 1978).

committee in support of Douglas. But the majority followed the sentiments Winston had uncorked to their logical extreme and chose Breckenridge, the candidate who most clearly signaled that secession would be the only appropriate response should Lincoln win. Three months later, when delegates to the state convention voted to secede, they drafted a constitution whose only significant new clauses prohibited virtually any type of governmental subsidy to business.

Lincoln and Generic American Inventive Genius

When Abraham Lincoln sought to brand Douglas and Buchanan as kingly aristocrats capable of orchestrating a conspiracy on behalf of a slave power, he thus had more in mind than the Dred Scott decision; he was doing something more than playing to deep-rooted popular anxieties about government corruption. Lincoln recognized in Douglas a brand of politics that he had spent his entire political life countering, with scarcely little success. Time and again Lincoln had seen his agenda and those of his heroes such as Henry Clay overwhelmed by politicians who played to populist sentiments for rapid expansion and limited government. War, "the most oppressive of all Kingly oppressions," had typically provided their most convenient rallying cry.[67] Now these men had substituted fanciful transportation and communications schemes for military campaigns.

For Lincoln, who had lived virtually all of his years at the crossroads of slavery and freedom on the expanding frontier, this brand of politics had always been joined most readily to the slave economy. But Lincoln understood that such politics thrived wherever wealth accumulated in the hands of people with no sustained ties to a particular place and where the vast majority of the electorate remained outside the sphere of economic activity that was the source of that wealth. The tumultuous events of the 1850s had brought these basic contours of society and politics into sharper relief than ever before throughout the United States, but nowhere more vividly than in the cotton South. Lincoln could not in his wildest imagination have devised a more colorful characterization of the phenomenon than John Winston. By highlighting the connections between Douglas and Southerners such as Winston and branding them all as merchant elites with ties to European aristocracy, Lincoln hoped to drive a wedge between the Democratic leadership and its mass constituency.[68] His own party would then offer the masses

[67] The comment comes from Lincoln's letter to William H. Herndon, February 15, 1848.

[68] James Oakes, *Slavery and Freedom: An Interpretation of the Old South* (New York: Knopf, 1990), has argued persuasively that the fervor over internal improvements in the slave states during the 1850s was no mere Southern gloss on a national phenomenon. By this he means that despite obvious similarities such as the importance of local rivalries and the reluctance to provide substantial direct aid, we cannot in the end comprehend the Southern debates over internal improvements apart from

easy access to a broad middle class, providing they accepted a measure of responsible government activism as the essential means to that end.

Lincoln brought these many themes together in a remarkable speech entitled "On Discoveries and Inventions," which he gave on several occasions in the winter of 1858–59. Anxious to keep himself in the public eye following his narrow defeat at the hands of Douglas, Lincoln had decided to try his lot at the professional speaking circuit rather than return to his law practice. For the first time in his life he prepared a speech for repeated delivery to paying audiences. Lincoln well understood, moreover, that this first extended statement since the previous summer's debates would mark a critical step in reestablishing himself with the public. Though sometimes dismissed as an inferior example of his prose, the speech reflects his considered opinion on the eve of his drive to the presidency.[69]

Lincoln began by lampooning the idea of Young America. Mimicking Douglas, he spoke as if Young America was an actual person. Lincoln denied Douglas's nation-man his youth, however, portraying him not as an aggressive young entrepreneurial builder but rather as an aging gentleman of leisure "with men, and things, everywhere, ministering unto him." (The verb "to minister," a favorite usage of Lincoln's, simultaneously conveyed an image of someone who expected devotion from others and raised the specter of European aristocracy and foreign officialdom.) Lincoln then launched into a brilliant satiric description of the finery that adorned this man:

> Look at his apparel, and you shall see cotton fabrics from Manchester and Lowell; flax-linen from Ireland; wood-cloth from Spain; silk from France; furs from the Arctic regions, with a buffalo-robe from the Rocky Mountains, as a general outsider. At his table, besides plain bread and meat made at home, are sugar from Louisiana; coffee and fruits from the tropics; salt from Turk's Island; fish from New-foundland; tea from China, and spices from the Indies. The Whale of the Pacific furnishes his candlelight; he has a diamond ring from Brazil; a gold-watch from California, and a Spanish cigar from Havanna. He not only has a present supply of all these, and much more; but thousands of hands are engaged in producing fresh supplies, and other thousands, in bringing them to him. The iron horse is panting, and impatient, to carry him everywhere, in no time; and the lightening [sic] stands ready harnessed to take and bring his tidings in a trifle less than no time.

the region's commitment to slavery. But Lincoln was surely also correct to see that debates over internal improvements outside the South contained elements similar to those that slavery imparted to the subject within it. For many Northern merchant capitalists shared the same essential vision as their slaveholding brethren in cities such as Mobile and Charleston. They sought large-scale railroads linking an international commercial empire.

[69] Lincoln, "Speech on Discoveries and Inventions," Jacksonville, Decatur, and Springfield, February 11, 1859. An exception who reads the speech as offering especially significant insight into Lincoln is J. David Greenstone, *The Lincoln Persuasion*, esp. pp. 278–280.

With a light hand, Lincoln had sketched the international economy, associated it repeatedly with ocean-going trade, branded its participants as decadent consumers living off the labors of anonymous "hands," and linked it to the transcontinental railroad and transatlantic telegraph. He then proceeded to ridicule the appetite of Young America for new land. "As Plato had for the immortality of the soul, so Young America has 'a pleasing hope – a fond desire – a longing after' territory. He has a great passion – a perfect rage – for the '*new*.'" Dripping with sarcasm, Lincoln described the source of Young America's hunger:

> He is a great friend of humanity; and his desire for land is not selfish, but merely an impulse to extend the area of freedom. He is very anxious to fight for the liberation of enslaved nations and colonies, provided, always, they *have* land, and have *not* any liking for his interference. As to those who have no land, and would be glad for help from any quarter, he considers, *they* can afford to wait a few hundred years longer.

Before leaving this ravenous beast in peace, Lincoln returned again to the metaphor of learning, discovery, and invention:

> In knowledge he is particularly rich. He knows all that can possibly be known; inclines to believe in spiritual rappings, and is the unquestioned inventor of "*Manifest Destiny*." His horror is for all that is old, particularly "Old Fogy"; if there be any thing old which he can endure, it is only old whiskey and old tobacco.

With characteristic deftness, Lincoln then shifted from humor to the most fundamental of principles. First he identified the skeptical Adam, resisting new pleasures in the Garden of Eden, as the original Old Fogy. Having thus laid claim to the Biblical human rights tradition, Lincoln quickly joined his subject to the Declaration of Independence. Free speech and liberty, he told the crowd, were the greatest of all inventions. By fostering "observation, reflection, and experiment," they served as the springboards for all creative acts. Nowhere, asserted Lincoln, had these qualities taken hold more firmly or permeated more deeply into the population than in the infant United States. Older societies created habits that suppressed or clouded the free thinking that gave rise to innovation. Lincoln drew out the contrast fully in a concluding passage that rings with the cadences and allusions of his address at Gettysburg four years later:

> It is difficult for us, *now* and *here*, to conceive how strong this slavery of the mind was; and how long it did, of necessity, take, to break its shackles, and to get a habit of freedom of thought, established. It is, in this connection, a curious fact that a new country is most favorable – almost necessary – to the immancipation of thought, and the consequent advancement of civilization and the arts.... We, here in America, *think* we discover, and invent, and improve, faster than any of [our predecessor nations]. *They* may think this arrogance; but they cannot deny that Russia has called on us to build steam-boats and railroads.... In anciently inhabited countries, the dust of ages – a real downright old-fogyism – seems to

settle upon, and smother the intellects and energies of man. It is in this view that I have mentioned the discovery of America as an event greatly favoring and facilitating useful discoveries and inventions.

Thus the genuine Young America lay not in some unrealized future but in the universal sustaining principles of the Declaration, and the path of progress that flowed from it could be found not in imported finery and grandiose projects, but in the simple generic inventions produced by ordinary citizens. These were the technologies most appropriate for a democratic nation of modest producers and freeholders, not the grand telegraphs and railroads that so captivated Douglas.

Lincoln and the Republicans harbored no illusions that such rhetoric would win them support in the South, at least in the short run. They did not even bother to place their ticket on the ballot in Alabama and other Black Belt states. For as long as slavery continued to expand, no politician could hope to win over the masses of Southern whites to the developmental vision. The Southern brand of internal improvement simply offered no inducements to the poor masses. Skewed toward cotton production and investments in slave capital, it failed to generate the economic diversification that might have drawn subsistence farmers and the landless more willingly into the labor market. Nothing demonstrated the predicament more clearly than the aborted attempts to exploit the rich mineral deposits of north-central Alabama. Despite extensive geological surveys and considerable boosterism during the 1850s, virtually no capital flowed into the region. At the time of secession Alabama manufacturing consisted almost entirely of sawmills, gristmills, and small artisanal enterprises such as blacksmithing.[70]

The situation would almost certainly change, virtually everyone sensed, if the South were denied access to additional lands. Escalating prices for land and slaves would further raise the threshold of entry into cotton culture, leaving mounting numbers of Southerners among the ranks of the hillcountry subsistence farmers or the landless. Capital then might shift into new economic endeavors in order to take advantage of the labor market, and the captive poor might accept such "dependent" positions as the best alternative. This scenario seemed likely enough that slaveholding ideologists developed an elaborate theory of "wage slavery," which posited that wage labor was as degrading and debilitating as slavery itself.[71] But even in the absence of such propaganda and the racist ideology that often accompanied

---

[70] Thornton, *Politics and Power*, pp. 278–280. On the failure to exploit mineral resources throughout the slave South, see Jonathan M. Wiener, *Social Origins of the New South* (Baton Rouge: Louisiana State University Press, 1978), and Wright, *Old South, New South*, pp. 27–29.

[71] Lincoln dismissed the idea of wage slavery with the simple observation that a wage system is motivated by hope, not the rod, and that this makes all the difference. Abraham Lincoln, "Fragment on Free Labor," September 17, 1859.

it, poor whites in the South had little reason to swallow the Republican medicine and accept confinement willingly. The passage from subsistence to small-scale commercial farming or wage labor would almost certainly involve considerable sacrifice in the short run. New Englanders had made the transition only under the duress of economic displacement caused by the Erie Canal.[72] Perhaps someday rural Southerners would reach the point where they, too, perceived greater integration into the market economy and the specialization it entailed as the best path to the ideal of self-improving citizenship Lincoln embraced so warmly. Lincoln himself held out hope that that day would dawn as soon as the slaveholding elite lost its grip on the region. As President, he would press for rapid reintegration of the South into the Union, so long as its leadership pledged to create a society free of slavery. But until such a social revolution occurred, one could expect non-slaveholding white Southerners to cast their lot with politicians promising unrestricted expansion and limited government, to the immediate benefit of commercial elites throughout the nation.

MIXED OUTCOMES: REPUBLICAN REVOLUTION AND EXTRACTIVE BOOM

Lincoln's startling victory in the presidential race of 1860 did indeed spark a socioeconomic revolution, though not precisely the one he had imagined. The established Southern leadership, sensing the threat to their long-term survival Lincoln presented, promptly withdrew from the Union, precipitating the Civil War. Republicans suddenly found themselves holding the reins of power in the midst of extraordinary social upheaval. Faced with the pressing task of conducting the war and enjoying a substantial majority in Congress, they embarked on a series of policies that significantly reoriented economic activity in every region. Aggregate statistics, which suggest the war actually interrupted the overall growth trends established during the boom of the late 1840s and 1850s, mask the startling shifts that occurred between regions and sectors. In reality, the war induced a huge transfer of wealth from the South to the North, primarily by destroying property in slaves. Across the North, moreover, significant new nodes of activity took hold, most noticeably in the heavy manufacturing sector of the East (now protected by high tariffs) and in the sprawling commercial agriculture of the prairie West (now opened to rapid settlement by the Homestead Act). Each of those nodes owed much of its prosperity to the continuing boom in railroad construction, which took a decided turn toward the North during the Republican heyday. Numerous

---

[72] The growth of manufacturing in Massachusetts occurred only after the opening of the Erie Canal had undercut the livelihood of farmers. See Goldin and Sokoloff, "Women, Children, and Industrialization."

new lines stretching across the expanding northern tier, many built with the aid of federal land grants, literally formed a bridge between the world of heavy industry and the booming agricultural sector.[73]

The precise character of these changes emerges most clearly by considering the dynamics of Western agriculture. Jeremy Atack, an economic historian who in general is quite skeptical of the notion that the war induced substantial growth or otherwise significantly altered the course of the American economy, notes that Northern prairie agriculture grew quite rapidly during the war and immediately after.[74] While impressive in size, that growth occurred without significant improvements in total factor productivity, the measure used by economists to relate output to the basic inputs of land, labor, and capital. In fact, farmers on the prairie used land quite profligately, adding little or no fertilizer and putting scant effort toward finding seed varieties that grew best in the prairie soil and climate. Even though many farmers benefited from the initial fertility obtained by breaking and cultivating virgin land, overall yields per acre in agriculture increased hardly at all. Growth came instead from bringing more land into cultivation and from using less labor per acre to do it. Those changes resulted from the increasing use of

---

[73] For an excellent summary of wartime developments in Northern economy and politics, see Phillip S. Paludan, *"A People's Contest": The Union and Civil War, 1861–1865* (New York: Harper and Row), pp. 85–197. On the emergence of the Midwest–Northeast Republican coalition and the continental economy, see James Livingston, *Pragmatism and the Political Economy of Cultural Revolution, 1850–1940* (Chapel Hill: University of North Carolina Press, 1994), pp. 24–40. Some argue that these developments may have occurred without the rise of the Republican Party and the Civil War. Political historians, for instance, point out that the surge of voters in the agricultural Midwest was well under way even before the Homestead Act, and that those voters helped propel Lincoln into the presidency. Yet Lincoln won with less than 40 percent of the popular vote, the smallest percentage ever. Republicans enlarged their base into a narrow national majority only after his election and the subsequent torturous adjustments of war and Reconstruction. The major policy measures that held the Republican coalition together – high tariffs, gold-backed paper currency, Negro suffrage, and the war itself – all occurred during the revolutionary period of diminished Southern representation. See Richard Franklin Bensel, *Yankee Leviathan: The Origins of Central State Authority in America, 1859–1877* (New York: Cambridge University Press, 1990). It is conceivable, as some economic historians point out, that those Republican policies merely diverted resources prematurely into otherwise unremunerative activities, creating a temporary distortion that steadily diminished with the passage of time. Railroads, coal, and Western agriculture, after all, would lead the economy into recession during the 1870s. Aside from an agricultural boom in California during the 1880s, these sectors failed to sustain the phenomenal returns of the Civil War era during the closing two decades of the century. Yet surely half a century is an enormous period of time for an economy to return to equilibrium. An awful lot of history can be made in the interim. For a useful summary of the many arguments about the economic effects of the war, see Atack and Passell, *New Economic View*, ch. 13.

[74] Atack and Passell, *New Economic View*, pp. 373 and 402–426.

heavy machinery, both directly in the form of agricultural implements and indirectly in the form of railroads that enabled farmers to reach more distant markets. Use of machinery soared with the wartime shortage of labor and with the increased demand for foodstuffs from soldiers and from workers in manufacturing. The lands opened during the war reinforced the trend, because machinery worked most effectively on large plots of flat prairie such as those made available by the railroads receiving federal land grants. Returns on capital invested in agriculture, already a healthy 8.5 percent during the 1850s, jumped to 10.1 percent in the 1860s and to a remarkable 13.4 percent during the 1870s, despite devastation of the highly profitable Southern plantation sector. Capital devoted to annual production of staple crops, rather than held as livestock or real estate, generated the largest returns, especially during the wartime decade of the 1860s.[75]

While those returns flowed in large part from the comparative advantages derived from applying machinery to vast tracts of land, Midwestern farmers could not have capitalized fully on those advantages without improvements in rail transportation that gave them ready access to world markets. Spurred in part by generous federal land grants, Midwesterners engaged in feverish competition to build rail lines in their region. By 1871, grain and livestock might arrive in Chicago via any of four lines from Iowa alone. Meanwhile, established railroads in the East cobbled together through lines connecting the Windy City with the Atlantic. Before the Civil War, 90 percent of the grain traveling eastward from Chicago went by ship; after it, the percentage shipped by rail seldom fell below 50, even though lake rates were generally 15 to 20 percent lower than rail rates except during peak harvest season.[76] For a few years shortly after the return to peace, Midwestern grain farmers enjoyed a glorious heyday when the cost of transporting grain from Chicago to London actually fell well below the difference in price between the two locations. Since the cost of shipping across the Atlantic actually remained slightly higher than the price difference between New York and London, Chicago gained this advantageous position because of the several through rail lines that now stretched across the Old Northwest to East Coast ports. Not surprisingly, large quantities of Midwestern grain soon flowed into Europe, helping spark further European investment in Western railroads. Such swings in price differentials between the major grain markets gradually diminished as the transport network grew more routinized, so that by the mid-1870s price differences corresponded almost precisely with transport charges. But prices remained highly volatile during the hectic period when railroads were still assembling their machines, and individuals with a speculative bent could

---

75 Robert W. Fogel and Jack Rutner, "The Efficiency Effects of Federal Land Policy, 1850–1900," in William Aydelotte et al., eds., *Dimensions of Quantitative Research in History* (Princeton: Princeton University Press, 1972), pp. 390–418.

76 Cronon, *Nature's Metropolis*, p. 87.

make small fortunes by holding grain and playing the swings in price to their advantage.[77] Not surprisingly, grain elevator operators and futures traders became ready targets of criticism from the legions of farmers for whom the swings in price often produced less fortunate results. Complaints mounted, too, from those who failed to obtain adequate rail services, either because a promised line failed to materialize or because an established one charged rates that customers lacking alternative outlets considered excessive.[78]

Something of the same story held true in the second great cluster of extractive enterprises in the Northern economy, the coal and steel complex centered around the state of Pennsylvania. As in the case of Western agriculture, ripples of change in these sectors had appeared before the war, as producers in Philadelphia and New York learned to utilize the anthracite coal found in eastern Pennsylvania.[79] During the war and the subsequent decade, the metal trades continued to grow at a spectacular pace while also reorienting their activities around new products, processes, and materials. Riding the demand of the railroad industry and benefiting as well from demand for producers' goods such as agricultural machinery, the metal producers and machine builders grew so rapidly that overall growth trends in manufacturing had resumed their prewar levels within a decade of the conflict, despite the extraordinary disruptions caused by the war in many branches of manufacturing.[80] Though much of their wartime output itself was destroyed by the war, the metals industries went through a vital learning process. Firms and workers developed new techniques not only in the production of metals, but also in the fabrication of machine tools, locomotives, and other essential components of heavy industry. The steel industry, compelled by demand for stronger rails from lines heavily burdened by wartime transport, took its first steps toward utilizing the Bessemer process. Producers and fabricators alike also gradually mastered the complexities of using the soft bituminous coal found west of the Alleghenies and made available by construction of new rail lines. With the wartime Congress, moreover, the metal industries at last secured the tariffs that would give them an opportunity to sustain such learning long after the war ended. As in the case of agriculture, these changes did not

---

77   C. Knick Harley, "Transportation, the World Wheat Trade, and the Kuznets Cycle, 1850–1913," *Explorations in Economic History* 17 (1980): 218–250, and Morton Rothstein, "America in the International Rivalry for the British Wheat Market, 1860–1914," *Mississippi Valley Historical Review* 47 (1960): 401–418.

78   Cronon, *Nature's Metropolis*, pp. 120–142, and George H. Miller, *Railroads and the Granger Laws* (Madison: University of Wisconsin Press, 1971). For an especially insightful treatment of the turn from promotion to resentment in one Western state, see William Deverell, *Railroad Crossing: Californians and the Railroad, 1850–1910* (Berkeley: University of California Press, 1994), chs. 1 and 2.

79   Chandler, "Anthracite."

80   Stephen Salsbury, "The Effect of the Civil War on American Industrial Development," in Ralph Andreano, ed., *The Economic Impact of the American Civil War* (Cambridge, Mass.: Schenkman, 1962), pp. 161–168.

immediately provide significant improvements in total factor productivity. The industries routinely used materials wastefully and no doubt suffered serious setbacks in the course of learning new techniques. Growth resulted largely from mobilizing increasing amounts of capital toward equipment that extracted, transported, and processed raw materials with less labor. Railroads themselves may well have been the most important piece of equipment in that endeavor.[81]

These tumultuous economic changes occurring across the northern tier of states produced a world that Abraham Lincoln could not have anticipated and would not have fully approved. The extractive economy was a complex hybrid of the one Lincoln had envisioned and those he had opposed. On the positive side, that economy operated exclusively on free labor. It included small farmers subsidized by government land policies and manufacturers protected by higher tariffs, which in turn diminished trade in goods manufactured abroad and to a degree undermined what Lincoln considered the corrosive influence of international merchants. Much of this fit the old Whig ideals of an ordered internal commerce among small proprietors. Now, however, the bonds of mutual dependence operated on a continental scale. Midwestern farmers and Eastern manufacturers interacted across vast distances through impersonal networks of commerce and through an increasingly strained political alliance in the national Republican party. For rather than endlessly replicating itself in small communities capable of nurturing a more diverse range of activities, American society had with the aid of the railroads reconstructed itself as an internally focused empire, with vast regions concentrating much of their energies on certain types of enterprise.[82]

The country could still justly be described as an agricultural republic. In 1880, even in the North well over four out of ten Americans still lived on farms, and agricultural products accounted for some 47 percent of economic output from the region.[83] But the nature of agricultural production differed markedly from the image of the sturdy yeomen settlers engaged in local commerce and improvement that Lincoln likely imagined. The Western farmers who swelled the ranks of the Republican Party had in many respects come to resemble the slaveholding cotton growers of the antebellum South more closely than the subsistence-oriented small farmers of the North. Most Westerners concentrated their energies on growing staple commodities to be sold in distant markets. They earned their returns primarily by turning virgin soil, not by fertilizing or enriching it. They moved frequently, yet gleaned only a small proportion of their profits from appreciating land values. And though they invested in machinery rather than slaves, Western farmers utilized comparatively large amounts of capital. Some of the most widely celebrated

---

[81] Abramowitz, "Search for the Sources of Growth."
[82] Livingston, *Pragmatism*, aptly characterizes the new economy as "continental industrialization."
[83] Atack and Passell, *New Economic View*, p. 402.

agricultural ventures, such as the wheat farms of Minnesota's Red River Valley, operated on a scale and with a degree of organization that surpassed those of the largest antebellum cotton and rice plantations.[84]

In the old agricultural empire of the South itself, meanwhile, considerable change ran against the trends toward concentrated, capital-intensive production.[85] With the end of slavery, agriculture shifted dramatically toward smaller units of production, as freedmen and upcountry whites alike quickly entered into sharecropping agreements. Though the new arrangements often tied indebted producers to landholders and merchant creditors, they drew far more Southerners than ever before into the nexus of trade. Local commercial activity and land development occurred on a scale not previously experienced in the South, as capitalists acted as landlords rather than laborlords.[86] Small inland railroad crossroads such as Atlanta, Birmingham and Chattanooga, having acquired new prominence during the war as the Confederacy struggled to supply armies located on its periphery with food and munitions, grew rapidly with the return to peace. New rail lines, some initially built and operated by invading Union soldiers, connected these warehousing and manufacturing centers in the deep South with emergent urban centers to the north such as Richmond and Nashville. Groups of financiers associated with the Pennsylvania Railroad and the Baltimore and Ohio competed to secure through routes from the upcountry to outlets in the Northeast, while ambitious Southern investors looked to send goods overland to emergent ports on the coast of Virginia. Even merchants in Charleston and Mobile, seeing their opulent coastal trading centers stagnating with loss of the trade in slaves and cotton, now invested in enterprises located along the railroad corridor running from southwest to northeast along the Piedmont.[87]

Yet if the war initiated something of the transformation Lincoln had imagined with the end of slavery, change in the South remained circumscribed by customs of culture and commerce. Though the various sharecropping arrangements provided African-Americans with considerably more autonomy than they had possessed under slavery, the region's commitment to producing cotton for a depressed world market undercut much of their gains. Declining prices saddled all sharecroppers with persistently disappointing returns

---

[84] Bruchey, *Enterprise*, pp. 294–295.

[85] This statement considers slaves to have been a form of capital.

[86] The usage is that of Wright, *Old South, New South*, ch. 2. On Southern agriculture after the war, see also Atack and Passell, *New Economic View*, pp. 376–401.

[87] Don H. Doyle, *New Men, New Cities, New South: Atlanta, Nashville, Charleston, Mobile, 1860–1910* (Chapel Hill: University of North Carolina Press, 1990); Russell Duncan, *Entrepreneur for Equality: Governor Rufus Bullock, Commerce, and Race in Post–Civil War Georgia* (Athens: University of Georgia Press, 1994); and Mark Wahlgren Summers, *Railroads, Reconstruction, and the Gospel of Prosperity: Aid under the Radical Republicans, 1865–1877* (Princeton: Princeton University Press, 1984).

and locked many into a cycle of debt. Virulent racism plagued Southern politics, creating problems for railroad promoters who, like their counterparts in the West, already faced considerable resistance from local interests who resented the transformations their enterprises wrought or who wished to capture more of the returns for themselves. Republican Governor Rufus Bullock of Georgia, who had come South as agent for Adams Express just prior to the war and along with fellow entrepreneur Hannibal I. Kimball had pursued a vigorous program of state-supported railroad building radiating from Atlanta, fled both his office and the state when angry white Democrats took control of the statehouse in 1871. Klansmen loosed their venom upon emergent railroading centers such as Alamance County, North Carolina. Brandishing hickory sticks in honor of Andrew Jackson, they clubbed black railroad workers and their white sympathizers.[88] While such attacks failed to stop the rapid reorientation of the Southern economy entirely, they undercut racial harmony, consigned freedmen to a distinctly inferior social status, stemmed the flow of outside capital, and impeded cultural and economic integration with other regions. For decades to come, the South remained economically isolated from the North and West, a low-wage region in a high-wage nation.[89]

The rapidly growing Northern manufacturing sector might have provided Lincoln some measure of consolation. Tariffs had curbed imports, enabling artisans in established domestic trades to flourish while others gained footholds in emergent infant industries. Yet here, too, Lincoln would have found ample cause for concern. For amidst the many small artisanal workshops had sprouted a few enterprises of a far different character. John D. Rockefeller's oil refineries at Cleveland and Andrew Carnegie's steel works at Pittsburgh operated on a scale that few could have imagined in 1860. These enterprises imposed a degree of concentration over their vital young industries that far surpassed anything prevailing in Europe. The steel industry of the United States, with just thirteen plants operating twenty-seven Bessemer converters, produced nearly as much steel as Great Britain, which had well over a hundred converters.[90] Such highly concentrated enterprises necessarily looked toward distant markets, thus driving the course of economic development still further away from local concerns and steering discussions of economic policy toward matters such as tariffs and finance. The spectacular wealth those enterprises generated for their owners, moreover, fostered just the sort of fascination with opulence that Lincoln had lampooned in his debates with Douglas.

[88]   Duncan, *Entrepreneur for Equality*, and Scott Reynolds Nelson, *Iron Confederacies: Southern Railways, Klan Violence, and Reconstruction* (Chapel Hill: University of North Carolina Press, 1999).

[89]   The phrase is again from Wright, *Old South, New South*.

[90]   Elting E. Morison, *Men, Machines, and Modern Times* (Cambridge, Mass.: MIT Press, 1966), p. 184.

Despite the growing prominence of these giant enterprises and the speculative fervor they helped encourage, the economy of the postwar decade did fit the Whig middle class ideal in one important respect: It was dominated by proprietorships. Family farms remained overwhelmingly the most common unit of economic organization. Most manufactured goods were still produced by artisans in workshops of modest size and sold through jobbers and small stores run by independent merchants. Virtually no brands had yet established a national identity, and chain retailers such as Montgomery Ward and Sears, Roebuck had only just made their appearance. Even the few large enterprises that had recently arisen in the processing industries were wholly owned by their proprietors. Men such as Carnegie and Rockefeller resembled overblown local barons, ensconced in mansions perched atop the highest points in town, overseeing their personal fiefdoms and spouting aphorisms about the virtues of hard work and personal character. They personally never absorbed the faceless bureaucratic ethic of the corporate order their enterprises ultimately did so much to create.[91]

The only significant corporate enterprises in the United States of the 1870s were the railroads themselves. As such, they occupied a far different place in society than corporations of a later era. Citizens and courts still held railroads to be unique creations of the commonweal, operating in the public purpose under special charters that conveyed specific privileges and in return carried certain obligations. The day of general incorporation laws and statutory regulation lay in the future, and with them the clear sense of separation between ownership and control that would become the hallmark of corporate capitalism.[92] Most of the public still entrusted railroad managers to act with a sense of benevolent stewardship. The great scandals of the Grant administration were widely interpreted as the product of a few corrupted souls rather than as a signal that government might need to maintain closer supervision over the magnificent spoils it had created.[93] When Charles Francis Adams, Jr.,

---

[91] On the proprietary character of late-nineteenth-century enterprise, see Louis Galambos and Joseph Pratt, *The Rise of the Corporate Commonwealth: United States Business and Public Policy in the Twentieth Century* (New York: Basic, 1988), ch. 2. On Carnegie, see Joseph Frazier Wall, *Andrew Carnegie* (New York: Oxford University Press, 1970), and Harold Livesay, *Andrew Carnegie and the Rise of Big Business* (Boston: Little, Brown, 1975). On Rockefeller, see Ron Chernow, *Titan: The Life of John D. Rockefeller, Sr.* (New York: Random House, 1998).

[92] Thomas K. McCraw, *Prophets of Regulation* (Cambridge, Mass.: Harvard University Press, 1984).

[93] Ari Hoogenboom, "Did Gilded Age Scandals Bring Reform?," in Abraham S. Eisenstadt, Ari Hoogenboom, and Hans L. Trefousse, eds., *Before Watergate: Problems of Corruption in American Society* (Brooklyn: Brooklyn College Press, 1978), pp. 125–142; Morton Keller, "Corruption in America: Continuity and Change," in Eisenstadt et al., eds., *Before Watergate*, pp. 7–19; Wallace D. Farnham," 'The Weakened Spring of Government': A Study in Nineteenth-Century American History," *American Historical Review* 68 (1963): 662–680; and McCormick, *Party Period*, chs. 6 and 9.

and his brother Henry published *Chapters of Erie*, their famous expose on the financial collapse of the Erie Railroad in 1871, they laid the blame on the speculative excesses of its financiers and board of directors. These young Brahmins, grandsons of John Quincy Adams and children of the man who had served Abraham Lincoln as ambassador to Great Britain, could not yet confront their world as a product of impersonal systemic forces.[94]

Such reluctance to adjust policies and expectations in the face of extraordinary change betrayed a fundamental feature of American society as the United States approached its centennial. During the previous three decades the nation had experienced a remarkable transformation, passing, as historian John Higham once put it, "from boundlessness to consolidation."[95] Yet most of its citizens remained locked in an earlier frame of reference. Of all the world's developed capitalist nations, the United States was the least inclined to construct instruments of government capable of confronting the new reality. Having briefly assembled a set of policies that generated a boom in railroad construction of virtually unmatched proportions, Americans in most regions remained unwilling to grant government agencies the power necessary to monitor the institutions that resulted. Government at virtually every level and in almost every locale remained firmly joined to party politics, a mechanism that had evolved to distribute spoils, not to administer to the results. Nor had the events of midcentury done anything to erode the virulent sectionalism that had long worked to undercut efforts to build administrative capacities at the national level.[96]

These features of American society and politics corresponded in many ways with conditions prevailing among the railroads themselves. Though railroads stood out at the time of the centennial as giant enterprises, they did not yet exhibit the highly bureaucratized character or the refined administrative expertise that would become their hallmarks during the closing decades of the nineteenth century. Most lines remained firmly tied to the developmental agenda, in which the largest returns came from mobilizing

---

94　Charles Francis Adams, Jr., and Henry Adams, *Chapters of Erie and Other Essays* (Boston, 1871); McCormick, *Party Period*, pp. 325–326; Edward Chase Kirkland, *Charles Francis Adams, Jr., 1835–1915: The Patrician at Bay* (Cambridge, Mass.: Harvard University Press, 1965); McCraw, *Prophets of Regulation*, ch. 1.

95　John Higham, *From Boundlessness to Consolidation: The Transformation of American Culture, 1848–1860* (Ann Arbor: William L. Clements Library, 1969).

96　Morton Keller, *Affairs of State: Public Life in Late Nineteenth Century America* (Cambridge, Mass.: Harvard University Press, 1977); Stephen Skowronek, *Building a New American State: The Expansion of National Administrative Capacities, 1877–1920* (New York: Cambridge University Press, 1982); McCormick, *Party Period*; and Bensel, *Yankee Leviathan*. On the enduring impediment sectionalism posed to the development of national administrative capabilities, see David M. Potter, *The South and the Concurrent Majority* (Baton Rouge: Louisiana State University Press, 1972), and Richard Franklin Bensel, *Sectionalism and American Political Development, 1880–1980* (Madison: University of Wisconsin Press, 1984).

capital toward real estate and ancillary activities that sprouted along new routes. The war-induced boom had superheated that endeavor, expanding its scale and channeling investments toward lucrative extractive enterprises such as stockyards, steel mills, and mines. But in the context of the world economy, American railroads stood out as they always had, as significantly undercapitalized facilities built quickly and cheaply and operated recklessly. Railroading practices and railroading technology, as we see in the chapters to follow, thus reflected the unique blend of opportunities presented by American political economy to foster certain styles of development, just as they had when Abraham Lincoln first entered politics some thirty years before.

2

Acquiring Technology:
Insider Innovation

Throughout this tumultuous developmental period, American railroads possessed little of the ordered, systematic character that would later become their hallmark. The early lines were essentially grand experiments. Their founders took a new, European invention – the combination of steam locomotive, fixed rails, and a train of carriages or wagons – and scrambled to adapt it to different sets of conditions.[1] Short on capital and labor, with long stretches of sparsely settled territory to cross and a comparatively weak industrial base on which to draw, these early builders constructed serviceable prototypes of what would eventually emerge as a distinctly American style of railroad. Though railroads stood out in the context of the American economy as highly capitalized institutions of great technical complexity, in comparison to railroads in other countries they appeared shoddy and underbuilt (Fig. 2.1).[2] To European eyes, the American lines were primitive affairs, built quickly and cheaply and operated with insufficient care. A delegation of European technicians who visited the United States on the eve of the New York Crystal Palace Exhibition of 1853 gave the railroads little more than a passing mention in their reports.[3] Though the Civil War pumped new

---

[1] Thomas Parke Hughes, "A Technological Frontier: The Railway," in Bruce Mazlish, ed., *The Railroad and the Space Program: An Exploration in Historical Analogy* (Cambridge, Mass.: MIT Press, 1965), pp. 53–73.

[2] One authority aptly characterizes the entire antebellum period as "still an era of railroad infancy, both in magnitude and technology." Albert Fishlow, *American Railroads and the Transformation of the Ante-Bellum Economy* (Cambridge, Mass.: Harvard University Press, 1965), p. 13. For a classic treatment emphasizing the slipshod character of early American transport, including railroads, see Daniel S. Boorstin, *The Americans: The National Experience* (New York: Random House, 1965), pp. 97–107.

[3] Nathan Rosenberg, ed., *The American System of Manufactures: The Report of the Committee on the Machinery of the United States 1855, and the Special Reports*

Figure 2.1. Hanover Junction, Pennsylvania, c. 1860. Such lightweight rails and equipment were characteristic of American railroading during its early decades. *Courtesy*: Library of Congress.

resources into railroading and imparted a new emphasis in some quarters on handling traffic efficiently, the conflict in many ways accentuated the slipshod character of the industry. New subsidized railroads emerged rapidly in the remote West, while war-ravaged established firms such the Pennsylvania and the B&O underwent continual hasty repair and scrambled to secure links with the upstarts.

Though these pioneering lines may have appeared primitive to many observers, the task of acquiring technologies and assembling the first machines posed an enormous challenge. Even the most modest of railroads constituted a technical assembly of virtually unparalleled complexity in its day. The rail itself, a seemingly simple item, continually taxed the capabilities of the American iron and steel industry. Those rails crossed bridges and entered stations that were widely celebrated as marvels in structural engineering. Over them passed a stunning array of cars built to steadily increasing dimension, each assembled from numerous components and in some cases embellished with devices intended to provide comforts found only in the most luxurious settings. Linked by couplers of rugged yet intricate design and later by hoses

of George Wallis and Joseph Whitworth 1854 (Edinburgh: Edinburgh University Press, 1969).

used to operate sophisticated air brakes, the cars were attached to one of the most complex and emotion-inspiring mechanical assemblages ever devised, the steam locomotive. Built and maintained by shopworkers and skilled mechanics who formed the "high-tech" community of the nineteenth century, locomotives came in a wide variety of designs and incorporated refinements that enabled them to grow not just heavier but proportionally more powerful. The trains pulled by these behemoths moved through the rail network governed by signals and switches that remained at the frontiers of innovation in electromechanical equipment for half a century.

The managers charged with assembling these complex machines in forms appropriate for their particular locales could draw on a wide variety of sources. The machine shops and other maintenance facilities located at periodic intervals along their lines provided an invaluable source of knowledge and techniques. In addition to repairing a wide array of motive power, rolling stock, and other equipment, the skilled machinists and shopworkers in many of these facilities could, if necessary, build entire locomotives and cars from scratch. Some shops operated their own foundries, giving railroads direct access to the frequently mysterious and rapidly evolving world of metallurgy.[4] Management had much to learn as well from the engineers and firemen who drove the locomotives, for these men retained considerable discretion over the outfitting and operation of their assigned equipment.[5] The reservoir of potential techniques extended well beyond the railroads' own employment rolls, as any number of supply businesses grew up to service the needs of the industry.[6] A handful of locomotive builders, led by the substantial works of Baldwin and American, supplied motive power to many lines.[7] Passenger cars came from a variety of sources, most notably the palace car works of George Pullman. In addition to these sources that dedicated their entire energies to the railroads, the industry also enjoyed the benefits of several technical efforts of a more general character. The iron and steel industry, which developed in close association with the railroads, continued to lean heavily on their demand throughout the period under study.[8] Producers of lubricants, paints, fuels, and numerous other commodities likewise found vibrant markets in the railroad industry. With their complex yet readily accessible facilities and their sizable potential demand, railroads also

---

4 On early railroad machine shops, see Fishlow, *American Railroads*, pp. 130–131 and 149–155.
5 Walter Licht, *Working for the Railroad: The Organization of Work in the Nineteenth Century* (Princeton: Princeton University Press, 1983).
6 Glenn Porter and Harold C. Livesay, *Merchants and Manufacturers: Studies in the Changing Structure of Nineteenth-Century Marketing* (Baltimore: Johns Hopkins University Press, 1971), chs. 5 and 6.
7 John K. Brown, *The Baldwin Locomotive Works, 1831–1915* (Baltimore: Johns Hopkins University Press, 1995).
8 Peter Temin, *Iron and Steel in Nineteenth Century America: An Economic Inquiry* (Cambridge, Mass.: MIT Press, 1964).

tantalized the community of independent inventors, and the ledgers of the patent office swelled with devices invented for their use.[9]

The task of surveying this sea of techniques and assembling a railroad appropriate for the particular locale usually fell to a small cadre of managers at the highest levels of each line.[10] Often boards of directors took an active hand in arranging contracts for equipment such as cars, locomotives, rails, and even individual devices such as brakes and couplers. As engines of development and providers of an essential service, railroads in many cases cultivated unusually close relationships with suppliers. Exchanges commonly involved capital investment and transport as well as the purchase of goods, and deals frequently worked to the direct financial benefit of the managers themselves. Eager to capitalize on such opportunities and to reap the large returns made possible by joining the basic technology of railroading with lucrative extractive enterprises, these managers typically cared far more about securing reliable sources of supply than about obtaining the latest untried devices. Few formal mechanisms for monitoring and selecting new technology existed, and changes took place in a highly informal and frequently idiosyncratic manner. Experiment and analysis occurred sporadically, usually in direct response to specific crises, and generally took the form of discrete trials. Executives directed few resources toward sustained technical refinement or toward undertaking thorough changes in procedure that might yield improvements in productivity.[11]

While choices of technologies often reflected immediate local concerns and opportunities, a spirit of shared adventure prevailed as railroad executives groped their way toward assembling the individual machines. Technical personnel moved readily from one firm to another, and lines shared information widely. Critical modifications to the European technology, such as the swing truck designed by John Jervis to help locomotives negotiate the tight curves common on America's mountainous routes, diffused freely through the industry.[12] Competition among lines focused overwhelmingly on the race to raise capital, extend lines westward, and develop vibrant commerce and enterprise in the territory served. Even in the comparatively infrequent circumstances when railroads competed directly for traffic between the same

[9] See Chapter 3.
[10] On the acquisition of technology during the early decades of railroading at one line, see Stephen Salsbury, *The State, the Investor, and the Railroad: The Boston and Albany, 1825–1867* (Cambridge, Mass.: Harvard University Press, 1967), esp. pp. 82, 106–109, 175–178, 190–192, 235, 262–263, and 272–273.
[11] These assessments, developed more fully below, bear some resemblance to those put forth in the pioneering analysis of Thomas C. Cochran, *Railroad Leaders, 1845–1890: The Business Mind in Action* (Cambridge, Mass.: Harvard University Press, 1953), pp. 141–148.
[12] Elting E. Morison, *From Know-How to Nowhere: The Development of American Technology* (New York: Basic, 1974), pp. 40–71, and Boorstin, *The National Experience*, pp. 105–106.

cities, managers did not perceive breakthrough technologies or a stream of lesser innovations as likely avenues for gaining significant competitive advantage. One needed to build a sturdy line, run it smoothly, and strike wise deals with customers, not monopolize new techniques. These sensibilities pervaded the industry virtually from the start, imparting to railroading a strong dose of conservatism and skepticism regarding new technology even as it pressed against the frontiers of American technical capabilities.[13]

Technical change in these circumstances occurred through diverse channels and processes that might best be characterized, to borrow a phrase from historian Naomi Lamoreaux, as "insider innovation."[14] Though we can detect elements of a vibrant market for railroad technology, with individual managers uniquely configuring their isolated systems using elements selected from a variety of sources, several factors distorted the workings of those market mechanisms. The course of innovation in the industry depended to a considerable degree upon the personalities of key railroad executives and their technical assistants, whose choices often reflected a mix of motives that went beyond mere technical accomplishment. As the case of steel rails examined in this chapter demonstrates, we cannot fully comprehend the path of change without considering the role of local circumstances and personality, including an ability to capitalize on opportunities to promote industrial development. While individual managers could exert substantial influence in particular cases, with their willingness to cooperate on technical matters and their substantial in-house expertise, railroads could also coordinate actions in ways that undercut the opportunities for inventors to sell their products on the open market. These features of technical change become apparent in the following chapter, which examines in detail how railroads interacted with inventors and the patent system.

PERSONAL PREFERENCES, TRUSTED EXPERTS

Arrangements at the Pennsylvania Railroad, which can be traced through the minutes of its board of directors, clearly reveal the personal nature of

[13] "Nineteenth-century American locomotive building was distinguished by conservatism," notes the foremost authority on the subject. "The understandable tendency to retain successful designs should be regarded as an intelligent conservatism." John H. White, Jr., *American Locomotives: An Engineering History, 1830–1880* (Baltimore: Johns Hopkins University Press, 1968), pp. 4–5. "Lest any false impressions be made," White then cautioned, "it should be emphasized that while no revolution in basic locomotive design was tolerated, the nineteenth century was alive with experiment."

[14] The phrase comes from Naomi Lamoreaux, *Insider Lending: Banks, Personal Connections, and Economic Development in Industrial New England* (Cambridge: Cambridge University Press and NBER, 1996), which emphasizes the importance of kinship ties and other close relations in the early-nineteenth-century economy.

decisions regarding technology during the middle decades of the nineteenth century. As the directors contemplated their first significant building spree in April 1847, they proposed to place responsibility in the hands of a chief engineer and two associates, each of whom would take charge of one of two divisions. The board filled the three positions, paying salaries of $3,000 to the associates and $4,000 to the chief engineer. This latter post fell to J. Edgar Thomson, veteran of the Georgia State Railroad and several other early civil engineering works. Before accepting the Pennsylvania's offer, Thomson insisted he have full responsibility for all hiring and firing, including the associate engineers. Early the following year, Thomson installed his friend and previous associate Herman Haupt in the new position of principal assistant engineer. Several months into his tenure, Thomson also had the procedures for allocating contracts altered, so that he rather than the board would enter all contracts subsequent to those covering initial construction of the road. In May 1848, the board gave him permission to draw up to $10,000 directly from the treasury at any time, without specific authorization.[15]

These arrangements gave Thomson great latitude in choosing equipment for the line. In April 1848, he personally arranged the purchase of the first seventy-five freight cars for $5,000, and for several years thereafter the board appears to have acted routinely on his advice when obtaining additional rolling stock.[16] The same procedures held true in the case of motive power. Between 1848 and early 1851 Thomson placed orders with a variety of locomotive manufacturers. From the start, he showed a strong preference for the machines made by the firm of Matthias Baldwin in Philadelphia, which received orders for eight locomotives in early 1850 and for another ten in early 1851.[17]

With this latter contract, which Thomson later explained he had entered verbally "during his visit to the seashore last summer," Thomson apparently overstepped his bounds. The board took the extraordinary measure of noting in its minutes that Thomson had acted even though it "had not authorized the

---

[15] Pennsylvania Railroad, Minutes of the Board of Directors (hereafter, PRR Board Minutes), vol. 1, April 9 and 28, September 8, and October 13, 1847; January 12 and May 10, 1848. These minutes are available in microform at the Hagley Museum and Library, Wilmington, Delaware. On Thomson, see James A. Ward, *J. Edgar Thomson: Master of the Pennsylvania* (Westport, Conn.: Greenwood Press, 1980). On the Pennsylvania, see George H. Burgess and Miles C. Kennedy, *Centennial History of the Pennsylvania Railroad Company, 1846–1946* (Philadelphia: Pennsylvania Railroad Company, 1949).

[16] PRR Board Minutes, April 5 and 26, 1848; January 30, 1850 (vol. 1, p. 246); May 23, 1850 (vol. 1, p. 288); and May 29, 1850 (vol. 1, p. 289).

[17] PRR Board Minutes, September 27, 1848 (vol. 1, pp. 118–119); October 18, 1848 (vol. 1, p. 121); April 18, 1849 (vol. 1, p.165); January 30, 1850 (vol. 1, p. 246), February 20, 1850 (vol. 1, p. 256); April 30, 1851 (vol. 1, p. 431). Burgess and Kennedy claim that twenty-three of the twenty-six locomotives purchased by the Pennsylvania in 1849–50 came from Baldwin, with the other three coming from Norris. They also claim the railroad first turned to Baldwin in 1846 at the advice of Thomson. Burgess and Kennedy, *Centennial History*, pp. 709–711.

Chief Engineer to enter into any fresh contract," and the authority granted him had "been already consummated and the engines delivered some time since."[18] A few weeks after recording this censure, the board announced a new plan of organization stipulating that while the general superintendent could direct expenditures for maintenance and operations, "all expenditures for additional buildings, cars, machinery, and apparatus shall be first sanctioned by the Board and all important contracts shall be submitted to the Board before being closed."[19] This assertion of authority followed hard upon a decision to separate the job of general superintendent, which Thomson had held since the Pennsylvania began operations in 1849, from that of chief engineer. Though Thomson claimed when he relinquished the post of general superintendent to Haupt in January of 1851 that he had planned all along to do so once construction of the main line had been completed, the board had passed a resolution expressing its desire to separate the positions several weeks earlier.[20] The board further exhibited its determination to recapture control over acquiring technology that summer when it asked Haupt for a report describing all locomotives in use and stating their carrying capacity.[21] Not long after, the board directed its secretary to maintain a record of all patents licensed to the Pennsylvania.[22]

While these steps restored a measure of fiscal accountability over affairs at the Pennsylvania – something any reasonable stockholder surely had a right to expect – they did little to ease the burdens of mastering unfamiliar techniques or to reduce the prominence of key personalities. Monthly trips over the line by two of its members hardly put the board in a position to pass judgment on the many technologies involved in railroading.[23] When the board constituted a special committee in 1853 to look into the possibility of acquiring a license for a telegraph system, for instance, its technically naive members initially rejected the decade-old system of Samuel Morse simply because they could not comprehend the code.[24] After gaining some experience with an alternative to the Morse device, a few members of the board insisted the company consult a "scientific expert" before finalizing its choice. In the end, the Pennsylvania bought a Morse system and hired the consultant to superintend it.[25] In circumstances such as these, figures such as Haupt and

---

18 PRR Board Minutes, April 30, 1851 (vol. 1, p. 431).

19 PRR Board Minutes, May 2, 1851 (vol. 1, pp. 434–440). Two months later, the board made clear that the general superintendent also could not sell real estate without its permission. PRR Board Minutes, July 23, 1851 (vol. 1, p. 480).

20 PRR Board Minutes, June 8, 1849; November 7, 1850 (vol. 1, p. 345); and January 8, 1851 (vol. 1, p. 373).

21 PRR Board Minutes, Minutes of the Road Committee, August 21, 1851.

22 PRR Board Minutes, November 5, 1851 (vol. 2, p. 53).

23 The board set up a rotating schedule for such visits early in 1851. PRR Board Minutes, Minutes of Road Committee, February 5, 1851.

24 PRR Board Minutes, Special Committee on the Telegraph, April 6, 1853.

25 Ibid., September 12, 1853; January 4, 1854, (vol. 2, p. 422); August 23, 1855 (vol. 3, p. 92); and September 19, 1855 (vol. 3, p. 102).

Thomson would inevitably continue to exercise considerable influence, simply because their first-hand experience with building and operating the line imparted a knowledge their superiors could not hope to match.

Indeed, whatever fall from grace Thomson may have experienced in 1851 proved to be temporary. Over the course of the subsequent decade, he reestablished a firm grip on the Pennsylvania's affairs, eventually rising to the presidency and a prominent spot on the board. In this capacity, Thomson came to exercise an authority that combined the discretionary power of a proprietary capitalist with the managerial capacities characteristic of the modern chief executive officer. Through his position on the board and its influential Committee on Supplies, he assumed a large hand in negotiating important contracts and acquisitions such as those involving Bessemer steel rails (an innovation discussed in more detail below).[26] Meanwhile, Thomson gained an added measure of control over routine technical matters by consolidating responsibility for maintenance and repair in the hands of key personnel located in a central shop facility at Altoona. In the late 1850s, he closed the old engineering department and replaced it with a resident engineer, who supervised the maintenance of way department and reported to the general superintendent. This arrangement, noted the board, gave "the General Superintendent a proper and more immediate control."[27] Similar benefits presumably accrued in the realm of locomotives and rolling stock when the Pennsylvania designated a master of machinery, also located at Altoona. Available records do not reveal definitively when the Pennsylvania first created this job, but when the general superintendent nominated John P. Laird to the post in 1862, the board minutes noted he would fill a vacancy.[28]

While one can perceive in these developments a tendency toward increasing bureaucracy at the Pennsylvania, the primary focus stayed on the task of assembling the basic machine, and this remained a highly personal affair that often involved top management working through a minimal hierarchy. As discussed in more detail below, Thomson would play an instrumental role in acquiring steel rails for the Pennsylvania during the Civil War and the major rebuilding and expansion that followed. To carry out that aggressive construction program, Thomson effectively resurrected the engineering department. He brought Wilson back to Philadelphia and installed him

[26]   PRR Board Minutes, Minutes of the Road Committee, September 7, 1856 (vol. 3, p. 174) and September 2, 1857 (vol. 3, p. 255).

[27]   PRR Board Minutes, December 19, 1856 (vol. 3, p. 201) and December 22, 1858 (vol. 3, p. 384); PRR Board Minutes, Minutes of the Road Committee, December 18, 1858. The quote comes from the Road Committee minutes. The changes took effect January 1, 1859, with William Haskell Wilson assuming the position of resident engineer with a salary of $3,000 and a house at Altoona.

[28]   PRR Board Minutes, June 11, 1862 (vol. 4, p. 188). The board minutes of April 29, 1868 (vol. 5, p. 226) identified Alexander J. Cassatt, future president of the Pennsylvania, as the superintendent of motive power and machinery, located at Altoona.

as chief engineer for construction and consulting engineer, while placing another man in charge of maintenance of way. At about this same time, Thomson organized a formal supply department, which gave him a means of monitoring the materials his line was then acquiring in unprecedented quantity.[29] Though this department would eventually work to disassociate top managers from personal involvement in purchasing decisions, prior to Thomson's death in 1874 it appears to have facilitated his efforts to direct purchases toward enterprises in which he and other high-level Pennsylvania executives held a proprietary stake.

Top managers at other lines exhibited similar tendencies in their approaches to technology. Robert Harris, chief operating officer of the Chicago, Burlington and Quincy during the 1860s and much of the 1870s, left behind a correspondence rich with evidence of his deep involvement with technical matters. An admitted enthusiast for new technology, Harris corresponded frequently with inventors, providing testimonials and occasionally offering hints about how best to promote their devices.[30] Harris regularly passed circulars advertising new devices on to his subordinates and solicited their opinions, and when Burlington employees wrote to their chief about ideas of their own, he gave them a considered judgment on their technical merits and sometimes even coached them on marketing strategies. On two occasions during the early 1870s, Harris personally set up inventors in the Burlington's facilities and encouraged them to develop patentable inventions.[31] Unlike Thomson, who lived and worked in Philadelphia and thus interacted regularly with fellow board members and other major investors, Harris reported to a group of financiers in distant Boston headed by John Murray Forbes and James F. Joy. This distance did not necessarily insulate Harris from the sort

[29] PRR Board Minutes, January 30, 1866 (vol. 5, p. 24) and February 7, 1866 (vol. 5, p. 26). Three years later, the Pennsylvania appointed Enoch Lewis to the newly created post of Purchasing Agent. PRR Board Minutes, May 3, 1869 (vol. 5, p. 296).

[30] Robert Harris's letterbooks and many other of his papers can be found in the papers of the Chicago, Burlington and Quincy Railroad at the Newberry Library in Chicago (hereafter, CBQ Papers). Much of his correspondence pertaining to inventions can be found in the subject file identified by the code 33 1870 2.5. Other examples include: Harris to W. W. Wilcox, October 18, 1867, CBQ Papers, 3H4.1, 11: 22; to Col. Miller, May 2, 1868, CBQ Papers, 3H4.1, 12: 302; to Col. Miller, May 7, 1868, CBQ Papers, 3H4.1, 12: 327; to J. F. Joy, May 11, 1868, CBQ Papers, 3H4.1, 12: 338–340; to Thomas Swingard, March 22, 1869, CBQ Papers, 3H4.1, 15: 259; to P. S. Henning, June 4, 1869, CBQ Papers, 3H4.1, 16: 239; to Col. C. G. Hammond, November 15, 1869, CBQ Papers, 3H4.1, 18: 92; and to C. E. Perkins, November 16, 1869, CBQ Papers, 3H4.1, 18: 104–107. On one occasion, Harris advised an inventor not to rest his hopes on the testimonial "of one who is known to be so ready to entertain novelties as I am." R. Harris to J. A. Sleeper, August 8, 1872, CBQ Papers, 3H4.1, 28: 116–18.

[31] R. Harris to F. H. Tubbs, June 17, 1868, CBQ Papers, 3H4.1, 12:501 and June 1, 1870, CBQ Papers, 3H4.1, 20: 287–88; to W. W. Wilcox, May 7, 1869, CBQ Papers, 3H4.1, 16: 38; and to J. Q. A. Bean, June 20, 1870, CBQ Papers, 3H4.1, 20: 378.

of meddling that nagged Thomson, however, as board members required Harris consult with them regarding all significant purchases. On occasion, Joy reminded Harris to pay attention to certain manufacturers when allotting contracts for items such as locomotives and rails.[32] Harris also acted as a conduit between the Boston group and executives in charge of Burlington subsidiaries and other Western lines in which they had a financial stake. Charles Perkins, who had charge of the Burlington's lines in Nebraska and eventually succeeded Harris, routinely consulted Harris about technical matters.

John Work Garrett, whose tenure with the Baltimore and Ohio paralleled that of Thomson and Harris at their lines, seldom exhibited the same perceptive attention to technical detail, much to the detriment of his company. Still, Garrett engaged in active correspondence with his personal assistants about certain patents and maintained a close watch over some technical matters.[33] His correspondence includes numerous exchanges about technical issues with Isaac Hinckley, president of the neighboring Philadelphia, Wilmington and Baltimore Railroad. Though Garrett sometimes moaned about the number of advertising circulars that flowed into his office from inventors, he dutifully forwarded them to technical experts such as Thatcher Perkins, who served as master mechanic at the B&O during much of the 1850s and 1860s, and occasionally even pressed his staff to conduct trials of devices.[34]

As railroads grew larger and top management shouldered more burdens, master mechanics such as Thatcher Perkins often came to assume primary responsibility for monitoring new technology.[35] The precise degree of freedom possessed by each master mechanic varied according to the degree of involvement of top officials of the road. The men who first assumed these posts often had as their supervisors individuals who, like Thomson at the Pennsylvania, had been in charge of the initial construction and outfitting of the line. Though these executives relinquished daily responsibility for mechanical affairs after the road began operating, as people with broad technical experience they often remained interested in the details of the mechanical features

---

[32] For example, see R. Harris to J. F. Joy, November 11, 1867, CBQ Papers, 3H4.1.

[33] Archives of the Baltimore and Ohio Railroad, MS 1925, held at the Maryland Historical Society, Baltimore (henceforth, B&O Papers) and the letters of John Work Garrett, MS 2003, also held at the Maryland Historical Society (henceforth, Garrett Papers). See, especially, Garrett Papers, Box 2, Sub. 10 and Box 94, Sub. 32846, and B&O Papers, Patents and Inventions File. On early acquisition of locomotives at the B&O, see Edward Hungerford, *The Story of the Baltimore and Ohio Railroad, 1827–1927* (New York: G.P. Putnam and Sons, 1928), vol. 1, pp. 69–79, 96–113, 143–146, 181–182, and 217–231, and vol. 2, pp. 81–98.

[34] Thatcher Perkins to Garrett, June 23, 1860, Patents and Inventions File, B&O Papers.

[35] The role and activities of master mechanics can be discerned from the early correspondence of Robert Harris of the Burlington and Garrett of the B&O, from the Board Minutes of the Pennsylvania, and from Monte Calvert, *The Mechanical Engineer in America, 1830–1910* (Baltimore: Johns Hopkins Press, 1967).

of railroading. When a colleague from another road sought guidance in choosing a man for the job, Harris advised him to find someone who "has his own views, but will carry out yours whenever you desire."[36] Harris's successor, Charles Perkins, nearly always delegated much responsibility for technology to his subordinates.[37] General Manager John E. Wootten of the Philadelphia and Reading went against the trend. During the 1860s and 1870s he served as his own master mechanic, monitoring railroad technology and patents with a verve surpassing even that of Harris at the Burlington.[38]

Master mechanics attained a central position in technical affairs by melding their personal expertise in mechanical technology with the dictates of growing bureaucracies. Most of the men who occupied these posts rose from the ranks of the machinists who worked in railroad maintenance shops. They generally distinguished themselves from their peers through a combination of managerial talents and technical accomplishments in design. Even after attaining their positions in management, the master mechanics typically remained in the shops, usually holding court in a drafting room located in the largest repair facility. From there they could supervise work on rolling stock, locomotives, and any articles the railroad manufactured itself, while also monitoring equipment performance and designing refinements as necessary. Operating outside the daily purview of top executives yet positioned to see patterns that individual shop workers and locomotive operators scattered along the route could not, master mechanics acquired a unique brand of knowledge that gave them enormous influence over the course of innovation at their firms. And because master mechanics saw how equipment functioned under the stress of actual operations and supervised shopworkers who frequently rebuilt cars and locomotives from the ground up, their understanding of railroad technology often surpassed even that of the original suppliers. Locomotive builders such as Baldwin soon learned to work from drawings and specifications submitted by the railroad mechanics.

Master mechanics and their subordinates formed an informal but effective network of technical experts capable of subjecting new technology to rigorous review. Within each company, master mechanics regularly exchanged opinions with other mechanics scattered through the various shops along the line. When considering a specific change in some aspect of a locomotive, they often also consulted the locomotive engineers, who typically assumed substantial responsibility for the maintenance and performance of their pet machines. In the case of the air brake, master mechanics at several lines even

[36] R. Harris to C. W. Mead, November 13, 1876, CBQ Papers, 3H4.1.
[37] For example, see the exchanges between Harris and Perkins regarding use of the Westinghouse Air Brake on passenger trains: R. Harris to Perkins, April 21 and 25 and November 11 and 14, 1870; CBQ Papers, 3H4.1.
[38] Wootten's letters are in the archives of the Philadelphia and Reading Railroad held at the Hagley Museum and Library, Wilmington, Delaware, Acc. 1451 (henceforth, Reading Papers).

solicited opinions from brakemen and division superintendents.[39] In addition to these exchanges with their coworkers, railroad mechanics actively engaged in correspondence and discussion with their colleagues at other lines and at trusted suppliers.[40] Though prior to the Civil War no formal organizations existed through which mechanics could meet and exchange ideas, railroad mechanics traveled frequently to one another's shops and to those of key supply firms.[41] In a process analogous to that occurring in the machine tool industry, where firms often transferred lessons learned in one branch of manufacturing to other settings, major locomotive builders came to operate something like central clearinghouses for much railroad innovation.[42] As various railroads submitted designs incorporating one novel device or another, builders effectively accumulated an inventory of experimental knowledge they could pass along to other customers. Brochures from firms such as Baldwin often contained long lists of appliances with which the builder had gained experience.[43]

The beginnings of a rudimentary technical press further aided exchanges among the community of railroad mechanics but played less of a role than the more informal processes. Technical treatises and journals appeared occasionally. The most enduring of the early journals, Henry Varnum Poor's *American Railway Journal*, focused more on traffic statistics and rates than

---

[39] Numerous examples of railroad management soliciting information on devices from employees holding a variety of positions can be found in the Burlington Archives. For statements of policy on this procedure, see Harris to Jauriet, August 8, 1871, CBQ Papers, 3H4.1 and Stone to Perkins, April 25, 1889, CBQ Papers, 3P4.57.

[40] Historians have frequently identified such openness as a characteristic feature of American mechanics in other industries during this period. See Brooke Hindle, *Technology in Early America: Needs and Opportunities for Study* (Chapel Hill: University of North Carolina Press, 1966) and *Emulation and Invention* (New York: New York University Press, 1981); Bruce Sinclair, *Philadelphia's Philosopher Mechanics: A History of the Franklin Institute, 1824–1865* (Baltimore: Johns Hopkins University Press, 1974); Eugene S. Ferguson, *The Early Engineering Reminiscences (1815–1840) of George Escol Summers* (Washington, D.C.: Smithsonian Institution Press, 1965); "On the Origin and Development of American Mechanical 'Know-How,'" *Midcontinent American Studies Journal* 3 (Fall 1962): 3–15; and "The American-ness of American Technology," *Technology and Culture* 20 (1979): 3–24; Anthony F. C. Wallace, *Rockdale* (New York: Knopf, 1978); and Carroll Pursell, *Early Stationary Steam Engines in America: A Study in the Migration of a Technology* (Washington, D.C.: Smithsonian Institution Press, 1969).

[41] Railroad executives regularly authorized trips by mechanics to examine devices on other roads. For example, see Stone to F. W. Webb, May 1, 1889, CBQ 3H5.42, Stone to Perkins, May 13, 1889, CBQ 3P4.57, and Potter to Stone, March 7, 1886, CBQ 3P6.14.

[42] Nathan Rosenberg, "Technological Change in the Machine Tool Industry, 1840–1910," *Journal of Economic History* 23 (1963): 414–443.

[43] Letters from locomotive manufacturers of this sort can be found in the incoming correspondence of railroad presidents and other incoming correspondence in each of the collections cited in this study. See, especially, the Patents and Inventions File, B&O Papers; CBQ Papers, 33 1870 2.5 and 33 1880 2.1.

on technical matters.[44] During the 1850s Alexander Lyman Holley published in cooperation with Zerah Colburn a technical journal on railroading, but this journal folded when Holley turned his attention to the steel industry.[45] More generalized journals such as *Scientific American* and the *Journal of the Franklin Institute* filled some of the void, but mechanics got along without an established specialized journal until after the Civil War, when trade journals such as the *Railroad Gazette* first made their appearance. Even then, such journals often resembled composite trade catalogs, with feature stories on particular devices or practices and page after page of advertisements for patented innovations.[46]

The fragmented character of the early technical press reflected a fundamental feature of the way master mechanics themselves approached technical change. Unlike the college-trained engineering executives who would assume much responsibility for railroad technology during the last quarter of the nineteenth century, mechanics did not for the most part attempt to develop a theoretical understanding of their enterprise. Most mechanics achieved their professional status by dint of their designs and organizational abilities rather than analyses based on engineering principles. Like inventors and the creators of the patent system, they conceived of technical change as occurring in the form of discrete devices and designs rather than through the accumulation of generalized knowledge. Though one can find theoretical treatises pertaining to railroading dating from this period, their impact on actual practice appears limited. Mechanics seldom dealt directly with scientific experts who devoted attention to railroad affairs. Railroads may occasionally have tapped such knowledge indirectly by using new devices that incorporated the ideas of scientists, but mechanics rarely showed much interest in comprehending the underlying scientific principles. The essential technical knowledge of American railroading remained embedded in artifacts and equipment.

These attitudes toward science and theory were apparent in the case of a device known as the injector. Invented in 1858 by French engineer Henri Giffard, the injector fed water into the boiler of the locomotive by the use of a series of nozzles. Giffard based his invention on the scientific training he received in the French technical schools, and the injector in turn became the focus of scientific investigation into the flow of steam.[47] American railroad mechanics and engineers, however, paid little attention to this theoretical discussion. They valued the injector for its simplicity, which necessitated far

44 Alfred D. Chandler, Jr., *Henry Varnum Poor: Business Editor, Analyst and Reformer* (Cambridge, Mass.: Harvard University Press, 1956).

45 Jeanne McHugh, *Alexander Lyman Holley and the Makers of Steel* (Baltimore: Johns Hopkins University Press, 1980).

46 David A. Hounshell, "Public Relations or Public Understanding?: The American Industries Series in *Scientific American*," *Technology and Culture* 21 (1980): 589–593.

47 Eda Fowlks Kranakis, "The French Connection: Giffard's Injector and the Nature of Heat," *Technology and Culture* 23 (1982): 3–28.

fewer repairs than the force pump they had previously used, and because it saved water and thus reduced the need for stops. Railroads limited their experiments with injectors to measuring the amount of water used with and without the device. After one such test, the Burlington decided to place injectors on one side of the locomotive and retain the force pump on the other for insurance.[48] The Burlington eventually participated in a theoretical study of the device two decades later, but even at that late date its technical staff simply supplied a professor at the Massachusetts Institute of Technology with information on the injector.[49]

The simple comparative trials of the injector and the force pump exemplified the sort of testing commonly conducted by master mechanics. Locomotives were the most complicated, important, and expensive pieces of machinery used by the railroads, and most master mechanics had earned their jobs because of their knowledge of them. Locomotive technology held forth a few readily identifiable targets for improvement. Virtually everyone connected with railroading could easily appreciate the benefit of conserving water. So, too, could they recognize the value of obtaining the most heat while burning the least fuel and generating as little smoke as possible. Studies of stationary steam engines had established a tradition of research into these subjects and had generated a body of knowledge upon which practical railroad mechanics might draw and to which they might contribute. Locomotives also stirred interest among more theoretically inclined experimenters interested in the nature of heat engines.[50] Yet at railroads themselves, investigations into these aspects of locomotive performance likewise took place haphazardly, as individual master mechanics evaluated specific devices and changes in design within the context of their particular operating conditions.

An early example of this approach to research occurred during the 1850s, when railroads first substituted coal for wood as locomotive fuel. Railroads in the anthracite region, such as the Reading, initiated experiments with coal in an effort to use the cheap fuel readily available along its route. The research itself involved little more than tinkering with different fire boxes and trying out various ways of tending the fire.[51] Once a consensus on the proper techniques had emerged, news of these methods spread from the anthracite region to other areas through informal channels. Along the way, mechanics

[48] R. Harris to A. Blood, December 16, 1868; R. Harris to F. B. Grant, July 14, 1869; and R. Harris to J. F. Joy, August 26, 1869; CBQ Papers, 3H5.24.

[49] H. B. Stone to Gaetano Lanza, November 11, 1888, and January 10, 1889; Stone to E. M. Herr, November 6, 1888, CBQ Papers, 3H5.24; and G. W. Rhodes to Stone, March 19, 1889, CBQ Papers, 3R2.1.

[50] On the growing expertise on stationary steam engines, see Pursell, *Early Stationary Steam Engines*. On European developments, see M. C. Duffy, "Mechanics, Thermodynamics and Locomotive Design: The Machine-Ensemble and the Development of Industrial Thermodynamics," *History and Technology* 1 (1983): 45–78.

[51] John H. White, Jr., "James Millholland and Early Railroad Engineering," U.S. National Museum *Bulletin* 252, no. 69, pp. 1–36, Washington, D.C., 1967.

in eastern Pennsylvania devised ways of burning the softer bituminous coal mined in that part of the state. By the late 1860s these techniques had reached the Burlington and other roads radiating south and west from Chicago.[52] Innovative boiler designs intended to reduce the smoke emitted by locomotives originated and diffused in similar fashion during the 1860s.

Because information spread so freely among executives and mechanics on different roads and among suppliers, these disparate tests produced an accumulated body of common knowledge. Yet though studies of fuel and smoke consumption generated considerable insight into the question of locomotive efficiency, railroads were slow to codify the results in ways that might have encouraged a sustained general inquiry into the subject. Testing proceeded in an irregular and uncoordinated fashion that in retrospect seemed wasteful. Reflecting on the situation years later, Perkins of the Burlington rued that so much information gained through occasional experiments conducted on his road had been lost for wont of careful record-keeping.[53]

THE SWITCH TO STEEL RAILS

An especially telling example of the ways technical change occurred during the era of insider innovation involves the decision to substitute steel rails for iron. On its surface, the choice between iron and steel might seem a simple, straightforward one. Rails were an essential item that constituted a significant element on the annual balance sheet of every line. Managers such as J. Edgar Thomson strove continually to obtain the best quality for the lowest cost. Since railroads generally purchased their rails from outside producers on the open market, this search involved staying abreast of available products and keeping an eye out for reliable sources of supply. Steel rails would, in this view, appear as simply a new alternative on the market. Railroads could choose steel rails over iron in much the same way a person with a plumbing problem might choose copper over galvanized pipe. They would assess their needs (in terms of quantity and proposed use), consider features such as how long each type would last, compare prices, and buy. Innovation would, in sum, amount to little more than intelligent shopping.

To a certain extent, this view holds true. Railroads typically learned about steel rails in the course of shopping for iron rails, and considerations of relative wear and cost figured prominently in their decisions to substitute steel for iron. Yet even the most superficial examination of the switch suggests that it was considerably more complicated. Various railroads initiated the change at different times and proceeded at such widely varying rates that

---

[52] On diffusion of coal-burning locomotives to the Burlington, see Nicolls to Charles E. Perkins, December 19, 1867, Reading Archives and numerous letters in the files of Robert Harris, 1868–1873, CBQ Papers, 3H4.1.

[53] Perkins to Higginson, December 29, 1892, CBQ Papers, 3P4.58.

we cannot date the change precisely. One can speak only of a period of innovation stretching from the early 1860s to approximately 1880.[54] Even during this broad period, moreover, railroads did not behave according to the simple market mechanism sketched above. Economic historians Jeremy Atack and Jan K. Brueckner found that a simple cost-minimization model based on the railroads' estimates of rail life, the cost of borrowing, and rail prices cannot explain the railroads' early actions regarding steel rails. Such a model predicts that by 1880, some 66 percent of all railroad track in the United States would have been steel, while in fact only 30 percent was. Only after 1880 did railroads behave in the fashion the model predicts.[55]

What complicated the switch from iron to steel rails? Atack and Brueckner attempted to answer that question by developing a more sophisticated model and testing it against the known behavior of forty-four railroads. This approach revealed a strong correlation between the intensity with which a railroad used its track – a factor which also incorporated the expected lifespan of steel rails and the relative price of steel and iron – and the extent to which it adopted steel rails by 1880. Two other factors correlated less strongly with extensive use of steel rails. Railroads with large revenue, which Atack and Brueckner used as a measure of the size of the firm, were more likely to switch.[56] Lines with steel mills close to their tracks and iron mills

[54]   The dating of the initial switch from iron to steel varies from study to study. Scholars agree that the change began with the Pennsylvania Railroad in either 1863 or 1864. Albert Fishlow, "Productivity and Technological Change in the Railroad Sector, 1840–1910," in National Bureau of Economic Research, *Output, Employment, and Productivity in the United States after 1800* (New York: NBER, Columbia University Press, 1966), pp. 583–646, suggests 1890 as a cut-off date, as does David Paul Marple, "Technology and Organization: Steel Rail Innovation and Railroad Survivorship in the American Manufacturing Region, 1860–1890" (Ph.D. dissertation, University of Cincinnati, 1981). Elting E. Morison, *Men, Machines, and Modern Times* (Cambridge, Mass.: MIT Press, 1966), ch. 6, believes the period of development of the steel industry was complete by 1880. Studies by Jeremy Atack and Jan K. Brueckner, "Steel Rails and American Railroads, 1867–1880," *Explorations in Economic History* 19 (1982): 339–359, and "Steel Rails and American Railroads, 1867–1880: A Reply to Harley," *Explorations in Economic History* 20 (1983): 258–262, also use the 1880 cut-off. Atack and Brueckner note that the price of steel had fallen below that of iron by 1883 and that by the end of the 1880s over 80 percent of the nation's rail track was steel, whereas only 30 percent was steel at the outset of the decade. Thomas J. Misa, *Nation of Steel: The Making of Modern America, 1865–1925* (Baltimore: Johns Hopkins University Press, 1995), pp. 1–43, concurs that railroads and rail makers had worked out the crucial elements of the switch to steel by 1880.

[55]   Atack and Brueckner, "Steel Rails" (1982), pp. 339–359.

[56]   The relationship between the size of a railroad and its tendency to innovate has long fascinated historians of railroad technology. Most evidence indicates that large railroads were more likely to innovate. For example, see Edwin Mansfield, "Innovation and Technical Change in the Railroad Industry," in NBER Universities–National Bureau Committee for Economic Research, Special Conference No. 17, *Transportation Economics* (New York: Columbia University Press, 1965), and Jacob Schmookler, "Changes in Industry and in the State of Knowledge as Determinants of Industrial Invention," in NBER Universities–National Bureau Committee for Economic Research,

far, which the authors saw as the only possible source of variation in price differential of iron and steel between railroads, also adopted slightly more steel rails than average. (Conversely, those with steel mills far from their routes and iron mills close were more likely to continue using iron.) Other factors, such as the cost of borrowing money and the proportion of tracks built before 1867, had at most an ambiguous effect on the decision to switch to steel.

The findings of Atack and Brueckner point to the importance of particular, local factors in shaping the course of innovation in rail technology. Their work suggests that the specific operational characteristics of a railroad (in particular, the intensity of track use) and its proximity to suppliers may have been the critical elements influencing change. In terms of the shopping analogy, their findings indicate that a railroad's assessment of its own particular needs and opportunities appears more complex than previously appreciated and more important than other factors such as comparative prices.

If we probe beneath the aggregate data and examine the actions of a few railroad companies in detail, we gain further insight into the ways local factors and elements other than direct cost comparison influenced the switch to steel at individual lines. Studies of the Pennsylvania, the Baltimore and Ohio, and the Burlington confirm the overwhelming importance of intensity of track use to the innovation and show how and why this factor played such a key role. The experiences of these three firms likewise highlight the important role proximity to suppliers played in the conversion to steel. When examined in detail, however, the behaviors of these lines reveal that the geographical linkages between producers and consumers of rails involved factors that went far beyond cost variations attributable to differences in transport charges. The desire to share in the bonanza made possible by the patented Bessemer steel process, through direct investments or by fostering new mills that would ship raw materials and finished goods over one's route, profoundly influenced the behavior of individual managers and shaped the course of innovation.

The Pennsylvania

No railroad executive took a more active role in the emergent Bessemer industry than J. Edgar Thomson of the Pennsylvania. Owing largely to his initiative, the Pennsylvania became the first American railroad to try steel rails and to use them in significant quantity. In 1862 Thomson traveled to England, where railroads had used steel rails for many years, to investigate their manufacture, performance, and cost. Thomson purchased a few hundred tons of

The Rate and Direction of Inventive Activity: Economic and Social Factors (Princeton: Princeton University Press, 1962), pp. 195–232. While my research cannot resolve the issue for the case of steel rails, it does suggest that large railroads often innovated early.

cast steel rails for trial in heavily used sections of the Pennsylvania's tracks.[57] The company laid these rails in 1864 and at the same time tried limited quantities of iron rails with steel wearing surfaces.[58] During the following year the Pennsylvania added 100 more tons of crucible steel rails to the test sections and installed 270 tons of Bessemer steel rails.[59] By 1866, Thomson and others at the Pennsylvania were convinced the new types of rails outperformed the old. Steel rails, Thomson estimated, lasted eight times longer than iron while costing only twice as much. The company considered steeled rails, which they believed extended the life of an iron rail three-fold and cost only 25 percent more, "a valuable article as an intermediate between steel and ordinary iron rails."[60] Though Chief Engineer William Haskell Wilson indicated he would continue to compare iron and steel in identical service, Thomson reported confidently to stockholders, "The general introduction of steel rails is now wholly a commercial question, in which the cost of the increased capital required for their purchase becomes the chief impediment to their general adoption."[61]

In rapidly arriving at this assessment of the technical qualities of steel rails, Thomson and his colleagues at the Pennsylvania were confronting urgent problems with iron rails. Thomson conveyed this problem-solving orientation in his annual reports to Pennsylvania stockholders.[62] Iron rails, he noted, wore out at an alarming rate. At some stations and in other heavily used sections, the railroad replaced them every six months. These frequent renewals raised materials and labor costs and disrupted service at a time when the Civil War had placed unprecedented demands upon his line and infused its operations with a heightened sense of urgency. While acknowledging that railroads such as the Pennsylvania taxed rails severely by running more and more weight over them at higher speeds, an indignant Thomson accused rail manufacturers of selling a product designed solely to lower the initial cost of rails.[63] In his report for 1863, the beleaguered executive disclosed his plans to try rails obtained from British sources and openly challenged American iron manufacturers to produce a better product.

---

[57] *Annual Report of the Pennsylvania Railroad Company* (henceforth, PRR *Annual Report*) 20 (1866), p. 25.

[58] PRR *Annual Report*, 17 (1863), pp. 13–14; 20 (1866), p. 27; and 21 (1867), p. 47. Some confusion persists about whether the Pennsylvania laid its English steel rails in 1863 or 1864, but a careful reading of the annual reports convinces me that they were laid in 1864. Steel-surfaced iron rails were a new product introduced in Europe and offered by some American mills. Manufacturers produced them either by treating a finished iron rail with heat and sending the head of the rail through rollers (a process that produced what were known as "steeled" rails) or by placing a bar of steel on top of the bars of iron which were rolled into rails (these were known as "steel-headed" rails).

[59] PRR *Annual Report* 20 (1866), pp. 63–64.   [60] Ibid., p. 26.

[61] Ibid., pp. 26 and 64.   [62] PRR *Annual Report* 17 (1863), p. 13.

[63] Ibid. and 20 (1866), p. 26.

In first considering steel rails, then, the Pennsylvania sought to solve problems of rail wear and breakage that arose in particular sections of track where more and more business was carried. The Pennsylvania did not anticipate an increase in traffic, assess the needs of its entire system, and plan a wholesale conversion to steel. The impetus for change came from problems that arose when the railroad found itself using certain portions of the system very intensively. Later, as Thomson began to purchase steel in larger quantities, the Pennsylvania would concentrate the new rails in its main line, where heavy traffic most frequently created problems and where broken rails disrupted service most severely. The company replaced worn rails in side tracks and branches with old rails that had been rerolled.[64] "While the business of a line is small," Thomson advised stockholders, "it will still be economy [sic] to use iron rails . . . until the cost of producing steel is reduced to its minimum."[65]

Though the desire to meet a potential operating crisis clearly provided the initial stimulus, the switch to steel soon came to involve other factors that spoke more to what Thomson had referred to in his report of 1866 as the "commercial question." Despite his expressed intent in that report to convert main line track to steel in the course of annual maintenance, Thomson did not immediately place large orders with English steel rail makers. The Pennsylvania ordered only 1,541 tons of steel rails in 1866 and another 3,455 tons the following year. Meanwhile, the railroad installed 15,830 tons of iron rails in 1866 and another 13,400 tons in 1867. Though the majority of these iron rails were rerolled, at least 7,000 tons were purchased new. Ignoring its announced policy of replacing annual wear and tear with steel, the Pennsylvania actually used 2,000 more tons of new iron rails than steel during these two years.[66]

While Thomson in his reports to stockholders emphasized his desire to conserve capital and maintain a high dividend, this deviation from stated policy probably had more to do with his budding involvement with the American Bessemer steel industry and a new venture known as the Pennsylvania Steel Company. When first broaching the subject of steel rails in his report of 1863, Thomson had predicted that Americans would soon manufacture steel rails and that prices would surely fall as domestic mills grew larger and gained experience with ores and production processes. As he laid plans to test imported steel and chastised domestic mills for their inferior product, Thomson raised the possibility that his railroad would erect rail manufacturing works if necessary to secure better-quality rails.[67] Though subsequent

---

64 Rerolled iron rails were made by placing new iron on the top and bottom of old rails and sending them through rollers. This process enabled railroads to recycle the iron in their rails and produced a rail only slightly inferior to those made entirely from new iron.

65 PRR *Annual Report* 20 (1866), p. 26.

66 PRR *Annual Report* 20 (1866) and 21 (1867).

67 PRR *Annual Report* 17 (1863), p. 14.

reports did not refer explicitly to the project, Thomson had in fact taken steps by late 1865 to construct a Bessemer mill along his firm's tracks in eastern Pennsylvania.[68] Thomson arranged for his railroad to contribute some $600,000 to the venture, or about one third of the required capital, and he and Pennsylvania Railroad vice-president Thomas A. Scott invested substantial amounts of their personal funds as well. Thomson and Scott assumed positions on the steel company's board of directors, while Samuel Felton, an active member of the railroad's board, took charge as president of Pennsylvania Steel.

Pennsylvania Steel made its first steel ingots in 1867 and the following year rolled 481 tons of steel rails. Output increased in 1869 to 7,097 tons, or nearly three quarters of the projected annual capacity.[69] Though the new steel company bid on at least one contract with the Baltimore and Ohio that year, the Pennsylvania Railroad consumed the bulk of this output. When the mill began turning out rails in volume, Thomson implemented the policy he had sketched earlier of buying steel and rerolling iron. Thereafter steel purchases rose steadily while the amount expended for new iron rapidly dwindled to nothing. Nearly all of the new steel came from American producers, and prior to 1871 only the Pennsylvania Steel Company could meet the demands.[70]

In committing his own resources and those of the Pennsylvania Railroad to this nascent steel enterprise, Thomson acted in part out of a desire to secure a ready and reliable supply of critically important materials. As Elting Morison has described so eloquently, the American Bessemer steel industry could not have gotten off the ground without the active support of the railroads. With no other segment of the economy ready to consume its products and with established ironworks reluctant to rebuild their facilities around the new technique, railroads such as the Pennsylvania needed to take a proactive role in the steel industry if they wished to harvest the fruits of Bessemer's innovation.

In supporting the new industry, however, Thomson and his colleagues hardly acted solely out of necessity. The new technology also offered them an enticing investment opportunity. In their capacity as managers of the railroad, executives such as Thomson and Scott could ensure that the new mill found a healthy market for its products. Pennsylvania Steel posed an especially ripe opportunity, moreover, because the government in Washington afforded it unusually strong measures of protection. With the South removed from Congress, Northern Republicans had forged an alliance built around subsidies for economic development. Western agriculturalists received cheap land, which they used in part to subsidize rapid construction of railroads,

---

[68] Morison, *Men, Machines, and Modern Times*, p. 141.   [69] Ibid., p. 168.
[70] PRR *Annual Report* (1867–1869); Morison, *Men, Machines, and Modern Times*, pp. 162–177.

while more established industrial areas to the east benefited from increased tariffs on imported manufactures. Duties on iron and steel, for instance, rose to nearly fifty cents on the dollar.

In addition to providing this tariff protection, Republicans in Congress and in the federal courts stood steadfast in their commitment to upholding patent rights such as those covering the Bessemer process. Individuals such as Alexander Lyman Holley, a railroad trade editor who had acquired rights to a patent essential to controlling that process, operated with confidence they could regulate entry into their industry and reap healthy returns on their investments. Until those patents expired in 1876, Holley took an active hand in every Bessemer steel plant built in the United States, including Pennsylvania Steel. The dozen firms he helped found joined informally in a pool known as the Bessemer Association, which met annually to set production quotas and prices. During the life of the patents, estimates Morison, members earned an average annual return of 30 percent on the capital they had invested.[71]

In certain respects, arrangements such as this grew naturally out of established customs in the railroad industry. Managers had routinely invested in companies that supplied their lines with goods since the beginning of the first railroads.[72] But the political and economic conditions induced by the Civil War had superheated the practice. Whereas such linkages had once seemed a natural and unremarkable offshoot of experimental ventures designed to foster diverse local commerce, they now provided a basis for industrial empires capable of generating stunning financial windfalls. During the postwar economic boom of the late 1860s, executives at various points in the Pennsylvania system exploited several similar opportunities to invest in firms that supplied patented articles to the burgeoning national railroad industry. Andrew Carnegie, overseeing operations in the West, arranged for the engineering department to obtain structural components from his Keystone Bridge Company. Robert Pitcairn, in charge of the terminal facilities around Pittsburgh, invested heavily in the Westinghouse Air Brake Company, whose factory sat across from the terminal and built devices the Pennsylvania helped become standard equipment on railroad passenger trains. Thomson himself funneled major purchase orders to Baldwin, of which he owned a substantial stake. His lieutenant Thomas Scott was among many top executives who profited from investment in the Empire Car Line, a trust that owned much of the Pennsylvania's rolling stock. Many high-ranking officials at the Pennsylvania had acquired great wealth by this practice. Using their inside knowledge of the railroad industry, they cut the risk of investing in new

---

[71] Morison, *Men, Machines, and Modern Times*, p. 169–175. See also Misa, *Nation of Steel*, pp. 1–44.

[72] For a description of this process on one railroad, see Salsbury, *Boston and Albany*.

enterprises. In the process, they fostered the development of new railroad technology.[73]

Whether the railroads themselves stood to benefit so handsomely from such inside arrangements and close coupling with their suppliers was not quite so clear. To the extent that the profits of the steel company came solely at the expense of the Pennsylvania Railroad, the railroad (and those among its stockholders who were not privy to the inside deal) would derive no benefit other than the improved performance obtained from rails it could not have acquired from other sources. Meanwhile, such insider arrangements opened possibilities for all sorts of chicanery. Managers such as Thomson and Scott could enter contracts that effectively shifted income from the railroad to the supply enterprises in which they held substantial personal stakes. Within months of Thomson's death in 1874, the Pennsylvania's board implemented new policies expressly designed to restrict the sort of insider trading that had characterized his administration. The board added new layers of upper-level management and created new standing committees. It also prohibited board members from voting on contracts involving firms with which they were involved.[74] Soon it applied this same standard to managers as well. "The Officers of the Company will be expected to devote their time to the duties of the official position held with this Company," stated an edict of September 1874, "and shall not be at liberty to accept official positions with corporations other than those controlled by this Company – unless by the assent of the Board of Directors."[75] The board gave managers until the first of the new year to separate themselves from arrangements with outsiders. When several failed to meet the deadline by the following June, it specifically directed them to take action or leave the Pennsylvania. This group included G. W. Barker, a division superintendent who operated as an agent for the Pullman Palace Car Company in New York, and Robert Pitcairn, the distinguished superintendent of the Pittsburgh Division who had refused to step down from a vice-presidency with the Westinghouse Air Brake Company, a firm he had supported since its founding in 1869.

While railroads such as the Pennsylvania might grow increasingly suspicious of relationships that blurred allegiances and responsibilities, they nevertheless had ample incentive to see healthy enterprises develop along their routes. For if businesses such as Pennsylvania Steel and Westinghouse Air Brake sold significant amounts of their output to other lines, the railroad might reap substantial dividends in the form of increased demand for its transportation services. Steel mills, especially, shipped large quantities of raw materials into their works and sent out heavy finished goods. As

[73] A lively account of these activates by Pennsylvania Railroad executives can be found in Harold C. Livesay, *Andrew Carnegie and the Rise of Big Business* (Boston: Little, Brown, 1975), pp. 45–58.

[74] PRR Board Minutes, June 29, 1874 (vol. 6, pp. 312–315).

[75] Ibid., September 23, 1874 (vol. 6, p. 371).

Morison notes, railroads as a group charged steel makers $8.26 million in freight charges in 1879 alone.[76] With lines being extended rapidly into regions of the country that lacked coal reserves and other materials necessary to produce steel, established railroads such as the Pennsylvania were well positioned to leverage their natural advantages and promote the development of industry along their routes on an unprecedented scale. Prospects seemed all the brighter given the subsidies offered by the federal government for railroad construction in the industrially undeveloped West and South.

During the early 1870s, two more enterprises with close ties to the Pennsylvania constructed Bessemer plants at locations along the railroad's main lines in the Keystone State. Cambria Iron Company, an established ironworks located in Johnston, Pennsylvania, started production of Bessemer steel rails in 1871. A year later, Andrew Carnegie's new steel works near Pittsburgh became the last of the dozen firms to join the Bessemer Association. The owners of Cambria had longstanding ties with their associates at the Pennsylvania. Though Carnegie was beginning to distance himself from his erstwhile employer, his years with the Pennsylvania had fostered deep ties to the Pittsburgh industrial community, and as a protégé of Thomson and Scott he was well versed in the ways of inside investments. Together with Pennsylvania Steel, these new ventures gave the railroad direct access to a quarter of the Bessemer facilities in the United States and to an even larger share of the steel industry's capacity.

Through adept bargaining, the Pennsylvania could in these circumstances reap the benefits of competition among suppliers while still promoting industrial development in the territory it served. Using its influence as a large buyer in a limited market and its power as a shipper of materials to the mills, each year the Pennsylvania negotiated a price for rails with each of the three firms. Generally, it ended up dividing its order among them. Because the steel firms were linked closely by the Bessemer Association, these negotiations had a significant influence on prices and production levels around the country. At meetings of the association, Pennsylvania representatives sought to keep the three mills free from the production restrictions that saddled other rail makers.[77] These restrictions would not have prevented the three mills from meeting the needs of the Pennsylvania, but the railroad stood to gain large sums from shipping charges if the plants kept producing.

Relationships between the Pennsylvania and the steel makers took another turn when Carnegie opened his mammoth Edgar Thomson works in 1875, just as the patents that had bound the association were about to expire. Carnegie had chafed under what he viewed as the unwarranted restrictiveness of the patent association. Much to the disgust of Thomson and Scott, he had threatened to bolt with the association and sell rails cheaper than the price

---

[76] Morison, *Men, Machines, and Modern Times*, pp. 175–176.
[77] Ibid., pp. 172–176.

agreed upon if its members refused to grant him a larger share of the steel market. Anticipating an era of intense price competition when the association dissolved, Carnegie took care to ensure his new facility would be served not only by the Pennsylvania, but also by its great rival, the Baltimore and Ohio. The arrangement gave Carnegie bargaining leverage that mills such as Cambria and Pennsylvania Steel could not match. The resulting savings in transport charges helped make Carnegie the low-cost provider of steel rails, and he used this advantage to build production volumes and achieve additional economies that kept him at the forefront of the industry for the remainder of the century.[78]

Carnegie's rise in some respects spelled the end to insider innovation of the sort illustrated by the founding of Pennsylvania Steel. As described in Chapter 6, the Pennsylvania, like other railroads, found itself purchasing rails in a highly contentious market from firms in which it held no direct financial stake. Yet even if executives at the Pennsylvania may have regretted they could not charge Carnegie more for their services, their line surely reaped enormous dividends as the steel magnate built an enterprise of enormous proportions in the heart of the territory their railroad served. In this sense, the Pennsylvania's support of the embryonic industry left a legacy of vital importance to its long-term interests.

The Baltimore and Ohio

The significance of those benefits becomes apparent when considered in light of events at the Baltimore and Ohio, the railroad Andrew Carnegie played off against the Pennsylvania in 1875. The B&O traced a substantially different path during the formative years of the steel industry, though those differences were not at first apparent. Like the Pennsylvania, the B&O carried a rapidly increasing volume of traffic over its lines during the early 1860s.[79] The B&O, too, experienced troubles with its iron rails as traffic increased. Searching for a more desirable product, the company bought new rails from a variety of American and English producers and had substantial quantities of old rails rerolled by several different firms.[80] In arranging these deals, the B&O learned from its English merchant supply houses about steel and steel-topped rails. In 1863, the same year Thomson began to test steel rails, B&O president John W. Garrett obtained a sample of English steel-topped rails.[81]

Following this early action, Garrett moved far more deliberately than Thomson. Rather than traveling to Europe, he continued to negotiate rail contracts from a distance through established supply houses. They offered

[78] Livesay, *Andrew Carnegie*, pp. 93–106.
[79] On operations at the B&O, see Hungerford, *Baltimore and Ohio*.
[80] Records of these purchases can be found in the B&O Papers and the Garrett Papers. See especially the B&O Papers, Iron and Steel Subject File.
[81] Benjamin F. French to John W. Garrett, August 8, 1863, B&O Papers.

him small lots of steel rails for trial in 1865 and heavily promoted larger quantities the following year, claiming that steel costing $105 per ton would outwear the best iron, which cost $80 per ton, ten to one.[82] Garrett declined their offers and between July 1865 and March 1866 bought 16,500 tons of English iron rails for extensive repairs to tracks damaged during the Civil War.[83] Though Garrett eventually tried a small quantity of steel rails in 1867, managers at the B&O decisively refused to make a wholesale switch to steel.[84] Vice-President John King, informing Garrett in the summer of 1867 that President Isaac Hinckley of the Philadelphia, Wilmington and Baltimore Railroad planned to lower his company's dividend from 10 to 6 percent in order to pay for the change, deemed the policy unwise. The amount saved by reducing the dividend, King noted, "will not go very far" toward buying steel rails.[85] Garrett apparently concurred, for he continued to buy iron rails from English exporters.[86]

The B&O did not buy a significant quantity of steel rails until 1869, when it purchased 2,000 tons of John Brown steel rails, the most famous English make.[87] Even then, Garrett established no firm policy of buying steel rails. The railroad ordered only small quantities in 1870 and 1871, and on at least one occasion Garrett chose extra-quality iron rails over steel rails.[88] He committed himself fully to steel only in 1872. That summer Garrett asked his master of machinery to confer with him about the "substitution of steel for rails wherever practical and economical."[89] He began to purchase large quantities of steel rails from a leading English exporter and by June 1874 had contracted for 32,500 tons. Several thousand tons of steel rails made their way into the B&O's tracks each year for the remainder of the decade.[90]

Though this pace by no means put the B&O at the tail end among American railroads, it marked a significant contrast with the vaunted competitor to its immediate north. By the time Garrett finally committed to steel, the Pennsylvania Railroad had converted much of its main line to steel, helped found a large steel mill, and begun to funnel significant amounts of

[82] French to Garrett, July 10, 1865, and March 26, 1866; Heyerdahl, Kettell and Company to Garrett, December 24, 1866; B&O Papers.

[83] Contracts for this steel from December 1866 can be found in B&O Papers, Iron and Steel Subject File.

[84] A. M. Lampson and Company to Garrett, June 4, 1867, B&O Papers.

[85] John King to Garrett, July 24, 1867, Garrett Papers, box 23, subject 342, no. 1.

[86] Contracts and correspondence relating to these purchases can be found in B&O Papers.

[87] Naylor and Company to Garrett, March 1, 1869; Garrett to Naylor and Company, March 16, 1869; B&O Papers.

[88] William R. Hart to Garrett, September 30, 1870, B&O Papers. The B&O did place small additional orders for steel rails in 1869 and 1870.

[89] Memo from Garrett, 1872, Garrett Papers, box 2, subject 10, no. 1.

[90] These figures were obtained from miscellaneous correspondence and documents in B&O Papers and Garrett Papers.

business to two other Bessemer mills located along its line. The B&O, meanwhile, continued to obtain rails from overseas through its old merchant suppliers.

The divergence in policy between the two railroads almost certainly did not result from different needs. Both companies sustained substantial damages to their tracks during the Civil War. Like the Pennsylvania, the B&O found that its increased volume of traffic destroyed rails and seriously disrupted service. On occasion B&O officials complained that the disruptions resulting from the poor rails caused the company to lose business to the Pennsylvania and asked Garrett for steel rails.[91] Once the B&O decided to switch to steel, it proceeded as had the Pennsylvania, installing the steel rail in heavily used sections of the main line and using rerolled iron elsewhere.[92] Clearly, the same consideration – worn and broken rails caused by heavy use of certain sections of track – motivated both railroads to convert from iron to steel.

A more likely explanation for the differences in policy lies in the financial condition of the B&O. The railroad emerged from the trials of the Civil War in a weak position and never recovered fully before the Panic of 1873 hit. The Pennsylvania weathered both events more successfully. Throughout their early discussions about steel rails, B&O managers concentrated intensely on initial cost while showing remarkably little concern with the long-term performance of steel. Garrett repeatedly quibbled with merchants over prices and chose iron instead of steel simply to save a few dollars. King opposed reducing the dividend in part because he believed profits were so low that the B&O could not afford steel even if it paid out a smaller share to its stockholders. As late as 1873 King wrote to Garrett that the B&O should "use the best quality iron rails, because we cannot afford steel."[93]

There is more to the story, however, than comparative impoverishment. Garrett made his choices regarding steel amidst the same complex blend of development strategies and investment opportunities that informed those of his counterpart Thomson at the Pennsylvania. Like its northern neighbor, the B&O stretched westward from a major East Coast port through the coal-rich Allegheny Mountains and across the farm belt of the Old Northwest to Chicago. It had much the same chances as the Pennsylvania to promote industrial enterprises in its Eastern sections. In determining whether to commit to steel, Garrett thus had far more to consider than price and performance. He needed to take into account how his actions would affect the battle among trunk line railroads to capitalize on the explosive opportunities opened by the sectional conflict.

---

[91] E. K. Hyndman to Garrett, January 16, 1880, B&O Papers.
[92] The railroad's policy toward putting steel rails in the main line was expressed clearly in a letter from William Keyser to Garrett, October 2, 1879, B&O Papers. Tables included with correspondence in these manuscripts show that the railroad did concentrate steel in the main line.
[93] King to Garrett, April 23, 1873, B&O Papers.

By the time Garrett overcame his initial hesitance and began to place substantial orders for steel rails, Thomson and the Pennsylvania had already made significant inroads in fostering the Bessemer industry. When Garrett in the fall of 1869 entertained offers to supply the B&O with several thousand tons of rails competitive in quality and price with the best British product, Pennsylvania Steel had nearly reached its annual production level of 10,000 tons. The new enterprise submitted a bid to the B&O. Garrett declined this offer and purchased English rails instead.[94] In making this choice, Garrett gained a slight savings in initial cost and avoided giving the rival Pennsylvania Railroad his business. But in shunning a domestic supplier in favor of an imported product made from an older technology, Garrett also risked alienating the founders of a nascent industry with enormous potential. Without the cooperation of Holley and other influential figures, Garrett could not hope to influence the development of the domestic steel industry in a manner that would benefit the B&O, either by enabling the railroad to build a steel mill of its own or by having others establish mills along its route. Garrett persisted in buying rails abroad for several years, moreover, even after he had committed to using steel and the Pennsylvania had relaxed its close ties with Pennsylvania Steel and begun to distribute its orders among other mills it served.

While Garrett shunned domestic steel producers and continued to obtain most of his rails from abroad, he unwisely committed B&O resources toward building a new iron rail mill at Cumberland, Maryland, where its main line passed through the Allegheny Mountains on its way to Pittsburgh. Garrett and some members of the B&O board had considered building such a mill during the early sixties, before they or anyone else had heard of steel rails. The idea languished until the end of the decade, however, when Garrett dispatched an ironmaker by the name of John Davis to Cumberland. Since early 1867, Davis had operated a small mill the B&O had opened in Baltimore to supply its shops with specialized shapes of iron. The mill had saved the railroad an estimated $20 per ton.[95] Garrett looked for Davis to perform similar feats with the mill at Cumberland, from which he hoped to obtain both new and rerolled iron rails at substantially less than current market prices. Obviously a pet project, Garrett monitored the work with unusual vigilance. He demanded that weekly reports showing daily production levels be sent to his office in Baltimore and berated his subordinates if they contained any discrepancies or related any problems.[96] Thankfully for Davis,

94 Phiney E. Chase to Garrett, October 27, 1869; Chase to Garrett, November 8, 1869; B&O Papers.
95 John C. Davis to Garrett, May 4, 1867; Davis to Garrett, May 29, 1867, January 2 and February 5, 1868; B&O Papers.
96 Garrett to Davis, March 6, 1871, Garrett Papers, box 2, subject 10, no 1. For examples of these reports and Garrett's notations about them, see B&O Papers, Iron and Steel Subject File.

the work proceeded smoothly. In September of 1870 he reported to Garrett, "I will certainly be ready to make rails by the first of January."[97] By April he had ten puddling furnaces operating, and the mill was turning out about 450 tons of iron rails per week.[98]

Despite this impressive performance, the iron mill at Cumberland testified more to Garrett's desperation than to his prescience. Garrett clearly erred in committing his railroad so heavily to this virtually outmoded project. Within a year after the mill opened, the B&O ordered large quantities of steel rails from England and began using the Cumberland plant exclusively for rerolling iron rails, which were laid in branches and lightly used sections.[99] Meanwhile, Garrett had certainly done little to curry the favor of domestic producers or to build traffic volume for the B&O. Indeed, his commitment to the mill reflected a characteristic flaw in his thinking about the railroad. Rather than pursue policies that generated business for his line, Garrett concentrated in his development policies on creating a fully integrated railroad that would perform all the essential functions of transportation itself.[100] Garrett viewed the mill as a means of obtaining key materials reliably and at low cost. He looked to reap savings by withdrawing from direct involvement in the market, rather than to promote a firm that might succeed in the market and generate trade for his railroad.

When Garrett finally began to purchase American steel rails in 1874, the significance of the traffic issue only gradually became clear to him. He entered the domestic market confidently, telling a subordinate "the manufacturers should desire to sell to the B&O as it may lead to important transactions hereafter."[101] In fact, the B&O's bargaining position proved much weaker than Garrett anticipated. Steel producers, with their output regulated by the Bessemer Association, did not always rush to secure contracts with the recalcitrant B&O. Once the steel makers had received yearly orders near the capacity of their mills, they spurned customers who were not willing to pay a premium. Garrett found himself in this position on several occasions.[102]

[97] Davis to Garrett, September 9, 1870, B&O Papers.

[98] Davis to Garrett, April 25, 1871, B&O Papers.

[99] Discussion of rerolling rails at Cumberland is contained in Davis to Garrett, November 5, 1872; Keyser to Garrett, August 4, 1875; and numerous letters between Keyser and Garrett, June–September 1876; B&O Papers.

[100] Among other major projects, he added a steamboat line to the B&O system and constructed an extensive port facility at Baltimore. Alfred D. Chandler, Jr., drawing on Hungerford, *Baltimore and Ohio*, has also noted this characteristic of Garrett's management. See Alfred D. Chandler, Jr., *The Visible Hand: The Managerial Revolution in American Business* (Cambridge, Mass.: Harvard University Press), p. 157.

[101] Keyser to Garrett, December 30, 1874; Garrett to Keyser, December 30, 1874; B&O Papers.

[102] Garrett's annual negotiations for steel rails can be followed in his correspondence, B&O Papers.

Even when demand for rails dropped or construction of new mills increased output and steel manufacturers sought business, the B&O encountered a crucial limitation in its bargaining strength. Garrett discovered this in 1876. With the panic reducing demand for rails and therefore their price, he looked to obtain American rails at a bargain price. Garrett entertained bids from two producers – Pennsylvania Steel and Carnegie's Edgar Thomson Works – and freely informed each of the other's offer.[103] The managers of Pennsylvania Steel responded by quoting a price of $59 per ton, an introductory offer they considered "extremely low" and asked Garrett to keep "strictly confidential."[104] Carnegie proved more difficult to manipulate. He offered to produce 7,000 tons at $66 per ton and told Garrett, "We make this offer to prevent a threatened stoppage of our works during the winter, a matter in which you are interested as all the coke and much of the coal and other material consumed is transported over your line."[105] Carnegie had met Garrett's effort to incite a bidding war by stressing what the B&O's president had so long neglected: the importance to the railroad of traffic going to and from the steel mills. The ploy worked. Garrett, who previously had purchased rails at the lowest available price, ordered rails from both Carnegie and Pennsylvania Steel, though he limited his orders to a thousand tons apiece.[106]

Garrett learned this lesson from Carnegie on several subsequent occasions during his few remaining years at the helm of the B&O. The frequently acrimonious exchanges between the two men reached a crescendo in 1879, when after years of cutting back on rail purchases the B&O implemented an extensive program of track improvement.[107] That January, Garrett and his assistant, William Keyser, arranged for Carnegie to supply 12,000 tons of steel rails in steady allotments by October.[108] The railroad paid $41 per ton, a price Keyser and Garrett found satisfactory once they determined the Pennsylvania Railroad had paid the same.[109] Relationships between the B&O and Carnegie again deteriorated in midsummer, however, when the railroad on short notice asked for additional rails in November. Before they had fully resolved this issue, the two parties entered negotiations over rails for 1880, when the B&O wanted 25,000 tons.[110] An aggressive Garrett again sought to engage Carnegie and Pennsylvania Steel in a bidding war.

[103] Charles E. Hinchman to Garrett, January 8, 1876; Hinchman to Garrett, January 24, 1876; Keyser to Garrett, February 16, 1876; Hinchman to Garrett, February 26, 1876; and Keyser to Garrett, March 6, 1876; B&O Papers.
[104] Hinchman to Garrett, February 26, 1876, B&O Papers.
[105] Andrew Carnegie to Garrett, November 13, 1875, B&O Papers.
[106] Hinchman to Garrett, February 26, 1876; Keyser to Garrett, March 6, 1876; B&O Papers.
[107] John Bradshaw to Garrett, November 18, 1878; Bradshaw to Garrett, January 6, 1879; B&O Papers.
[108] Keyser to Garrett, January 8, 1879, B&O Papers.
[109] Keyser to Garrett, January 30, March 31, and April 22, 1879; B&O Papers.
[110] Keyser to Garrett, October 17, 1879, B&O Papers.

Through this tactic he succeeded in August in obtaining 1,000 tons of rails from Carnegie and 2,000 from Pennsylvania Steel at $45.50 per ton, $2.50 less than Carnegie had initially asked.[111]

As the tense negotiations continued, Garrett deployed a new bargaining tool: He threatened to produce his own steel rails at Cumberland. B&O managers had discussed the possibility of converting the mill to steel production for several years, without apparent effect.[112] Now Garrett gave the idea much more serious consideration. He and Keyser personally investigated the possibility of importing blooms of English steel, which the B&O would then roll into rails at Cumberland.[113] Garrett also coordinated a survey of modern methods of steel manufacture, including practices used at major mills in Pennsylvania and the West. Keyser looked seriously at the possibility of bypassing the Bessemer interests by utilizing the new Siemens–Martin process, which he planned to install at Cumberland without notifying its European patent holders.[114]

Carnegie responded forcefully to Garrett's tactics. Determined to drive up the price of rails amid the postdepression rise in demand, in October he rejected a B&O offer of $56 per ton and held out for $60, even though the Pennsylvania Railroad had placed large orders with Cambria and Pennsylvania Steel at $48 per ton just six weeks earlier.[115] He threatened to raise the price still further in 1880, and in February followed through on this pledge and demanded $80 per ton.[116] Carnegie accompanied these offers with letters warning the B&O not to produce its own steel. He cautioned Garrett against overestimating the profits of steel makers and advised him that it would cost $250,000 to produce steel at Cumberland. Adopting a high moral tone, Carnegie questioned "whether it was just the fair, high-toned thing for a powerful rail way organization – with an empire before it to develop – to pounce down upon" the rail manufacturers who "after years

[111]   Garrett to L. S. Bent, July 1879; William P. Shinn to Garrett, August 20, 1879; Bent to Garrett, August 21, 1879; Shinn to Garrett, August 26, 1879; Garrett to King, August 26, 1879; contract with Pennsylvania Steel Company, August 27, 1879; B&O Papers.

[112]   Keyser to Garrett, November 20, 1875, and March 3, 1879; B&O Papers.

[113]   Keyser to Garrett, September 17, 1879; Garrett to Ramsden, September 24, 1879; Ramsden to Garrett, September 27, 1879; Keyser to Garrett, October 22, 1879; Hart to Garrett, October 25 and November 6, 1879; B&O Papers.

[114]   Keyser to Garrett, July 14, 1879, B&O Papers; Keyser to Garrett, August 7, 1879; Keyser to Garrett August 8, 1879; William Palmer (president, Colorado Coal and Iron Company and Denver and Rio Grande Railroad) to Garrett, December 28, 1879; Garrett Papers, Box 94, Subject 32846. These letters reveal that the B&O sought to use the Siemens–Martin process as a means of circumventing the Bessemer Association's control of the Bessemer patents. Keyser planned to use the Siemens–Martin patents secretly, without notifying their owners.

[115]   A. Carnegie to Garrett, October 22, 1879; King to Garrett, November 6, 1879; B&O Papers.

[116]   A. Carnegie to Garrett, October 28, 1879; Thomas Carnegie to Garrett, February 5, 1880; A. Carnegie to Garrett, February 3, 19, and 21, 1880; B&O Papers.

of struggle, begin to see daylight." Above all, Carnegie stressed the mutual advantage to the B&O and his steel company of having rails produced at the Edgar Thomson Works. "The tonnage of our various works," he wrote, "will far exceed one million tons per annum as soon as the new blast furnaces are in blast. Our blast furnaces alone will consume every day about 35,000 bushels of coke, 800 tons of ore, etc. Now a great portion of that, and certainly all the coke and lime, should come over your line and would do so were you our customer. Not one pound ever will, if we can help it, if your great rival [the Pennsylvania Railroad] seeks its prosperity through the prosperity of the manufacturing concerns on its line, as it has hitherto, and I think, most wisely done, and if you decide to become our competitor."[117]

With characteristic bluntness and perception, Carnegie had in this letter focused on the crucial factor that shaped the B&O's actions during the period of steel rail innovation and differentiated them from those of the Pennsylvania. The Pennsylvania, as Carnegie noted, had long fostered manufacturing interests along its line and had seen the new technology of steel rails as an opportunity to continue this practice. The B&O, on the other hand, had shown surprising insensitivity to this opportunity. Carnegie, with his enormous plant situated on the tracks of both railroads, now challenged Garrett to recognize the importance of the steel industry's traffic to the B&O's business.

In a real sense, this challenge culminated the early period of the steel rail innovation at the B&O. The confrontation between Carnegie and Garrett ended in a compromise that reflected Garrett's new appreciation for the traffic issue. The B&O, unable to obtain blooms of steel or manufacture its own, abandoned its plans to produce steel rails at Cumberland. Garrett no longer tried to integrate backward into rail production. At the same time, he withstood Carnegie's threats and accused the steel maker of having already discriminated against the B&O in shipping raw materials over the Pennsylvania. Garrett noted that the mutuality of interests flowed in both directions. Carnegie ultimately received the railroad's order for rails, but he failed to drive the price to $80 and settled instead for as little as $65.[118] In subsequent years, negotiations for steel rails followed a similar pattern, with both the railroad and the steel makers acknowledging the mutuality of interests between them.

The Chicago, Burlington and Quincy

Stretching westward from Chicago across the corn belt of Iowa and Nebraska, the Chicago, Burlington and Quincy Railroad provides an important source of comparison with its Eastern counterparts. The Burlington

---

[117] A. Carnegie to Garrett, August 11, 1879, B&O Papers.
[118] A. Carnegie to Garrett, February 21 and March 19, 1880; Garrett to Keyser, March 22, 1880; King to Garrett, March 31, 1880; A. Carnegie to Garrett, April 23, 1880; B&O Papers.

first tried steel rails in 1867, the same time as the B&O. Robert Harris, the company's top executive in the West, and James F. Joy, its president in Boston, obtained 300 tons from an English maker and laid them in a heavily used three-mile section of track. The company also laid fifty tons of steel rails Joy obtained from a small mill in New York.[119] Two years of trial convinced Harris of the value of using steel rails. "The great economy in the use of steel rail has been so fully shown by our experience, as well as by that of other roads," he wrote Joy, "I would recommend that a portion of the tracks be relaid with it each year."[120] When Joy expressed his willingness to adopt steel "as fast as circumstances will allow," Harris encouraged him to order large quantities and told a colleague, "I hope this means at the rate of from twenty to thirty miles a year."[121]

Like executives on other railroads, Harris especially valued the use of steel rails as a remedy for broken rails in tracks carrying a heavy volume of business. In response to a national poll, he wrote, "We have no doubt that within a few years steel rails will be exclusively used on roads having large traffic."[122] He complained to his counterpart at the Michigan Central that iron rails wore out far too quickly and hoped that by switching to steel his firm would "be relieved of the annoyances . . . which we both are now experiencing."[123] Harris plotted a strategy of placing steel rails in "those portions of the road subjected to the greatest wear," such as at junctions and throughout the main line.[124] He planned to use rerolled iron in lesser-used sections and avoid buying any new iron in hopes the price of steel would fall below that of iron.[125]

By 1871, then, the Burlington had reached precisely the same position as the B&O. Convinced of the superiority of steel rails and prepared to install them in its main line, the railroad needed only to obtain large quantities of steel rails and begin replacing the iron. Unlike the B&O, however, the Burlington moved promptly and steadily toward that objective. In 1871, the board of directors provided rails for fifty miles of track. Harris laid nearly eighty more miles the following year and continued at that rate, or slightly greater, through much of the decade. The Burlington charged the amount expended for steel in excess of the cost of iron to its new construction account.

---

[119]   Robert Harris to N. N. Irons, December 11, 1867, and R. Harris to James F. Joy, January 11, 1868, CBQ Papers, 3H4.1. On the Burlington's early steel rail orders, see also Richard C. Overton, *Burlington Route: History of the Burlington Lines* (New York: Alfred A. Knopf, 1965), pp. 106, 151, 163, and 175.

[120]   Harris to Joy, May 27, 1870, CBQ Papers, 3H4.1, 2: 232–242.

[121]   Harris to George H. Nettleton, July 11, 1870; Harris to Joy, July 11, 1870; CBQ Papers, 3H4.1, 20: 496–498.

[122]   Harris reply to questionnaire, November 29, 1869, CBQ Papers, 3H4.1, 18: 222–225.

[123]   Harris to Nettleton, July 11, 1870, CBQ Papers, 3H4.1, 20: 496–497.

[124]   Chicago, Burlington and Quincy Railroad, *Annual Report for 1872*, February 26, 1873, p. 37.

[125]   Harris to Charles E. Perkins, December 5, 1876, CBQ Papers, 3H4.4, p. 34.

In a typical year, this amounted to about $150,000, which represented about 60 percent of the total cost of the rails and just under half of the total expended for new construction.[126]

The Burlington obtained these rails without any of the complications that characterized the purchases by the Eastern roads. At no time did the Burlington attempt to build or purchase its own rail plant. The company concentrated on purchasing rails in the open market, and Harris continually sought bids from as many producers as possible. The Burlington obtained rails from both English and American mills. Within the United States, the railroad contracted for steel rails with two mills in Chicago but also gave its business to several Eastern mills located on the Pennsylvania's tracks.[127] When the Burlington placed large orders with Chicago's Union Rolling Mill, Andrew Carnegie accused the railroad of discriminating against his mill. Harris responded by asking him for bids and claiming, "I think I can say that no mills near Chicago will have any preference over those more distant. We have no entangling alliances that interfere with our contracting with those who can do the best for us."[128]

Throughout the period of innovation, then, the CB&Q acted as an ordinary consumer. Harris approached the subject with characteristic zeal, but he pursued steel rails strictly as a solution to a technical problem, not as an opportunity to secure a source of materials or build up traffic. Harris and his colleagues had good reasons for maintaining the attitude of a consumer. Unlike the Pennsylvania, they did not need to support new steel mills in order to obtain rails. By 1871 several mills could supply them with steel rails. Nor did the Burlington have to worry about helping a competitor by purchasing steel from mills served by another railroad. None of the railroads paralleling the Burlington's route had steel mills on their line, and the CB&Q maintained friendly relations with the Eastern roads that did.

The geographical location of the Burlington severely restricted its opportunities to promote the development of mills along its own route. The regions served by the CB&Q lacked the raw materials necessary for steel production. Two mills did locate in Chicago, but they did so to gain access to Western markets, not raw materials. By cultivating a relationship with these mills the CB&Q could hope to ship finished rails to Western railroads, but the Burlington would ship rails westward from Chicago whether they originated in the Windy City or in Pennsylvania.

Even if opportunities to promote mills along the line had arisen, it is unlikely that Harris would have seized them. Prior to the 1880s, the Burlington showed little inclination to support new industry along its line.

---

[126] Chicago, Burlington and Quincy Railroad, *Annual Report for 1872*, February 26, 1873, p. 37.

[127] The Burlington's orders of steel rails during the early 1870s can be traced in the correspondence of R. Harris. For example, see R. Harris to Perkins, November 17, 1876, CBQ Papers, 3H4.4.

[128] Harris to Andrew Carnegie, October 25, 1876, CBQ Papers, 3H4.2.

The company concentrated its colonization efforts on fostering agricultural development.[129] In obtaining its own equipment, the Burlington dealt with Eastern firms which often were connected with members of the board of directors and other investors in the railroad.[130] When manufacturers of railroad products asked the Burlington for support to locate along its route, the railroad showed little enthusiasm.[131] Even when the region grew more industrialized and the Burlington's links to the East dissipated, the railroad did not actively support industry. As late as 1883 its executives complained that the CB&Q lagged well behind its Western rivals in this regard and urged President Charles E. Perkins to establish a policy of promoting industrial development.[132] Perkins gradually heeded their advice and supported, among other projects, a steel mill located on the Burlington's extension into Colorado.[133]

THE LUMPY DEMAND FOR INNOVATION

The experiences of these three railroads with steel rails suggest why models of innovation based on straightforward cost and performance comparisons fail to capture the full complexity of technical change in railroading during the mid-nineteenth century. Though managers at each line showed early enthusiasm for steel rails and paid them close attention, in no case did they turn to steel rails as a comprehensive alternative to iron. Rather, they deployed steel rails as a remedy for pressing problems created by increasing traffic in heavily used locations. Intensive use of certain parts of the system, not a gradual increase in traffic throughout the network, generated the initial interest in steel and shaped the railroads' approach to it for many years. None of these railroads ever made a system-wide study of the volume of traffic and its effect on rails. They simply tested steel and then tried to get as much steel as possible into the heavily used parts of their system. At least one of the railroads – the Burlington – replaced steel in its main track with

[129] Richard C. Overton, *Burlington West: A Colonization History of the Burlington Railroad* (Cambridge, Mass.: Harvard University Press, 1941).

[130] On the Burlington's connections with Eastern capital, see Arthur M. Johnson and Barry E. Supple, *Boston Capitalists and Western Railroads* (Cambridge, Mass.: Harvard University Press, 1967).

[131] For examples of the Burlington's refusal to support industrial firms, see R. Harris to John S. David, March 22, 1873, CBQ Papers, 3H4.1; Potter to Perkins, February 4, 1882, CBQ Papers, 3P6.16; and T. S. Howland to Geo. H. Edwards, March 22, 1897, CBQ Papers, 3P4.

[132] G. Harris to Perkins, March 12, 1891, and June 23, 1892, CBQ Papers, 3P4.51.

[133] W. L. Brown to G. W. Rhodes, November 18, 1885, CB&Q Lab Reports, vol. 6, pp. 235–238. This letter reports the results of tests that had been requested by Robert McClure, the Burlington's consulting engineer, of steel produced by the Pueblo Steel Rail Company and suggests that McClure was in the process of evaluating the steel mill after the Burlington had purchased it.

newer, heavier steel rails long before it removed all of the iron rails from its tracks.[134]

This practice of innovating in direct response to localized crises characterized much technological change in the railroad industry. Railroads used various parts of their expanding systems in vastly different fashions. Many miles of track carried little traffic, while others shouldered the bulk of the rapidly increasing business. The problems that arose in the course of operating these busy sections continually challenged railroad managers and absorbed the energies of those who created new railroad technology. Though new construction continued to pose fresh challenges for civil engineers, heavily used sections such as the Pennsylvania Railroad's main line constituted the technical frontier for the managers and mechanics who concerned themselves with moving trains through the system. Consequently, new techniques often emerged as solutions for what were in fact quite localized phenomena. Incentives to adopt even such a seemingly simple and undifferentiated innovation as steel rails varied dramatically not only among firms, but also within them. As a result, demand for new technology exhibited a lumpy quality not readily perceived in aggregate statistics.

Demand assumed an especially complex character in cases such as steel rails because broader business concerns impinged on the decision to innovate. The sheer size of the railroads led them to view steel rails in a different light than ordinary consumers would have. Railroads might choose to invest in the new industry themselves, or they might build their own mill in order to secure a supply of an essential material. Above all, railroads might see in steel the potential to develop the transportation business of their enterprise. With enormous plants and high fixed costs, large railroads in particular focused on building and sustaining a heavy volume of traffic. Because they consumed large quantities of raw materials and manufactured bulky finished products, rail mills presented a particularly attractive means of building up trade. The switch from iron to steel gave railroads the opportunity to relocate rail mills to their benefit. Once they became established, the flow of traffic to and from the mills discouraged railroads from acting as simple consumers and contracting freely with all producers. Railroads wanted to build their own traffic as much as possible and avoid bolstering the business of a competitor.

These factors produced different outcomes at the three firms. Variations arose in part because local geographic conditions presented distinct opportunities. The Pennsylvania, located in the iron and coal-rich regions of the Keystone State, could easily foster the development of steel along its route. The B&O did not pass through as much of the steel region, but it did carry coal and coke to the important metalworking center of Pittsburgh.

---

[134] Atack and Brueckner, "Steel Rails" (1982), who focus on the gross mileage of each railroad and do not distinguish between heavily and lightly used sections, hypothesized that all steel was used to replace iron prior to 1880.

The Chicago, Burlington and Quincy, on the other hand, stood west of the steel-producing regions and had little chance of fostering the industry along its line.[135]

Though geographical differences contributed, managerial strategies also proved decisive. Managers at the Chicago, Burlington and Quincy, despite a keen interest in new technology, concentrated on building up agriculture in their region. Although its absentee owners were involved with industrial concerns in the East, they did little to promote industry along the railroad even when opportunities presented themselves. The B&O, despite more favorable geographic circumstances, also neglected the opportunity to build up traffic. Under the leadership of John W. Garrett, it pursued the slightly different goal of creating a fully integrated transportation company. Meanwhile, managers at the neighboring Pennsylvania Railroad seized the day. Although perhaps motivated initially by opportunities to attain great personal wealth, by supporting the rail plants along their line and collecting revenue from shipping materials to and from these mills, they effectively cut the cost of innovation for the railroad. In the process, the Pennsylvania fostered the development of a vast, technologically intensive industry concentrated in the region it served.

Few innovations of the nineteenth century opened possibilities to leverage technical change quite so dramatically as in the case of Bessemer steel, of course. Rails absorbed extraordinary amounts of capital, and the technology introduced by Bessemer and refined by Holley offered profound improvements over prior techniques. Still, a remarkable number of prominent technical innovations in railroading during this period exhibited at least some of the same basic characteristics as the switch to steel rails. Enterprises such as George Westinghouse's air brake company and George Pullman's palace car works sprang to life with assistance from inside investors at lines such as the Pennsylvania and the Burlington.[136] Capitalizing on strong patent positions, these firms sold inventions to an industry that had suddenly exploded to national proportions. The factories built to produce these innovations became cornerstones of industrial development in their regions, often to the benefit of the lines that helped create them. Yet as in the case of Carnegie and the B&O, these enterprises and their cantankerous founders soon came to be thorns in the sides of rail executives who found themselves dependent upon their products. This becomes clear when we consider the place of the patent system in the world of insider innovation.

[135]   The experience of another large railroad, the New York Central, provides another example of the importance of geographical location to a railroad's actions regarding steel rails. The New York Central established no close contacts with American steel producers. The railroad purchased 12,000 tons of English steel as late as 1879. Morison attributes this to the geographical position of the New York Central. See Morison, *Men, Machines, and Modern Times*, p. 186.

[136]   The information on the air brake comes from Chapter 3.

3

Patent Problems: Inventors and the Market for Technology

Nearly four decades before the first steam railroad operated in the United States, the Revolutionary generation of political leaders established a mechanism intended to stimulate the creation and diffusion of new technology. At Philadelphia, they incorporated into the Constitution a clause stipulating that the federal government should encourage "science and the useful arts." The patent clause, as it has since been known, struck an uneasy compromise between competing philosophies of political economy. In endowing the central government with authority to grant monopolies, it preserved a touch of mercantilism in what was rapidly becoming a Smithian world. Thomas Jefferson, an inventor of no small accomplishment, was among the many who looked with suspicion upon such an exercise of government power. When as Secretary of State he took responsibility for first administering the system, Jefferson held inventors to such high standards of novelty and utility that only three received patents during the first year.[1] Yet even the most ardent watchdogs of centralized power could console themselves in knowing that the ultimate test of patented technologies would come not in the halls of government but in the marketplace and the courts. For a patent in and of itself conveyed no rewards or special privileges. Inventors did not receive a bounty based on the perceived utility of their handiwork. Rather, a patent merely extended to creative individuals a legal claim upon those who wished

[1] Hugo Meier, "Technology and Democracy, 1800–1860," *Mississippi Valley Historical Review* 43 (1957): 618–640; I. Bernard Cohen, *Science and the Founding Fathers: Science in the Political Thought of Thomas Jefferson, Benjamin Franklin, John Adams, and James Madison* (New York: Norton, 1995), pp. 237–243; Eugene S. Ferguson, *Oliver Evans: Inventive Genius of the American Industrial Revolution* (Greenville, Del.: Hagley Museum, 1980), pp. 52–59; Brooke Hindle, *Emulation and Invention* (New York: New York University Press, 1981), pp. 16–23 and 42–43; and Morgan Sherwood, "The Origins and Development of the American Patent System," *American Scientist* 71 (1983): 500–506.

to use their novelties. The market would determine the number of takers and the amount they were willing to pay.

By the time railroading came of age half a century later, Americans had gained considerable experience with the market for patented inventions. Jefferson's stringent enforcement of criteria for novelty and utility had soon given way to far more liberal practices. For several decades, the patent office approved applications so routinely it functioned more as a registry than a judge of novelty. The resulting flow of patents stimulated both lively trade and feverish litigation, as federal courts assumed the burden of resolving conflicting claims and upholding the property rights of legitimate inventors. Some notorious cases left inventors such as steamboating pioneers Oliver Evans and John Fitch unrewarded and bitter. But other individuals, such as the machine-tool designer Thomas Blanchard, showed how a mix of creativity, business savvy, and legal acumen could yield steady returns from the market for invention. The outlook for inventors grew still brighter after 1836, when Congress revised the patent statutes to provide for more thorough examination and allocated funds for an elaborate new home for the patent office. These measures imparted a substance and legitimacy to the market for technical novelties that would make the American patent system the envy of inventors around the world.[2]

Though the men who built and managed American railroads had charge of what was arguably the most significant of all technological innovations of the day, they participated in this market for inventions not as suppliers or sellers but as consumers. The railroad itself – the fundamental synthesis of steam, wheel, and rail – was widely considered a generic technology freely available in the public domain.[3] Railroad pioneers succeeded not by attempting to monopolize that basic invention but by mobilizing capital toward it. The monopolies they sought were those of geography or territory, not technique, and they turned to government for the protections offered by corporate charters rather than for those conveyed by the patent system. Nor were railroad executives inclined to seek competitive advantage by retaining

[2] Hindle, *Emulation and Invention*; Ferguson, *Oliver Evans*; Carolyn C. Cooper, *Shaping Invention: Thomas Blanchard's Machinery and Patent Management in Nineteenth-Century America* (New York: Columbia University Press, 1991); Steven Lubar, "The Transformation of Antebellum Patent Law," *Technology and Culture* 32 (1991): 932–959; B. Zorina Khan, "Property Rights and Patent Litigation in Early Nineteenth-Century America," *Journal of Economic History* 55 (1995): 58–97; Kenneth L. Sokoloff and B. Zorina Khan, "The Democratization of Invention during Early Industrialization: Evidence from the United States," *Journal of Economic History* 50 (1990): 363–378; and Robert C. Post, *Physics, Patents, and Politics: A Biography of Charles Grafton Page* (New York: Science History Publications, 1976).

[3] Despite the efforts of a few ambitious souls, the basic techniques of steam railroading were never subject to serious patent protection. Certainly by the time most railroad ventures got under way, investors could operate with confidence that no one would later stake a claim for the fundamental synthesis of steam, wheel, and rail.

exclusive rights to improvements in the various components that made up a railroad system. Sensing that in this experimental stage they had more to gain by openness than secrecy, railroads generally exchanged technical information quite freely. Even key consulting experts to the railroads, such as the remarkable John Jervis, often let their improvised solutions to the challenges of railroading in North America slip into a common pool of techniques.[4] These men and the various lines that employed them functioned something like a community of scientists conducting concurrent experiments in a number of different laboratories. Managers applied the same basic technique to a variety of conditions, made useful adaptations, and circulated the results among their peers.

Yet if those who had charge of the railroads saw little purpose in staking claims to new technology, the same could not be said of the numerous skilled mechanics and other creative technicians who inevitably clustered around the industry. Each of the many components that comprised a railroad – the cars and locomotives (each complex technical assemblies in their own right), the bridges and other structures, even the rail itself – presented a ripe opportunity for inventing and patenting. Virtually anyone with a modicum of technical ability who rode the trains or simply watched their operation could conceive of possible improvements. Scores of inventors and firms from an array of economic sectors, enticed by the technical challenges and by the potential returns of a large lucrative market, offered railroads a stream of promising technical improvements. In time, established railroad supply companies emerged, each anxious like merchants in all lines of business to sustain a flow of proprietary items to their clientele.[5] British railroading, which one historian has aptly characterized as a "complex of invention" in its own right, offered yet another source of patented refinements, as the case of Bessemer rails demonstrated so vividly.[6] The many skilled shopworkers who performed routine maintenance and other essential tasks for the railroads added to the pool of patented technologies.

Throughout the antebellum period, railroading accounted for a disproportionate share of patents. Year after year, the list of new patents published in the annual report of the Commissioner of Patents contained increasing numbers of devices under the headings "Civil Engineering and Architecture" and "Land Conveyance." Most of them pertained to railroads. In 1852, the Patent Office introduced a separate category for inventions devised specifically for

---

4 Jervis contributed such valuable novelties as the swing truck, which helped locomotives negotiate the sharply curved routes built along rivers and mountain passes. See Elting E. Morison, *From Know-How to Nowhere: The Development of American Technology* (New York: Basic, 1974), ch. 3.

5 On the railroad supply industry, see Glenn Porter and Harold C. Livesay, *Merchants and Manufacturers: Studies in the Changing Structure of Nineteenth-Century Marketing* (Baltimore: Johns Hopkins University Press, 1971).

6 P. L. Payne, *Rubber and Railways in the Nineteenth Century* (Liverpool, 1961).

railroading. By the end of the Civil War, the number of patents included in this classification had risen from fifty to over 500 per year.[7] Because railroads operated complex facilities and performed a broad array of activities, moreover, they deployed numerous other technologies listed under categories ranging from paints, lubricants, and building materials to pumps, office machinery, and electrical equipment.

This remarkable level of inventive activity apparently occurred without significant direct impetus from the railroads themselves. In a pioneering study of patenting activity, economic historian Jacob Schmookler had little success when he attempted to draw connections between railroad behavior and the rate and direction of inventive activity. Schmookler hypothesized that in a situation where most technology came from suppliers – either individual inventors working independently or for the railroads or employees of established supply firms – inventive activity would vary as railroads expended money on supplies and thus pumped resources to the generators of technology. In boom times railroad workers would have more money to spend on tinkering and suppliers would have more income to invest in developing new technology. Though Schmookler found that bursts of patenting did indeed appear to follow spurts of investment in equipment and supplies, the correlation was not terribly strong. In the end he acknowledged that "in an industry as large as railroading inventors probably are continually recognizing problems."[8]

Railroad corporations of the mid-nineteenth century thus occupied a position in the market for technology their managers found at once enviable

---

[7] Statistics on patents come from Reports of the Commissioner of Patents, which appear annually in the collected documents of the U.S. House of Representatives and the U.S. Senate. For the years discussed here, these reports contain only sketchy information on the number of patents granted for railroad inventions. The commissioner provided itemized tabulations of patents sporadically, and the categories used often did not identify clearly those patents that served the railroads. The figure cited for 1852 comes from the "Report of the Commissioner of Patents for 1852," U.S. Senate, 32d Cong., 2d sess., Executive Document no. 55, p. 438. That for 1865 appears in the "Report of the Commissioner of Patents for 1865," U.S. House of Representatives, 39th Cong., 1st sess., Executive Document no. 52, p. 18.

[8] Jacob Schmookler, "Changes in Industry and in the State of Knowledge as Determinants of Industrial Invention," in NBER Universities–National Bureau Committee for Economic Research, *The Rate and Direction of Inventive Activity: Economic and Social Factors* (Princeton: Princeton University Press, 1962), pp. 195–232, quote from p. 215. Even if the connection between expenditures on devices and inventive activity had proved significant, it would not have demonstrated that railroads tried consciously to influence the generation of new technology. Investment through the purchase of supplies hardly constitutes an active policy of fostering innovation. With the exception of a few significant innovations such as steel rails and possibly the air brake, railroads did not invest directly to outside inventors. In these cases railroads supported proven technologies and sought primarily to build their own business, not to promote innovation.

and irritating. As they struggled to assemble from many components the particular variants of the basic railroading innovation most suitable for their local conditions, railroad executives had at their disposal a remarkable array of technical alternatives. They could rest assured that the market for new technology would generate an ample supply of novelties, without direct intervention on their part. The mechanism designed by the Founders had seemingly come to flourish most vigorously in a technical realm unlike any its creators had witnessed or perhaps even anticipated. Yet the very vitality of the system could also prove problematical for the railroads. As the number of patented technologies expanded nearly exponentially, managers faced an increasingly difficult challenge in trying to assess the alternatives. Many struggled to obtain reliable judgments about the technical merits and legal status of literally hundreds of new devices. Lacking trade associations and other formal mechanisms of cooperative analysis, most managers entrusted this task to key individuals who monitored the market and conducted trials of specific devices. Though aggressive managers such as those at the Pennsylvania might occasionally turn the power of a patent in their favor, as in the case of Holley and Bessemer steel, as consumers of patented technologies railroads more frequently found themselves on the defensive. The mounting array of patents constituted an expanding minefield of potential lawsuits and financial liabilities.

During the decade following the Civil War, railroads and the patent system raced forward on a collision course. As rapid growth raised new technical challenges for railroads and placed a mounting premium on maintaining standards across systems of vastly greater proportions, the patent office grew still more liberal in its grants. With the number of patents proliferating at unimaginable speed, newly created government commissions directed attention to safety appliances and other technologies intended to protect the public, fueling interest in specific patented devices and sometimes threatening railroads with legislation mandating their use. To make matters worse, federal judges seeking to assess damages in a variety of cases pertaining to the railroads articulated a new legal doctrine that dramatically increased payments to patent holders. Taken together, these developments left railroads exposed to new liabilities of unprecedented scale and scope, as clever inventors could now leverage their patent power much more effectively. Eventually, as discussed in the chapter to follow, railroads responded with pioneering collective action aimed at altering patent law and reshaping the market for technology in their industry. Through organized campaigns that occupied leading figures in American politics and jurisprudence, they eventually reached a new accommodation with the system created by the Founders and paved the way for a new era of innovation in railroading. Those remedies came only after a long ordeal, however, during which railroads discovered just how vulnerable they had become.

THE INSIDE MARKET FOR RAILROAD INVENTION

On its surface, the railroad industry of the mid-nineteenth century appears to have fostered just the sort of market in technical novelty the designers of the patent system intended. Considerable evidence suggests patentees and railroads engaged in market transactions very much like those we would envision under the ideal. Advertising circulars and printed brochures describing patented devices streamed into the offices of railroad executives from independent inventors and established supply firms.[9] Though such unsolicited materials no doubt frequently met with indifference, quite a few managers paid them serious attention. Circulars often included lists of firms that had tried the device and testimonials from railroad managers. Master mechanics often put devices through rigorous tests.

Yet in several fundamental respects, railroading always existed in tension with the mechanisms of technical change envisioned by the patent system. As demonstrated in the previous chapter, railroads often selected technologies for reasons that had more to do with local investment opportunities than with performance. When railroads did enter the market for patented technology, moreover, they did so from an unusually strong bargaining position. Because railroads operated their own machine shops and foundries for purposes of maintenance and repair, they often possessed skills that enabled them to develop their own solutions to technical problems. When the B&O grew irritated at paying a supplier for its journal boxes, it asked one of its own mechanics to devise an alternative. Within weeks, the railroad had negotiated a much more favorable agreement with the supplier.[10] Individuals such as John Wootten of the Reading considered it something of a badge of honor that he could devise his own solution to any technical challenge.[11] As an institution, the Pennsylvania Railroad exhibited a similar hubris, with considerable justification.[12] When the Road Committee of the

[9] Many advertising circulars and the reactions of railroad executives to them can be found in Patents and Inventions File, Archives of the Baltimore and Ohio Railroad, MS 1925, held at the Maryland Historical Society, Baltimore (henceforth, B&O Papers) and in the incoming correspondence of Robert Harris and T. J. Potter in the Archives of the Chicago, Burlington and Quincy Railroad at the Newberry Library in Chicago (henceforth, CBQ Papers).

[10] Patents and Invention File, B&O Papers, contains many letters pertaining to the innovation, known as the Lightner journal box. J. C. Davis to John King, Jr., n.d., provides a useful summary of the case.

[11] Letterbooks of John E. Wootten, Archives of the Philadelphia and Reading Railroad, Hagley Museum and Library, Wilmington, Delaware, Acc. 1451 (henceforth, Reading Papers). See also James L. Holton, "John Wootten: Locomotive Pioneer," *Historical Review of Berks County* (Summer 1978): 97–107.

[12] Roads such as the Burlington, itself much admired among Western roads for its technical competence, routinely looked to the Pennsylvania for guidance on technical matters. See CBQ Papers.

Pennsylvania considered purchasing a patent for a car ventilator designed by one H. J. Rattan in 1867 – to cite one example of its attitude – the railroad dispatched one of its mechanics to the Patent Office to investigate the subject of ventilating cars. Though the problem had attracted the labors of many inventors, the mechanic concluded that given six months' time the Pennsylvania could develop a better ventilator than any then available. "In the mean time request the able mechanics employed at the various shops of the Company to exercise their wits and talents to produce such improvements as may be of service to this company which pays them so well for their time and attention to its interests," noted the board minutes upon receiving this report. "Pride alone should prevent them from allowing any outsider from surpassing them in inventions to subserve the interests of this Company, their employer."[13]

Railroads could operate with such confidence because the inherent complexity and expense of their technical systems erected substantial impediments in the path of outside inventors. Most patentees simply had no means to test and evaluate their creations without gaining access to the lines themselves. Securing the cooperation of proud mechanics such as Wootten and the B&O's Thatcher Perkins was no easy matter. "My many years experience in Rail Road Machinery teaches me, that many new things when first got up bids fair to make a revelation in that part of the machinery, but after a few years practice at last it was found to be an improvement over the left shoulder (that is anything but an improvement)," wrote the skeptical Perkins when his boss John Garrett asked him to review a patented axle box. "Therefore I have learned to be very causcious [*sic*] about said or said to be patents." Not wishing to appear a mere obstructionist, Perkins elaborated. "Do not understand me to say I think Rail Road machinery is at a point called perfection, it is far from it," he wrote, "but what I wish to say is that experience and close observation will tell what any improvement is." Having staked his claim that technical authority ultimately lay in the minds of men such as himself, Perkins concluded with a note of deference. "And at the same time," he hastily closed, "it will give me pleasure to try any new piece of machinery that you may direct."[14]

Should outsiders be so fortunate as to get past these gatekeepers and gain admittance to the inner sanctum, they faced the strong possibility of having their ideas expropriated by their hosts. Such was certainly true in the case of a Mr. Rich, inventor of a device to consume smoke emitted from locomotives. Both the Pennsylvania Railroad and the Philadelphia and Reading,

13 Pennsylvania Railroad, Minutes of the Board of Directors (henceforth, PRR Board Minutes), April 18, 1866, 5: 47; May 2, 1866, 5: 50; April 19, 1866, 5: 67; and March 6, 1867, 5: 108. These records are available on microfilm at the Hagley Museum and Library, Wilmington, Delaware.

14 Thatcher Perkins to Garrett, June 23, 1860, Patents and Inventions File, B&O Papers.

faced with pressure from municipalities to reduce smoke, took the unusual step of inviting the inventor to come to their shops and test his appliance on a locomotive. Although it must have seemed that the golden door of opportunity was opening for him, these experiments proved costly to the unfortunate Mr. Rich. Not only did the railroads decline to purchase his patented concept, but he was killed in an accident during experiments on the Pennsylvania. As his heirs sued unsuccessfully for both personal damages and patent infringement, subsequent tests conducted at the Pennsylvania pointed to alternative means of modifying fireboxes and decreasing emissions.[15]

The skilled personnel who worked in the railroad shops and operated the locomotives occupied an ambiguous position between employee and independent inventor. Though railroad executives seldom encouraged employees to obtain patents, most recognized that patents were an important source of personal esteem and potential reward for their mechanics. Managers walked a fine line, sometimes offering assistance and reward to these men, while at other times expressing the idea that modification and experiment were essential parts of the job. James Millholland, who preceded Wootten as master mechanic at the Philadelphia and Reading, received $1,000 from his employer in 1850 in payment for rights to all his inventions.[16] Available records do not indicate whether this payment covered the actual market value of the patents or if Millholland retained the right to charge his employer and others for subsequent inventions, but the round sum suggests it may well have been intended simply as a bonus for loyal and productive service. Such appears to have been the case when the board of Pennsylvania agreed in 1866 to compensate master of machinery John P. Laird with $3,000 in railroad bonds "for the use of his patented improvement in fire boxes of locomotive engines of the Pennsylvania Railroad." The sum was given, noted the board, "as an acknowledgment of his efforts to improve the character and efficiency of the locomotives and rolling stock belonging to the company."[17]

[15] On experiments with the Rich device at the Pennsylvania Railroad, see Henry C. Carey to the President and Board of Directors of the Pennsylvania Railroad Company, January 15, 1875; H. M. Phillips to Carey, April 1875; Tucker and Sellers to Carey and Thomas Scott, December 23, 1874; and A. J. Cassatt to Tucker and Sellers, January 11, 1875; Papers Pertaining to Matters Brought before the Board of Directors of the Pennsylvania Railroad (henceforth, PRR Board Papers), Hagley Museum and Library, Wilmington, Delaware, Acc. 1807. On tests of the device at the Reading, see G. A. Nicolls to Carey, May 1, 1871; Nicolls to J. E. Wootten, May 1, 1871; Nicolls to Carey, May 26, 1871; S. Jeffrey to Nicolls, July 12, 1871; Nicolls to Wootten, September 14, 1871; T. H. Wilson to Wootten, September 18, 1871; Wootten to Franklin B. Gowen, November 18, December 14 and 21, 1871, and April 6, 1872; Reading Papers.

[16] Managers Minutes, March 15, 1850, Board of Directors Minute Book, Book C, p. 9, Reading Papers.

[17] PRR Board Minutes, March 7, 1866, 5: 29.

By no means had such payments become a standard condition of employment at the Reading, the Pennsylvania, or elsewhere in the industry. A mechanic who had worked for the B&O for three decades informed president John Garrett in 1872 that he was resigning and joining another road because the B&O had never compensated him for a switch and crossing now used extensively.[18] Robert Harris of the Burlington encountered a similar case three years later. "There seems to me to be a reasonableness in the position, sometimes taken, that one in the employ of a Railroad Co. has no rightful claim upon that Co. for a patent fee upon an article introduced or invented in the prosecution of his ordinary duties to the Co.," Harris wrote to a former employee who had requested payment for use of his patented device. "To be sure the patent laws do not recognize any such idea, but it would seem reasonable that to the performance of the duties of any position one's best efforts and ingenuity should be given."[19] Because the man had left the Burlington's service, Harris did "not want to be tenacious on a point of this kind." He offered a modest sum of five dollars per car up to a total of $350. Though on occasion Harris paid similar premiums to other creative employees, he seems in general to have assumed a gentleman's agreement would prevail in such circumstances, with the railroad paying for the patent application and the inventor granting his employer unlimited use of the device in return. The railroad then left the employee free to sell licenses to other companies, but gave him no special assistance. When his successor, Charles Perkins, neglected to pay the fees for one employee, a close subordinate corrected the oversight and told Perkins that "our practice in this matter has been uniform for a number of years back, and several patents have been taken out under it."[20]

When railroads dealt with inventors outside their own employ, they virtually always preferred to obtain licenses rather than buying patented products on the open market. The Pennsylvania, especially, exhibited this tendency early and pursued it relentlessly, and other railroads followed suit.[21] Most licensing agreements called for railroads to pay a flat fee in exchange for rights to manufacture themselves or to obtain from other sources unlimited quantities of a patented article. Fees sometimes varied depending upon the size of the road, with lines paying a given amount per mile operated or some other criteria. On occasion, railroads agreed to pay a royalty on each device used.

[18]   Frank Thiemeyer to Garrett, May 27, 1872, Letters of John Work Garrett, Maryland Historical Society, Baltimore, MS 2003 (henceforth, Garrett Papers), Box 86, Sub. 10110.

[19]   R. Harris to C. M. Higginson, November 6, 1875, CBQ Papers, 3H4.1.

[20]   R. Harris to F. H. Tubbs, June 17, 1868, and to C. M. Higginson, January 6, 1875; CBQ Papers, 3H4.1; Henry B. Strong to C. E. Perkins, November 1, 1888, CBQ Papers, 3P4.57.

[21]   Minutes of the Meetings of the Board of Directors and Associated Reports, PRR Board Papers.

Whatever the precise terms, by obtaining a license early in the life of a patent, railroads acquired a measure of insurance against liabilities. With rights to use a patent secured, a railroad remained free to adopt the innovation at its own pace, without worry that a supplier would discontinue production or raise prices. This consideration was especially important because railroads often incorporated devices into complex assemblies. Lines could easily grow dependent upon particular technologies that meshed tightly with other components in the larger system. Though inventors and railroads debated whether the phenomenon resulted from trial discounts granted at the beginning of the monopoly period or from extortionist rates demanded later on, most people involved with railroad technology agreed that license fees increased during the life of a patent.[22]

In addition to providing protection should a claim prove valuable, licenses enabled railroads to take advantage of the manufacturing abilities of their own shops and those of the major manufacturers and foundries along their lines. Railroads could thus provide work to their shop forces during idle periods and promote industrial development in their territories. In the process, moreover, railroads anticipated that techniques covered by licenses would soon be modified in ways that rendered them generic. Only by retaining exclusive control of their patents and integrating forward into production could inventors avoid having railroads absorb new techniques into the pool of inside knowledge that resided within those technical facilities. So great was the desire to internalize new techniques that the Pennsylvania even pressed to obtain a license from George Westinghouse, an inventor who had located his manufacturing facilities along its tracks and who had received funding from several of the railroad's Pittsburgh executives.[23]

The ultimate intent of railroads was apparent in their willingness to forego paying any fee and risk infringement. Latecomers who encountered escalating prices were especially prone to flaunt claims of patentees. Instead of paying what they considered an inflated fee, railroads would infringe and claim the lower fee as the established one if taken to court. With each passing year in a patent's life, moreover, the possibility arose that another patent covering a similar principle would come to light. If this happened, railroads stopped paying fees and left the inventors to battle over the question of priority. This practice had become so routine by 1872 that Harris told an

---

[22] U.S. Senate, "Arguments before the Committees on Patents of the Senate and the House of Representatives in Support of and Suggesting Amendments to Bills (S. 300 and H. R. 1612) to Amend the Statutes in Relation to Patents, and for Other Purposes," 45th Cong., 2d sess., Miscellaneous Document no. 50 (henceforth, Senate Arguments or House Arguments).

[23] Minutes of the Meeting of the Road Committee, December 22, 1869; January 12 and 21, and February 9, 1870; George Westinghouse, Jr., to D. H. Williams, November 13, 1869; and David H. Williams to J. Edgar Thomson, December 12, 1869; PRR Board Papers.

employee who had invented a new grain door, "[Y]ou should buy [another inventor] out before selling your door to other railroads; otherwise, with two claims, roads will use doors and pay for neither."[24] When inventors did sue, railroads almost always successfully negotiated lump sum settlements for little or nothing more than if they had purchased a license initially. At the B&O, for example, only two out of dozens of patent disputes went before the courts between 1840 and 1879.[25]

Railroads further cut the risks of dealing in an open market of unfamiliar inventors by cultivating ongoing relationships with a few key suppliers. As the case of steel rails suggests, railroad technology continually stretched the limits of American capabilities in metallurgy and machining. Lines sought out suppliers who could provide quality workmanship and materials in timely fashion. An ability to generate novelties mattered far less than a willingness to conform to exacting requests from knowledgeable customers. With railroads willing to run the risk of missing a superior technique in exchange for gaining the security of knowing they would obtain a reliable and predictable product, firms such as Baldwin thrived by cultivating a record of dependability and responsiveness. Such established suppliers would not risk alienating customers by demanding large patent fees. When railroads manufactured articles in their own facilities for another road, such as the B&O, which built locomotives for other railroads, they sold only the work performed and did not attempt to profit from the novelty of the product.[26]

These unusual characteristics of relations among railroads, suppliers, and employees, combined with the systemic nature of railroad technology and the distinctive aspects of competition among railroads, produced an environment in which innovation can hardly be described as flowing from free competition among inventors seeking to meet the demands of a broad market. This was quite obvious in the case of steel rails and the Bessemer process. But it was true as well even when the innovations involved less significant technical devices and patented appliances. Even in this arena, which on the surface appeared quite hospitable to the so-called independent inventor, the process of technical change in railroading exhibited many qualities of the sort characterized above as "insider innovation."[27] Information about railroad technology flowed among a network of interested and unequal parties whose

---

[24]   Robert Harris to Bassler, April 4, 1872, vol. 26, p. 498, CBQ Papers, 3H4.1.
[25]   J. H. B. Latrobe to J. W. Garrett, January 29, 1879, Patents and Inventions File, B&O Papers.
[26]   Edward Hungerford, *The Story of the Baltimore and Ohio Railroad, 1827–1927* (New York: G. P. Putnam and Sons, 1928), vol. 1, pp. 77–113, 143–146, and 217–231, and vol. 2, pp. 81–98.
[27]   The phrase, as discussed in Chapter 2, comes from Naomi Lamoreaux, *Insider Lending: Banks, Personal Connections, and Economic Development in Industrial New England* (Cambridge: Cambridge University Press and NBER, 1996).

perspectives and decisions regarding technical innovations involved a complex mix of motives. Outside inventors and suppliers of railroad technology operated in a world of extraordinarily well-educated customers who could easily fend for themselves if provoked. Though the railroad industry fostered a climate of experiment and trial capable of subjecting new technologies to a rigorous market test, success often came to those with advantages that went beyond mere technical accomplishment.

PROBLEM PATENTS I: DOUBLE-ACTING BRAKES AND THE DOCTRINE OF SAVINGS

Though railroads seemingly held many advantages in this inside market for technology, patents remained a major source of concern to their executives. As lines grew and deployed more devices in ever larger quantities, managers such as the Burlington's Harris felt increasingly exposed to potential risks from patents. Not only did executives have to monitor a broader array of techniques; they also accumulated significantly larger liabilities. As the stakes increased, railroads could no longer rest assured that they could easily and inexpensively settle with inventors who held strong patent positions. With so much to gain, patent holders might marshal considerable resources in defense of claims, as railroads would soon discover in the course of several extended disputes with especially formidable opponents.

By far the most significant of these cases involved a technology known as "double-acting" brakes. Such brakes, which first appeared around midcentury and within a dozen years had become almost universal in both freight and passenger service, enabled a brakeman to apply retarding force simultaneously to both trucks of wheels on a car by turning a single brake wheel. With the new rigging, railroads could apply brakes to twice as many wheels in a given amount of time, stopping trains faster, or they could maintain the previous level of braking performance with fewer brakemen. Railroads could accomplish this effect by adding familiar mechanical linkages, arranged any number of different ways, to their existing brakes. Most companies converted their fleets in a piecemeal fashion as cars came into the shops for repairs. The innovation soon lost its novelty and became an accepted feature of railroad technology. In many respects, then, double-acting brakes could serve as a prototype for the anonymous sort of innovation that characterized so much technological change in the railroad industry.[28]

Like many such innovations of the period, double-acting brakes had in fact been patented. Indeed, between 1849 and 1853 the United States Patent Office had issued three separate patents covering the double-acting principle

---

[28]   On these technical developments, see John J. Harrower, *History of the Eastern Railroad Association* (Eastern Railroad Association, October 25, 1905), pp. 26–30.

and had also granted a reissue on the first of the three.[29] Upon granting the initial patent (no. 6762) to Nehemiah Hodge in October 1849, the examiner emphasized that Hodge's arrangement could be applied easily to existing cars and brakes, unlike previous inventions that had also enabled brakemen to activate brakes on both trucks with equal force using wheels at either end of a car. Hodge had apparently left room for improvement, however, because two years later, in November 1851, Francis A. Stevens received a patent (no. 8552) for "railroad car brakes" that included a combination of levers arranged so that "each wheel of both trucks...[was] retarded with a uniform force." Then, in July 1852, the patent office issued yet another patent (no. 9109) for a system that connected brakes on both trucks with operating windlasses using vibrating levers in order to "significantly apply the brakes of both trucks." L. F. Thompson and A. G. Bachelder, who had first applied for the patent in 1847, received credit for this invention, but the patent came to be known by the name of their assignee, Henry Tanner. When Hodge applied for and received a reissue (no. 231) in March 1853, his new patent stressed the use of windlasses and discussed a feature known as parallelism, which ensured that the brake rubbers on each wheel of a truck wore evenly, suggesting that equal braking pressure was applied to each wheel with Hodge's brake as well as Stevens's.

This complex web of claims began to baffle railroad management even before the patent office had finished weaving it. In December 1851, with his application still pending, Tanner threatened to bring suit against the Pennsylvania Railroad. The Pennsylvania's board, which in characteristic fashion had already obtained a license from Hodge, initially rebuffed the latecomer and proceeded to apply brakes to numerous cars.[30] Four years later, however, the board reversed field and negotiated a licensing agreement with Thomas Sayles, who had purchased the Tanner patent in July 1855.[31] The change in policy at the Pennsylvania followed a similar action by the B&O. Managers at that line had begun deploying double-acting brakes under licensing arrangement with Stevens, but in February 1854 had obtained a

[29] References to the brake patents appear in the Reports of the Commissioner of Patents for 1849–53. On the Hodge patent, no. 6762, granted October 2, 1849, see the report for 1849, U.S. House of Representatives, 31st Cong., 1st sess., Executive Document no. 20, esp. pp. 428–29. On the Stevens patent, no. 8552, granted November 25, 1851, see the report for 1851, U.S. Senate, 32d Cong., 1st sess., Executive Document no. 118, esp. p. 286. On the Tanner patent, no. 9109, granted July 6, 1852, see the report for 1852, U.S. Senate, 32d Cong., 2d sess., Executive Document no. 55. For the Hodge reissue, no. 231, granted March 1, 1853, see the report for 1853, U.S. Senate, 33d Cong., 1st sess., Executive Document no. 27, esp. p. 483.

[30] Harrower, *History of the Eastern Railroad Association*, pp. 26–30, and PRR Board Minutes 2 (November 19, 1851), p. 64.

[31] PRR Board Minutes 3 (November 28, 1855), p. 115. Later testimony suggests this occurred after Sayles won a suit against the Erie Railroad, following which he settled with many roads for a license fee of $10 per mile. See House Arguments, p. 397.

license for the Tanner patent from a Mr. A. Enigh after determining that the Tanner claim "overrides" the others.[32] In the West, the Chicago, Burlington and Quincy followed the lead of the Pennsylvania and obtained a license to the Tanner patent. Other roads, most notably the Chicago and North Western, acquired rights to use the Stevens.[33]

Though railroads had shown what Robert Harris would have considered an uncharacteristic degree of caution in bothering to obtain rights to disputed patents, they still had not freed themselves from the specter of infringement. Much to their astonishment, a series of lawsuits involving the brake patents hit the railroads between 1859 and 1862. Management at the B&O first got wind of the problem when one of its subsidiaries received a letter charging it with infringing Hodge's patent.[34] Puzzled executives, who presumed the Tanner patent for which they had obtained a license superseded other claims involving double-acting brakes, asked a specialist in railroad patent law to look into the matter. The expert, John Cochran, investigated the case for several months and to his apparent surprise uncovered signs of a conspiracy. "There appears to me to be a kind of connivance of three of these brake patentees, Tanner, Stevens, and Hodge," Cochran reported in September 1860, "for no matter which of these patents a party may purchase the other two claim an infringement, but not at the same time, the third one generally waits till the second one has got his claim allowed and then he steps in and trys [sic] to make it appear that his patent is essential to the other two!"[35] A letter from Thomas Sayles to B&O President John Garrett soon confirmed Cochran's suspicions. Sayles now owned an interest in all three patents. Declaring that the Stevens and Hodge patents infringed the Tanner, he offered to settle with the subsidiary line if it bought a separate license for the Tanner patent.[36]

While managers in the East negotiated with what were proving to be much more formidable opponents than customary, those in the West found themselves confronting those same patent agents in the federal courts of Chicago. Mr. Enigh, who had originally licensed the B&O to use the Tanner patent, now sued the Burlington for infringing the Stevens patent.[37] Meanwhile,

---

[32] "Notes to File," dated 1854, Patents and Invention File, B&O Papers.

[33] The actions of Western roads with regard to "double-acting" brakes can be inferred from subsequent legislative arguments, as discussed in House and Senate Arguments, and from *Railway Co. v. Sayles*, 97 U.S. 554 (1878).

[34] S. S. Hayes to W. G. Harrison, November 9, 1854, and Duane Williams to Northwestern Virginia Railway Company, January 1859, Patents and Inventions File, B&O Papers.

[35] J. Cochrane to H. W. Evans, September 25, 1860, Patents and Inventions File, B&O Papers.

[36] Thomas Sayles to J. W. Garrett, October 3, 1860, B&O Papers.

[37] H. Tanner to J. W. Garrett, March 25, 1862; J. H. B. Latrobe to J. W. Garrett, January 15, 1866; John Cochrane to J. Anderson, March 7, 1866; J. H. B. Latrobe to J. W. Garrett, July 3, 1866; John Cochrane to J. W. Garrett, July 4, 1866; and U.S. Supreme Court to Baltimore and Ohio Railroad Company, March 23, 1868; B&O Papers.

Sayles pressed suit against the Chicago and North Western for infringing the Tanner patent.[38] To Cochran, the prospect of joint suits was appalling. Agents for either Tanner or Stevens should go to court and get the other patent overturned, he complained, because two valid patents could not exist for the same thing. Instead, the patent owners "agreed among themselves to extort money from railroad companies under the pretense of a patent which they know must be invalid."[39] The strategy, however appalling, proved effective in the Chicago courtrooms. In 1865, Sayles achieved the first of what would prove to be a series of victories upholding the Tanner patent.[40] The following year Enigh won his case against the Burlington, which was told to pay damages of $25 per car for each year it had used double-acting brakes.[41] To make matters worse, the patent office then routinely extended the patents of Stevens and Hodge for another seven years.[42]

The rulings out of Chicago reverberated through the entire railroad industry, for in reaching their assessments of damages, federal judges there had evoked a new doctrine with far-reaching implications.[43] Traditionally, courts had arrived at damage figures by determining the profits patent holders made through sales of their inventions to consumers who had not infringed. Those convicted of infringement paid three times the profits the patent holders would have earned had they sold the product themselves. In situations where the patent holders sold licenses instead of finished products, damages totaled three times the established license fee. Problems arose under this method of assessing damages when infringement occurred without the patent holder having sold sufficient numbers of either licenses or finished products to establish a market price. What, then, was the value of the invention? Very early in the history of patent litigation, courts in equity facing this situation began treating infringers as trustees for the plaintiffs of all that

---

[38] *Railway Company v. Sayles.*   [39] John Cochrane, "Report," n.d., B&O Papers.

[40] *Railway Company v. Sayles.*

[41] J. H. B. Latrobe to J. W. Garrett, January 15, 1866; U.S. Supreme Court to Baltimore and Ohio Railroad Company, March 23, 1868; and James R. Doolittle to J. W. Garrett, May 16, 1870; B&O Papers.

[42] Latrobe to Garrett, July 3 and 4, 1866, and Cochran to Garrett, July 4, 1866, Patents and Inventions File, B&O Papers, and Harrower, *History of the Eastern Railroad Association*, pp. 28–30. Additional information on the extensions of 1866 can be found in official documents generated when the patent holders petitioned Congress for a second extension seven years later. See U.S. House of Representatives, "Report of the Committee on Patents," March 2, 1875, 43d Cong., 2d sess., Report no. 274, and U.S. Senate, "Reports of the Committee on Patents," February 4, 1873, 42d Cong., 3d sess., Report no. 369, and June 20, 1874, 43d Cong., 1st sess., Report no. 471.

[43] In addition to Senate and House Arguments, this summary and my subsequent discussion of cases and legislation involving the doctrine of savings is based largely on U.S. House of Representatives, "Report of the Committee on Patents," March 2, 1875, 43d Cong., 2d sess., rept. 274; and U.S. Senate, "Reports of the Committee on Patents," February 4, 1873, 42d Cong., 3d sess., rept. 369; June 2, 1874, 43d Cong., 1st sess., rept. 471; and March 5, 1878, 45th Cong., 2d sess., rept. 116.

they had gained through the unauthorized use of the invention.[44] In other words, patent holders would receive all profits the infringers had generated through sales of the patented article. Again, the market would ultimately set the value of the invention.

But what about cases in which the patent covered a process rather than a product, or when the infringer made and used patented articles but never sold them on the open market? The U.S. Supreme Court confronted just such a situation in the case of *Mowry v. Whitney*.[45] Determining that Whitney had illicitly used a patented process to manufacture railroad car wheels, the court calculated profits not on the basis of revenue and expenses but on "the gain in advantage or economy between the old method...and the new." In other words, it had based its award on the savings the infringer had derived from employing the patented process. The full import of this method of assessing damages emerged in the subsequent case of *Mevs v. Conover*, when the Supreme Court awarded damages based on an accounting of savings even though the infringer had lost money in his business.[46] Widely publicized by the Patent Office and the press, the Mevs decision sparked a wave of proceedings in equity. One notorious example, known as the swedge block cases, struck especially close to railroads.[47] Several lines had tried repairing deformed rails in their tracks by hammering them against metal blocks containing an imprint of the proper shape. Courts awarded damages on the basis that the technique saved labor costs, even though railroads claimed the reshaped rails wore so poorly that in the end they would have saved money by simply tearing out the worn rails and substituting new ones. This ruling came from Thomas Drummond, the same circuit court judge who heard the cases involving double-acting brakes.

The doctrine of savings posed a serious financial threat to railroads. Coming at a time when they had just begun to recognize how exposed their cavalier practices regarding licenses had left them, the doctrine threatened to saddle railroads with damages far greater than they had ever imagined. After winning his initial suit against the Chicago and North Western Railroad, for instance, Sayles sought compensation for savings in brakemen's wages and wheel wear totaling some $455 per car per year. Eventually embraced by Judge Drummond in December 1873, this formula taxed the Chicago and North Western nearly $64,000 for just a five-year period. Even after Drummond substantially reduced the allowance for wheel wear two years

44 *Livingston v. Woodworth*, 56 U.S. 546 (1853); *Dean v. Mason*, 61 U.S. 198 (1857); and *Goodyear v. Providence Rubber Company*, 10 F. Cas. 712 (1864).

45 14 Wall 620 (1872), reversing *Whitney v. Mowry* 29 F. Cas. 1105 (1870).

46 131 U.S. 142 (1877), affirming *Conover v. Mers* 6 F. Cas. 322 (1868) and *Conover v. Mers* 11 Blachf. 197 (1873).

47 *Cawood Patent*, 94 U.S. 695, reversing in part *Turrill v. Illinois Central Railroad Company*, 24 F. Cas. 383 (C.C.N.D.Ill. 1867), 24 F. Cas. 385 (1871), and 24 F. Cas. 387 (1873).

later, patent attorneys claimed railroads would owe some $45 million in damages assessed on this basis for the Tanner claim alone, with appeal to the U.S. Supreme Court the only remaining avenue for relief.[48] As the string of cases leading to the savings doctrine suggested, moreover, other patent holders would apparently have little difficulty convincing judges that conditions in railroading did not establish fair market value for their work and that an assessment based on savings was required. Railroads could reasonably anticipate a flood of lawsuits involving patents stretching back two decades or more, followed by an endless stream of disputes in the future as they accumulated new liabilities. This possibility seemed all the more likely because the patent office, starved by Congress of funds to pay examiners, had significantly relaxed its standards. In 1847, when Thompson and Batchelder first applied for the Tanner patent, the office had issued 572 patents out of 1,531 applications filed (37%). A quarter-century later, when that patent was upheld in Chicago, the office issued 13,033 patents out of 19,472 applications (67%).[49]

As the magnitude of their plight became clear, executives throughout the industry scrambled to get a hold on the situation. At the Philadelphia and Reading, for instance, General Manager Nicolls wrote to master mechanic James Millholland inquiring about the brake patents immediately after Sayles won his first case.[50] Those more familiar with the cases took steps to marshal a collaborative response. Attorney Cochran launched a venture known as the Railway Protective Agency, which in return for annual dues promised to monitor all patents pertaining to railroads and to conduct common defenses if disputes went to trial. Though B&O President John Garrett subscribed to the service and wrote a number of testimonial letters on its behalf, his counterparts at other lines generally preferred to stick with established counsel.[51]

---

[48] *Railway Company v. Sayles*, pp. 556–557; House Arguments, p. 229; and Harrower, *History of the Eastern Railroad Association*, pp. 23, 29. Later, Harris admitted the defense in these trials had not always been conducted as well as it should have. Harris to Isaac Hinckley, December 12, 1876, CBQ Papers, 3H4.2, 2: 255–58.

[49] U.S. House of Representatives, 42d Congress, 2d sess., Report of the Commissioner of Patents for 1871, Ex. Doc. 86, p. 8.

[50] Nicolls to J. Millholland, July 19, 1865, Reading Archives.

[51] Henry Tyson to J. Garrett, August 8, 1859; John Cochrane to Garrett, August 9, 1859; January 4 and 9, September 29, October 3, 1861; and October 10, 1864; and Cochrane to Evans, October 12 and 26, 1861; Garrett Papers, box 76, subject 4178. The Pennsylvania Railroad, for one, refused to support Cochran. At the recommendation of the line's general superintendent, its board decided in October 1862 against aiding Cochran in fighting renewal of Lightner patent for axle boxes. PRR Board Minutes, 4 (October 8, 1862), p. 218. In the years immediately preceding and following, the Pennsylvania's board had referred matters pertaining to patents to Mr. Cuyler, solicitor. PRR Board Minutes, 4 (October 21, 1861), pp. 69 and 71, and 4 (March 18, 1863), p. 289. Later in the same decade, the board would consult with J. H. B. Latrobe, its general counsel, who also corresponded with John Garrett of the B&O about patents and various legal matters.

When executives from a variety of railroads gathered at the inaugural meeting of the National Railway Convention in October 1866, however, they laid plans for two similar organizations to be managed by railroads themselves.[52] Isaac Hinckley, president of the Philadelphia, Wilmington and Baltimore Railroad, circulated copies of a draft constitution for the Eastern Railroad Association. President D. L. Harris of the Connecticut River Railroad, noted Hinckley, had agreed to conduct its business affairs and to coordinate the flow of information among members. Soon Hinckley had persuaded Garrett and executives from most of the major east–west trunk lines to join.[53] Major railroads headquartered in Chicago, led by Harris, formed a companion organization. By 1876, the Western Railroad Association (WRA) included eighty-one lines operating 32,000 miles of track.[54]

Created and managed by chief executives from some of the most respected railroads, these associations constituted pioneering ventures in interfirm cooperation. Lines would pay annual fees, assessed in proportion to earnings, and in return receive full legal services, including consultation on the legal status of all inventions. In the event of a trial, patent experts employed by the

[52] Proceedings from the convention published the following May recalled that in early 1866 New England railroads had joined to conduct a common defense in a suit involving the brake patent of one C. B. Turner. Formal constitutions establishing more permanent organizations of broader scope, the proceedings noted, were still being circulated among prospective members. *Proceedings of the National Railroad Convention* (New York, 1867), pp. 20–22. I am indebted to Professor Colleen Dunlavy of the University of Wisconsin for this reference. On the efforts to form national railroad organizations, see Colleen A. Dunlavy, *Politics and Industrialization: Early Railroads in the United States and Prussia* (Princeton: Princeton University Press, 1994), pp. 245–254, and "Organizing Railroad Interests: The Creation of National Railroad Associations in the United States and Prussia," *Business and Economic History* 19, series 2 (1990): 133–142. See also Isaac Hinckley to J. W. Garrett, April 1, 1867, Garrett Papers, box 86, subject 9614, and Harrower, *History of the Eastern Railroad Association*, pp. 22–30.

[53] Harrower, *History of the Eastern Railroad Association*, pp. 22–25; Isaac Hinckley to Garrett, April 1, 1867, and "Copy of the Constitution of the Eastern Railroad Association (February 6, 1867)," Garrett Papers, box 86, subject 9614. Because the association was politically controversial, it kept a low profile, and precise data regarding membership is scarce. In 1879, Hinckley informed Garrett that nearly every major line in the East belonged to the ERA. Isaac Hinckley to J. W. Garrett, July 24, 1879, Garrett Papers, box 86, subject 9614.

[54] R. Harris to C. W. Mead, October 16, 1869, and Harris to O. S. Lyford, September 27, 1873, CBQ Papers, 3H4.1; and *Annual Reports of the Executive Committee of the Eastern Railroad Association to the Members* (henceforth, *ERA Annual Reports*) 3 (1870), p. 7. For a full account of Harris's leadership of the Western Railroad Association, see letter book in CBQ Papers, 9W5.2. Precise dating of the birth of the WRA is difficult. Official histories indicate that it came into existence with the ERA, but the earliest explicit reference to the association in the papers of Robert Harris is the letter to Mead dated October 16, 1869. U.S. Senate membership data comes from *Senate Arguments*, pp. 191–92.

associations would develop common defenses for the entire group. An executive council consisting of representatives from several member companies – usually executives who took an interest in technical affairs or possessed some legal expertise – would meet semiannually to guide the direction of the group. More than simple cost-sharing arrangements, the patent associations were designed to undercut what railroads perceived to be a "divide and conquer" strategy, in which speculators used credibility gained by quietly reaching settlements with a few lines to extract large settlements from the majority of companies. Members consented to follow the instructions of the association when dealing with any patent holder. Any firm caught entering into an agreement with an individual currently bringing suit against another member would sacrifice its rights to defense by the association. Members also agreed to provide any information they possessed regarding disputed technologies and to keep associations informed of any invention and experiment taking place in their own shops that might be used to undermine patent claims.[55]

The strategy behind the associations clearly reflected recent experience with the brake cases, and there is little doubt those cases provided the immediate stimulus for these collaborative ventures. Lawyers who had argued the cases immediately filled the only full-time positions in the associations and occupied them for many years thereafter. They promptly set to work preparing an appeal in the Stevens case, which reached the Supreme Court in 1868, and continued to devote much of their time to further appeals and other trials involving the brake patents until well into the 1880s. Proponents such as Harris and Hinckley corresponded frequently with one another about the conduct of the trials and used the continuing specter of the brake cases to recruit new members.[56] Harris's successor at the Burlington, Charles Perkins, considered them the primary reason for belonging.[57] The brake cases also figured prominently in a sustained effort by association lobbyists to reform the patent laws, as discussed in more detail below.

Yet in entering into these extraordinary collaborative arrangements, railroad managers clearly understood that the rulings in Chicago had

---

[55] Eastern Railroad Association, "Constitution," February 6, 1867, copy in Garrett Papers, box 86, subject 9614. On the assessment of fees, also see Harrower, *History of the Eastern Railroad Association*, p. 31.

[56] On recruitment, see Isaac Hinckley to Garrett, February 14, 1873, Garrett Papers, box 86, subject 9614; R. Harris to O. S. Lyford, September 27, 1873, CBQ Papers, 3H4.1; and R. Harris to Robert Robinson, September 4, 1874, CBQ Papers, 9W5.2. For commentary on the trials, see R. Harris to Isaac Hinckley, June 7, 1873, CBQ Papers, 3H4.1, 31: 235, and August 9, 1873, CBQ Papers, 3H4.1, 31: 586; and Isaac Hinckley to R. Harris, December 14, 1876, CBQ Papers, 3H4.6, box 3.

[57] R. Harris to C. W. Mead, October 16, 1869, CBQ Papers, 3H4.1, 17: 470–71 and to O. S. Lyford, September 27, 1873, CBQ Papers, 3H4.1, 32: 251–52; R. Harris to C. E. Perkins, April 18, 1876, CBQ Papers, 3H4.2; and W. B. Strong to C. E. Perkins, May 12, 1876, CBQ Papers, 3P4.4.

implications well beyond the matter of brakes. Executives feared that enterprising agents such as Sayles and Enigh might easily expose numerous other hidden patent liabilities. At the B&O, for example, Garrett was involved at the time in lengthy disputes with speculators who owned patent rights for a type of car axle and for a method of manufacturing car wheels.[58] In 1867, managers at the Pennsylvania felt compelled to dispatch their mechanics to the patent office before pursuing work on ventilators. The mechanics returned confident in their abilities to design a better ventilator. But who could be certain the "jumble of patents" they had found did not contain the seed of an infringement suit that might negate their efforts and cost the Pennsylvania dearly? Could the sea of accumulated claims effectively block railroads from reaping the inventive talents of their own expertise?

The question was not an idle one, as Harris of the Burlington discovered the following year when he found himself facing precisely such a predicament. Harris had for some time monitored and encouraged some experiments with novel fireboxes conducted by C. F. Jauriet, a Burlington employee who in 1871 would become the firm's master mechanic.[59] Early on in this work, Jauriet apparently took out a patent, with the usual approval and assistance of Harris.[60] The device performed well enough for Harris to request its use on new locomotives under construction at the Burlington's suppliers and to promote it among colleagues responsible for other roads in the Burlington system. This recommendation came back to haunt Harris in the spring of 1868. Burlington Director James F. Joy wrote from Boston complaining that Mr. Mead, head of the Hannibal and St. Joseph Railroad, had been threatened with expensive litigation for infringing the Jauriet patent. A contrite Harris assured Joy he had secured full rights to the patent for the CB&Q. But he confessed that the inventor, short on funds, had fallen into the hands of a Mr. Chittenden, a patent dealer notorious for his activities in connection with the sewing machine and gas industries. Anxious to protect the man to whom he would soon assign principal responsibility for all technical affairs at the CB&Q, Harris explained to both Joy and Mead that if Jauriet had retained control over the patent, he certainly would have granted permission to use the device without charge throughout the system.[61] The mistake had occurred, however, and Harris had seen his customary policies regarding innovation and patents blow up in his face. The following year he included the Jauriet fire box, along with

58 Patents and Inventions File, B&O Papers.
59 R. Harris to Mr. Jauriet, October 8, 1869, CBQ Papers, 3H4.1, 17: 438, and August 8, 1871, CBQ Papers, 3H4.1, 24: 434–435.
60 R. Harris to C. E. Perkins, June 4, 1868, CBQ Papers, 3H4.1, 12: 441, and to O. S. Lyford, July 29, 1872, CBQ Papers, 3H4.1, 27: 491.
61 R. Harris to J. F. Joy, March 6, 1868, CBQ Papers, 3H4.1, 12: 69–70, and to C. W. Mead, March 7, 1868, CBQ Papers, 3H4.1, 12: 81–82.

brakes and the swedge block, as the principal issues standing before the WRA.[62]

The Jauriet episode vividly illustrates why railroad executives felt so vulnerable in the face of the patent cases of the 1860s and why they looked to the patent associations for relief. At the time Harris received the inquiry from Joy, the CB&Q had not even bothered to maintain a centralized list of licensing agreements with patentees.[63] Such lax policies, borne of an age when railroad technology had emerged in highly local contexts through the efforts of individual mechanics, now left railroads exposed to significant liabilities they could not readily identify. The ignorance and informality that early on had imparted a useful generic quality to railroad technology had been turned against railroads by aggressive agents. Managers such as Harris, caught off-guard, realized belatedly that they would need to maintain close watch over inventive activities or risk losing access to channels of innovation they had come to take for granted. Upon promoting Jauriet to master mechanic in 1871, a chastened Harris would stipulate that Jauriet submit no new designs to manufacturers without first giving them to Harris.[64]

Railroads would eventually impose a measure of control over the market for patents, but in 1868 such an outcome was anything but obvious. That summer, the WRA lost its appeal to the Supreme Court in the Stevens case. Faced with the prospect of paying Enigh royalties of $25 per car per year for a device nearly two decades old, Garrett and other prominent members of the ERA decided to launch yet another appeal.[65] Meanwhile, Sayles stood ready to claim even larger damage settlements as the Tanner case remained before the federal courts in Chicago. Two days before Christmas, Harris received word from a subordinate of yet another disputed patent. Doubtless still reeling from the Jauriet fiasco, the exasperated Harris stamped a fitting epitaph upon what for him had been a dismal year. "Patents and passes," he scrawled angrily across the letter before returning it, "will be the death of me!"

PROBLEM PATENTS II: SAFETY APPLIANCES AND THE LURE OF TECHNOLOGY

When Harris sang this lament, he had yet to encounter serious troubles involving one area of railroad technology in which patents figured unusually

---

[62] R. Harris to C. W. Mead, October 16, 1869, CBQ Papers, 3H4.1, 17: 470–71.

[63] A list of licenses, prepared at Harris's request when he discovered the lapse in 1872, can be found in the CBQ Papers, f32.4.

[64] R. Harris to Mr. Jauriet, August 8, 1871, CBQ Papers, 3H4.1, 24: 434–35.

[65] James R. Doolittle to J. W. Garrett, May 16, 1870, B&O Papers. In 1882, the Supreme Court denied this appeal as well, and the WRA advised the Pennsylvania to settle for a fixed fee of $25,000. George Harding to Wayne McVeagh, December 4, 1882; A. McCallum to Hon. James A. Logan, January 3, 1883; and John Scott to Geo. Roberts, January 9, 1883; PRR Board Papers.

prominently. From its beginnings, steam transport had stirred public concern about nuisances such as noise, smoke, and accidents. During the 1830s, frequent boiler explosions on steamboats had prompted some of the earliest state and federal legislation intended to remedy the negative consequences of new technology.[66] Railroads brought the dirt and perils of steam into congested urban areas. In an effort to minimize costly transhipments, lines typically penetrated right to the old waterfront, often passing through newer business and residential areas along the way. Tracks in Baltimore, for instance, ran down the middle of bustling commercial strips such as Howard Street throughout most of the nineteenth century. Only with the coming of smoke-free electric traction during the 1890s did the B&O at last replace the surface lines with a tunnel beneath the street. By then, the number of deaths and serious injuries attributable to railroad grade crossings and mishaps at stations had reached the astonishing total of over 4,500 per year nationwide.[67]

Communities and individuals sought relief from the obvious perils of railroading through a variety of means. Much of the response came in the form of legal actions taken by individuals seeking compensation for damages. Reports from state and federal courts of the mid-nineteenth century contain a thicket of legal rulings in tort cases so tangled it defies easy generalization. Railroads skirted some of their greatest potential liabilities when courts consistently passed responsibility for accidents onto railroad employees under the doctrines of contributory negligence and the fellow servant principle. Such cases left aggrieved parties with hollow victories, since they stood little chance of collecting significant payments from brakemen or other railroad workers. Disputes involving excessive noise and smoke, nuisances for which railroads could not so easily pass the blame, yielded no clear legal doctrine.[68]

In addition to the constant threat of private lawsuits, railroads faced a myriad of local ordinances restricting their operations.[69] Most towns imposed

---

[66] John G. Burke, "Bursting Boilers and the Federal Power," *Technology and Culture* 7 (1966): 1–23.

[67] U.S. Interstate Commerce Commission, *Eighth Annual Report on the Statistics of Railways in the United States* (Washington: Government Printing Office, 1896), pp. 84 and 95. Some 525 people died at grade crossings alone during the year ending June 30, 1895, all but 20 of whom were neither passengers nor employees of the railroads; another 499 were killed at stations.

[68] For attempts to untangle the legal thicket, see Christine Rosen, "Differing Perceptions of the Value of Pollution Abatement Across Time and Place: Balancing Doctrine in Pollution Nuisance Law, 1840–1906," *Law and History Review* 11 (1993): 303–381; "Businessmen Against Pollution in Late Nineteenth Century Chicago," *Business History Review* 71 (1995): 387–396; and "Noisome, Noxious, and Offensive Vapors, Fumes and Stenches in American Towns and Cities, 1840–1865," *Historical Geography* 25 (1997): 49–82.

[69] David O. Stowell, *Streets, Railroads, and the Great Strike of 1877* (Chicago: University of Chicago Press, 1999).

speed limits, and many banned transport entirely on Sundays or late at night. Though seemingly little more than innocuous encouragements toward common courtesy, such laws often created costly bottlenecks for lines seeking to push more traffic through increasingly congested networks. Managers chafed against the restrictions and often flaunted them during busy periods. When the aspiring young Andrew Carnegie took responsibility for moving trains through the Pennsylvania's crowded lines around Pittsburgh, for instance, he immediately authorized round-the-clock operations.[70] Western roads such as the Burlington eased congestion during harvest season and other periods of peak demand by running trains on Sundays.[71]

Brazen managers could take such chances and challenge local authorities with little anxiety during the developmental boom of the fifties and early sixties. So long as communities and states engaged in fierce competition to attract new lines, few risked driving away outside capital with unfriendly restrictions or overzealous enforcement.[72] The federalist system drove regulations addressing nuisances, like those pertaining to finance and rates, toward a least common denominator.[73] Following the Civil War, however, years of frustrating experiences with costly bankruptcies and unbuilt lines cooled enthusiasm for railroad investment and sparked an angry backlash. Grangers and other voters rebelled at the prospect of raising taxes to pay off bonds used to fund lines that had never come into existence.[74]

While courts and legislatures continued to struggle for many years with the financial hangover from the earlier investment binge, the public increasingly turned its focus away from finance and toward matters pertaining to railroad service.[75] As with most consumer-oriented movements, much of the attention went toward prices. Newly created state commissions, drawing on common-law powers giving states the right to regulate certain types of businesses affecting the public interest, carved a role adjudicating rate

---

[70] Harold C. Livesay, *Andrew Carnegie and the Rise of Big Business* (Boston: Little, Brown, 1975), pp. 31–32.

[71] On the introduction of Sunday trains, see Walter Licht, *Working for the Railroad: The Organization of Work in the Nineteenth Century* (Princeton: Princeton University Press, 1983), and CBQ Papers.

[72] George H. Miller, *Railroads and the Granger Laws* (Madison: University of Wisconsin Press, 1971).

[73] Harry N. Scheiber, "Federalism and the American Economic Order, 1789–1910," *Law and Society Review* 10 (1975): 57–118.

[74] Charles Fairman, *Reconstruction and Reunion, 1864–1888: History of the Supreme Court of the United States, Part One* (New York: Macmillan, 1971), chs. 17 and 18.

[75] Lee Benson, quoting the railroad economist Arthur Hadley, observes that in both the United States and Europe the emphasis in railroad regulation shifted between 1870 and 1873 from investor-oriented legislation to shipper-oriented legislation. Lee Benson, *Merchants, Farmers, and Railroads: Railroad Regulation and New York Politics, 1850–1887* (Cambridge, Mass.: Harvard University Press, 1955), pp. 292–293.

disputes.[76] In Congress, a special commission headed by Senator William Windom, a prominent member of the Minnesota Grange, investigated transport rates between the Midwest and the Eastern Seaboard. Following publication of its report in 1873, a bill proposing to create a national railway commission received serious consideration.[77]

The renewed conflict between railroads and their growing ranks of detractors inevitably spilled over into the area of nuisances as well. Operating amid an increasingly hostile political environment, railroads could not afford to alienate the public further by appearing callous or indifferent to the disruptions and calamities they caused. New organizations such as the Grange and the state regulatory commissions, moreover, could direct attention toward those nuisances on a scale never before seen. No longer could railroads proceed with the confidence of knowing their battles over nuisances would take place in local forums of government or in isolated courtrooms against plaintiffs of comparatively limited means. A single isolated but dramatic accident, if brought beneath the spotlight of an official state inquiry, might prompt an ongoing national debate.

Just such an incident occurred at Revere, Massachusetts, in August 1871, when a train plowed into the rear of another packed with tourists making a holiday excursion to the beach. The lightweight cars, loosely joined with link-and-pin couplers, telescoped into one another. Some twenty-nine passengers died in the fiery wreckage, and another fifty-seven were injured.[78] The disaster was the first significant wreck to occur since the Massachusetts legislature in 1869 had created a state railroad commission and appointed Charles Francis Adams, Jr., to its head. This young Brahmin, grandson of former President John Quincy Adams and son of the United States ambassador to Britain during the Civil War, had recently come to prominence in public affairs when he and his brother Henry penned a widely published exposé of the financially troubled Erie Railroad. The piece exemplified Adams's commitment to the so-called sunshine approach to regulation. He believed in the power of publicity, rather than compulsory legislation, to remedy the evils of the industry.[79]

[76] Miller, *Railroads and the Granger Laws*; Benson, *Merchants*; and Edward Chase Kirkland, *Industry Comes of Age: Business, Labor, and Public Policy, 1860–1897* (New York: Holt, Rinehart, and Winston, 1961), chs. 3–6.

[77] Margaret Susan Thompson, *The "Spider's Web": Congress and Lobbying in the Age of Grant* (Ithaca: Cornell University Press, 1985), pp. 265–266.

[78] Edward Chase Kirkland, *Charles Francis Adams, Jr., 1835–1915: The Patrician at Bay* (Cambridge, Mass.: Harvard University Press, 1965), pp. 51–52, and Thomas K. McCraw, *Prophets of Regulation* (Cambridge, Mass.: Harvard University Press, 1984), pp. 26–28.

[79] Charles Francis Adams, Jr., and Henry Adams, *Chapters of Erie and Other Essays* (Boston, 1871); Kirkland, *Charles Francis Adams, Jr.*; McCraw, *Prophets of Regulation*, ch. 1.

In the wake of the accident at Revere, Adams set to work in characteristic fashion, writing two reports on the incident. In one, intended primarily for the railroads, Adams attributed the accident to sloppy procedures and improper clarification of responsibilities. He stressed the need for rule books that would anticipate all operational conditions and advised that they be kept on file with the state commission. In other words, he made an appeal for greater order. Adams directed his second report to the public, which he feared had reached a state of panic in the wake of the disaster. With it, Adams sought to restore confidence. He cited statistics showing how rail travel in Massachusetts was still safer than in most other states and was growing steadily safer over time when considered on a per capita basis. Perhaps sensing that such numbers offered a weak antidote to sensational news stories describing the travails of victims, Adams then noted hopefully that several new appliances offered the potential for dramatically improved safety. He promised the commission would sponsor trials of a few, including air brakes, tight-fitting couplers, and automatic electric signals. To the public, Adams held out the lure of technology.[80]

With these reports, Adams gave new definition to the safety issue. His two conceptions of railroad safety – one grounded in the mundane appeal of order, the other steeped in the promising lure of technology – would shape the contours of debate about railroad safety and its regulation throughout the Gilded Age and Progressive era. Virtually all public discussions of railroad safety during the next half-century owed something to them. In his own subsequent reports on accidents, which appeared periodically during the 1870s and eventually were gathered together in an influential book, Adams revealed clearly that his personal sentiments regarding safety rested firmly with the appeal to order. His analyses of accidents repeatedly focused on administrative neglect and on the failures of management to establish routines and ensure that employees followed them correctly. By relentlessly drawing attention to these issues and publishing statistics on actual performance, Adams thought, he could compel railroads to bring a more concerted effort to the task of running trains safely.

Among the public, however, Adams had sparked widespread interest in safety appliances. Air brakes and close-fitting automatic couplers, as well as certain types of signals, were alluring devices. They were technical marvels that held forth the promise of seemingly absolute, fail-safe protection,

---

[80] Charles Francis Adams, Jr., *Notes on Railroad Accidents* (New York: Putnam's Sons, 1879); McGraw, *Prophets*, pp. 25–31; Kirkland, *Charles Francis Adams, Jr.*, pp. 51–54; and Edward Chase Kirkland, *Men, Cities, and Transportation: A Study in New England History, 1820–1900* (Cambridge, Mass.: Harvard University Press, 1948), vol. 2, ch. 15. See also Mark Aldrich, *Safety First: Technology, Labor, and Business in the Building of American Worker Safety, 1870–1939* (Baltimore: Johns Hopkins University Press, 1997), ch. 1.

without dependence on human performance or on the complicated sets of rules Adams emphasized.[81] In the cases of automatic brakes and signals, the appliances accomplished this by utilizing mysterious new forces such as compressed air and electricity. The fact that most of these technical novelties were covered by patents seemed only to heighten public interest. In an age that frequently revered inventors, patents gave brakes and couplers an identity and an aura that much railroad technology did not carry. People spoke constantly of "patent" brakes and "patent" couplers and often referred to entire areas of technology by a single name, as in "Westinghouse brakes" and "Janney couplers," despite the fact that several alternative devices existed in each field. We can detect little public interest or enthusiasm for countless other technologies – shock-absorbing springs, bearings made from alloys that did not so easily overheat and deform, wheels and rails that did not crack or split so readily, hand grips, and running boards – all of which made enormous contributions to improved safety but were not controlled by patents. Congress would not mandate the use of such simple, generic technologies as sill steps, running boards, and ladders on freight cars until 1910, nearly two decades after it passed legislation requiring automatic brakes and couplers on freight trains.[82]

Calls for legislation mandating the use of automatic brakes, couplers, and signals, on the other hand, surfaced almost immediately after the accident at Revere. Adams raised the prospect himself in his annual report of January 1872, but in keeping with his "sunshine" approach to regulation he concluded that compulsory legislation "would be of very doubtful expediency."[83] Numerous other state commissions entertained the idea, however, and in 1873 Representative Andrew King introduced a bill to Congress calling for all passenger trains to have continuous brakes by 1875.[84]

The prospect of having to deploy large numbers of patented safety devices, just as courts and the Congress seemed intent on enforcing the patent laws by rewarding unprecedented damage claims, came as a rude shock to the railroads. Industry representatives rushed to put forth the railroad perspective in both the general press and the trade literature. Spokesmen for the railroads typically expressed sympathy with the drive for safety but argued that

---

[81] Even the sober editors of the *New York Times* expressed such sentiments. In the wake of Adams's report, they called for compulsory legislation requiring automatic brakes. *New York Times*, April 2, 1872, p. 4. "The great aim in railroad management," wrote the editors later that year, "should be to so utilize all mechanical inventions that little or no dependence need be placed on unskilled men." *New York Times*, October 27, 1872, p. 4.

[82] U.S. Interstate Commerce Commission (henceforth, ICC), "Summary History of Legislation Regarding Safety Appliances," n.d. (c. 1896), mss. copy in ICC Library, Washington, D.C.; ICC, *Annual Reports*, vol. 22 (1908) and vol. 24 (1910).

[83] Massachusetts, *Third Annual Report of the Board of Railroad Commissioners* (1872).

[84] ICC, "Summary History of Legislation."

legislation should "make safety the requirement without troubling ourselves with the means." (One proposed alternative called for laws that would make railroads responsible for all damages.) Editors denied that lawmakers could "judge the value and necessity of inventions" and warned that "legislators should not be too positive that they can at once solve problems that have taxed professional railway men for years."[85] Trade press editors frequently questioned the wisdom of compelling railroads to adopt specific devices covered by patents, a concern Adams shared. He argued such laws would reward monopolists and freeze further development.[86]

Aside from an Illinois statute requiring automatic couplers, public agitation in the wake of the accident at Revere ultimately produced no new safety laws during the 1870s.[87] Yet there can be no doubt railroads felt intense pressure throughout the decade from the mounting clamor for safety appliances. The threat of legislation hung constantly over them in many forums. As railroads well knew, moreover, the traveling public could easily vote with its pocketbooks if it failed to find satisfaction in political forums. When a few pioneering lines advertised that their equipment employed one device or another, managers at other roads felt powerless to resist emulating them. In the end, railroads would head off regulation not so much by argument as by acquiescence.

Harris and Electric Signaling

Once again, the ordeals of Robert Harris at the Burlington provide unusually rich insight into the burdens rail executives experienced as they faced the harsh glare of Adams's sunshine. During the 1860s, before the full impact of the brake cases had become clear to him, Harris had shown considerable enthusiasm for new safety devices. Upon learning about the Miller platform, a new and much safer method of joining passenger cars, Harris cultivated a close relationship with the inventor and publicized his creation widely.[88] He did the same for George Westinghouse, Jr., and his air brake not long after that device made its appearance in 1869.[89] The year before that, Harris put up company funds when the Burlington's superintendent of the telegraph, F. H. Tubbs, sought a patent for an electric crossing signal he

---

85 Sentiments such as these can be found regularly in the two major trade journals of this period, *Railway Age* and *Railroad Gazette*. The quotes here come from *Railway Age*, 1 (1876), p. 189, and 2 (1877), p. 642

86 Kirkland, *Charles Francis Adams, Jr.*, p. 53.

87 ICC, "Summary History of Legislation."

88 R. Harris to W. W. Wilcox, October 18, 1867; R. Harris to Thomas Swingard, March 22, 1869; R. Harris to P. S. Henning, June 4, 1869; R. Harris to Col. C. G. Hammond, November 15, 1869; R. Harris to C. E. Perkins, November 16, 1869; R. Harris to J. F. Joy, May 11, 1868; and R. Harris to Col. Miller, May 2, 7, and 13, 1868; CBQ Papers, 3H4.1.

89 This episode is discussed in more detail below.

had designed. Harris monitored Tubbs's inventive endeavors over the next few years and consulted with him on several occasions about the use of such signals at trouble spots on the Burlington's route.[90] In February 1871, he pressed Tubbs to take the initiative in approaching his counterparts at other lines about installing signals at points where their tracks intersected the Burlington's.[91]

The case of signaling illustrates especially well why Harris, despite what appears an admirable record in matters pertaining to safety, found himself feeling quite vulnerable as the movement for railroad safety mobilized during the seventies. Signaling technology attained particularly swift notoriety in the aftermath of Revere. Adams and other early investigators recognized immediately that the sort of rear-end collision occurring there would in all likelihood have been prevented had the Eastern Railroad deployed a technique known as block signaling to govern the movements of its trains. Railroads operating in block fashion divided the track into short sections, or blocks, and prohibited any train from entering a block until the previous train had exited. If rigidly enforced, this method provided much surer protection than the more commonly used time-interval procedure, in which lines attempted to keep trains separated by spacing their departures across time.[92]

American lines generally lagged behind their European counterparts in utilizing block operations, but by the end of the Civil War, many railroads had come to employ their regular stations in a sort of informal block arrangement. Station agents would not permit a locomotive engineer to depart until they received word via telegraph that the train ahead had cleared the next station. In a few exceptional cases, lines had built special stations at regular intervals along their routes and manned them with operators whose sole responsibility was to monitor the signal. A pioneering installation along the main line of the Philadelphia and Reading, which ran frequent heavy coal trains down its curvy, mountainous route from the anthracite fields to the Quaker City, was garnering considerable attention in railroad circles

[90]   R. Harris to Wilcox, December 6, 1867; R. Harris to Hitchcock, August 16, 1870; and R. Harris to C. Latimer, July 17, 1873; CBQ Papers, 3H4.1.

[91]   For examples of the Burlington initiating discussions of crossing signals, see R. Harris to F. H. Tubbs, February 11, 1871, CBQ Papers, 3H4.1.

[92]   The term "block signals" was in fact something of a misnomer, for station agents could and often did operate block systems without signals of any sort. They literally passed instructions directly to each locomotive driver via written train orders. This method had the added benefit of providing an official record that supervisors could use to trace responsibility in the event of a problem. As a convenience and added measure of protection, however, railroads often installed simple, hand-operated semaphore signals at each station. Agents set the blades at one of three angles in order to indicate "stop," "go," or "proceed with caution." Signal operators along the Philadelphia and Reading accomplished the same end by displaying blue and white discs in various combinations.

at the time of the Revere wreck.[93] But few American railroads faced such arduous operating conditions as the Reading, and the sort of dedicated signaling systems it employed remained rare. (Even the technically progressive Pennsylvania would not install signal towers along its unusually busy lines from New York through Philadelphia to Pittsburgh until 1876.[94]) In the crush of actual service, moreover, station agents and signal operators often resorted to so-called permissive operations, in which they routinely let trains proceed with caution into a block so long as sufficient time had passed, even if they had not received word about the progress of the previous train. When Adams stressed the importance of writing and enforcing rules, he frequently had in mind the need for explicit instructions governing operating procedures in this permissive mode.

While railroads remained circumspect about the virtues of absolute block signaling, safety advocates seized upon it as a surefire means of preventing rear-end collisions. In their zeal to obtain absolute protection, moreover, some safety proponents expressed interest in the possibility of combining block methods with the sort of electromechanical mechanisms used by inventors such as Tubbs to activate their crossing signals. If such arrangements could somehow enable trains themselves to activate the signals, the block system would function without dependence on human operators (other than locomotive engineers who needed to respond to the signal). Such "automatic" signals might also discourage or even eliminate permissive operations, since locomotive engineers would presumably act on the assumption a "stop" signal really meant an obstruction lay ahead, rather than being left to wonder whether an operator had neglected to send back word that the previous train had cleared the block.

For automatic electric block signals to be used with such confidence, of course, they would need to be built to high standards of reliability. In retrospect, we know that task would prove extremely difficult. Frequent problems with false stops, together with several other factors (discussed in Chapter 8), caused railroads and safety regulators to shy away from automatic electric block signals until the early twentieth century. National surveys in 1900 revealed that fewer than 2,300 miles of track were equipped with automatic signals.[95] Yet three decades earlier, when the techniques were still untested and antirailroad sentiment ran high, this outcome was anything but obvious to railroad executives such as Harris. In June 1871, two months before the accident at Revere, his own superintendent of the telegraph had approached

93 This system is described in G. Nicolls to C. E. Smith, August 8, 1864, vol. 670, pp. 19–20 and 23–26, and Angus Mcleod to W. F. Merrill, November 6, 1890, vol. 605, pp. 378–379, Reading Papers.

94 *Annual Reports of the Pennsylvania Railroad Company* (henceforth, PRR *Annual Reports*) 28 (1874), p. 123; 29 (1875), pp. 34, 117, and 127; and 30 (1876), p. 31.

95 Braman B. Adams, *The Block System of Signaling on American Railroads* (New York, 1901), pp. 170–171.

Harris about the possibility of operating a block system by using the crossing signals scattered along the Burlington's route. Harris decided against the idea.[96] Apparently he did not dismiss the prospect altogether, however, for that November, at about the time Adams issued his reports on the incident at Revere, Harris sent Tubbs on a tour of Eastern railroads in order to gain familiarity with the latest signaling technology.[97] A year later, he again arranged funding so that Tubbs could patent a signal of his own design.[98]

The available records do not reveal with absolute certainty what Harris had in mind in taking these steps. Perhaps he had no real interest in block operations and was merely indulging a valuable employee with a yen to invent. Like Adams and most railroad managers of his era, Harris tended to look first toward organizational remedies to congestion rather than to technological ones. He liked to tell, with amusement but no apparent regret, how his company had not used the telegraph until 1864, fully twenty years after Morse first demonstrated the device.[99] But this story also resonated with a healthy dose of nostalgia, as if Harris could not quite believe just how far removed from those halcyon days the Burlington had grown. The postwar boom had placed unprecedented demands on the system. Not only did the Burlington run more trains; competition forced it to run them faster. Like most railroad managers, Harris was loathe to meet those challenges by increasing speeds. He periodically warned his division managers to limit freight trains to the prescribed speed of 15 miles per hour, and he set a maximum speed of 40 miles per hour.[100] Charles Perkins, who had charge of operating trains through the Burlington system in Nebraska, followed this dictum so zealously that on at least one occasion even Harris objected.[101] With such constraints on speed, the Burlington needed to eliminate as much dead time as possible and keep trains in motion if it hoped to compete in lucrative markets served by fast freight and express stock trains.

Signals could help in this endeavor. Not only might they prevent the occasional disruptive accident, but on a routine basis they would also help engineers avoid unnecessary stops. When railroads such as the Pennsylvania at last deployed automatic block systems during the 1890s, they would do so to keep trains moving, not to provide more secure protection.[102] In 1873,

96 R. Harris to F. H. Tubbs, June 7, 1871, CBQ Papers, 3H4.1.
97 Open letter from R. Harris to executives of Eastern railroads, November 15, 1871, and R. Harris to F. H. Tubbs, May 15 and June 22, 1871, CBQ Papers, 3H4.1.
98 R. Harris to Tubbs, June 22, 1871; October 19 and November 8, 1872; CBQ Papers, 3H4.1.
99 R. Harris to M. S. Foote, February 19, 1874, CBQ Papers, 3H4.1.
100 For example, see R. Harris to Potter, August 4, 1875, and R. Harris to Hitchcock, October 1, 1875, CBQ Papers, 3H4.1.
101 R. Harris to Perkins, December 15, 1869, CBQ Papers, 3H4.1, 18: 361.
102 See discussion below in Chapter 8 and George H. Burgess and Miles C. Kennedy, *Centennial History of the Pennsylvania Railroad Company* (Philadelphia: Pennsylvania Railroad, 1949), p. 494.

Harris emphasized this same benefit when urging a fellow rail executive to help pay for an automatic crossing gate at one intersection. Such signals reduced delays, he stressed, by eliminating the need to stop routinely at all crossings.[103] By reducing the need for stops, moreover, signals also held out the promise of lower operating expenses, because steam locomotives consumed much of their fuel and placed great strains on track and other equipment during starting. Such considerations may not have corresponded with those of safety advocates, but they nonetheless gave Harris good reason to show an interest in automatic signals.

Harris also had good reason to be concerned about patents. Signaling presented aspiring inventors with an enticing opportunity. With a minimum of investment, tinkerers could devise novelties that might earn a handsome profit and provide an invaluable public service to boot. The emerging science and technology of electricity, moreover, seemed to hold forth endless possibilities. The telegraph industry had long since demonstrated how electricity could reliably be used to achieve effects across long distances. The industry had also given rise to a substantial community of independent inventors, including the young Thomas Edison as well as hundreds of less conspicuous figures such as the Burlington's Tubbs. This group busily worked to generate larger quantities of electricity and to use it to power lights or to propel machines such as stock tickers and even locomotives. Numerous inventors seemingly far removed from the railroads used their knowledge of electricity to design signaling apparatus. A steady stream of pamphlets describing new, patented safety gates flowed into the offices of the Burlington and other American railroads.[104] Some gates automatically closed when a train approached, others required the operation of a signalman. Blockades varied, and inventors added countless permutations of bells, lights, whistles, and other warning devices. One manufacturer surveyed the vast number of devices and dryly noted, "There is something about signals very fascinating to the inventive faculty."[105]

---

[103]   R. Harris to C. Latimer, July 17, 1873, CBQ Papers, 3H4.1, and Perkins to G. Harris, February 2, 1890, CBQ Papers, 3P4.1. The Burlington and most other railroads would ultimately deploy interlocking signal apparatus at crossings and other track junction points. This technology used mechanical or electrical connections to link signals and switches in yards and other busy spots in ways that prevented the switchman from sending two trains over the same crossing or junction or from setting a switch against an approaching train. Interlocking apparatus did not garner significant notoriety in the United States until 1876, when the British firm Saxby and Farmer exhibited their device at the Centennial Exhibition in Philadelphia.

[104]   Examples of these pamphlets can be found in the archives of the Burlington, B&O, and Reading. See, in particular, the Garrett Papers, box 21, subject 289, and box 22, subject 316.

[105]   The Johnson Railroad Signal Company, *Catalogue of Interlocking and Railroad Signaling Appliances* (Rahway, N.J.: Johnson Railroad Signaling Company, 1889), p. 5, Pamphlet Collection, Hagley Museum and Library.

Executives such as Harris faced a daunting task in trying to wade through this pool of patented signaling devices. Many of the appliances drew on techniques that fell outside the familiar realm of the machine shop and the expertise of the master mechanic. Over the years, railroad management had persistently encountered difficulty in assessing innovations involving electricity. Members of railroad boards of directors found themselves over-matched, for instance, by the technical complexity of the telegraph. Though telegraph companies ran wires along their rights-of-way from the time of Samuel Morse's invention in 1844, railroads did not utilize the innovation in their own operations for at least another seven years.[106] The Pennsylvania's board of directors had spent three years puzzling over various devices before finally deciding to purchase a Morse system in 1855.[107] At most railroads, the superintendent of the telegraph long remained the only trusted consultant in matters pertaining to electricity, as Tubbs was at the Burlington.[108] As late as 1889, top executives at the Burlington routinely told manufacturers of electrical devices that "our superintendent of the telegraph has complete charge of all electrical matters."[109] With so little sound advice available to guide them, executives such as Harris and their subordinates remained unchar-acteristically dependent upon outside inventors when considering electrical apparatus.

Because electrical devices originated outside the technical realm encom-passed by master mechanics, they were also less subject to the centralized administrative controls that increasingly characterized innovation involving locomotives and mechanical technology. Responsibility for crossing signals and warning devices generally fell to division superintendents and operating personnel who had little connection to the network of shop workers and mechanics. The choice to install those devices, moreover, often took place under duress. When the surge in traffic had begun to strain the Burlington, for instance, Harris had generally behaved reactively, adding devices spo-radically as problems arose rather than pursuing any sort of systematic initiative. Discussions of specific signaling installations in his extensive cor-respondence almost always included references to accidents at that point in the track. His early "policy" regarding signals was perhaps best expressed in a scrawled note to an underling following an accident on the Burlington in 1870: "Anything but collisions! If it is semaphores by the dozen or flagmen

[106] Robert L. Thompson, *Wiring a Continent: The History of the Telegraph Industry in the United States, 1832–1866* (Princeton: Princeton University Press, 1947), pp. 205–208.

[107] PRR Board Minutes, Special Committee on the Telegraph, April 6 and September 12, 1853; January 4, 1854, 2: 422; August 23, 1855, 3: 92; and September 19, 1855, 3: 102.

[108] R. Harris to M. S. Foote, February 19, 1874, CBQ Papers, 3H4.1.

[109] Stone to Clancy, October 31, 1889, CBQ Papers, 3H5.24.

by the hundred!"[110] Not surprisingly, managers operating under such orders neglected to keep close tabs over which signals they used. When Perkins took over from Harris and inquired in 1878 about who supplied the Burlington with crossing gates and manual signals, he was alarmed to learn that employees on different parts of the system had been left to purchase their personal favorites.[111] The situation left the Burlington exposed to the sorts of hidden patent liabilities that had come to haunt railroads in the brake cases.

The same beguiling electromechanical techniques used to activate the patented crossing gates, moreover, would likely come into play as inventors tackled the problems of automatic block signaling. Indeed, the man who would ultimately receive credit for inventing automatic block signals, William Robinson, was already actively engaged in just such an effort when Tubbs suggested the possibility to Harris in June 1871. An obscure figure, Robinson had taught school and gradually established himself in the developing oil business of Western Pennsylvania after graduating from Wesleyan University in Connecticut in 1865.[112] Sometime during this formative period Robinson designed an automatic crossing gate, which he exhibited at the American Institute Fair in New York in 1870. During that same year Robinson used his automatic gate in conjunction with block signals on a short section of the Philadelphia and Erie Railroad.[113] Such appears to have been the state of his work when Adams drew attention to automatic signals and Robert Harris dispatched his superintendent of the telegraph to investigate signaling systems in the East.

Sometime the following year, in 1872, Robinson patented a critical refinement known as the closed circuit. Rather than use the wheels of a train entering a block to complete a previously open electrical loop and activate the signal, the new arrangement used the wheels to short the flow of current in a completed circuit. The signal moved to the "stop" position when a train entered the block circuit and deprived the device of current, then returned to the "clear" setting when the train exited the block and the flow of current resumed. The closed circuit gave Robinson's signals a fail-safe quality. If the battery was depleted or a wire became dislodged, they would indicate "stop." Though railroads which subsequently tried such arrangements would complain about frequent false stops, the fail-safe feature appealed to

[110] R. Harris to Hitchcock, August 16, 1870, CBQ Papers, 3H4.1.

[111] Tubbs to C. M. Higginson, January 28, 1878; Higginson to Perkins, January 29, 1878; and W. Beckwith to Perkins, February 1, 1878; CBQ Papers, 33 1870 2.5.

[112] The following discussion of Robinson's work is based on *Dictionary of American Biography* (henceforth, *DAB*), vol. 16, p. 56, and Signal Section of the American Railroad Association, *The Invention of the Track Circuit* (New York: American Railroad Association, 1922), which contains excerpts from recollections Robinson recorded in 1906.

[113] "Ashbel Welch," *DAB*, vol. 19, pp. 618–619.

the sensibilities of safety advocates seeking absolute protection. With this important patent secured, Robinson formed a Pennsylvania corporation in 1873 with the expressed intent of manufacturing and installing all types of railroad signals. Two years later he relocated to New England, where Adams was conducting his tests of safety appliances.[114]

Viewed in light of these developments, we can more readily comprehend why Harris acted as he did in supporting Tubbs. Even before the accident at Revere, Harris was at once intrigued by the possibilities signaling techniques held for relieving congestion and preventing accidents, yet uncertain about the patent liabilities they might entail. The public clamor for automatic block signaling in the wake of the accident gave this quiet dilemma urgency. The safety movement threatened to compel railroads to deploy signaling devices in ways they almost certainly would not choose on their own accord, and it stimulated a burst of patenting activity on the part of outsiders such as Robinson that increased the chances of infringement. Unless Tubbs could patent his own signals and make them available to the Burlington, or at least through his experiments provide grounds for the WRA to dispute the claims of other inventors, Harris faced the prospect of becoming dependent upon an outside patent holder.

Westinghouse and the Air Brake

Robert Harris's discomfort regarding signals could hardly have been soothed by his concurrent experiences with another safety appliance and its crusty

---

[114] "William Robinson," *DAB*, vol. 16, p. 56. Whether Robinson made this move in order to capitalize on the publicity of the public trials is not entirely clear, but his departure from the railroad-rich Keystone State does suggest that he had more than a little difficulty in interesting railroads themselves in his patented devices. Pennsylvania was home both to some of American railroading's most technically progressive lines and to some of its most advanced signaling installations. The Philadelphia and Reading, for instance, had garnered accolades not just for its novel discs, but because it was one of the few lines that had built signal towers distinct from its regular stations. A year after Robinson left the state, the Pennsylvania Railroad began operating a similar dedicated system of block signal towers along its main routes from New York through Philadelphia to Pittsburgh. Though these celebrated installations seemed ideal candidates for Robinson's automatic devices, both lines chose instead to use manual signals operated by signalmen. Nor did Robinson apparently enjoy much greater success outside the Keystone State. As late as the summer of 1876, the editors of *Scientific American* noted that a track circuit designed by Robinson and installed "for a short time past" by the Boston, Lowell and Nashua Railroad "appears to solve the long sought problem of making the rails serve as conducting wires in an electrical circuit governing the signal mechanism." *Scientific American* 35, series 1 (July 29, 1876): 66. When Robinson sold his patents and his business in 1881, key personnel at the Burlington indicated to the new proprietor that they had not so much as heard of the closed circuit. Their confession betrayed both their indifference and their vulnerability.

inventor. Of the various safety devices thrust into the public limelight by the Revere disaster, none proved more vexing for railroad management than the automatic air brake. Invented in 1869 by George Westinghouse, Jr., a young Civil War veteran who had grown up amid the machine shops of Schenectady, New York, the air brake enabled locomotive engineers to activate brakes on each car of a train almost instantaneously, simply by pulling a lever in the cab of the locomotive.[115] In contrast to double-acting brakes, which multiplied the effectiveness of brakemen, air brakes removed these workers from the system altogether. Responsibility for stopping the train rested solely in the hands of the engineer, a breed of employee whom the traveling public generally held in much higher regard than trainmen. In this respect, air brakes resembled automatic electric signals, which delegated to machines tasks previously performed by signalmen. As did Robinson, moreover, Westinghouse soon incorporated a fail-safe feature into his design. In a process analogous to the switch from the open to the closed circuit, he revised his system so that the brakes came on not when the pipe running the length of the train filled with air, but when the pressure in the pipe dropped. If the pipe leaked or the compressor failed, or if a car separated from the rest of the train, the brakes activated automatically (Fig. 3.1a and b).

Air brakes possessed many of the same characteristics that made electric signals so problematical for the railroads. To safety advocates, the brakes held out the potential of seemingly absolute protection, with little reliance on human frailty or negligence. But they accomplished this by utilizing complicated, expensive technologies that fell outside the established expertise of railroads. Aside from its use on a few civil engineering projects such as the Mont Cenis Tunnel and the Brooklyn Bridge, compressed air was still virtually unknown when Westinghouse devised his braking system. Though mechanics at several railroads had experimented for years with brakes that also would have given engineers direct control over their trains, they had pursued avenues that relied on springs, levers, chains, and other mechanical connections.[116] Railroad personnel found the compressed air devices so unfamiliar and complex that Westinghouse had to provide training cars to

---

[115] For details on the air brake and an analysis of Westinghouse's career as an inventor, see Steven W. Usselman, "Air Brakes for Freight Trains: Technological Innovation in the American Railroad Industry, 1869–1900," *Business History Review* 58 (1984): 30–50, and "From Novelty to Utility: George Westinghouse and the Business of Innovation during the Age of Edison," *Business History Review* 66 (1992): 251–304.

[116] For some examples, see the Garrett Papers, box 82, subject 7130, and the letters of Robert Harris, CBQ Papers, 3H4.1. One exception to the preponderance of mechanical arrangements, devised by the Burlington's superintendent of the telegraph with the assistance of an outsider named Ohmsted, utilized electromagnetism. R. Harris to F. H. Tubbs, June 17, 1868, CBQ Papers, 3H4.1, 12: 501; R. Harris to Mr. Hitchcock, December 23, 1868, CBQ Papers, 3H4.1, 14: 192; and R. Harris to Whom It May Concern, March 29, 1869, CBQ Papers, 3H4.1, 15: 323.

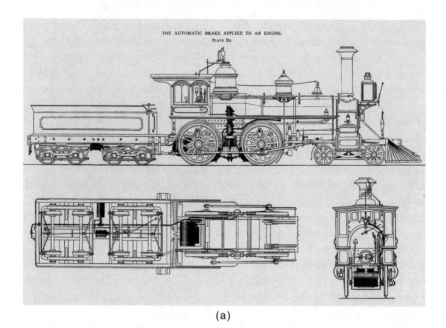

(a)

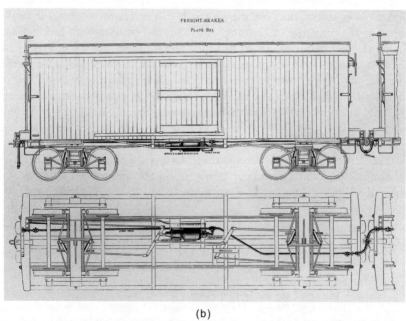

(b)

Figure 3.1. The Westinghouse automatic air brake linked brakes on individual cars in a train to controls located on the locomotive via pipes, hoses, and patented couplings. *Courtesy*: Hagley Museum and Library Pamphlet Collection.

explain how to operate and maintain his brakes.[117] Such service and sophisticated equipment did not come cheap. The compressor and other appliances mounted on the locomotive cost nearly $400 alone. Westinghouse charged another $50 for the devices added to each car, and because any car lacking this equipment would interrupt the flow of air, railroads had to apply air brakes to all cars if they wished to gain the full advantages of the device and put their customers completely at ease.

The air brake created something of a public sensation even before the awful tragedy at Revere. Just two months after their initial trial, the inventor negotiated his first sales of air brakes to the Pennsylvania Railroad. In seeking to persuade Pennsylvania President J. Edgar Thomson to give his device a try, Westinghouse informed him that "the Chicago and North Western and Michigan Central Railroad Companies have already adopted it, and other Western Roads will probably do the same, with a view of making its use a feature in their advertising material."[118] The Burlington's Harris quickly jumped on the bandwagon and by his own account soon became the most enthusiastic supporter of the Westinghouse brake among executives in the West.[119] When a skeptical Perkins steadfastly resisted his desire to get air brakes installed on Burlington trains in Nebraska, Harris testily echoed the inventor's sentiments about the public relations value of early adoption. "I have no doubt that it will be made a subject of reference in advertisements," he wrote, "and that whether the traveling public would really be more safe or not, they would *think* so."[120]

As Westinghouse gained an initial foothold for his device, railroads tried in their customary fashion to minimize the value of his patent monopoly. The Pennsylvania, always quick to recognize the potential of a new technology and supremely confident of its own abilities to master it, purchased a few brakes and then asked Westinghouse for a license to manufacture them. The inventor refused. He would grant no licenses, Westinghouse explained in a letter to executives at the Pennsylvania, because he wished to maintain uniformity in his system. Uniformity would be essential, he noted, so that railroads could interchange equipment with brakes.[121]

In making this argument, Westinghouse deftly melded his own self-interest with the concerns of railroad executives. Robert Harris made the same point about uniformity when seeking permission from his directors to overrule

[117] "Air Brake Instruction Cars," *Santa Fe Employees' Magazine* 1 (July 1907): 197.

[118] George Westinghouse, Jr., to E. H. Williams, November 13, 1869, and David H. Williams to J. Edgar Thomson, December 12, 1869; PRR Board Papers.

[119] For example, see Harris's and Perkins's discussion of the Westinghouse Air Brake for passenger trains, R. Harris to Perkins, April 21 and 25, November 11 and 14, 1870; CBQ Papers, 3H4.1.

[120] R. Harris to C. E. Perkins, April 25, 1870, CBQ Papers, 3H4.1, 20: 26–27.

[121] George Westinghouse, Jr., to E. H. Williams, November 13, 1869, and David H. Williams to J. Edgar Thomson, December 12, 1869; PRR Board Papers.

Perkins and buy air brakes for the entire Burlington system.[122] Providing for uniformity would later prove an important obstacle to using air brakes in freight service, where trains were often comprised of cars belonging to many different lines.[123] But in 1869, when air brakes would fill the vast, untapped market of passenger service, in which firms seldom interchanged cars, Westinghouse certainly had more in mind than easy exchange of equipment. The young inventor had already learned through personal experience the importance of maintaining control over patents for railroad technology. His first professional invention, a "frog" designed to keep trains from derailing at junctions, had slipped immediately into the pool of anonymous railroad innovations. Westinghouse assumed, quite reasonably, given the ample evidence provided by other examples of railroad innovation, that licenses would lead to diversity of equipment. As railroads gained first-hand experience with manufacturing brakes, they would also acquire the understanding necessary to alter their design. As expertise gravitated from his own shops to those of the railroads, as his customers patented their own refinements, control would slip from Westinghouse's hands. Westinghouse would not let this happen. For the remainder of the century, he sold complete brakes at a fixed price and granted no rebates to an industry where they were exceedingly common.[124]

Railroads did not take long to recognize they faced a formidable opponent in George Westinghouse. Rebuffed executives at the Pennsylvania decided to give up the fight and make the best of a bad situation. In a classic example of the sort of insider dealing in patented technology characteristic of the Pennsylvania at the time, high-ranking managers invested personal funds in Westinghouse's company and arranged for him to relocate his factory directly across the street from the railroad's main shops and roundhouse in Pittsburgh.[125] Meanwhile, other lines were left to search for alternatives that would undermine Westinghouse's control. At the Philadelphia and Reading, master mechanic and general manager John Wootten solicited opinions from the Pennsylvania and other Eastern roads in June of 1872 and submitted a full report on alternative automatic brakes to the company president.[126] After some preliminary experiments, the Reading obtained

[122] R. Harris to J. F. Joy, November 16, 1870, CBQ Papers, 3H4.1, 21: 513–514.
[123] Usselman, "Air Brakes."
[124] Documents in the manuscript collections of railroads I have studied consistently quote a price of $325 per locomotive and $100 per car between 1869 and 1875.
[125] Internal history of WABCO obtained from Cy Hosmer. Robert Pitcairn, who had charge of the Pennsylvania's sprawling Pittsburgh operations, was particularly active in these maneuvers. The freight yards burned to the ground during the tumultuous labor uprisings of 1877.
[126] J. E. Wootten to G. Clinton Gardner, June 4, 1872, 966: 671–672; J. E. Wootten to H. L. Brown, June 10, 1872, 966: 693; J. E. Wootten to H. L. Brown, June 20, 1872, 971: 34; and J. E. Wootten to Franklin Gowen, June 24, 1872, 971: 49–55; Reading Papers.

rights from the Smith Brake Company to manufacture vacuum brakes, and by January 1874 it had placed them on nine locomotives and thirty-seven cars.[127] "We are not putting any new air brakes on passenger trains now," Wootten notified his superior. Then, revealing his ultimate objective, he added, "we have been recently experimenting with a vacuum brake *of our own design.*"[128]

Vacuum brakes presented an especially promising avenue for undermining Westinghouse, and many prominent figures in the railroad industry besides Wootten scrambled to take advantage.[129] Charles Francis Adams, Jr., arranged for a comparative trial of the two braking systems on the Eastern Railroad in April 1873.[130] Adams, who had previously expressed his fear that the safety movement would reward monopolists, hoped to establish whether the vacuum system presented a viable alternative. The trial apparently impressed many New England roads, for in November of 1874 Wootten learned that "the Boston and Maine, the Boston and Albany, and the Grand Trunk... have discarded the Westinghouse and adopted the Vacuum."[131] This news came from Isaac Hinckley, the president of the Philadelphia, Wilmington and Baltimore Railroad, who had long taken an active role in monitoring patents for the ERA. Harris, his counterpart among Western executives and with the WRA, took up the call as well. "I look for great results from the vacuum brake – greater even than from the Westinghouse," Harris wrote in November 1873, just prior to arranging for Smith's agent

[127] J. E. Wootten to Franklin Gowen, December 9, 1872, 975: 1; J. E. Wootten to R. E. Ricker, December 30, 1872, 975: 89; J. E. Wootten to Franklin Gowen, January 3, 1873, 975: 260; and H. F. Kenney to G. A. Nicolls, January 29, 1874, Air Brake File, Reading Papers. The Reading began using vacuum brakes in regular service in February 1873. According to statistics Kenney provided from September 1872, the Reading had placed air brakes on only ten of its locomotives and forty-two of its cars. On adoption of the Westinghouse brake at the Reading, see J. E. Wootten to Morris Sellers, June 28, 1871, 966: 12; J. E. Wootten to C. M. Cresson, August 9, 1871, 966: 50; Mr. Nicolls to J. E. Wootten, December 5, 1871, 704: 389; J. E. Wootten to Mr. Nicolls, December 6, 1871, 966: 231; J. E. Wootten to Mr. Nicolls, December 7, 1871, Nicolls in-letters; Nicolls to J. E. Wootten, December 9, 1871, 704: 411; and J. E. Wootten to Ralph Bagaley, December 20, 1871, 966: 253; Reading Papers.

[128] J.E.W. to G. A. Nicolls, January 27, 1874, Air Brake File, Reading Papers. Emphasis added.

[129] Instead of compressing air and reducing the pressure to activate the brakes, this system created a vacuum and used the pressure of the atmosphere to power the brakes. Vacuum brakes provided the same performance features as air brakes and seemed likely to require less maintenance, since they operated at lower pressure. In Europe, where vacuum brakes would become the standard, railroads showed a preference for the low-pressure system almost immediately.

[130] Westinghouse Air Brake Company, printed circular announcing trial, copy in Air Brake File, Reading Papers.

[131] Isaac Hinckley to J. E. Wootten, November 9, 1874, Nicolls in-letters, Reading Papers. Hinckley claimed that these companies saved over 50 percent in maintenance costs by switching to the vacuum brake.

to conduct a trial of the vacuum device on a Burlington train.[132] Meanwhile the Master Car-Builders Association (MCBA), a recently formed trade group consisting of representatives from railroads and their prominent suppliers, laid plans to conduct its own public trial of the two braking systems.[133]

Despite these extraordinary efforts, however, railroads ultimately foundered in their attempts to undermine Westinghouse. In little more than another year's time, the vacuum brake was a dead letter in the United States, and virtually all passenger trains had air brakes. Westinghouse accomplished this reversal primarily through a relentless patent fight. The inventor had built up a formidable array of patents, including a basic one covering continuous brakes operated by compressed air, which he could plausibly argue encompassed the vacuum principle. Whenever railroads expressed interest in vacuum brakes, Westinghouse appeared with threats of infringement suits. When Wootten first inquired about vacuum brakes in December of 1872, Smith and his agent admitted they were not "sure about the validity of their patents."[134] That very day, Westinghouse sent word he would drop by to speak with executives at the Reading.[135] A year later Harris reneged on his plan to try the Smith brake when, three days after agreeing to the test, "Westinghouse stopped by . . . and warned that if we try the vacuum, even experimentally, he will bring suit."[136]

When railroad executives persisted in obtaining vacuum brakes, Westinghouse offered to supply them cheaper himself, all while insisting the air brake outperformed its rival. "Mr. Westinghouse offers, if we decide upon the use of the Vacuum Brake, to furnish it at a much lower rate than the Smith Brake," Wootten reported.[137] The brazen inventor shortly thereafter sent the Reading a printed invitation to the trial conducted by the Massachusetts Railroad Commission.[138] An exasperated Harris, who still wished to try a vacuum brake system and arranged for Westinghouse to provide one in the summer of 1874, could not resist lecturing his reluctant supplier. "What one should not do must sometimes be proven by experiment as well as what one should do," he wrote in apparent rebuttal to Westinghouse's unsolicited advice to forego the trial. "We get most of our knowledge by paying for it, and in this light the investment in the vacuum brake will not be 'thrown away!'"[139]

[132] R. Harris to J. N. A. Griswold, November 29, 1873, CBQ Papers, 3H4.1, 32: 549, and R. Harris to R. E. Ricker, December 20, 1873, CBQ Papers, 3H4.1, 33: 78.
[133] *Annual Report of the Master Car-Builders' Association for 1875.*
[134] J. E. Wootten to Franklin Gowen, December 9, 1872, vol. 975, p. 1, Reading Papers.
[135] J. E. Wootten to Franklin Gowen, December 9, 1872, vol. 971, p. 687, Reading Papers.
[136] R. Harris to R. E. Ricker, December 23, 1873, CBQ Papers, 3H4.1, 33: 92.
[137] J. E. Wootten to Franklin Gowen, January 30, 1873, vol. 975, p. 260, Reading Papers.
[138] Copy in Air Brake File, Reading Papers.
[139] R. Harris to Geo. Westinghouse, Jr., August 26, 1874, CBQ Papers, 3H4.1, 34: 503–504.

Westinghouse met enough resistance from Harris and others of his ilk that in early 1875 he purchased the Smith company and its patents.[140] This action abruptly terminated diffusion of the vacuum device. The MCBA, determining that a test of two appliances manufactured by a single firm would have no meaning, dropped its plans for a comparative trial.[141] The MCBA would not formally evaluate brakes until the famous trials at Burlington in 1886, the year Westinghouse's original patents expired. Meanwhile, Westinghouse conducted his own comparison, declared the air brake superior, and in 1876 discontinued production of vacuum brakes.[142] He had for all intents and purposes secured a monopoly over a technology most Americans had come to consider indispensable for railroad passenger service.

Robert Harris, burned once again by his generosity toward inventors, was left searching forlornly for relief from the clutches of a man he had initially supported with such enthusiasm. "Do you use Westinghouse," he inquired of a mechanic at the neighboring Chicago and Alton Railroad in the summer of 1875, "and can you make any improvement upon his apparatus without his permission and cooperation?"[143] Harris asked lawyers at the WRA to look into the matter and offered to give the mechanic's arrangement a trial.[144] But these desperate moves were for naught. A few years later, when managers at the Pennsylvania considered adding air brakes and automatic couplers to some of their freight equipment, they again approached Westinghouse about obtaining a license. The inventor would not budge.[145] Not long after that, in 1881, Westinghouse announced he had purchased rights to

140   *Railroad Gazette* 7 (February 6, 1875): 36.
141   *Annual Report of the Master Car-Builders' Association for 1875.*
142   *Railroad Gazette* 8 (April 14, 1876): 159–61, and 8 (April 21, 1876): 176.
143   R. Harris to J. R. Reniff, July 15, 1875, CBQ Papers, 3H4.1, 37: 330.
144   R. Harris to J. R. Reniff, August 7, 1875, CBQ Papers, 3H4.1, 37: 495, and October 21, 1875, CBQ Papers, 3H4.1, 38: 255. Harris put the steam braking system of one S. N. Goodale on a par with Westinghouse and noted that neither was "perfect beyond possible improvement." R. Harris to F. E. Sickels, February 3, 1873, CBQ Papers, 3H4.1, 30: 174. In 1871, Goodale had offered his brake for trial to the B&O. See Garrett Papers, box 82, subject 7130.
145   PRR Board Minutes, Supplies Committee Minutes, October 17, 1878; May 22, June 19, November 20, and December 18, 1879; January 22, April 21, June 28, and August 20, 1880, and PRR Board Minutes, December 22, 1880, vol. 9, p. 140. That managers at the Pennsylvania desired to circumvent patents for brakes and couplers before adding them to freight equipment is evident from the reports of a committee of top management at the line from 1880. The reports expressed the Pennsylvania's intent to obtain automatic couplers for freight cars, if it could find a "modified Janney coupler." The line abandoned the effort after "a party was sent to the Patent Office ... to secure data necessary to make a report in regard to the different inventions" and returned to inform the committee that "there is such a mass of invention and so mixed that it would take six months to get the desired information, and we much doubt whether when secured it would be of any real value." Association of Transportation Officers, Minutes, January 14, March 18, and May 12, 1880; and January 8, 1881; PRR Papers.

William Robinson's signaling patents, including that covering the fundamental fail-safe principle of the closed circuit. With this purchase he would soon build an enterprise, the Union Switch and Signal Company, that would be as formidable in automatic signals as the Westinghouse Air Brake Company was in automatic brakes.

THE INTOLERABLE RISKS OF PROPRIETARY CAPITALISM

The ordeals Robert Harris experienced in confronting figures such as George Westinghouse were no mere nuisances of the sort routinely encountered by all managers of large enterprises. The travails involving patents reflected a basic disjuncture that had developed between railroading and the prevailing constructs of American political economy. For nearly five decades, as executives such as Harris and J. Edgar Thomson of the Pennsylvania had engaged the basic challenge of assembling their railroads, they had operated in a world consisting overwhelmingly of small proprietors oriented toward local markets. As the enterprises for which they had responsibility grew into the most technically complex facilities of their day, these pioneering managers came to bridge two worlds. While retaining the individual autonomy and personal involvement of the owner-operators who supervised most enterprises of the period, they acquired something of the managerial reach characteristic of later generations of corporate bureaucrats. For a time, these circumstances bestowed enormous power and influence upon railroad managers. As the case of steel rails discussed in the previous chapter suggests, Thomson and his associates at the Pennsylvania had learned how to exploit the combined leverage provided by the grand developmental ventures they managed and by the patent system to generate great personal wealth and substantial profits for their firms. Now, with assistance from a patent system designed with small proprietors in mind and from a public deeply concerned about the aggregated power of railroads, men such as Westinghouse had turned the tables. Much as Andrew Carnegie had reversed the bargaining position between railroads and steel producers by locating his steel mill at the convergence of the Pennsylvania and the B&O, Westinghouse had found a way to extract large profits from the market for patented railroad technology. A bevy of other inventors, aided by the doctrine of savings, appeared poised to duplicate the feat.

The disputes over patents thus in many respects heralded the passage of railroading into a new era. With the task of assembling the basic machines largely complete, railroads such as the Pennsylvania and the Burlington assumed the character of established enterprises, in which managers would concentrate on utilizing those machines most effectively to provide transport services. The developmental function, which had so occupied managers such as Harris and Thomson, would give way to a new concern with moving equipment smoothly and economically through the networks of tracks and ancillary facilities. By the end of the 1870s, these longtime railroad leaders and their contemporary John Work Garrett of the B&O all would have relinquished control of their lines to a new generation of managers. Their successors would bring a new outlook to railroading. Consciously abandoning the insider dealing and deep personal involvement characteristic of men such as Thomson, the new breed would instill an ethic of impersonal administrative expertise. Possessing little of the entrepreneurial spirit and creativity associated with inventors such as Westinghouse or his contemporary Thomas Edison, they turned with enthusiasm to the careful analyses provided by the mounting numbers of professional engineers.

Yet while railroads stood poised to enter a new age, the larger society in which they operated remained firmly rooted in the realm of proprietary capitalism. The American economy still consisted largely of small proprietorships, and the instruments and ideals of American politics still betrayed a vision of society grounded in the image of small holders operating in local but competitive markets. Perhaps nothing captured those ideals more effectively than the image of the independent inventor, ready to sell the fruits of his labors in a market fostered by the patent system. As the nation approached its centennial, much of its populace stood ready to celebrate with spectacular displays of inventive accomplishment, including exhibits by Westinghouse and a host of other railroad suppliers. Meanwhile, the railroads that would carry visitors to the centennial exhibition at Philadelphia increasingly perceived the patent system as an anachronism whose hidden liabilities might undermine efforts to provide more efficient transport. In the quarter-century to come, the men responsible for managing the railroads would find ways to surmount that obstacle and to create alternative pathways of innovation in their industry. In the process, they would fashion an alternative vision of American political economy as well.

PART II

Running the Machine,
1876–1904

The grand developmental epic of American railroading reached its denouement with the extraordinary postbellum boom of the Northern and Western economy. The ensuing financial collapse of the mid-1870s ushered in a dramatically different era. No longer able to reap the easy bonanza initially made possible by the marriage of railroad technology to virgin land and resources, railroads faced increasingly intense competition for traffic that might travel over any of several highly capitalized routes. Government, which had long been a source of subsidy for railroads, now threatened them with regulation that would further intensify the pressures to cut fares and shave costs. Though new frontiers would open during the 1880s in the Pacific Northwest and to a lesser extent in the Gulf Coast region, the paramount concern of American railroading was now to utilize existing facilities fully and keep costs low. Railroads tried to attract a large and steady volume of traffic and push it through their network of tracks as smoothly as possible.

The passage from expansive development to operational stewardship dramatically altered the paths of technical change in the railroad industry. The new objectives imparted an emphasis on standardization and routine that often bordered on the obsessive. Managers sought to diminish the degree of personal autonomy that had long characterized railroad innovation and to impose order over their technical affairs through bureaucratic control. They withdrew from direct investments in their suppliers and turned responsibility for technology over to salaried engineers who appreciated the importance of uniformity and happily pursued incremental change that functioned within the existing system. Through laboratory experiment and controlled study of actual practice, these academically trained professionals substituted sustained analysis for the hit-and-miss approach of inventors and mechanics. Cooperation in technical affairs grew more formalized and extensive, as lines exchanged equipment and forged alliances that facilitated uninterrupted long-distance transport. Engineers from competing lines, together with representatives from major suppliers, negotiated technical specifications through trade associations and professional organizations that soon came to function as the centers of technical knowledge in the industry. Patents diminished in importance, as first railroad managers and then Congress and the federal courts accepted the notion that technical improvements would flow primarily from the continual efforts of engineers, not from the sporadic accomplishments of inventors.

The rise of engineers to prominence in American railroading during the last quarter of the nineteenth century produced a situation rife with paradox. On the surface, railroading seemed to lack the technical vitality and spirit of experimentation that had characterized its first half-century. Yet in reality the pace of innovation quickened. Though railroads now seldom provided Americans with the spectacular bursts of productive efficiency made possible by the initial substitution of rails and engines for roads and horses or canals and flatboats, the railroad industry itself attained far more impressive improvements in productivity than ever before. Railroads achieved this success, moreover, precisely *because* they constricted the realm of technical possibilities and pursued one grand objective with single-minded purpose. By laying down clear ground rules about operations and shunning innovations that threatened to disrupt those rules, railroads channeled the collective energies of the engineering community into a few vital areas. Engineers thrived in such a well-defined environment. With so much already decided on and worked out, they could readily draw on their abilities to optimize performance and apply those skills across a realm far vaster than any other of the day. Inventors and mechanics, in contrast, chafed against the constraints imposed by system and bureaucracy. A handful of successful inventors managed to bypass the reluctant railroads and pitch their products directly to consumers seeking improved safety and comfort or custom services. But these exceptions seldom contributed significant economies to the railroads themselves. For railroads of the late nineteenth century, less innovation was more.

By the turn of the twentieth century, this formula had proved so successful that railroad executives and many other observers heralded engineering as offering a new means of organizing technical and economic affairs. Celebrated in exhibits at world's fairs and in many other venues, railroad engineering pointed in the eyes of many toward a more ordered and fruitful method of resolving conflict than those provided by either unregulated markets or politics. Engineering became enshrined. Few yet recognized that railroading itself had begun to confront a dramatically new set of circumstances calling for significant departures in management and technology.

4

Patent Remedies: Politics, Jurisprudence, and Procedure

Though the impetus for reshaping the paths of innovation in American railroading originated from forces that transcended the immediate problems with patents, railroad managers could not succeed in imposing new discipline over technology without resolving the nagging uncertainties regarding the patent system. By the mid-1870s, the ongoing struggles with the likes of Westinghouse and Sayles had pushed executives such as Robert Harris well beyond the point of exasperation. Managers recognized that the disputes involving these patents posed a fundamental threat to their industry. For at root, the attempts to regulate safety and to allocate damages in patent cases pointed to a common issue of basic importance for the emerging corporate age: Should credit for improvements in productivity and performance go primarily to inventors or to the corporate managers who ran the complex machine? Who offered the surer path to safety? Who responded more effectively to public demand? These questions, in turn, touched upon the very nature of markets and the role of government in structuring incentives. The persistent tension inherent in the patent system, which purported to serve the public interest by granting monopoly privileges to individuals, came under renewed scrutiny. Indeed, that tension seemed in many respects to encapsulate the fundamental concerns of an age in which legislatures and courts wrestled continually with questions about the authority of state and federal governments to create and regulate monopolies.

The magnitude of the patent issues became clear when railroads, having encountered more and more difficulty with the patent system and having suffered recurrent setbacks in court, turned to the political arena for relief. At a time when financial panic and economic depression had pushed antirailroad sentiment to unprecedented heights, managers through their patent associations conducted a sustained campaign to revise the patent laws. This pioneering effort at industry-wide lobbying sparked vehement debate in Congress and the press, as politicians, the legal community, and others connected with the patent system struggled to reconcile its mechanisms with the structures of modern railroading. Their arguments open a remarkable window into the ways Americans conceived of technology and innovation at the dawn of the corporate age. The outcomes helped pave the way for a new era of technical change in the industry that stood at the forefront of the new economic order.

PATENT REFORMS AND REFORM POLITICS

Railroads first entered the political fray in early 1874, when they attempted to block Sayles from obtaining a second seven-year extension of the Tanner patent from Congress. The Burlington's Harris took the lead in mobilizing a lobbying effort to defeat the measure. He directed Squire M. Whipple, a longtime advocate for the two railroad patent associations, to appear before the Senate Committee on Patents in Washington.[1] When the committee initially reported favorably on the application for extension, Harris immediately wrote influential members of the Burlington's board and several fellow executives at other lines encouraging them to approach key members of the Senate about defeating the measure.[2] "Cannot some influence be brought upon those who have no pecuniary interest at stake, to show up in the Senate the inconsistency of clamoring about transportation reform whilst they are loading down the transportation agencies with extended patents upon which millions are claimed[?]" Harris asked his colleague D. L. Harris of the Eastern Railroad Association in a lengthier missive. "Not being a politician I don't know how such a point would take, but from my practical standpoint it would seem to me to be effective."[3] Whether the lobbying effort deserves the credit remains uncertain, but railroads did indeed find relief on just such grounds as Harris delineated when a new Congress reassembled later in 1874. The reconstituted Senate Committee on Patents, noting Sayles had already collected some $60,000 in damages and stood ready to receive substantially more, reversed course and decided against extending the Tanner patent. Several months later the House Committee on Patents

[1] R. Harris to S. M. Whipple, December 27, 1873, Papers of the Chicago, Burlington and Quincy Railroad, Newberry Library, Chicago (henceforth, CBQ Papers), 3H4.1, 33: 111, and S. M. Whipple, "Testimony before Congress Concerning Extension of the Tanner Brake Patent," printed circular, n.d., copy in CBQ Papers, 33 1870 2.5.

[2] U.S. Senate, "Report of the Committee on Patents," February 4, 1873, 42d Congress, 3d sess., report no. 369. For direct evidence of the lobbying campaign, see Robert Harris to Gen. J. A. Craig, February 3, 1874, CBQ Papers, 9W5.2; Robert Harris to Chas. Paine, February 3, 1874, CBQ Papers, 9W5.2; Robert Harris to Geo. Willard, February 3, 1874, CBQ Papers, 9W5.2; and Isaac Hinckley to J. W. Garrett, February 14, 1873, Papers of John Work Garrett, Ms. 2003, Maryland Historical Society, Baltimore (henceforth, Garrett Papers), box 86, subject 9614.

[3] Robert Harris to D. L. Harris, February 3, 1874, CBQ Papers, 9W5.2.

followed suit, explicitly citing rulings of Judge Drummond that it claimed would cost railroads $4.5 million in one year and $31 million over seven years.[4]

Buoyed by this success in Congress but still frustrated in court, lawyers working for the Western Railroad Association next drafted a comprehensive bill to revise the patent laws. Its primary author was George Payson, a lawyer who had argued the swedge block cases on behalf of the Chicago and Alton Railroad and had been hired by Harris in 1874 to work full-time for the WRA on the brake cases and other pending litigation. The bill drafted by Payson contained a variety of provisions intended to stymie the machinations of speculators such as Sayles and to revoke the doctrine of savings.[5] Its opening section proposed a statute of limitations prohibiting infringement suits based on claims dating back more than a single year. Other provisions required any patent holder actively marketing a patented product, as demonstrated through the existence of circulars or other advertising material, to press suit and take testimony without delay if a user inquired about potential infringement. No longer would plaintiffs be allowed to drag their feet while infringers unknowingly accumulated vast liabilities. Another section permitted anyone to use an invention, without fear of damages if later found in infringement, simply by posting a bond. Yet another required holders of patents to pay renewal fees at prescribed intervals of every few years or forfeit their rights. This practice, common in European patent systems of the time, would in the eyes of its supporters clear useless patents off the books and prevent speculators from suing over patents that had apparently been abandoned.

While most parts of the bill focused on ways to diminish the chances of users infringing patents across long periods of time, its critical second section homed in on the question of how courts should assess damages in cases where infringement did occur. Whenever possible, it stated, courts should seek to identify an established license fee or to determine profits made through manufacture and sale of the device. In cases where a patent was used in the course of conducting another business, courts should make no attempt to assess the profits or savings derived by the infringer. Instead, Payson stipulated, "the court and jury should take into consideration the time, labor,

---

4   U.S. House of Representatives, "Report of the Committee on Patents," March 2, 1875, 43d Cong., 2d sess., report no. 274, and U.S. Senate, "Report of the Committee on Patents," June 20, 1874, 43d Cong., 1st sess., report no. 471.

5   On the proposed revisions to the patent laws, see "Some Suggestions as to an Amendment of the Patent Law," n.d., printed circular in Patents and Inventions File, Papers of the Baltimore and Ohio Railroad, Ms. 1925, Maryland Historical Society, Baltimore (henceforth, B&O Papers) and U.S. Senate, "Arguments before the Committees on Patents of the Senate and the House of Representatives in Support of and Suggesting Amendments to Bills (S. 300 and H.R. 1612) to Amend the Statutes in Relation to Patents, and for Other Purposes," 45th Cong., 2d sess., miscellaneous document no. 50 (henceforth, Senate Arguments or House Arguments).

ingenuity, and experience involved in making the invention" when awarding damages.[6] Under this provision, the legal system would in effect determine a license fee based on the effort and creativity of the inventor rather than on the benefits users derived. Though Payson in revised versions of the bill would retreat from identifying explicitly the factors courts and juries should consider when determining appropriate compensation, he remained insistent they should avoid an account of savings and concentrate on establishing a reasonable license fee. This was, he told the House Committee on Patents, "What I deem to be the very heart and soul of this bill."[7]

Responsibility for shepherding the bill through Congress fell primarily to John H. Raymond, longtime secretary-treasurer of the WRA. His strategy called for the bill to slip as quietly through Congress as possible. Rather than route it through one of the Committees on Patents, which had recently heard the controversial petitions for renewing the Tanner patent and surely would have recognized Payson's proposal for the sweeping reform it was, he had Representative Stephen A. Hurlbut of Illinois send it to the House Judiciary Committee in December 1875.[8] The bill prompted little discussion there and moved without fanfare to the floor of the House, where it passed without debate during the closing session at the end of January 1877.[9] Robert Harris, who had arranged passage for Raymond to Washington two weeks before, immediately wired Illinois Senator R. J. Oglesby, asking him to support the measure when it reached the Senate.[10] With the unsuspecting Senate preoccupied with resolving the disputed presidential election of the previous November, prospects for passage looked good. Only the eleventh-hour opposition of New York's Roscoe Conkling, then at the height of his influence among Senate Republicans, kept the bill from becoming law at that point.[11]

During these early political maneuvers, railroads garnered considerable support from an unlikely ally. Grangers, the very group that had done so much to carry the cause of railroad regulation into Congress, had mobilized a campaign to relieve their rural constituents of what they considered the unjust burdens of the patent system. Farmers in the South and West, who had long harbored resentment toward the patent system, chafed at having to

---

6   House Arguments, p. 370.
7   Ibid., p. 367. Payson "surrendered the point [about explicitly stating the basis of establishing a fee] in draughting, with other gentlemen, the present bill, and left it in the form in which it now is, as the other gentlemen were afraid to hamper the court and jury." Ibid., p. 370.
8   Ibid., p. 226.
9   *New York Times*, January 31, 1877, p. 2, and House and Senate Arguments.
10 R. Harris to John King, January 16, 1877, CBQ Papers, 9W5.2, and Harris to Hon. R. J. Oglesby, January 31, 1877, CBQ Papers, 3H4.2, 2: 414.
11 At hearings held the following year on a revised version of the bill, a member of the House committee noted that "[Hurlbut's] bill would have passed had it not been for the opposition of one Senator." House Arguments, p. 438. Based on additional evidence discussed below, that senator was almost certainly Conkling.

pay premiums for patented articles manufactured in Chicago and the East. One especially galling case, which proved particularly important in paving the way for railroad success in the House of Representatives, involved the sewing machine. Owners of key patents had pooled their rights in an effort to block competitive manufacturers. Machines made under license from Elias Howe and Isaac Singer sold for $70 or $80, whereas those manufactured illicitly cost half as much. These cheaper sewing machines constituted what historian Hal S. Barron calls the "big ticket item" for Montgomery Wards, the pioneering retailer who had gained the trust and admiration of many rural Americans by bypassing middlemen and marketing directly to farmers through the Grange cooperatives. When the same Congress that initially approved the second reissue of the Tanner patent agreed to extend those of Elias Howe in late 1872, Wards and the Grangers reacted with outrage. The agrarian press implored farmers to vote the offending members out of office in November of 1874.[12] Though many factors played into the result, of course, the election indeed sent a decidedly more agrarian element to Washington, including a House controlled for the first time since the Civil War by the Democratic Party. At the opening of the next session, the new House Committee on Patents not only reversed the decision to extend the Howe patents; it also rejected out of hand a bill proposing all patents issued prior to 1861 be reissued without debate upon payment of a $100 fee.[13]

While the sewing machine aroused broad resistance to the patent system among rural Americans, controversies involving two other patents drew farmers into even greater sympathy with the complaints voiced by the railroads. These disputes involved patents covering the swing gate (a hinged gate used to shunt and separate livestock) and the driven well (a pipe driven into the earth to obtain water). Wells and gates of these basic types had become familiar sights on American farms, especially in the arid West, where they met basic needs by simple, inexpensive means virtually anyone could readily comprehend. Sometime around 1875, farmers began receiving letters claiming use of the driven well infringed a patent originally issued in 1868 and extended by Congress three years later. Anyone using such wells needed to pay $50, the letters claimed, or defend themselves in federal courts. When courts upheld the patent and its extension, owners of rights to the swing gate and several other commonplace devices sent similar letters alleging infringement.[14] Hapless farmers complained they had no

---

[12] On the sewing machine patents, see Hal S. Barron, *Mixed Harvest: The Second Great Transformation in the Rural North, 1870–1930* (Chapel Hill: University of North Carolina Press, 1997), p. 172.

[13] House of Representatives, "Report of the Committee on Patents," April 8, 1874, 43d Congress, 1st sess., report no. 389.

[14] These patents were the source of frequent petition to Congress during the late 1870s. Their history is traced in *Scientific American* 56 (1887): 352, which claims it was almost an axiom that reissues could not be sustained until the driven well reissue of May 19, 1871, was upheld by the Supreme Court.

choice but to pay, since the cost of travel to the federal courts alone made the prospects of mounting a legal defense prohibitively expensive.

The driven well case exerted a psychological and symbolic impact far beyond its economic significance for individual farmers. The case tapped deep-felt resentments among rural Westerners over Eastern insensitivities to the natural hardships and isolation of the West. If a person could not hammer a pipe into the ground to obtain water without bringing down the force of the federal government, they asked, what *could* one do? That government, moreover, seemed to have lent its authority and cooperation to what amounted to nothing more than rapacious speculators, or "patent sharks," as they were called by many, who bought the rights to the creations of others and used them to prey upon "innocent," isolated farmers unable to defend themselves before the law. Grangers and several state legislatures petitioned Congress to pass "innocent purchaser provisions," which would exempt from infringement suits and damage payments anyone who used a patented device unknowingly. The statute of limitations and other measures contained in the railroad bill served much the same purpose. "The interests of the Railroads of the Country in this matter, fortunately for them, are identical with those of the people at large," explained Raymond to the B&O's Garrett when asking for assistance with lobbying, "both being *users* and not vendors of patents."[15]

Support from the Grangers and association with their innocent purchaser provisions may ultimately have worked against the railroads, however, for it aroused defenders of the patent system and drew the railroad reform initiative into the vortex of a political storm. In the eyes of men such as Conkling and the editors of *Scientific American*, a journal steadfastly devoted to advancing the interests of independent inventors, the Granger bills constituted reckless and unwarranted assaults upon fundamental rights of property. These men recoiled at the notion that infringers could escape liability simply by pleading ignorance. "Under this theory," noted the chairman of the Committee on Patents when one such proposed amendment came before the full Senate, "the best patent advisor of a corporation or a manufacturing company would be the lawyer who knew the least law and would always advise his clients that there was no existing patent."[16]

Innocent purchaser bills, moreover, carried a great deal of baggage that transcended the immediate issue of patents. In stamping such bills with the "innocent purchaser" label, Grangers plucked a tense chord in the tumultuous politics that gripped American life during the depression of the 1870s. The term cleverly turned back at courts and the financial community a notion that had consistently frustrated rural states and municipalities in their struggles to escape the burdens of ill-advised bond issues used to finance railroads

---

[15]   J. H. Raymond to Garrett May 11, 1878, Patents and Inventions File, B&O Papers.

[16]   *Congressional Record* (henceforth, *CR*), 45th Cong., 3d sess., 8 (December 18, 1878): 296–297. The speaker was Senator Booth of California.

and other projects in the 1850s and 1860s. In case after case, federal judges had denied states the right to default on bond payments, on grounds the bonds had since fallen into the hands of "innocent purchasers." States could not penalize people who had bought bonds in good faith on the open market, courts maintained, even in cases where the bonds had been issued under improper authority. The rule applied even if officers of the companies receiving the funds had squandered them on fraudulent contracts with cronies who never completed the railroad, as had been the case with the federally funded Union Pacific and the notorious Credit Mobilier construction syndicate. Investors who might be located in Europe or the East, explained judges, could not be held responsible for knowing about such local circumstances affecting bond issues. They had a right to presume state and local governments would fulfill their obligations. These principles should prevail even if the claimant, as in one early precedent-setting case, was none other than J. Edgar Thomson, president of the Pennsylvania Railroad. Such was the opinion of the overwhelming majority of federal judges, including Thomas Drummond of the Chicago Circuit, who issued the opinion upholding Thomson's claims.[17]

In linking patents with bonds, Grangers also indirectly tied the disputes over patents to the intense arguments taking place over the money supply. Those inclined to praise courts for upholding the rights of railroad bond-holders were also likely to sing the praises of "hard money" and to insist upon rapid retirement of greenbacks and orderly repayment of government war bonds in specie. The decidedly sectional cast of the disputes over monetary policy further reinforced the symbolic ties with the patent issue, because Westerners and Southerners had long branded the Patent Office as a New England bastion.[18] In the hands of the Grangers, patent reform thus became

---

[17] The authority on railroad bond cases is Charles Fairman, *Reconstruction and Reunion, 1864–1888: History of the Supreme Court of the United States, Part One* (New York: Macmillan, 1971), chs. 17 and 18. "For a season," writes Fairman, "cases on municipal bonds bulked larger than any other category of the Court's business. Chiefly these were bonds issued to purchase stock in order to encourage the building of a railroad. In our period the Court decided some two hundred cases on these railroad aid bonds" (p. 918). The phrase "innocent holders" appeared as early as 1853 in a case before the Pennsylvania Supreme Court. Judge John F. Dillon, who was at the center of jurisprudence involving bonds in his capacity as chief justice of the Iowa Supreme Court from 1862 to 1869 and as the federal circuit judge in the Eighth District for ten years after that, wrote an influential treatise on bonds in 1872. In it he condemned much of the jurisprudence, but noted that "it will be well if it shall teach municipalities the lesson that if, having power to do so, they issue negotiable securities, they cannot escape if these find their way into the hands of innocent purchasers." Quoted in Fairman, *Reconstruction*, p. 947.

[18] Ari Hoogenboom, *The Presidency of Rutherford B. Hayes* (Lawrence: University Press of Kansas, 1988), p. 117, notes this resentment and observes that "fewer than one in five [of the eighty-eight] examiners came from west of the Mississippi and South of the Potomac and Ohio Rivers. Even the Old Northwest was slighted."

enmeshed with the complex issues of public finance, monopoly power, judicial authority, and economic nationalism that underlay so much of the conflicts of this tumultuous decade. To achieve their own reforms, railroads would have to get past this minefield.

As Payson and Raymond prepared to resubmit their bill to a new Congress, a number of influential politicians and patent attorneys who opposed the innocent purchaser provisions exhibited at least some willingness to help them find their way. A group of distinguished patent lawyers located in and around Boston took an especially prominent role. The group included J. J. Storrow, who later would argue for the Bell Telephone Company in the most notorious patent case of the late nineteenth century. Storrow would eventually introduce the revised bill before the House Committee on Patents, and his arguments there would provide the basis for an official report summarizing the hearings. Another influential voice was that of Chauncey Smith. A contributor of several important articles on the history of the patent system and its functions during the late nineteenth century, Smith circulated the initial bill among the Boston legal community in the summer of 1877, then spent a week in Chicago that September working with Payson and Raymond and another dozen attorneys to revise it. He was joined there by Henry D. Hyde, head of the New England Textile Association, which performed functions for the textile manufacturers similar to those the WRA carried out for the railroads. Both Smith and Hyde testified extensively on behalf of the revised bill before both the House and Senate committees.[19] This circle of Yankee attorneys also included Bainbridge Wadleigh, a New Hampshireite who had been sent to the U.S. Senate in 1872 and immediately appointed to a place on the Committee on Patents. The revised bill would carry his name.

Virtually all of these men belonged to the emerging community of reform politicians, known variously as Liberal Republicans among their admirers or Mugwumps to their detractors, who had grown alienated from President Grant and party regulars such as Conkling and James Blaine. Decrying what they saw as excessive corruption in the wake of scandals such as Credit Mobilier, the reformers had nominated the old Republican editor Horace Greeley to run against Grant in 1872. Perhaps their truest standard-bearer, however, might well have been Representative James Garfield of Ohio, an articulate young Republican who would attain the presidency in 1880. "We

---

[19]   Evidence on the role of these men in revising the patent bill comes from House and Senate Arguments. Smith notes that he was invited to Chicago by Payson and Raymond (p. 17), and Storrow states that "a dozen men meeting seven days in Chicago revised the bill" (p. 265). Payson observes in discussing the stipulations regarding determination of a license fee that he "surrendered the point in draughting, with other gentlemen, the present bill" (p. 370). Albert Walker, attorney for Sayles, complains that Smith excluded him from the deliberations "beginning last September 20" (pp. 403–404). A good example of their sentiments is Chauncey Smith, "A Century of Patent Law," *Quarterly Journal of Economics* 5 (1891): 44–69.

are rapidly reaching that period when the two great political parties must dissolve their present organizations," Garfield wrote to a colleague in 1872. Four years later, Garfield still eagerly anticipated the day when "in the south as in the north men may seek their party on the great commercial and industrial questions."[20]

Such comments betrayed the fundamental precepts binding the diverse reformers. These men were anxious to close a door on the chaos of the war era and get on with what they saw as the serious business of making peace with the new economic order. They were quick to give up the fight over civil rights, for instance, if it meant securing a stable currency. Though their ranks included many forceful advocates of free trade, most accepted tariffs and other subsidies to industry as expedients necessary to help a young nation compete in world markets. Comfortable with corporate business but recognizing it called for new measures of supervision, these younger men had little patience for what they perceived to be the irrelevance and distractions of machine politics. They looked to do away with politics based on distributing benefits at the local level, so that they could build a new, national order grounded in expert administration. As with the Adams brothers in *Chapters of Erie*, reformers usually perched loftily above the fray, condemning speculators for their crassness while admiring managers for their competence. "There was nothing remotely revolutionary about them," observed historian John G. Sproat in his pioneering study of the breed, "for they had no quarrel with capitalism and the industrial revolution, and they were uncompromising defenders of private property."[21]

For men of this ilk, the mounting furor over patents constituted just the sort of economic growing pain that required careful, measured response from informed policy makers and experts. Reformers would not for a moment entertain notions advanced by Grangers and others who questioned the

[20] Quoted in Margaret Susan Thompson, *The "Spider's Web: Congress and Lobbying in the Age of Grant* (Ithaca: Cornell University Press), p. 113.

[21] John G. Sproat, *"The Best Men": Liberal Reformers in the Gilded Age* (New York: Oxford University Press, 1968), p. 10. Other useful portraits of the reformers can be found in David Montgomery, *Beyond Equality: Labor and the Radical Republicans, 1862–1872* (New York: Knopf, 1967); William Gillette, *Retreat from Reconstruction, 1869–1879* (Baton Rouge: Louisiana University Press, 1979); Michael McGerr, *The Decline of Popular Politics* (New York: Oxford University Press, 1986); and Eric Foner, *Reconstruction* (New York: Harper and Row, 1988), chs. 10–12. On the enthusiasm of reformers for administrative expertise, see Stephen Skowronek, *Building a New American State: The Expansion of National Administrative Capacities, 1877–1920* (New York: Cambridge University Press, 1982), pp. 132–138. Skowronek cites Henry Carter Adams, Charles Francis Adams, Jr., Simon Sterne of New York's Hepburn Committee, and Arthur Hadley as examples. For a detailed look at one of these figures, see A. W. Coats, "Henry Carter Adams: A Case Study in the Emergence of the Social Sciences in the United States, 1850–1900," *American Studies* 2 (1961): 177–197. See also Gordon S. Wood, "The Massachusetts Mugwumps," *New England Quarterly* 33 (1960): 435–451.

fundamental beneficence of the system. "As to the abolition of the Patent system, which has of late been influentially advocated," wrote Greeley two years before his run for the presidency, "I shall be more easily reconciled to it when I learn that it is to be swiftly followed by a repudiation of *all* rights of property whatever."[22] Similar paeans to the patent system appeared periodically in the liberal press of the day. The *New York Times*, a paper sympathetic to the reform cause and persistently critical of party regulars such as Conkling, dismissed claims that the system had little influence on inventors. The system should be preserved and celebrated, its editors steadfastly insisted, for it served the public interest by encouraging the diffusion of technologies that improved the general welfare. The paper portrayed advocates of innocent purchaser provisions as narrow-minded men who in their zeal to protect one group – farmers – failed to grasp the nuances of the patent system.[23]

While defending the system from what they perceived as intemperate attacks by agrarians, liberal editors acknowledged the need for reforms of the sort proposed by railroads. The *Times* followed the Wadleigh bill closely and endorsed it repeatedly.[24] E. L. Godkin of *The Nation* likewise embraced the cause of patent reform, on grounds it would protect manufacturers who too often found themselves harassed by parties claiming infringement of "old patents." Under current law, observed the ardent nationalist, nothing could prevent a citizen of Great Britain from acquiring obscure American patent rights and using them to hound any rivals for international trade. Something must be done to clear these old patents off the books and ease this onerous burden on American producers. Godkin recommended Congress add more examiners, so the Patent Office could provide stricter reviews and issue fewer patents. He also suggested it create a board of experts that would make definitive legal rulings about novelty, rather than leaving courts free to constantly review the issue of priority and Congress free to consider extensions. By placing greater responsibility in the hands

[22] Horace Greeley, *Essays Designed to Elucidate the Science of Political Economy, While Serving to Explain and Defend the Policy of Protection to Home Industry, as a System of National Cooperation for the Elevation of Labor* (1870; rpt., New York: Arno, 1972), p. 52.

[23] The *Times* monitored patent policies and cases quite closely throughout the late nineteenth century. Its editors persistently defended the system while calling for greater professionalization of its staff. Even during the long controversy over the telephone patents, when the paper took the popular antimonopoly side against the Bell Company, its editors still retained their trust in experts. They attributed Bell's ability to extend its patent monopoly to poor administration of the Patent Office. With an inadequate staff (despite a healthy budget surplus), the office granted patents without sufficient inquiry into technical novelty, then allowed a huge backlog of conflicting applications to drag on without resolution. This diagnosis echoed a recurrent theme in the *Times*'s editorials: that the office needed more expert examiners who would grant far fewer patents. The editors sounded this theme at every opportunity.

[24] For editorials supporting the bill, see *New York Times*, July 14, 1878, p. 6; December 21, 1878, p. 4; and January 11, 1879, p. 4.

of experts, Congress would insulate the patent system from the suffocating influence of party politics, which too often spilled over into the judiciary as well. Godkin took care to set the cause of patent reform apart from the crass, contentious politics practiced by agrarian interests and party regulars. His editorials mentioned neither the Grangers and their innocent purchaser doctrines nor the railroads, preferring instead the less specific reference to "manufacturing."[25]

The New England attorneys who joined with representatives of the railroad patent associations during summer 1877 clearly shared the basic sensibilities of the reform community. Operating in the region of the country which received the most patents and consequently was the scene of most patent litigation, the New Englanders comported themselves as self-appointed stewards of the patent system. In their testimony before congressional committees, Smith and Storrow always began with heartfelt tributes to the patent system and to the inventive genius they believed it fostered. "All men should know," Wadleigh flatly stated when introducing his bill to the full Senate, "that they cannot be permitted to retain any profits realized by the use of another's patented invention without his consent."[26] Such pronouncements struck a decidedly more emphatic tone in defense of the system than more tepid remarks by Raymond and Payson. While Raymond endorsed a complete ban on reissues and extensions, Wadleigh refused to cater to popular resentment and spent valuable time pressing for clauses permitting inventors to obtain new claims in certain circumstances.[27]

Sensitive to Western and Southern criticism that the system served New England manufacturing interests, men such as Smith, Storrow, and Wadleigh sought to amend the laws without opening the way for more radical changes. Whereas railroad lawyers besieged by costly lawsuits had welcomed relief in any form, including innocent purchaser provisions, these reformers viewed such populist notions as fundamental threats to the patent system that must be defeated at all costs. Often they couched their support for the revised railroad bill in preservationist terms. "One reason for this legislation," Smith told the House committee in veiled reference to the Grangers, "is to preserve the patent system from reformers who seek to revise the laws 'solely with reference to some special hardship.'"[28] In his opening remarks to the Senate, Wadleigh stressed the importance of patents in foreign competition, then

---

[25] "The Necessity of Patent-Law Reform," *The Nation* 18 (January 8, 1874): 22–33, and "Our Patent System," *The Nation* 23 (October 16, 1876): 260–261.

[26] U.S. Senate, "Report from the Committee on Patents to Accompany Bill S. 300," March 5, 1878, 45th Cong., 2d sess., report no. 116, p. 4.

[27] On Raymond, see Senate Arguments, p. 108. On the debates over reissues on the Senate floor, see *CR* 8 (January 17, 1879): 527–530, and 8 (January 20, 1879): 567–568.

[28] House Arguments, p. 421.

quickly pointed to the potential threat from more radical reform measures.[29] "I do not come here as representing a section of the people who cry out against the patent laws," Henry Hyde of the Textile Manufacturers Association assured the Senate committee. "We believe in them."[30]

Reformers generally embraced with little hesitation those sections of the railroad bill intended to reduce the number of suits occurring late in the life of a patent. Virtually everyone testifying in support of the bill, including former Commissioner of Patents M. D. Leggett and a number of prominent patent attorneys, praised the idea of charging periodic renewal fees.[31] Most also endorsed the statute of limitations, though reformers pressed to extend it beyond the single year stipulated by Payson in the original bill.[32] Reformers were less thoroughly convinced about the desirability of the bill's other provisions, including section two and its stipulations regarding the doctrine of savings and a license fee. Neither Hyde nor Leggett, for instance, openly endorsed section two, though Hyde did provide some evidence from the shoe industry to buttress arguments in its behalf. The group that had gathered in Chicago, uncomfortable with the way Payson had seemingly tied the hands of courts, had mulled over the section at great length in an effort to develop more flexible language. In the end, they had agreed simply to strike passages expressly identifying factors courts should take into account in arriving at a license fee. When the bill came before the Senate Committee on Patents, its own sponsor questioned whether the section compelled judges and juries to arrive at a license fee, or whether it left them free to assess damages more broadly. Wadleigh and some others expressed surprise when Raymond indicated the clause referred to a fee and not to damages. Only after the railroad representative insisted the bill must leave no ambiguity in this regard did the sponsoring senator reluctantly agree to add new language specifying that courts should concentrate on establishing an appropriate fee.[33]

RATIONALE: INNOVATION IN A CORPORATE ECONOMY

Despite their initial hesitancy to embrace section two, Liberals ultimately expended much of their energies on behalf of the bill in fashioning an elaborate defense of its basic provisions. In lengthy testimony before the congressional Committees on Patents during the winter of 1877–78, summarized

---

[29] CR 8 (January 9, 1879): 379–384.   [30] Senate Arguments, p. 94.

[31] Ibid., pp. 101–105.

[32] The group assembled in Chicago decided upon a period of four years, which Storrow endorsed and the congressional committees both approved. House Arguments, p. 343. Wadleigh and several other Liberal members of the Senate committee later voted in favor of a last-minute amendment on the floor of the Senate proposing to extend the statute of limitations another two years, but lost out to an alliance of Westerners and Southerners. CR 8 (January 23, 1879): 660.

[33] Senate Arguments, p. 115.

by Wadleigh in a trenchant report and rehashed a year later on the floor of the Senate, they strove to explain how structural changes in the economy had created situations that baffled judges and juries in patent cases. In the process, reformers articulated a sophisticated explanation of how the patent system functioned in an economy growing increasingly populated with large institutions. They effectively asked Americans to reconceptualize the nature of technical change and to reassess how the benefits of new technology flowed to consumers.

The Chicago courts, in the opinion of the New Englanders, had opened a can of worms with the savings doctrine. Storrow traced the series of rulings through which they had arrived at the doctrine and characterized the judges as having acted "unadvisedly."[34] At points, his critique seemed based merely on practical difficulties. Experience had demonstrated courts could not possibly assess savings in complex business situations, both Storrow and Smith emphasized, and any bill attempting to prescribe methods of ascertaining savings would founder in a morass of accounting details. But as Wadleigh's summary made especially clear, reformers also questioned the fundamental philosophy upon which the doctrine rested. Wadleigh sought to expose two fallacies regarding the benefits provided by new technology he believed lay behind the doctrine of savings.

The first and most important fallacy pertained to the flow of returns from technological innovations promising reduced expenses. "The certain and almost immediate effect of a patented labor-saving invention is that it diminishes the cost of the product to the consumer," Wadleigh confidently asserted. "The consumer has gained not just by the diminished cost due to the use of the invention after the expiration of the patent, but by an immediate cheapening, for it has been shown by figures drawn from many branches of industry that the royalties commonly received seldom exceed five percent of the actual saving immediately realized; so that, if an invention cheapens the product one dollar, the patentee generally receives five or ten cents of it, and the community at large gains the rest."[35] Direct evidence of this phenomenon came from Hyde, who discussed at length how a new pegging machine for attaching soles to uppers had resulted in a precipitous drop in the price of shoes.[36] By passing all savings resulting from an invention back to the patentee, Wadleigh suggested, the doctrine of savings worked against "the inevitable laws of trade." For if inventors priced their devices so as to reclaim all savings resulting from their use, no one would ever adopt an invention.

This was all the more true because the process of innovation clearly involved risks on the part of the user of an invention as well as on the part of the inventor. Did users, asked Wadleigh, deserve no credit for creating the conditions of use? Did all of the economies gained through innovation result

---

[34] House Arguments, pp. 343–347.
[35] U.S. Senate, "Report to Accompany Bill S. 300," pp. 3–5.
[36] House Arguments, pp. 300–305.

from the act of invention, or did some come from economical manufacture on the part of the infringer? How could courts be certain users of a patented device would not have acted differently, and perhaps more economically, had they known they were infringing? In assessing profits in earlier cases, the Supreme Court had emphasized that "it compensates one party and punishes another; it makes the wrong-doer liable for *actual*, not possible gains," Storrow and Wadleigh insisted, quoting from an opinion issued by the high court in a dispute involving the Goodyear rubber patents. "The controlling consideration is that he shall not profit by his wrong."[37] When courts began to equate savings with profits, Wadleigh emphasized in his summary of Storrow's remarks, they lost sight of the fundamental goal of infringement cases, which was to keep infringers from taking what otherwise would have gone to the inventor. By equating the complex process of innovation with the simple act of invention, courts unfairly skewed the rewards of innovation toward inventors and away from consumers.

In addition to harboring this fundamental misunderstanding about the flow of returns from innovation, the doctrine of savings perpetuated a second common misconception: that new technology merely provided savings over existing practice. In reality, Wadleigh noted, many new technologies performed novel functions and conveyed benefits such as "increased ease and convenience." Repeating examples originally highlighted by Storrow in testimony, Wadleigh mentioned "an electric fire-alarm for a city, a safety switch for a railroad, or an improved car-ventilator" as inventions of this sort.[38] "The use of these would not bring any direct saving, and would not lead to any profit which could be ascertained by any technical process of accountancy," Wadleigh wrote. "This bill declares that the courts shall not attempt to do what cannot be done successfully, but in such cases shall award a gross sum for the damages."[39] Senator Thomas Morgan of Alabama, Wadleigh's colleague on the committee, elaborated further on this point when defending the bill before the full Senate. In many instances, Morgan insisted, users deployed technologies of this sort "without evil intent" but "to serve life and property.... They are compelled, often, to use the patent to save themselves from great censure, and even from criminal responsibility."[40]

Viewed in light of such analysis, railroads, manufacturers, and other users of patented technologies appeared not so much as villains expropriating the fruits of inventors but as intermediaries who in the course of providing a product or service conveyed the benefits of invention to the public. Patentees who sought compensation under the doctrine of savings, in contrast, looked more like greedy individuals who tried to withhold those benefits or extort

---

[37]   *Goodyear v. Providence Rubber Co.*, 9 Wallace, p. 788; quoted by Wadleigh in U.S. Senate, "Report to Accompany Bill S. 300," p. 4.

[38]   U.S. Senate, "Report to Accompany Bill S. 300," p. 5, and House Arguments, p. 347.

[39]   U.S. Senate, "Report to Accompany Bill S. 300," p. 6.

[40]   CR 8 (January 7, 1879): 351.

a king's ransom for them. "In the introduction of inventions to the public use the case rarely, if ever, occurs where an inventor is able to place in his own pocket any considerable amount of the value which the community derives from his invention," the diplomatic Chauncey Smith told the Senate committee, capturing the essence of the argument in a single phrase. Any law which attempts to allow this must "involve in some way some lurking fallacy."[41] A few days earlier, the railroad lobbyist Raymond expressed the same idea more crudely. "It is a mistaken idea that pervades almost every provision of the patent law," he told the senators, "that the inventor should be compensated for his invention in the measure of its value to the public."[42]

How, then, *should* inventors be compensated? They should receive "a gross sum for the damages," in Wadleigh's phrase, or an appropriate license fee, as Raymond and Payson preferred it. "What the inventor wants and should have *is a certain and reasonable reward*," Raymond testified. "By making this reward just and reasonable the public will be better satisfied; the growing hostility to patents will be allayed; the users of patented inventions will be more numerous, and will pay for such use far more willingly; and the temptation to buy patents for the purposes of speculation be in a great measure done away with."[43] His colleague Payson made much the same argument, but justified it in terms of historical change in the size and structure of the market. "You must remember that the evils in regard to patent property have gone on increasing... not simply in proportion to the population, but far in excess thereof," Payson reminded the House committee. "You will please remember that the license fee, which forty or fifty years ago might have been a very inadequate reward to the inventor, will today enable him to live like a prince."[44] If owners of the Tanner patent received payment from all lines based upon a license fee already paid by some, he noted by way of example, they would recover between $350,000 and $700,000.[45]

Stephen Hurlbut, the experienced politician, advanced a similar argument in terms his agrarian colleagues perhaps found more amenable. Given the final word before the House committee even though he had lost his seat in Congress, Hurlbut insisted the bill would ensure creative individuals a just reward, while taking away "the thing that demoralizes that class of industry more than anything I know of, and that is the gambling notion of the enormous, unwise, and improper profits to be derived." Hurlbut went on to link the large rewards captured under the doctrine of savings to the moral decay many believed had run rampant in the Age of Grant. "If I am correct in my observation, the great evil of our society now, and which has been the great evil for ten or fifteen years – and it pervades all society – is this undue and unsound desire, which amounts to a mania among the people, to grow

[41] Senate Arguments, p. 45.   [42] Ibid., pp. 113–114.
[43] House Arguments, p. 244.
[44] Ibid., p. 371.   [45] Ibid., p. 370.

suddenly rich without work. I think that is at the bottom of nearly all our social troubles. I think that the present patent law as it is administered – not in the law itself, but as it is administered – tends to create that appetite, and foster that gambling spirit. I think it holds out the same temptation in the instances of these enormous profits, that have been made from time to time, that are held out by the lottery."[46] For Hurlbut, it followed that in passing this bill "you will have done more for the development of the country than has been done by any one measure that I know of that has occurred within the last ten years."[47]

In advancing these arguments, advocates of patent reform tried to suppress references to the railroad industry and to portray the bill as a series of technical refinements reflecting the broad consensus of expert opinion. In organizing their lobbying efforts, spokesmen for the railroads took special care to avoid giving the impression they spoke narrowly in their own interests. "It is exceedingly desirable to have [the bill] become a law," wrote ERA President D. L. Harris to John Garrett as the House committee deliberated. "Will you quietly do what you can in its aid by personal letters to your friends in Congress, urging them IN BEHALF OF MANUFACTURERS AND USERS OF MACHINERY to give the Bill favorable consideration[?]"[48] Raymond encouraged WRA members to lobby quietly on behalf of the bill but cautioned them not to appear as if they opposed the whole patent system.[49] Hurlbut admitted under hostile questioning that he came before the House on behalf of the WRA, but he characterized the association as a cooperative legal agency rather than as a lobbying organization and claimed he had responded initially at the request of heavy manufacturers in his district.[50] Payson sought to establish the same point in concluding his testimony before the House committee. "I wish to repel, with the utmost earnestness with which I am capable, the stigma sought to be cast upon us, that this is an attempt upon the part of a few infringers, men who have no interest in patent law, to get rid of the effects of their infringements," he declared solemnly. "We are aiming at the greatest good for the greatest number."[51] In a transparent attempt to curry favor with Grangers, Raymond praised legislators for refusing to extend the sewing machine patents and deplored notorious patent monopolies on agricultural machinery and Paris Green, an insecticide used by cotton farmers.[52]

---

[46] Ibid., p. 439.　　[47] Ibid., p. 442.

[48] D. L. Harris to Garrett, February 16, 1878, Patents and Invention File, B&O Papers. Emphasis in original.

[49] Circular from J. H. Raymond, November 26, 1878, CBQ Papers, 33 1870 7.6. See also J. H. Raymond to Garrett, May 11, 1878, Patents and Invention File, B&O Papers.

[50] House Arguments, pp. 438–442.　　[51] Ibid., p. 372.

[52] Ibid., pp. 242–243. Raymond also stressed the Paris Green case before the Senate. See Senate Arguments, pp. 116–117.

Try as they might, however, those testifying on behalf of the bill could not escape the long shadow cast by the railroads. When tracing the origins of the doctrine of savings, for instance, Wadleigh could hardly disguise the simple truth that most of the key cases underlying the doctrine involved the railroads. In illustrating his point about the nonpecuniary benefits of many inventions, the senator cited two prominent examples from railroading. At congressional hearings, railroad patent attorneys found themselves face to face with attorneys representing Sayles, Westinghouse, and others who held a direct stake in disputed railroad patents. Confronted with men they had battled unsuccessfully in court for many years, Payson and Raymond occasionally lapsed into the impassioned tones of the advocate, laying bare in the process the growing contempt railroads felt for the patent system.

"This whole country for the last ten years has been patent-mad, courts and all," the intemperate Raymond told the Senate Committee on Patents, describing the origins of the doctrine of savings in terms decidedly different from Storrow and Wadleigh. "They have treated patentees as they would treat idiots and insane people, and as they used to treat married women. They have built up a series of rules, wherein they prostitute the doctrine of trusts entirely as the measure of damages for recovery, and it will take them ten years to get over it by their own operation."[53] Raymond portrayed Judge Drummond as feeling handcuffed when assessing damages in the key cases involving railroads. In the swedge block case, according to Raymond, Drummond "had reduced the decree from $1,700,000 to $416,000, and said he felt himself bound by the rules of the court and by the statute, and he admitted that that was a ridiculous decree, and said he would have reduced it more if he could."[54] Payson likewise characterized Drummond as "finding himself in the grasp of the law" when he set damages in the brake cases.[55] The usually more restrained Payson may have surpassed even Raymond with his frenzied rhetoric when reflecting upon the doctrine Drummond found himself compelled to uphold. "I will defy any gentleman, present or absent, to find for me a single instance where a rule of recovery for damages, for any species of injury, has ever been adopted in any country in Christendom, civilized or uncivilized, that begins for enormity, for absurdity, for tyranny, to furnish a parallel to the rule of recovery which has for many years prevailed in the courts of the United States in patent cases," he told the House committee. "I can find no words strong enough to express my utter abhorrence and detestation of this sort of judicial legislation."[56]

---

[53] Senate Arguments, p. 120. Raymond later opened his prepared remarks to the House Committee on Patents with a similar reference to "insane people and married women." In describing the reasons for revising the system before this committee, Raymond characterized "the rules which obtain in ascertaining the measure of damages in patent litigation" as "the greatest injustice now being perpetrated in the name of law." House Arguments, p. 229.

[54] Senate Arguments, p. 120.   [55] House Arguments, p. 369.   [56] Ibid., p. 367.

Passions ran even hotter when the subject turned from savings to safety appliances and other patented devices offering improved comfort and convenience. Improvements of this sort included the conspicuous contributions of Pullman and Westinghouse, who Raymond singled out for special criticism. While admitting the two entrepreneurs had invested "perhaps a million dollars or more" in the manufacture of their products, Raymond accused them and "perhaps some dozen others" of attempting "to maintain what I call a close monopoly of the patent." The idea did not rest easy with Raymond. "It is an infliction upon the public, that I will not attempt to measure, that Mr. Pullman or his company should have, by virtue of anything...a monopoly upon using sleeping cars in this country, and that we are forced to make such contracts with him as please him, or else respond to him in damages for the infringement of his patent," Raymond complained to the Senate committee (see Fig. 4.1). "I do not characterize it as a credit mobilier in the disgraceful sense of the word, but it is a credit mobilier in every good sense of the word. It is a fifth wheel. It is a ring within a ring. I have been trying to demonstrate the fact that it is the right duty of the railroad companies to do their own business, and it does not belong to the Pullman Palace Car Company, or any fast freight-line, or any extraneous company. Why should Mr. Pullman, by reason of having a patent on the triangular space in the roof for the upper berth...prevent the railroads from using any kind of sleeping cars that the public will accept[?]"[57]

This bitter outburst occurred shortly after Raymond had exchanged barbs with George H. Christy, lawyer for Westinghouse. Christy complained about clauses requiring patent holders to take testimony and pursue infringement suits promptly. These obligations would place insurmountable burdens upon inventors such as his client, who at the time he invented the air brake lacked sufficient funds even to pay the fees required to obtain his initial caveat.[58] Showing no sympathy, Raymond turned his ire upon the now famous inventor. "Take the Westinghouse brake: why should we be obliged to buy any power brake of Westinghouse or Lockridge or Eames or Smith, and, in order to be able to protect the lives and property of the people, pay them $150 for what it costs them $10 or $12 to make in the first instance, and then be obliged to buy every part that wears out, whether the piston or the rubber tube, from the manufactory of the patentee, and pay him a like profit? To be sure, we are doing our best to get the money out of the people that we have to pay; but I say it is an outrage, and that so far from receiving such profits upon the manufacturing, they ought to receive a reasonable patent royalty, and be subject to the competition in manufacturing that characterizes all other branches of trade."[59]

[57] Senate Arguments, pp. 114–115.
[58] Ibid., pp. 89–91, and House Arguments, pp. 259–260.
[59] Senate Arguments, pp. 114–115.

Figure 4.1. Interior of early Pullman palace car, c. 1869. A patent for the triangular sleeping space above the curtained reclining chairs particularly irritated railroad attorneys. *Courtesy*: Library of Congress.

This last point got to the nub of the matter. For above all else, railroads wanted to establish in testimony that considerable technical change occurred independently of the patent system, in the ordinary course of conducting business. Some people testifying on behalf of the revised bill, such as Henry Hyde of the Textile Manufacturers Association, went so far as to assert that inventors created technologies out of an innate desire rather than in response to patents or other economic inducements.[60] Though Payson and Raymond likely sympathized with that view, they offered more measured assessments. "I am not one of those who share the growing belief that there is no necessity for or commensurate benefit from a patent system, and who favor its entire repeal (which class of persons is much larger than is generally supposed)," Raymond declared before the House committee. "Nor do I sympathize," he immediately added, "with those other extremists who attribute all progress in science and the useful arts to the patents issued upon improvements and the law permitting and regulating the same."[61] Payson likewise assured the House committee that he did not propose repealing the patent laws, while insisting, "At the same time, I am very far from sharing in the opinion of others, that the patent law is the principal element of our national prosperity."[62] These double-edged remarks echoed those made at Senate hearings. "Although we are told eloquently of the offices performed by the patent laws in attaining our present civilization, yet their exact measure in this respect is never given as except in the glowing terms of glittering generalities," Raymond told Wadleigh's committee. "That they perform important offices in this respect, none should deny; that they perform principal and primary offices, none should believe."[63]

Through comments such as these, railroad spokesmen managed to give credit to the patent system for stimulating invention, while also preserving ample room for inventiveness occurring outside its mechanisms. "All inventions run in lines," Raymond stated confidently, offering senators a brief tutorial on the nature of technical change. "There is a certain progress and steady improvement in all the arts, and...not by virtue of the patent law exclusively. These lines of invention are what is called 'the art.'"[64] Such a portrait of innovation very much served the interests of railroads, of course, and Raymond found ways to embellish upon it elsewhere in his testimony. In describing the WRA to the House committee, for instance, he noted that in addition to representing railroads as the largest users of patents, the association also served "secondarily the small number of railroad officers and employees comprising the inventors of the more valuable of the improvements we use."[65] While subtly laying claim for railroad employees to the more worthy contributions to "the art," Raymond diminished those of outsiders. "In the army of inventions that are presented to the railroad companies," he noted condescendingly, "the man has simply the broad seal of the

---

[60] House Arguments, pp. 300–305.   [61] Ibid., p. 228.   [62] Ibid., p. 372.
[63] Senate Arguments, p. 112.   [64] Ibid., p. 110.   [65] House Arguments, p. 226.

United States in his hands, and wants us to manufacture and introduce the article."[66]

The image of the amateurish outsider using a sketchily drawn patent claim to hold hostage the community of railroading experts captured the sympathy of reformers such as Wadleigh. At one point in his committee hearings, the senator characterized the Tanner invention "as a very simple one indeed" and advised as "I believe it was in evidence that this brake was invented by several workmen in railroad shops, who did not apply for a patent, and it went into use on those roads."[67] But for railroads to find relief from the patent system, they needed to persuade more than Wadleigh and his liberal colleagues. Their arguments must win support from majorities in both houses of Congress or meet with approval before the Supreme Court, whose justices had yet to issue their rulings in the brake case appeals.

CONGRESS AND THE COURTS

Matters came to a head in both forums during 1878. That April, the House passed the revised patent bill without debate, and Wadleigh read a slightly different version into the record of the Senate. In June, the senator agreed reluctantly to postpone consideration of the bill until December, a move that editors at the *New York Times* later credited with seriously damaging the chances of reform. In the interim, the Senate ordered several thousand more copies of Wadleigh's report and the accompanying testimony printed and distributed, fueling public debate.[68] Editors of *Scientific American*, who two years before had still identified "the Western Grangers" as "the chief opponents to the patent system," now branded the revised legislation as the handiwork of "covetous corporations" and regularly deplored the practice of railroads combining in defense against independent inventors.[69] Hundreds of inventors and representatives of firms such as the Providence Tool Company rallied to the cause and swamped Congress with letters opposing the proposed revisions.[70]

---

[66] Senate Arguments, p. 128.   [67] Ibid., pp. 32 and 38.

[68] On April 26, 1878, the House adopted without debate a bill prohibiting consideration of economy or savings unless the patented object was sold. See *Scientific American* 38 (May 18, 1878): 306, and *Journal of the U.S. Senate*, 45th Senate, 2d sess., April 1 and 29, 1878. Looking back on these events, the *New York Times* would later note that Congress had made a crucial mistake by not acting on the bill the previous spring. *New York Times*, July 14, 1878, p. 6.

[69] *Scientific American* 36 (March 17, 1877): 161; 37 (December 15, 1877): 368; and 38 (April 13, 1878): 224.

[70] When the revised bill reached the Senate, virtually the first response came from Senator Allen Thurman, who said: "My attention has been called to this bill by a great many letters. I do not propose to understand it.... There is a controversy as I understand between the railroad companies on the one side and inventors on the other ... There is some provision in this bill in respect to which has excited a great deal of interest

Meanwhile, events in national politics reached a fever pitch, often with surprising implications for the patent cases. The long dispute over Credit Mobilier came to a head, as the Supreme Court considered the right of Congress to collect damages from the Union Pacific in compensation for fraudulent contracts the railroad had joined with suppliers. The list of suppliers included not only the building contractors and owners of coal lands located along the route, but also the Pullman Palace Car Company. An especially vitriolic fight over state bonds in Missouri created such an uproar that in summer 1878 residents of that state held a special convention in conjunction with the ordinary Democratic Party gathering simply to denounce the federal courts. The Supreme Court responded by authorizing a special tax to repay the bondholders. The primary beneficiary was plaintiff Elisha Foote, a prominent Republican who in the late 1860s had served as Commissioner of Patents.[71] At congressional hearings that winter, Foote had offered an extended critique of the proposed patent reform bill, whose second section he believed would gut the patent system.[72]

By the time the Wadleigh bill at last came before the full Senate in December 1878, it faced a body charged with uncertainty and excitement.[73] Congresses habitually reserved much of their business for these pressurized "lame duck" sessions between the fall elections and the swearing in of a new Congress in early March.[74] The startling results of that November's voting, which had secured Democrats control of the Senate, compounded the usual sense of urgency. For the first time since before the Civil War, Democrats would control both houses when the next Congress convened. Senate Republicans, though badly divided as always, had a last opportunity to close

both among inventors and among the railroad companies." *CR* 8 (December 11, 1878): 89.

[71] On cases involving the Union Pacific, see Charles Fairman, *History of the Supreme Court of the United States*, vol. 7: *Reconstruction and Reunion, 1864–1888, Part Two* (New York: Macmillan, 1987), pp. 589–646. In May 1878, Congress passed a measure calling for federally funded railroads to build such a fund by paying a tax of 25 percent on earnings (calculated before dividends) and by foregoing the whole amount of charges for services rendered to the government, rather than merely half the charges as originally agreed. Whether this measure represented a slap at railroads or a further subsidy for bondholders, or both, was not entirely clear. But it kept the issue of bonds in the forefront of politics. In an agonizing decision issued in the fall term of 1878, Justice Miller made clear that the government had a legal right to sue and left no question that the contracts were fraudulent. He invited innocent stockholders to pursue relief in equity proceedings, while letting it be known that the most powerful stockholders were by no means innocent. Yet even Miller could not approve the payment of compensation to government, for the government was in this case not a stockholder but a creditor who under terms of the bond issue was not owed payment for another thirty years.

[72] House Arguments, pp. 408–419.   [73] *CR* 8 (December 11, 1878): 89–91.

[74] David J. Rothman, *Politics and Power: The United States Senate, 1869–1901* (Cambridge, Mass.: Harvard University Press, 1966), pp. 79 and 82–83.

ranks and produce legislation on pressing issues such as the currency and civil rights. "It can take but little time," Wadleigh assured colleagues anxious to table his bill and proceed to other matters, as "there can be no extended debate whatever." James Blaine, powerful leader of the so-called Half-Breed element of the Republicans, immediately registered his skepticism. "The senator underrates the capacity of the Senate of the United States," drolly responded the prophetic Blaine, "when he thinks there cannot be an extended debate on his measure, or on any other."[75]

In fact, the bill would occupy weeks of debate, as Wadleigh and his cohort of liberal supporters attempted to navigate the treacherous course through a divided Senate.[76] First, Grangers blasted the bill for failing to address the concerns of farmers. Members of the patent committee, loathe to embrace the innocent purchaser approach, eventually placated the Grangers by drafting an amendment that would prevent plaintiffs from recovering court costs when damages from infringement totaled less than $50. This measure would discourage nuisance suits that plagued farmers without affecting more substantial disputes such as those involving the railroads and manufacturers. Advocates of reform then encountered Roscoe Conkling, the man who had scuttled the efforts of Raymond two years before. For nearly two weeks after the holiday recess, amid pleas to move on to other matters and with time for conference with the House dwindling, the New Yorker and a small cohort of his Stalwart allies engaged Wadleigh and other reformers in an extended debate about the intricacies of the doctrine of savings.

The exchanges between these groups betrayed the distinctive blend of political rhetoric and judicial reasoning characteristic of the Gilded Age Senate as it confronted the emergent corporate order. Conkling and many of those who joined him were deeply engaged in patent law, either as judges or in their private legal practices. David Davis of Illinois, who had joined the Senate in March 1877 after nearly fifteen years on the Supreme Court, had helped decide many of the critical patent cases of the era and had participated directly in the celebrated brake cases before Judge Drummond in Chicago, which fell within his circuit. Stanley Matthews of Ohio would assume a place on the high court within another two years. William D. Whyte of Maryland, another member of the dissenting eight, had represented Conover in the famous case against Mevs that had helped established the doctrine of savings. Conkling, who once declined President Grant's offer to be nominated for the post of Chief Justice, had himself recently defended the Remington

---

[75] *CR* 8 (December 13, 1878): 170.

[76] The group of Liberals from the patent committee who actively supported the bill on the floor of the Senate included Newton Booth of California, Isaac Christiancy of Michigan, George Frisbee Hoar of Massachusetts, and Thomas Morgan of Alabama. Christiancy had recently come to the Senate after years on the Michigan Supreme Court. See Rothman, *Politics and Power*, p. 30.

Arms Manufacturing Company and another manufacturer in two prominent infringement suits.[77]

Conkling relentlessly homed in on the central premise advanced by Wadleigh that courts in certain circumstances could not reasonably ascertain the savings derived from an invention. The New Yorker refused to accept without question that conditions in railroading and in large manufacturing enterprises differed so substantially from those prevailing among smaller firms. Like a skilled cross-examiner, Conkling posed an array of hypothetical situations in which users incorporated patented technologies into their products, then asked Wadleigh to explain why the same reasoning did not apply to those cases. Why did a railroad that manufactured its own locomotives and incorporated into them patented devices deserve relief under the bill, Conkling wondered, while a blacksmith who used a new alloy to harden parts or who unwittingly placed a patented axle upon a wagon he built and sold did not deserve such relief?

This scenario and others posed by Conkling compelled reformers to draw distinctions they could not always easily explain. Wadleigh floundered repeatedly and fell back upon rehashing examples such as the swedge block. A flustered George Frisbee Hoar, the young senator from Massachusetts who would carry the Liberal banner for decades to come, noted huffily that one could always pick a law apart by raising arcane hypotheticals, then launched into a ringing tribute to the patent system and raised the specter of radical reform. Only the aging Isaac Christiancy offered an effective response. Conkling's examples, he claimed, further illustrated the difficulties of assessing savings. His blacksmith would receive protection under the bill, Christiancy insisted, and so would farmers. Deny the exemption for users of patented articles, on the other hand, "and every purchaser of a mowing machine, every purchaser of a patented plow, every purchaser of any farming implement, although he purchases in good faith, will be responsible not only for the real damages but for all the profits it can be shown he has made."[78]

---

[77] Alfred R. Conkling, *The Life and Letters of Roscoe Conkling, Orator, Statesman, Advocate* (New York: Charles L. Webster, 1889), pp. 491–493 and 571–573. Both cases bore many markings of the sorts of complaints registered by railroads. In the Remington suit, decided in August 1875, an independent inventor sought at the last moment before his rights to an 1857 patent for a breech-loading rifle expired to sustain a complaint against an established manufacturer who had accumulated significant liability. Conkling had his successful argument in the case reprinted and widely circulated. In the summer of 1878, with the Wadleigh bill pending, Conkling had thrust himself into an effort to make a special appeal to Judge Blatchford of the New York circuit on behalf of an alleged infringer of a patent for nickel-plating. Here, too, Conkling confronted a situation characteristic of railroads, in which a firm used a process rather than making a product for the open market, and once again he argued on behalf of the alleged infringer.

[78] *CR* 8 (January 17, 1879): 522.

When pressed in this way, Conkling abandoned his prosecutorial style and resorted to more highly politicized rhetoric. "The bill is objectionable because the distinction the Senator now points out is made, and made not in favor of the innocent, the defenseless, the people who need protection, but made in favor of exactly those persons who do not need it," the New Yorker responded to Christiancy. "It is an exemption of aggregated capital, of powerful combinations, of intelligent persons from a rule of law which in the same bill we propose to visit upon the ignorant, the weak, and those who accidentally become subject to it."[79] Later, Conkling honed his criticism, targeting the specific forces he believed lay behind the proposed reforms. "Who are excluded?" he asked of the clause limiting an account of savings. "We know not from this bill, but from other information of which we cannot fail to take notice we do know who the excluded parties are, namely the strong, the rich, the powerful, the owners of aggregated capital, the great mill-owners, the railway corporations of the country."[80] Similar rhetoric came from Davis, who throughout his long political career had cultivated a reputation for defending the rights of the underdog against organized interests. Along with fellow Lincoln appointees Samuel F. Miller and Stephen J. Field, Davis had persistently dissented from Supreme Court decisions upholding railroad bond issues. To his way of thinking, the second section of Wadleigh's bill constituted nothing less than a license for railroads to infringe patents at will. Davis implored his colleagues to recognize the section as the handiwork of "monopoly power" exercised by combinations of patent users whose "concentrated power is sufficient to ruin any patentee who attempts to bring them to public account."[81]

While indisputably hyperbolic, such attacks fit within a coherent ideology of political economy. Historians have often portrayed Conkling and his followers as quintessentially political animals whose contests with rivals such as Blaine and Garfield were largely personal.[82] But in reality, the Republican Stalwarts actually staked out a distinctive stance regarding the emerging corporate order. Unlike Blaine, who often did the railroads' bidding and operated beneath a lingering cloud of scandal, Conkling persistently

---

[79] *CR* 8 (January 15, 1879): 460.   [80] *CR* 8 (January 17, 1879): 523.

[81] *CR* 8 (December 19, 1878): 305.

[82] For such an assessment, see John A. Garraty, *The New Commonwealth, 1877–1890* (New York: Harper and Row, 1968), p. 239. "The division of congressional Republicans into Stalwarts and Half-Breeds did not separate members according to principle," writes Garraty. "The Stalwarts were merely the personal friends of Senator Roscoe Conkling of New York, dedicated to the frustration of the ambitions of Conkling's enemy, James G. Blaine of Maine. The conflict between these two men, each talented and attractive but incapable of subordinating his dislike of the other to the interest of the country or the party, was entirely personal." Rothman, *Politics and Power*, pp. 26–35, acknowledges Conkling's power in the wake of the Liberal Republican uprising but identifies no prevailing coherent ideology among the Stalwarts and attributes no substantive policies to them.

resisted the carriers, who considered him incorruptible.[83] In ways perhaps less blatant than Blaine and his followers, reformers such as Garfield, Hoar, and Wadleigh sought in the eyes of Conkling to reach an accommodation with economic forces and interests the New Yorker could not stomach.[84] While Conkling in decrying those interests could sound much like the Grangers, he deployed such antimonopoly rhetoric not on behalf of Western and Southern farmers but in defense of small proprietors, craftsmen, and independent inventors. He raised the image of the skilled blacksmith assembling a wagon for sale in the local community, not that of the innocent farmer falling victim to speculators.[85]

Conkling sought to preserve the patent system, in sum, because he remained firmly anchored in the world of the proprietary capitalist that lay at the foundation of that system. For him, railroads and other corporations appeared not as the vanguard of a new age, but as deviant creations of an older world they now threatened to destroy. These "aggregations of capital,"

[83]   Railroad magnate Collis Huntington advised his partners that Conkling "would take nothing from us while...in Congress." See Rothman, *Politics and Power*, pp. 196–197. Lee Benson, *Merchants, Farmers, and Railroads: Railroad Regulation and New York Politics, 1850–1887* (Cambridge, Mass.: Harvard University Press, 1955), pp. 156–160, emphasizes that Conkling was much more resistant to railroads and other organized economic interests than either Blaine and the Half-Breeds or Garfield and the Liberal Republicans. Conkling gave Chauncey Depew, notorious lobbyist for the New York Central, a "sharp going over" at the hearings of Windom Committee in 1873, when Congress first considered the subject of railroad regulation at length. He retained his animosity to the Central and other "corporate monopolies" until he resigned from Congress in 1881.

[84]   Both Conkling and Blaine chafed at reformers who targeted machine politics and thus threatened their personal power. But while Blaine often fell into alliance with Liberals on crucial economic issues, Conkling attracted the ire of Godkin and others in the reform community for failing to defend with sufficient vigor pet liberal causes such as a strong currency. Benson, *Merchants*, p. 158. In 1881, Conkling would stage a dramatic exit from the political scene, resigning his post in the Senate after engaging in a notorious showdown with James Garfield, the reform prince who had recently gained the presidency. Because the immediate source of the dispute involved appointments to the New York Customs House, a key bastion in Conkling's political network, one can easily interpret the episode as the last gasp of a machine politician. Rothman, *Politics and Power*, pp. 32–35. Yet as the issue of patent reform suggests, Conkling's differences with reformers could extend as well to "the great commercial and industrial questions" Garfield considered the real business of the day.

[85]   Indeed, when William Windom proposed amendments intended to protect innocent purchasers, Conkling broke with Davis and quietly supported efforts by Wadleigh to defeat or weaken it. *CR* 8 (January 20, 1879): 571, and 8 (January 23, 1879): 659. When a similar innocent purchaser bill passed by the House at the start of the next session reached the Senate floor in early 1881, Conkling again actively opposed it. After ridiculing Windom for getting a lot of mileage out of the pump case, Conkling noted sarcastically, "I want to sympathize all around with all the people who like to borrow the inventions of somebody else and use them and not pay for them." *CR* 11 (February 23, 1881): 1794.

with their power to disrupt both markets and politics, were the true monopolists of the day. Those who ran interference for them, whether reformer or Half-Breed, deserved the highest censure. Conkling had greater sympathy for Grangers, who rebelled against corporate power and often celebrated the values of the independent capitalist. But agrarians were willing to take liberties with patents and bond issues and other essential rights to property that underlay the world of the proprietary capitalist as well as the corporation. Conkling would not follow them down this path. And though Conkling never enjoyed the support of anything close to a majority of his colleagues in Congress, he managed to defeat attempts to alter the patent laws. For when the Wadleigh bill at last cleared the Senate, supported by reformers and by a large block of Grangers, little time remained for meaningful consideration of it in the House. Though a revised version emerged from the House committee on patents three days before the close of the session, a vote to suspend the rules and consider it narrowly failed.[86]

Yet if a small tribunal in the Senate could block railroads from securing a legislative remedy to their problems by altering the patent laws, a handful of justices on the Supreme Court might offer at least a measure of relief through their interpretations of those laws. Indeed, by the time Wadleigh's bill died in the House, the court had already demonstrated in key cases a willingness to embrace the arguments advanced by railroads and their liberal supporters. The first of those rulings came in October 1878, when with the patent legislation pending and the Senate debate still two months away, the Supreme Court at last handed down its decision in the Tanner case.[87] Rather than confront the issue of the doctrine of savings directly, the justices based their decision on association arguments that railroads had easily found alternatives to the Tanner method of linking brakes. Some lines, they claimed, had tried out several arrangements for linking brakes on an experimental basis prior to the time Mr. Tanner obtained his patent. These experiments, in the opinion of the railroads, demonstrated that the idea of linking brakes was "in the air" at the time and thus did not deserve broad coverage in a patent. The Court agreed. Though the experimental devices were "not so perfect as that of [Tanner]" and though railroads had never actually patented them, noted the justices in reversing a series of rulings by lower courts, their use invalidated Tanner's claim to have achieved a basic principle. "Like almost all other inventions," confidently wrote Justice Bradley of an innovation that had occurred three decades earlier, "that of double brakes came when, in the progress of mechanical improvement, it was needed; and being sought by many minds, it is not wonderful that it was developed in different and independent forms." Expressing a philosophy of

---

[86] CR 8 (January 24, 1879): 717, 723; 8 (February 6, 1879): 1069; 8 (February 8, 1879): 1146; and 8 (March 1, 1879): 2257–2259.
[87] Circular from J. H. Raymond, November 26, 1878, CBQ Papers, 33 1870 7.6.

technical change in which the railroads and others who employed patented technologies could find great comfort, he continued, "if the advance towards the thing desired is gradual, and proceeds step by step, so that no one can claim the complete whole, then each is entitled only to the specific form of device which he produces."[88]

In taking this approach, the justices did not absolve railroads of all liability in the brake cases. Railroads using certain forms of double-acting brakes needed to pay appropriate royalties to the owners of the patent covering the particular arrangement they deployed. The Court made this clear in 1882, when it ruled that the Baltimore and Ohio owed the owner of the Stevens patent for use of the Stevens arrangement. In the wake of that decision, the ERA advised the Pennsylvania, which had also used the Stevens device, to settle for a fixed fee of $25,000.[89] But with its insistence in the Tanner case that several patents for double-acting brakes could exist independently of one another, the Court blocked holders of one brake patent from claiming infringement by those who used a different arrangement. The Court rejected claims advanced by Sayles and his representatives in Court and before Congress that the three brake patents constituted an interdependent system analogous to a horse, stirrup, and bit, in which each component was worthless without the other two. Use of one patented arrangement, the justices ruled, did not necessarily entail use of another. By the same token, no railroad could escape liability by claiming that a license for one patent gave it carte blanche to use any and all forms of double-acting brakes.

Though the Court based its ruling in the Tanner case on technical details specific to double-acting brakes, the decision had broad implications for railroad technology. As Bradley's telling reference to "almost all other inventions" suggests, the circumstances involved in the brake cases were hardly unusual. With so many inventors and mechanics at work in railroad shops and in those of their suppliers, most devices deployed by railroads appeared in numerous patented forms. By declining to insist that one patent be given priority over all others and by refusing to deem one form or arrangement essential to another, the Court signaled its intent to restrict the scope and power of patent monopolies. The ruling carried particular weight because its author, Justice Bradley, had carved a role as the foremost expert on the Court in patent cases.[90]

---

[88] *Railway Co. v. Sayles*, U.S. Reports, vol. 97 (October 1878), pp. 556–557.

[89] George Harding to Wayne McVeagh, December 4, 1882; A. McCallum to Hon. James A. Logan, January 3, 1883; and John Scott to Geo. Roberts, January 9, 1883; Papers Pertaining to Matters Brought before the Board of Directors of the Pennsylvania Railroad (henceforth, PRR Board Papers), Hagley Museum and Library, Wilmington, Delaware, Acc. 1807.

[90] See Fairman, *Reconstruction and Reunion, Part Two*, pp. 117–127. Bradley had worked as chief counsel for the Camden and Amboy Railroad before being appointed

A few years later, the justices elaborated on this theory of innovation and made clearer its implications for the sort of speculative behavior exhibited in the Tanner case:

> The process of development in manufactures creates a constant demand for new appliances, which the skill of the ordinary head-workmen and engineers is generally adequate to devise, and which, indeed, are the natural and proper outgrowth of such development. Each step forward prepares the way for the next, and each is usually taken by spontaneous trials in a hundred different places. To grant a single party a monopoly of every slight advance made, except where the exercise of invention somewhat above ordinary mechanical or engineering skill is distinctly shown, is unjust in principle and injurious in its consequences....
>
> It was never the object of [the patent] laws to grant a monopoly for every trifling device, every shadow of a shade of an idea, which would naturally and spontaneously occur to any skilled mechanic or operator in the ordinary progress of manufacturers. Such an indiscriminate creation of exclusive privileges tends rather to obstruct than to stimulate invention.
>
> It creates a class of speculative schemers, who make it their business to watch the advancing wave of improvement and gather its foam in the form of patented monopolies, which enable them to lay a heavy tax upon the industry of the country without contributing anything to the real advancement of the art. It embarrasses the honest pursuit of business with fears and apprehensions of concealed liens and unknown liabilities to law suits and vexatious accountings for profits made in good faith.[91]

COORDINATED RESPONSE

With this rationale, the Supreme Court effectively sanctioned the sorts of legal arguments that the railroad patent associations would almost always be capable of advancing. With access to nearly all companies and with individual firms taking great care to document their technical activities, the

> to the Court, and it is easy to see in his ruling evidence of railroad influence on the Court. Yet the long record of Bradley's jurisprudence suggests he acted on other principles. In a variety of decisions, including several that went against the desires of railroads, Bradley consistently exhibited a discomfort with monopoly. In the famous Slaughterhouse cases and in several rulings pertaining to the rights of states to regulate railroads, including the landmark case of *Munn v. Illinois* (1877), Bradley exhibited a willingness to place curbs upon businesses he believed operated with monopoly power. In one lesser-known example with ironic connections to the brake cases, Bradley refused to excuse a railroad from liability for an injury to a passenger, on grounds that travelers had no real choice but to use the railroad. The plaintiff was none other than Stevens, owner of the brake patents.

[91] The case was *Atlantic Works vs. Brady*, decided March 5, 1883, and quoted in *Annual Report of the Executive Committee of the Eastern Railroad Association* 19 (1885), p. 16 (henceforth, *ERA Annual Reports*).

lawyers at the ERA and the WRA could readily establish precedence and undermine broad claims pertaining to virtually any aspect of technology.[92] Since courts retained the right to review questions pertaining to originality at every stage of appeal, the railroads stood an excellent chance of escaping liability at some point in the judicial process. With courts willing to consider techniques that had not been patented as evidence of priority, moreover, the associations or their members would not have to take out patents themselves in order to accomplish their goal. (Though as a precaution they often did so, making sure that the individuals holding the rights turned them over to an association member.) Railroads needed only to pool information and to keep a united front in their dealings with patent holders.[93]

During the years the Supreme Court embraced this understanding of invention, railroads took steps to ensure that information about technical change in their industry flowed through routinized channels. In the wake of the Tanner decision of 1878, the patent associations and their members tightened control over use and acquisition of patented technologies. At the Burlington, where Robert Harris some years earlier had instructed his mechanics to submit all new designs to him for approval, C. E. Perkins forcefully extended the policy to cover all devices used by the railroad. "In order to avoid trouble from infringement of patents I think best that from this date no new device or improvement whatever should be used in any department of this company until it has been submitted to me with full drawings and descriptions for investigation as to whether it infringes upon some already existing patent," Perkins wrote to his assistant T. J. Potter. "Such preliminary investigation is necessary to avoid suits and damages on account of infringements, and this order applies to every new device, however slight the alleged improvement may be, and whether the same has been patented or not. Improvements invented by employees of the Company are included in this order."[94]

Also in the fall of 1878, a special committee of the Pennsylvania's board again reviewed procedures used by their line to obtain materials and supplies. On its recommendation, the board reestablished the position of Purchasing

---

[92] By 1876, the WRA already included 81 lines operating 32,000 miles of track. Senate Arguments, pp. 191–92. Within a year of the Tanner decision, nearly every major line in the East belonged to the ERA. Isaac Hinckley to J. W. Garrett, July 24, 1879, Garrett Papers, box 86, subject 9614.

[93] In 1878 the ERA amended its constitution to provide stronger sanctions against firms that negotiated their own agreements with holders of disputed patents. The secretary of the association complained that such deals lent credence to the claims of inventors and hurt the chances for success in court. "To obtain the best results," he cautioned, "the members of the Association must act as a unit, and it is believed that this unity of action has been the true cause of our success heretofore." *ERA Annual Report* 12 (1878–1879): 8–9.

[94] C. E. Perkins to T. J. Potter, May 15, 1878, CBQ Papers, 3P6.21.

Agent, which had fallen by the wayside earlier in the decade.[95] The man filling this post would coordinate all purchasing activities of the various departments and geographical divisions of the entire Pennsylvania system. He would prevent officers within the system from negotiating separate contracts for the same material or from ordering different items to be used for identical purposes. Other railroads, including the Burlington, added purchasing agents for the same reasons at about the same time as the Pennsylvania.[96]

As individual companies imposed greater control over the acquisition of technologies, the patent associations took steps to secure closer ties among their members. The ERA amended its constitution in 1878 to provide stronger sanctions against firms that negotiated their own agreements with holders of disputed patents. By striking their own deals, explained the secretary of the association in justifying the reforms, individual members lent credence to the claims of inventors and hurt the chances for success in court. "To obtain the best results," he cautioned, "the members of the Association must act as a unit, and it is believed that this unity of action has been the true cause of our success heretofore."[97] The secretaries encouraged railroads to submit devices developed in their own shops to the associations, who would arrange for patenting and add them to the rolls of techniques members could deploy without fear of liability. The ERA included this patenting service as part of its membership, and the WRA performed the function for a nominal fee.[98] The secretaries also urged members to submit any appliance or technique they proposed to use for routine clearance by their staffs. By the early eighties, inquiries of this sort constituted the most frequent item of business.[99] With the information he provided, observed the ERA secretary,

---

95 Minutes of the Board of Directors of the Pennsylvania Railroad, microform available at the Hagley Museum and Library, Wilmington, Delaware (henceforth, PRR Board Minutes), 8 (May 8, 1878): 104; 8 (November 13, 1878): 75–76; and 8 (January 22, 1879): 201.

96 The Burlington bolstered the authority of its purchasing agent and appointed a man to the office in 1877. See Higginson to Perkins, January 31, June 5, and December 1, 1877; CBQ Papers, 3P4.4. The B&O reviewed its purchasing policies in similar fashion in 1875 as a cost-cutting measure in the face of the depression. See Garrett Papers, box 69, subject 3851. On the creation of purchasing agents and their role in the railroad industry, see Glenn Porter and Harold C. Livesay, *Merchants and Manufacturers: Studies in the Changing Structure of Nineteenth-Century Marketing* (Baltimore: Johns Hopkins University Press, 1971), pp. 104–106, and Alfred D. Chandler, Jr., *The Visible Hand: The Managerial Revolution in American Business* (Cambridge, Mass.: Harvard University Press, 1977), p. 105.

97 *ERA Annual Report* 12 (1878–1879): 8–9.

98 *ERA Annual Reports* 16 (1882): 14; 18 (1884): 13; and 20 (1886): 24. For an example of this patenting service, see Geo. Chalender to Perkins, August 6, 1878; Potter to E. D. Barbour, October 15, 1878; J. H. Raymond to Barbour, October 17, 1878; Chalender to Barbour, November 9, 1878; Potter to Barbour, October 23, 1878; and Raymond to Barbour, December 7, 1878; CBQ Papers, 33 1870 2.5.

99 *ERA Annual Reports* beginning with 15 (1881): 13; esp. 20 (1886): 22.

a railroad executive "may determine whether the patent is worth the price asked for the right to use the invention covered by it; or he may learn that he can use the device without paying anything for it. Or it may be made apparent to him that, with the exercise of normal mechanical skill, the patent may be evaded by alterations in the construction of the device."[100]

With railroads sharing legal costs and freely exchanging information about patents and experiments, patent holders faced a daunting task in exploiting their rights. No longer could they count on gaining legitimacy by quietly entering into separate deals with individual lines. If patent holders pressed suit, they confronted association lawyers who could draw on the experiences of many lines to build a formidable case undermining the legitimacy of the patents. The power of the associations became evident with two early successes they achieved in the area of firebox design. Happily for Robert Harris, the WRA found a way around the Jauriet patent. The particulars remain obscure, but apparently the association surveyed railroads about their experiments with fireboxes and found precedence for Jauriet's arrangement. With the basis for a possible legal victory in hand, the association negotiated very favorable terms with Mr. Chittenden. "The Association saved us $10,000 in the Jauriet case alone," a relieved Harris wrote to a prospective member.[101] ERA secretary D. L. Harris achieved similar success when faced with a suit over patents covering a common method of securing boiler tubes within a locomotive. Harris canvassed members, asking for any evidence that someone before 1860 had used "ferrule of copper or other soft metal applied to the exterior of the iron flue tubes, between them and the tube sheet, for the purpose of making a better joint." An executive from the Philadelphia and Reading replied with testimony from master mechanic John Wootten and three other employees that they had used the method prior to the date of the patent.[102]

Not surprisingly, the number of claims brought against railroads dropped dramatically under these circumstances. The ERA carried only one suit to trial during its first six years, and except for a brief spurt in the late 1870s, the association rarely found itself in court.[103] "During the last three years," its secretary reported in 1887, "only four suits for infringement of patents have been brought against our members," and all but one was "unimportant, commenced by the patentees themselves, and of a local nature."[104] Frustrated

---

[100] *ERA Annual Reports* 20 (1886): 23.

[101] R. Harris to Robert Robinson, September 4, 1874, CBQ Papers, 9W5.2, and J. H. Raymond to R. Harris, July 3, 1874, CBQ Papers, 33 1870 2.5. Raymond, Secretary of the Western Railroad Association, reported on the legal status of three patents for fireboxes.

[102] D. L. Harris to Nicholls [*sic*], March 22, 1876, and Nicolls to D. L. Harris, March 30, 1876, Papers of the Philadelphia and Reading Railroad, Hagley Museum and Library, Acc. 1451.

[103] *ERA Annual Reports* 6 (1873): 5, and 19 (1885): 1 and 4.

[104] *ERA Annual Report* 21 (1887): 26.

inventors, unable or unwilling to pursue their claims individually, channeled their fight into collective assaults on the associations themselves. In a rare display of concerted action, they banded together under the auspices of the Inventors Protective Agency. Originally formed to lobby Congress in opposition to the proposed patent reforms, this group later challenged the legality of the railroad associations.[105] But these efforts went for naught. Courts persistently upheld the rights of railroads to combine in their defenses in patent cases, and during the early 1890s Congress twice rejected petitions that would have declared the ERA and WRA in violation of the antitrust laws.[106] Ironically, perhaps the biggest threat to the associations came ultimately from their own success. With virtually no litigation afoot, some railroad executives began to question their utility.[107]

Perhaps driven by the bureaucratic instinct for self-preservation, staffs at the associations subtly redefined their focus as the number of claims dropped. Newsletters and reports increasingly provided advice of a narrowly technical nature, with little or no reference to legal issues.[108] During the mid-1870s, the ERA acquired testing apparatus similar to that used in the mechanical laboratories that some railroads had recently opened and also provided funds to support extensive tests of drawbars using the newly developed dynamometer car of P. H. Dudley.[109] Harris refused to authorize such activities during his tenure with the WRA.[110] The man who replaced him as the Burlington's representative, however, went so far as to suggest the WRA might support itself by providing inventors with technical evaluations of experimental devices.[111] A handful of inventors even advertised that the association had approved their products.[112] In pursuing such activities, lawyers who worked for the associations tread a fine line between advancing the interests of inventors and acquiring knowledge that would preserve the freedom of railroads to

[105] On the formation of these inventors' groups, see *Scientific American* during 1879 and arguments over patent reform. On the petitions to Congress, see *New York Times*, October 21, 1883, p. 3; October 23, 1883, p. 8; and October 24, 1883, p. 4.

[106] *ERA Annual Reports*; *New York Times*, May 8, 1892, p. 20; *Scientific American* 62 (May 3, 1890): 176, and 66 (March 12, 1892): 160–61; and William K. Tubman, *Petition to the Congress of the United States* (New York, 1894).

[107] The executive was the Burlington's Perkins, whose vice-president promptly reminded him of why the associations mattered and paid the annual dues. Potter to Perkins, January 1, 1883, CBQ Papers, 3P4.56.

[108] The files of the B&O and the Chicago, Burlington and Quincy contain numerous examples of their work in this regard. On these activities at the Burlington, see especially the letterbooks of Robert Harris, CBQ Papers, 3H4.1 and 9W5.2; the letterbooks of C. E. Perkins, CBQ Papers, 3P4.4; and the in-letters of T. J. Potter, CBQ Papers, 3P6.21. At the B&O, see Patents and Inventions File, B&O Papers.

[109] *ERA Annual Reports* 10 (1877): 11–13.

[110] Robert Harris to Riehle Bros., February 18, 1878, CBQ Papers, 3H4.2, 4: 87.

[111] E. D. Barbour to C. E. Perkins, January 14, 1879, CBQ Papers, 3P4.4.

[112] Examples of advertising circulars proclaiming ERA support for the product can be found in the Burlington Archives.

innovate without liability. The longtime secretary of the ERA, S. M. Whipple, was forced to resign in 1878 after he allowed a patent holder (and, events later revealed, business partner) to use his name and that of the association in advertising.[113] The Burlington's representative returned from one meeting of the WRA with a warning that some manufacturers had begun to get one device certified, then offer a different version for sale.[114]

These trends culminated in the mid-eighties when the secretary of the ERA floated the idea of creating a Bureau of Inventions, whose staff would pass judgment on the technical merits as well as the legal status of all new devices.[115] To no one's surprise, railroads stopped short of this, for the very idea ran counter to the association's primary objectives of reducing the importance and visibility of patented technologies. As discussed in the chapters to follow, railroads preferred to leave the business of evaluating technology to engineering organizations and trade associations, where their own employees and representatives of established suppliers coordinated studies and reached considered judgments. Interestingly, the constitutions of these organizations expressly prohibited the advocacy of specific, patented articles in their specifications and standards. Their members conceived of problems to be worked out, not inventions to be made. To them, as to Justice Bradley, innovation in railroading flowed steadily if inconspicuously from the routine.

---

[113] A. McCallum, Secretary of the Eastern Railroad Association, printed circular, February 1879, B&O Papers.

[114] H. B. Stone to T. J. Potter, January 18, 1886, CBQ Papers, 3P6.37.

[115] *ERA Annual Report* 15 (1882): 13, and "Should the Railroads of this Country Establish an Experimental Station," offprint from *The Railway Master Mechanic* (1886), copy in CBQ Papers, 3P6.37. H. B. Stone to T. J. Potter, September 22, 1886; E. W. Lewis to J. F. Barnard, September 18, 1886; CBQ Papers, 3P6.37.

5

Mastering Technology,
Channeling Change

When railroads first entered into cooperative agreements designed to undercut the patent system, they were in large measure responding to specific crises associated with particular devices. By the time those troubling cases reached their climax, however, the patent associations had come to fill a vital niche in a much broader effort by management to assert some control over railroad technology. Through a variety of measures, managers sought to take the image of technical change they had advanced in their legal arguments and secure it as an institutionalized reality. This effort involved not merely taking precautions to avoid the pitfalls of the patent system, but also developing policies and procedures necessary to sustain ongoing innovation of a more anonymous character. Managers faced with rapidly changing competitive conditions looked to channel technical efforts toward certain identifiable objectives. Steering clear of radical departures in technique that might disrupt routines, they mobilized a cadre of technical experts capable of subjecting established techniques to analyses of unprecedented rigor and thoroughness. Master mechanics at individual lines increasingly gave way to professionally trained engineers ensconced in bureaucracies capable of imposing technical standards throughout the firm. These bureaucrats looked toward trade associations and professional engineering societies as forums for encouraging sustained cooperative study of select technical problems that affected the entire industry. Through coordinated analysis and action, they sought to contain innovation and render it routine.

THE CHANGING FACE OF COMPETITION

The new departures in railroad policies regarding technology and innovation stemmed from fundamental changes in the economics of the railroad industry, which in turn resulted from changes in the larger economic environment in which railroads operated. The long developmental epic of American railroading came to an abrupt end during the economic crisis of the 1870s. The panic itself had much to do with the change, if for no other reason than it turned off the spigot of European capital.[1] But the effects of the collapse extended well beyond the specifics of finance. The panic sobered up the railroad industry and the extractive economy in which it was embedded, fundamentally altering the psychology that had sustained them. Many who had made fortunes from the great extractive bonanza, such as Charles Francis Adams, Jr., recalled the depression as the turning point in their lives. The panic laid bare the contradictions between the sober industriousness that men such as Adams extolled in their rhetoric and the get-rich-quick realities of their financial affairs.[2]

Though observers such as Adams continued to interpret economic matters largely in terms of character and personality, the transition that occurred during the 1870s actually owed a great deal to fundamental changes in the structure of the economy. After years of intensive investment, the central nodes of the extractive economy had come to yield far less spectacular returns. During the fifties and sixties, wheat farmers on the American plains had enjoyed such enormous competitive advantages that they appear to have exerted substantial influence over the price of grain in London. By the mid-seventies, these farmers had settled into the more customary position of price-takers. Unable to block entry into their business or otherwise restrict output, they now stood exposed to the shifting fortunes of an international marketplace they could not control. More than ever, they had come to resemble their cotton-growing brethren to the south, though to their relative good fortune the price of wheat generally held firmer than that of cotton.[3]

The nonagricultural sectors of the extractive economy followed much the same scenario. The steel industry, deprived of its protective umbrella when fundamental patents covering the Bessemer process expired in 1876, entered an age of fierce price competition. Once the golden goose of railroad insiders, the industry was transformed suddenly into an unforgiving domain hospitable only to such relentless economizers as Andrew Carnegie.[4] The

---

[1] On diminished foreign investment, see Stanley Lebergott, *The Americans: An Economic Record* (New York: Norton, 1984), pp. 278–279, and Leland Jenks, "Railroads as an Economic Force in American Development," in Joseph T. Lambie and R. V. Clemence, *Economic Change in America: Readings in the Economic History of the United States* (Harrisburg, Pa.: Stackpole Co., 1954).

[2] On Adams's ambivalence as an investor, see Edward Chase Kirkland, *Charles Francis Adams, Jr., 1835–1915: The Patrician at Bay* (Cambridge, Mass.: Harvard University Press, 1965), pp. 75–80.

[3] Jeremy Atack and Peter Passell, *A New Economic View of American History*, 2nd ed. (New York: Norton, 1994), ch. 15.

[4] Harold C. Livesay, *Andrew Carnegie and the Rise of Big Business* (Boston: Little, Brown, 1975), and Thomas J. Misa, *A Nation of Steel: The Making of Modern America, 1865–1925* (Baltimore: Johns Hopkins University Press, 1995), chs. 1 and 4.

oil empire of John D. Rockefeller passed through a similar transition, as did the anthracite industry of eastern Pennsylvania. Faced with mounting competition from kerosene and from the vast bituminous coal deposits located to the west, the anthracite barons saw the value of their once lucrative holdings rapidly depleted. They slipped into recession even before the panic, then teetered on the brink of bankruptcy for the rest of the century.[5] The ranching and silver bonanzas of the Far West played themselves out with even more stunning rapidity. Silver grew so common following discovery of Nevada's Comstock lode that within just a few years Congress refused to coin it. The numbers of animals on the Western grasslands soared so rapidly that prices for meat dropped precipitously. Like others who had cast their lot with the extractive boom, Westerners had fallen victim to their own success.[6]

As the centerpieces of the extractive economy, railroads felt the effects of its maturation most forcefully of all. A failed attempt by railroads to generate additional capital in the European bond market triggered the panic, and several major lines fell into receivership during the remainder of the decade. Some of the financial travails followed directly from those of the major shippers and suppliers with whom the railroads had developed such close ties. The Erie, for instance, would have stood a better chance of surviving the managerial blunders documented by Adams had the anthracite region through which much of the line passed not fallen on such hard times. Two other notorious receiverships of the late nineteenth century would involve the Philadelphia and Reading Railroad, a line that not only served the anthracite region but itself owned substantial coal reserves there.[7] Diminished returns from investments in steel companies stung managers at the Pennsylvania Railroad and at the Baltimore and Ohio, setting in motion a series of events that helped push the latter into a brief bankruptcy of its own.[8] Those responsible for running many Western lines found that land sales and colonization work occupied fewer of their attentions and generated much less of their revenue.[9] Ambitious ventures in economic development, long the

---

5   Anthony F. C. Wallace, *St. Clair: A Nineteenth Century Coal Town's Experience with a Disaster-Prone Industry* (New York: Knopf, 1981).

6   Stuart Bruchey, *Enterprise: The Dynamic Economy of a Free People* (Cambridge, Mass.: Harvard University Press, 1990), ch. 10.

7   On receiverships at the anthracite roads, see Stuart Daggett, *Railroad Reorganization* (Cambridge, Mass.: Harvard University Press, 1908), pp. 50–51 and 75–100.

8   Ibid., pp. 14–28. See also Edward Hungerford, *The Story of the Baltimore and Ohio Railroad, 1827–1927* (1928; rpt., New York: Arno, 1972), pp. 121–144, 163–179, and 199–218. On the financial history of the Pennsylvania during this period, see George H. Burgess and Miles C. Kennedy, *Centennial History of the Pennsylvania Railroad Company* (Philadelphia: Pennsylvania Railroad Company, 1948), esp. pp. 341–383.

9   Richard C. Overton, *Burlington West: A Colonization History of the Burlington Railroad* (New York: Russell and Russell, 1941).

lucrative lifeblood of the railroad industry, appeared more and more like costly albatrosses.

As diminishing investment opportunities narrowed their potential sources of income, railroads also found themselves facing intensified competition in the market for transportation services. Years of massive land grants and liberal investment had left segments of the industry overbuilt and vulnerable. As with so much else in mid-nineteenth-century America, the situation was illustrated most vividly by Chicago. In 1846, the city's one railroad had existed only on paper. A quarter-century later grains and animals might arrive in the Windy City on any of four major railroads from Iowa alone. Once there, several established trunk lines and a phalanx of lake vessels stood ready to carry the fruits of the Great Plains onward to the Atlantic. Farmers and other Western producers might, moreover, choose to bypass Chicago entirely and send their trade through older shipping centers such as St. Louis or newer ones such as Kansas City and Minneapolis. These competing companies and urban networks constituted an astounding aggregation of capital, much of which was chasing what was increasingly a single integrated market for shipping services. When falling agricultural prices suppressed the volume of trade, railroads thus found themselves subject to price competition of a sort few areas of the economy had yet experienced. Frantic to defray at least some of their interest obligations and other fixed costs, which accumulated even if track and equipment stood empty and idle, lines lured shippers with generous rebates and other steep discounts. Some zealous managers compounded their financial difficulties by failing even to cover the costs of operating the trains.[10]

Railroads responded with pooling arrangements intended to buttress prices and with wage cuts aimed at shaving costs. Neither approach proved tenable. Pooling was less a forward-looking response to changed realities than a poorly conceived attempt to perpetuate the past. Most pools formed around the concept of natural territories, which held that lines possessed special claims to conduct business originating in the lands they had originally developed. Members would carry traffic in proportion to the produce generated by those lands.[11] Like similar agreements designed to restrict competition and bolster prices in other branches of trade and industry, these pacts soon disintegrated, as lines lowered rates by offering rebates and other

[10]   William Cronon, *Nature's Metropolis: Chicago and the Great West* (New York: Norton, 1991), chs. 2 and 3. On the industry generally, see Alfred D. Chandler, Jr., *The Visible Hand: The Managerial Revolution in American Business* (Cambridge, Mass.: Harvard University Press, 1977), chs. 3–5.

[11]   Julius Grodinsky, *The Iowa Pool: A Study in Railroad Competition, 1870–1884* (Chicago: University of Chicago Press, 1950). Albert Fink coordinated a pool of Eastern roads on a slightly more sophisticated basis, with attention to the capital markets and the diversity of business. See D. T. Gilchrist, "Albert Fink and the Pooling System," *Business History Review* 34 (1960): 24–49.

unpublished discounts. Meanwhile, workers grew increasingly angry over sustained wage cuts. A series of destructive strikes during the summer of 1877, though suppressed, left railroads chastened and fearful toward labor. As economic fortunes turned in subsequent years, railroads found themselves competing with the booming manufacturing sector for skilled workers, whose real wages increased steadily.[12]

Railroads of the late nineteenth century thus faced a harsh reality. The transportation service they provided, like many of the goods they carried, was increasingly becoming a commodity. Over the thirty-year course of the extractive epic, virtually all American institutions and technologies had evolved in response to one overriding objective: to encourage an ever smoother and more continuous flow of wheat, coal, lumber, oil, and other undifferentiated bulk goods across vast distances. The great fortunes of the era had been made at what historian William Cronon aptly calls the sticking points: the grain elevators, stockyards, lumber docks, refineries, Bessemer converters, and other intermediate stations where raw materials arrived to be stored, sorted, or processed into bulk goods.[13] The large enterprises that arose at these points of constriction initially established themselves by dramatically reducing the time and expense incurred along the path from land to market. Grain elevators, for instance, eliminated the costly step of bagging and labeling each farmer's produce. But once such enterprises had achieved the breakthrough economies made possible by high-volume throughput, they themselves came to be perceived as the major obstructions to the smooth flow of commerce, and the market economy wasted little time in turning its transforming energies upon them.

As the essential conveyor belts that linked the nodes of processing and production, railroads constituted the most prominent and menacing potential bottlenecks of all. Like most of the other intermediaries, railroads performed a function so vital as to be deemed indispensable. They were protected from the sort of wholesale displacement suffered by the rural storekeepers who had once bagged grain. But railroads could not insulate themselves from the relentless pressure of competition, which steadily wore away the magnitude of their initial advantages and eroded their capacity for profit. Clever industrialists such as Carnegie learned to locate their enterprises at major junctions, where they could play one line against another and bargain down rates.[14]

What market processes failed to accomplish, moreover, political action threatened to complete. The few sticking points that persisted became targets of political reform. Pooling and other strategies intended to temper the effects of competition met with substantial opposition from a public that resented

---

[12] On railroad labor, see Chapter 8 below.
[13] Cronon, *Nature's Metropolis*.
[14] On railroad rates, see Alfred D. Chandler, Jr., ed., *The Railroads: The Nation's First Big Business* (New York: Harcourt, Brace, and World, 1965).

their seeming arbitrariness and distrusted their anticompetitive elements. Criticism mounted over fare structures that often charged more for goods shipped shorter distances to the same destination. By the mid-seventies, legislatures in most states had created railroad commissions. The most powerful could be found in Midwestern grain regions. Under pressure from the Grangers and other organized interests, legislators in Iowa and several neighboring states vested their commissioners with authority to set maximum rates charged by grain elevator operators and to adjudicate disputes in which shippers claimed railroads exploited local monopolies with high fares.[15] When the Supreme Court embraced such measures in its landmark case of *Munn v. Illinois* in 1877, the commodification of the Western agricultural economy was complete.[16] Henceforth, profits would hinge almost entirely upon competitive advantages derived from operational efficiency.

Few comprehended the changing situation more clearly than Charles Perkins, an executive who had cut his teeth building and operating the Iowa lines of the Chicago, Burlington and Quincy Railroad. In a famous memorandum penned sometime after he had assumed responsibility for the entire CB&Q system around 1880, Perkins explained the changing character of railroading. He divided problems of railroad management into two classes – those concerning "business" or "traffic" and those relating to "the economical maintenance of the *machine*" – and correlated the two types of questions with stages in railroad development. During "the first stage, where the volume of traffic is not sufficient to make necessary, or to warrant, the highest degree of physical efficiency," Perkins explained, "the first class of questions must be of paramount importance." Under these circumstances, top managers could afford to handle daily operations or maintenance themselves, at a level "far below perfection." With onset of "the second stage, where the volume of traffic is so great as not only to warrant the expenditure, but also to make it economical to maintain the physical efficiency at the highest point," chief officers must "leave questions [of maintenance of the machine] to men who have been specially educated in the exact sciences of civil and mechanical engineering." Perkins concluded succinctly. "The proper economical maintenance of a road in the first stage is not an exact science," he wrote, "while that of a road in the second stage is, and scientific methods which would be unnecessary and extravagant on the one, may become necessary and economical on the other."[17]

---

[15] George H. Miller, *Railroads and the Granger Laws* (Madison: University of Wisconsin Press, 1971).

[16] Cronon, *Nature's Metropolis*, pp. 132–142. See also Harry Scheiber, "The Road to *Munn*: Eminent Domain and the Concept of Public Purpose in the State Courts," *Perspectives in American History* 7 (1971): 327–402, and Charles Fairman, *History of the Supreme Court of the United States*, vol. 7: *Reconstruction and Reunion, 1864–1888, Part Two* (New York: Macmillan, 1987), pp. 679–768.

[17] Charles E. Perkins, "Memorandum on Organization," n.d. (ca. 1885), Papers of the Chicago, Burlington and Quincy Railroad (henceforth, CBQ Papers), Newberry

Perkins's analysis captured the essence of a passage that characterized the entire railroad industry of the last quarter of the nineteenth century. A substantial portion of the traffic on virtually every line, regardless of age, would flow long distances and be susceptible to intense price competition (see Fig. 5.1). The new manufacturing and warehousing facilities that sprang up along their lines presented railroads with few opportunities to exploit feedback relationships of the sort that had once generated such stunning returns. Lines faced a future in which they would handle larger volumes of traffic that generated significantly smaller profit margins. Servicing this business would require large infusions of capital and substantial indebtedness, which in turn would bring close monitoring of operations by the financial markets. Responsible managers could not ignore the constant burden of meeting their debt obligations and providing a steady return to investors who might easily shift their money elsewhere in the booming manufacturing economy. Increasingly, moreover, managers at the most ably run lines faced competition from railroads that had fallen into receivership and been temporarily relieved of those burdens.[18]

Library, Chicago, 3P6.36. To some extent, of course, Perkins's comments reflected the particular circumstances of the Chicago, Burlington and Quincy. One of the four major lines that had joined the Iowa Pool, the CB&Q had recently felt the deleterious effects of the passage from developmental boomtime to competitive transport with full force. Railroads at the Northwestern and Southwestern frontiers still stood squarely within the developmental stage. James J. Hill's Great Northern Railroad, for instance, had barely begun to tap the vast timber and mineral resources of the Northern plains and Rockies. For a useful analysis of such regional differences in railroad investment during the late nineteenth century, see James Reed Golden, "Investment Behavior by United States Railroads, 1870–1914," Ph.D. dissertation, Harvard University, 1971. Older railroads to the east, on the other hand, had already acquired some of the machine-like characteristics to which Perkins aspired. Perkins routinely advised his subordinates to consult with their counterparts at the Pennsylvania Railroad, a line whose sophisticated techniques earned it the sobriquet "Railroad University." Nor should one exaggerate the degree to which development policies and local service diminished in strategic importance as competition for through traffic increased. Managers at the Burlington later chided Perkins for not having done more to foster industrial enterprises along its Western lines. Other established firms such as the Pennsylvania still sought through a variety of incentives to facilitate construction of manufacturing plants and other businesses along their routes. And while emergent enterprises might receive steep discounts, the persistent complaints of many other shippers suggest that railroads may still have derived much of their profits from isolated customers who lacked alternative outlets. Rate schedules and classifications grew seemingly ever more complex, and the traffic departments responsible for them became more prominent components in the managerial structures of many lines. Cost-based pricing remained the elusive goal of reformers, while managers such as Perkins defended the rights of railroads to "charge what the market will bear."

[18] On the dynamics of fixed costs, see Chandler, *Visible Hand*, and Gerald Berk, *Alternative Tracks: The Constitution of American Industrial Order, 1865–1917* (Baltimore: Johns Hopkins University Press, 1994).

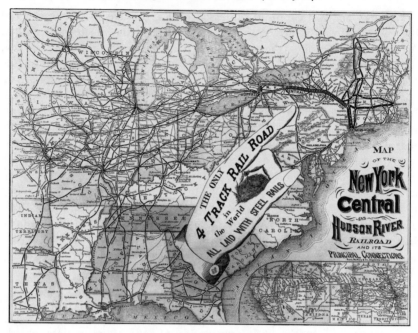

Figure 5.1. An 1876 map of the New York Central points to the massive investment in its main east–west trunk line to the Midwest. The hand obscures competitors such as the Pennsylvania and the Baltimore and Ohio, while major through routes from Chicago to the Gulf of Mexico via the Illinois Central appear as lesser lines. *Courtesy:* Library of Congress.

Potential regulation posed a constant threat, keeping managers on the defensive and forcing them ever closer toward cost-based pricing. With passage of the Interstate Commerce Act in 1887, Congress assumed responsibility for some of the regulatory functions previously administered by the states. Though this timid and laxly enforced measure disappointed many reformers and has sometimes even been interpreted as a "victory" for the railroads, it signaled the continuing vitality of a political movement that worked inexorably to diminish the autonomy of railroads in setting rates. No longer permitted even to attempt pooling, railroads turned toward mergers in an effort to gain some relief from competitive pressures. The wave of consolidation saddled many lines with additional debt, and the giant enterprises that resulted exacerbated public concerns about fairness and brought increased pressures for regulation.[19]

[19] George H. Miller, *Railroads and the Granger Laws* (Madison: University of Wisconsin Press, 1971); Ari and Olive Hoogenboom, *A History of the ICC: From Panacea to Palliative* (New York: Norton, 1976); Morton Keller, *Affairs of State: Public Life in Late Nineteenth Century America* (Cambridge, Mass.: Harvard University

These political and financial machinations absorbed extraordinary energies at the time and rightly occupy center stage in much of the best railroad history, but in the end they failed to relieve the incessant pressures railroad managers felt to contain costs and gain control over their sprawling, complex, hastily built enterprises. Ultimately, this burden was borne principally by the less conspicuous efforts of managers to operate their roads more efficiently – to use capital more effectively – while handling steadily increasing volumes of traffic. This was the constant, overarching objective, so obvious and pervasive to those involved that it hardly needed stating. And it was, essentially, a technical problem.

As Perkins suggested and historians have subsequently confirmed, railroads had much to gain simply by standardizing and routinizing what they already did. The image of a smoothly operating machine was an ideal, not a reality. Trains did not actually run with such clock-like precision as the appeal for standard time might suggest.[20] Nor did railroads govern their affairs in quite so ordered a manner as the managerial treatises and organizational charts would indicate. However routine railroad operations might have appeared at the time, and however logical they might seem in retrospect, those attributes did not emerge automatically, and they did not take hold immediately. Managers still had much to learn about the initial, system-originating invention that was the railroad. They still struggled to regulate the performance of that first, grand innovation. American railroading during the last quarter of the nineteenth century was a vast training ground, in which not only managers but virtually everyone connected to the railways sought to grasp the full implications of the transition Perkins had described.

Though railroads accomplished a great deal through changes in management and organization, innovation of this sort could not alone meet the demands to move larger amounts of traffic with greater economy. Technological change remained essential, too. As ever-increasing volumes of bulk commodities moved over the lines, the existing structure literally broke under the strain. Trains collided or sat interminably on sidings. Locomotives stalled under the weight of heavier loads. Trains broke apart. Rails crumbled. No amount of reorganization or clever scheduling could make

Press, 1977); Stephen Skowronek, *Building a New American State: The Expansion of National Administrative Capacities, 1877–1920* (New York: Cambridge University Press, 1982); and Thomas K. McCraw, *Prophets of Regulation* (Cambridge, Mass.: Harvard University Press, 1984).

[20] Though often attributed to railroads, the drive to create uniform time zones actually came primarily from scientists who wanted to coordinate observations made across great distances. The scientific community recruited the support of railroads in order to gain public attention and increase their political clout. Ian R. Bartky, "The Adoption of Standard Time," *Technology and Culture* 30 (1989): 25–56. See also Carlene Stephens, "'The Most Reliable Time': William Bond, the New England Railroads, and Time Awareness in 19th-Century America," *Technology and Culture* 30 (1989): 1–24.

Figure 5.2. Four trains traverse the main line of the New York Central at Little Falls, New York, c. 1890. *Courtesy*: Library of Congress.

such problems disappear. Their remedies demanded changes in technology. Without it, the flood of traffic would simply have overwhelmed the capacity of the system.

While technical change continued to play a vitally important role in the railroad industry, the passage from a developmental epic to a managerial one dramatically altered the nature of such innovation. Potential improvements would now be measured not by their ability to generate new business for the railroad or by the returns they might provide investors but strictly by their ability to reduce operating costs. Innovation must provide economies while conforming to the constraints of the established system. An observer from 1876 or even 1846, transformed suddenly to the turn of the twentieth century, would certainly have had no difficulty identifying the basic physical components of a railroad. Steam locomotives still pulled coaches and cars along metal rails mounted on wooden ties set in gravel. But while the basic technologies retained their recognizable shapes and forms, their scale increased dramatically. Locomotives of much greater power pulled longer trains of cars, each carrying several times more tons of freight than those of an earlier generation, over steel rails that in places weighed three times as much as the typical iron rail of Civil War vintage (Fig. 5.2). As railroads sent more and more of these behemoths over their most important routes, they built huge maintenance facilities, switchyards, and terminals and devised countless methods for utilizing such facilities more intensively. All of this helped generate extraordinary improvements in productivity and dramatically drive down the cost of rail transportation.[21]

Railroad managers of the late nineteenth century thus did more than merely run the machine. They replaced an early, crude machine with one of vastly greater power and sophistication and ran the new one harder than the old. Their success hinged largely upon a sustained effort to gain a fuller and more reliable understanding of the basic technologies that made up the complex systems. Through a variety of means, railroads heightened their involvement with the process of technical innovation, refining technology and channeling change in ways that enhanced performance without disturbing the smooth working of the machine.

MANAGERIAL REFORMS

The drive to assert greater control over railroad technologies began during the mid-1870s with important managerial reforms introduced at several influential lines. Firms such as the Pennsylvania and the Burlington shifted overall responsibility for rolling stock and motive power to central offices headed by officers who sought to standardize equipment. Engineers and scientists trained in new methods of analysis soon joined these staff departments. Working in conjunction with central purchasing agents, they effectively took charge of acquiring new technology. Together, these measures gradually began to transform innovation in railroading from a local, particular phenomenon in which personality held sway into a more bureaucratic exercise conducted by engineering professionals who typically expressed their opinions in general, abstract terms.

The changes in approach to technology typically were heralded by appointment of a staff executive – usually called the superintendent of motive power – who would have authority over all technical matters regarding equipment for the entire system. Unlike the master mechanics of an earlier day, who typically worked in the major shop facilities, these administrators usually maintained offices at corporate headquarters, where they mingled regularly with top management and the corporate staff. The superintendents of motive power spent their days attending meetings and pushing paper, not handling machinery. They sought to establish broad policies and to enforce them throughout complex systems that might stretch across half the

[21] Albert Fishlow, "Productivity and Technological Change in the Railroad Sector, 1840–1910," National Bureau of Economic Research, *Output, Employment, and Productivity in the United States after 1800* (New York: NBER, Columbia University Press, 1966), pp. 583–646.

nation and contain tens of thousands of miles of track. The superintendents assembled substantial staffs and sat atop a hierarchy of employees that stretched downward through assistant superintendents of motive power to master mechanics on each division. Rather than exercise their own creativity, these master mechanics now were expected to implement corporate policies and to keep the superintendent of motive power informed of the results.[22]

Railroads created these staff offices not out of a desire to promote change but in an effort to establish control over an increasingly unwieldy collection of equipment and personnel. The primary goal was to foster order and routine across a broader front. Defining the duties of its general superintendent of motive power in its bylaws of 1882, the Pennsylvania Railroad declared, "He shall furnish others with standards and instructions required to insure a perfect uniformity in construction and repairs of all the company's rolling stock and machinery."[23] Other railroads asked their superintendents of motive power to perform similar duties.

The desire to instill uniformity did not spring forth out of the blue, of course. As discussed in previous chapters, lines had long recognized the benefits of stabilizing locomotive designs. Managers such as Robert Harris and J. Edgar Thomson hesitated to switch suppliers out of fear they would disrupt established routines and complicate maintenance. Prior to the 1870s, however, efforts to achieve uniformity depended largely upon the highly personal judgments exercised by master mechanics and on the inside relations railroads often developed with key suppliers. Superintendents of motive power and other managers now sought to transcend the local and the personal. By drawing up formal technical specifications, expressed in terms of general principles and standard measures and without reference to particular devices or patents, they found a way to instill uniformity while weaning railroads from dependency on particular suppliers and specific personnel.[24]

---

[22] On the appointment of superintendents of motive power, see the Minutes of the Board of Directors of the Pennsylvania Railroad (henceforth, PRR Board Minutes), Hagley Museum and Library, Wilmington, Delaware, 5 (September 19, 1866): 68, and R. Harris to Jauriet, August 8, 1871, Archives of the Chicago, Burlington and Quincy Railroad (henceforth, CBQ Papers), Newberry Library, Chicago, 3H4.

[23] PRR Board Minutes, 10 (September 13, 1882): 68.

[24] Carl Condit, *The Railroad and the City: A Technological and Urbanistic History of Cincinnati* (Columbus: Ohio State University Press, 1977), pp. 64–66, cites the Pennsylvania Railroad's purchase of bridge components from the Keystone Bridge Company in 1876 as establishing the principle under which railroads wrote specifications "of the now universal form in which the kind and the quality of materials, the criteria of performance and workmanship, the obligations of the contractors, the loading factors, allowable stresses, wind pressure, and the testing procedures are given in full and precise terms allowing no ambiguity of interpretation and no deviation from the standards set forth." Keystone Bridge, in which Andrew Carnegie held a large share, had exemplified the sort of insider dealing that prevailed at the Pennsylvania just a few years before.

New devices complicated the effort to standardize existing technology, and superintendents of motive power generally put less emphasis on them than their predecessors. Personally, the new administrators did not view themselves as inventors, nor did they especially value the inventive ability of their master mechanics and skilled operators. In many cases, the new superintendents of motive power actively sought to limit the freedom of employees to tinker and invent. Most companies, for instance, removed locomotive engineers from direct control of a single engine and no longer granted them much input into decisions regarding changes.[25] At the Burlington, which had once held semiannual meetings to solicit and evaluate new technical ideas, Charles Perkins in 1880 strictly prohibited employees from working on new technology on company time in company shops.[26] Later in the decade the Burlington resurrected the idea of regular meetings where its mechanics would share new ideas they had tested. But now these meetings were intended not to promote change but to contain it. By having the mechanics tinker a bit before sharing their ideas with peers, Superintendent of Motive Power Godfrey Rhodes explained to his superiors, he hoped to keep them from raising speculative proposals that fueled group enthusiasm and would "certainly bring about unlimited experimenting and [make it] exceedingly difficult . . . to maintain even a pretense of standards." The ploy worked, as mechanics seldom suggested any changes. Rhodes then used the meetings to review company policies and reemphasize the importance of uniformity.[27]

Managers at the Pennsylvania tried various organizational schemes intended to limit experiment and to channel technical activity toward uniformity and routine. One enduring arrangement, known as the Association of Transportation Officers, captured the prevailing spirit especially well.[28] Like many of the changes discussed here, its roots went back to the mid-1870s. Beginning in 1875 and for several years thereafter, superintendents in charge of operating the various divisions of the Pennsylvania met two or three times yearly with general superintendents from the corporate staff such as Theodore N. Ely, the general superintendent of motive power. The Pennsylvania's general manager, Frank Thomson, chaired the meetings, and its general agent, Charles E. Pugh, acted as secretary. The group sought to reach agreement about standard practices that should prevail throughout the sprawling

---

25 On the autonomy of locomotive engineers, see James H. Ducker, *Men of the Steel Rails: Workers on the Atchison, Topeka, and Santa Fe Railroad, 1869–1900* (Lincoln: University of Nebraska Press, 1983), p. 57, and Walter Licht, *Working for the Railroad: The Organization of Work in the Nineteenth Century* (Princeton: Princeton University Press, 1983).

26 C. E. Perkins, "Memorandum," March 27, 1880, CBQ Papers, 3P6.36.

27 Rhodes to Besler, November 22, 1887, CBQ Papers, 3P4.51, and Rhodes to C. M. Higginson, January 2, 1892, CBQ Papers, 3R2.1.

28 The activities of this group and its antecedents can be traced in the files of the Association of Transportation Officers of the Pennsylvania Railroad (henceforth, PRR ATO Files), Papers of the Pennsylvania Railroad, Hagley Museum and Library, accession 1807. See especially, "Speech at A.T.O. Dinner, 1910."

Pennsylvania system. Ely, for instance, chaired a committee charged with investigating prevailing signaling practices, studying available devices, and recommending rules for use on all lines. With the outbreak of the labor strife that culminated in violent strikes in summer 1877, attention turned largely to matters such as standard personnel forms, uniform rules for operating trains, and a proposed insurance scheme. Once that crisis passed, however, the group again focused upon matters of a more strictly technical character.[29]

In the spring of 1879, officers of the Pennsylvania formally christened the group the Association of Transportation Officers (ATO) and drafted a new set of bylaws. Though the general manager remained as president, the new arrangements sought to foster a spirit of open inquiry, without regard to hierarchy. A vice-president, secretary, and three directors would be drawn from the membership at large, which would now include assistant superintendents of motive power, general agents, engineers of maintenance of way, and principal assistant engineers from the various divisions and subsidiary lines. Most members assumed positions on one of three standing committees: maintenance of way, motive power, and conducting transportation. The object of the newly constituted group would be "the general improvement of the Pennsylvania Railroad Company's Service, the professional advancement of its members in the science of Railway Management, and the encouragement of social intercourse with each other."[30] To this end, members would gather on a quarterly basis for a day of meetings spent considering highly technical committee reports, followed by a group dinner that might conclude with cigars and song. With the general manager firmly ensconced in the chair, these gatherings could hardly be characterized as exercises in democracy. But the founders strove to temper any authoritarian tendencies with frequent gestures toward cooperation. Financial officers and other high-ranking managers who did not belong to the group, for instance, could attend only as guests at the invitation of ATO directors who might occupy posts far down the corporate hierarchy. The work of the association proceeded when members submitted questions, some of which were referred by the secretary to committees for systematic study and report. The plan of organization, Thomson stressed, "endeavored . . . to combine with the official character of the Association, the entire freedom of expression of individual opinions of each of its members."[31] In tone and structure, the ATO bore a strong resemblance to a professional engineering society, though one devoted exclusively to topics arising at the Pennsylvania Railroad.[32]

[29] "Minutes of the Superintendents Meetings, 1877–1879," PRR ATO Files.
[30] "Constitution," Minutes of the Association of Transportation Officers, May 20, 1879, PRR ATO Files.
[31] Minutes, May 20, 1879, PRR ATO Files.
[32] For an excellent study of one such engineering society founded at about the same time as the ATO, see Bruce Sinclair, *A Centennial History of the American Society of Mechanical Engineers, 1880–1980* (Toronto: University of Toronto Press, 1980).

Like those societies, the ATO aspired above all to foster consensus opinions that could be expressed in the form of technical standards. The few existing records from its early years indicate that committees generally attempted to resolve nagging problems through coordinated study culminating in a report containing recommendations. If approved, the report effectively constituted a standard, one which appeared to have percolated up from below rather than being dictated from the corporate office. In cases such as signaling, the ATO often constituted special committees that not only brought together representatives from various geographic areas, but also transcended functional divisions among the officers. Executives in charge of running the trains mingled with those who would maintain the signals, while mechanical experts such as Ely passed judgment on the merits of various devices.[33] This ability to bridge bureaucratic lines would prove especially important during the 1890s, when a reborn ATO assumed a major role in shaping policies at the Pennsylvania.[34]

INTERFIRM COOPERATION

The desire to instill uniformity, promote routine, and facilitate uninterrupted movement throughout large systems ultimately spilled beyond the boundaries of individual firms. Superintendents of motive power such as Ely and Rhodes increasingly carried the crusade to national bodies such as trade associations and technical societies. A trade group known as the Master Car-Builders Association (MCBA) rose to particular prominence. Its roots went back to the mid-1860s, when representatives from a number of New York railroad companies met to discuss rules governing the exchange of freight cars.[35] In an effort to reduce congestion and avoid costly transfers, these railroads had begun to accept cars owned by other companies and to pass their own rolling stock along to adjoining lines. The practice kept goods and equipment flowing more smoothly but raised some troubling managerial challenges regarding the cars. Roads needed collectively to formulate procedures for monitoring rental charges and for allocating maintenance costs.[36]

Maintenance, which often stimulated the drive for standardization within individual systems, posed particularly tricky problems. Without some

---

[33] "Minutes of the Conducting Transportation Committee," January 14, 1880, PRR ATO Files.

[34] On the resurgence of the association in 1893, see PRR ATO Files, box 1, files 4 and 2, and "Speech at A.T.O. Dinner, 1910." For detailed studies of the ATO in action, see Part III below.

[35] The history and activities of this group can be traced through the *Annual Reports of the Master Car-Builders' Association* (henceforth, *MCBA Reports*).

[36] The standard source on these developments is George Rogers Taylor and Irene D. Neu, *The American Railroad Network, 1861–1890* (Cambridge, Mass.: Harvard University Press, 1956).

reasonable assurance they would be compensated, roads had little incentive to make repairs on cars owned by other lines. To develop acceptable compensation schemes, lines needed to agree upon appropriate charges for various repairs. This in turn compelled them to reach agreement about standards of quality for workmanship and for equipment placed upon the cars. Even if they agreed to defer most substantial repairs until a car returned to its home shops, lines needed to consider uniform standards for parts that broke frequently and catastrophically, such as wheels and axles, and for materials used in routine service, such as lubricating oils and bearing alloys. Without standards for devices such as couplers and drawbars, moreover, railroads could not hope to link cars from separate firms into a common train.

As railroads throughout the country standardized their gauges and followed the lead of the New Yorkers, the issues posed by the practice of interchanging equipment grew to national proportions. By the late 1870s, a fifty-car freight train might include cars owned by twenty or more railroads.[37] As one of the few established forums for interfirm cooperation and standards-setting, the MCBA assumed an ever more prominent place in discussions of railroad technology. By the beginning of the 1880s the group included representatives from all major car builders and from the motive power departments of most railroads in the United States. Member railroads owned nearly a million freight cars – about forty times the number used in passenger service.[38] The association convened annually and maintained standing committees to consider technical matters such as automatic couplers and the heights of drawbars. Matthias Forney, editor of the influential trade paper *Railroad Gazette*, acted as its secretary and regularly published reports on its activities.

A good example of the mounting importance of the MCBA comes from its long engagement with the subject of air brakes for freight trains. The association formed a standing committee on continuous brakes in 1877, almost as soon as a few lines in the West first began experimenting with Westinghouse brakes on freight trains (see Chapter 8). The committee held regular discussions at annual meetings, circulated questionnaires among railroads and car builders from around the country, and maintained contact with representatives from Westinghouse and other manufacturers of brakes.[39] For a number of years, however, these efforts yielded no clear standard for continuous freight brakes. Members persistently disagreed over the costs and benefits of using air brakes in freight service. The association stuck with an

---

[37]   *New York Times*, March 21, 1879.

[38]   *MCBA Reports*, 1885, indicate that member railroads owned over 800,000 freight cars. U.S. Interstate Commerce Commission, *Annual Statistics on the Railroads of the United States* (henceforth, *ICC Statistics*), list slightly over one million freight cars in 1889 and nearly 1.3 million in 1894.

[39]   *Railroad Gazette* 15 (March 30, 1883): 191, and 16 (April 18, 1884): 293; and *MCBA Reports*, 1884.

early, arbitrary figure that a brake should cost no more than $25 per car, even after several railroads had paid twice that amount. These discrepancies regarding costs resulted in large measure from Westinghouse's dominance. Railroads suspected the inventor charged a substantial premium for his patent monopoly, and without a basis for comparison they had no way to determine otherwise. MCBA bylaws, moreover, expressly prohibited association standards from endorsing specific devices.[40] Until the basic Westinghouse patent of 1869 expired, the association found it virtually impossible to set a standard that did not constitute an endorsement of the Westinghouse product.

Another reason for the failure to move toward a standard lay in the organizational structure of the MCBA. The founders of the association had hoped to create a forum where railroad mechanics could discuss equipment, reach a consensus, and make recommendations that members would follow voluntarily.[41] The system may have worked among a few railroads in upstate New York, but it broke down as the MCBA expanded to a national level. With diverse new members from around the country each offering their opinions, the association seldom arrived at a clear consensus. In addition to introducing regional differences, the enlarged membership brought together railroads of dramatically different size. Large firms saw little reason to engage in discussions and to enter into agreements on an equal basis with smaller, less influential companies. In the early 1880s they pressed to revise the constitution so that members received votes in proportion to the number of cars they owned. Organized in this way, the power structure of the association would reflect the distribution of economic might within the industry as a whole. Smaller firms, which often pleaded poverty when faced with a proposed specification, would no longer be able to squelch the desires of the giants and keep the MCBA from adopting a standard. The measure passed in 1882.[42]

This fundamental change in organization had an immediate effect on association policies regarding automatic brakes. Previously, members of the brake committee had come from lesser roads that lacked significant clout or special experience with automatic brakes. Shortly after the reorganization of 1882, representatives from the Central Pacific and the Santa Fe, two Western railroads with considerable experience and financial investment in using air brakes on freight trains, joined the committee.[43] They were chaired by another new member, Godfrey Rhodes, the highly respected superintendent of motive power at the Burlington. At the time of his appointment, managers at the Burlington had recently begun to consider applying air brakes to

40 *MCBA Reports*, 1875–1884.   41 *MCBA Reports*, 1867.
42 Printed circular from the Committee on the Reorganization of the Master Car-Builders Association and Stone to Potter, April 17, 1882, Air Brake File, CBQ Papers. See also *MCBA Reports*, 1882.
43 *Railroad Gazette* 16 (November 14, 1884): 816.

large numbers of freight cars. Rhodes had solicited opinions from colleagues throughout the industry and had started conducting technical trials using two twenty-five-car trains equipped with Westinghouse brakes. On the basis of preliminary results, Rhodes and several of his colleagues at the Burlington strongly advocated converting their entire fleet to air brakes. Top management nixed the idea, however, in large part out of concern their investment would be frittered away as cars owned by the CB&Q were dispersed through the national network. Rhodes saw the revitalized brake committee as a forum through which the Burlington might press for coordinated action by major carriers throughout the industry. His bosses agreed and encouraged him to pursue a leadership role within the MCBA.[44]

At Rhodes's initiative, the reorganized brake committee soon asserted itself as the central clearinghouse for discussion of air brakes in freight service. Its principal instrument was a widely publicized series of trials sponsored by the MCBA and conducted on the CB&Q's tracks near Burlington, Iowa. Members of the MCBA had suggested as early as 1880 that trials of brakes on fifty-car trains would help railroads determine the merits of continuous brakes for freight service.[45] Calls for such tests surfaced again after representatives of the Pennsylvania Railroad tempered an otherwise optimistic report to the MCBA in 1884 with a warning that the brakes caused shocks when used to slow long trains on steep grades.[46] Trials failed to materialize, however, until Rhodes assumed control of the new committee and committed the resources of the CB&Q to the endeavor. In October 1885, as Rhodes and his superiors scrambled to learn more about the problems with shocks, the MCBA committee announced it would conduct trials that December at Burlington. When rival suppliers complained that the short notice gave Westinghouse an insurmountable advantage, the committee convened representatives from six brake manufacturers and established rules for trials to be held the following July. The brake companies agreed to bring fifty-car trains equipped with their products to Burlington. The CB&Q pledged to

---

[44] Potter to Stone, June 28, 1884, and Stone to Potter, July 5, 1884, Air Brake File, CBQ Papers. Rhodes assumed the chairmanship of the committee. See *Railroad Gazette* 16 (November 14, 1884): 816.

[45] *MCBA Reports*, 1880.

[46] *MCBA Reports*, 1884. The Pennsylvania had installed air brakes on cars used to transport livestock, an especially valuable cargo that needed to be moved quickly. See *MCBA Reports*, 1882, and Potter to Stone, June 28, 1884, Air Brake File, CBQ Papers. News of the problem with shocks reached upper-level management at the Burlington in late 1885. Vice-President Potter and General Manager Harlan Stone wrote to their colleagues on Western railroads and to Westinghouse requesting information on the trouble. They received conflicting information in return. In some cases, officials from the same company offered contradictory opinions. Westinghouse defended its product and provided testimonials to the virtues of its product from the president of the Union Pacific. See Stone to Potter, January 27, 1886, and accompanying materials, Air Brake File, CBQ Papers.

provide locomotives, use of its repair shops, and the services of Rhodes, who volunteered to coordinate the trials. Rhodes arranged for members of the brake committee and other technical experts to visit Burlington and ride in a car containing a dynamometer and other testing apparatus that would be attached to the rear of each train undergoing test. Matthias Forney would cover the proceedings for *Railroad Gazette*, and Rhodes would prepare summaries to be published with the annual reports of the MCBA.

The trials that began in July 1886 had an impact far beyond anything Rhodes could have imagined.[47] When the initial runs revealed serious problems with all brakes during emergency stops, Rhodes and the MCBA convened a second series of trials in May of 1887. Amidst great hoopla and press coverage, representatives from throughout the industry gathered to see fifty-car trains equipped with brakes from various manufacturers put through an exhaustive series of trials. On the basis of these tests and the design changes they stimulated, the brake committee issued a new set of recommended technical standards in 1888. Though the MCBA still lacked the authority to compel all railroads to follow these recommendations, its thoroughness and reach commanded widespread respect. When Congress passed legislation in 1893 mandating the use of continuous brakes and automatic couplers in freight service, it basically embraced the MCBA standards for both devices.[48] The measure signaled that the MCBA had established itself as a forum where technical experts could reach definitive assessments of broad influence and applicability.[49]

TESTING AND RESEARCH

The Burlington brake trials exemplified a new style of testing and research that flourished in the railroad industry of the late nineteenth century. As with the administrative reforms and the emphasis on uniformity, developments in this area owed a great deal to what had come before. Considerable

---

[47] The best source of information on the Burlington brake trials is *Railroad Gazette*, which covered every aspect from planning through the writing of new standards. See especially 18 (May 7, 1886): 309; 18 (June 18, 1886): 426; 18 (July 30, 1886): 521–523; 19 (January 7, 1887): 3; 19 (October 17, 1887): 653; 19 (November 11, 1887): 729 and 734; 20 (June 1, 1888): 346; and 20 (June 15, 1888): 390. Additional information on the trials comes from *MCBA Reports* for 1887 and 1888.

[48] See Chapter 8.

[49] In his famous defense of railroad managerial practices in the wake of the Eastern Rate Case of 1910–1911, economist William J. Cunningham cited the work of the MCBA on air brakes in praising railroads for their frequent exchanges of technical information. Railroads "are unique in having so few secrets concerning operating methods," wrote Cunningham, "and in their willingness to tell of, hear about, and profit by their mutual experiences." William J. Cunningnam, "Scientific Management in the Operation of Railroads," *Quarterly Journal of Economics* 25 (May 1911): 539–561, quote from p. 557.

experiment still took place haphazardly as mechanics confronted particular difficulties that arose at individual lines. Investigators often focused at least initially on the performance of specific devices, as was the case at Burlington. Yet in several respects, inquiries into technical matters acquired a fundamentally different character during the 1870s and after. Mechanics and others conducting studies of specific technologies increasingly drew upon general theory and a broad record of systematically gathered data when addressing their particular problems. Their inquiries, moreover, now often blossomed into investigations of a broader character. Frequently, they resulted in publications and presentations before engineering societies, so that results became incorporated into an expanding pool of knowledge expressed in terms that transcended particular applications.

A good example of this transition comes from the work of John E. Wootten, the longtime master mechanic and general manager of the Philadelphia and Reading. Throughout much of the 1870s, Wootten struggled to design a locomotive that would burn the powdered refuse, known as culm, that accumulated at the many anthracite collieries located along his company's lines.[50] The prospect of burning culm, which collieries considered a useless nuisance, had long enticed railroads operating in the anthracite region. No one, however, had yet designed a firebox that would burn this fuel and produce sufficient heat to power a locomotive or some other large mechanical device. Wootten, recently given full charge over locomotives and machinery at the Reading, took up the challenge with characteristic verve and confidence. Utilizing his own considerable mechanical skill and drawing freely upon the assistance of his shopworkers and the skilled enginemen and firemen of the Reading, he tinkered continually with numerous arrangements for burning the culm in existing locomotives. Wootten also solicited information from mechanics at other railroads in the anthracite region who had tried to burn culm, and he carried on an extensive correspondence with the captains of steamships who had attempted to use the enticing but recalcitrant fuel.

Aside from his thoroughness, in drawing upon these resources Wootten did not distinguish his activities substantially from those of numerous other cases of inventive behavior during the heyday of the master mechanics. He departed more significantly from the norm, however, when he also asked friends at nearby universities to share their knowledge on the heat of different fuels and the power of steam. These university associates agreed to conduct experiments with culm and to share the results with Wootten.[51] In part on the

---

[50] George M. Hart, "History of the Locomotives of the Reading Company," *Railway and Locomotive Historical Society Bulletin* 67 (May 1946): 36–41, and James L. Holton, "John Wootten: Locomotive Pioneer," *Historical Review of Berks County* (Summer 1978): 97–107.

[51] Extensive correspondence concerning the development of culm-burning locomotives at the Reading can be found in the papers of John E. Wootten, in the Papers of the Philadelphia and Reading Railroad (henceforth, Reading Papers), Hagley

basis of their findings, Wootten determined that with an enlarged surface area a culm fire could generate sufficient heat to power a locomotive. He solved this problem by extending the grate of the firebox across the full width of the locomotive and back under the cab. With close attention from a trained fireman, a locomotive with this enlarged fire area could attain unprecedented speeds. The Reading built numerous locomotives in the new design and used them for many years.[52]

News of this success diffused to other mechanics in the railroad industry through a variety of channels. *Railroad Gazette* published engravings and an article on the locomotive, while Wootten himself sold the engines to many companies and personally supervised their initial runs. Wootten dutifully answered inquiries about the use of culm, consulting to the Baltimore and Ohio and the Pennsylvania, among others, and also monitored tests of his locomotive design with conventional fuels such as bituminous coal. With their reflection of self-interest and intense personal involvement, these activities bore the basic marks of an approach to innovation that had long characterized railroading. Indeed, Wootten grew so involved with this project and the Reading invested so heavily in his locomotives that its receivers grew suspicious. They accused Wootten of pursuing his own inventive activities at the expense of the company and even brought in technical experts in an unsuccessful effort to discredit the locomotive.[53] These charges lacked merit, however, not just because the locomotives performed admirably, but also because Wootten's efforts often were directed not at furthering his personal fortune but at developing theoretical insights into the performance of heat engines. He remained in close contact with academic researchers as well as with respected railroad authorities such as Theodore Ely of the Pennsylvania.[54] As a result, Wootten found himself at the center of a network of investigators seeking to comprehend combustion in more abstract terms. In this respect, his activities heralded a new era in railroad research.

Numerous other cases from the late nineteenth century exhibited a similar pattern, in which research and testing prompted by a specific problem occurring in a limited context eventually blossomed into a wide-ranging investigation into a subject of general interest that transcended particular circumstances. The air brake trials at Burlington, for instance, began with a clear objective of resolving concerns about shocks and identifying potential alternatives to Westinghouse. In the course of evaluating specific devices,

---

Museum and Library, Wilmington, Delaware, accession 1451. See also "Report of the General Manager," *Annual Reports of the Philadelphia and Reading Railroad Company* (henceforth, *Reading Annual Reports*), 1877.

[52] Hart, "History of the Locomotives of the Reading Company."

[53] After some struggle Wootten survived these indictments, and the engine became an integral part of railroading in the anthracite district. *Reading Annual Reports*, 1881–1883, esp. 1881, pp. 85–100.

[54] Correspondence of John E. Wootten, Reading Papers, accession 1451.

however, the assembled experts gathered unprecedented data relating braking force, stopping distance, and several other variables. Subsequent refinements in brake design owed a great deal to theories derived from this data. The brake trials also sparked a related inquiry into the relationship between the amount of slack in a train and the power needed to start it, a subject which became integral to locomotive design as trains grew longer and heavier.[55] In similar fashion, the Burlington and other lines developed theoretical insights into heating and ventilating in the course of conducting comparative trials of car heating systems. The trials took place after inventors developed new heaters and governments threatened the railroads with legislation requiring them. Toward the end of the century, the Burlington and other railroads carefully studied chemical methods of preserving cross ties – a technique that had been suggested for many years – when they confronted a serious shortage of wood.[56] In an especially telling example discussed in more detail in the following chapter, concern generated by a sudden rash of broken steel rails developed into a sustained inquiry into the wearing properties of steel and other metals.

Because systematic investigations and analyses generally followed upon particular crises, the new approach to testing and research developed in fits and starts over the course of the late nineteenth century. Looking back in 1892 at the periodic testing the Burlington had conducted during the previous three decades, Charles Perkins rued that much information had been lost because careful records had not been kept.[57] Yet even in the absence of a coordinated, programmatic effort, a common methodology of testing steadily took hold. Mechanics grew accustomed to accompanying their evaluations of technologies with quantitative evidence of the sort readers of engineering journals and attendees at meetings of engineering societies expected.

A key element encouraging these trends was the development of new testing machines and tools of analysis. Dynamometers of the sort deployed at Burlington, for instance, became a standard feature of railroading during the 1870s. Individuals such as P. H. Dudley built highly respected consulting practices by traveling to different lines and making tests of their locomotives using a car outfitted with the device. The Eastern Railroad Association, interested in evaluating how certain patented technologies affected

55 Perkins to Stone, April 28, 1887, CBQ Papers, 3P6.37, and *Railroad Gazette* 18 (August 6, 1886): 540–541; 18 (August 13, 1886): 559–560; 18 (August 20, 1886): 578–579; and 19 (January 28, 1887): 60–61.

56 Numerous references to these tests can be found in the papers of Charles E. Perkins, CBQ Papers, 3P4.1, 3P4.51, and 3P4. 58. On railroad research into chemical preservation of wood, see Sherry H. Olson, *The Depletion Myth: A History of Railroad Use of Timber* (Cambridge, Mass.: Harvard University Press, 1971), and "Report of the Maintenance of Way Committee," November 5, 1895, pp. 32–81, PRR ATO Files.

57 Perkins to Higginson, December 29, 1892, CBQ Papers, 3P4.58.

locomotive performance, contributed funds to support Dudley.[58] Soon major railroads equipped cars of their own with the testing equipment and began making considerable use of dynamometers to measure, for example, the tractive force of locomotives and the force needed to stop a train (Fig. 5.3).[59] Once railroads had invested in these costly dynamometer cars, mechanics had an incentive to find additional topics to study with them, and the sort of data the testing machines provided gradually became an expected feature of studies of railroad technology.

LABORATORIES AND TESTING FACILITIES

New testing equipment also figured prominently in perhaps the most significant development in railroad research: the founding of formal laboratories for physical and chemical analysis staffed by professionally trained experts. The Pennsylvania initiated this movement in the early 1870s when it consolidated its study of mechanical engineering problems in a new bureau of experiments located at its Altoona shops. The company replaced the bureau in 1874 with a Department of Physical Tests, which though located at Altoona fell directly under the authority of Superintendent of Motive Power Theodore N. Ely. Soon Ely bypassed the master mechanic at Altoona entirely and placed this facility under John W. Cloud, a formally trained mechanical engineer who assumed the title "mechanical engineer." The Pennsylvania provided Cloud with some commercially available apparatus for testing the strength of metals and other materials and collected a small library of engineering and railroad journals for his department.[60] In November of the following year, Charles B. Dudley joined the small staff in the testing department. A Ph.D. chemist recently graduated from Yale's Sheffield Scientific School, Dudley organized a chemical laboratory to supplement the new mechanical engineering facility.[61]

---

[58] On P. H. Dudley, see Minutes of Road Committee, March 26, 1877, PRR Board Minutes; and A. J. Cassatt to W. P. Shinn, May 1, 1877, and Cassatt to Joseph Lesley, February 12, 1879, Papers Concerning Matters Coming before the Board of Directors of the Pennsylvania Railroad (henceforth, PRR Board Papers), Hagley Museum and Library, Wilmington, Delaware. On the importance of dynamometers to engineering analysis during this period, see Edward W. Constant, "Scientific Theory and Technological Testability: Science, Dynamometers, and Water Turbines in the 19th Century," *Technology and Culture* 24 (1983): 183–198.

[59] By January 1880, the Pennsylvania had acquired its own dynamometer car. See Minutes of the Conducting Transportation Committee, January 14, 1880, PRR ATO Files.

[60] "Departments of Chemical and Physical Tests (Historical)," Typescript Report, c. 1914, PRR Papers, accession 1807, box 661.

[61] "Departments of Physical and Chemical Tests (Historical)," pp. 5–7; "Testing Materials at Altoona," *Railroad Gazette* 14 (August 4, 1882): 467–468; Theodore N. Ely, "Charles B. Dudley as a Railroad Man," *Memorial Volume Commemorative of*

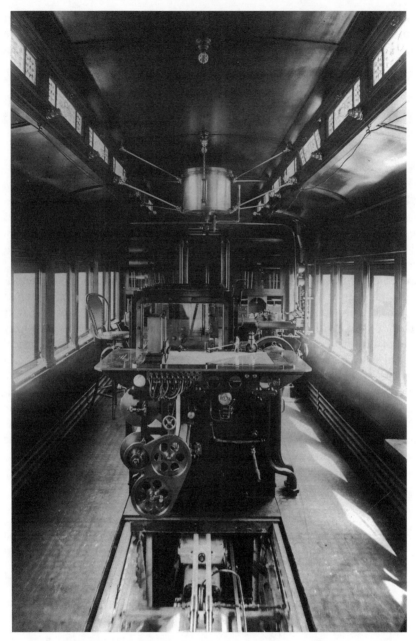

Figure 5.3. A dynamometer car of the Pennsylvania Railroad, c. 1900. *Courtesy*: Hagley Museum and Library.

Ely, who by all accounts originated the idea, apparently launched these ventures with no clear idea of what they would accomplish. Looking back years later, he characterized the decision to create the test department as an "experiment" and stressed that the company had authorized "an engineering laboratory in its broadest sense."[62] The choice of Dudley – a general experimentalist fresh out of college with no direct experience in railroad affairs – reflected the unspecified character of the new testing facility.[63] Dudley later claimed that the Pennsylvania granted Ely permission to hire him "more as a concession and as an experiment than with any faith or belief that the scheme would prove to be permanent or valuable."[64] For half a decade, the testing facilities occupied an unused corner in an old building at the shops. The original equipment cost well under $2,000, and operating costs consisted of a few thousand more in salaries and about $100 worth of supplies.[65]

the Life and Life-Work of Charles Benjamin Dudley, Ph.D. (Philadelphia: American Society for Testing Materials, n.d.), pp. 50–57; and PRR Board Minutes, 21 (January 12, 1910): 88–89.

[62] Ely, "Charles B. Dudley as a Railroad Man," p. 51.

[63] How Ely selected Charles Dudley to head the laboratory remains a mystery. Ely probably circulated news of the Pennsylvania's interest in hiring a chemist among an informal network of engineers and scientists in Philadelphia. Coleman Sellers, a member of an influential family in that network, apparently recommended Dudley. What is clear is that in hiring Dudley the Pennsylvania obtained a chemist with a general knowledge of chemistry and a familiarity with many analytical techniques, but without any experience working on the specific chemical questions that had troubled the railroad in the past. In fact, Dudley had little experience with any problems that had arisen outside of a laboratory on a university campus. He had graduated from Sheffield, where he wrote a dissertation entitled, "On Lithium; and a Glass Made with Lithium," just one year before. After graduating he had worked as an assistant to Dr. George F. Barker, a physicist at the University of Pennsylvania. Dudley had resigned that position and accepted a teaching post at a New England prep school when Sellers recommended him to Ely as a suitable candidate for the job at the Pennsylvania Railroad. For biographical information on Dudley, see ASTM, *Memorial Volume*, and R. W. Raymond, "Biographical Notice of Charles B. Dudley, Ph.D.," *Transactions of the American Institute of Mining and Metallurgical Engineers* 41 (1911): 837–851.

[64] C. B. Dudley and F. N. Pease, "Chemistry Applied to Railroads: What the Chemist Does," *Railroad and Engineering Journal* 63 (December 1889): 554–557.

[65] Information on the cost of establishing and operating a railroad laboratory can be found in "Department of Physical and Chemical Tests (Historical)," pp. 2–7, and the Annual Reports of the Laboratory (henceforth, PRR Lab Reports) and of the Test Room or Test Department (henceforth, PRR Test Reports), Annual Report Papers, Motive Power Department, PRR Papers, accession 1810. These annual reports cover the years 1885–1907. By 1887, annual expenses for the chemical laboratory had reached approximately $12,000, with roughly three quarters going to salaries and the remainder to materials. After holding steady for nearly a decade, they doubled between 1895 and 1902, then grew more modestly. Comparable figures for the Burlington can be found in Quereau to Forsyth, December 1 and 15, 1893; inventory dated May 5, 1901; and Max Wickhorst to L. S. Storrs, January 1, 1905; Laboratory Notebooks, CBQ Papers.

While undeniably modest and perhaps lacking a clear sense of purpose, these pioneering laboratories did not take shape out of thin air. In several respects, they fit squarely within emergent trends that garnered considerable attention in American industry at the time. The U.S. Government Testing Board, which had responsibility for assessing materials purchased by the navy and other federal agencies, had with the cooperation of Robert Thurston of Stevens Institute of Technology just opened a laboratory containing machines designed by Thurston and a few other engineers.[66] Ely appeared to mimic this widely publicized venture when outfitting his lab. All but one of the testing machines purchased by the Pennsylvania prior to 1879 came from Thurston, and Dudley joined the railroad shortly after Thurston began supplementing his physical tests with chemical analyses.[67] Dudley came to the Pennsylvania at the recommendation of famed machinist William Sellers. Owner of several speciality metal works located in and around Philadelphia, Sellers was a major proponent of bringing the methods of scientific investigation and analysis to bear upon craft procedures. Several years earlier, he had orchestrated efforts by the Franklin Institute to establish standards for screw threads, which the Pennsylvania promptly adopted. At his Midvale Steel Works, two young Yale graduates with degrees in chemistry had launched a series of careful, exhaustive studies of the materials and methods used to make steel rails and tires. They would be joined in 1878 by the young Frederick Winslow Taylor, the future "Father of Scientific Management," who had dropped out of Stevens despite a stellar record and would soon set to work studying tool steels.[68]

The early work at the Pennsylvania bore much in common with the activities taking place at Midvale. The foundry at Altoona had begun casting steel car wheels shortly before Cloud arrived, and he devoted a great deal of his time to testing samples of the material that went into them. Gradually, Cloud came to perform similar bending and breaking tests on metals used in items such as boilers, springs, axles, brake chains, and crank pins. Such analyses rapidly became the bread-and-butter activity of the physical laboratory. The Pennsylvania spent nearly $3,000 in 1879 to acquire a machine capable of performing tests on larger samples and erected it in a building outfitted

[66]   Robert Julius Kwik, "The Functions of Applied Science and the Mechanical Laboratory during the Period of Formation of the Profession of Mechanical Engineering, as Exemplified in the Career of Robert Henry Thurston, 1839–1903," (Ph.D. dissertation, University of Pennsylvania, 1974); Robert J. Kwik, "Between Science and Society: The Engineering Career of Robert Henry Thurston," Massachusetts Institute of Technology, *Technology Studies Bulletin* 3 (May 1974): 66–75; "Robert Thurston," *Dictionary of American Biography* (henceforth, *D.A.B.*), vol. 18, pp. 518–520; and Robert H. Thurston, *Memoirs and Professional Reports*, n.d.

[67]   "Departments of Chemical and Physical Tests (Historical)," pp. 2–7.

[68]   See Robert Kanigel, *The One Best Way: Frederick Winslow Taylor and the Enigma of Efficiency* (New York: Viking Penguin, 1997), pp. 178–179.

especially for the test department. Subsequent reports from the physical laboratory always featured an account of the number of samples tested on this machine and of the savings that accrued from identifying faulty materials in timely fashion.[69]

Dudley took a bit longer to establish a niche for his chemical laboratory but ultimately traced a similar course toward routine analysis of purchased materials and supplies. During his first few years at the Pennsylvania, Dudley acted something like an in-house consultant, bringing his techniques of chemical analysis to bear upon a number of technical problems that arose in the course of running the railroad. He spent much of his first eighteen months, for instance, attempting to determine why the valves on locomotive boilers clogged so frequently. Toward the end of the 1870s, in an episode discussed more fully in the next chapter, he undertook a study intended to reveal why some steel rails wore more rapidly than others. Trained in the basic methods of scientific experiment, Dudley collected random samples of any materials that might contribute to these problems and performed chemical analyses of them, then correlated his findings to the observed performance. When seeking an answer to the problems with clogged boiler valves, for instance, he analyzed the mineral content of water from various sources used in the boilers and also determined the amounts of impurities in the tallows used to lubricate the valves. In the case of rails, he looked for possible variations between the chemical constituents of rails that wore more or less rapidly. In similar fashion, Dudley analyzed the contents of oils the Pennsylvania used in its lamps, searching for clues to why some burned cleaner than others.[70]

The sort of knowledge Dudley accumulated through these early studies soon drew him into alliance with the purchasing agent, whose authority the Pennsylvania bolstered in late 1878. In another example of the intensified drive for uniformity that pervaded the railroad at the time, this officer would coordinate all purchasing activities of the various departments and geographical divisions of the entire system. Dudley's work dovetailed readily with this mission. In several cases, his investigations revealed that supplies such as lubricants and lighting oil contained adulterants that lay at the roots of the problems. By prescribing a preferred formula and analyzing samples from purchased lots, the Pennsylvania could identify such potential sources

---

[69] PRR Test Reports. By 1886, the value of material tested annually exceeded $1.5 million, with slightly over half of that amount tested in the Test Room and the remainder evaluated at the place of manufacture. By 1892, those amounts had doubled. They fell drastically with the onset of depression the following year and did not regain their 1892 levels until 1898. Five years later, the value of material tested surpassed $12 million, with nearly three quarters of that amount tested at the place of manufacture.

[70] "Departments of Chemical and Physical Tests (Historical)," pp. 3–6; "Testing Materials at Altoona," *Railroad Gazette* 14 (August 4, 1882): 467–468; and Dudley and Pease, "Chemistry Applied to Railroads: What the Chemist Does," pp. 554 and 556.

of difficulty in advance. As this practice grew routine, the purchasing agent began publishing the formulae as official specifications and letting suppliers know that the railroad would reject any lots that deviated from the stipulated amounts.

In addition to providing a check against unscrupulous suppliers, such specifications provided the purchasing agent with an important tool in his struggle to impose uniformity throughout the Pennsylvania system. Under the old, decentralized system of purchasing, individual managers had grown accustomed to selecting supplies and products based largely on their personal preferences. Dudley and his chemical analyses, like the apparatus for testing metals in the physical laboratory, in effect functioned as a neutral arbiter. They provided the purchasing agent with independent and impersonal assessments he could easily invoke when managers disagreed with his choice of material for a certain purpose. As Dudley would later explain in papers before the American Chemical Society, the goal was not to produce the most accurate analyses possible, but to provide consistent assessments from one time to the next.

During the remaining years of the 1880s – his most productive period – Dudley set out to extend the practice of purchasing according to specifications to as many products as possible. Though operational problems generally still first drew him to a topic, Dudley consistently expanded his inquiries into exhaustive studies covering all varieties of materials that might have contributed to the problem. He would then suggest detailed guidelines for an entire line of products, and the purchasing agent would issue specifications based on his advice. When shock-absorbing springs on railroad cars began to break with alarming frequency, for example, Dudley analyzed the steel used in the springs and recommended a certain type of steel for that application. This work, which flowed in part out of Dudley's investigations of steel rails, in turn prompted him to devise specifications for all steel and cast-iron products purchased by the railroad.[71] Similarly, a study of metal alloys used in bearings led Dudley to devise specifications for all alloys employed by the Pennsylvania.[72] The same pattern appeared outside the realm of metals. In an attempt to settle a dispute among employees over why the varnish had worn off a car, Dudley analyzed the soap used to scrub cars. Discovering that an adulterant in the soap had damaged the varnish, Dudley proceeded to study all soaps used by the Pennsylvania and issue specifications for each one.[73] On another occasion a problem with one type of red paint

---

[71] Dudley and Pease, "Chemistry Applied to the Railroads: Steel for Springs," *American Railroad and Engineering Journal* 66 (1892): 13–16.

[72] Dudley and Pease, "Chemistry Applied to Railroads: Bearing Metals," *American Railroad and Engineering Journal* 66 (1892): 86–89.

[73] Dudley and Pease, "Chemistry Applied to Railroads: Soap," *American Railroad and Engineering Journal* 65 (1890): 492–494 and 551–554.

that faded badly when applied to wooden cars prompted Dudley to develop standards for all paints.[74]

By proceeding in this fashion, Dudley had by 1889 secured a well-defined role for the chemical laboratory in the management of the Pennsylvania Railroad. The established character of the lab emerged clearly in a series of articles Dudley and his assistant, F. N. Pease, wrote for the *Railroad and Engineering Journal*.[75] Naming their series "Chemistry Applied to Railroads," Dudley and Pease described in detail the work done in their laboratory at the Pennsylvania. They portrayed the facility as an established institution built firmly on the foundation of making and enforcing specifications. By 1889, they reported, the Pennsylvania regularly purchased twenty-five products according to chemical specifications drawn up by Dudley in collaboration with the purchasing agent. To enforce these specifications the company maintained an expanded laboratory facility and employed several additional personnel. Under Dudley's supervision this staff performed over 25,000 chemical analyses each year, making it perhaps the largest analytical chemistry laboratory in the country.

Informed observers had long since detected the benefits of the facilities at the Pennsylvania and begun to emulate them. An 1880 article in the *Railroad Gazette* described activities at the test department in glowing terms, and another published two years later concluded that the laboratory "proves that science, as a method of investigation, is fully recognized as having a place in railroad affairs."[76] Such facilities, its author confidently declared, would soon become standard in the railroad industry. The Burlington, in characteristic fashion, followed the Pennsylvania nearly from the start. In October 1876 it hired a mechanical engineer and a chemist and set up laboratory facilities for both in its main shops at Aurora, Illinois. The Burlington acquired a machine to test the viscosity of oils and one to bend metals. Two years later, again following the Pennsylvania, it added a testing machine capable of handling larger samples.[77] The Burlington's purchasing agent, C. M. Higginson, had since 1873 conducted extensive tests of coal similar to some performed by Cloud at the Pennsylvania in 1876. He took an immediate interest in the testing facilities and soon became the staunchest advocate of the chemical laboratory as well. Higginson assumed direct

74 Dudley and Pease, "Chemistry Applied to Railroads: Paint Specifications," *American Railroad and Engineering Journal* 65 (1891): 251–254.

75 Dudley and Pease, "Chemistry Applied to Railroads" series.

76 "Testing Materials at Altoona," *Railroad Gazette* 14 (August 4, 1882): 467–468. The 1880 article is quoted at length in "Departments of Chemical and Physical Tests (Historical)," pp. 9–11.

77 Most information in this chapter regarding the laboratory at the Burlington comes from the Laboratory Notebooks, CBQ Papers. On the origins of the lab, see also C. M. Higginson to Perkins, December 29, 1876, January 31, June 5, and December 1, 1877; and W. Strong to Perkins, January 2, 1877; CBQ Papers, 3P4.4.

responsibility for the routine operations of both, and the chemist and mechanical engineer addressed all their reports to him. Under his direction the
chemist at the Burlington duplicated Dudley's work step by step, and the
testing department issued specifications for most of the products covered by
Pennsylvania specifications.[78] By 1883, the practice of purchasing materials
based on specifications had become so established that the Burlington extended the work of Higginson and the laboratory to cover purchases by its
branch lines.[79]

Several more railroads followed suit during the 1880s, as assistants trained
in the laboratories of the two pioneers moved on to set up testing facilities and laboratories at other companies. The Burlington sent alumni of
its testing facilities to the Chicago and Northwestern as early as 1881, and
Dudley's assistants left to join the Philadelphia and Reading, among others.[80]
By 1889, at least nine railroads employed chemists and maintained testing
facilities.[81] As at the Pennsylvania, these facilities devoted most of their time
and energy to setting and enforcing specifications.[82] Chemists and mechanical engineers working for the railroads, aided in part by their common roots,
rapidly developed a group consciousness centered around these tasks. They
corresponded frequently and began to hold annual meetings at which they
discussed new specifications and methods of analysis.[83] Some cultivated spe-
cialities in certain areas. Walter Lee Brown of the Burlington, for example,
looked forward to sharing his work on qualitative analysis and testing heavy
petroleum lubricating oil with his fellow railroad chemists.[84] Mechanical

[78] Higginson to Perkins, December 29, 1876, January 31, June 5, and December 1, 1877;
      and Strong to Perkins, January 2, 1877; CBQ Papers, 3P4.4; C. M. Higginson to
      C. E. Perkins, June 5, 1877, CBQ Papers, 3P4.4; George Chalender to C. E. Perkins,
      April 26, 1878, CBQ Papers, 3P4.4; and Laboratory Notebooks, CBQ Papers.

[79] See extensive correspondence in CBQ Papers, 3P4.56.

[80] W. L. Brown to Rhodes, January 1, 1881, Laboratory Notebooks, vol. 10, pp. 190–
      224, CBQ Papers; A. McLeod to L. B. Paxson, January 8, 1889, and December 6,
      1890, and Paxson to McLeod, October 29, 1890, Reading Papers, accession 1451.

[81] Dudley and Pease, "Chemistry Applied to Railroads: What the Chemist Does," p. 554.
      The mechanical engineer of the Burlington in 1890 listed the following railroads as
      having laboratories: Pennsylvania; Burlington; Chicago and North Western; Chicago,
      Milwaukee and St. Paul; Baltimore and Ohio; Union Pacific; Southern Pacific; Philadel-
      phia and Reading; Lehigh Valley; and New York and Western. Sargent to Rhodes, May
      24, 1890, Laboratory Notebooks, vol. A8, p. 4, CBQ Papers.

[82] The chemist at the Philadelphia and Reading, who also served as the storekeeper,
      listed this as his principal function. On the laboratory at the Philadelphia and Read-
      ing, see O. S. Doolittle to Theodore Vorhees, March 22, 1893; Paxson to McLeod,
      October 29, 1890; and Doolittle to Vorhees, June 15, 1893; Reading Papers, accession
      1520.

[83] Brown to various railroad chemists, 1885 and 1886, Laboratory Notebooks, vol. 10,
      CBQ Papers.

[84] Brown to Geo. M. Davidson, July 6, 1886, Laboratory Notebooks, vol. 10, p. 59, and
      Brown to T. W. Robinson, May 14, 1887, Laboratory Notebooks, vol. 10, p. 145,
      CBQ Papers.

engineers in the testing departments likewise contributed many professional papers on new methods of analysis.[85]

While routine analyses performed in connection with purchasing materials rapidly became the raison d'etre of most railroad laboratories, the chemists and mechanical engineers also contributed to the developing tradition of testing when they assisted in occasional tests of new technology. By the mid-1880s, Dudley had established ongoing programs for examining products such as storage batteries, fire extinguishers, paints, greases, and a variety of lighting systems used to illuminate cars, tracks, and buildings. He personally designed and patented a carburetor system of lighting. After testing it against a number of alternatives over the course of several years, Dudley and General Superintendent of Motive Power Theodore Ely deemed his system superior in cost, performance, and safety. At various times, the laboratory staff at the Pennsylvania conducted thorough studies of subjects ranging from use of chemical solvents in cleaning upholstery to ways of packing ice in refrigerator cars to techniques for transporting black powder. Most years, the lab staged comparative tests of several novel appliances used in some feature of railroad practice. Targets of investigation included not only items such as wheels and axles, but also such general-purpose technologies as acetylene torches, hydraulic jacks, water filters, and septic tanks. After devoting substantial effort throughout much of the 1890s to investigating various methods of heating and ventilating passenger cars, in 1899 Dudley issued a standard design for placement of air ducts in the cars.[86]

The mechanical engineer at the Pennsylvania likewise grew deeply involved with testing various pieces of equipment used by the railroad. Not surprisingly, locomotives captured much of his attention. By 1884, the mechanical engineer had established a set of standard protocols for testing locomotive boiler pressures under different conditions.[87] Before long, the railroad created a distinct Test Department to carry out studies of locomotives when burning different grades of coal or using various lubricants, sealants, and devices intended to boost performance. Often, the employees in this department collaborated with chemists in the laboratory, who supplemented the road tests with analyses of coals, oils, and other chemical products used on the locomotives.[88] In 1903, the Pennsylvania formally placed responsibility for these activities in the hands of an employee, designated the engineer of

[85] Report of the Physical Laboratory, F. W. Sargent to G. W. Rhodes, April 5, 1890, Laboratory Notebooks, vol. A7, pp. 270–280, CBQ Papers.

[86] PRR Lab Reports; "Departments of Chemical and Physical Tests (Historical)," pp. 13–15; "Testing Materials at Altoona," *Railroad Gazette* 14 (August 4, 1882): 467–468; Dudley and Pease, "Chemistry Applied to Railroads: What the Chemist Does," p. 556; Dudley and Pease, "Chemistry Applied to Railroads: The Ventilation of Passenger Cars," *American Engineer and Railroad Journal* 73 (1898): 191–193.

[87] "Department of Chemical and Physical Tests (Historical)," p. 12.

[88] PRR Test Reports.

tests, who reported directly to the general superintendent of motive power along with the chemist and the mechanical engineer.[89]

Executives at the Pennsylvania and many other lines identified the laboratories and testing departments as important drawing cards in the recruitment of young scientists and engineers. As early as 1880, *Railroad Gazette* noted that the experimental department usually "becomes a training school for subordinate officers."[90] New graduates of scientific and technical schools were offered jobs as "special apprentices" in the labs, where they would find a familiar environment and perhaps work on the same problems and with the same equipment they had used in college laboratories (Fig. 5.4). Applicants requested these positions even though they paid little.[91] "There is now such a large and increasing class of educated young men, many of whom can afford to spend from one to five years in practical training with little or no compensation," observed the *Gazette*, "that the salaries of assistants in such a department are a very small item."

Over time, railroads came to view the laboratories as ideal entry points on the path to careers in management. New graduates refined their drafting and analytical techniques in the laboratories and test facilities while beginning to familiarize themselves with all aspects of railroading. Within months of arriving at the railroad, the young recruits would move from the lab to some mechanical or even commercial department. Both the Pennsylvania and the Burlington relied heavily on such men for their managerial talent. By the 1890s, most Pennsylvania division superintendents and master mechanics had served as special apprentices, and many executives not directly involved with machinery had spent time in the testing facilities and laboratory as well.[92] The laboratory became so important to recruitment and training at the Burlington that when an economizing Perkins threatened to cut back the facility during the depression of the 1890s, Superintendent of Motive Power Godfrey Rhodes objected on the grounds that it would harm the Burlington's technical reputation and undermine efforts in these areas. "The CBQ RR would never hold its present position in motive power matters among railroads were it not for the information it has gathered through its laboratory," Rhodes wrote. "It would be better to abandon the practice of starting young men in the mechanical department if they are to be discharged at every falling off in business."[93]

[89] Chas. Pugh to A. J. Cassatt, June 18, 1903, and W. W. Atterbury to Pugh, June 8, 1903, PRR Board Papers.

[90] *Railroad Gazette*, November 5, 1880, quoted in "Departments of Chemical and Physical Tests (Historical)," pp. 10–11.

[91] Perkins to Stone, June 28, 1887, CBQ Papers, 3P4.1.

[92] Numerous examples of the career paths of Pennsylvania Railroad executives who spent time in the laboratory can be found in documents concerning promotions contained in PRR Board Papers.

[93] Rhodes to J. D. Besler, June 2, 1893, CBQ Papers, 3P4.58.

Figure 5.4. Carrying on a tradition established some forty years earlier, an engineering apprentice operates equipment for testing metal in the Pennsylvania's mechanical engineering laboratory, 1917. *Courtesy*: Hagley Museum and Library.

While testing facilities at several lines came under similar scrutiny from economizing executives during the financial crises of the 1890s, they generally survived the cutbacks and came back stronger than ever. Though Perkins in reviewing possible areas to make cuts had inquired "whether we might not cut off entirely or materially curtail the laboratory at Aurora," Rhodes and Higginson managed to nurse the facility through the crisis until the tide turned in 1896.[94] The Burlington then expanded its standards-setting activities, adding a physical laboratory to its chemical facility. Testing

[94] Perkins to G. Harris, February 18, 1891, CBQ Papers, 3P4.1; G. Harris to Perkins, August 22, 1893, CBQ Papers, 3P4.51; Quereau to Forsyth, December 1, 1893, Laboratory Notebooks, vol. A14, pp. 310–314, CBQ Papers; and Carney to Forsyth, January 23, 1896, Laboratory Notebooks, vol. A17, pp. 420–426, CBQ Papers.

activities at the Pennsylvania slumped a bit with the onset of depression, but in 1896 the line completed improvements that tripled the size of its chemical laboratory.[95] Dudley and Pease curtailed their experimental work slightly but continued to develop new standard analytical techniques for use in connection with specifications.[96] By 1903, the Pennsylvania employed a laboratory staff of approximately twenty-five people and enforced forty-seven sets of chemical specifications.[97] Top executives at the Reading, besieged by a second bankruptcy, repeatedly turned down requests from the chemist for a higher salary and an expanded facility but did not eliminate them altogether.[98] Other companies, accepting specifications as a routine component of railroad operations, built their first separate laboratory facilities during the decade.[99]

The dialectic between innovations in test equipment and evolving methods of technical analysis also reached a new watershed in the 1890s with proposals to build plants for testing and evaluating locomotives in place. The initiative for constructing these test plants came from the growing community of professional engineers. Professor W. F. M. Goss, a mechanical engineer who played an instrumental role in founding departments of railway engineering at the University of Illinois and Purdue University, had devised a machine of this sort in the early 1890s for pedagogical and research purposes.[100] In 1894, several technical societies – the American Railroad Association, the American Society of Mechanical Engineers, the American Railroad Master Mechanics Association, and the Western Railroad Club – launched a cooperative effort to conduct a series of tests at his Purdue facility. Mechanics from the Pennsylvania, the Burlington, and the Chicago, Milwaukee and St. Paul agreed to coordinate a project comparing the performance of simple and compound locomotives under various conditions. To pay for the tests, they solicited contributions from railroads of thirty cents per locomotive

---

[95] PRR Lab Report, February 10, 1897.
[96] PRR Lab Reports; Dudley and Pease, "Chemistry Applied to Railroads: New Series – Chemical Methods," *American Engineer and Railroad Journal* 66–72 (1892–1898); and Dudley and Pease, "The Need of Standard Methods for the Analysis of Iron and Steel, with Some Proposed Standard Methods," *Journal of the American Chemical Society* 15 (1893): 501–541.
[97] Charles B. Dudley, "The Making of Specifications for Materials," *Proceedings of the American Society for Testing Materials* (henceforth, *ASTM Proceedings*) 3 (1903): p. 17.
[98] Paxson to McLeod, October 29, 1890; O. S. Doolittle to Vorhees, July 15, 1893; Vorhees to Doolittle, July 19, 1893; Doolittle to Vorhees, September 3, 1894; Vorhees to Doolittle, September 6, 1894; Reading Papers, accession 1520.
[99] On the activities of the Burlington laboratory during the nineties, see the Laboratory Notebooks, CBQ Papers.
[100] Bruce Seely, "Research, Engineering, and Science in American Engineering Colleges: 1900–1960," *Technology and Culture* 34 (1993): 347–348.

owned.[101] The project fizzled for a time, as executives at lines such as the financially strapped Philadelphia and Reading refused to contribute despite the urging of its superintendent of motive power.[102] For many years a small machine built by the Chicago and North Western in the early 1890s remained the only one owned by a railroad. With the return of prosperity toward the end of the decade, however, the plants took hold at various lines and universities. Management at the Pennsylvania agreed in 1902 to erect a test plant of unprecedented size in conjunction with the industrial exposition in St. Louis two years later. The line staged a highly publicized series of fuel tests at the fair, supervised by a team of advisors headed by Goss, and published the results in an elaborate book. When rebuilt at Altoona, the locomotive test plant became the centerpiece of the Pennsylvania's testing facilities.[103] Other railroads soon followed suit, adding similar plants during the first decade of the twentieth century. The chemist at the Burlington, for instance, reported in 1905 that "by far the most important study was of fuel" using that line's new plant.[104]

CHANNELING CHANGE

Over the course of the late nineteenth century, railroad managers thus developed a powerful set of tools for evaluating technology and monitoring the course of innovation in their industry. By establishing testing facilities and creating staffs of technical advisors linked by a technical press, trade associations, and engineering societies, railroads mobilized a large community of highly trained technical experts who had no responsibilities other than assessing the condition of railroad technology. At a time when rapid growth made traditional methods of personal exchange difficult to sustain even at

[101] Willard A. Smith and R. C. Blackall to T. Vorhees, December 24, 1894; "Proposed Shop Tests of Locomotives," printed pamphlet; Reading Papers, accession 1520; and *The Pennsylvania Railroad System at the Louisiana Purchase Exhibition: Locomotive Tests and Exhibits* (Philadelphia: Pennsylvania Railroad Company, 1905).

[102] Vorhees to Paxson, December 29, 1894; Paxson to Vorhees, January 2, 1895; and Vorhees to Smith, January 4, 1895; Reading Papers, accession 1520.

[103] On the creation of this plant, see V. P. Thomson and Theodore N. Ely, "Memorandum on Louisiana Purchase Exposition," June 10, 1903; V. P. Pugh to Pres. Cassatt, June 4, 1903; and Pugh to Cassatt, February 4, 1904; PRR Board Papers. For details on its operation in St. Louis and the role of Professor Goss, see PRR Motive Power Papers, box 717, folder 6; *The Pennsylvania Railroad System at the Louisiana Purchase Exhibition*; and Chapter 7 below. On its relocation to Altoona, see PRR Motive Power Papers, box 715, folder 3, and Chapter 9 below.

[104] Annual reports of the laboratory, Laboratory Notebooks, vol. A30 (January 23, 1902), pp. 158–169, and vol. A33 (March 23, 1903), p. 82, CBQ Papers; M. H. Wickhorst to Clark, March 8, 1904, Laboratory Notebooks, CBQ Papers; and Annual Report for 1903, Laboratory Notebooks, vol. A36, pp. 133–141, CBQ Papers.

individual lines, the language and analytical methods of engineering lifted discussions of technology to a more abstract plane, free from the peculiarities of particular devices and locales. Managers could readily exchange information about techniques gathered from across their industry, and they could implement desired changes in technology quickly throughout their sprawling enterprises. "The professionalization of the railroad manager increased the productivity of the American transportation system," states esteemed business historian Alfred Chandler unequivocally after pointing out the increasing prominence of engineers in railroad management. "Repeated discussions by the salaried managers of both organizational and technological innovations permitted their quick development and rapid adoption by American railroads."[105]

These benefits resulted not so much from a vast effort aimed at generating and promoting technical novelty but from attempts to focus technical efforts on a few areas of particular importance. Managers charged with responsibility for operating highly developed systems of great complexity had little interest in revolutionary change that might seriously disrupt established operations. They sought to gain small economies by incorporating minor innovations and refinements as smoothly and as fully as possible. This desire to optimize performance in the context of a fixed system and established practices drew railroads readily into alliance with the growing body of academically trained scientists and engineers and with the educational institutions that trained them. Engineers and scientists possessed just the sort of knowledge and orientation to problems that railroads needed. Their novel methods of analysis sought not to generate significant departures in technology but to evaluate existing practices and materials and to establish standards of performance. Laboratory facilities and testing equipment subjected materials to routine evaluation along well-established criteria. In a process familiar to those who study scientific and engineering research, the testing machines themselves came to circumscribe the areas of potential inquiry. Communities of experts formed around the tools of analysis, so that while a large number of people might participate in an inquiry, the range of questions remained quite narrow. To the extent high-level managers perceived the laboratories as centers of experiment and novelty, they deemed them suspect. Faced with a particularly acute financial crisis during the early 1890s, Charles Perkins advised a subordinate who proposed a test that "we cannot be experimenting" and suggested that "our policy is to let our richer neighbors in the East point the way for us."[106] Even at progressive lines such

---

[105] Chandler, *The Visible Hand*, p. 132.
[106] Perkins to Bates, October 19, 1891, CBQ Papers, 3P4.58. Perkins and other Burlington executives called for cutbacks in experiments in many letters, including Perkins to G. Harris, May 29, 1894, CBQ Papers, 3P4.58; Harris to Perkins, February 27, 1891, CBQ Papers, 3P4.51; and Stone to E. J. Swords, March 28, 1889, CBQ Papers, 3H5.24.

as the Pennsylvania, laboratories rarely assumed new responsibilities outside their established realm of standards-setting. No railroad turned to research and testing of new products as a possible avenue of escape from the woes of the depression.

While the turn toward engineering methods shifted analysis of railroad technology onto terms that transcended conditions at particular firms and in many respects depersonalized choices regarding technology, the institutional and organizational changes worked in some ways to centralize technical decision-making and to concentrate it in the hands of a few individuals. Matthias Forney, through his dual position as editor of *Railroad Gazette* and secretary of the Master Car Builders Association, exerted a strong influence over the flow of information and attitudes pertaining to innovation. The Pennsylvania Railroad and, in particular, General Superintendent of Motive Power Theodore N. Ely, assumed a position as the foremost expert in technical matters. Burlington President Charles Perkins described Ely as "the highest authority," and the CB&Q, along with nearly every other railroad, kept an eye turned to practices deployed by the Pennsylvania.[107] The Burlington itself became the leader in technical matters among the many Chicago roads.[108] By cooperating freely and allowing this informal hierarchy of expertise to develop, railroads avoided unnecessary duplication of research and kept the costs of evaluating and selecting techniques low. Railroads obtained similar benefits by concentrating their purchases of equipment and supplies in a handful of manufacturers. Executives looking for novel technology no longer scoured a diffuse market, but instead entrusted established firms such as Baldwin and Westinghouse with the task of finding and marketing the best available devices. In entering into such established relationships, railroads looked for reliability more than novelty. Producers and consumers of railroad technology engaged in sustained collaboration that encouraged ongoing refinement but perhaps placed less emphasis on radical departures from routine.

As discussed more fully in Part III, these policies may have led managers to overlook innovations that would have been tried and used widely in an earlier era. Relying on the judgment of experts at a few railroads and suppliers was a cheap and efficient way to evaluate innovation across a narrow spectrum; it was not a policy designed to ensure that the best ideas came to fruition. Rather than many inventions being tried and some ultimately

---

[107] Perkins to Mrs. E. G. Low and to T. N. Ely, September 21, 1897, CBQ Papers, 3P4.1.

[108] An example that showed both CB&Q prominence among the Chicago roads and the Burlington's respect for the technical expertise of the Pennsylvania involved tests of heating and lighting systems in the 1880s and 1890s, when Perkins organized cooperative tests among the Chicago roads and monitored closely investigations on the Pennsylvania. See Perkins to Stone, April 28 and June 29, 1887, CBQ Papers, 3P4.1; Perkins to G. Harris, January 16, 1893, CBQ Papers, 3P4.58; and G. Harris to Perkins, January 24, 1893, CBQ Papers, 3P4.51.

surviving and becoming common, most inventions never received a trial. But in the competitive conditions of the late nineteenth century, managers were willing to risk missing the benefits of a dramatic innovation if they could incorporate minor changes without difficulty while maintaining efficient operations. The potential returns from such a course could be great, as we can see by examining the case of steel rails in some detail.

6

Standardizing Steel Rails:
Engineered Innovation

Perhaps no area of technology better reflected the turn toward engineered innovation and the process of negotiated improvement through technical specifications than the sustained efforts by railroads to obtain heavier and more durable steel rails. According to the systematic assessment of economic historian Albert Fishlow, changes in rails contributed a larger share to railroad productivity improvements between 1870 and 1910 than any other technology.[1] By the end of that period, he concludes, railroads were saving an estimated $479 million per year by using the stronger and more durable steel rails then available in place of iron rails of 1870 quality and price. Some of those savings accrued directly from the superior capacity of steel to resist wear. A section of track laid with steel rails lasted significantly longer for less cost than a similarly used section laid with iron. But most of the benefits identified by Fishlow flowed indirectly from changes associated with the increased strength of the rail. Steel rails could, quite simply, support heavier locomotives and cars without breaking, and trains made up of such equipment carried passengers and freight at substantially lower costs per mile than their lighter predecessors. Innovation in rail technology thus was a great facilitator. It eliminated a potentially debilitating constraint and paved the way, so to speak, for a mode of operations made possible by a host of additional innovations in management and machinery.

Contrary to what a comparison of 1870 iron rails with steel rails of 1910 might imply, railroads derived only part of this dramatic improvement in

---

[1] Albert Fishlow, "Productivity and Technological Change in the Railroad Sector, 1840–1910," National Bureau of Economic Research, *Output, Employment, and Productivity in the United States after 1800* (New York: NBER, Columbia University Press, 1966), pp. 583–646.

performance from their initial switch from iron to steel.[2] The steel rails lines first substituted for iron beginning in the late 1860s differed considerably from those which carried the heavy traffic of a half century later. Rails changed in two interdependent ways between 1870 and 1910. Considerable refinement occurred through the sustained efforts of steel makers who continually revised methods of manufacture in ways that substantially altered the finished product. Manufacturers speeded up the rolling process, utilized different ores, and learned innumerable ways of manipulating the metal. This sustained exercise in learning by doing helped drive down the price of rails and often improved their quality, thus offering railroads substantial gains in productivity to be had simply through the purchase of rails. A second area of change involved efforts initiated by the railroads to alter the shape of the rails. The weight of a typical new main-line steel rail increased in steady increments, so that by the turn of the twentieth century such a rail weighed 100 pounds per yard, nearly double that of one installed during the late 1860s. Rails of each weight came in numerous shapes, moreover, with various designs distributing the metal in significantly different proportions within the basic I-form.

Though the first of these paths of innovation was associated largely with suppliers and the latter was typically initiated at the behest of the railroads, their parallel pursuit drew the two parties into increasingly close collaboration over the course of the late nineteenth century. Because both railroads and steel makers labored under conditions of ignorance, in which they lacked fundamental understanding about the factors influencing rail performance, neither could proceed in complete isolation from the other. If a manufacturer seeking economies in production used a different ore or treated the hot steel in a new manner, the resulting rail might cause problems that railroads would discover only after months or even years of use. By the same token, a new shape of rail might introduce unanticipated complications for the manufacturer and require special processing at the mill, and the resulting product might ultimately prove inferior to the older design. If they hoped to overcome these difficulties, producers and consumers needed to link their experiences more closely and systematically. The two sides needed to develop reliable means of correlating changes in design and in manufacturing with performance of the rails in actual service. Railroads and manufacturers would have to pool information about phenomena neither could fully ascertain themselves, and they would have to develop a way to express their understanding of those phenomena on more theoretical grounds, with agreed-upon tests and a common language. Until they cooperated in this fashion, manufacturers

[2] Fishlow readily concedes that his macroeconomic focus cannot tell us why railroads acted as they did or even whether their managers accurately perceived the effects the innovations he studies would have. To ascertain the course of technical change and the motivations behind it, he recommends an "assault upon the specifics." Fishlow, "Productivity," p. 645.

and the railroads stood little chance of discovering and mastering the crucial interactions between the shape of the rail, the method of manufacture, and the quality of the material.[3]

Though with hindsight we can readily perceive the benefits of cooperation, those engaged in manufacturing and using steel rails came to appreciate them only gradually. Their collaboration developed haltingly and at times grudgingly, compelled in large measure by a shared desire to overcome the mutual affliction of ignorance. Rails represented the single largest routine capital expenditure on most railroad balance sheets, and they accounted for virtually the entire output of the steel industry. Annual negotiations for rail contracts, as discussed in Chapter 2, often involved testy exchanges among executives at the highest levels. Having only recently extracted themselves from tight financial relationships, railroads and suppliers initially lacked forums in which they might discuss technical matters with some measure of insulation from immediate pecuniary concerns. Emergent groups of professional engineers offered one outlet, but these nascent communities of experts had not yet developed the apparatus necessary to foster a sustained, cooperative approach. They had only just begun to develop a common methodology of testing that might provide a more theoretical basis for comprehending rail performance, and they lacked established procedures for translating such understanding into workable technical specifications.

FIRST STEPS: DUDLEY AND THE PENNSYLVANIA

The first tentative steps toward collaboration took place during the mid-1870s, at about the time the original Bessemer Association collapsed and managers at railroads such as the Pennsylvania divested themselves of direct investments in their steel suppliers. Perhaps not coincidentally, concerns began to surface among rail executives about this same time regarding the strength and durability of steel rails. When executives such as J. Edgar Thomson had first begun substituting steel for iron, they had expected the investment to set them free from concern over rails for an extended period. Extrapolating from short-term tests of steel in trouble spots, railroads projected long life for the rails in ordinary service. Estimates varied, but the prediction of an executive for the Chicago, Burlington and Quincy that the new rails would last at least a generation, or twenty years, fell about in the middle.[4]

---

[3] For an interesting analysis of the state of knowledge in iron-making, with particular emphasis on the difficulty in establishing specifications, see Robert B. Gordon, "Materials for Manufacturing: The Response of the Connecticut Iron Industry to Technological Change and Limited Resources," *Technology and Culture* 24 (1983): 602–634.

[4] Robert Harris to Frank B. Crandon, August 26, 1875, Papers of the Chicago, Burlington and Quincy Railroad, Newberry Library, Chicago (henceforth, CBQ Papers), 3H4.1.

Once railroads had used steel rails for several years and had an opportunity to monitor their performance in actual service, however, executives began to temper their assessments with mild criticism. Amid growing concern, a committee of the American Society of Civil Engineers (ASCE), whose membership included many railroad engineers in charge of maintenance of way, conducted a survey of railroad officials to determine how much steel had been laid, how much traffic it had carried, and how its performance compared with that of iron.[5] The committee's reports, issued between 1874 and 1876, indicated that most railroad officials believed steel superior to iron, but not by so large a margin as originally thought. Some respondents complained that steel rails had broken unusually often. More frequently, officials expressed disappointment with the durability of steel. Respondents from the Pennsylvania and some other early innovators reported that their first steel rails had begun to need replacement, ten years earlier than originally anticipated. Several officials suspected, moreover, that newer steel might wear out even faster.

This pioneering survey marked a significant departure in relations between railroads and the steel industry. By collecting and publicizing the experiences of many companies, the ASCE report heightened awareness of the variable wearing quality of steel rails. The ASCE committee, moreover, offered railroads some practical advice about how to address the problem: Pay closer attention to the shape of the rails. Previously, the mills had dictated the form of the rails, and naturally they had chosen shapes that were easily manufactured. The committee urged railroads to assert themselves and demand that more steel be put in the head of the rail. This would concentrate the metal at the point of greatest wear and lead to longer life.[6]

Steel manufacturers watched with considerable interest as their product came under attack. Alexander Holley, who had designed virtually every Bessemer rail plant in the country and stood as the undisputed technical leader of the steel industry, responded coyly to the ASCE suggestion that railroads demand different shapes of rails. Manufacturers would happily produce complex rail shapes, Holley commented at an 1875 meeting of the ASCE, because these yielded higher profits than simpler

5 Ashbel Welch, "On the Form, Weight, Manufacture, and Life of Rails," *Transactions of the American Society of Civil Engineers* (henceforth, *ASCE Transactions*) 3 (June 10, 1874): 87–110; O. Chanute, "Notes on the Weight of Rails and the Breaking of Iron Rails," *ASCE Transactions* 3 (June 10, 1974): 111–117; Ashbel Welch, "On the Form, Weight, Manufacture, and Life of Rails," *ASCE Transactions* 4 (May 5, 1875): 136–141; and Ashbel Welch, "On the Form, Weight, Manufacture, and Life of Rails," *ASCE Transactions* 5 (June 15, 1876): 327–329.
6 Ashbel Welch, "On the Form, Weight, Manufacture, and Life of Rails," *ASCE Transactions* 5 (June 15, 1876): 327–329, and Ashbel Welch, "Comparative Economy of Steel Rails with Light and Heavy Heads," *ASCE Transactions* 10 (June 15, 1881): 251–274.

designs.[7] This glib reply, however, was probably intended to deflect attention from genuine concerns among manufacturers, who worried that growing doubts about the superiority of steel would drive down its price. If they hoped to keep the price of all ferrous metals from converging, steel producers needed some definitive basis for distinguishing their product from alternatives.

Using the American Institute of Mining and Metallurgical Engineers (AIME) as their forum, Holley and his expert colleagues among steel makers had for some time pursued this goal. In a series of technical papers, they attempted to develop new methods of characterizing the quality of material that went into the rail. A paper presented at the AIME annual meeting in 1872 by John B. Pease, superintendent of the Pennsylvania Steel Works, typified these efforts.[8] Pease identified the crucial advantage of steel as its greater "hardness," which he defined as the ability to resist wear without breaking due to excessive brittleness. To guarantee a full return on their investment, railroads and manufacturers alike needed to ensure that the steel in their rails had sufficient hardness.

While Pease cleared up some nagging problems with definitions and established a basis for discussion, his report exposed a glaring weakness that would plague the metallurgical community for years to come. As subsequent debate indicated, Pease had left a key issue unresolved: How might the degree of hardness be determined? Pease conceded that the only sure test was performance in actual service. But because steel rails lasted so many years, this could hardly serve as a practical guide when purchasing rails.[9] Railroads and manufacturers needed short-term tests. They had agreed on a check, known as a drop test, to determine whether the rail was brittle and would break.[10] A quick test of the long-term wearing qualities of rails, however, remained unknown.

Metallurgical engineers discussed two possible avenues. Physical tests, such as those recently developed by Robert Thurston with his machines for measuring the force required to bend metal components, might be used to predict the long-term wearing performance of rails.[11] A second, more

7   See Holley's comments in response to the ASCE rail committee's report, *ASCE Transactions* 4 (May 5, 1875): 223.

8   John B. Pease, "The Manufacture of Iron and Steel Rails," *Transactions of the American Institute of Mining and Metallurgical Engineers* (henceforth, *AIME Transactions*) 1 (May 1871–February 1873): 162–169.

9   Ibid., p. 163.

10 As its name suggests, this test involved dropping a heavy weight from a predetermined height onto a sample rail. If the rail broke, it failed the test.

11 Robert Julius Kwik, "The Function of Applied Science and the Mechanical Laboratory during the Period of Formation of the Profession of Mechanical Engineering, as Exemplified in the Career of Robert Henry Thurston, 1839–1903" (Ph.D. dissertation, University of Pennsylvania, 1974); Robert J. Kwik, "Between Science and Society: The Engineering Career of Robert Henry Thurston," Massachusetts Institute

promising possibility lay in the chemistry of metals. Pease expressed hope that he or another investigator would soon identify a chemical formula for hardness. Holley picked up on this idea in an address to the AIME in 1873, when he predicted that specifications for rails would most likely come in the form of a chemical formula.[12] Several members of the AIME, including both Pease and Holley, presented papers at subsequent meetings seeking to identify the chemical composition of steel.[13]

While these early papers and discussions taking place at the two engineering societies in some respects heralded a new approach to railroad technology, they also contained seeds of difficulties that would persist to some degree for the next quarter-century. In the first place, tremendous gaps in fundamental understanding existed among both groups. The ASCE survey revealed how little substantive data railroads had accumulated relating the volume of traffic to the wear of rails. On the other side, metallurgists clearly lacked a theoretical explanation for the behavior of steel. They had only recently begun to investigate the physical and chemical properties of the material, and they had no firm basis upon which to evaluate its long-term performance. This knowledge would come slowly.[14]

In addition to these fundamental gaps in understanding, the preliminary discussions revealed a huge gulf in the way manufacturers and railroads approached the subject. Though both parties had turned toward professional engineering societies as forums of action, the two organizations pursued the issue from entirely independent points of view. The ASCE focused on shape and wear, while the AIME concentrated on chemistry and hardness. Each society, moreover, remained firmly associated with one side of the dispute. Even Holley, who had brokered relations between railroads and suppliers during the early years of the Bessemer industry and as a consultant maintained a degree of detachment from any particular mill, managed to sound more confrontational than conciliatory. Though he stressed the importance of opening lines of communication between producers and consumers and personally attended meetings of both societies, Holley placed the onus firmly

of Technology *Technology Studies*, Bulletin no. 3 (May 1974): 66–75; *Dictionary of American Biography* (New York: Scribner, 1958), vol. 18, pp. 518–520; and Robert H. Thurston, *Memoirs and Professional Reports* (New York: American Society of Mechanical Engineers, n.d.).

12   A. L. Holley, "Tests of Steel," *AIME Transactions* 2 (May 1873–February 1874): 116–122.

13   A. L. Holley, "What Is Steel?," *AIME Transactions* 4 (May 1875–February 1876): 138–149; John B. Pease, "Iron and Carbon, Mechanically and Chemically Considered," *AIME Transactions* 4 (May 1875–February 1876): 157–178; Professor Frederick Prime, Jr., "What Steel Is," *AIME Transactions* 4 (May 1875–February 1876): 328–339; and Andrew S. McCreath, "Determination of Carbon in Iron and Steel," *AIME Transactions* 5 (May 1875–February 1876): 575–579.

14   Cyril Stanley Smith, *A History of Metallography: The Development of Ideas on the Structure of Metal before 1890* (Chicago: University of Chicago Press, 1960).

on the railroads. They must decide what hardness they desired in a rail, Holley insisted, then translate that hardness into terms rail manufacturers could understand and use.

During the latter years of the 1870s, railroads began to pick up this challenge. As usual, the Pennsylvania took the lead. With its early and substantial investment in steel rails, the Pennsylvania stood to lose more than most railroads if the rails failed sooner than anticipated, and through its long experience the line had collected more information about rail performance than any other company. The Pennsylvania had also established the fundamental precedents for negotiating with rail manufacturers. After observing a number of steel rails break at the joint in 1868, company president J. Edgar Thomson had forced rail makers to drill instead of punch the holes for the joints.[15] Gradually the Pennsylvania gained more protection against breakage, until its contracts for rails routinely provided for a railroad employee to examine new rails at the mill for obvious defects and to conduct a drop test of selected samples. The contracts also contained a guarantee against breakage caused by defects overlooked by the inspector.[16] By the late 1870s, railroads such as the Chicago, Burlington and Quincy had copied the Pennsylvania contracts, though smaller firms with less purchasing power generally remained subject to the dictates of the manufacturers.[17]

While the Pennsylvania's long experience with steel rails provided the motive and stature to meet Holley's challenge, its recently created chemical laboratory and mechanical testing facility gave the line the means to gather the necessary technical data. As noted above, the mechanical engineer regularly tested faulty materials using the machines in the physical laboratory, and Charles Dudley performed chemical analyses of the same materials. Broken rails were one of the materials routinely tested.[18] Sometime around 1876, Dudley broadened and reoriented his work on rails. Rather than merely analyzing broken rails that happened to make their way into the lab, Dudley systematically collected worn rails, recording their position in the track.

[15] Report of John A. Wilson, Chief Engineer of Maintenance of Way, *Annual Report of the Pennsylvania Railroad Company* (henceforth, *PRR Annual Report*) 22 (1868): 47.

[16] *PRR Annual Reports* and *Railroad Gazette* 8 (September 29, 1876): 426.

[17] Examples of rail contracts similar to those of the Pennsylvania can be found in the Papers of the Baltimore and Ohio Railroad, Maryland Historical Society, Baltimore, Ms. 1925; the Papers of the Philadelphia and Reading Railroad, Hagley Museum and Library, Wilmington, Delaware, accession 1407; and the CBQ Papers. For example, see C. M. Higginson to C. E. Perkins, November 10, 1876; W. B. Strong to Perkins, December 4, 1876; and Beckwith to Perkins, May 21, 1878; CBQ Papers, 3P4.4; and contracts from the N. Chicago Rolling Mill (dated December 4, 1876) and Cambria Iron Works (dated December 12, 1879), CBQ Papers, 33 1870 5.1.

[18] Theodore N. Ely, "Charles Dudley as a Railroad Man," in *Memorial Volume Commemorative of the Life and Life-Work of Charles Benjamin Dudley, Ph.D.* (Philadelphia: American Society for Testing Materials, n.d.), pp. 50–57.

After determining the amount of traffic they had carried, he sketched the rails to show the degree and nature of the wear. Dudley then had physical and chemical tests performed on the rails and related the data to the wearing qualities he had observed.

These pioneering studies clearly marked a direct response to the calls of Holley, Pease, and others in the AIME. Dudley had joined this organization shortly after arriving at the Pennsylvania, and between 1878 and 1881 he presented his results in several formal papers delivered at its annual meetings. The heart of his papers consisted of a chemical formula for the best steel rails. The formula prescribed proper levels of four impurities – phosphorus, silicon, carbon, and manganese – which Dudley called "hardeners." In a separate paper, which he soon abandoned, Dudley condensed this array of numbers into a single, summary total of "hardness units."[19]

Dudley's papers immediately sparked controversy that would have prolonged effects on the development of steel rails and the process of standards-setting. In extensive discussions that filled well over a hundred pages of the AIME's transactions, the audience questioned Dudley's work on two counts.[20] First, they attacked his scientific techniques and conclusions. Dudley had taken a radical stance; he argued that what were known as chemically "soft" rails actually wore longer than harder rails. This position, which eventually proved incorrect, challenged the conventional wisdom that held steel's hardness responsible for its superiority over iron. Few metallurgists agreed with Dudley. Detractors criticized nearly every aspect of his procedures, from how he selected the rails to his methods of chemical and statistical analysis. For the next several years many papers on these subjects were presented at AIME meetings.[21]

Other critics skipped over the details of Dudley's work and questioned the fundamental premise that railroads should collect data systematically in

[19] Charles B. Dudley, "The Chemical Composition and Physical Properties of Steel Rails," *AIME Transactions* 7 (May 1878–February 1879): 172–201; Dudley, "Does the Wearing Power of Steel Rails Increase with the Hardness of the Steel?," *AIME Transactions* 7 (May 1878–February 1879): 202–205; and Dudley, "The Wearing Capacity of Steel Rails in Relation to their Chemical Composition and Physical Properties," *AIME Transactions* 9 (May 1880–February 1881): 321–360.

[20] "Discussion of Dr. Charles B. Dudley's Papers on Steel Rails, Read at the Lake George Meeting, October 1878," *AIME Transactions* 7 (May 1878–February 1879): 357–413, and "Discussion on Steel Rails," *AIME Transactions* 9 (May 1880–February 1881): 529–608.

[21] Among the papers appearing in the wake of Dudley's studies were William Kent, "Manganese Determination in Steel," *AIME Transactions* 10 (May 1881–February 1882): 101–111; Magnus Troilius, "Chemical Methods for Analyzing Rail-Steel," *AIME Transactions* 10 (May 1881–February 1882): 162–187; comments by John W. Cabot, *AIME Transactions* 10 (May 1881–February 1882): 302–304; and Alexandre Pourcel, "Notes on the Relation of Manganese and Carbon in Iron and Steel," *AIME Transactions* 11 (May 1882–February 1883): 197–201.

order to tell the manufacturers how to produce better rails. Despite Dudley's caveat that his formula was merely a recommendation, rail makers vigorously objected to what they viewed as an unwarranted intrusion by a major railroad into their affairs. Led by the respected Philadelphia manufacturer William Sellers, the steel producers told the railroads to set criteria for desired performance but to leave the details of meeting those criteria up to the manufacturers.[22] Apparently Alexander Holley's vision was not widely shared, for none of these critics acknowledged the potential benefit of combining knowledge of the material with a record of performance in actual service. The AIME remained a long way from establishing standards and providing guidance on how to improve the rails.

Amidst these sometimes impassioned exchanges, a rail inspector by the name of C. P. Sandberg delivered an exhaustive paper that captured the attitudes of most AIME members.[23] Drawing on his extensive experience in American and European mills, Sandberg argued that railroads should obtain rail contracts specifying nothing more than a visual inspection for defects supplemented by a drop test of selected rails and a guarantee against breakage. Sandberg criticized the move for more precise specifications, which he predicted would tie railroads to a few mills willing to follow narrow guidelines, thus limiting competition for contracts and driving up the price of rails. Sandberg singled out Dudley's proposed chemical formula as a specific example. Several manufacturers had refused requests for rails made according to Dudley's formula, Sandberg reported, because they could not produce them with existing equipment.

ENGINEERING EMERGENT: THE BURLINGTON
DURING THE 1880s

Despite this setback, at least some railroads remained undeterred in their efforts to impose greater authority over manufacturers. At the Burlington, Purchasing Agent C. M. Higginson headed a special committee convened by President C. E. Perkins in 1878 to study the matter of steel rails.[24] Higginson had recently taken charge of the new laboratory facilities at the Burlington, and he directed its staff to conduct studies similar to those Dudley was performing at the Pennsylvania. "We have to go a little slow as the mills have had everything their way so long that they are quite independent," Higginson cautioned Perkins when forwarding some preliminary results,

[22] "Discussion on Steel Rails," *AIME Transactions* 9 (May 1880–February 1881): 529–608.

[23] C. P. Sandberg, "Rail Specifications and Rail Inspection in Europe," *AIME Transactions* 9 (May 1880–February 1881): 193–248.

[24] On problems with steel rails at the Burlington, see the report of the company's rail committee, dated September 12, 1878, CBQ Papers, 33 1870 2.2.

"but we are getting ready to tighten our hold."[25] In subsequent months Higginson hired a full-time rail inspector and wrote contracts containing a guarantee against breakage and stipulating that rails be examined for flaws by the Burlington at the mills.[26] The Burlington stopped short of issuing chemical specifications, which in the unchallenged assessment of one of its managers were proving "a delusion and a snare."[27] But Perkins remained committed to the idea of developing some sort of detailed rail specifications and anticipated they would soon be forthcoming. "The time will doubtless come," he wrote Vice-President T. J. Potter in November of 1882, "when the great railroad corporations will require rails to be made to their own specification . . . without guarantee."[28]

Not all of Perkins's subordinates concurred with his assessment or welcomed the prospect. Robert McClure, the company's longtime chief engineer, argued that railroads just needed a way of quickly testing the wearing ability of sample rails before they accepted large orders. Early in 1883, he designed a machine for the purpose and submitted drawings to Perkins for review. General Manager Harlan B. Stone and others in the Burlington hierarchy intervened and convinced Perkins the device would not work.[29] While some of McClure's critics desired to see alternative tests developed, Stone found the entire exercise misguided and superfluous. Expressing a view that likely gave voice to the sentiments of many of his colleagues, Stone insisted railroads could influence manufacturers only by exercising their purchasing power in the marketplace. He recommended "that we treat the makers of [steel rails] in the same way we would treat the makers of any other poor material, viz: not to buy of them until they give us something better."[30]

Disagreements over the potential benefits of rail specifications inevitably became entangled with parallel discussions taking place about the pros and cons of redesigning the shapes of the rails and making them heavier. High-ranking Burlington officials harbored doubts about their rail patterns from the moment Higginson first tackled the subject of rail purchases in 1878. Many among them, including Higginson himself, were tempted to follow the suggestion advanced in the ASCE report of 1876 and shift metal from the flange of the rail into its head. After considerable soul-searching, however, Higginson and Perkins had agreed to continue ordering rails in an older

---

[25] Higginson to Robert Harris, March 5, 1878, CBQ Papers, 3H4.6, and Higginson to Perkins, September 5, 1878, CBQ Papers, 3P4.4.

[26] Potter to Perkins, June 13, 1880, CBQ Papers, 3P6.16; Perkins to Potter, April 8, 1882, CBQ Papers, 3P6.36; and Perkins to Potter, October 5, 1883, CBQ Papers, 3P4.56.

[27] McClure to Potter, June 24, 1884, CBQ Papers, 33 1880 2.61.

[28] Perkins to Potter, November 29, 1882, CBQ Papers, 33 1880 2.61.

[29] McClure to Potter, January 2, 1883; Perkins to Potter, January 28, 1883; McClure to Potter, January 29, 1883; and Stone to Potter, February 15, 1883; CBQ Papers; 33 1880 2.61.

[30] Stone to Potter, July 8, 1884, CBQ Papers, 33 1880 2.61.

pattern they had copied from the Pennsylvania.[31] The Burlington pursued this conservative course and persisted in it for several years in part because experience had convinced railroads and manufacturers that rails made from different sets of rolls required slightly different treatment during manufacturing. To avoid the delays and problems that occurred while manufacturers learned these craft secrets, as well as the added expense mills charged for their trouble, most railroads tended to work with established shapes. But in addition to raising concerns about how mills might react, proposed changes in rail shape also caused considerable consternation among Burlington managers responsible for maintaining track and equipment. Rail joints already constituted probably the single most vexing problem in track maintenance, one which would surely grow worse if the joints involved rails of different shape. To minimize such occurrences, the Burlington would have to install large stretches of the new track instead of replacing individual rails as they broke or wore out. As men from the car departments hastened to point out, moreover, wheel flanges on cars and locomotives might also wear unusually rapidly if they traveled along rails of varying shape.[32]

Together, these considerations pointed to a fundamental and discomforting truth about steel rails. Though seemingly the simplest of technologies, rails in fact formed the central component in a complex and expensive technical system, one which included not only the rails and rolling stock of the railroads but also the massive integrated mills owned and operated by steel makers such as Carnegie. Any changes in the shape of the humble rail reverberated throughout that giant technical complex. As is often the case with potential innovation, the deadening inertia of the system threatened to freeze rail design.

Even in the face of this sizable impediment to change, however, rail executives such as Perkins and his colleagues at the Burlington could not afford to stand pat for long. The mounting volume of traffic simply compelled them to find stronger rails. With no dramatic breakthroughs in the quality of the basic material on the horizon, changing the shape seemed the only avenue available. Early in 1884, Perkins embarked on what would prove to be a decade-long effort to increase the heft of the rail laid in the most heavily used stretches of the Burlington system.

The venture got off to a false start. No sooner had chief engineer McClure begun designing the new sections than several high-ranking CB&Q officials,

[31] Higginson to Perkins, October 4, 1878, CBQ Papers, 33 1870 2.2. In subsequent years the Burlington frequently opted to buy the familiar Pennsylvania Railroad sections. For example, see Perkins to William Irving, December 26, 1885, CBQ Papers, 3P4.1.

[32] An early discussion at the Burlington on the problems with changing sections can be followed in correspondence contained in CBQ Papers, 33 1870 2.2. See, especially, J. D. Besler to Potter, June 9, 1878; Beckwith to Perkins, June 11, 1878; Besler to Potter, June 29 and August 2, 1878; Higginson to Potter, September 13, 1878; and Higginson to Perkins, October 4, 1878.

including at least one member of the board of directors, questioned the wisdom of putting more metal into each yard of rail so long as doubts persisted about the basic quality of the steel coming from the mills.[33] They suggested Perkins let steel manufacturers work out their problems with the material before burdening them with unfamiliar sections. Apparently heeding their advice, Perkins moved more deliberately, dispatching McClure to England to gather information about specifications, sections, joints, and prices.[34] This move appeared especially prescient when a sudden rash of crushed rails seriously disrupted service on the Burlington's lines in January 1885. As exasperated managers hurriedly traced the failures to a recent batch of rails from Andrew Carnegie's Edgar Thomson works, Perkins at Stone's encouragement ordered 10,000 tons of steel rails from an English mill.[35] This purchase no doubt helped Perkins negotiate a settlement with Carnegie, who after lengthy discussions and many visits from Burlington personnel, reluctantly agreed to replace the rails. The negotiations dragged on because Carnegie, concerned about maintaining the reputation of his product, insisted the formal settlement contain a clause explaining that an error in processing, not an inherent problem with the raw material, had produced the faulty rails.[36]

The Burlington emerged from this crisis with a new perspective on what Perkins had come to call "the steel rail conundrum." Ironically, managers at the railroad had grown more sympathetic to the plight of the manufacturers. "Our people were badly frightened last year about American rail," Burlington vice president T. J. Potter admitted to Perkins when reflecting on the hectic events in July 1886. "While the rail that Carnegie sold the CB&Q was not good, it was not so bad as Stone and Merrill thought it was."[37] Even General Manager Stone, while continuing to advocate that the Burlington exercise its purchasing power to influence manufactures, exhibited at least some inkling toward conciliation. While Stone credited the decision to purchase foreign rails with "stirring up the American steel makers," he advised that subsequent orders be placed with American mills.[38]

33 Chas. J. Paine to Perkins, April 16, 1884; Perkins to Potter, April 22, 1884; and Perkins to Paine, April 22, 1884; CBQ Papers, 33 1880 2.61.
34 Perkins to McClure, October 21, 1884, CBQ Papers, 3P6.36, and Perkins to Potter, December 11, 1884, CBQ Papers, 3P4.1.
35 Potter to Perkins, March 20, 1885, CBQ Papers, 3P4.56; Perkins to Potter, April 7, 1885, CBQ Papers, 3P4.1; Stone to Potter, April 8, 1885, and Potter to Perkins, April 15, 1885, CBQ Papers, 33 1880 2.62; Perkins to Potter, May 12, 1885, CBQ Papers, 3P4.1; Potter to Perkins, May 26, 1885, CBQ Papers, 3P4.56; and Perkins to T. S. Howland, October 31, 1885; Perkins to John L. Gardner, October 31, 1885; Gardner to Naylor & Co., November 9 and 10, 1885; CBQ Papers; 33 1880 2.62.
36 Wirt Dexter to Perkins, April 11, 1885, and Potter to Perkins, April 13, 1885, CBQ Papers, 33 1880 2.62.
37 Potter to Perkins, July 23, 1886, CBQ Papers, 33 1880 2.62.
38 Stone to Potter, July 21, 1886, CBQ Papers, 33 1880 2.62.

Beyond their renewed commitment to doing business with domestic suppliers, Burlington managers possessed newfound appreciation for the value of linking knowledge of the manufacturing process with the performance and design of steel rails. Perkins signaled as much when in early 1887 he assigned responsibility for studying the rail situation and devising new sections to a young engineer by the name of Frederic A. Delano.[39] In contrast to McClure, who had worked his way up through the maintenance of way department and acquired a thorough hands-on knowledge of railroading, Delano had recently come to the Burlington straight from college. His career at the railroad has many hallmarks of a golden boy. Right from the start, Perkins took an unusually close personal interest in his progress, making sure Delano received a special appointment in the prestigious drafting room. Later, Perkins would place Delano in charge of reorganizing the company's vast Chicago stockyards. Early in the twentieth century, Delano would become the Burlington's superintendent of motive power.[40]

Delano approached the rail problem in dramatically different fashion than McClure, who continued to work on his own sections. When McClure thought about changing the rails, he worried primarily about fitting the new designs into the existing system of railroad operations he had developed through years of service to the Burlington.[41] He solicited opinion from subordinates who dealt with track maintenance and repair on a daily basis about what shape they preferred. When they complained that past changes in section had caused wheel flanges to wear rapidly, McClure focused much of his attention on the interaction of the car and locomotive wheels with the rails. When he looked for guidance from outside the Burlington, McClure turned naturally to the ASCE, which had traditionally approached the rail question as a structural problem rather than a chemical or metallurgical one. During the period McClure worked on his sections, the ASCE had embarked on an ambitious study of rail and flange wear. Reacting to criticism voiced in 1883 at the Master Car-Builders Association that new rail shapes caused wheels to wear unacceptably fast, the ASCE formed a committee in 1885 to study the matter. Over the course of the next several years, this group solicited unprecedentedly extensive, detailed records on the subject

[39] Perkins to Potter, September 18, 1885, CBQ Papers, 33 1880 2.63; T. S. Howland to Delano, February 10, 1887, CBQ Papers, 3P4.1; and Perkins to Stone, December 7, 1887, CBQ Papers, 3P4.1.

[40] On Delano's career with the CBQ and Perkins's personal interest in it, see Potter to Perkins, December 8, 1886; CBQ 3P4.56; Perkins to Potter, July 14, 1886; Perkins to Stone, April 26, 1889, January 8 and 27, 1890; and Perkins to G. Harris, May 5, 1892; CBQ 3P4.1; and G. Harris to Howland, June 21 and 24, 1901; CBQ 3P4.51.

[41] McClure's approach to the rail question can be followed in great detail in the correspondence contained in CBQ Papers, 33 1880 2.63. See especially his report of January 10, 1887, and the response from his colleagues.

from railroad trackmen throughout the country.[42] It also published several technical papers examining the complex dynamics between wheel and rail, a subject that captivated the theoretically inclined engineers who increasingly populated the ASCE and other engineering societies. Though McClure appears not to have contributed directly to this literature, his sections reflected the long-standing ASCE preference for thickening the rail head.

Delano drew his inspiration from entirely different sources. Paying little or no heed to the scattered testimony of experienced trackmen, he reviewed all available statistical evidence on the life of steel rails and made extensive use of laboratory tests of rails. These included not only the bending tests and chemical analyses pioneered a decade before at the Pennsylvania, but newer techniques of metallography, which used chemical etchings of cross-sections to reveal the fine metallic structure of broken rails. Delano learned of such techniques by reading extensively in the technical literature, especially that developed by metallurgists in the AIME, to whom he would present papers in 1888 and 1889.[43] Above all, Delano heeded the concerns of manufacturers. For several months before sitting down to the drafting table, he visited rail mills in the Chicago area almost daily.[44]

Approaching the rail problem in this way, Delano came to focus upon elements that hardly concerned McClure. Likely inspired by the work of metallurgists such as William Metcalf, who in a "classical" paper read before the AIME in 1887 had surveyed the known relations between raw materials, manufacturing techniques, and the performance of metals, Delano concentrated on designing sections that manufacturers could produce reliably using conventional methods.[45] Delano had become convinced that years of following the ASCE recommendations had created rails with so much metal in their heads that manufacturers could not provide the "working" necessary to make the metal homogenous. The heavy rails crumbled and flaked because the metal in their heads contained coarse pockets. Delano redistributed metal from the head to other parts of the rail and also made the

---

[42]   On the efforts of the MCBA and the ASCE on the issue of wheel wear, see "Preliminary Report on the Committee on the Proper Relation to Each Other of the Sections of Wheels and Rails," *ASCE Transactions* 19 (July–December 1888): 1–54, and "Final Report of the Committee on the Proper Relation to Each Other of the Sections of Wheels and Rails," *ASCE Transactions* 21 (July–December 1889): 223–302.

[43]   Perkins to Stone, January 3, 1888, CBQ Papers, 3P4.1; Frederic A. Delano, "Certain Conditions in the Manufacture of Steel Rails, Which May Greatly Influence Their Life in Service," *AIME Transactions* 16 (May 1887–February 1888): 594–601; and Frederic A. Delano, "Rail-Sections," *AIME Transactions* 17 (May 1888–February 1889): 421–426.

[44]   Information on Delano's activities comes from CBQ Papers, 3H5.24.

[45]   William Metcalf, "Steel; Its Properties; Its Use in Structures and Heavy Guns," *ASCE Transactions* 16 (1887): 283. Robert W. Hunt, a central figure in rail technology discussed below, reflected on the significance of Metcalf's paper to the rail industry in his "Finishing Temperatures for Steel Rails," *AIME Transactions* 31 (1901): 458–465.

head wider, producing sections of dramatically thinner profile than prevailing designs such as those advocated by McClure.[46]

Like Charles Dudley a decade earlier, Delano in his attempt to bridge the gap between railroads and steel makers had produced a radical departure from accepted practice. And like Dudley, he met with mixed success at best. The competing designs of Delano and McClure left the Burlington's Perkins in a pinch. Anxious to substitute new 85-pound rails for the existing 66-pound rail in his busiest tracks but disturbed by the obvious discrepancies between the two designs, Perkins circulated the blueprints among his subordinates during fall 1888. Predictably, middle management split over the two sets of standards. Younger engineers such as those in the laboratory and the drafting room generally preferred Delano's designs, while managers who had risen from the ranks of practical trackmen sympathized with McClure's concerns about wheel and flange wear.[47] Though reluctant to go against the advice of his chief engineer, Perkins in summer 1889 ordered 6,000 tons of rails in Delano's 85-pound pattern and several thousand tons of lighter-weight rails in Delano's sections.[48] Less than half a year later, the Burlington backed hastily away from this course. When the broad heads of Delano's rails apparently caused wheels to wear unusually fast, Perkins agreed to conduct a trial to ascertain the comparative wearing properties of the two designs.[49] Burlington managers soon concluded that any orders in the near term would have to call for McClure's section and that future purchases of any significant quantity would likely stipulate an entirely different design.[50]

Despite the disappointing initial results, the approach to the steel rail conundrum that Delano embodied had gained considerable favor with Perkins and many other executives at the Burlington and elsewhere in the railroad industry. Perkins not only chose Delano's sections over those of his chief engineer. He also established a Bureau of Rail and Rail-Joint Inspection, Tests and Records and appointed Delano to the post of chief rail inspector.[51] When transferring Delano from the rail inspection bureau to another trouble spot, Perkins reaffirmed his commitment to the policy of purchasing rails according to specifications. "It is of the greatest importance," he wrote Vice-President George Harris, "that we should not allow any ground we

[46] Delano described his rail sections to the AIME in Delano, "Certain Conditions in the Manufacture of Steel Rails" and "Rail-Sections."

[47] For response to the proposed sections, see CBQ Papers, 3H5.24.

[48] Perkins to Stone, July 29, 1889; Perkins to McClure, August 2, 1889; and Perkins to Irving, August 2, 1889; CBQ Papers; 3P4.1.

[49] Stone to Irving, January 20, 1890, CBQ Papers, 3H5.24.

[50] Harris to Perkins, September 11, 1891, CBQ Papers, 3P4.51; Harris to Merrill, February 16, 1892; Merrill to Harris, February 17, 1892; and Harris to Perkins, February 20, 1892; CBQ Papers; 3P4.51; and Perkins to Harris, February 23, 1892, CBQ Papers, 3P4.58.

[51] On Delano's appointment as chief rail inspector, see Stone to Delano, November 15, 1888, CBQ Papers, 3H5.24.

have gained in this rail problem to be lost." Harris immediately arranged for C. M. Higginson to continue Delano's work.[52]

Delano's efforts also met with a favorable response in the broader engineering community. His papers before the AIME complemented studies conducted by several other highly respected figures. P. H. Dudley, who with his pioneering use of the dynograph car had established a reputation as a fine analytical railroad engineer, presented a paper at about the same time describing rail sections he had recently designed for the New York Central.[53] Like Delano, Dudley focused on the inadequate working of the metal in the head of the rail. Another influential figure, Robert W. Hunt, praised the efforts of Dudley and Delano.[54] Hunt operated the most widely respected of the consulting firms that inspected rails at the mills for various railroads. He, too, had come to appreciate the importance of matching rail design with manufacturing techniques. Hunt drew connections between analyses of rails and the findings of William Metcalf and researchers who had studied structural steel and other products with applications outside the railroad industry. Their results, like those of Delano, all pointed toward the working of the metal as a key to performance.[55] If Delano and other analysts and engineers employed by railroads had not yet quite fully succeeded in designing a better rail, then at least they had taken large strides toward organizing a broad research effort around key technical factors. In the process, they

---

[52] Perkins to Delano, July 8, 1890, CBQ Papers, 3P4.1; Perkins to Harris, July 8, 1890; Harris to Perkins, July 10, 1890; and Perkins to Harris, October 2, 1890; CBQ Papers; 3P4.58.

[53] P. H. Dudley, "The Wear of Rails as Related to Their Section," *AIME Transactions* 18 (May 1889–February 1890): 228–242, and P. H. Dudley, "A System of Rail-Sections in Series," *AIME Transactions* 18 (May 1889–February 1890): 763–798.

[54] Robert W. Hunt, "Proposed Rail Sections," *AIME Transactions* 17 (May 1888–February 1889): 778–785, and Hunt, "Specifications for Steel Rails of Heavy Sections Manufactured West of the Alleghenies," *AIME Transactions* 25 (February 1895–October 1895): 653–660.

[55] In addition, metallurgists and others had begun to understand the significance of Sorby's microscopic analysis of the structure of steel. This understanding came about only when rail users familiarized themselves with production. James C. Baylor, "Microscopic Analysis of the Structure of Iron and Steel," *AIME Transactions* 11 (May 1882–February 1883): 261–274; F. Lynwood Garrison, "The Microscopic Structure of Car-Wheel Iron," *AIME Transactions* 14 (June 1885–May 1886): 913–919; and Garrison, "Microscopic Structure of Steel Rails," *AIME Transactions* 15 (May 1886–February 1887): 761–767. On later microscopic investigations of steel rails, see James E. Howard, "Some Results of the Tests of Steel Rails in Progress at Watertown Arsenal," *Proceedings of the American Society for Testing Materials* (henceforth, *ASTM Proceedings*) 8 (1908): 53–73; Henry Fay, "A Microscopic Investigation of Broken Steel Rails: Manganese as a Source of Danger," *ASTM Proceedings* 8 (1908): 73–93; and Howard, "Strength and Endurance of Steel Rails," *Proceedings of the American Railways Engineering and Maintenance of Way Association* (henceforth, *AREMWA Proceedings*) 9 (1908): 109–127. For a modern metallurgist's analysis of metallurgy in the late nineteenth century, see Smith, *A History of Metallography*.

had gained the confidence of their employers and the attention of the steel mills.

INDUSTRY-WIDE STANDARDS

As a community of investigators coalesced around the issue of providing sufficient working of the metal, the primary locus of action on rails shifted from individual lines to engineering societies and other intermediaries. Men such as Robert Hunt assumed an especially prominent role in spearheading a drive to create industry-wide specifications for rails. Unlike Delano and P. H. Dudley, who each represented the interests of a particular railroad, Hunt and the handful of consulting rail inspectors occupied a true intermediary position between railroads and the steel producers. Working full-time on the rail problem and spending most of their time at the mills, these consultants gained the respect of producers as well as consumers. In the eyes of many engineers, Hunt and his brethren represented a new ideal: the independent expert devoted to solving a technical problem to the benefit of all parties. Such men provided a mechanism for establishing standards that was previously lacking.[56]

Hunt at first moved guardedly into the arena of standards-setting. When Delano and Dudley presented their designs, he joined the chorus lamenting the opportunities engineers had squandered over the years to promote specifications, but expressed doubts about the possibility of establishing standard rail sections anytime soon. Hunt refused to offer his own designs as a basis for discussion. His attitude changed, however, as the ASCE committee investigating wheel and flange wear began issuing its findings. At long last, engineers now had available a large body of data systematically documenting the performance of various rails in actual service, evidence of a sort Delano and others had previously found lacking for want of adequate controls.[57] To its surprise, moreover, the ASCE committee detected widespread agreement among railroads about the proper shape of rails.[58] Even steel producers

---

[56] On the rise of consulting engineers, see Monte Calvert, *The Mechanical Engineer in America, 1830–1910: Professional Cultures in Conflict* (Baltimore: Johns Hopkins University Press, 1967). On the growth of standards-setting among professional engineers, see Bruce Sinclair, *Centennial History of the American Society of Mechanical Engineers, 1880–1980* (Toronto: University of Toronto Press, 1980).

[57] On the efforts of the MCBA and the ASCE regarding the issue of wheel wear, see "Preliminary Report on the Committee on the Proper Relation to Each Other of the Sections of Wheels and Rails," *ASCE Transactions* 19 (July–December 1888): 1–54, and "Final Report of the Committee on the Proper Relation to Each Other of the Sections of Wheels and Rails," *ASCE Transactions* 21 (July–December 1889): 223–302; and Delano, "Certain Conditions in the Manufacture of Steel Rails," p. 599.

[58] On the movement of the ASCE to establish standards, see "Progress Report of the Committee on Standard Rail Sections," *ASCE Transactions* 24 (January–June 1891): 1–12.

now conceded that standard rail sections might offer some advantages. By concentrating on a few shapes, a representative from Carnegie told the assembled engineers at a meeting of the ASCE in 1889, manufacturers could better control inventory and distribute production more evenly.[59]

When the newly invigorated ASCE committee regrouped with the express goal of establishing rail specifications, Hunt rose to lead the effort. He returned to the AIME in 1889 to offer his designs for consideration, and shortly thereafter the ASCE appointed him to its rail committee.[60] Within months, he had become its secretary. This assignment placed Hunt at the center of an emerging network of expertise about rails, and during the next few years he used his appointment as a platform for coordinating the flow of information among railroads and steel producers about preferred shapes and methods of manufacture. His committee report, issued early in 1893, contained sections for rails of several different weights and offered general advice pertaining to manufacturing procedures.[61] Two years later, Hunt proposed adding chemical guidelines and a stipulation requiring that all batches of rails satisfy a drop test. Clauses to this effect were soon appended to the specifications.[62]

Though official policy prohibited the ASCE from openly sanctioning specific technical advice, the rail sections and the guidelines for manufacture contained in these committee reports rapidly acquired the status of industry-wide standards. At the Burlington, for instance, Perkins reoriented his policies regarding rails almost as soon as Hunt began tackling the rail issue for the ASCE. The Burlington turned responsibility for rail inspections over to outside consulting services and postponed further purchases of new sections until Hunt's committee issued its report. Perkins then chose the ASCE 75-pound section as a compromise between the old 66-pound rail and the proposed 85-pound sections of McClure and Delano, while also ordering rails made in the ASCE's 65-pound section to replace the 66-pound rail used in the Burlington's lesser-used Western tracks.[63] So many other lines followed suit that by 1895 Hunt could crow that the shapes prescribed by his

---

59 See comments of William R. Jones in response to the final report of the ASCE committee on wheel wear, *ASCE Transactions* 21 (July–December 1889): 279–280.

60 Robert W. Hunt, "Steel Rails, and Specifications for Their Manufacture," *AIME Transactions* 17 (May 1888–February 1889): 226–248, and Robert W. Hunt, "Proposed Rail-Sections," *AIME Transactions* 17 (May 1888–February 1889): 778–785.

61 "Final Report of the Committee on Standard Rail-Sections," *ASCE Transactions* 28 (January–June 1893): 425–444.

62 Robert W. Hunt, "Specifications for Steel Rails of Heavy Sections Manufactured West of the Alleghenies," *AIME Transactions* 25 (February–October 1895): 653–660, provides information on the details of the ASCE standard sections and these revisions.

63 G. Harris to Perkins, October 3, 1890; Harris to Perkins, September 12, 1893; G. Harris to Perkins, January 3, 1893; and Harris to Perkins, January 15, 1895; CBQ Papers; 3P4.51; Perkins to George Harris, March 10, 1893, CBQ Papers, 3P4.58; and Perkins to Besler, January 3, 1898, and Besler to Perkins, January 4, 1898, CBQ Papers, 3P4.91.

committee "have been largely adopted already by the railroads of the country, and promise soon to be absolutely the standard American sections."[64] By 1901, some 84 of 128 railroads surveyed by the AIME purchased rails of ASCE design.[65] The same survey indicated that three quarters of the rails produced by several major manufacturers, including Carnegie, met ASCE specifications. A few mills that supplied primarily the Pennsylvania, the New York Central, and other Eastern carriers who issued their own specifications produced less than half of their total output in the ASCE sections.[66] But outside the Northeast, the ASCE sections reigned supreme. Even the Pennsylvania's own Lines West of Pittsburgh preferred the ASCE sections.

While publication of the ASCE sections and guidelines regarding manufacturing marked a significant watershed in the development of rail standards, Hunt's committee skirted some critically important issues. As a series of recommendations not even officially sanctioned by the association, the guidelines regarding chemical composition, manufacturing procedures, and sample testing lacked teeth. In many cases, mills and railroads that claimed to be observing the ASCE standards in reality made use only of the sections, while not rigidly following the suggestions regarding manufacturing.[67] With the financial constraints imposed by the panic encouraging railroads to focus on low price rather than high quality, most lines picked selectively from among the recommendations, incorporating only certain provisions into their contracts.[68]

In at least one vitally important matter, moreover, the ASCE offered no guidance whatsoever. As metallurgists developed a firmer and fuller understanding of the relations between manufacturing and performance, they began to recognize that the temperature at which metal was worked, not just the extent of the working, dramatically affected the quality of steel.[69] To obtain the fine-grained metallic structure necessary for strength and durability, many analysts suspected, manufacturers needed to roll rails at lower temperature during the final stages of processing. Providing for cooler rolling posed little difficulty in the case of lightweight rails, because their

---

[64] Hunt, "Specifications for Steel Rails of Heavy Sections Manufactured West of the Alleghenies," p. 654. See also Hunt's comments in *AREMWA Proceedings* 1 (1900): 125.

[65] *AREMWA Proceedings* 2 (1901): 189.

[66] William R. Webster, "The Present Situation as to Specifications for Steel Rails," *AIME Transactions* 33 (1902): 164–170.

[67] Discussion of the Committee on Rail, *AREMWA Proceedings* 6 (1905): 188–189, and 7 (1906): 566–567.

[68] *ASTM Proceedings* 1, no. 11 (May 1900): 101–105, and Robert W. Hunt, "Brief Note on Rail Specifications," *AIME Transactions* 27 (February–July 1897): 139–141.

[69] The role of temperature in determining the quality of the rails was first put on public record by a manufacturer, John W. Cabot of the Bessemer Steel Company, in his paper "The Influence of Temperature in Steel-Making on the Behavior of the Ingots in Rolling," *AIME Transactions* 14 (June 1885–May 1886): 84–88.

temperature fell in the normal course of processing as they moved from the furnace to the final roll. Heavier rails, however, retained more heat and did not cool adequately. As economizing mill operators speeded up the manufacturing process, moreover, they reduced the temperature drop still further.[70]

The issue of finishing temperature held the potential to spark disputes between railroads and steel makers far more acrimonious than those provoked by earlier matters such as changing the shape of rail. In redesigning their sections to ensure adequate working of the metal in the head, Delano and others had operated largely within the framework of existing manufacturing techniques. Manufacturers attempting to produce rails in the new forms needed only to replace the rolls in their equipment and to learn tricks for dealing with the problems that inevitably accompanied new rolls. In seeking to obtain rails rolled at lower temperature, railroads proposed to interfere more substantially in affairs at the mills. Cost-conscious manufacturers had constructed tightly integrated plants in which rails moved quickly through a virtually continuous series of rollers. They could not finish heavier rails at cooler temperatures without slowing down production or altering their plants in ways that allowed rails to rest between passes through the rollers. Not surprisingly, mills insisted on charging a premium for such service. Producers and consumers of heavy rails thus found themselves at loggerheads, with railroads unable to obtain the change they desired without mills incurring substantial increases in cost.[71]

The issue of finishing temperature abated for most of the 1890s while hard times forced railroads to buy light rails or have their original steel rerolled. The Burlington, for instance, received a lukewarm response when it asked producers to finish its experimental 85-pound rails at cooler temperatures, but the dispute passed when Perkins switched to 75-pound rails.[72] Meanwhile, experiences with rerolled steel rails added to the mounting body of evidence in favor of lower finishing temperatures. During rerolling, rails were shaved, heated, and put through the finishing steps again. In an effort to save fuel, companies that specialized in this highly competitive trade experimented with heating the rails as little as possible. Not only did their success demonstrate that rails could be rolled at cooler temperatures; the resulting product also seemed to break considerably less often than new heavier rails finished at higher temperature.[73]

---

[70] Hunt, "Finishing Temperatures."

[71] For a perceptive retrospective analysis of the conflicts between manufacturers and railroads on this issue, see the letter from Thomas H. Johnson to William R. Webster, published in *AREMWA Proceedings* 6 (1905): 177–178.

[72] Stone to Irving, January 20, 1890, CBQ Papers, 3H5.24; Perkins to G. Harris, September 9 and 26, 1891; January 5 and March 10, 1893; CBQ Papers, 3P4.58; and G. Harris to Perkins, September 11, 1891, CBQ Papers, 3P4.51.

[73] Hunt, "Finishing Temperatures," and comments by George B. Woodworth, *AIME Transactions* 31 (1901): 970.

When prosperity returned toward the end of the century and railroads sought heavier rails in larger quantities, the temperature question burst dramatically to the fore. A rash of rail failures swept through the industry beginning in 1899, as the heavy new rails crumbled under the strain of unprecedented traffic volume.[74] Leading producers and consumers scrambled to get a grip on the problems. Carnegie and a few other manufacturers reluctantly experimented with letting the rails cool slightly before sending them through the rolls a final time. Railroads liked the results but still balked at the idea of paying a premium price for what mills deemed special treatment.[75] The Pennsylvania, which in 1898 had embarked on a major program of capital improvements calling for large purchases of heavy rails, pressed forward with an effort to require mills to finish the new rails at lower heat. The railroad's chief rail inspector, E. F. Kenney, visited the Cambria mills in search of a means of ensuring that rails were finished at what he considered the proper temperature. Unable to ascertain the temperature of the metal inside the head directly during manufacture, Kenney settled instead upon periodically measuring the overall length of the rails, which shrank as they cooled. Working with the manufacturers, Kenney devised a schedule prescribing the amounts mills should allow rails of each shape to shrink before final passage through the rolls.[76] In 1901, the Pennsylvania introduced a "shrinkage clause" into its rail contracts, and at least one other company pressed to incorporate the requirement into its contracts as well.[77]

As individual firms sought to gain control of the situation, engineers in the ASCE and other public forums struggled to provide guidance for the industry as a whole. As before, Hunt and fellow consulting rail inspectors such as William R. Webster took the lead in trying to steer a course between railroads and the steel makers. The task looked daunting, for in addition to wrestling with the volatile issue of finishing temperature, these men would have to negotiate a terrain that had grown considerably more cluttered with engineering organizations. In addition to the AIME and the ASCE, two newly formed technical societies had staked a claim on the process of establishing rail specifications. The American Society for Testing Materials (ASTM), a group dedicated to setting standards for all sorts of industrial products, formed a committee on rails at the time of its founding in 1899. A year later, railroad engineers responsible for track construction and maintenance congregated in the new American Railroad Engineering and Maintenance of Way Association (AREMWA). A committee of its members immediately set about drawing up rail specifications as well.

74 Report of the Committee on Rails, *AREMWA Transactions* 1 (1900): 117–118.
75 Comments of William R. Webster, *AIME Transactions* 31 (1901): 971; comments of Robert Trimble, *AREMWA Proceedings* 2 (1901): 200; and Hunt, "Finishing Temperatures," pp. 461–464.
76 *ASTM Proceedings* 2 (1902): 95.
77 Comments of C. S. Churchill, *AREMWA Proceedings* 2 (1901): 188–218.

While ostensibly committed to fostering the sort of collaboration necessary for reaching consensus standards, these upstarts actually threatened to
undermine the delicate mechanisms men like Hunt and Webster had nur-
tured during the previous decade. The ASTM committee on rails quickly
gained a reputation as a bastion of manufacturers. Though Webster chaired
the group and Hunt also served, three representatives from steel companies
comprised the majority.[78] Ignoring the pressing problems with heavier sections, the committee initially adopted specifications that differed little from
the 1893 recommendations of the ASCE. The ASTM guidelines did not even
include clauses pertaining to chemical composition and the drop test. An indignant Hunt left the committee within a year of his appointment, declaring
that an organization so dominated by manufacturers should not set national
standards.

AREMWA initially seemed no more likely a candidate to assume the role
of neutral arbiter and standard-setter. Dominated by individuals employed
by railroads, the association engaged the standards issue largely out of a perceived need to combat the producers and counter the ASTM.[79] Convinced
that the ASCE guidelines carried inadequate force, AREMWA members resolved that their standards should be more than a collection of technical
recommendations from which railroads could pick and choose at will. They
looked for standards to express shared goals that all members would insist
upon when negotiating with producers. Only by acting in concert could railroads successfully match the bargaining power of the mills, especially now
that major producers had consolidated to form the enormous United States
Steel Corporation.[80]

During the opening years of the new century, men such as Webster and
Hunt scrambled to suppress the obvious biases in these new organizations
and to restore a climate stressing cooperation rather than confrontation. The
consulting rail inspectors shared the prevailing opinion within AREMWA
that standards should express more than mere guidelines, and they also
firmly believed those standards must address the touchy issues regarding
temperature and methods of manufacture. These stances enabled both Hunt
and Webster to secure appointments to the AREMWA committee on rails,
with the latter serving as chair despite his continuing association with the
ASTM. Webster moved quickly to temper the more extreme elements of the
AREMWA committee, which consisted primarily of rail inspectors employed
by railroads, and steered the group toward the intermediary role previously
cultivated by the established engineering societies. As soon as the AREMWA
began discussing rail specifications, Webster wrote to the ASCE proposing

[78] *ASTM Proceedings* 1, no. 6 (November 1899): 60–61.
[79] Hunt, "Finishing Temperatures," and *AREMWA Proceedings* 2 (1901): 188–218.
[80] Report of the Committee on Rails, *AREMWA Proceedings* 1 (1900): 112–133, pro-
      vides a clear explanation of the association's view of specifications.

it form a committee to revisit its own recommendations. The civil engineers not only approved the idea; they appointed Webster to the committee. This coup helped Webster supplant the belligerent posturing of an interest group with the dispassionate aura of a community of engineering experts. Working in alliance with the ASCE, the AREMWA committee methodically gathered data on the performance of rails built to ASCE guidelines and systematically investigated the troubles with heavy rails. It paid particular attention to a recent paper by Hunt and to Kenney's ongoing work for the Pennsylvania Railroad regarding proper finishing temperatures. By 1903, AREMWA had formally approved rail standards covering the familiar territory of the ASCE recommendations and also incorporating the Pennsylvania's shrinkage clause.[81]

Securing the support of the ASTM and the manufacturers posed a stiffer challenge. Pursuing a parallel strategy to that which served him so effectively among railroaders, Webster attempted to build a bridge between the established professional engineering community and the more cantankerous industrial interests who formed the ASTM. In 1901, he appeared before the AIME and urged the institute to take an active role in advising the ASTM and other groups engaged in drawing specifications for rails and other metallurgical products. The following year he convinced the AIME to support AREMWA's proposed specifications regarding the temperature at rolling. Webster reported that he had already received favorable comments from members of the ASCE rail committee about the proposed changes, and he predicted the ASTM would go along when its committee on rails met to review the standards in late 1902.[82]

Webster's confidence in gaining ASTM approval reflected a significant change in the membership and orientation of that organization. Though manufacturers retained considerable influence within the society, representatives of consumers had come to share power. In a gesture that spoke volumes about the new mood, none other than Charles Benjamin Dudley of the Pennsylvania Railroad had assumed the presidency of the ASTM in early 1902. A veteran of over a quarter-century of service to the railroads and a recent past president of the American Chemical Society, Dudley had overcome his early embarrassment in advocating soft rails to become an avowed authority on the practice of purchasing according to specifications. During his four consecutive two-year terms as its president, Dudley would launch the ASTM well on its way to becoming the preeminent body for industrial standards in the United States. The rail issue, a matter of personal interest as well

[81] Reports of the Committee on Rails, *AREMWA Proceedings* 1 (1900): 112–133, and 2 (1901): 188–218.

[82] William R. Webster, "Specifications for Steel Rails," *AIME Transactions* 31 (1901): 449–458, and Webster, "The Present Situation as to Specifications for Steel Rails," *AIME Transactions* 33 (1902): 164–170.

as high visibility and large financial stakes, figured prominently in those efforts. Under his leadership, the ASTM committee on rails rapidly acquired a
balance of interests that gave it new respect as a forum for standards-setting,
as some of the manufacturers relinquished their posts to representatives from
railroads.[83]

The revamped committee quickly reached consensus on the matters of rail
sections, chemical formulae, and drop tests for breakage. Everyone agreed
that the key questions now involved heat treatment during manufacture
and the structure of the metal. Convinced that high finishing temperatures
had caused the rash of failures of heavy rails, representatives from railroads
pushed hard to incorporate the shrinkage clause into the ASTM specifications. Manufacturers resisted. Some objected on practical grounds, questioning whether shrinkage accurately reflected temperature or claiming that
allowances appropriate for conditions at one mill might be impossible to obtain at another where the rolls were closer together.[84] Others looked past the
details and raised doubts about the very idea of prescribing new methods of
manufacture in an industry-wide standard. Representatives from Carnegie
and from Maryland Steel asserted that such specifications should merely codify "standard practice," not compel adoption of novel practices such as waiting for the rails to shrink. Manufacturers did not mind complying with a new
specification put forth by an individual railroad, such as Kenney's requests
regarding finishing temperature, because "when the Pennsylvania Railroad
makes a mistake, the inspector lets it hang up in the air, while he takes his
rails, for the power that wrote the specification can modify it on a moment's
notice." But an organization such as the ASTM was obliged to move cau-
tiously and avoid mistakes, because "when we as a society...proclaim a
certain shrinkage clause, we cannot modify it without long debate and the
lapse of many months."[85] Representatives from the railroads dismissed this
conservative stance and embraced the proposed specifications as a mechanism for promoting engineered improvement of rails. "If we do not specify
a colder treatment for rails, how are we engineers going to get rails finished
that way," asked Kenney, "and if we do not get them, how are we to obtain
any information as to their wear?"[86]

These exchanges, characteristic of an approach to technical change that
had taken firm hold in the rail industry of the early twentieth century, resulted in yet another compromise. The ASTM committee agreed to table
the proposal and delay incorporating the AREMWA specifications into its
own standards until manufacturers had gained more experience with the
shrinkage clause. Three years later, a subcommittee consisting primarily of

[83] The changing character of the ASTM and its committee on rails can be followed in
      ASTM Proceedings.
[84] "Discussion of Proposed AREMWA Standards," *ASTM Proceedings* 2 (1902): 23–49.
[85] Comments of H. H. Campbell, *ASTM Proceedings* 2 (1902): 95.
[86] Comments of E. F. Kenney, *ASTM Proceedings* 2 (1902): 93.

representatives of the Pennsylvania Railroad and two major steel producers convened to reconsider the proposal, and in 1906 the ASTM incorporated a shrinkage clause into its specifications. Though the ASTM persisted in giving individual manufacturers greater leeway in handling the material and letting the rails cool, this move brought the various industry-wide standards into close agreement. Except for some minor variations in chemical formulae, the ASCE standards duplicated those of the AREMWA, and all three sets contained the same basic elements.[87] Webster and Hunt moved freely among the groups, stressing the common ground and urging the societies to resolve the few remaining differences.[88] All parties understood that contracts for rails would incorporate detailed specifications similar to those published by these national institutions, and that any proposed changes in rail design or manufacture would undergo close scrutiny by engineers in those forums.

SYSTEMATIZING INNOVATION

In developing the means to refine steel rails through negotiated standards, railroads of the late nineteenth century adapted the process of technological innovation to a business environment characterized by large corporations operating expensive, established technological systems. Railroads poured resources into the rail problem because stronger, more durable rails offered them a ready avenue for improving the carrying capacity of their systems without drastically altering the configuration of those systems. To a greater degree than with any previous innovation, railroads utilized controlled testing by engineers and other analytical techniques for facilitating incremental change. In the course of these efforts, railroads came to realize that the production of improved rails also depended on the technological systems of the rail manufacturers. They developed a process for setting specifications that facilitated cooperation between producers and consumers and enabled engineers from railroads and from suppliers of steel rails to focus intensively on the problems of working out changes within the constraints of existing practice.

The development of industry-wide standards did not completely eliminate the haggling that had long characterized the annual purchases of rails. Nor did the practice of drafting industry-wide technical specifications reduce negotiations between mills and railroads strictly to mere matters of price. Specific contracts often compromised various provisions of the standards in order to accommodate conditions at a particular mill or the

---

[87] *ASTM Proceedings*, 1902–1906.

[88] Discussion of the Committee on Rail, *AREMWA Proceedings* 7 (1906): 572, and Report of the Committee on Rail, *AREMWA Proceedings* 9 (1908): 431.

pocketbook of an individual railroad.[89] Inspectors at the mills, facing urgent and unanticipated circumstances, sometimes looked the other way. Changes in industry-wide standards, moreover, continued to reflect the experiences of large companies who pressed against the technical frontiers and exercised their purchasing clout to gain concessions that most railroads could not attain. The engineering societies decided upon a standard 100-pound rail section, for example, only after the Pennsylvania had established specifications for rails of that weight.[90] When problems arose with those sections, as discussed in more detail in Chapter 9, the Pennsylvania in a moment of crisis even threatened briefly to abandon its specifications entirely and return to a system in which mills supplied rails as they saw fit and took responsibility for the consequences.

Still, railroads and steel producers had by the turn of the twentieth century constructed a new framework that buffered engineering experts from the market and left them free to address technical problems. Producers and consumers had familiarized themselves with all aspects of rail production and use and had established clear areas of agreement and dispute. As a result, manufacturers and consumers confronted problems such as those with heavy sections more quickly than they otherwise would have. The principal engineering societies all issued standard sections for 100-pound rails shortly after the first such rails were produced. For all but the large, precedent-setting railroads, industry specifications provided guidance in dealing with issues they previously had confronted independently. An entirely new approach to innovation – one that emphasized cooperation, careful experiment by engineers, and controlled change that did not disrupt the economic equilibrium – had arrived.

This new departure in managing technological change had implications far beyond the steel rail issue. As railroads solidified relationships with producers of most of their essential technology and entrusted academically trained engineers with the responsibility of operating and maintaining their systems, the approach grew increasingly characteristic of technological innovation throughout the industry. Successful introduction of devices such as the air brake, as discussed in the previous chapter, occurred only after railroads worked out a means of coordinating change so as not to disrupt their systems. Changes in locomotives occurred in much the same way, as railroads drafted specifications that served as a medium of exchange with one or two trusted suppliers. Beyond this, the business of drafting specifications exemplified a way of thinking about technology that permeated virtually every aspect of

[89]   Discussions of the Committee on Rail, *AREMWA Proceedings* 6 (1905): 188–189, and 7 (1906): 566–567.

[90]   Progress on standards for hundred-pound rails can be followed in the transactions and proceedings of the ASTM, ASCE, AIME, and AREMWA during the first decade of the twentieth century. On the prominence of the Pennsylvania Railroad's design, see, especially, the comments of R. W. Hunt in *ASTM Proceedings* 7 (1907): 94.

railroad management during the last quarter of the nineteenth century. As managers grappled with the challenges of running their machines, they grew steadily more enamored with the apparent potential of engineering values and methods to substitute for the more harried and less predictable affairs of market competition. Engineers and engineering, as embodied in the process of negotiated specifications, acquired an almost mystical appeal.

7

Engineering Enshrined

In summer 1904, Henry Adams made what has undoubtedly become the most discussed visit to a world's fair in the annals of American letters. Adams, now the reigning elder of America's most distinguished Brahmin families, had recently returned from a long sojourn in Europe. While there he had indulged his fascination with medieval culture, in part by making a thorough tour of the French Gothic cathedrals. Now Adams left Washington for St. Louis to observe the vast spectacle of the Louisiana Purchase Exposition, which had been organized in commemoration of Thomas Jefferson's masterful negotiations with the French a century before. Riding the rails back to the East, Adams conceived what has come to serve as the touchstone of his memoirs, a chapter comparing the enthralling power exerted by the image of the Virgin Mary over medieval society with the almost mystical enchantment of the dynamo in modern American affairs. For Adams, the self-regenerating dynamo, which drew its own power back into itself in order to distribute still greater power to the vast array of lights and machines of the fair, served as an almost ideal icon for the capacity of modern society to organize itself around the single concept of productive efficiency, until society itself seemed to function as a giant machine.[1]

Though the dynamo provided a particularly apt metaphor that looked ahead to the emerging world of electricity, one senses in Adams's recounting of his trip that he was no less inspired by the more established machine that

[1] Henry Adams, *The Education of Henry Adams: An Autobiography* (Boston: Houghton, Mifflin, 1918), pp. 378–390. Adams drafted the essay in 1906 and published it privately in 1907. Though he referred to the Paris Exposition of 1900, Adams visited several world's fairs of the period. He delayed his annual sojourn to Paris in order to travel to St. Louis, and gave a full report on the exhibition to Mrs. Theodore Roosevelt in the White House upon his return to Washington. For his sentiments, see J. C. Levenson et al., *The Letters of Henry Adams*, 6 vols. (Cambridge, Mass.: Harvard University Press, 1988), vol. 5, pp. 533–534 and 586–590.

carried him to and from the fair. In 1904, railroads remained the supreme example of organized productive effort. Only in that year had the amount of capital invested in the entire industrial manufacturing sector of the American economy come to surpass that invested in railroads.[2] Though the recent merger wave had created a handful of business institutions larger than the biggest railroads, the giant transportation alliances still first came to mind when one thought of the corporations and trusts that occupied so much attention in public affairs of the day. During the very year of the fair, the Supreme Court handed down its decision in the Northern Securities case, in which by the slimmest of margins it sided with President Theodore Roosevelt and the government in breaking up the powerful alliance of financiers J. P. Morgan and E. H. Harriman that dominated railroads in the Northwest.[3] Meanwhile, Congress pondered far-reaching legislation intended to place the transportation behemoths under an unprecedented degree of government supervision.

Among the nation's railroads, none commanded more prominent attention or projected a more machine-like efficiency than the giant Pennsylvania. This sprawling system – the largest corporation and biggest employer in America, public or private, before the formation of U.S. Steel in 1901 – had remained relatively untainted by the sorts of financial manipulations associated with lines owned by the likes of Harriman, the Vanderbilts, and Jay Gould. Compared with them, the Pennsylvania appeared to have grown organically, earning through single-minded devotion to the task of moving traffic its self-styled moniker, "The Standard Railroad of America" (Fig. 7.1). No visitor to the fair at St. Louis could have failed to notice the Pennsylvania or to grasp something of the machine-like image it cultivated. The Pennsylvania System had long held a commanding presence in the Gateway City, its western terminus. During the 1870s, Pennsylvania-affiliated lines had been the first to cross the Mississippi there, and in subsequent decades the system had done much to rejuvenate St. Louis as a Midwestern entrepot capable of rivaling Chicago.[4] The vast majority of those approaching the fair from the East, like Adams, would arrive over Pennsylvania tracks. The exhibition thus presented the Pennsylvania's officers with a golden opportunity, and they took care to mount a display of unusual quality and impact. One of the line's four vice-presidents, F. D. Casanave,

[2] Simon Kuznets, *Capital in the American Economy, Its Formation and Financing* (Princeton: Princeton University Press, 1961), and Lance E. Davis, "Savings and Investment," in Glenn Porter, ed., *Encyclopedia of American Economic History* (New York: Charles Scribner's Sons, 1980), vol. 1, p. 192.

[3] Martin J. Sklar, *The Corporate Reconstruction of American Capitalism, 1890–1916: The Market, the Law, and Politics* (Cambridge: Cambridge University Press, 1988), pp. 134–142 and 182.

[4] William Cronon, *Nature's Metropolis: Chicago and the Great West* (New York: Norton, 1991), pp. 295–309.

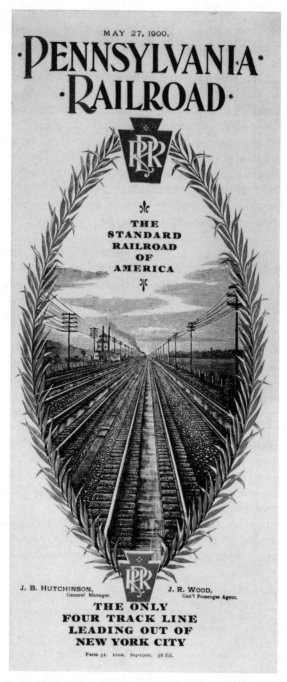

Figure 7.1. Pennsylvania Railroad timetable, 1900. *Courtesy*: Library of Congress.

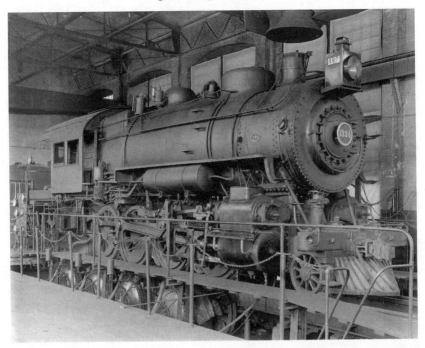

Figure 7.2. The locomotive testing plant, centerpiece of the Pennsylvania's exhibit at the 1904 Louisiana Purchase Exposition in St. Louis, was later relocated to Altoona. *Courtesy*: Hagley Museum and Library.

temporarily relinquished his post in order to take charge of the St. Louis project.[5]

At the center of the Pennsylvania's exhibit stood an icon to rival Adams's dynamo: a giant plant for testing locomotives (Fig. 7.2). To view this new marvel, the first of its kind, visitors entered a long, narrow building standing

---

[5] On the creation of this plant, see V. P. Thomson and Theodore N. Ely, "Memorandum on Louisiana Purchase Exposition," June 10, 1903; V. P. Pugh to Pres. Cassatt, June 4, 1903; and Pugh to Cassatt, February 4, 1904; Papers Concerning Matters Coming before the Board of Directors of the Pennsylvania Railroad (henceforth, PRR Board Papers), Hagley Museum and Library, Wilmington, Delaware. All told, the Pennsylvania's board authorized expenditures of nearly $200,000 on the exhibit. For details on its operation in St. Louis and the role of Casanave, see Files of the Association of Transportation Officers of the Pennsylvania Railroad (henceforth, PRR ATO Files), Hagley Museum and Library, Wilmington, Delaware, accession 1807, box 717, folder 6; "St. Louis Test Facility" File, Engineer of Tests Papers (henceforth, PRR Engineer of Tests Papers), Motive Power Department Papers (henceforth, PRR Motive Power Papers), PRR Papers, accession 1810, Hagley Museum and Library, Wilmington, Delaware; and *The Pennsylvania Railroad System at the Louisiana Purchase Exhibition* (Philadelphia: Pennsylvania Railroad Company, 1905).

several stories high. Overhead ran an enormous steel-framed walking crane capable of hoisting a steam locomotive – even one of the mammoth new Atlantic-type engines recently introduced by the Pennsylvania – and carrying it into position above a set of massive rollers. Once lowered into place, the locomotive could be run in place, its wheels revolving and complex mechanisms churning at the same pace as when pulling trains at top speed down a main-line track. Visitors looked on as if suspended in space and time, now able to observe and ponder the source of the awesome power that previously they had experienced only as a passing blur.

Here, in the enclosed confines of a laboratory, that power was being tamed and mastered. Amid the hiss and roar, a team of Pennsylvania employees quietly proceeded with the deliberate business of measuring fuel consumption, changing tractive resistance, and recording the pulling power of their captured mechanical patient. One man did nothing but record temperatures, using thermometers whose accuracy had been verified by the Bureau of Standards in Washington. A chemist took samples of all fuels and lubricants for analysis. Periodically, the technicians stopped the locomotive, replaced or readjusted one of its many components, then proceeded with another test. The work went forward according to a rigid schedule determined months in advance under the guidance of a board that included technical experts from many of the world's largest railroads and equipment suppliers. It was headed by Professor F. M. Goss, director of the new Department of Railway Engineering at Purdue University. At the conclusion of the fair, as visitors learned from brochures and placards, Professor Goss and the Pennsylvania's expert technicians would publish a full tabulated record of all results. The plant itself would be dismantled and rebuilt in a new building at the railroad's mechanical laboratory in Altoona, Pennsylvania, where it would continue to provide "unprecedented data of immense utility to anyone who valued safe and economical transportation."[6]

With its ability to combine the exhilarating experience of the machine with the methodical methods of the engineer, the locomotive testing plant was perhaps the ideal shrine to what Cecelia Tichi has called the Gear and Girder Age.[7] The frequent public celebrations of engineering accomplishments during these forty years around the turn of the century, as Tichi notes, tended to emphasize dynamic artifacts and soaring structures. Visitors exiting the test plant, for instance, would encounter a set of full-scale models showing structural features of the Pennsylvania's spectacular terminal being built in Manhattan, including cross-sections of tunnels that would carry trains

[6] V. P. Thomson and Theodore N. Ely, "Memorandum on Louisiana Purchase Exposition," June 10, 1903, PRR Board Papers.

[7] Cecilia Tichi, *Shifting Gears: Technology, Literature, and Culture in Modernist America* (Chapel Hill: University of North Carolina Press, 1987).

Figure 7.3. Display featuring tunnels beneath the Hudson River into Pennsylvania Station, Louisiana Purchase Exposition, St. Louis, 1904. *Courtesy:* Hagley Museum and Library.

beneath the Hudson River and portions of its many lattice stairways built from structural steel components (Fig. 7.3). Most portrayals of engineers during this period similarly evoked images of independent heroic figures such as Gustav Eiffel, whose tower inspired many elements in the design of Penn Station. In reality, of course, most engineers worked anonymously in large organizations, methodically performing the calculations, studies, and routines that together constituted the most powerful machine of all. With the test plant, the Pennsylvania had found a way to expose this essential foundation of technicians and reveal something of their methods, while retaining the more popular, universal appeal of the thundering locomotive.[8]

---

[8] In authorizing the exhibit, the board emphasized that "the plant could be made an attraction from a spectacular point of view by giving notice in the Exposition Bulletin that at a certain hour on a certain day a locomotive at the Testing Plant would be run at the rate of, say, seventy miles per hour. The experience at other exhibitions has

The plant would, in the opinion of the line's board of directors, "illustrate better than could be done in any other way the progressive tendency of the Pennsylvania System."[9]

If we wish to understand the railroad industry of the late nineteenth century, and if we hope to comprehend the troubles that lay ahead for the industry in the decades to follow, we must capture something of the spirit that informed this monumental shrine to engineering in St. Louis. To a world steeped in the exhilarating pleasures and ready diversions provided by a plethora of consumer products and inventive novelties, modern engineering often seems a mundane affair, made all the more so by its thorough but quiet effectiveness. For those who attended the exhibit at St. Louis, however, engineering itself possessed the thrill of novelty. Equipped with a new methodology and infused with the self-conscious outlook of crusaders, engineers in railroading and a few other settings had taken hold of one problem after another, until they had imposed a degree of standardization and routine never before seen on such a grand scale. The achievement combined the dispassionate authority of scientific investigation with the exciting appeal of inventive novelty; for these pioneering engineers were inventors not of a new device or clever amusement but of a powerful methodology grounded in the universal principles of science.[10]

By the turn into the twentieth century, virtually everyone associated with railroading had caught something of the enthusiasm. Managers, financiers, informed observers, and ultimately the public at large grew entranced by the possibilities opened by engineering methods. Though grounded in concrete accomplishments, the commitment to engineering ultimately went beyond a mere rational response to economic and technical conditions facing the railroad industry as it passed into maturity. As engineers came increasingly to define the major problems confronting the railroads, as their methods and outlook permeated every corner of the industry, engineering acquired a mystique. Only later, as the conditions facing railroads turned once more, would some of these individuals come to realize that the enchantments of

---

been that exhibits of this character attract large crowds." V. P. Thomson to C. M. P. Theodore N. Ely, "Louisiana Purchase Exposition, St. Louis, 1904," June 10, 1903, PRR Board Papers.

9 Ibid. The board was confident the exhibit "would appeal to all classes of visitors to the Exposition – shareholders of the Pennsylvania Lines, technical engineers, and railroad officials, as well as the general public."

10 For an especially astute analysis, see Edwin T. Layton, Jr., *The Revolt of the Engineers: Social Responsibility and the American Engineering Profession* (Cleveland: Case Western Reserve University Press, 1971). On the widespread enthusiasm for engineering efficiency, see Samuel P. Hays, *Conservation and the Gospel of Efficiency: The Progressive Conservation Movement, 1890–1920* (Cambridge, Mass.: Harvard University Press, 1959), and Samuel Haber, *Efficiency and Uplift: Scientific Management in the Progressive Era* (Chicago: University of Chicago Press, 1964).

engineering blinded them to other possibilities and impeded their ability to respond more creatively to changing circumstances.

DUDLEY, THE PENNSYLVANIA, AND THE BACONIAN IDEAL

The locomotive testing plant marked the culmination of an endeavor that had begun at the Pennsylvania Railroad nearly three decades before, when the line first founded its chemical laboratory and testing facilities and hired Charles Benjamin Dudley as its chief chemist. As discussed in previous chapters, Dudley came to the Pennsylvania straight from his graduate training at Yale's Sheffield Scientific School, where he had earned a doctorate in chemistry. At the time, he became perhaps the first Ph.D. scientist employed full-time by an American corporation. Aged thirty-four and a veteran of the Civil War, which had left him permanently disabled, Dudley soon carved out a role at the Pennsylvania by writing specifications for chemical products. His activities attracted widespread interest, in part because Dudley himself published widely in the technical literature, and within a decade several other lines had emulated the Pennsylvania. In 1889, Dudley began publishing an exhaustive series of essays entitled "Chemistry Applied to Railroads," which documented his experiences at the Pennsylvania and discussed his philosophy regarding technical specifications. The material contained in these essays provided the basis for the Pennsylvania's exhibit at an earlier fair, the World's Columbia Exposition, held in Chicago in 1893. A few years later, Dudley served two terms as president of the American Chemical Society (ACS) during a critical moment in its history. While continuing to head the laboratory at the Pennsylvania, he devoted much of his final decade to the nascent American Society for Testing Materials. As its president from 1901 until his death eight years later, Dudley established the ASTM as the foremost body for creating industrial standards in the United States.[11]

Early in this illustrious career, Dudley paid a telling visit to yet another world's fair, the Centennial Exhibition in Philadelphia. On June 16, 1876, little more than half a year after going to work for the railroad, he joined a group of about seventy chemists who attended the fair and later met for dinner at the city's exclusive Union League Club. This gathering marked the first meeting outside New York City of the fledgling ACS, which had been formed just two months before.[12] The venue was fitting, for the fair at

[11]   On Dudley and the early history of the ASTM, see the *Proceedings of the American Society for Testing Materials* (henceforth, *ASTM Proceedings*) and *Memorial Volume Commemorative of the Life and Life-Work of Charles Benjamin Dudley, Ph.D.* (Philadelphia: American Society for Testing Materials, 1911).

[12]   Charles Albert Browne and Mary Elvira Weeks, *A History of the American Chemical Society: Seventy-Five Eventful Years* (Washington, D.C.: American Chemical Society, 1952), pp. 15–23. Dudley formally joined the ACS later that fall. See *American Chemist*

Philadelphia in many respects captured the essence of the relationship then flowering among science, technology, and an emergent industrial economy of national scale and scope. With Reconstruction about to end and the final defeat of the Native Americans in the West imminent, the centennial produced an orgy of tributes to American national purpose and achievement. Thousands traveled daily to witness the fair, most of them over the tracks of the Pennsylvania Railroad, which was headquartered in the City of Brotherly Love and was a major sponsor and exhibitor. There they saw spectacular displays of the country's emerging industrial prowess.

The Centennial Exhibition brought to life an ideal first articulated by Francis Bacon, the British bureaucrat-turned-philosopher of the early seventeenth century. Bacon had stressed that knowledge, when applied to the useful arts, produced power and accomplishment. The sort of knowledge he had in mind was that obtained through empirical scientific study, organized on a large scale and pursued in a systematic fashion. Rather than seeing science and utility as being at odds, Bacon saw them as a piece. In his eyes, utility did not mark a contamination or denigration of the scientific endeavor, but instead constituted its highest and ultimate expression. If that utilitarianism could be harnessed to national purpose, so much the better. Thus Bacon could celebrate his holy triumvirate of inventions – gunpowder, printing, and the magnetic compass – as fruits of scientific endeavor that surely heralded the progress of Northern Europeans beyond their ancestors and their southern and eastern contemporaries. For Bacon, the accumulation of knowledge was itself a workmanlike affair. It depended heavily on equipment and organization, and it occurred often in a practical context. Bacon called for the establishment of public institutions that would support a comprehensive effort to generate such knowledge. "The general staff of science had worked out the strategy of the campaign long before the commanders in the field had developed a tactics capable of carrying out the attack in detail," wrote Lewis Mumford in 1934 of Bacon and his seventeenth-century contemporaries. "The laboratories and technical museums of the twentieth century existed first as a thought in the mind of this philosophical courtier: nothing that we do or practice today would have surprised him."[13]

Those attending the fair at Philadelphia stood at the dawn of a new era, at just the moment when the field commanders first mobilized the mounting numbers of college-trained scientists and engineers and the institutions to which Mumford referred began taking shape. The fair itself marked a first step toward implementing the Baconian vision, and not surprisingly, the ranks of dignitaries whose visits were regularly noted in newspapers

---

7 (1876): 121 and 205. The dozen or so initiates also included Harvey W. Wiley and F. W. Clarke.

[13] Lewis Mumford, *Technics and Civilization* (New York: Harcourt Brace Jovanovich, 1934), p. 57. On Bacon, see Paolo Rossi, *Francis Bacon: From Magic to Science* (Chicago: University of Chicago Press, 1971).

and journals included many prominent scientists. William Thomson, the Cambridge physicist whose studies of electricity and thermodynamics would later lead to his being knighted Lord Kelvin, headed an official delegation from Europe and authored a report on its findings.[14] Among other things, the experience made Thomson an enthusiastic proponent of the American patent system. Thomson praised the United States Patent Office for making a genuine effort to certify the novelty of each application for letters patent, rather than merely registering the application, as was the practice in most other countries. In the eyes of Thomson, patent examinations provided something like peer review, in which a fellow expert certified a claim to discovery before the idea was circulated broadly.[15] Thomson, who had long been actively engaged in the telegraph industry, argued vehemently that without such a system of review European countries would almost certainly fall behind the United States in the race to develop the useful arts. Like Bacon, he drew no sharp divisions between science and utility, but saw the commonalities that underlay the means and the ends of each. And like Bacon, he drew clear connections between the organization of scientific and technical enterprise and the well-being of nations.

This same Baconian spirit stimulated perhaps the most dramatic development in American higher education of the day, the founding of the Johns Hopkins University in Baltimore, which also occurred in 1876. Heavily endowed (with a healthy dose of railroad money provided by the Garrett family, whose patriarch John Work Garrett was president of the Baltimore and Ohio and a close associate of the Baltimore merchant Johns Hopkins) and located in a city where Southerners felt at least as comfortable as Yankees, the new university set out expressly to mimic the German university model, with its emphasis on laboratory study, practical apprenticeship, and links to the commercial world. Two of Hopkins's most distinguished faculty, the chemist Ira Remsen and the physicist Henry Rowland, became outspoken advocates of the research university and of the scientific agenda in general. In 1880, Rowland issued the era's most famous defense of scientific research, his celebrated "plea for pure science."[16] This essay has with some justification been used to illustrate the difficulty American scientists had in gaining support for their pursuit of abstract, theoretical understanding in a nation biased toward

---

[14] Crosbie Smith and M. Norton Wise, *Energy and Empire: A Biographical Study of Lord Kelvin* (New York: Cambridge University Press, 1989).

[15] Many Americans, such as the electrical inventor Elihu Thomson, used the patent system virtually as a means of publication. See W. Bernard Carlson, *Innovation as a Social Process: Elihu Thomson and the Rise of General Electric, 1870–1900* (Cambridge: Cambridge University Press, 1991).

[16] For an interesting perspective, see David A. Hounshell, "Edison and the Pure Science Ideal in 19th Century America," *Science* 207 (1980): 612–617. Hounshell identifies George Barker, the same University of Pennsylvania professor who briefly employed Dudley and recommended him to the Pennsylvania Railroad, as a key link between Thomas Edison and the scientific community.

"practical" affairs. But Rowland's appeal and the founding of Johns Hopkins did not strive to isolate science in some ivory tower. Far from it. These were exercises in Baconism that sought to secure a place for science in the "real world." Or, perhaps more accurately, they sought to make that world more scientific. In preaching the virtues of a new method of understanding centered in the laboratory, Rowland and his colleagues sought to overcome resistance not just from people of a practical bent who shunned formal education, but also from people of letters who viewed education as a matter of theology and philosophy. Braced with confidence that their approach to education would yield material benefits as well as intellectual ones, they sought, as did the exhibitors at Philadelphia and Lord Kelvin in his embrace of the patent system, to link their agenda to the fate of an expanding nation.

At the time of the Philadelphia meeting, both Dudley (as agent for the Pennsylvania Railroad) and the founders of the ACS had embarked on ventures intended to bring the Baconian vision to fruition. Each would attempt to establish a role for chemists in the emerging national culture. Success would come when they had articulated clear standards of conduct and embedded them in organizations of national scope. For Dudley, this involved finding ways to make his expertise useful to the Pennsylvania and to the railroad industry at large on a sustained basis. For the pioneers at the ACS, it involved writing constitutions with clear membership standards, recruiting qualified members, sponsoring scholarship of a high caliber, and choosing appropriate leaders.

There can be little question about which of these two experiments yielded better results during the next decade and a half. The ACS was virtually still-born. While the chemistry profession exploded, its membership stagnated. Some of its most visionary and impassioned founders, frustrated by the dominance of a small clique of New Yorkers and their parochial concerns, had bolted from the ACS almost from the start.[17] In 1890, the society listed just 238 members, only eight more than in 1876.[18] Meanwhile, Dudley had plunged into affairs at the Pennsylvania and secured a role for chemists in railroading. By 1889, his laboratory at the Pennsylvania (Fig. 7.4) performed more than 20,000 chemical analyses annually, a level of activity comparable to that of the famed analytical laboratory of Arthur D. Little, another future ACS president and the virtual founder of chemical engineering in America.[19]

---

[17] Browne and Weeks, *History of the American Chemical Society*, pp. 26–40.
[18] Arnold Thackray et al., *Chemistry in America, 1876–1976: Historical Indicators* (Boston: D. Reidel, 1985).
[19] Annual Reports of the Chemical Laboratory (henceforth, PRR Lab Reports), 1885–1908, PRR Motive Power Papers. In 1907, the last year for which complete data exist, the chemical laboratory at the Pennsylvania employed twenty-five people, including sixteen chemists, and made nearly 100,000 determinations. In 1913, it employed thirty-three people, analyzed nearly 60,000 samples, and made nearly 300,000 determinations. See "Departments of Physical and Chemical Tests (Historical)," PRR

Figure 7.4. The new chemical laboratory of the Pennsylvania, opened in 1914, fulfilled the dreams of Charles Benjamin Dudley, who died in 1909 after a career of thirty-five years with the railroad. *Courtesy*: Hagley Museum and Library.

The Ideology of Specifications

Through a series of speeches and writings begun during that year, Dudley became an articulate spokesman for the engineering ideal as embodied in the process of establishing technical specifications. In a lengthy run of articles for the *Railroad and Engineering Journal*, Dudley and his assistant J. N. Pease at first merely documented their efforts to draft specifications for various products purchased by the Pennsylvania. By the time they wrote the concluding numbers of this series, however, Dudley and Pease had developed both a coherent universal prescription for purchasing according to specifications and a philosophical justification for the practice.[20] When developed in the proper spirit of cooperation, they argued, technical specifications captured the fundamental harmony among business management, engineering methodology, and the public good.

Papers, accession 1807, box 661. In 1909, Arthur D. Little had twenty-six technical employees. See Arthur D. Little to E. W. Nelson (Engineer of Tests, Pennsylvania Railroad), October 18, 1909, PRR Papers, accession 1807, box 714, folder 10.

[20] Dudley and Pease, "Chemistry Applied to Railroads: How to Make Specifications," *American Railroad and Engineering Journal* 66 (April 1892): 160–163.

Basing their theory on the twenty-five specifications they had written since the steel rail investigations, the two chemists stressed that workable specifications emerged only when all interested parties cooperated to conduct careful, impartial studies of the material under consideration. "Early in our work the making of specifications seemed to be the simplest of all things," they wrote in apparent reference to the steel rail case. "All that it was necessary to do, we thought, was to sit down and write what would give a satisfactory material, saying largely what might be regarded as common knowledge."[21] Dudley and Pease went on to explain that in practice all interested parties could seldom agree on what constituted a satisfactory material. Conflicts between producers who were concerned exclusively with manufacturing processes and consumers who focused on performance alone had led Dudley and Pease to revise their basic conception of what a specification entailed. In the central theme of these and subsequent writings on the subject, they declared that specifications should not be simply an effort on the part of consumers to tell manufacturers what they want, but "a mutual agreement between them as to what the material shall be."[22]

Succeeding articles laid out in great detail how manufacturers and consumers could arrive at such mutual agreement. Dudley and Pease paid particular attention to the sources of information that should be consulted. They emphasized the importance of testing the performance of the material in actual service and stressed that only consumers could conduct such studies. But Dudley and Pease also emphatically suggested that all manufacturers should be consulted when writing specifications. "We are strongly of the opinion," they wrote, "that any man who attempts to write a specification without any knowledge of the processes by which the material is made will make a serious blunder." The railroad chemists further advised that manufacturers should review the specifications before they take effect. "This method of consulting the manufacturers who are to furnish the material," they noted, "is entirely characteristic of all our later specifications, and we feel that it is essential."[23]

Ten years later, in a series of presidential addresses to the American Society for Testing Materials, Dudley made a greater effort than he had previously to demonstrate how his theory and practice of specifications benefited the public by offering financial returns to both consumers and producers. By purchasing goods according to technical specifications, he asserted, railroads had obtained better quality goods at lower prices, without reducing the profits of suppliers. In the absence of specifications, Dudley noted, railroads purchased goods "on price alone" in a market that included materials of varying quality. This free, open market worked to the disadvantage of both railroads and their most trusted suppliers. Railroads unknowingly obtained inferior goods at bloated prices, while "honest, competent" manufacturers

[21] Ibid., p. 160.   [22] Ibid., p. 161.   [23] Ibid., p. 162.

had to contend with "unfair competition" from the producers of these inferior goods. Rather than waiting passively for the rigors of competition in the open market to drive manufacturers of inferior goods out of business, railroads and trusted suppliers would prevent producers of shoddy goods from ever entering the market by arriving at mutually agreed upon standards of technical performance. Technical experts such as Dudley thus restructured the nature of competition, substituting scientific analysis and systematic assessments of performance for the waste of the unregulated market. Dudley characterized the resulting exchanges among railroads and quality manufacturers as "genuine competition."[24]

Dudley felt certain the switch from "unfair" to "genuine" competition benefited both consumers and producers. He boasted that because of his own work "a number of firms who formerly did quite a large business with railroads, have gone out of existence or have been forced to seek business in other fields than those which they formerly cultivated with such unfair profit to themselves."[25] Not all producers welcomed a system that hastened business failures, of course, and Dudley admitted that many railroad suppliers still found specifications "annoying and harassing." But he insisted that competent manufacturers endorsed efforts to eliminate producers of inferior goods. "Some manufacturers have asked that specifications be prepared," Dudley noted, "and one large producer, indeed, told us in conversation that the more difficult the specification, the better they liked it, on the ground that it limited the competition they would have in producing the product."[26]

In addition to providing these testimonials from his supporters, Dudley addressed critics who argued that the benefits of restructuring competition did not justify the cost of establishing specifications. In his experience, Dudley asserted, "prices show a strong tendency to drop below the figures prevailing at the time the specification was first issued."[27] Dudley hinted that genuine competition – the process of bidding on goods of standard quality from several different producers – pushed prices down. But he argued fundamentally that prices fell because manufacturing costs dropped. Specifications created stable markets in which there existed "steady demand" for "staple commodities," Dudley explained, thus enabling producers to plan their business activities more thoroughly. Better planning resulted in lower costs, which meant reduced prices for consumers without loss of profits for manufacturers.

By explaining and defending his system of specifications in terms of cooperation and order, Dudley placed the role he had forged in the mainstream of managerial changes taking place at the Pennsylvania and other railroads in

[24]   Charles B. Dudley, "The Making of Specifications for Materials," *ASTM Proceedings* 3 (1903): 15–34. See also, Dudley, "The Influence of Specifications on Commercial Products," *ASTM Proceedings* 4 (1904): 17–33.
[25]   Dudley, "Making of Specifications," p. 28.
[26]   Ibid., pp. 28–29.   [27]   Ibid., p. 29.

the last quarter of the nineteenth century. His arguments capture the essence of what historian Alfred D. Chandler, Jr., has characterized as the tendency of business managers during this period to substitute the "visible hand" of managerial experts for the invisible hand of Adam Smith's free market.[28] By establishing specifications, expert technicians such as Dudley would replace the unpredictability of the competitive marketplace with a more stable approach grounded in cooperative scientific and engineering study. Dudley's idea that consumers and producers could transcend their differences and derive mutual benefit from such practices anticipated the thinking of the most famous engineering standard-setter of the Progressive era, Frederick Winslow Taylor. Through his system of scientific management, Taylor believed he could transcend the conflicts between workers and their employers by steering attention toward scientifically derived standard procedures that generated financial benefits for both parties.[29] Like Taylor, whose roots as a professional engineer also went back to the Philadelphia metal trades of the 1870s, Dudley genuinely believed engineers could serve as neutral arbiters who through science and careful administration would skirt conflict and make a better world for everyone. Such sentiments, and the practice of standards-setting that embodied them, placed Dudley and his colleagues among railroad researchers at the forefront of a movement that historian Bruce Sinclair has aptly characterized as "the ideal expression of that drive for system that dominated American life in the years after 1880."[30]

Dudley and the ACS

The broad appeal of standards-setting helps explain why Dudley rose to the forefront of the ACS despite his comparatively undistinguished career as a scientist. When measured by the lasting contributions of his ideas to the discipline of chemistry, Dudley clearly falls short of many ACS presidents of the period. The paragraph summarizing his accomplishments in the official history of the society contains virtually no reference to intellectual merits

---

[28] Alfred D. Chandler, Jr., *The Visible Hand: The Managerial Revolution in the United States* (Cambridge, Mass.: Harvard University Press, 1977).

[29] Robert Kanigel, *The One Best Way: Frederick Winslow Taylor and the Enigma of Efficiency* (New York: Viking Penguin, 1997), and Martha Banta, *Taylored Lives: Narrative Productions in the Age of Taylor, Veblen, and Ford* (Chicago: University of Chicago Press, 1993), ch. 3. See also Layton, *Revolt of the Engineers*; Hays, *Conservation*; and Haber, *Efficiency and Uplift*.

[30] Bruce Sinclair, *A Centennial History of the American Society of Mechanical Engineers, 1880–1980* (Toronto: University of Toronto Press, 1980), and "At the Turn of a Screw: William Sellers, the Franklin Institute, and a Standard American Thread," *Technology and Culture* 10 (January 1969): 20–34. For an interesting treatment of this subject that complements my analysis of Dudley, see Theodore Porter, *Trust in Numbers: The Pursuit of Objectivity in Science and Public Life* (Princeton: Princeton University Press, 1995).

and achievements. Identifying Dudley as "Chief Chemist of the Pennsylvania Railroad, charter member of the ACS, and president of the ASTM," it cites his "exhaustive study of structural materials" and notes that he "investigated and improved the ventilation and sanitation of railway coaches and sleeping cars and the methods of safe transportation of explosives." The brief biography refers to "his standardized methods of analysis" but discloses no pioneering breakthroughs in technique or understanding.[31] A glance forward through the biographical sketches brings us to such distinguished scientific figures as Edward Morley, Ira Remsen, Arthur Noyes, Marston Bogert, Willis Whitney, and Wilder Bancroft, just in the dozen years following Dudley's tenure. Yet despite this rather paltry record of scientific accomplishment, the ACS tapped Dudley to serve two consecutive terms as president at a time when the society aspired to establish itself as the country's leading society for professional chemists.

Dudley assumed the reins of the ACS during the midst of a concerted campaign by certain dissatisfied members to break the hold of the New Yorkers who had dominated affairs of the society since its inception. Prominent figures such as F. W. Clark and Harvey Wiley, using the leverage provided by their influential Chemical Society of Washington and by their activities with Section C of the American Association for the Advancement of Science, compelled the ACS to either loosen itself from the grip of its New York members or to abandon all hope of serving as a legitimate national organization. Charles E. Munroe, a former Harvard colleague of the two renegades and who had remained an ACS member, opened a new Rhode Island section, paving the way for other regional organizations to establish a connection with the ACS while maintaining their distinct identity.[32] This move occurred while Munroe's father-in-law, George F. Barker, served as ACS president. A professor at the University of Pennsylvania, Barker had been at Yale when Dudley was a student there and had employed the young chemist as a laboratory assistant just prior to his taking the appointment with the Pennsylvania Railroad. Wiley himself assumed the presidency in 1893 and served two terms before relinquishing the post in 1895 to Edgar Fahs Smith, a younger faculty colleague of Barker's at Penn. Dudley succeeded Smith, serving two terms before giving way to Munroe.

Dudley thus took the helm of the ACS just as the revolt that would establish the society as the preeminent professional organization among American chemists reached its peak. During his tenure, the society wrote and adopted a new constitution that brought its governance structure in line with its national ambitions. The new constitution called for a board elected from the membership at large. An important provision, widely considered the key to successful passage, stipulated that the election would be conducted by

[31] Browne and Weeks, *History of the American Chemical Society*, pp. 446–447.
[32] Ibid., pp. 31–40.

precinct, with each of the geographical sections voting as a block and having its vote weighted in proportion to its share of total ACS membership. This federalist arrangement, familiar to anyone who had followed the workings of railroad trade groups such as the Master Car-Builders Association, assuaged fears that the largest block or a well-organized minority might dominate the affairs of the society.

By no means should Dudley be seen as the principal architect of the new constitution. If anyone deserves that accolade, it is Wiley, who chaired the subcommittee that drafted the document and had been at the forefront of the reform movement from its inception. Yet Dudley surely deserves some credit for its apparently smooth passage. One can hardly imagine a person better suited to the task of ushering such a document through an organization still trying to find its bearings among conflicting factions. Dudley had risen to prominence among chemists through his ability to fashion compromise. His scrupulous commitment to honest, open investigation gave him an authority that few could match. He was the sort of person whose motives seemed beyond question. (Dudley's infirmities, which the ACS biographer uncharacteristically made reference to in the sketch quoted above, might very well have added to this persona.) Dudley had fashioned this reputation not in the rarified retreat of some university, but in the world of commerce, where affairs were supposedly dominated by self-interest. He had a track record of intervening between conflicting interests and getting them to agree at least upon a common language and approach to negotiation. In establishing procedures and organizing bodies capable of drawing and enforcing specifications, Dudley and other engineering experts in the railroad industry had struggled successfully with precisely the same organizational issues confronting the ACS. Within the ACS, Dudley was ideally positioned to push along the currents of reform without causing undue alarm among those resistant to change. Though clearly in the reformist camp, Dudley was no extremist. Unlike other reformers, he apparently had never resigned from the ACS. He was, in sum, a proven facilitator with an unwavering commitment to building a healthy national society that would advance the cause of chemistry.

Beyond his proven political skills, Dudley offered the ACS a powerful exemplar of the broader Baconian mission that inspired its leadership. For despite all the jurisdictional squabbling and political posturing that characterized the ACS during the period of Dudley's presidency, the society remained engaged in a larger struggle that reflected broad consensus. It sought to establish a place for chemistry in national affairs. To accomplish this, the ACS needed first to recruit large numbers of the nation's chemists, then organize them so that they could speak with a common voice. Few better symbolized this effort than Dudley. Here was a chemist who had demonstrated the utility of his profession to the largest institution of the day and who had become through his writing a proselytizer for chemistry in other affairs as well. In his post with the railroad, Dudley was the rare chemist of his day who had an opportunity to link his work closely with physical tests and actual experience on a large scale. This unusual opportunity put him in a position to assert a place for chemistry in the analysis of mechanical and physical phenomena – something that foreshadowed the rise of physical chemistry during the decades ahead. Few people in the nineteenth century had attained anything close to such status and recognition for their chemistry.[33]

The intellectual content of that chemistry does not impress us today and did not earn him much esteem among chemists in his own time. The fact that Dudley used his second presidential address to defend "the dignity of analytical work" is the surest proof that its dignity was in some question.[34] No ACS president ever felt obliged to stand up and defend the dignity of a university research professorship. Even among analytical chemists, Dudley did not particularly distinguish himself through his contribution of new techniques or more accurate assays. A history of his lab prepared by the railroad itself freely acknowledged that his methods of analysis were not necessarily the most accurate, for what mattered most was simply that the tests agreed upon by the railroad and its suppliers be performed consistently.[35] Though Dudley wrote frequently about various procedures and tests, his contributions almost always codified the state of the art rather than advanced it. His first presidential address, for instance, merely lobbied for broader acceptance of the standard analytical methods he and Pease had developed.[36] In these respects, his work stands in sharp contrast to the generation of chemists, just coming into prominence at the time of his presidency, who would advance the ideas of physical chemistry and use them to produce analyses of ever greater accuracy.[37]

But to dwell on the differences between Dudley and the emergent physical chemists is to misread conditions in the chemical profession and elsewhere in the communities of science and engineering at the turn of the century. The fact that Dudley had achieved his prominence more through diligence

---

[33] Porter, *Trust in Numbers*, observes that rigid quantification of the sort exemplified by the organized pursuit of standards moved from engineering and politics into science, rather than the reverse. Dudley's growing prominence among chemists testifies to that process.

[34] Charles B. Dudley, "On the Dignity of Analytical Work," *Journal of the American Chemical Society* 20 (1898): 81–96.

[35] "There is a strong incentive to prefer precise and standardizable measures to highly accurate ones," notes Porter, *Trust in Numbers*, p. 29.

[36] Charles B. Dudley, "Some Present Possibilities in the Analysis of Iron and Steel," paper read before the American Chemical Society, Troy, New York, December 29, 1896. See also Charles B. Dudley and F. N. Pease, "The Need of Standard Methods for the Analysis of Iron and Steel, with Some Proposed Standard Methods," *Journal of the American Chemical Society* 15 (1893): 501–541.

[37] John W. Servos, *Physical Chemistry from Ostwald to Pauling: The Making of a Science in America* (Princeton: Princeton University Press, 1990).

and perseverance than sheer brilliance might well have enhanced his appeal for many of the chemists who stood poised to join the ACS, many of whom were analysts with positions in industry themselves.[38] The reformers expressly sought to reach out to this group. Dudley clearly stood out as a paragon among these analytical chemists. He held a Ph.D. (though from an American university, the first among ACS presidents with a doctorate whose degree was not obtained in Germany) and was a prolific publisher. Though a paid employee for two decades, he retained the title "chemist." (The letterhead of the Bureau for the Safe Transportation of Explosives, yet another organization Dudley served as president, identified the eight members of its executive committee. Among them were four vice-presidents of railroads, a general manager, a superintendent of transportation, and the assistant to the president of the Erie. At the top stood Dudley, identified simply as "Chemist, Pennsylvania Railroad.") His colleagues at the Pennsylvania unfailingly referred to him as "Doctor." His work and his articles and speeches had asserted a role for science as the new language of national commerce. Largely through the efforts of Dudley, commercial transactions between the most powerful business institutions of the day came to revolve around negotiated technical specifications, including chemical formulae.

ENGINEERING VALUES AND THE RAILROADS

Technical publications and professional service such as Charles Benjamin Dudley's, along with the displays at world's fairs that featured them, were public gestures consciously intended to advance railroad interests outside their own organizational boundaries. One might well wonder whether the enthusiasm for engineering methods expressed in these forums sincerely reflected a set of values broadly prevalent within the railroads themselves. More than a few historians of engineering have dwelled upon apparent conflicts occurring among engineers and their corporate employers or among college-trained engineers and an old school of mechanics who lacked such formal technical education.[39] Railroading certainly exhibited some conflict

---

[38] "Around 1900," observes Theodore Porter of another industry that employed large numbers of chemists, "the principal role of science in the pharmaceutical industry was not the development of new medicines, but testing and standardization." Porter, *Trust in Numbers*, p. 29. See also James Donnelly, "Consultants, Managers, Testing Slaves: Changing Roles for Chemists in the British Alkali Industry, 1850–1920," *Technology and Culture* 35 (1994): 100–128.

[39] Daniel Hovey Calhoun, *The American Civil Engineer: Origins and Conflict* (Cambridge, Mass.: MIT Press, 1960); Monte A. Calvert, *The Mechanical Engineer in America, 1830–1910: Professional Cultures in Conflict* (Baltimore: Johns Hopkins University Press, 1967); and Layton, *Revolt of the Engineers*. Peter Meiksins, "The 'Revolt of the Engineers' Reconsidered," *Technology and Culture* 29 (1988): 219–246, argues that most engineers fit quite comfortably within corporate bureaucracies and

of these sorts. Engineers anxious to conduct systematic investigations some-times found themselves frustrated by what they viewed as the conservatism of management. When the Burlington struggled to obtain higher quality rails during the 1880s, for instance, longtime vice-president T. J. Potter consis-tently favored the opinions of "experienced trackmen" over college-educated civil engineers.[40] During the financial crises of the 1890s, managers at even the most progressive roads sometimes expressed skepticism about the worth of testing engineers such as Dudley.

Yet the far more striking feature of the late nineteenth century is the re-markable harmony that developed between engineering methods and rail-roading. Railroad testing formed a solid core of problems around which the new engineering societies oriented themselves, and specialists in rail-road problems often attained significant stature within these professional groups. Young graduates flocked to the railroads, lured in part by special apprenticeships in the laboratories.[41] The academically trained mechani-cal engineers and chemists who took these posts seemed genuinely excited about working for the railroad. "The work is interesting," wrote chemist Walter Lee Brown of the Burlington to a young chemist who was consider-ing joining the railroad. "I think it is a good field for a young man and you work for a good company."[42] By the mid-nineties, schools such as Illinois and Purdue had created special departments devoted exclusively to railway engineering.

The good feelings cut both ways, as managers and high-ranking executives grew steadily more enamored with the potential of engineering methods to solve problems in all aspects of their businesses. "We have got to get more and more on to a scientific basis in the running of railroads," implored Charles Perkins of the Burlington when discussing new hires with his top assistants.[43] By sending models and records to university laboratories, Perkins cultivated relationships with professors whom he hoped would then send "their best graduates" to the railroad. Perkins urged his underlings "to take educated

were wary of the few exceptional figures in engineering societies who accentuated the differences between engineering and business.

40 T. J. Potter to C. E. Perkins, January 18, 1883, Papers of the Chicago, Burlington and Quincy Railroad (henceforth, CBQ Papers), 3P4.56.

41 See Chapter 5 above and Stuart Morris, "Stalled Professionalism: The Recruitment of Railway Officials in the United States 1885–1940," *Business History Review* 47 (1973): 317–334. For contemporary accounts emphasizing the value of engineering training in railroad hiring practices, see William J. Wilgus, "Making a Choice of a Profession, VIII – Railroading," *Cosmopolitan* 35 (1903): 462–465; J. Aubrey Tyson, "The Making of Railway Officials," *Munsey's Magazine* 30 (1904): 868–872; and A. J. County, "The Desireability of a College Education for Railroad Work," *Annals of the American Academy of Political and Social Science* 27 (1906): 128.

42 W. L. Brown to Ernst Speidel, May 18, 1885, Laboratory Notebooks (henceforth, CBQ Lab Books), vol. 10, p. 1, CBQ Papers.

43 Perkins to Harris, August 13, 1890, vol. 27, p. 481, CBQ Papers, 3P4.1.

men" when filling posts and often recommended recent graduates to them. While Perkins suggested in his famous memorandum on management that engineers should be kept out of the realm of traffic, their methods soon spread beyond the strictly technical aspects of railroading and came to encompass the business departments as well. Discussing college-trained engineers with his general manager in 1887, Perkins expressed his desire "to make use of some of these men in the commercial branch of our business."[44] Indeed, the only domain Perkins ultimately reserved for the older school of managers was rate-setting. A strict defender of the principle of setting rates according to what the market would bear, Perkins felt engineers had wrongly fostered the belief that rates could be determined from costs. "Men educated to an exact science, like civil engineering, are apt to carry its methods into everything they do," he told a railroad lobbyist, "and it is no doubt true that when it came to making railroad tariffs such men undertook to construct them on mathematical principles, instead of recognizing the fact that they must in the end be regulated by the laws of supply and demand."[45] In all other areas of railroad management, however, Perkins had no objections to the use of mathematical principles.

Executives attempted to get engineers into every branch of their enterprises because they recognized that the usefulness of the engineering approach was not limited to specific technical problems. The basic focus of most railroads – moving more goods through a fixed system – was essentially a grand problem that begged for the methodical, systematic analysis characteristic of engineering. The concern among managers with operating an established system and the ability of engineers and scientists to optimize performance within a known environment formed a fundamental basis of harmony between engineers and the railroads. Engineers would not build, create, or innovate. That work had been done. Engineers would use the scientific method to get the most out of an existing machine. They would do this not by contributing dramatic or clever new innovations, but by collecting and organizing information and using it to administer the daily operations of the railroad. What men such as Charles Dudley and Frederick Delano had done for narrowly technical subjects such as steel rails others would do for the railroad machine as a whole by keeping careful traffic statistics and utilizing seminal techniques such as cost accounting.

As these novel procedures diffused through quarters such as railroad traffic departments, managers not formally trained in engineering disciplines caught the enthusiasm for engineering methods. Freight agents for the Burlington plunged into new tasks such as filing traffic reports so zealously, observes historian Olivier Zunz, that they sometimes found it necessary to patch up relations with customers who had been alienated by their excessive attention

[44] Perkins to Stone, July 13, 1887, CBQ Papers, 3P4.1.
[45] Perkins to Mr. Joseph Nimmo, Jr., July 23, 1891, CBQ Papers, 3P4.1.

to bureaucratic procedures and rigorous enforcement of rules.[46] Agents, the sales force of railroading, at times seemed almost to elevate the pursuit of regularity and routine above that of profit itself. Their confusion was understandable, for with so much emphasis upon shipping basic commodities economically across long distances, the abstract goal of improved efficiency corresponded closely with the more concrete objective of profit-making. Engineers and managers could routinely pursue the former with full confidence they would contribute to the latter. Thus, engineering methods crept steadily into even the domain of rate-setting, which Perkins had identified as the last preserve of market mechanisms.

The mounting enthusiasm for engineering throughout the ranks of railroad management was perhaps most evident at the Pennsylvania and its revitalized Association of Transportation Officers (ATO). Operating essentially as an in-house engineering society, the ATO assumed steadily greater prominence during the 1890s, as executives looked to it as a critically important vehicle for establishing engineering standards within their sprawling empire.[47] Standing committees and special ad hoc commissions addressed a broad array of issues, from rail shapes to train speeds to the preferred colors for signal lights. Whatever the subject, members of the ATO pursued a common methodical approach, in which they sought to identify the basic parameters involved in each situation and to generate a mathematical formula that would dictate the prescribed course of action. During the spring of 1898, for instance, the Committee on Maintenance of Way set out to examine the prevailing practice of removing rails from passenger tracks to freight tracks and then to sidings and the scrap heap. Curious whether it might prove more economical to put new rails directly into the freight tracks, the committee hoped to produce "a simple and useful equation . . . that would be susceptible of comprehensive analysis, and that would be expressed in such terms as to render the several questions involved intelligible and capable of easy solution for all practicable purposes."[48] As was often the case, the committee encountered a frustrating shortage of reliable data. The Pennsylvania kept no records of the tonnage passing over particular tracks, lamented the report summarizing the study, nor could the line fully account for the expenses incurred when transferring rails to new locations. Undeterred, the committee recommended such records be kept in the future and meanwhile offered a formula pertaining

---

[46] Olivier Zunz, *Making America Corporate, 1870–1920* (Chicago: University of Chicago Press, 1990), ch. 2.

[47] On the resurgence of the ATO in 1893, see in particular "Minutes of the Meeting of the Association of the Transportation Officers of the Pennsylvania Railroad Held in the Gallery of the Art Club, Broad and Brighton Streets," June 23, 1893, PRR ATO Files, box 1, file 4.

[48] Report of the Maintenance of Way Committee, May 3, 1898, pp. 406–413, PRR ATO Files.

to the relative economy of using new or old rails in freight tracks at various prices.

Reports such as these betrayed both the aura engineering methods held among managers at the Pennsylvania and the wealth of opportunities railroading presented to individuals anxious to apply those methods. Time and again during the 1890s, executives convened to consider a problem, only to discover they lacked sufficient data to reach a definitive answer. Yet despite the frequent frustrations, managers remained committed to the engineering ideal. Indeed, the shortage of reliable data spurred them to embrace that ideal even more fully, as they sensed the enormous untapped potential for improving performance and yielding economy. The careful, restrained reports generated by the ATO during this period read like tributes to engineering methods, with authors consistently holding themselves rigidly to the standards of scientific investigation. While readily acknowledging the inconclusiveness of their studies, members of the ATO chose not to ponder the limits inherent to engineering analysis. They did not despair at the daunting prospect of identifying and measuring all relevant inputs governing the complex practical problems of railroading. Rather, managers looked forward with confidence to the day when they would possess sufficient data to generate the definitive solutions they desired.[49]

The recurrent appeal to impersonal authority grounded in scientific analysis that so informed the ATO and its ideology of standards-setting conflicted to a degree with the Pennsylvania's intensely hierarchical and militaristic style. Over the course of the late nineteenth century, however, the road melded the two managerial styles quite effectively. Basically, the Pennsylvania's executives came to see themselves as technical authorities who had earned their status in the corporate hierarchy by dint of their understanding of railroad practice. This was one reason why the issuing of technical standards carried an aura of importance that few outside the firm could fully grasp. Only the initiated understood that a Pennsylvania standard stood as the highest expression not just of an organization but of a community of shared values. When people in positions of leadership in that community spoke of discipline, as they often did, they liked to think of it as flowing from the technical requirements of the railroad system itself, not from individuals exercising authority. The Pennsylvania's elaborate structures of rules, which drastically narrowed the scope of managerial discretion, accentuated these machine-like qualities of its organizational culture.[50]

While few railroads absorbed the depersonalized engineering outlook quite so thoroughly as the Pennsylvania, by the turn into the twentieth century, the basic tenets expressed within the ATO had come to enjoy wide

[49] PRR ATO Files contain numerous examples of committee reports from this period.
[50] My thinking about the organizational culture of the Pennsylvania has been influenced by the work of Glenn Porter, who provided a draft of his manuscript on this subject.

currency among those interested in railroading and the larger economy. The esteemed Harvard economist Frederick W. Taussig captured the mood in a lengthy essay penned for the *Quarterly Journal of Economics* at the turn of the century.[51] "Nothing is more wonderful in the industrial history of the past generation than the new vista opened as to the possibilities of organization," declared the Austrian expatriate about his adopted land. "The increasing application of machinery has made it possible to reduce operations more and more to routine and system, and to lessen the need of independent judgement for every step. Technological education has supplied an array of trained, intelligent, and trustworthy assistants – engineers, chemists, mineralogists, electricians – to whom can be delegated a multitude of steps and processes that formerly needed the watchful eye of the master himself."[52] Taussig offered this glowing assessment under the deceptively simple title "The Iron Industry of the United States." In actuality, he intended to use the iron trade to illustrate what he believed to be the underlying bases of modern economic prosperity. In particular, Taussig wished to direct attention to the extraordinary achievements made possible by the pursuit of "routine and system" and to the cadre of technical experts who strove to attain them.

Toward the conclusion of his two-part essay, Taussig returned to this central theme once more. After again noting "the wonderful growth of technical and scientific education," he explained its significance at some length:

> The supply of intelligent and highly trained experts, to whom the management of departments and separate establishments can be intrusted with confidence, has facilitated the process of consolidation and the organization on a grand scale of widely unifying enterprises. It may be a question how far our scientific schools and institutes of technology have been successful in stirring invention and developing initiative talent. The prime essential for leadership seems to be here, as elsewhere in the intellectual world, inborn capacity. But the rapid spread and complete utilization of the best processes have been greatly promoted by them. They have been largely instrumental in enabling prompt advantage to be taken of chemical, metallurgical, and mechanical improvements in the iron and steel works. Their influence has shown itself no less in the railways, the great buildings, the textile works, the manufacturing establishments at large. Their efficacy in permeating all industry with the leaven of scientific training has been strengthened by the social conditions which have enabled them to attract from all classes the plentiful supply of mechanical talent. Hence American industry has shown not only the inventiveness and elasticity characteristic of the Yankee from early days, but that orderly and systematic utilization of applied science in which the Germans have hitherto been – perhaps still are – most successful.[53]

[51] F. W. Taussig, "The Iron Industry of the United States," *Quarterly Journal of Economics* 14 (1900): 143–170 and 475–508.
[52] Ibid., p. 158.   [53] Ibid., p. 488.

While Taussig believed engineers and scientists had made invaluable contributions "throughout the industrial field," he reserved perhaps his highest praise for American railroads. "The history of the American iron trade in the last thirty years is thus in no small part a history of transportation," the professor wrote after describing the flow of ore and coke across the nation. "And, clearly, this factor has not been peculiar to the iron industry. The perfecting of transportation has been almost the most remarkable of the mechanical triumphs of the United States." Again echoing the themes of order and routine, Taussig asserted flatly that "the efficiency of the railways has been brought to a point not approached elsewhere."[54] He then explained in some detail:

> In the carriage of iron ore and of coal the methods of railway transportation developed under the stress of eager competition have been utilized to the upmost.... At every step direct manual labor is avoided, and machines and machine-like devices enable huge quantities of ore to be moved at a cost astonishingly low.... At either end the railway has been raised to the maximum efficiency for the rapid and economical carriage of bulky freight. What has been done for grain, for cotton, for coal, for all the great staples, has been done here also, and here perhaps more effectively than anywhere else: the plant has been made larger and stronger, the paying weight increased in proportion to the dead weight, the ton-mile expense lessened by heavier rails, larger engines, longer trains, and easier grades, the mechanism for loading, unloading, transshipping perfected to the last degree until yet another stage towards perfection is invented.[55]

EFFICIENCY, NOT INVENTIVENESS

Though Frederick Taussig could hardly have intended it at the time, his assessment stamped a fitting epitaph on an extraordinary epoch in American railroading. In dwelling upon the themes of order and routine and in highlighting the contributions of professionally trained engineers, Taussig captured the essence of developments in the industry across the previous quarter-century. Engineers and railroad managers had indeed found a rich symbiosis in the maturing railroad industry of the late nineteenth century, a compatibility based on a commitment to optimum management of a system that, by and large, they considered given. Engineers thrived in the railroad industry, as they would later in areas such as electric power and communications, precisely because so much there had already been decided upon and worked out.[56] Accepting the constraints imposed by the machines they inherited from the early builders, they concentrated on the largely undifferentiated

[54] Ibid., p. 156.   [55] Ibid., pp. 156–157.
[56] Thomas P. Hughes, *Networks of Power: Electrification in Western Society, 1880–1930* (Baltimore: Johns Hopkins University Press, 1983), and *American Genesis: A Century of Invention and Technological Enthusiasm, 1870–1970* (New York: Penguin, 1989).

task of moving bulk commodities through a fixed but heftier system. Operating in such a well-defined environment, engineers could readily limit the parameters sufficiently to apply the optimization techniques on which their discipline rested. They energetically seized upon the job of comprehending the basic paradigm and achieving incremental improvements within it. The intense focus on standards and specifications, as Dudley and the managers who organized the exhibit in St. Louis clearly recognized, exemplified this sustained effort at refinement. Just as researchers such as Dudley and the mechanical engineers who operated the testing plant attempted to enhance technology within a largely fixed environment, engineers in managerial positions tried to optimize performance within the constraints of the existing railroad machine.

In coming to rely so heavily upon engineers, railroads fundamentally reoriented the relationship between technical activity and market incentives that had prevailed during the early decades of the industry. Members of the engineering community were far more likely to feel the economic incentives to innovate through the market for transportation services rather than through the market for patented inventions and novelties. Competitive market forces still motivated the pursuit of innovation. Indeed, engineers were generally more attuned to cost considerations than the inventors and mechanics of the previous generation had been. Because engineers never ventured far from established, measured routines, they never lost sight of the potential economic returns of their activities. Creatures of capital, they framed their objectives within the context of the entire system and routinely expressed their goals and accomplishments in terms that connected their particular tasks to the economic performance of the firm as a whole. This they did extraordinarily well.

While engineers and scientists proved adept at polishing the railroad machine, they showed less inclination than their mechanic predecessors to incur the risks associated with more innovative departures in technology. Extensive reliance on graduates of scientific schools and institutes of technology, as Taussig himself conceded, did not augur well for success "in stirring invention and developing initiative talent." The rise of research and testing, together with new administrative changes and patent policies, produced a closed circle of technical experts representing railroads and established suppliers who assumed responsibility for most railroad technology. To the extent this circle fostered a high degree of cooperation and reduced unnecessary duplication of effort, it likely provided some economies in selecting and evaluating new technology. But this tight community of technical experts was not so well suited to the tasks of identifying and promoting significant new avenues in railroad innovation. As Taussig understood, engineers and scientists emphasized control, order, and regularity, not change. They bound themselves together through mastery of a common methodology aimed at addressing a limited range of problems.

Executives did not encourage this new breed of technical expert to innovate, and the engineers and scientists did not make invention their top priority. Engineers often replaced master mechanics who had considered invention a central component of their professional activities. When through their research and testing engineers and scientists addressed technological change, they did not look for dramatic departures or bold innovations. Instead, they sought to understand existing practices more thoroughly and to improve them if possible through slow and careful refinement. When engineers assumed managerial positions that did not directly involve technical questions, they utilized their training in mathematics and the use of controlled experiment to optimize performance within the constraints of existing practice. In the process, they reinforced the conception of the railroads as a fixed system and accelerated the development of attitudes that limited the chances of innovation.

The overriding attention to system paid handsome dividends in the context of the late nineteenth century, when engineers encountered an industry just emerging from decades of feverish construction and focusing intently on moving standard commodities long distances. But perhaps inevitably, the emphasis on engineered routine drew railroads toward two potential dangers. First, in shunning the more fluid and less predictable selection mechanisms of the market for inventions, railroads insulated themselves from consumer tastes. Railroads thus closed themselves off from what in the American experience has persistently proven to be the source of the most dynamic or radical innovations. Second, in turning more and more of their affairs over to engineers, railroads ultimately risked confusing technical objectives with economic ones. As engineering language and methodology permeated ever more thoroughly through the industry, the distinction between technical efficiency and financial performance grew increasingly blurred. Managers, investors, and court-appointed receivers came to evaluate the condition of individual lines according to technical criteria and to describe the health of the industry as a whole in engineering terms. These potential liabilities would rapidly grow evident with the dawn of the new century, as railroads faced new challenges in the form of changing traffic patterns and a newly assertive federal government. By the time the Pennsylvania closed its exhibit in St. Louis and relocated the testing plant to its shops in Altoona, railroading had entered a new age calling for more radical departures. Yet as railroads would soon discover, the engineering ideology enshrined at St. Louis still cast a powerful spell over those who would give shape to their industry in the century ahead.

PART III

Friction in the Machine,
1904–1920

The fruitful marriage of engineering and railroading resulted from a particular set of conditions that amplified the potential benefits of engineering methods and masked their inherent limitations. The new century ushered in fundamental changes that would eventually cast the tensions inherent to engineering in a far different light. In the most significant watershed for American railroading since the depression of the 1870s, a wave of mergers and corporate reorganizations swept through the industry. Within a span of just a few years at the turn into the twentieth century, nearly two thirds of the nation's rail mileage fell under the control of seven large systems. Perhaps inevitably, the rapid drive toward consolidation rekindled lingering public concerns about railroad power and the fairness of rates. With encouragement from a new generation of political leaders headed by young President Theodore Roosevelt, calls for national regulation gained new strength and legitimacy. By 1906, when Congress passed the Hepburn Act, the Interstate Commerce Commission had gained unprecedented influence over rates, safety, and other aspects of railroading. Its role would grow steadily more prominent over the subsequent decade and a half.

As railroads confronted new challenges in the regulatory arena, they grappled as well with fundamental changes in the character of demand for their services. With the economic recovery from the depression of the mid-1890s, established lines and newly organized systems found themselves overwhelmed by an unprecedented surge in the volume of traffic. As the economy rapidly industrialized and the output of the manufacturing sector grew more diversified, moreover, much of the goods shipped by rail no longer conformed to patterns established during the late nineteenth century, when long-distance shipments of commodities had dominated. Local shipments and specialized services proliferated, placing enormous burdens on stations and yards already taxed by the sheer volume of business.

Under these conditions railroads often appeared far from the models of efficiency portrayed in their own publicity and described so glowingly by admirers such as the economist Frederick Taussig. The newly created systems, organized in large measure to facilitate long-distance movement of commodities, struggled to reorient themselves in light of the new tasks. Cars and locomotives purchased to handle the surge in traffic spent much of their time idling in clogged switch yards or on sidings. Massive investments in more powerful locomotives, larger cars, and heavier rails – long the golden triad of railroad innovation – no longer sustained the productivity improvements and rates of return railroads had grown accustomed to during the previous half-century. Organizational remedies of the sort touted by Taussig and other students of railroading, such as new rules intended to expedite the exchange of cars, failed to relieve the congestion. If railroads hoped to reach what Taussig had termed "the next stage of perfection," they would have to break away from the established course of change and embrace new technological departures such as electrification and sophisticated signaling. Innovativeness of such thoroughgoing character did not come easily to the railroads.

As the rigid railroad machine broke under the burdens of economic prosperity, faith in the engineering methodology that had so impressed Taussig crumbled as well. Even at lines known for their careful study and machine-like performance, such as the Pennsylvania, managers questioned the tenets of railroad operation as established under the doctrines of engineering. Preferences for technical refinement over inventiveness, for negotiation over free market exchange, for study and statistical analysis over accumulated experience and judgment – all hallmarks of the engineering epoch – came under new scrutiny from executives who could no longer achieve extraordinary economies through the single-minded pursuit of moving bulky goods through the system. Managers accustomed to evaluating performance according to engineering criteria now questioned the explanatory power of such measures. The engineering emphasis on cooperation and consensus, evident in everything from the specifications the Pennsylvania reached in conjunction with steel makers and other suppliers to the apprenticeship training program it used to recruit executives, gave way to a resurgent ideology stressing individual character, confrontation, and power.

These new attitudes placed heavy strains on relationships railroads had carefully cultivated during the late nineteenth century. Trusted suppliers and customers such as the steel companies publicly accused railroads of heavy-handedness. Most important of all, railroads found themselves increasingly at odds with their own employees. Executives had once drawn workers into their management system with concessions such as lucrative wage agreements and pension programs tied to seniority and rigid job classifications. Now railroad managers chafed against work rules and procedures they increasingly perceived as inflexible obstacles that dampened responsiveness and hindered innovation. Many looked to undercut worker power by actively reasserting managerial authority in the workplace or, less directly, by pursuing labor-saving technologies more vigorously than they had before. Management faced an uphill battle, however, in confronting a work force whose strength was buoyed by an accelerating demand for labor and by an organized political movement of growing sophistication and influence. Calls by the railroad brotherhoods for greater cooperation between management and labor resonated with those of reformers who trumpeted the virtues of stability and order.

Faced with mounting pressures for government regulation and shifting demands prompted by the changing structure of the economy, railroads gradually grew more responsive to public taste. Lines more readily accommodated customers wishing to ship products that required specialized services, and they showed new appreciation for the power of grand technical projects to spark public enthusiasm and win them support in political circles. Engineers certainly remained conspicuous in railroad management and in the image railroads sought to convey to the public. Indeed, the crisis of congestion prompted the industry to turn toward engineers more vigorously than ever. At the same time, however, many within the industry exhibited greater sensitivity to the potential conflicts between order and innovation and between engineering efficiency and financial performance.

Yet just as railroads began to move away from the old paradigm and build greater flexibility into their thinking about technology, government and the public embraced engineering methods more wholeheartedly than ever before. At a moment of massive economic restructuring, when few issues loomed larger in American life than the "trust question," the rhetoric and methods of engineering held profound appeal. Politicians and other influential public figures placed great hope in the apparent potential of engineering to provide a way past the divisiveness of class conflict and interest group politics. Just as engineers in settings such as the railroads had found ways to build consensus, so would technical experts operating in the public sector transcend social divisions and orient policy toward a common public interest. Under pressure from reformers holding these views, railroads grew ever more deeply embroiled in discussions of engineering efficiency, even as the primary locus of their concern shifted away from the operational considerations that had given rise to the concept.

American railroads at the opening of the twentieth century thus found themselves curiously out of synch with the emerging ethos of the day. At a time when most large business institutions were still in a stage of ascendancy, in which their most difficult task was to justify their extraordinary power by demonstrating the efficiencies they provided, railroads had entered a troubled state of maturity. Groping for remedies to problems without precedent in their industry or in any other, the men responsible for managing the railroads had just begun to perceive the essential limits of engineering. As they backed tentatively down the track that had until recently served them so effectively, however, railroads found themselves staring at a rampaging locomotive of public opinion steaming toward them along the very same line. At the Eastern Rate Case of 1910, the two forces collided. The advocate Louis Brandeis, trumpeting the virtues of engineering as embodied in Frederick Winslow Taylor's system of scientific management, frustrated railroads in their efforts to obtain a rate increase by branding them as inefficient. Several subsequent disputes over rate regulation shook the industry for another decade, until railroading eventually reached an awkward new equilibrium. Laws passed in the wake of World War I placed the industry on a rate-of-return basis, a form of regulation that accepted the premise that railroads constituted a unified system susceptible to comprehensive quantitative analysis. Though this enduring arrangement tempered the hostilities among railroads, their shippers, and their employees, it did little to address the complex challenges of an industry faced with the ongoing task of balancing efficiency and innovation.

8

Reluctant Innovators: The Annoying
Allure of Automatic Train Control

During the last quarter of the nineteenth century, American railroads had
at their disposal a variety of technological devices that held the potential to
eliminate dangerous procedures performed by trainmen and other workers
and in effect to automate the assembly and movement of trains through their
systems. Automatic air brakes and couplers, which reduced dependence on
brakemen in joining and stopping trains, had become standard features in
passenger service by the mid-1870s. Established suppliers stood ready and
eager to see them placed upon freight equipment. Inventors had also designed a variety of electromechanical appliances intended to activate signals
automatically and link them to one another in switchyards and along the
line. By the early 1880s, distinguished British firms and a number of domestic ones, including the recently formed Union Switch and Signal Company
of George Westinghouse, offered railroads a full array of signaling devices
and services.

Despite their apparent promise, however, none of these automatic devices
gained widespread acceptance among those responsible for moving freight
and passengers through the American railroad network. As discussed in
Chapter 3, most railroads applied automatic brakes and couplers to passenger trains quite reluctantly, conceding to make the switch only under intense
pressure from customers and from threatened legislation. Hand-operated
brakes and couplers remained the norm in freight operations for more than
another two decades, until federal legislation mandated the change to automatic devices at the start of the twentieth century. Automatic signaling
met with similar resistance. Aside from a few complex interlocking plants
installed at especially busy stations, railroads invested scant resources in
new signaling methods before the twentieth century. Most lines persisted
in governing the movement of both freight and passenger trains by simple,
hand-powered signals displayed from stations by dispatchers who received
orders via telegraph. Even the handful of railroads that had invested in signal

towers dedicated exclusively to implementing a rigid block system continued to rely overwhelmingly on manually operated signaling equipment. Of the approximately 200,000 miles of railroad track in the United States in 1900, only 27,000 were operated under block systems of any type, and fewer than 2,300 were equipped with automatic signals.[1]

The sluggish response to innovation in braking and signaling appears all the more remarkable in light of developments elsewhere in the American economy. At a time when escalating costs for skilled labor prompted employers in many segments of the economy to adopt labor-saving technology more eagerly than ever, railroads apparently shunned this course and persisted in using manual techniques. Rather than come down to us as examples of labor-saving innovation, automatic brakes and signals have fallen into a category of railroad technology known as "safety appliances." Their historical significance has generally been perceived to lie within the realm of public policy, where they became important features in the drive for legislation protecting workers, not in the realm of economic efficiency and performance.

The detailed account of innovation in braking and signaling presented in this chapter serves two broad purposes in the context of my larger inquiry. By examining in some detail the actions of railroads that experimented with braking and signaling and utilized these technical novelties in at least limited fashion before the government compelled them to do so, we gain deeper understanding of the thinking that informed all innovation in the railroad industry of the late nineteenth century.[2] These "paths seldom traveled" reveal more clearly how the technical changes that did occur resulted from choices exercised by railroad managers operating within a well-defined set of parameters. The cases of freight brakes and signals show how railroads in many respects pursued a path of least resistance, in which innovation served to enhance performance along a simple trajectory.

Unlike changes in rail shape or bearing alloys or firebox design, the technologies of continuous brakes and automatic signaling did not offer a single, clear benefit over established practice. None of them, for instance, were *simply* labor-saving devices. They also held forth the promise of other potential benefits such as improved safety and comfort or the ability to increase the speed of transit and thus offer a different quality of service. To capitalize on such potential, however, the innovator might very well find it necessary to make additional alterations to other elements of the established system, in effect setting off a cascade of change. All of this made calculation of the ultimate results of a proposed innovation extraordinarily difficult. There

[1] Braman B. Adams, *The Block System of Signaling on American Railroads* (New York: Railroad Gazette, 1901), pp. 170–171.

[2] For some suggestive ideas about the complexities involved in the selection and deployment of technologies affecting workplace safety, see Arthur F. McEvoy, "Working Environments: An Ecological Approach to Industrial Health and Safety," *Technology and Culture* 36 (1995): S145–S172.

was no single frontier against which these technologies worked and could be measured. Managers could not fully ascertain the costs and benefits until they had integrated these technologies fully into new routines. Consequently, those contemplating their use found themselves reconsidering the basic assumptions underlying railroad operations. Decisions to innovate in these areas thus involved an element of risk – a plunge into uncertainty – that did not occur in other cases.

Much of the uncertainty in these cases resulted from their potential implications for labor relations in the industry. The main course of innovation in railroading, of course, also had implications for labor – profound ones, at least when considered on the macroeconomic level. In bulking up, railroads substituted capital for labor. Longer, heavier trains pulled by bigger locomotives over track that needed less frequent repair – all added up to less labor required for each ton moved. Yet railroads managed to obtain these increasing returns from labor without directly confronting the issue of labor costs or vigorously pursuing labor-replacing technology. The labor-saving dimensions of change flowed incidentally from the attempt to handle more traffic without massive additional construction of parallel lines and other costly infrastructure. Railroads focused first on reducing their capital requirements, and saved labor in the process. The ultimate sources of much of the increased labor productivity, moreover, lay in the steel mills and in the locomotive and car works. When Andrew Carnegie introduced labor-replacing methods in his mills and confronted the steel makers at Homestead, railroads reaped the benefits in the form of lower prices for heavier rails, without significantly altering working conditions for their own employees. By designing their own locomotives but putting out the construction work, railroads could maintain control over a crucial technology while gradually reducing their own shop forces, which had traditionally been the source of much agitation in the industry.

In the case of air brakes and automatic block signals, railroads could not so easily skirt labor questions. These technologies invited direct comparisons between devices operated by a trainman or signalman with those activated automatically by the train itself. Even when railroads did not plan directly to eliminate jobs such as brakemen and dispatchers, by adopting these devices they might significantly alter procedures and work routines in unanticipated ways. The apparent labor-saving qualities of these technical innovations could not be understood apart from the larger system in which those technologies functioned.

While studies of braking and signaling help further elucidate the main course of innovation in late-nineteenth-century railroading, they also alert us to a fundamental transition that occurred around the turn of the twentieth century. A variety of factors, some resulting from internal dynamics and others imposed from outside, placed railroads under enormous strain, prompting them to question prevailing assumptions and to reassess their methods

of operation. In certain key cases, railroads experiencing a rapidly growing volume of traffic confronted operating conditions that would no longer
yield readily to tried-and-true remedies. Many lines also found themselves
responding to demands from customers for services that called for significant departures from normal procedures. Railroads facing these pressures
turned to technologies such as air brakes and automatic signals, despite
their previous reluctance and in spite of mounting concerns about labor,
even in the absence of government regulation. The changing regulatory
climate, which drew most of its energy from concerns about rates and finance rather than from a concern with safety per se, only added to these
pressures.

A study of braking and signaling, then, provides a bridge between two
epochs. It illustrates more vividly the contours of the engineering epoch that
characterized railroading during the last quarter of the nineteenth century,
while foreshadowing developments that would cause that ordered world to
come unhinged in the early twentieth.

AIR BRAKES IN FREIGHT SERVICE

By the mid-1870s, automatic air brakes had become an ubiquitous feature of
railroad passenger service. Virtually all passenger trains had them, and their
inventor, George Westinghouse, had earned fame and fortune. His Pittsburgh
factory supplied brakes to the entire industry. Recognizing that his initial
business would diminish as the market for passenger brakes grew saturated,
Westinghouse encouraged railroads to try his product on freight trains. A
trial on the Denver and Rio Grande Railroad during the summer of 1878 met
with favorable reviews in the trade literature. Application of air brakes to
freight trains, commented the editors of *Railroad Gazette*, was "only a matter
of time."[3] That time seemed short in coming when influential members of the
Pennsylvania's board of directors approached Westinghouse the following
spring about purchasing large numbers of brakes for freight equipment.[4] The
board also dispatched a special committee to investigate the possibility of

---

[3]   *Railroad Gazette* 10 (August 23, 1878): 417. The comment echoed an earlier one that
appeared in *Annual Report of the Proceedings of the Master Car-Builders' Association*
(henceforth, *MCBA Reports*), 1875. See also *Railway Age* 3 (August 29, 1878): 427,
and George Westinghouse, "Conception, Introduction, and Development of the Air
Brake," *Santa Fe Employees Magazine* 5 (September 1911): 35–43.

[4]   On negotiations between Westinghouse and the Pennsylvania, see Minutes of the
Meetings of the Committee on Supplies, May 1879 through August 1880, accompanying Minutes of the Meetings of the Board of Directors of the Pennsylvania Railroad (henceforth, PRR Board Minutes), Hagely Museum and Library, Wilmington,
Delaware. On similar negotiations at the Burlington, see Air Brake File, Papers of
the Chicago, Burlington and Quincy Railroad (henceforth, CBQ Papers), Newberry
Library, Chicago.

adopting automatic couplers for freight service.[5] Executives at the Burlington monitored the situation closely as well. When some freight cars owned by Western lines arrived at the Burlington system equipped with air brakes in 1883, Charles Perkins arranged to purchase brakes for a pair of twenty-five car freight trains and directed his subordinates to conduct rigorous trials.[6] The brakes performed well, and several key executives in the Burlington's operating departments became enthusiastic champions of their use in freight service. They advocated adding air brakes to all locomotives and to the entire fleet of some 15,000 freight cars over the next three or four years.[7]

Despite these auspicious omens, air brakes failed to take hold in many branches of railroad freight service during the 1880s and 1890s. After negotiating with Westinghouse for many months, both the Pennsylvania and the Burlington shelved their plans indefinitely. Most other railroads in the East and the Midwest followed the lead of these respected firms. Aside from those on a few lines in the mountainous Far West, where the difficulties of controlling trains on steep mountainous descents provided added inducements to substitute air brakes for hand brakes, train crews persisted in stopping freight trains with manual methods.[8] A government survey in 1893 revealed that fewer than 10 percent of the nation's freight cars had air brakes.[9] Even after the federal Safety Appliance Act of that year mandated use of air brakes in sufficient number to give engineers direct control over all freight trains, railroads moved very deliberately. In the early 1890s they adopted only between 30,000 and 40,000 air brakes per year, a rate that barely matched the annual additions of new cars to the total stock of freight equipment. Railroads lobbied successfully to push the original compliance date of 1898 back two more years, and even then in many cases added brakes to as few cars as the law allowed.[10]

5 Minutes of the Association of Transportation Officers of the Pennsylvania Railroad, January 14, March 18, and May 12, 1880, and January 8, 1881, Files of the Association of Transportation Officers of the Pennsylvania Railroad (henceforth, PRR ATO Files), Hagley Museum and Library, Wilmington, Delaware, Acc. 1810.

6 Westinghouse Air Brake Company to Chicago, Burlington and Quincy Railroad, November 21, 1883, Air Brake File, CBQ Papers.

7 William Forsyth to Godfrey W. Rhodes, May 31, 1884; W.A. Merrill to Harlan B. Stone, May 28, 1884; Stone to T. J. Potter, June 19, 1884; Potter to Stone, June 28, 1884; and Stone to Potter, July 5, 1884; Air Brake File, CBQ Papers.

8 *Railroad Gazette* 15 (August 24, 1883): 564, and 15 (February 2, 1883): 80, and Westinghouse, "Conception," p. 40. The Western companies adopting the air brake included the Central Pacific, Union Pacific, Santa Fe, and Northern Pacific.

9 United States Interstate Commerce Commission, *Annual Reports* (henceforth, *ICC Reports*), 1893; and *Railroad Gazette* 20 (October 12, 1888): 671, and 22 (March 21, 1890): 197.

10 The application of air brakes to freight trains following the Burlington trials can be followed in *ICC Reports*, 1889–1901, and United States Interstate Commerce Commission, *Annual Report on the Statistics of Railways in the United States* (henceforth, *ICC Statistics*), 1889–1901.

To a certain extent, this reluctance to deploy air brakes in freight service resulted from continuing concern about the high cost charged by the patent monopolist Westinghouse. As discussed in previous chapters, railroad managers had long chafed at having to pay premiums for patented technologies. When top management at the Pennsylvania Railroad expressed its desire to obtain automatic couplers for freight cars, for instance, it expressly predicated the move upon its success in finding a "modified Janney coupler." The line abandoned the effort after "a party was sent to the Patent Office . . . to secure data necessary to make a report in regard to the different inventions" and returned to inform the committee "there is such a mass of invention and so mixed that it would take six months to get the desired information, and we much doubt whether when secured it would be of any real value."[11] Considerable evidence suggests patents posed a similar obstacle in the case of automatic brakes. Both the Pennsylvania and the Burlington dropped their interest in air brakes during the 1880s only after Westinghouse persistently refused to issue licenses or to reduce prices.[12] The railroad patent associations challenged the validity of key Westinghouse patents, including one covering the hose couplings that linked brakes on each car to the rest of the braking system, which effectively prohibited railroads from mixing brakes manufactured by others into the Westinghouse system.[13] This effort failed to unseat Westinghouse, however, as did the public trials at Burlington, which the MCBA scheduled to coincide with expiration of his patents. Much to the disappointment of railroads, those trials actually ended up giving the inventor a chance to extend his patent control. When all brakes caused intolerable shocks on long trains during emergency stops, Westinghouse won the race to find a remedy. Altering the valvework in his existing braking systems so that brakes on each car fired nearly simultaneously, his firm devised the newly patented "quick action" air brake. Though Westinghouse lacked the sort of ironclad control provided by the patented hose coupling, patents covering the quick-action principle gave him a powerful competitive tool well into the twentieth century.[14]

---

[11]   Minutes, January 14, March 18, and May 12, 1880, and January 8, 1881, PRR ATO Files.

[12]   Minutes of the Meetings of the Committee on Supplies, May 1879 through August 1880, PRR Board Minutes; and Westinghouse Air Brake Company to Chicago, Burlington and Quincy Railroad, November 21, 1883, and George Westinghouse, Jr., to T. J. Potter, April 1, 1885; Air Brake File, CBQ Papers.

[13]   *Annual Report of the Executive Committee of the Eastern Railroad Association* 22 (1888): 27.

[14]   On the brake trials, see *Railroad Gazette* 19 (November 11, 1887): 729 and 734, and 20 (June 1, 1888): 346. On Westinghouse's continuing pursuit of patent control and negotiations with various railroads, see Godfrey Rhodes to C. M. Higginson, September 18, 1891, CBQ Papers, 3R2.1; Geo. Harris to C. E. Perkins, September 19 and 21, 1891, CBQ Papers, 3P4.51; Geo. Harris to T. S. Howland, September 28, 1891, CBQ Papers, 3P4.51; Geo. Harris to C. E. Perkins, October 3, 1891, CBQ

While patents certainly played an important role, the reluctance to deploy air brakes in freight service stemmed from other factors as well. For a variety of reasons, railroads could not easily assess the potential returns that might accrue from adding the devices. At the time Perkins of the Burlington authorized outfitting the two test trains in 1883, he asked General Manager Harlan Stone to prepare a report on the costs and benefits of using air brakes in freight service.[15] Stone's study yielded results far more ambiguous than those from the early technical trials. The initial expense of putting air brakes on the Burlington's 15,000 freight cars was clear. Westinghouse charged $50 per car for the equipment, and installation required another $42 per car, bringing the total outlay up to $1.38 million for the entire Burlington fleet.[16] Most other costs, however, were far more difficult to determine accurately until the air brake was actually employed in freight service. Stone hesitated, for instance, to estimate the annual cost of repairing 15,000 air brakes without having first set up and tried a program of routine maintenance. When his superiors insisted on attaining an estimate, Stone drew on his experience with air brakes in passenger service and on information obtained from the Western railroads to produce a figure of $2.50 per car, but he expressed serious doubts about the accuracy of this figure.[17]

Estimating the potential benefits of using air brakes in freight service proved especially problematical. Air brakes did not offer the sort of straightforward savings railroads attained from substituting superior materials or from making cars larger. Contrary to what their automatic operation might suggest, for instance, air brakes promised no savings in labor costs. Though the Westinghouse equipment eliminated the need for brakemen to scramble from car to car tightening brakes, it did not reduce the work force required to operate the trains, for the trainmen still needed to perform many

Papers, 3P4.51; H. H. Westinghouse to C. E. Perkins, December 7, 1891, CBQ Papers, 3P4.51; Godfrey Rhodes to Geo. Harris, December 10, 1891, CBQ Papers, 3P4.51; C. E. Perkins to Geo. Harris, December 11, 1891, CBQ Papers, 3P4.1, 31:240; C. E. Perkins to Geo. Westinghouse, December 11, 1891, CBQ Papers, 3P4.1, 31:241; Geo. Westinghouse to C. E. Perkins, December 14, 1891, CBQ Papers, 3P4.51; Godfrey Rhodes to Geo. Harris, December 14, 1891, CBQ Papers, 3R2.1; Mr. Quereaux to Mr. Forsyth, December 24, 1891, Laboratory Notebooks, A10:325–331, CBQ Papers; Geo. Harris to C. E. Perkins, December 28, 1891, CBQ Papers, 3P4.51; and Godfrey Rhodes to Geo. Harris, January 26, 1892, CBQ Papers, 3R2.1, and *Railroad Gazette* 26 (October 26, 1894): 740–741. For additional details, see Steven W. Usselman, "From Novelty to Order: George Westinghouse and the Business of Innovation during the Age of Edison," *Business History Review* 66 (1992): 251–304.

15 Westinghouse Air Brake Company to Chicago, Burlington and Quincy Railroad, November 21, 1883, Air Brake File, CBQ Papers.

16 Westinghouse Air Brake Company to Chicago, Burlington and Quincy Railroad, November 21, 1883; Rhodes to Stone, May 31 and June 18, 1884; Air Brake File, CBQ Papers.

17 Potter to Stone, June 28, 1884; Rhodes to Stone, July 2 and May 23, 1884; Stone to Potter, May 25, 1884; Air Brake File, CBQ Papers.

other functions such as throwing switches, checking equipment, and coupling cars. If anything, air brakes seemed likely to increase amounts spent on train crews, which would now have to check hose couplings and inspect the complex braking apparatus located on each car. These tasks so confounded brakemen that Westinghouse found it necessary to supply training cars and tutoring with each major sale.[18]

Unable to identify obvious direct savings, railroads contemplated more elusive benefits that might flow from the ability air brakes offered to stop trains faster and with greater smoothness and control. Western lines stood to gain substantial operating advantages from these qualities. Locomotive engineers preparing to descend steep grades in the Western mountains frequently paused their trains while brakemen lightly applied hand brakes on many cars, then stopped again at the bottom while the crew released the brakes. In addition to incurring such routine delays, trains on these routes often sustained flattened car wheels when anxious brakemen cranked down too hard during the descent and locked the wheels, causing them to slide rather than roll along the track.[19] Lines operating under less arduous circumstances lacked such clear incentives. At the Burlington, Stone predicted annual savings from reduced damages to equipment of $150,000, or roughly 10 percent of the total original investment. When pressed, however, he conceded that no one really knew precisely how many accidents air brakes would prevent or how much wear and tear to equipment they would eliminate.[20]

Advocates of air brakes at the Burlington and at lines to its east ultimately built their case around the potential returns from operating freight trains at increased speed. Proponents typically emphasized two possible benefits of faster travel. First, higher speeds would enable railroads to use facilities and personnel more effectively. Trains might travel greater distances in the same amount of time, thus increasing the work performed by the train crew and ultimately permitting railroads to expand their carrying capacity without purchasing additional cars and locomotives or laying more track. Second, high-speed transit without the customary accompanying jolts and risks of accident would enable railroads to capture lucrative areas of business. Stone cited the developing fast-freight industry as evidence of mounting demand for such service. He also noted that shorter shipping times would attract the

---

[18] *Railroad Gazette* 23 (March 27, 1891): 215. On these instruction cars, see "Air Brake Instruction Cars," *Santa Fe Employees' Magazine* 1 (July 1907): 197.

[19] Beginning with the demonstration on the Denver and Rio Grande in 1878, the Westinghouse company turned much of its attention to these railroads. Westinghouse developed a retaining valve that regulated the pressure in the air brake system during descents of these long grades. On the refinement for mountainous routes, see David G. Blaine, "The Importance of Being Able to Stop," *Trains* 35 (October 1975): 44–53.

[20] Rhodes to Stone, May 31, 1884; Stone to Potter, June 19, 1884; Air Brake File, CBQ Papers.

Figure 8.1. "The Fastest Time on Record: Photo'd by A. P. Yates, Syracuse, N.Y., May 10, 1893, when Engine 999 drawing the Empire State Express train, made the record of 112½ miles an hour." High-speed runs such as this stirred public interest but frustrated railroad management. *Courtesy:* Library of Congress.

business of fruit growers and others who shipped perishable goods over the rails.[21]

Neither of these arguments went unchallenged. The idea of running at increased speed flew in the face of established wisdom in the railroad industry. Most railroaders held it as an article of faith that higher speeds resulted in higher operating expenses, as trains consumed more fuel and caused tracks and equipment to wear more rapidly (Fig. 8.1). "It is not fully enough apprehended how speed enters into costs," cautioned Robert Harris of the

---

[21] This discussion of the debate over the benefits of increased speed is based on a variety of letters in the Air Brake File, CBQ Papers; on *MCBA Reports*, 1875–1888; and on assorted articles in *Railroad Gazette* and *Railway Age*. In his important study of technological innovation and productivity in the railroad industry, Albert Fishlow demonstrates that air brakes provided significantly lower gains in productivity than other innovations (such as steel rails). Fishlow further suggests that railroads acted rationally when they delayed equipping freight trains with air brakes. This analysis may be correct in hindsight, but both the public and private discussions among railroad managers indicate that at the time of the innovation these managers did not fully understand the economic effects the adoption of air brakes would produce. The process of innovation in the case of air brakes for freight trains cannot be interpreted simply in economic terms. Albert Fishlow, "Productivity and Technological Change in the Railroad Sector, 1840–1910," in National Bureau of Economic Research, *Output, Employment and Productivity in the United States after 1800* (New York: NBER and Columbia University Press, 1966), pp. 583–646.

Burlington in 1873 when dealing with prematurely worn rails in a section of track where trains reached unusually high speeds.[22] In the absence of compelling evidence to the contrary, executives persisted in this cautious approach for decades, preferring almost always to err on the side of slowness. Executives at the Pennsylvania, faced with mounting concerns about congestion on its main freight lines, asked a committee of its Association of Transportation Officers in 1895 to consider the most economical speed for freight trains. While freight cars could handle speeds above the prescribed rate of fifteen miles per hour, the committee cautioned, existing locomotives could not withstand such increases without "very greatly increased" costs of fuel and repairs. Perhaps, the committee allowed, engineers could push speeds to twenty-five miles per hour without excessive risk. But in the end it recommended the Pennsylvania retain a standard speed of fifteen miles per hour while seeking to obtain locomotives that would run more efficiently at higher speeds.[23] A similar study conducted at the Burlington five years later produced no more conclusive results. After extensive investigation, the man entrusted with this job complained about "the difficulties in the way of making even an approximate statement of the additional cost of running fast trains, as compared with an average rate of speed."[24] He eventually suggested that the best treatment of the subject could be found in a pamphlet written by Albert Fink a quarter-century earlier.[25] Revisiting the subject of train speeds once more in 1904, the ATO again puzzled despairingly over ascertaining the costs involved. "The effect of speed upon the various items of expense which enter into the cost per ton mile," declared the opening sentence of its two-page report on the subject, "is unknown."[26]

Arguments grounded in a desire to lure or retain business stood a better chance of persuading but still met with considerable resistance. Executives at the Burlington and elsewhere in the railroad industry consistently balked at demands from consumers to provide faster service and met them only grudgingly. Charles Perkins was reluctant even to accept a lucrative contract from the United States Post Office because he thought the emphasis on speed in mail delivery would foster bad habits and recklessness in other parts of the service. Perkins concurred with Burlington director John Murray Forbes, who saw no reason for the Post Office to ask the Burlington to run a fast mail train when the telegraph could better serve the need for fast communication. Perkins eventually accepted the contract, but only because he believed mail

[22]   R. Harris to A. J. Mattson, July 25, 1873, CBQ Papers, 3H4.1.
[23]   "Report of the Committee on Conducting Transportation," April 20, 1895, PRR ATO Files, box 1, file 22.
[24]   Howland to Delano, January 13, 1900, CBQ Papers, 3P4.1.
[25]   Howland to Perkins, January 16, 1890, CBQ Papers, 3P4.1.
[26]   "Report of the Committee on Conducting Transportation on 'For What Speed Should Slow Freight Trains Be Loaded as to Produce the Best Results in Cost per Ton Mile? For What Speed Should Fast Freight Trains Be Loaded to Produce the Best Results?'," May 2, 1904, PRR ATO Files, box 6.

trains made the railroad "more prominent" and "stronger with the public" and provided a learning exercise of some value to the passenger trade. "While a fast mail [train] may not be a necessity," he wrote Forbes, "there is all the time more and more pressure for faster passenger trains, and running a mail train for a year is a good means of educating our operatives to save time and it will also rather force us to more scientific methods which it is not easy to introduce till you are forced."[27]

Despite his obvious preference to run trains slowly, Perkins also struggled with mixed success to maintain control over speeds in certain branches of the freight business. In late 1884, with Burlington managers actively discussing the air brake, he lobbied among Midwestern lines to resist the spread of fast freight service.[28] The livestock business caused him recurrent headaches as well. Midwestern railroads such as the Burlington depended heavily upon shipments of this valuable product to the urban processing centers. Price wars erupted frequently, and railroads concocted many special services in an effort to attract drovers to their line. Because the animals either had to be fed in transit or lose valuable weight, speed presented a prime opportunity to attract business, and beginning in 1874 some Midwestern roads began offering express stock train service.[29] With the aid of the famous Iowa Pool, Robert Harris and other executives quelled this sort of rivalry for a time. Reflecting the widely shared consensus about speed, members of the pool resolved disputes over transit time more readily than those about rebates and other factors that disrupted their traffic agreements.[30] Express stock trains reappeared during the mid-1880s, however, as several Burlington competitors outfitted trains of stock cars with air brakes and close-fitting couplers and ran them at high speed. Some lines even attached sleeping cars for drovers who wished to accompany their animals to market.[31] When Perkins learned that one of his own stock trains had reached forty miles per hour, he chastised subordinates with the message, "We are all old enough to know better

27   Perkins to Forbes, March 13, 1884, CBQ Papers, 3F3.2.

28   Perkins to Potter, December 9, 1884, CBQ Papers, 3P4.1.

29   R. Harris to J. F. Barnard, March 5, 1874, CBQ Papers, 3H4.1.

30   Julius Grodinsky, *The Iowa Pool: A Study in Railroad Competition, 1870–94* (Chicago: University of Chicago Press, 1950).

31   Potter to Stone, September 16, 1885, CBQ Papers, 3P6.14, and Perkins to Potter, October 20, 1885, CBQ Papers, 3P6.36. "If thought best, the air brake can be dispensed with and thus save a large part of the estimated cost," conceded Traffic Agent E. Ripley when lobbying in 1889 for outfitting more stock cars in such fashion, "but the car will be much inferior to the private cars which mostly are equipped with air." E. Ripley to Henry B. Stone, February 12, 1889, CBQ Papers, 3P4.57. General Manager Stone "strongly recommended" such cars have air brakes as well as automatic couplers. "I make an especial point of the air brakes," he wrote Perkins, "not only because of their advantage in operating, but because all other Palace stock cars have these brakes, and if we attempt to furnish a car without air-brakes, we shall afford to our competitors, a strong point, and one visible to everyone, against us." Henry B. Stone to C.E. Perkins, February 19, 1889, CBQ Papers, 3P4.57.

than to engage in such senseless contests of speed which can prove nothing, cost money, and involve unnecessary risk."[32] Over the next several months, Burlington managers met several times with executives of competing lines in an effort to discontinue the express service and control train speeds.[33] The stock train issue reared its head once more during the early 1890s, when the Burlington again joined many other railroads in restricting speeds between the West Coast and Chicago.[34]

When division managers at the Pennsylvania learned of the competition among Chicago firms to run such trains, they uniformly expressed relief at not having to provide similar services. In the eyes of these executives – the most respected operating managers in the industry – prudence called for railroads to move freight slowly and methodically at their own discretion.[35] Yet even managers at the Pennsylvania conceded the need to run at high speed under certain conditions. The ATO committee of 1895, though clearly reluctant to deviate from established practice and run trains faster, acknowledged that a full account of the speed question must also consider "the necessity for high speed in order to meet competition, and other commercial necessities." It is "absolutely necessary" to run above twenty-five miles per hour in certain branches of service, its report conceded, while also acknowledging "occasions when certain classes of equipment must be moved at comparatively high speeds in order to meet the demand for cars," such as westbound coke on the Pittsburgh Division. Still, the committee remained doubtful whether such practices yielded genuine returns. "Whether this increased cost [in fuel and repairs] has been counterbalanced by increased earnings in the shape of increased patronage," it noted with obvious skepticism, "your committee [are] unable to determine."[36]

Even in those rare cases where the overall time of freight transit decreased, railroads did not necessarily increase the speed of trains. Lines sought first to reduce the amount of time trains stood idle, rather than to increase the speed while in motion. The general manager of the Burlington understood this approach clearly. Recognizing that "there is more and more of a demand

[32] Perkins to Potter, October 20, 1885, CBQ Papers, 3P6.36.

[33] Potter to Stone, October 26, 1885, CBQ Papers, 3P6.13; Stone to Potter, October 31, 1885, CBQ Papers, 6.36; Potter to Perkins, November 2 and November 14, 1885, CBQ Papers, 3P4.56; and Perkins to Potter, November 13, 1885, CBQ Papers, 3P6.36.

[34] Calvert to Holdrege, December 18, 1889; Pendleton to Ripley, December 27, 1889, and January 2, 1890; Ripley to Stone, December 30, 1889; Thomas Miller to Holdrege, January 3, 1890; Holdrege to Stone, January 4, 1890; and Merrill to Stone, January 22, 1890; CBQ Papers, 3P4.57; and G. Harris to Perkins, September 16 and 29, 1890; and April 10, 1893; CBQ Papers, 3P4.51.

[35] "Report of Committee on Conducting Transportation on the Relationship Existing Between the Present Practice of Classification and the Proposed Adoption for General Use of Freight Train Air-Brakes," c. 1894, PRR ATO Files, box 1, file 11.

[36] "Report of the Committee on Conducting Transportation," April 20, 1895, PRR ATO Files, box 1, file 22.

for good time on stock and higher classes of freight," he explained that, "to do this successfully, and not run trains at excessive rates of speed, it is necessary to keep trains moving, and not lying on side-tracks at meeting points."[37] Perkins concurred with his subordinate. When arranging for the fast mail train, he told his assistant, "The time lost in stops is what we want to get rid of."[38] This is what Perkins meant when he spoke of introducing "scientific methods" into railroad operations.

Like virtually all American railroads of the late nineteenth century, the Burlington had considerable room for improvement in this regard. Though the challenges posed by running fast passenger trains captured more attention from the public, then and now, railroads understood that the freight business presented them with problems of much greater complexity. Freight operations took place on a grander scale and involved a much greater diversity of products and tasks. Passenger trains might travel rapidly and meet tight schedules, but they generally stayed together as coherent units for long stretches of time, traveling the same route over and over again, with regular crews and routine inspections. Many freight trains, in contrast, were continually reshuffled as crews picked up cars from various sidings and dropped them off at others. Demand for services varied widely, making routine elusive. Railroads faced a daunting task in trying to impose order in this vast, diverse, fluid realm. But the very difficulty of the task meant it offered innumerable opportunities for improvement.

A great deal could be accomplished without resort to technology at all. Railroads could clear considerable space in their networks and avoid unnecessary delays simply by taking greater care when assembling trains and by scheduling train movements more shrewdly. Freight agents and traffic departments, which once functioned strictly to generate business, devoted more and more of their time to recording and analyzing data pertaining to the flow of goods through the system.[39] Pursuing the ultimate goal of operating fewer trains but carrying more traffic, managers focused ever more intently on composing trains in ways that minimized the number of empty cars and added more goods to each train. The "train-load" – the ratio of tonnage actually carried to total capacity – became ever more firmly established as the crucial measure of operating performance.[40] Fewer but heavier trains, quickly and smoothly assembled, would move slowly but steadily through a less congested system.

In addition to paying closer heed to planning and coordinating the flow of traffic, railroads went to considerable lengths during the last quarter of

---

37 Stone to Potter, January 11, 1884, CBQ Papers, 3P6.37.
38 Perkins to Potter, March 12, 1884, CBQ Papers, 3P6.36.
39 Olivier Zunz, *Making America Corporate, 1870–1920* (Chicago: University of Chicago Press, 1990), ch. 2.
40 For an example of the use of train loads in evaluating service, see G. Harris to Holdrege, November 9, 1900, CBQ Papers, 3P4.51.

the nineteenth century to secure the active cooperation of their employees. Workers remained an essential element in the operating system, especially on the freight side, where flexibility and an ability to adjust to unusual circumstances counted for so much. No workers were more important in these respects than those who ran the trains themselves. Railroads treated this group gingerly, especially after the disruptive strikes of 1877.[41] They paid trainmen well – much better than the shop workers and trackmen – and attempted to foster a sense of professionalism by formalizing work rules and grievance procedures and by encouraging the formation of mutual insurance programs.[42] Historian Walter Licht found that workers, perhaps even more than managers, advocated these steps toward greater bureaucratization of labor–management relations.[43] Though managers may have preferred the flexibility and discretionary power of a less formal relationship, the emphasis on rules fitted easily with their fundamental goal of creating a disciplined work force that would follow prescribed procedures. Railroads tolerated the conservative brotherhoods that arose during the closing decades of the century, using them to help enforce rules and secure the dependable employees who would not disrupt the smooth operation of their lines. The contracts the brotherhoods negotiated through collective bargaining, notes a historian who studied labor at the Santa Fe, usually "encompassed few alterations in independent company policy.... Management's basic desire was to maintain a steady, productive work force."[44] Railroad managers sought to achieve this goal as cheaply as possible, of course, and disputes over wage levels precipitated frequent strikes (Fig. 8.2). But on the whole railroads were willing to pay competitive wages, and sometimes better, in order to keep and maintain a reliable work force.[45]

[41]   Philip S. Foner, *The Great Labor Uprising of 1877* (New York: Monad Press, 1977), and Nick Salvatore, "Railroad Workers and the Great Strike of 1877: The View from a Small Midwest City," *Labor History* 21 (1980): 522–545.

[42]   Dan Mater, "The Development and Operation of the Railroad Seniority System," *Journal of Business of the University of Chicago* 13 (1940): 387–419. "Doubtless railroad managements finally came to realize that, while seniority would entail a partial surrender of their prerogative of job allocation, the loss therefrom might be compensated by a decrease in the extremely high rate of labor turnover," notes Mater on p. 16, citing sentiments expressed in *Railroad Gazette* in 1880.

[43]   Walter Licht, *Working for the Railroad: The Organization of Work in the Nineteenth Century* (Princeton, N.J.: Princeton University Press, 1983), p. 125.

[44]   James H. Ducker, *Men of the Steel Rails: Workers on the Atchison, Topeka, and Santa Fe Railroad, 1869–1900* (Lincoln: University of Nebraska Press, 1983), quotes from pp. 114 and 125.

[45]   In addition to Ducker, *Men of the Steel Rails*, see Nick Salvatore, *Eugene V. Debs: Citizen and Socialist* (Urbana: University of Illinois University Press, 1982); Shelton Stromquist, *A Generation of Boomers: The Pattern of Railroad Labor Conflict in Nineteenth-Century America* (Urbana: University of Illinois Press, 1987); and Richard Schneirov et al., eds., *The Pullman Strike and the Crisis of the 1890s: Essays on Labor*

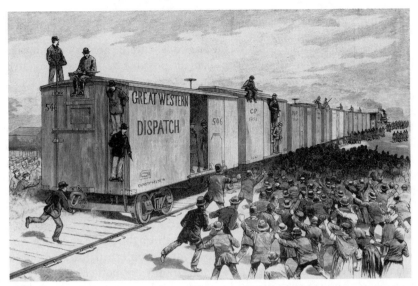

Figure 8.2. During the strike of 1886, one of many labor disputes of the period, National Guardsmen mounted cars equipped with hand brakes and link-and-pin couplers. *Courtesy:* Library of Congress.

Railroad managers of the late nineteenth century thus implicitly weighed new technologies against a broad set of alternatives that might involve little or no new technical content. The unrelenting efforts to bulk up the basic technical components of railroading, with larger locomotives tugging more cars of greater capacity over rails containing increasing amounts of metal, by and large complemented the administrative initiatives. They helped keep the number of trains to a minimum, and they enhanced the productivity of labor without directly altering work structures and routines. Crews accustomed to being compensated for a daily run between two points would perform roughly the same tasks at the same pace, but haul considerably more cargo in the process. (A major source of disgruntlement leading to the labor violence of the 1870s had been the double-heading of trains,

and Politics (Urbana and Chicago: University of Illinois Press, 1999). Andrew Dawson, "The Paradox of Dynamic Technological Change and the Labor Aristocracy in the United States, 1880–1914," *Labor History* 20 (1979): 325–351, suggests that conditions in railroading may well have followed patterns prevalent throughout much of the American economy. See also Alexander James Field, "Land Abundance, Interest/Profit Rates, and Nineteenth-Century American and British Technology," *Journal of Economic History* 43 (1983): 405–431. On an industry with close parallels to railroading, see Logan Hovis and Jeremy Mouat, "Miners, Engineers, and the Transformation of Work in the Western Mining Industry, 1880–1930," *Technology and Culture* 37 (1996): 429–456.

a measure whose motivation was too obviously the reduction of labor costs.)

Air brakes, in contrast, often seemed at odds with the goals of administrative reforms. Though the higher speeds made possible by air brakes might in certain circumstances enable trains to make up lost time and maintain schedules, railroads perceived little advantage in incorporating faster travel into ordinary operations. The potential benefits of increased speed simply did not seem worth the risks of disrupting routines and fomenting disgruntlement among employees. To gain the full benefits from the air brakes, moreover, railroads would have to make certain all cars outfitted with the equipment were switched to the front of each train, so that the pipes and hoses connecting the brakes to the air supply on the locomotive would not be interrupted. The extra switching confounded efforts to assemble trains more smoothly into various classifications and also burdened train crews with added tasks. An extensive survey of practices prevailing throughout the industry, conducted privately in 1894 by the Pennsylvania, confirmed fears among its management that many train crews would simply not bother with the extra movements. Though the railroad brotherhoods had by then supported new legislation mandating use of air brakes, in practice crews often left the air brakes disconnected while continuing to use hand brakes to slow and stop their trains. Though freights traveling on the Pennsylvania's busiest eastern divisions on average contained at least a quarter or more cars with air brakes, at most only 30 percent of those brakes were actually in use. On several divisions, crews left at least four out of five equipped cars disconnected, so that on average well under 5 percent of cars in each train had working air brakes. This level of performance lagged behind that of some other lines, conceded the authors of the report, but "until these outside roads attacked the problem with an arbitrary order, the difficulties brought forward seemed insurmountable."[46] Only by confronting their workers directly, and risking reprisals, could the Pennsylvania and other railroads capitalize on their investment in air brakes.

The switching issue proved all the more vexing because railroads interchanged freight cars so extensively with other lines. This practice – an administrative reform designed to eliminate the need to transfer goods between cars and thus to facilitate movement through the rail network – meant that even lines purchasing air brakes for their entire fleets might not avoid the problems of assembling trains in ways that utilized the costly equipment. Executives such as the Burlington's Perkins raised this concern repeatedly when refusing to equip his freight cars with air brakes during the 1880s. Such fears remained a primary obstacle to innovation even after the MCBA issued industry standards for automatic braking equipment in 1888. While

[46] "Report on Freight Train Air-Brakes," c. 1894, PRR ATO Files, box 1, file 11.

these standards ensured that lines adopting brakes would choose devices capable of attaching to one another, the MCBA could not compel railroads to make the switch to automatic equipment.

For any number of reasons, then, air brakes remained something of a rarity in routine freight operations throughout most of the nineteenth century. For a long while, lines outside the Far West restricted their use to premium services such as express stock trains, fast freight, and refrigerated shipments, in which speed figured prominently and trains typically stayed together as a unit.[47] Aside from a fifty-car train it equipped for Westinghouse to use at the Burlington trials, prior to 1888 the Pennsylvania added air brakes just to fifty stock cars (in spring 1881) and to 100 refrigerator cars (in June 1886). Air brakes grew decidedly more common following the trials at Burlington. In 1888, managers at the Pennsylvania decided to place them on all stock cars and box cars newly purchased for use on their lines east of Pittsburgh. Two years later the Pennsylvania began installing air brakes on such cars as they came in for repair, and in 1892 it extended the purchase policy to all types of new freight cars used throughout its system. By then, the Pennsylvania owned more than 10,000 freight cars equipped with air brakes.[48] All Burlington stock cars had air brakes by 1894, and 30 percent of its total fleet was likewise equipped. The New York Central was adding brakes to nearly 300 freight cars a month at that point. Managers at these lines and several others reported that their employees had overcome their initial resistance and now willingly expended the effort necessary to get air brakes attached to the locomotives.[49] Yet as the Pennsylvania well understood, use of the air brake could easily complicate freight movements, especially in cases where trains consisted of cars originating from diverse locations.

By the time these railroads acquired air brakes in significant quantities, moreover, firms could no longer assess their worth strictly on technical and economic grounds, for in the wake of the trials at Burlington the public had turned its attention toward the question of railroad safety. Buoyed by

---

47 Because trains on Western lines often traveled long distances without adding new cars, they avoided the switching problems that plagued railroads in more congested areas. The Western companies had a further advantage because their common ownership tied them together and facilitated simultaneous action on the air brake and other aspects of the interchangeability issue.

48 Theo. N. Ely to F. L. Sheppard, December 7, 1888, and July 8, 1890; and Theo. N. Ely to J. M. Wallis, August 23, 1892; plus attachments; Records of the Motive Power Department (henceforth, PRR Motive Power Records), Altoona Office Files, Pennsylvania Railroad Papers, Hagley Museum and Library, Wilmington, Delaware, Acc. 1810. Between January 1, 1888, and January 1, 1892, the number of Pennsylvania freight cars equipped with air brakes increased from 486 to 10,104; the number equipped with automatic couplers grew from 436 to 12,076.

49 "Report on Freight Train Air-Brakes," c. 1894, PRR ATO Files, box 1, file 11.

growing antirailroad sentiment that led to passage of the federal Interstate Commerce Act (1887) and the Sherman Anti-Trust Act (1890), humanitarian reformers concerned with the safety of railroad workers campaigned for legislation requiring railroads to equip freight trains with continuous brakes and automatic couplers.[50] The reformers initially drafted bills at the state level, but the interchange of cars among railroads from many different states forced them to seek national legislation from Congress. In March 1889 the state railroad commissioners urged the Interstate Commerce Commission (ICC), the national regulatory agency Congress had established two years earlier, to advocate such legislation.[51] Three months later the ICC received a similar request signed by over 10,000 members of the Brotherhood of Railroad Brakemen, a recently formed union that enabled brakemen for the first time to voice their grievances collectively.[52] These petition drives attracted considerable attention, and the campaign for railroad safety rapidly acquired the support of a public that harbored strong opposition to the power of the railroads. Faced with this public pressure, Congress began holding hearings in 1890 on several bills that proposed federal laws pertaining to railroad safety equipment.

Railroads initially opposed efforts to legislate railroad safety. Even superintendents of motive power from the few railroads that had ordered large numbers of air brakes testified against the proposed laws. Claiming they would adopt the safety appliances in due course without interference from Congress, railroads steered debate toward a court-based approach and away from a legislative one. Rather than prescribe blanket requirements compelling railroads to deploy a supposed means to improved safety, railroads argued, why not let courts assess responsibility for damages in particular cases? Such arguments, which railroads had evoked with success in resisting proposed state safety laws since the early 1870s, worked to the interest of railroads because judges had long since knitted together a series of rules

---

[50] The best sources on the legislative process are the hearings Congress held on the proposed laws, transcripts of which can be found in U.S. House of Representatives, *Miscellaneous Documents,* 51st Cong., 1st sess., report nos. 142 and 145; U.S. House of Representatives, 52nd Cong., 1st sess., report no. 1678; and U.S. Senate, "Reports from the Committee on Interstate Commerce," 52nd Cong., 1st sess., report no. 1049. See also *ICC Reports,* 1889–1893, and the *New York Times.* On the railroad safety movement more generally, see Charles Hugh Clark, "The Railroad Safety Movement in the United States, 1869 to 1893" (Ph.D. dissertation, University of Illinois, 1966); Charles H. Clark, "The Development of the Semi-Automatic Freight-Car Coupler, 1863–1893," *Technology and Culture* 13 (1972): 170–208; Kurt Wetzel, "Railroad Management's Response to Operating Employees Accidents, 1890–1913," *Labor History* 21 (1980): 351–368; and Mark Aldrich, *Safety First: Technology, Labor, and Business in the Building of American Work Safety, 1870–1939* (Baltimore: Johns Hopkins University Press, 1997), ch. 1.

[51] U.S. Senate, "Reports from the Committee on Interstate Commerce," 52nd Cong., 1st sess., report no. 1049, pp. 1–5.

[52] *ICC Reports,* 1889, pp. 338–339.

that effectively cut most workers off from relief in court. The doctrine of assumed risk, for example, shifted the burden of maintaining safe practices from employer to employee so long as the former had adequately informed the latter of the dangers inherent in the task. Its close cousin, the doctrine of contributory negligence, left employees responsible for their own fate if they had failed to observe a rule or in any way contributed to their own injury. The fellow-servant rule absolved employers in cases where a colleague of the injured party had caused the accident. Yet another inheritance from the common law prohibited relatives of deceased victims from filing suits on their behalf. Though state legislatures and sympathetic judges had started to open holes in this thicket of legal obstacles, railroads still preferred to take their chances in court.[53]

By the time of the 1892 presidential campaign, when the candidates from both major parties advocated safety legislation, railroads recognized that the growing public support for legislation dwarfed any opposition they could muster. They then set their sights on obtaining the most favorable bill possible. With the help of their old friend Senator Cullom, who had

[53] Lawrence M. Friedman, *A History of American Law* (New York: Simon and Schuster, 1973), pp. 410–424; Christopher L. Tomlins, "A Mysterious Power: Industrial Accidents and the Legal Construction of Employment Relations in Massachusetts, 1800–1850," *Law and History Review* 6 (1988): 375–438, and *Law, Labor, and Ideology in the Early American Republic* (Cambridge: Cambridge University Press, 1993), ch. 10; Eric Tucker, *Administering Danger in the Workplace: The Law and Politics of Occupational Health and Safety in Ontario, 1850–1920* (Toronto: University of Toronto Press, 1990); and Jonathon Simon, "For the Government of Its Servants: Law and Disciplinary Power in the Work Place, 1870–1906," *Studies in Law, Politics, and Society* 13 (1993): 105–136. By 1874, notes Friedman, legislatures in Georgia, Wyoming, Iowa, and Kansas had all passed statutes giving railroad workers the right to recover damages from their employers even if a fellow servant had contributed to the accident. Another dozen states had adopted similar statutes by 1908, according to historian Harry Weiss, and many others had modified the fellow-servant rule in ways that gave workers greater chances at recovering damages. The ban on liability suits in cases involving death had been abolished in thirty-nine states by 1904. Ten states by 1896 had outlawed contracts that called for employees to waive their rights to sue, and another seventeen took similar action during the next dozen years. Harry Weiss, "Employers' Liability and Workmen's Compensation," in John R. Commons et al., *History of Labor in the United States, 1896–1932*, vol. 3 (New York, 1935), pp. 564–610, esp. pp. 568–569. On the growing number of injury cases receiving favorable treatment in the courts, see Friedman, *History of American Law*, and Edward D. Berkowitz and Kim McQuaid, *Creating the Welfare State: The Political Economy of 20th-Century Reform* (Lawrence: University of Kansas Press, 1988, 1992), p. 44, who report data showing that the number of workmen's compensation cases rose from 92 to 736 per year between 1875 and 1905. A sample of those cases showed that jurors decided in favor of employers only 98 times out of 1,043. On the possibility that workers in the absence of legislation received higher wages in return for incurring increased risk, see Price V. Fishback and Shawn Everett Kantor, " 'Square Deal' or Raw Deal? Market Compensation for Workplace Disamenities, 1884–1903," *Journal of Economic History* 52 (1992): 826–848.

been instrumental in curbing more extreme proposals for rate regulation, they helped fix attention on an act that narrowly specified the use of safety appliances and did not open the door for more general action. Regulation of safety appliances offered a convenient means of addressing the problem without establishing government administrative capacity to investigate operating procedures or otherwise assert a more prominent influence over railroad practices. Most railroad managers testifying at the hearings concentrated on assuring the eventual law designated desirable standards for the equipment. Railroads succeeded in this aim, and the Safety Appliance Act that became law in 1893 effectively required the railroads to meet MCBA standards for continuous brakes and automatic couplers by the end of 1898. Lines need only place brakes on sufficient numbers of cars at the front of the train to enable the locomotive engineer to stop without assistance from brakemen.[54] Courts would remain the primary forum for resolving worker safety issues, though with the act in place railroads would now stand liable in cases where they failed to provide the necessary safety equipment.[55]

Though many railroads ultimately embraced the Safety Appliance Act as the lesser of evils, their support for the bill by no means heralded any significant change in thinking about the merits of automatic brakes in freight service. The act basically embraced current practice by the best firms and helped railroads ensure standardization and a level playing field. For several years railroads continued to adopt air brakes at a pace that just kept up with production of new cars. Laboring under the burdens of economic recession and still struggling to get around Westinghouse, they appealed successfully for a two-year extension of the designated time limit. Congress upped the requirement for brakes when it agreed to slip the original deadline, so that by 1903 all freight cars would be required to have self-couplers, and half in every train were to be equipped with automatic brakes.[56] Only during the two years before the second deadline, after Congress refused to grant another extension, did most railroads equip significant proportions of their freight car fleets with air brakes.[57]

[54] U.S. House of Representatives, Miscellaneous Documents, 51st Cong. 1st sess., report nos. 142 and 145; U.S. House of Representatives, 52nd Cong., 1st sess., report no. 1678; and U.S. Senate, "Reports from the Committee on Interstate Commerce," 52nd Cong., lst sess., report no. 1049. Additional examples of railroad opposition to safety legislation appear in *Railroad Gazette*, 1887–1893.

[55] Friedman, *History of American Law*, p. 420.

[56] U.S. Interstate Commerce Commission, "Summary History of Legislation Regarding Safety Appliances," n.d. (c. 1896), mss. copy in ICC Library, Washington, D.C., and *ICC Reports*, 1893–1907.

[57] The response to the Safety Appliance Act can be followed in the *ICC Reports*, 1893–1907. In asking for an extension of the act, many railroads complained that the depression of the mid-1890s had prevented them from purchasing air brakes for freight trains.

SIGNALING TECHNOLOGY

Developments in railroad signaling technology traced a course similar in many respects to that of automatic brakes on freight trains. A variety of novel signaling methods received widespread notoriety during the mid-1870s, as railroads and state commissioners investigated the field quite intensively following the disaster at Revere. They examined the merits of a variety of signaling devices, including semaphores and crossing gates activated automatically by trains via electrical track circuit and interlocking machines designed to coordinate signal settings and switch movements. During this period railroads also grasped the essentials of block methods, in which trains proceeded through successive segments of track governed by signals. When deployed in its absolute form, with trains strictly prohibited from entering each block of track until the previous train had vacated, this "space interval" system provided a level of assurance against collision that no dispatching or "time interval" system could achieve. If the signals governing the blocks operated via track circuit, such an absolute block system seemingly provided automatic "fail safe" protection, without reliance on human operators other than the men who ran the locomotives and observed the signals.

While techniques such as automatic block signaling and interlocking devices held out the promise to safety advocates of greater security against accident, in the eyes of railroads, these technologies also represented potential means of improving the smooth flow of goods and passengers through their systems. "The public saw in signaling the possibilities for greater safety," recalled a signal engineer for the Burlington in his textbook of 1909; "the railroads saw opportunities for both safety and efficiency in operation."[58] For most of the nineteenth century, questions of efficiency took precedence. Following the initial burst of interest during the 1870s, public pressure to require signaling technology built considerably slower than it did in the case of automatic brakes. Long after passengers demanded trains have good brakes, they still did not expect to be protected by automatic signals along routes that might traverse thousands of miles. Nor did the labor unions and the movement for railroad safety look to signaling for relief, for the number of employee deaths and injuries caused by collisions paled when compared with those resulting from switching, coupling, and braking. Because lines

---

[58] Edward Everett King, *Railway Signaling* (New York: McGraw-Hill, 1921), p. 2. In this volume, when discussing the use of automatic signals on single track lines, King elaborated on this idea. "Automatic block signals provide for efficiency and safety in operation on a single-track road as well as on a double-track line. When a single-track line reaches the point of congestion, the installation of automatic block signals will relieve the congestion and postpone the day when double-tracking becomes necessary. The installation of the signals requires very little time, expense and labor in comparison with the construction of a double track. Some roads report that the capacity of a single track has been increased by 20% with the installation of automatic block signals." King, *Railway Signaling*, p. 249.

retained full responsibility for monitoring movement of trains over their own tracks, moreover, signaling did not raise troubling questions about interchangeability of the sort that stimulated talk at trade associations and other industry-wide venues in the cases of air brakes and couplers. Individual railroads thus remained free throughout the nineteenth century to install signals largely on their own terms, much as they did with air brakes in freight service prior to passage of the Safety Appliance Act.

Left to their own devices, railroads acted with something less than zealous enthusiasm. Managers at the Chicago, Burlington and Quincy Railroad pursued a policy typical of many railroads. The Burlington showed early interest in crossing gates during the 1870s but added them sporadically.[59] After supporting some experiments conducted by its superintendent of the telegraph during the early 1870s, the Burlington gave little attention to electric signaling until 1881, when it tried a limited installation from the newly formed Union Switch and Signal Company.[60] The Burlington did not invest substantial sums in electric signals until 1884, when it purchased an extensive interlocking facility to monitor the movement of trains in and out of its Chicago yards.[61] Though the CB&Q added a smattering of interlocking devices at crossings during the next few years, the large plant at Chicago remained an isolated exception until the 1890s, when the railroad embarked on a program to outfit many major crossings with interlocking equipment.[62] The Burlington used no block signals prior to the twentieth century aside from those on its extraordinarily busy stretch of some forty miles between Chicago and its yards at Aurora, where the signals helped space trains arriving at the interlocking plants.[63] The CB&Q converted those blocks to automatic signals in 1901, but chose to use manual devices as it placed other stretches of track under block operation during the early twentieth century.[64] Even this limited program placed the Burlington at the forefront of signaling innovators among Midwestern lines. More often than

---

59 R. Harris to Wilcox, December 6, 1867; R. Harris to Hitchcock, August 16, 1870; and R. Harris to C. Latimer, July 17, 1873; CBQ Papers, 3H4.1.
60 Union Switch and Signal Company (F. S. Guerber) to T. J. Potter, August 23, 1881; O. E. Stewart to Potter, August 31, 1881; Potter to J. D. Besler, September 1, 1881; F. C. Rice to Besler, September 3, 1881; and Besler to Potter, September 4, 1881; CBQ Papers, 3P6.21.
61 Robert McClure to Potter, June 4, 1884, CBQ Papers, 3P4.56.
62 C. E. Perkins to H. B. Stone, March 12, May 8 and 15, 1890; and Perkins to G. Harris, June 28 and July 11, 1892; CBQ Papers, 3P4.1.
63 McClure to Potter, June 4, 1884, CBQ Papers, 3P4.56.
64 Stone to Perkins, July 2, 1889, CBQ Papers, 3P4.57; Perkins to F. A. Delano, January 25, 1890, CBQ Papers, 3P4.1; and G. Harris to Perkins, June 29, 1901, CBQ Papers, 3P4.51. The Burlington's chief signal engineer, John Latimer, wrote a textbook in 1909 that argued repeatedly for the superiority of manual over automatic block signaling. See James Brandt Latimer, *Railway Signaling in Theory and Practice* (Chicago: Mackenzie-Klink, 1909).

not, managers from the CB&Q initiated discussions with other companies about interlocking signals at mutual crossings, and Burlington officials noted that neighboring railroads followed their lead in trying automatic electric signals.[65]

Eastern companies, acting independently of the Burlington, proceeded in much the same fashion. They first installed crossing gates and some isolated interlocking devices, then purchased extensive, complicated interlocking facilities for their busiest terminals. The Pennsylvania began installing interlocking signals at crossings and switches around 1880, when it acquired some devices from the leading British supplier, Saxby and Farmer, which had exhibited interlocking devices at the Centennial Exhibition in Philadelphia.[66] Later in the 1880s, the Pennsylvania contracted with the Union Switch and Signal Company for complex interlocking systems governing movements at its new passenger terminals in Philadelphia and New York. At about the same time, the Philadelphia and Reading also had the experts from Westinghouse install new interlocking plants at its major terminals.[67]

These same railroads also pioneered in use of signals along their busy main lines. During the Civil War, the Reading mounted hand-operated signals on towers located at curves and other dangerous spots along its mountainous route. Though apparently not operated in strict block fashion for another two decades or more, these distinctive blue and white discs marked a pioneering use of signals along the line and attracted considerable attention in the industry.[68] The Pennsylvania took the lead in true block signaling. By 1876, the line had established a rigidly operated manual block system, with signals spaced regularly along the route regardless of station location, from New York through Philadelphia to Pittsburgh.[69] These routes all had multiple tracks on which trains traveled in one direction only. Attendants in the towers, linked by telegraph, regulated the movement of trains by displaying a stop signal when a train passed their station and changing it to "go"

---

[65] For examples of the Burlington initiating discussions of crossing signals, see Perkins to G. Harris, June 28, 1892, CBQ Papers, 3P4.1, and G. Harris to Perkins, June 29, 1901, CBQ Papers, 3P4.51.

[66] "Report of the Committee on Signals," January 14, 1880, PRR ATO Files. On interlockings in general, see Latimer, *Railway Signaling*, pp. 35–247, and Adams, *Block System*, pp. 173–214.

[67] On developments in signaling connected with stations in New York City, see Carl W. Condit, *The Port of New York*, 2 vols. (Chicago: University of Chicago Press, 1980–1981).

[68] On using these signals in block fashion, see A. McLeod to W. F. Merrill, November 6, 1890, vol. 604, pp. 378–379, Papers of the Philadelphia and Reading Railroad Company (henceforth, Reading Papers), Hagley Museum and Library, Wilmington, Delaware, Acc. 1451, and *Annual Reports of the Philadelphia and Reading Railroad Company* (1894), pp. 14–15; (1895), p. 13; and (1896), p. 8.

[69] *Annual Reports of the Pennsylvania Railroad Company* (henceforth, *PRR Annual Reports*), 28 (1874), p. 123; 29 (1875), pp. 34, 117, and 127; and 30 (1876), p. 31.

when they learned that the train had passed the next tower.[70] In constructing this network of stations dedicated exclusively to signaling and operating it in this fashion, the Pennsylvania jumped ahead of the rest of the industry by at least a decade. No other American railroad had a similar system prior to 1885, and even then most lines installed blocks only in certain busy stretches.[71]

The Pennsylvania pioneered again at the end of the century when it converted block stations along several hundred miles of its routes to automatic operation.[72] Reports at the time hailed these facilities as representing the new state of the art, and soon several other lines besides the Burlington followed suit. Railroads converted over 1,000 miles to automatic control in 1901 alone, bringing the total amount of rail route governed by the automatic block system to 2,300 miles.[73] When the ICC conducted its first survey of signaling practices in 1907, it found nearly 11,000 miles equipped with automatic block signals.[74] As in the case of automatic brakes a decade before, however, this increased use of automatic block signaling occurred under cloud of threatened legislation from Congress, which began in 1901 to consider requests from the ICC and some of its members to require the block system. Five years later, Congress authorized the regulatory agency to conduct a special study of "block signals and appliances for the automatic control of trains," and in 1907 it created a Block Signal and Train Control Board to help carry out the task.

Explanations for this sluggish pace of change in signaling point to much the same mix of factors that discouraged railroads from making more extensive use of air brakes in freight service. As tools for increasing the flow of trains through the system, signaling technologies in effect competed with alternatives such as heavier trains, stronger rails, and shrewder scheduling. All of these helped keep congestion to a minimum and enabled railroads to maintain slower speeds, thus reducing pressures that served as the primary inducements to deploy comprehensive changes in signaling such as the block system. A report from the Pennsylvania's Association of Transportation Officers in 1898 regarding new steel-framed boxcars (Fig. 8.3) expressed prevailing attitudes quite succinctly: "The rates are declining and will continue to decline, and the only way to offset the decline is to decrease the cost

---

[70] Adams, *Block System*, pp. 7–23. In 1901, the 105-mile stretch from Philadelphia to Harrisburg contained 51 sections.

[71] U.S. Senate, "Report of the Interstate Commerce Commission on Block-Signal Systems and Appliances for the Automatic Control of Railway Trains," 59th Cong., 2d sess., document no. 342, pp. 6–7.

[72] George H. Burgess and Miles C. Kennedy, *Centennial History of the Pennsylvania Railroad Company* (Philadelphia: Pennsylvania Railroad Company, 1949), p. 494.

[73] Adams, *Block System*, pp. 170–171.

[74] U.S. Interstate Commerce Commission, "Final Report of the Block Signal and Train Control Board to the Interstate Commerce Commission," June 29, 1912, p. 7.

(a)

(b)

Figure 8.3. Built on a steel frame and equipped with air brakes, the typical new Pennsylvania boxcar at the turn of the century carried 100,000 lbs., nearly double the capacity of those built just a few years earlier. *Courtesy*: Hagley Museum and Library.

of handling; the only way to decrease the cost of handling is to increase the paying load; the only way to increase the paying load is by the construction of equipment that will carry a greater load."[75] Railroads operating with this

[75] "Joint Report of the Committee on Conducting Transportation and Committee of Motive Power on the Subject of 'Iron Freight Cars,'" November 2, 1898, p. 6, PRR ATO Files, box 4, file 142.

mindset typically looked to signaling only under duress, and when they did so, they encountered troubling issues involving labor and work routines. The increasing use of signals at the turn of the twentieth century constituted a departure from the preferred course of action. It heralded a breakdown in the established paradigm of railroad operations and a loss of autonomy for railroad management.

Throughout much of the nineteenth century, railroads turned to signals primarily as tools to prevent accidents and to facilitate smoother movement at trouble spots, not as a means of facilitating high speeds.[76] Crossing gates and interlocking plants, like the expensive new stations and freight yards they frequently accompanied, prevented collisions and reduced delays in extraordinarily congested areas. In addition to providing relief from especially dangerous circumstances, interlocking signals and crossing gates helped keep trains in motion because most states required trains come to complete stops at intersections without them (Fig. 8.4). Adding interlocking signals at such spots "effects a saving not only in the time element involved," observed one treatise on railroad signaling, "but also in the expense of operation in stopping and starting trains." A 1905 analysis by a signal engineer for the Chicago and North Western Railway Company, explained this same source, demonstrated that "a road could economically install an interlocking plant where there were between 16 and 20 trains a day" simply on the basis of reduced expenses incurred from starting and stopping.[77] Railroads also frequently interlocked signals with switches at sidings and passing tracks, so that drivers of approaching trains had ample time to adjust their speed accordingly and avoid unnecessary delays.

To keep trains moving across heavily used bridges and other places where frequent trains traveled in both directions over the same track, many lines embraced a method known as the staff system. Locomotive drivers and conductors approaching such a section of track each grabbed half of a rod or staff from an attendant as they passed, then tossed the pieces into a bin when they reached the other end. Another attendant collected the pieces and inserted the reassembled staff into a machine, which reset the signals to clear and released a locking mechanism, permitting the attendants to obtain another staff. The linked machines would not release a second staff or reset the signals so long as the first staff remained in use. Railroads embraced this method not merely for the security it provided against collision, but also because it eliminated the need for locomotive engineers to come to a complete stop and obtain a written train order before entering such dangerous stretches. A survey conducted by the Pennsylvania revealed that on most

[76]   R. Harris to C. Latimer, July 17, 1873, CBQ Papers, 3H4.1, and Perkins to G. Harris, February 2, 1890, CBQ Papers, 3P4.1.
[77]   King, *Railway Signaling*, pp. 22–23.

Figure 8.4. Isolated interlocking signal plants, such as this one deployed by the Chicago and Alton, c.1901, kept trains moving at crossings and junctions. *Courtesy*: Library of Congress.

lines enginemen and conductors could receive the staff and deposit it in the bin while traveling as fast as thirty miles an hour.[78]

Early semaphore systems likewise served in large measure to keep trains from having to stop at dangerous spots along the route. Companies such as the Reading and the Pennsylvania deployed semaphores along lines that traversed mountainous routes with frequent obstructed views. A signalman

[78] A. Feldpauche to E. D. Nelson, June 8, 1905, plus attachments, Engineer of Tests Papers (henceforth, PRR Engineer of Tests Papers), box 722, folder 14, PRR Papers, Hagley Museum and Library, Wilmington, Delaware, Acc. 1807.

located at a bend in the track could in effect look ahead in either direction and with his semaphore send word of what he saw back to the engineer of an approaching train. Other railroads added semaphores sporadically at hazardous locations as traffic increased and accidents occurred.[79] Lines also installed semaphores at way stations so that trainmen did not have to stop unnecessarily if dispatchers had no orders for them. Blades set at caution indicated crews should slacken speed and snatch orders from a hoop without coming to a standstill.

The Pennsylvania's signal installation of 1876 apparently constitutes something of an exception to general practice, as the railroad seems to have originally seen these semaphores as providing the sort of absolute protection against collisions that advocates of the block system intended. Operators changed the signals to clear not when a train disappeared from view but when they received word via telegraph that it had cleared the next signal. Over time, however, managers at the Pennsylvania came to see the signals less as a form of insurance against accident and more as an active tool for keeping trains moving along the line. The change in thinking came through clearly in an 1893 report intended to "form the foundation of the art of signaling on the Pennsylvania Railroad." Its authors, emphasizing that their report offered "a radical change in regard to the function of signals," called for the Pennsylvania to abandon its "unwritten axiom . . . that 'signals govern tracks'" and replace it with a frank admission that "signals are primarily for the purpose of controlling or indicating the movement of *TRAINS*." In making this recommendation, the committee argued that the shift in approach had already begun in practice. "There is certainly a tendency in handling the traffic on busy lines," it observed, "to make the signals a quick and positive means of conveying information or orders to trains."[80]

This change in attitude grew at least in part out of practical problems that built up under the early block system. As the number of trains increased and more blocks filled up, trains began to encounter stop signals with intolerable frequency. Members of the signal committee identified "the question of reducing the number of red signals displayed to an approaching train" as "one of two subjects that have been brought regularly before [us]."[81] Pressure mounted to clear blocks more rapidly by running at faster speeds. Railroads did not like to run trains fast, however, and in any event block signals placed limits on speed because engineers would overrun them if traveling

[79]   E. P. Ripley to Stone, March 2, 1889, CBQ Papers, 3P4.57; Nicolls to C. E. Smith, August 6, 1864, vol. 670, pp. 19–20, and McLeod to Merrill, November 6, 1890, vol. 605, pp. 378–379, Reading Papers; and Burgess and Kennedy,*Centennial History of the Pennsylvania Railroad*, p. 494.

[80]   "Report of the Committee on Interlocking and Block Signals," October 24, 1893, PRR ATO Files, box 1, file 16.

[81]   "Report of the Committee on Interlocking and Block Signals," November 21, 1894, PRR ATO Files, box 2, file 35.

too fast. The Pennsylvania dealt cleverly with this situation by installing an additional semaphore blade at each tower. These "distant" or "caution" signals informed locomotive engineers about the status of the block beyond the one they were about to enter. Though safety advocates sometimes interpreted such signals as providing an extra measure of insurance, the Pennsylvania clearly deployed them so that locomotive engineers would not have to travel in anticipation of stopping at signals that might in fact be set in their favor. When a subsequent report on signaling suggested the Pennsylvania require engineers to slack their speed upon encountering a distant signal set to caution, managers objected that the practice would defeat the entire purpose of signals, which was "to pass the maximum traffic over the road at the greatest speed."[82] Even with the addition of distant signals, however, by the early 1890s stop signals disrupted train movements so severely that the Pennsylvania actually abandoned the absolute block system. For a number of years, management allowed the system to operate permissively, with trains entering occupied blocks after waiting a prescribed amount of time.[83]

As these experiences at the Pennsylvania suggest, block operations hardly constituted the choice of first resort for railroads contemplating ways to move more traffic through their systems. Indeed, railroads generally turned to the block system only when faced with precisely the circumstances they worked so hard to avoid: having to operate increasing numbers of trains traveling at higher speeds. Blocks held special appeal under these circumstances not only because faster trains required greater distances to stop, but because when traveling under the time-interval system, high-speed trains also effectively occupied much longer stretches of track. Two freights traveling at fifteen miles per hour could maintain a five-minute interval while being separated by as little as a mile and a quarter. A pair of passenger trains running at sixty miles per hour seeking to maintain the same five-minute spacing, on the other hand, would occupy five miles of track or more. If passengers and freights traveling at these characteristic speeds attempted to use the same

---

[82] This phrase comes from a 1905 letter from General Manager W. W. Atterbury to President A. J. Cassatt explaining the function of automatic signals. "As the function of the automatic signal is to pass the maximum traffic over the road at the greatest speed consistent with safety," Atterbury wrote, "it follows that each train should be kept at its maximum speed over as great a portion of the road as possible." W. W. Atterbury to A. J. Cassatt, April 4, 1905, PRR ATO Files, box 7, file 413. The report of 1893 stressed that the general plan for signaling applied to "lines where a large traffic is handled and where speed and safety are the ends sought." "Report of the Committee on Interlocking and Block Signals," October 24, 1893, PRR ATO Files, box 1, file 16.

[83] After stating emphatically that "the permissive block signal cannot be defended under any perfect signal system," the authors of the 1893 report acknowledged "the necessity under present conditions for a permissive block system." "Report of the Committee on Interlocking and Block Signals," October 24, 1893, PRR ATO Files, box 1, file 16.

track under the time interval system, the passenger trains might well find themselves having to wait for long periods in order to avoid overtaking slower moving freights. Variable speed operations proved so complex that on especially busy routes, railroads such as the Pennsylvania built a second pair of parallel tracks reserved exclusively for passenger traffic. Other lines added more and more sidings, so that freights could readily pull out of the way of faster passenger trains.[84] So long as trains continued to move under the time-interval method, however, faster trains threatened rapidly to absorb such added track capacity. Because the most highly congested lines generally ran through densely settled urban areas or through rugged mountainous terrain, moreover, railroads could not add still more tracks without incurring steep charges for real estate and construction.

Railroads turned to block signals as a means to escape this constraint and pack more trains into their existing networks. With blocks spaced every two miles, a ten-mile stretch of track might conceivably hold as many as five trains, even if those trains traveled as rapidly as sixty miles per hour. Roads could increase capacity still further by adding even more signals and shortening the blocks. In theory, blocks could shrink to as small as the length of a train plus the distance required to stop. Block signals, whether manual or automatic, thus functioned in the eyes of railroads primarily as a capital-saving technology. "From a humanitarian standpoint the block system is to be regarded simply as a safeguard against collisions of trains," explained the ICC signal board in 1907, "but it is much more than that, for it is an effective means of increasing the capacity of a railroad" that "serves, in some degree, to postpone the day when additional main tracks must be built at great expense."[85] Members of the board reluctantly acknowledged that such cost considerations served as the primary motivator behind the rise of block methods. "On a few roads...," they noted ruefully, "farseeing and discriminating managers who saw that the potential value of the space-interval principle was greater than appeared from the cold calculations based on volume of traffic and on the earnings or expenses for single years, introduced the telegraph block system on lines where the volume of traffic did not compel its introduction. That is to say, the trains were not so frequent as to require a shortening of the time interval to increase the capacity of the road."[86]

Labor and the Economics of Block Signals

Even with the incentives produced by faster and more frequent trains, the decision to install a block system did not come easily. In either their manual

---

[84] One informed contemporary investigator reported that between 1894 and 1904, the mileage of track devoted to sidings, second tracks, and yards increased 50 percent, while the amount of new single track railroad grew just 20 percent. See M. O. Lorenz, "Constant and Variable Railroad Expenditures and the Distance Tariff," *Quarterly Journal of Economics* 21 (1907): 287.

[85] U.S. Senate, "Report on Block Signals," p. 11.   [86] Ibid., pp. 7–8.

or automatic form, dedicated block signals entailed considerable expense. Manual signal towers of the sort used by the Pennsylvania cost about $500 to build. A simple, manually controlled semaphore powered by electricity or compressed air, together with the necessary telegraph instruments, added roughly another $60 to $85 per tower to the initial investment. Wire and batteries ran about $45 to $55 per mile if copper was used, perhaps $20 less if a railroad chose iron wire instead. With stations spaced three miles apart, a typical distance used by the ICC in its cost estimates, total installation charges for a manual system at the beginning of the twentieth century added up to approximately $200 per mile.[87] (New rails weighing 100 pounds per yard and costing $35 per ton, by way of comparison, would involve an expense in excess of $6,000 per mile.) By utilizing existing station buildings as signal towers, a line could reduce the necessary capital outlay still further.

While comparatively inexpensive to install, manual systems saddled railroads with significant ongoing operating expenses. At prevailing wage rates in 1901, railroads paid approximately $100 per month to keep a simple signal station operating round the clock. If the signal station also included a track switch, labor costs jumped substantially, as switchmen worked eight hours per day rather than twelve and earned about 20 percent more per month than signal operators.[88] At this rate, observed the ICC of the manual method in its annual report for 1902, "on nearly or not quite every railroad not now using a block system it would require an increase of 25% more or less in the force of signalmen (or telegraph operators) employed, and therefore is looked upon as expensive in operation."[89] The ICC concurred with these estimates of labor costs in its extensive report on block signals of 1907. The commissioners estimated annual expenditures for labor and maintenance of between $1,200 and $1,500 for each manual signal tower. On its hypothetical installation with dedicated signal towers spaced every three miles, this put annual costs for a manual block system at between $400 and $500 per mile. Shorten the blocks to two miles, as the Pennsylvania had done on its busiest routes, and these annual costs reached totals of some $600 to $750 per mile. Even the ICC considered such an expense "very high."[90]

[87] Adams, *Block System*, pp. 23–24. Adams reported that towers built on the Erie Railroad in 1887 also cost $500, not including equipment. In 1907, the ICC estimated a cost of $500 per tower including the telegraph and signal apparatus, which they reported cost $75. Given the pains commissioners took to keep estimates as low as possible and the escalating costs of construction during the early twentieth century, a figure of $500 plus equipment seems more reasonable. U.S. Senate, "Report on Block Signals," p. 10.
[88] Adams calculated labor charges using standards for signalmen of $45 to $55 per month for twelve hours per day, seven days per week and for switchmen of $50 to $70 per month for eight hours per day, seven days per week. Adams, *Block System*, pp. 23–24.
[89] *ICC Report* 16 (December 15, 1902): 68.
[90] U.S. Senate, "Report on Block Signals," p. 11.

Considerable evidence suggests that the high cost of labor significantly discouraged railroads from deploying the manual block system. When the ICC first endorsed the block system during the opening years of the twentieth century, it repeatedly sought to temper concerns about associated labor costs. "The assertion that this increase [in wages] is necessarily large or burdensome, in proportion to the number of trains run, has never been substantiated by evidence," argued the commissioners in their report for 1904. "One railroad manager is reported saying that on one of his principal lines of several hundred miles the increase in the pay rolls was only 3% – certainly a moderate sum to pay."[91] Commissioners suggested lines could reduce labor charges by assigning responsibilities for the block signals to existing station agents. If such men were too busy to perform the task, the road could without great hardship provide an assistant, who would certainly find ways to make himself useful in other tasks besides signaling. If traffic were too light to justify keeping a man on duty round the clock, the line could close selected stations at night and lengthen the blocks.[92] Such advice suggests railroads viewed labor costs as a significant obstacle. Railroads had a similar reaction to the Hours of Service Act, which stipulated that signalmen could not work longer than nine hours at a stretch unless the railroad received special exemption from the ICC. Over fifty companies requested exemptions the moment the law took effect in March 1908. The ICC, which had campaigned for the law, summarily denied them all, and within months the Signal Board detected a dramatic drop in the rate of adoption of the block system. The number of miles operated under the manual block system actually decreased for the year, as some roads switched to automatic methods in order to save labor costs.[93]

Railroads interested in signaling technology tried in a variety of ways to sidestep the expense of labor or at least keep it to a minimum. In a move that grew characteristic of the entire industry, for instance, the Philadelphia and Reading early on adopted a policy of filling the post of signal operator with men who had been disabled in the war or in railroad service.[94] Managers believed such individuals, in addition to working for less money, were ideally suited to a task that required little skill but demanded great diligence. At grade crossings, attendants watched for trains and lowered a gate or rang a bell as the train passed, then raised the gate and waited for the next train to approach. The crossing gate attendants worked twelve-hour shifts and sometimes waited hours for a train to pass. Signalmen located in towers

---

[91]   *ICC Report* 18 (December 19, 1904): 99.   [92]   Ibid., pp. 100–102.

[93]   *ICC Reports* 21 (December 23, 1907): 132; 22 (December 24, 1908): 307; and 23 (December 21, 1909): 49; and Latimer, *Railway Signaling*, p. 348.

[94]   Nicolls to C. E. Smith, August 6, 1864, vol. 670, pp. 19–20 and 23–26, and McLeod to Merrill, November 6, 1890, vol. 605, pp. 378–379, Reading Papers; and U.S. Interstate Commerce Commission, "Reports of the Block Signal and Train Control Board to the Interstate Commerce Commission," 1907–1912.

at dangerous points performed similarly, turning their signals to the danger position after a train passed, setting the signal to caution when the train disappeared from sight, and returning the signal to the clear position after a prescribed period of time. The practice of assigning such posts to injured workers grew so common at the Reading and other railroads that many came to view the job of signalman as a central peg in a kind of informal pension program. Injured employees expected to receive positions as signalmen, and they accepted these jobs in lieu of any other settlement. Railroads recognized that through this practice they headed off a potential area of dispute with workers, who might have pressed more vigorously for other compensation had the signaling jobs not been available.[95] With thousands of employees injured on the railroads each year, railroads could not easily abandon this informal pension arrangement. When the ICC Signal Board convened in 1907, it clearly expected many signaling jobs to be filled by injured workers, and it advised managers on how best to deal with the old-timers.[96]

Railroads could not so readily tap the pool of disabled workers in the case of block signaling, however, for the block signal operator needed to be an accomplished telegrapher. Rather than drawing on a source of cheap labor, railroads contemplating the block system thus found themselves competing for skills that demanded a premium. In the opinion of the Burlington's Latimer, at least, this proved a significant stumbling block. "As long as there was no accepted method of communication between stations except by telegraph, the introduction of manual block systems was seriously retarded by the scarcity of telegraph operators," he declared flatly in his 1909 textbook. "Professional telegraph operators who would accept positions as block operators at the wages which railroads could afford to pay for such service were, as a rule, beginners – young men who expected, as soon as they became proficient enough, to be able to secure better pay in other positions."[97]

Lines confronting this tight labor market actively looked to substitute alternative means of communicating between signal stations. In 1887, for example, the Erie experimented with using a simple bell-ringing mechanism in signal towers along its forty-seven-mile stretch of blocked track. According to Braman Adams, author of a 1901 book on railroad signaling, the line took this step so that "in an emergency new signalmen could be obtained at shorter notice." Though Adams did not specify the nature of such an emergency, it seems likely given the timing of the experiment that the Erie's managers acted out of concern the telegraphers might go on strike or abet other striking workers by refusing to run the trains. Adams believed that the bell-ringing mechanism, like other alternatives to the telegraph, "at the

---

[95] Licht, *Working for the Railroad*, p. 202.
[96] "Second Report of the Block Signal and Train Control Board," November 22, 1909, p. 11.
[97] Latimer, *Railway Signaling*, pp. 353–354.

present time . . . gives little or no advantage, in the matter of wages, because telegraph operators with considerable experience can generally be hired for the same pay that is required to secure non-telegraphers of the requisite mental equipment and moral character to perform duties of signalmen."[98] This assessment may well have represented a plea to upgrade the quality of the signalmen, however, rather than a report on the state of wages. For Adams himself noted that the Santa Fe, which had placed several hundred miles of track under block operation during the previous two years, used telephones at fourteen of its 153 stations and paid the men who operated them $10 per month less than telegraphers.[99]

The idea of using telephones in place of telegraphs was not unique to the Santa Fe. A special committee convened by the Pennsylvania in 1897 considered the possibility at great length. Its extensive survey of railroad industry practices revealed that though the Burlington had begun experimenting with telephones at one place in its system and the Pennsylvania's own lines west of Pittsburgh used them exclusively to direct switching operations in large yards, virtually no lines used telephones routinely in dispatching or block signaling. Respondents expressed concern that telephones were not reliable and were not capable of handling numerous apparatus simultaneously. Most important, phones were liable to create misunderstanding since they did not produce a precise written record of communication. Dismissing these criticisms as reflecting a "natural prejudice against innovation," the committee recommended the Pennsylvania try using phones in mainline operations, though it cautioned that orders should be read back letter by letter in order to leave a written record, as the Burlington was doing in its trials.[100]

Top management at the Pennsylvania, apparently concerned about continuing uncertainty regarding the telephone patents, chose not to pursue this course until January 1904. General Manager W. W. Atterbury then authorized gradual conversion to the telephone at stations that did not handle a large volume of business.[101] A subsequent report of October 1905 indicated the switch was "going forward quickly."[102] When Atterbury surveyed his superintendents in spring 1908, he received enthusiastic responses. "Our aim has been to use the telephone for both train operations and commercial purposes," reported G. W. Creighton, general superintendent of the Eastern Pennsylvania Division. "It serves as a complete substitute for the telegraph, having in mind the elimination of the telegraph operator as a necessary class of employees in any part of our operations."[103] The Pennsylvania's

---

98   Adams, *Block System*, pp. 26–27.   99   Ibid., p. 57.
100   "Report of the Committee on the Telegraph," November 22, 1897, PRR ATO Files, box 5.
101   PRR ATO Files, box 5, file 263.
102   "Joint Report of the Committee on Train Rules and the Committee on the Telegraph," October 30, 1905, PRR ATO Files, box 6, file 325.
103   G. W. Creighton to W. W. Atterbury, June 4, 1908, PRR ATO Files, box 5, file 263.

superintendent of the telegraph, J. B. Fisher, also expressed enthusiasm for the labor-saving potential of the telephone. "There are other good reasons for the use of the telephone, not the least of which is the broader field it opens for securing competent operators and competent dispatchers," he wrote. "Under the present system a train dispatcher must of necessity be a telegraph operator. With the telephone he need not be, but bright, brainy young men, with a knowledge of practical railroad work can be developed into telephone train dispatchers very quickly."[104]

The experiences of the Pennsylvania with telephones evidently reflected larger trends throughout the industry. Latimer of the Burlington concluded his 1909 study with an optimistic outlook for the future of manual block signaling. He based his judgment primarily upon recent experience with the telephone. "The introduction of the telephone for block purposes has made it possible for railroads to use a different and more permanent class of men for this work," he reported, "which is bound to result in more efficient service in the future."[105] The ICC detected the trend as well. "For the year 1909 the Commission has asked for information covering the use of the telephone in the operation of trains," it reported in December of that year. "It appears that the telephone is to large extent displacing the telegraph, not only in block-signal work but in train dispatching as well."[106]

Automatic Devices

Automatic signals, activated by track circuit and powered by electromagnets, electric motors, or compressed air, offered yet another technological alternative to manual operation. Pioneers in block signaling such as the Pennsylvania and the Burlington experimented with these sorts of devices as early as the 1880s, at about the time the Erie tried its bell mechanism. The Pennsylvania obtained a few devices from George Westinghouse's new Union Switch and Signal Company in 1881 and installed them at selected sites. These test sections remained isolated exceptions until the late 1890s, however, when the Pennsylvania converted its intensively used tracks between Philadelphia and New York and from Philadelphia west to Paoli from manual to automatic signals. Managers at the Burlington considered using automatic signals in 1886, almost as soon as they instituted block operations on the busy section from Chicago to Aurora.[107] They arranged for Union Switch and Signal to install an experimental station on a trial basis and studied offers from rival

---

[104] J. B. Fisher (Supt Telegraph) to W. W. Atterbury, May 26, 1908, PRR ATO Files, box 5, file 263.

[105] Latimer, *Railway Signaling*, pp. 353–354.

[106] *ICC Report* 23 (December 21, 1909): 49.

[107] Potter to Stone, February 15, 1886, CBQ Papers, 3P6.13; Stone to Potter, February 17, 1886, CBQ Papers, 3P6.37; Perkins to Potter, February 25, 1886, CBQ Papers, 3P4.1; and Potter to Stone, March 5, 1886, CBQ Papers, 3P6.14.

manufacturers who complained of having been excluded from bidding for the contract.[108] After considerable discussion, Burlington management implemented a manual block system for that section of track. The railroad did not again try automatic electric block signals until 1901, and even then it installed them only on the extraordinarily congested run from Chicago to Aurora.[109]

Though evidence is slim, several factors reminiscent of the air brake case probably influenced thinking at these lines regarding automatic signals. Railroads contemplating the purchase of advanced signaling devices ran headlong into none other than George Westinghouse, the entrepreneur who had proven so formidable in the market for automatic brakes. During the interim when most railroads had adopted air brakes for passenger service but few had purchased them for freight trains, Westinghouse had moved into the signaling business. In 1881 he had acquired rights to a fundamental patent governing electric circuits that ran through railroad track and utilized trains to activate signals.[110] This initial patent protection, combined with his experience in marketing to railroads, gave Westinghouse a leg up on competitors that he did not soon relinquish. Union Switch and Signal won pilot contracts to build complex interlocking plants at several new stations during the late 1880s and early 1890s. These jobs gave the firm vital practical experience with the sort of custom work involved in the signaling business and also helped broaden its base of expertise. By scrupulously obtaining patents on the countless innovations devised in the field, the company could keep imitators at bay and ensure its control of those devices that eventually proved to have the greatest utility and applicability. Following this course, Westinghouse steadily secured another stronghold in the railroad supply trades.[111] Though his presence brought stability and substance to a line of enterprise previously dominated by unknown upstarts, railroads did not warm quickly to the idea of becoming dependent upon another of his complex patented products.

---

[108] Potter to Perkins, April 18, 1886, CBQ Papers, 3P4.56; Potter to Stone, April 30 and May 13, 1886, CBQ Papers, 3P6.13; and Stone to Potter, October 29, 1886, CBQ Papers, 3P6.37.

[109] Stone to Perkins, July 2, 1889, CBQ Papers, 3P4.57; Perkins to F. A. Delano, January 25, 1890, CBQ Papers, 3P4.1; and G. Harris to Perkins, June 29, 1901, CBQ Papers, 3P4.51.

[110] Signal Section of the American Railroad Association, *The Invention of the Electric Track Circuit* (New York, 1922); Mary Brignano and Hax McCullough, *The Search for Safety: A History of Railroad Signals and the People Who Made Them* (Pittsburgh: American Standard Company for the Union Switch and Signal Company, 1981); and Union Switch and Signal Company (F. S. Guerber, agent) to T. J. Potter, August 23, 1881, CBQ Papers, 3P6.21.

[111] Henry G. Prout, *A Life of George Westinghouse* (New York: American Society of Mechanical Engineers, 1921), lists and describes many patents pertaining to signaling taken out by Westinghouse during the last fifteen years of the nineteenth century, when one might expect the inventor's energies to be monopolized by electric power.

In addition to concerns about patents, questions lingered during this early period about the reliability of automatic signaling. Electric signal systems depended for successful operation on subtle changes in voltages, and any number of problems could inadvertently create these changes or cause intended changes to go undetected. "If automatic signaling could be relied upon always it would probably be accepted as the most satisfactory and would certainly be the least expensive [block signaling system]," declared one signal manufacturer in his 1889 catalog, "but unfortunately it cannot always be relied upon, and when it does fail there is no one to tell an engineer that it has failed." Once engine men realized signals frequently showed stop when they should show clear, the catalog continued, they "regard the signal with suspicion and either run so slowly as to lose time or run with reckless disregard of what the signal shows."[112] Managers at the Burlington believed even the simplest electric interlocking would require a full-time employee for maintenance. The Union Switch and Signal Company sent an expert to install each interlocking and offered to let the railroad employ the man until its managers were satisfied the signals were reliable and easily maintained, but questions about reliability remained an obstacle to innovation for many years.[113]

As railroads and suppliers such as Westinghouse gained experience with electrical interlocking devices and crossing gates, concerns about maintenance and reliability faded, and first costs became the primary obstacle for those considering automatic block signals. "The decreased cost and improvement of automatic block signals will in all probability in the near future make possible the absolute block system," wrote the Pennsylvania signals committee in 1893, "where the question of expense now makes it practically impossible of adoption."[114] Concern about costs remained high even after the Pennsylvania installed automatic devices on a limited basis in late 1890s. "The automatic system is costly to install," stated the ICC succinctly in its annual report for 1902, "and so is looked upon by the managers of most lines of light traffic as an unwarranted luxury."[115] The report of the ICC signal board in 1907 reiterated the point. Automatic block signals remained a rarity until recent years, noted the board, because "the cost of installation of apparatus and fixtures was high, as was also the cost of inspection and maintenance; therefore, only companies enjoying a heavy and profitable traffic deemed it wise to equip their lines with automatic signals."[116]

Based on the limited experience of railroads to that time, the signal board estimated that automatic signals "have involved expenditures of from $1,500

[112] Johnson Signal Company, *Catalogue*, p. 12.
[113] Perkins to Stone, March 18, 1882, and Stone to Potter, March 27 and April 25, 1882, CBQ Papers, 3P6.21.
[114] "Report of the Committee on Interlocking and Block Signals," October 24, 1893, PRR ATO Files, box 1, file 16.
[115] *ICC Report* 16 (December 15, 1902): 68.
[116] U.S. Senate, "Report on Block Signals," p. 7.

and $3,000 a mile of double-track road."[117] On a hundred-mile stretch with signals every three miles, automatic signals would cost at least $125,000 more to install than a manual block system. If one compared the most economical manual facilities with the most expensive automatic ones, the difference in first costs could climb as high as $275,000, or nearly $3,000 per mile. With annual expenditures for maintenance of just $25 to $40 per mile and no additional wage payments to operators (compared with yearly expenditures on wages and repairs of from $400 to $500 per mile for the manual signals), a railroad could potentially recoup its investment in automatic devices in as little as two and a half years and would certainly do so within seven years (not counting interest charges and depreciation).[118] Shorten the distance between signals to just two miles, as lines had done in especially congested corridors, and the cost comparison swung increasingly in favor of automatics. Though a premium automatic system would cost nearly $2,700 more per mile than the best manual signals under these circumstances, railroads could expect annual savings to repay the difference in under five years.[119] At that rate, the ICC suggested, railroads would almost certainly choose automatic devices.[120]

As the ICC well understood, however, choices of signal systems in reality rarely hinged strictly on such apparently straightforward cost comparisons. Only in rare instances had lines fully committed to operating block systems using signal facilities dedicated exclusively to that task. Most railroads patched together block systems using a mix of existing station signals, interlocking devices at switch points and sidings, and perhaps some isolated semaphores along the line. Even the Pennsylvania, moreover, did not resort to automatic devices strictly out of a desire to lower labor costs. A careful look at available company records suggests that its managers turned to automatic signals when they perceived the mounting volume of traffic had simply overwhelmed the capabilities of the old manual system.

---

[117] Ibid., p. 10.

[118] Ibid. The estimate for an automatic system is based on ICC estimates for maintenance of $75 to $125 per signal.

[119] Using the high-end figure of $3,000 per mile, an automatic system for such a line would have cost $300,000 to install. Fifty-one manual stations along the same route outfitted with the best equipment would cost a mere $640 apiece, for a total of $32,640, or a savings of nearly $270,000. Annual operating expenses for the manual system, however, would have exceeded those of the automatic signals by nearly $60,000 to upward of $75,000 per year. Under these conditions railroads would recover the additional investment in even the most expensive automatic devices within four and a half years.

[120] "Where trains are so frequent that a time interval of five minutes or more can not be tolerated, the automatic system is now generally deemed the only suitable system, because where trains must follow one another as closely as once in five minutes the block signals must be not over two miles apart; and with this interval the cost of the manual block system would be very high." U.S. Senate, "Report on Block Signals," p. 11.

Having reluctantly agreed to operate their manual block system permissively in an effort to overcome what they considered an intolerable number of stop signals, managers at the Pennsylvania soon discovered that employees could not handle the complexities involved. A report issued in 1896 documented an alarming number of dangerous mistakes resulting from improper setting of distant signals. Its authors emphatically stressed the urgent need for additional rules governing permissive blocking with distant signals. So pressing was the problem that the signals committee suspended all action on thirteen points previously under review in order to meet jointly with the committee on rules and draft new instructions. "The Committee are, I believe, unanimously of the opinion that we are in need of some general rules governing the movement of trains by signal," reported the chairman of the signals committee to the secretary of the ATO in his summary of the meeting. Apparently fearful of upsetting passengers, shippers, and perhaps the workers themselves, the chairman steered clear of adding details about why the Pennsylvania deemed it necessary to institute new rules of this sort "in a report to the Association which might fall into the hands of outside parties." But the officers responsible for signaling left no doubt of their resolve to stipulate new procedures. "It hardly seems right that we should have rules covering the general railway practice, and omit to provide rules for perhaps the most important conditions under which our traffic is handled."[121]

New rules and permissive operations were clearly stopgap measures in the eyes of the committee, however, for all of its reports pointed to new technology as the ultimate remedy. As early as 1893, the committee expressed its eager anticipation of the time when financial considerations permitted use of "automatic signals" and "the absolute block."[122] The following year the committee identified "reducing the cost of interlocking, so that it may be put in more general use as soon as practicable" as the second most pressing matter under its review.[123] In addition to enabling engineers to proceed across switches and other dangerous points without slacking speed, interlocking arrangements could be used to connect home and distant signals, thus relieving tower men from the burdens of having to relay changes in the state of their blocks to two signal operators back up the line. Two years later, in 1896, the committee considering new rules suggested that perhaps the Pennsylvania should link home and distant signals by track circuit. "There are many other appliances which could be provided which would make signaling more safe," the committee went on to note in an apparent reference to the automatic block, "but as these would involve a considerable outlay

---

[121] N. Trump (Chairman, Signal Committee) to S. M. Prevost (President, ATO), October 29, 1896, PRR ATO Files, box 1, file 16.

[122] "Report of the Committee on Interlocking and Block Signals," October 24, 1893, PRR ATO Files, box 1, file 16.

[123] "Report of the Committee on Interlocking and Block Signals," November 21, 1894, PRR ATO Files, box 2, file 35.

of money, it seems important that the necessary rules should be made and enforced."[124] With the return to prosperity during the next two years, the Pennsylvania began making the switch to automatic signals as part of its major program of capital improvements. By 1901, it had converted towers along over 500 miles of its route.[125]

In the assessment of executives at the Pennsylvania, then, automatic signals opened possibilities managers considered simply unattainable through other means. Manual signals, no matter how frequent, could not handle the number of heavy freight trains and fast passenger trains the Pennsylvania wished to push through its busiest tracks. Machines replaced men not because they saved money, but because they performed tasks the men could not.

That judgment, of course, reflected certain attitudes and assumptions about the work force. British railroads faced circumstances in their passenger services similar to those confronting the Pennsylvania, yet managed to persist in using manual signals.[126] Though observers pointed to the lower wage rates in Britain as a contributing factor, they ultimately emphasized the quality of the work force as the key element accounting for the differences. By all accounts, British signalmen were better trained and more experienced than their American counterparts. "The facts of the accident records justify a strong presumption that American signalmen are not so carefully selected nor so well trained as those of England," declared the ICC signal board in seeking to explain the national differences.

> The average signalman in America is young, and has had, probably from six months to two years instruction – not systematic instruction – under another signalman, whose superiority to the student is entirely due to what he has learned by experience and not at all to methodical and authoritative instruction. The average block signalman in England, on the contrary, has served as such from five to twenty-five years and has been through a long course in a signal cabin as a "booking boy," or as an assistant, before being trusted with full charge of the block signals. This difference in personnel of the signalmen of the two countries undoubtedly explains in large measure the nearer approach to perfection of the block signal service in England.[127]

[124] N. Trump (Chairman, Signal Committee) to S. M. Prevost (President ATO), October 29, 1896, PRR ATO Files, box 1, file 16.

[125] "Report of the Committee on Train Rules," October 29, 1898, PRR ATO Files, box 1, file 6, and Adams, *Block System*, p. 165.

[126] "Automatic block signals were invented in America and have been developed on American railroads," observed the Interstate Commerce Commission in its report to Congress. "Although man-operated block signals had been used for some years on English railroads, with their denser traffic, more frequent stations, and lower expenses for attendants, automatic block signals found more pronounced favor in this country." U.S. Senate, "Report on Block Signals," p. 7.

[127] Ibid., p. 14.

A prominent American signal engineer captured the differences in pithier fashion. "In this country we spend millions in an endeavor to make our apparatus fool proof," he wrote, "while in England they spend hundreds to eliminate the fool, and appear to get better results."[128] Perhaps signalmen receiving better training – and better pay – would have handled the job of operating home and distant signals simultaneously on the busy Pennsylvania tracks.

While much public discussion in the United States about the "human element" focused upon the signal operators, use of automatic signaling actually directed attention away from signalmen and toward train crews, who now stood as the sole remaining humans responsible for the safe movement of trains. Safety advocates and many others associated with the railroad industry worried that engineers would race past a signal set to stop. For railroads, the situation raised a troubling issue of accountability. Under manual operations, managers had relied on engineers and signalmen to provide a mutual check against error. Now an engineer could pass a stop signal without being observed and blame mechanical malfunction of the signal if something went wrong as a result. With much trepidation, the Pennsylvania and several other lines resorted to so-called surprise tests, in which inspectors set signals to stop and secretly observed how the train crews responded. Those caught running past a signal were subject to various disciplinary actions, including suspension or even firing. These tests and disciplinary procedures continually stirred controversy. Braman Adams and other influential figures in the ICC deemed them essential elements in any automatic system, but a survey conducted by the Pennsylvania in 1906 revealed significant opposition to the tests among railroad managers, who feared the surprise checks alienated skilled locomotive engineers and inflamed worker protest. Following publication of a series of essays about railroad discipline in the *Atlantic Monthly* during 1908, executives at the Pennsylvania again subjected disciplinary practices at their line to widespread review. In the end, a committee studying the matter recommended merely that the tests be renamed "efficiency tests." "The term 'efficiency' seems more dignified and satisfactory than the word 'surprise,'" noted the managers, "and should give less offense."[129] That October, the Pennsylvania's new Publicity Bureau issued a press release bragging that train crews observed signals correctly in 99.25 percent of the 3,255 "signal 'efficiency' tests" performed in August.[130] A few years later, signal engineers at the Pennsylvania tried to stymie public pressure demanding that railroads deploy new devices capable of stopping a train automatically should it pass a red signal.

[128] Latimer, *Railway Signaling*, p. 350.
[129] G. W. Creighton to W. W. Atterbury, January 28, 1908, PRR ATO Files, box 9, file 493.
[130] Pennsylvania Railroad Company, "Information for the Press," October 16, 1908, PRR Engineer of Tests Papers, box 153, folder 28.

The managers preferred instead to deploy speed controllers that generated a retrievable record documenting how engineers handled their locomotives.[131]

Ironically, the desire to save labor costs may have figured more prominently on the remote lines of the Far West than in the crowded conditions implied by the ICC cost comparison. While the Pennsylvania gathered much of the limelight, the less densely traveled lines traversing the prairies and deserts actually made far more extensive use of automatic signals during the opening years of the twentieth century. The Santa Fe, for instance, had placed several hundred miles of track under block operation by 1901.[132] Between them, the Union Pacific system and the Southern Pacific Company operated over 4,000 miles of track under automatic signals by 1907.[133] Apparently desirous of gaining the added protection provided by block signaling, these lines simply found it impractical to man isolated signaling stations in remote areas, where operators had no other responsibilities to keep them occupied. Several long single-track lines traversing lightly settled territory in the East likewise turned to automatic block devices beginning around 1904. Here the occasional automatic semaphores functioned strictly as a safeguard to supplement the dispatching methods required to coordinate the movement of trains in opposite directions.[134]

Examples such as these suggest that automatic signals eventually took hold not so much as a substitute for labor and as a means actively to reduce labor costs but as a way of providing greater security against accidents without incurring so large a cost as new manual towers would have entailed. In most circumstances, trains continued to move through the railroad network governed by the dispatching system, with locomotive engineers receiving orders from station agents located along the line. Block signals, whether manual or automatic, provided an added measure of insurance. Only in rare circumstances did railroads turn the task of monitoring train movements entirely over to mechanical devices, with locomotive engineers proceeding from automatic signal to automatic signal. Especially in freight service, lines preferred to retain the flexibility inherent in the dispatching method. "One of the chief arguments in the favor of automatic signals is that a great operating expense – the wages paid to manual block operators – may be saved by their use," observed Latimer in 1909. "In actual practice this rarely if ever

---

[131] A. H. Rudd to C. D. Young, June 24, 1913; K. D. Kavanaugh to C. D. Young, July 1, 1913; C. D. Young to A. H. Rudd, July 2, 1913; and A. H. Rudd to C. D. Young, July 3, 1913; PRR Engineer of Tests Papers, box 723, folder 16.

[132] Adams, *Block System*, p. 57.

[133] "Second Report of the Block Signal and Train Control Board to the Interstate Commerce Commission," November 22, 1909, p. 10.

[134] On such use of block signals, see A. Feldpauche to E. D. Nelson, June 8, 1905, plus attachments, PRR Engineer of Tests Papers, box 722, folder 14. Some roads with "considerable investment" used automatic devices just to back up old time-interval rules; see U.S. Senate, "Report on Block Signals," p. 7.

works out.... I have known several cases where automatic signals were put in and operators discharged, who in a month or two had to be re-employed in order to keep the business moving at all satisfactorily."[135] Lines generally allowed most freight trains and even some passenger trains to observe the block signals permissively, pausing for a time at a red signal and proceeding into the occupied block at slower speed. Used in these ways, block signals must be seen primarily as a response to the growing demand for safety rather than as a tool deployed by managers to move trains aggressively and economically through the system. We cannot ultimately comprehend the rise of automatic block signaling, then, without considering the role of government in stimulating demand for greater safety.

REGULATION REVISTED

Public interest in signaling technology grew steadily with the dawn of the new century. In 1901, Congress passed a law requiring railroads to submit statistics regarding accidents. Published by the ICC in its *Report* of 1902, these statistics constituted "the first authentic record [in the matter of collisions and derailments] relating to the railroads of the whole country." Noting that "the publication of official data has drawn renewed attention to the subject," the commissioners suggested that the block system of signaling provided the best remedy for collisions.[136] The following year, Representative John J. Esch of Wisconsin introduced legislation requiring railroads to deploy the block system in all passenger operations. The ICC immediately endorsed this proposal, which basically copied a British law of 1889, and added a recommendation that the commission be given power to supervise the railroads and ensure compliance.[137] In its reports of subsequent years the ICC again lobbied emphatically for the bill and also asked for the power to investigate accidents.[138] President Theodore Roosevelt joined the crusade and called for passage of the legislation in his annual messages to Congress of 1904 and 1905.[139]

As with earlier campaigns to regulate railroad safety, these efforts to assert government influence over procedures for handling trains drew added force and energy from concurrent debates taking place over the role of government

---

[135] Latimer, *Railway Signaling*, pp. 302-303.
[136] *ICC Report* 16 (December 15, 1902): 64–69.
[137] "Reports of Block Signal and Train Control Board to the Interstate Commerce Committee," 1908–1912.
[138] *ICC Reports* 17 (December 15, 1903): 102–104; 18 (December 19, 1904): 98–99; and 19 (December 14, 1905): 77–78.
[139] Report from the Committee on Interstate and Foreign Commerce to the U.S. House of Representatives, "Block Signals and Appliances for the Automatic Control of Railway Trains," House Report No. 4637, 59th Cong., 1st sess.; and U.S. Senate, "Report on Block Signals," p. 25.

in setting rates. During the late nineteenth century, the Supreme Court had essentially deprived the ICC of authority in this vital matter. The Court's rulings sparked enormous controversy and fomented a renewed cry for legislative action. Congress tabled a bill in 1901 that would have provided the ICC with limited rate-making powers, but two years later it granted the commission authority to prosecute railroads offering rebates or other discounts from their published fares. Congress then proceeded to consider legislation permitting the ICC to set maximum rates and granting it more authority to investigate and monitor railroad finance. When the House and Senate split on this matter, President Roosevelt decided to throw himself strongly in support of a measure giving the ICC broad authority, at precisely the same moment he endorsed the regulation requiring block signals.[140]

Congress took action on both the rate question and the issue of block signals in 1906. With regard to rates, it passed the Hepburn Act, which basically embraced the positions Roosevelt had advocated regarding commission oversight of rates and finance but left open the possibility courts would continue to review ICC decisions. In the matter of signals, Congress directed the ICC to investigate "block signals and appliances for the automatic control of trains" and asked it to make recommendations regarding legislation.[141] Neither measure, it soon became clear, put matters fully to rest. In each case, Congress had bolstered the administrative responsibilities of the ICC without defining its authority precisely. In effect, the bills established an institutional framework for further debate and action. While leaving much unresolved, the political developments of 1906 nevertheless marked a significant watershed in the development of railroad signaling and methods of handling trains. By dealing with signaling in parallel with the volatile rate question, Congress raised public consciousness of the subject of train handling and established the ICC as a focal point for further discussions of it.

During the next few years, as the ICC attempted to capitalize on its new authority, the agency struggled to move beyond an approach to safety based on laws requiring particular technological devices and to substitute for it one grounded upon the power to supervise and inspect actual railroad practice. This change in strategy emerged in part out of experience gained in the course of implementing the safety appliance law. Though Congress had required that freight trains have self-couplers and large numbers of continuous brakes by the opening year of the new century, the number of deaths and injuries due to coupling and braking had remained at appalling levels. Statistics revealed that for the year ending June 30, 1904, some 3,632 railroad workers (one out of 357) had been killed in service. Another 67,067 (one out of 19) had been injured. For trainmen, the ratios stood at one out of 120 dead and one out

---

[140] Stephen Skowronek, *Building a New American State: The Expansion of National Administrative Capacities, 1877–1920* (New York: Cambridge University Press, 1982), pp. 248–256.

[141] U.S. Senate, "Report on Block Signals," p. 25; and Skowronek, *Building*, p. 256.

of nine injured. Amazingly, the casualty statistics had actually deteriorated from a decade earlier, when one trainmen out of every 156 had been killed in service and one out of 12 had received serious injury.[142] This shocking rate of carnage had diminished only after 1904, when with congressional approval government inspectors had begun visiting railroads and supervising maintenance and use of the required safety devices.[143]

Even before it received authority to investigate signals, the ICC tried to make as much use as possible out of the limited powers of inspection it had obtained in connection with the safety appliance law. Commissioners regularly attached summary statements from its air-brake and coupler inspectors to their annual reports and drew attention in the body of these reports to comments the inspectors had made about issues pertaining to the general matter of safety. Often these remarks highlighted the importance of personnel, training, and discipline in the safe conduct of railroad transportation. The commission also continued to press for the right to investigate accidents, and on occasion it reported informally on wrecks that had garnered widespread public notoriety (Fig. 8.5).

The resolution of 1906 held ambiguous implications for this approach to safety. Congress had given the commission authority to investigate, report, and recommend on a subject it had previously addressed only informally. That subject, moreover, touched upon the very matters of rules, discipline, and operational procedures that commissioners had come to see as essential to safe transportation. The ICC might conceivably use the resolution to obtain additional supervisory authority over railroad operations. As the commissioners pointed out in their response to Congress, enforcement of a law requiring the block system would require regular government inspection of train-handling methods, since manual block systems were only as effective as the rules and procedures that defined and governed them.[144]

But the resolution from Congress also contained strong overtones of the conventional, technology-centered approach to safety regulation. The first stirring of public interest in laws mandating block signaling coincided with publication of Braman Adams's *The Block System* (1901). Adams lavished praise upon recent developments at the Pennsylvania and left no doubt that its automatic devices constituted the finest system in the land. Not surprisingly, many seized upon the new technology as the latest step in pursuit of that glorious ideal: fully automatic control of trains.[145] Tellingly, the resolution

[142] U.S. House, "Report on Block Signals," p. 3. Some 1,823 workers (one in 428) were killed in service on American railroads during the year ending June 30, 1894, and another 23,422 (one in 33) were seriously injured.

[143] *ICC Report* 19 (December 14, 1905): 168–173.

[144] U.S. Senate, "Report on Block Signals," p. 25.

[145] Modern signal engineers regard the complete elimination of human action from train control as a desirable, if ultimately unattainable, goal. For an example of the views of modern signal engineers, see M. Mashour, *Human Factors in Signaling Systems: Specific Applications to Railway Signaling* (New York: John Wiley and Sons, 1974).

Figure 8.5. ICC inspectors examine a wreck on the Maine Central Railroad, c. 1912. An air brake hose dangles from the upended car, which carries the stencil "United States Safety Appliance Standards." *Courtesy*: Library of Congress.

from Congress referred to "block signals," not the "block system." The commission pointed this discrepancy out to Congress in its initial response, and in subsequent reports the signal board and the ICC spoke always of the block system. Commissioners persistently made clear that they considered a manual block system essential, an automatic block system nice but superfluous.[146] Still, if construed narrowly, the resolution might easily divert the ICC away from its emerging emphasis on inspection and supervision and turn it back toward technological remedies.

The conflict between these approaches to safety was apparent from the moment the ICC first responded to the block signal resolution in 1907, and it continued to influence all actions and discussions pertaining to government regulation of train-handling for at least another half-dozen years after that (see the ICC slogan in Fig. 8.6). Nothing demonstrated this more clearly than the experiences of the commission when it tried to carry out its charge to investigate "appliances for the automatic control of trains." Faced with the task of evaluating numerous devices whose merits had not yet been

[146] ICC, "Report of the Block Signal and Train Control Board," 2 (November 22, 1909), pp. 8 and 31; 3 (November 22, 1910): 13; and 4 (December 26, 1911): 6–9.

Figure 8.6. An ICC slogan in 1919 captured a basic tension that had informed discussions of railroad safety ever since the accident at Revere, half a century before. *Courtesy*: Hagley Museum and Library.

demonstrated through actual practice, the ICC requested special funds to conduct tests, and in July 1907 it received authorization from Congress to create the Block Signal and Train Control Board to carry out the task. When inventors persuaded Congress to require this board to examine *any* prospective invention pertaining to railroad safety, the floodgates opened. Within a year, the board had received nearly 500 techniques for consideration, and hundreds more followed. Members dutifully responded to each submission, even though in a typical year "only twelve plans, devices, or processes have been found . . . to be of sufficient merit to warrant . . . giving them any encouragement."[147] (This result could hardly have come as a surprise to railroads, who years before had come to rely on two suppliers for such devices.) "Inventive faculty and business ability," noted the board ruefully in its report of 1910, "seldom go hand in hand."[148] Board members lamented they could not provide inventors with the financial assistance necessary to develop promising ideas, and a majority recommended the ICC establish a permanent board for this purpose. But the commission seemed anxious to extricate itself from this charade and move toward a broader consideration of signaling practice.

While the ICC labored under this unsolicited burden, it struggled to maintain public focus on the block system and the broader issue of safety. But even when the commission discussed the block system, it often had difficulty getting past the matter of technology. Many people looked upon the block system not as a method but as a set of novel devices such as those at the Pennsylvania, which appeared to provide absolute safety through technological means. Despite its intentions, the ICC in many ways reinforced the tendency to think first about technology. In response to the resolution asking for an investigation of block signals, the commission in 1907 had two consultants produce a report on the subject. One was Adams, and the other was C. C. Anthony, who for the previous eleven years had served as supervisor of signals at the Pennsylvania. Though these authors carefully defined the block system as a method and described its various forms and the extent of its use in actual practice, they dwelled at length on the most sophisticated installations. The influence of developments at the Pennsylvania loomed especially large. Because the report was an official government document that could not advocate particular devices, moreover, the authors referred to these developments in generic terms and used the passive voice when discussing them. Rather than portraying automatic block signals as a specific response to a particular set of circumstances, the report characterized them as "the highest exemplification of the art" and noted that they "are

[147]   Ibid., esp. 4 (December 26, 1911). Quote from *ICC Report* 22 (December 24, 1908): 53.

[148]   ICC, "Report of the Block Signal and Train Control Board," 3 (November 22, 1910): 24.

superseding the telegraph block system to some extent, and seem destined to do so increasingly in the future."[149]

In an effort to make the strongest case possible for a mandatory requirement while retaining their tone of impartial investigation, the authors tried as they surveyed techniques to identify as many arguments in favor of adoption of the block system as they could. This led them into detailed discussions of costs of various systems and extended ruminations about the potential of block methods to increase capacity and provide other economic benefits. Consequently, the report ended up possessing an encyclopedic quality. It lacked the morally compelling sense of urgency a reformer might have brought to the safety issue, and its thorough, considered judgments of the economic costs and benefits of various installations could hardly have served to direct attention away from technology and build support for the ICC's preferred approach to regulation.

Perhaps the strongest points made in favor of inspection and supervision in the consultants' study and subsequent ICC reports were those pertaining to personnel. Commissioners repeatedly directed attention to the role of management and workers in administering the block system and recurrently stressed the importance of proper training and supervision of signalmen.[150] In reporting on a tour of signaling facilities around the country, the committee emphasized errors in discipline, not the quality of the machinery. Often these arguments came in the form of a comparison with Great Britain, where government inspectors regularly examined manual signaling practices to ensure that railroads indeed enforced the procedures necessary to sustain block movements.[151]

But here the ICC encountered a dilemma. For in emphasizing the need for a well-trained, disciplined work force subject to government oversight, the commissioners also lent support to those who saw automatic technology as the key to improving safety. This dilemma regarding labor was brought home to the ICC with the surprising effect of the Hours of Service Act. Hoping to ease the burdens upon workers such as signalmen, a majority of commissioners supported this bill, then found to their consternation that the act prompted some railroads to abandon the block system and shifted attention toward automatic technology.[152]

Perhaps nothing illustrated the difficulties facing the signal board and the ICC more clearly than the subject of automatic stops. In an effort to emphasize the importance of inspection and to direct interest toward manual forms of the block system, commissioners cautioned that automatic signals did not

149   U.S. Senate, "Report on Block Signals," p. 22.
150   Ibid., esp. pp. 14, 17, and 28; and *ICC Report* 23 (December 21, 1909): 50.
151   ICC, "Report of the Block Signal and Train Control Board," 1908–1912, and U.S. Senate, "Report on Block Signals," esp. p. 14.
152   *ICC Reports* 21 (December 23, 1907): 132; 22 (December 24, 1908): 307; and 23 (December 21, 1909): 49; and Latimer, *Railway Signaling*, p. 348.

provide the fail-safe protection many imagined, since engineers could still run through them. Almost immediately, cries arose that locomotives should be outfitted with "automatic stops" to protect against that possibility. "Every great accident due to an engineman's fault," skeptical commissioners sighed in one report, "is followed by a strong public demand for the introduction of automatic train stopping devices."[153] Inventors responded with countless arrangements they claimed would do the trick. Though a few urban transit systems had tried such devices on an experimental basis, none had yet proved satisfactory. Too often these temperamental appliances had stopped trains inadvertently, creating more danger than they had been designed to prevent. Railroads traditionally had placed far more hope on "surprise tests" than on automatic stops, and the ICC concurred.[154] But for those obsessed with substituting mechanical devices for human judgment, the technology of automatic stops could not be ignored. The ICC devoted precious time and energy to investigating the matter even though at the time only a fraction of the nation's rail system had block signals of any sort and a rare few among those used automatic systems.

For those who had hoped the resolution regarding block signals would lead to a significant enlargement of government authority over the movement of trains, the experiences of 1906–11 were a great disappointment. They had fallen victim to the American predilection to focus on technological devices rather than on the entire system in which those devices functioned. Ironically, the developments at the Pennsylvania, which safety advocates could only have praised, had worked against their efforts to achieve more systematic reform.

These frustrations spilled over in the Signal Board's report for 1911. Authored by three of the board's four members, this report boldly declared that "the time has come in this country to inaugurate a system of supervision over interstate roads somewhat similar in character to that now administrated through the British Board of Trade." The report called for laws that would give a supervisory agency regulatory authority over "the details of construction, maintenance, and operation of all interstate roads, so far as concerns safety of railroad travel and employment." Clearly frustrated with

---

[153]   U.S. Senate, "Report on Block Signals," p. 26.
[154]   For attitudes at the Pennsylvania, see G. W. Creighton to W. W. Atterbury, January 28, 1908; R. M. Patterson (Superintendent of Freight Transportation) to Atterbury, February 18, 1908; and Thomas E. Reilly (Superintendent of the Telegraph) to Patterson, February 10, 1908; PRR ATO Files, box 9, file 493. For ICC praise of surprise tests as "progressive," see *ICC Report* 16 (February 15, 1902): 303–311, and U.S. Senate, "Report on Block Signals," p. 17. On automatic stops, see "Reports of the Block Signal and Train Control Board," esp. 4 (December 26, 1911), and A. H. Rudd to C. D. Young, June 24 and July 3, 1913, PRR Engineer of Tests Papers, box 723, folder 16. For another perspective, see Mark Aldrich, "Combating the Collision Horror: The Interstate Commerce Commission and Automatic Train Control, 1900–1939," *Technology and Culture* 34 (1993): 49–77, and Aldrich, *Safety First*, ch. 5.

its experience of the previous "four and one-half years of special study, investigation, and observation," the board stressed that the actual study of devices and methods should be left to railroads. The ICC should concentrate on watching over actual practice. "The railroads are well organized to represent their own interests, as are also their employees," the report observed in justifying this course, "but the public must look to governmental agency to protect its interests."[155] The ICC thus sought to pull back from the technical details, distance itself from railroads and their workers, and assume the post of a watchdog operating strictly on behalf of consumers.

The lone dissenter from this position was Braman B. Adams, the trade journal editor, who had joined the Signal Board after his initial stint as a consultant. Adams submitted a minority report in which he criticized the idea of an inspection board and defended an approach to safety based upon the power of publicity to hold managers accountable. "Beyond publicity we enter an untried field," Adams warned, echoing sentiments voiced by another Adams nearly forty years before, following the accident at Revere. "If and whenever an agent of the Government decides what a railway officer shall do, the State assumes some degree of responsibility for the acts of such officer." Adams argued that any experts employed by the government in such a broad supervisory capacity would need a level of experience commensurate with that of the general manager of a major railroad. Until the ICC hired such men and trained them, a prospect Adams clearly considered highly unlikely, Congress should simply require the block system.[156]

In advocating this course, Adams and the railroad interests for whom he spoke fell back again on the strategy they had pursued years before, when passage of a law pertaining to automatic brakes and couplers appeared unavoidable. Railroads would accept a mandate calling for block operations while avoiding provisions for the inspections necessary to give teeth to that requirement. Such an approach to safety legislation would be especially inoffensive to railroads in the case of signaling technology, for by stipulating the block system rather than block signals, the law would leave railroads free to choose from a variety of methods, including permissive operations. Railroads thus could satisfy the public demand for action without having to spend money on the sort of automatic system deployed by the Pennsylvania to address its unusual operating conditions and without opening the door to widespread meddling in their daily operations by government inspectors. In this sense, the flexibility inherent to the term "block system" very much worked to the advantage of railroads.[157]

155 ICC, "Fourth Report of the Block Signal and Train Control Board," December 26, 1911, pp. 12–18, quotes from pp. 14 and 16.
156 Ibid., pp. 18–22. Quote from p. 20.
157 At least some influential railroad executives had already come around to the position endorsed by the majority of the signal board. "It is unfortunate," wrote Superintendent of Freight Transportation R. M. Patterson to General Manager Atterbury when

At the time Adams expressed his difference of opinion with his fellow members of the signal board, a decade of debate over accident prevention and the block system had revealed several policy alternatives. One approach, advocated by a significant segment of the public, was to require that railroads adopt particular technologies. Most of those responsible for administering regulation no longer viewed this approach as sufficient to ensure safety. Indeed, in the case of the block system they saw the focus on technology as distracting from real reform. These regulators preferred a law that focused instead on the block method. Above all, they sought broad supervisory powers and administrative authority. Adams, who from the perspective of his fellow board members had sympathies more for the railroads than for the public, opposed both regulation mandating specific technologies and expansion of government supervisory authority. He sought to restrict the role of government to that of publicist. In supporting a law requiring the block method, Adams moved only slightly away from that position. For as he well understood, the term block system covered a range of options, including permissive application. Railroads would retain broad discretion over their operations.

In its actual policies, Congress had pursued an approach of intensified publicity. It allowed the ICC to gather information about accidents, to survey existing practices regarding the block system, and to evaluate and publicize technical developments. Congress had not passed legislation requiring the block system. Nor had it significantly expanded the power of the ICC to inspect and supervise ordinary practice.[158] The arguments submitted by the majority of the Signal Board did not prompt Congress to alter its course significantly. In fact, Congress closed down the Signal Board after 1912 and created a Division of Safety, which took over responsibility for the tasks already authorized under existing statutes, such as gathering statistics, inspecting devices required under the safety appliance law, and investigating accidents. Congress dropped the routine evaluation of prospective safety devices, though in 1913 it authorized an emergency allocation to renew studies of automatic stops. Despite a fervent plea from the Signal Board, which

ruminating at length upon the matter of signaling and safety regulation in 1908, "that we have not a Board of Trade in this country to force all the American roads to a better system, even if it costs more and the public had to pay higher rates for more safety." R. M. Patterson to W. W. Atterbury, February 18, 1908, PRR ATO Files, box 9, file 493. Much like the signal board, Patterson cited the power of organized labor, which he believed undermined traditional forms of employee discipline, as a reason for embracing government regulation of safety.

[158] In 1910, Congress granted the ICC authority to investigate accidents in addition to collecting accident statistics. In subsequent years, however, commissioners complained that the available funds permitted them to carry out only a few accident investigations each year. See U.S. Interstate Commerce Commission, "Reports of the Chief of the Division of Safety to the Interstate Commerce Commission" (henceforth, "ICC Safety Reports"), 1913–1915.

claimed in its final report that "railways have been slow in adopting the block system" and labeled the absence of a requirement a "failure of Government," Congress did not require the block system, and continued instead to rely on its expanded powers of publicity.[159]

This approach left railroads free to employ the block system in a selective fashion. Between 1901 and 1915, most came to use some form of the system in their passenger operations. In 1901, Adams reported that under 27,000 miles of road were being operated under the block system, and of those fewer than 2,300 miles had automatic signals. Many companies used the method permissively, and some lines employed the block system only during foggy weather or other exceptional circumstances.[160] By 1912, railroads had equipped 20,334 miles of track with automatic electric signals.[161] Three years later, those figures had risen to 96,609 miles under the block system and 29,864 miles with automatic signals. "The block system is in use on the entire passenger mileage of the important roads of the country," declared the ICC that year, "and the activities of these roads in signal work now consist principally of substituting modern for antiquated equipment and improving operating conditions and practices."[162] Conversion to the block system had not, however, entailed a wholesale switch from one system to another. Most freight operations still took place under the dispatching method or in a permissive fashion. In the end, fifteen years of experimentation by individual lines and another fifteen of political haggling had resulted in a hybridized system for governing the movement of trains. Over 60 percent of the country's railroad mileage still operated under the older dispatching system, and those that used the block system employed it in a wide variety of forms. Few railroads had revised their methods of governing the movement of trains as radically as the Pennsylvania.

RELUCTANT INNOVATORS

The long, convoluted paths of innovation in freight braking and signaling traversed courses stretching from one epoch of railroad technology to another emergent era of far greater complexity. So long as railroads had ready alternatives for handling the increasing volume of traffic and remained free from outside influence, they shunned or resisted air brakes in freight service and automatic signals. Complex and expensive, these technologies raised troubling issues regarding labor and work routines that railroads preferred

---

[159] "ICC Safety Reports," 1913–1915, and ICC, "Final Report of the Block Signal and Train Control Board," June 29, 1912, p. 22.

[160] Adams, *Block System*, pp. 170–171.

[161] ICC, "Final Report of the Block Signal and Train Control Board," June 29, 1912, p. 7.

[162] "ICC Safety Report for 1915," pp. 18–19.

to avoid. Lines turned to these techniques only when confronted with circumstances outside the ordinary. Railroads first applied air brakes to freight cars, for instance, only when they could no longer stem demand from select shippers who sought special services such as express stock trains. The Pennsylvania installed automatic block signals, a move one veteran manager characterized as "a thorough revolution in railway practice," only after the increasing speed and frequency of its trains overwhelmed the capabilities of its established methods. Neither technique spread outside these isolated circumstances and diffused through the industry until government threatened railroads with mandates. Even then, railroads turned the laws in ways that minimized the degree of change.

The spread of air brakes in freight service and of automatic signaling thus heralded the passage of railroading into a new era. No longer could managers concentrate simply on refining certain basic technologies in ways that enabled them to push more traffic through a bulkier but otherwise stagnant system. Demands from an increasingly diverse array of shippers would present railroads with challenges unlike those they had confronted before. Those demands, together with the growing volume of traffic, created unprecedented congestion, especially at junctions and transfer points. Railroads could not overcome those burdens without departing more radically from established practices and resorting to novel technical remedies of uncertain merit. At the same time, government and railroad employees brought new pressures to bear upon railroads. Though motivated in large measure by concerns about rates and wages, the public and railroad workers ultimately exerted influence upon the choices of technologies as well. Thus, just as managers perceived the breakdown of established methods and struggled to construct a new paradigm, they lost a measure of autonomy. The full nature of their ordeal becomes clear when we examine the torturous disputes over rates that absorbed so much energy on the part of those engaged in railroading during the opening decades of the new century.

9

The Limits of Engineering: Rate
Regulation and the Course
of Innovation

At the very moment the ICC signal board advocated imposing an unprecedented degree of government oversight upon railroad operating procedures,
the commissioners themselves gathered in Washington to consider a matter of even more vital importance to American railroading. The occasion
was the Eastern or Advance Rate Case, in which the ICC would exercise its
new authority to set maximum rates for railroad transportation. Railroads
in the densely settled northeastern third of the nation had petitioned for
a 10 percent increase in all tariffs. As a parade of railroad executives and
their hired experts testified to the need for increased revenue, they came
under close scrutiny from Louis Brandeis, a savvy and experienced advocate retained by New England shippers and merchants who opposed the
proposed rate hike. Like a skilled prosecutor, Brandeis peppered one witness after another with detailed queries regarding costs. The insistent cross-
examiner attracted no special attention from the smothering press coverage, however, until he took the floor early that winter and proceeded to
march his own stable of experts before the commission. Railroads did not
in fact need the proposed rate increase, explained each authority in turn,
because they could raise the same amount of funds simply by eliminating
inefficiencies. The carriers could realize this startling savings – a million
dollars a day, in the convenient shorthand of the press – by employing
the methods of scientific management as espoused by engineering experts
such as Frederick Winslow Taylor and Harrington Emerson. The argument not only carried the day; it propelled Taylor and the ideas of scientific management into the national limelight, fueling an almost messianic
enthusiasm for the idea of improving efficiency through careful engineering
analysis.[1]

[1] For a recent account, see Robert Kanigel, *The One Best Way: Frederick Winslow Taylor
and the Enigma of Efficiency* (New York: Viking Penguin, 1997), pp. 429–436.

How had this happened? How could the railroads, who at the turn of the century had been held up as models of engineering efficiency, see themselves defeated just a decade later by a critic who accused them of inefficiency? One respected observer of the day, the economist William J. Cunningham, thought the answer lay in the element of surprise. "The most striking feature of the recent public hearings before the Interstate Commerce Commission," wrote Cunningham in the *Quarterly Journal of Economics* not long after the ICC denied the increase, was "Mr. Brandeis's clever turn in attacking the railroads in the quarter where attack was least expected."[2] Cunningham proceeded to argue that scientific management as described by Taylor and his associate Emerson, whose data from the Santa Fe Railroad Brandeis had cited with great effect at the hearings, could not easily be applied to railroads. The techniques espoused by Taylor and Emerson, observed Cunningham, had been developed in machine shops and other facilities engaged in the manufacture and assembly of finished goods. The shop facilities studied by Emerson at the Santa Fe, in contrast, did not manufacture cars and locomotives from scratch but instead merely repaired and maintained such equipment. Railroad shops played a supporting role in the much larger effort to provide transport services. In fulfilling that broader objective, moreover, railroads had pursued efficiency with a rigor Taylor would certainly admire. "After all," Cunningham observed, "there is little essential difference between the aims and accomplishments of scientific management as advocated by the new experts and scientific management as practiced by the exceptionally well-managed railroads. As a system, it means a careful study and analysis of each element of operation, and the application of the methods best adapted to bring about the best results under the given conditions. Many railroads are doing this successfully; others are doing it in part." As a result, net train load (the value of tonnage carried per train) had increased by 50 percent during the previous decade alone. Railroads did not need a new system, Cunningham concluded, but merely continued application of their old one.

Historians evaluating railroad rate regulation of the early twentieth century have often concurred with this assessment. In his Pulitzer Prize-winning study *Prophets of Regulation*, for instance, historian Thomas McCraw shows that Brandeis was an experienced trial lawyer who had consistently demonstrated an ability to win cases by surprising complacent opponents.[3] Like Cunningham, McCraw respects Brandeis more for his tactics than for

---

[2]   William J. Cunningham, "Scientific Management in the Operation of Railroads," *Quarterly Journal of Economics* 25 (May 1911): 539–561.

[3]   Thomas K. McCraw, *Prophets of Regulation* (Cambridge, Mass.: Harvard University Press, 1984). See also his "Rethinking the Trust Question," in Thomas K. McCraw, ed., *Regulation in Perspective* (Cambridge, Mass.: Harvard University Press, 1981), pp. 1–55.

the merits of his arguments. In McCraw's assessment, railroads stood at the center of an emerging corporate economy in which a core of large institutions generated the lion's share of economic growth by relentlessly pursuing the efficiencies of high-volume throughput. The shippers and other small business interests with whom Brandeis felt such close affinity and whose cause he served so effectively occupied what McCraw refers to as the periphery of that economy. Stuck in enterprises that did not or could not pursue the economies of high-volume throughput and efficient routine, they used politics to block the emerging tide of giant low-cost suppliers such as the railroads.

In evoking an image of railroad opponents as misguided and anachronistic, McCraw's analysis bears a strong resemblance to that presented by historian Albro Martin. In his provocative study *Enterprise Denied*, Martin brands railroad prosecutors such as Brandeis and the commissioners who embraced their arguments as "archaic progressives" who still thought of railroads as unopposed powerful institutions.[4] These men did not recognize that railroads of the early twentieth century faced extraordinary operational challenges and political opponents of great sophistication. Railroads, for their part, failed to alert commissioners as effectively as they might have to these realities. When Brandeis presented the panel with what the public took to be a plausible reason to side against the railroads, the commissioners seized it and denied the requested increase. The consequences, in Martin's assessment, were dire indeed. Capital fled to more attractive investments, leaving railroads unable to sustain the impressive programs of capital improvements they had pursued between 1898 and 1907. As a result, the industry could not reap the benefits of "a burgeoning technology [that] held out the promise of a hundred ways to hold down the operating ratio" and to increase productivity, and the railroads slipped into decline.

By situating the question of railroad rates within a larger discussion taking place in Progressive-era America about economic structure and the sources of efficiency, these studies have greatly enriched our understanding of railroad politics and of political economy in general. Earlier accounts had focused more on political outcomes than on the economic effects of regulation. Studies from the 1930s and 1940s, for instance, generally interpreted the establishment of regulatory agencies such as the ICC and the Federal Trade Commission as a priori evidence that liberal democracy (the people) had triumphed over concentrated economic power (big business).[5] Later, a younger

---

4   Albro Martin, *Enterprise Denied: Origins of the Decline of American Railroads, 1897–1917* (New York: Columbia University Press, 1971). See also his "The Troubled Subject of Railroad Regulation in the Gilded Age," *Journal of American History* 51 (1974): 339–371.
5   For an example of the institutional approach of particular relevance to this chapter, see I. L. Scharfman, *The Interstate Commerce Commission: A Study in Administrative Law and Procedure*, 5 vols. (New York: Commonwealth Fund, 1931–1937).

generation of historians turned this idea on its head. To these revisionists, the emerging government bureaucracies of the Cold War era appeared less like a source of countervailing power and more like unwarranted extensions of corporate influence into the public arena. Some influential figures, armed with detailed analyses of legislative history, went so far as to claim that the regulatory state had consciously been constructed by big business in a successful effort to close off more radical alternatives.[6] Critics responded with a spate of detailed studies tracing the origins of regulatory statutes at the state and federal level and emphasizing the conflicting objectives of various interests within the business community.[7] Though such works blunted the force of the revisionist argument, they remained focused on political outcomes rather than on the actual social and economic ramifications of regulation.

Yet while historians such as McCraw and Martin brought a welcome shift in emphasis, they may well have obscured some important elements of the story. In positing the railroads as unquestionable instruments of efficiency and in dismissing Brandeis's arguments as anachronistic or merely tactical, these authors skirt certain complexities raised by experiences of the Pennsylvania Railroad and of other lines during the years immediately preceding the rate case. Even in the absence of government intervention, railroad executives of the early twentieth century faced a set of challenges significantly different from those they had confronted so successfully during the previous few decades. Techniques that had facilitated steady improvements in productivity during the late nineteenth century no longer generated returns so readily. The task of accommodating a larger and more diverse volume

---

[6] The classic statement is Gabriel Kolko, *The Triumph of Conservatism: A Reinterpretation of American History, 1900–1916* (New York: Free Press, 1963) and *Railroads and Regulation, 1877–1916* (Princeton: Princeton University Press, 1965). See also James Weinstein, *The Corporate Ideal in the Liberal State, 1900–1918* (Boston: Beacon Press, 1968).

[7] Edward A. Purcell, Jr., "Ideas and Interests: Businessmen and the Interstate Commerce Act," *Journal of American History* 54 (1967): 561–578; K. Austin Kerr, *American Railroad Politics, 1914–1920: Rates, Wages, and Efficiency* (Pittsburgh: University of Pittsburgh Press, 1968); George H. Miller, *Railroads and the Granger Laws* (Madison: University of Wisconsin Press, 1971); and Richard H. K. Vietor, "Businessmen and the Political Economy: The Railroad Rate Controversy of 1905," *Journal of American History* 64 (1977): 47–66. The most careful works on the politics of regulation had in fact always stressed the multiplicity of interests that typically influenced legislation. See, for example, Arthur S. Link, *Woodrow Wilson and the Progressive Era, 1910–1917* (New York, 1954), and Richard Hofstadter, *The Age of Reform: From Bryan to F.D.R.* (New York, 1955). This approach also characterizes the more recent specialized studies of Stephen Skowronek, *Building a New American State: The Expansion of National Administrative Capacities, 1877–1920* (New York: Cambridge University Press, 1982), and Morton Keller, *Regulating a New Economy: Public Policy and Economic Change in America, 1900–1933* (Cambridge, Mass.: Harvard University Press, 1990).

of traffic called for bold new departures. As the previous chapter suggests, railroads found it necessary to alter established routines and to restructure their aging machines in ways that did not come easily. At the time of the rate case, managers had only begun to grasp the magnitude of the challenges before them. Still reeling from crises induced by the changing character of demands for their services, they had little confidence that the future held forth burgeoning opportunities to improve the operating ratio and enhance productivity in the fashion that observers such as Cunningham and F. W. Taussig had celebrated. Rather, they probed tentatively for ways to reorient their business activities toward meeting the demands of customers willing to pay a premium for specialized services.

Viewed in this light, the disputes over rate regulation appear not so much as anachronisms but as harbingers of a fundamental challenge that has persistently plagued business managers and policy makers throughout the twentieth century: the ongoing effort to reconcile the efficiency of routine with the potential dynamism of innovation. Time and again, in industries ranging from electric power to telecommunications to computing, government and business have grappled with the sticky problem of combining what the economist Frederick Taussig termed "the inventiveness and elasticity characteristic of the Yankee from early days" with "that orderly and systematic utilization of applied science in which the Germans have hitherto been . . . most successful."[8] Frequently, these delicate balancing acts have involved precisely the two sorts of challenges posed by railroading at the opening of the century. One variety of problem involves matters of maturity or obsolescence. Operators of large systems, like all people engaged in management, have struggled to recognize when their business or industry faced moments of transition, in which established technological trajectories and organizational paradigms produced diminishing returns, or novel breakthroughs presented new threats or opened potentially rewarding opportunities. The task of avoiding obsolescence and responding to changing circumstances can prove especially difficult in large, systems-based industries, which acquire substantial momentum in the form of fixed assets and, perhaps more important, expectations on the parts of operators and consumers.

Efforts to negotiate these critical junctures grow especially complicated when they meld with the second, more persistent issue faced by highly systematized organizations. This second characteristic feature involves the difficulty of building sufficient flexibility into the system to accommodate the particular needs of diverse customers. In meeting demands for customized services, railroads and other system operators often must resort to novelties

---

[8] F. W. Taussig, "The Iron Industry of the United States," *Quarterly Journal of Economics* 14 (1900): 488. See also F. W. Taussig, "Recent Discussions of Railway Management in Prussia," *Quarterly Journal of Economics* 9 (1895): 77–87. For further analysis, see Chapter 7.

that threaten to disrupt the pursuit of uniformity and routine so valued by engineers and managers. During the late nineteenth century, railroads frequently permitted service-oriented activities such as refrigerated shipments, express deliveries, and deluxe passenger travel to fall into the hands of outside concerns. Firms such as Pullman, Swift, and Westinghouse achieved success only after overcoming considerable resistance from railroads who favored uniformity-enhancing routine over product-differentiating innovation.[9]

Efforts to meet demands from individual customers involve more than novel technologies and diversified services. Pricing also matters. By manipulating rate schedules, managers and government can steer demand toward certain services and away from others. As the range of products and services increases, rate-making grows steadily more complicated. The task is especially difficult in system-based utilities such as railroading, where the distinct services share a common infrastructure and where access to the basic product at a reasonable price is considered a fundamental right of all consumers. In these circumstances, the challenge for managers and government alike has been to find mechanisms that conceive of consumer demand not simply as a homogeneous mass seeking standard performance at lower cost, but rather as a collection of interests wishing to have their individual needs met through innovative services, without sacrificing the steady drive for economy that keeps the basic price low.

This ongoing struggle, which to some degree had characterized railroading from its earliest days, first came to national prominence in American public life with the rate cases of the early twentieth century. Without benefit of precedent or obvious parallel to guide them, and with the remarkable performance of the engineering epoch still fresh in their minds, the public and the railroads attempted to construct new mechanisms for setting prices. The outcome, not fully apparent for another decade after Brandeis's triumph, would shape innovation in railroading and throughout the transport sector for half a century to come.

---

[9]   On Pullman, see Stanley Buder, *Pullman: An Experiment in Industrial Order and Community Planning, 1880–1930* (New York: Oxford University Press, 1967). On railroad resistance to meatpackers, see Mary Yeager, *Competition and Regulation: The Development of Oligopoly in the Meat Packing Industry* (Greenwich, Conn.: Greenwood Press, 1981). On the railroad express, see Peter Z. Grossman, *American Express: The Unofficial History of the People Who Built the Great Financial Empire* (New York: Crown, 1987), and "Golden Silence: Why the Express Chose Not to Incorporate," *Business and Economic History* 21, series 2 (1992): 300–306. On Westinghouse, see Steven W. Usselman, "From Novelty to Utility: George Westinghouse and Business of Innovation in the Age of Edison," *Business History Review* 66 (1992): 251–304. For an excellent introduction to American political economy that raises precisely this dichotomy, see Louis Galambos and Joseph Pratt, *The Rise of the Corporate Commonwealth: United States Business and Public Policy in the 20th Century* (New York: Basic, 1988).

THE RATE QUESTION

Disputes over rates were by no means new to railroading with the onset of the Progressive era. Rate regulation of some sort had been a part of the industry virtually from its inception, and during the late nineteenth century rate disputes had constituted the central component of what many Americans routinely referred to as "the railroad problem." As historian George Miller observed a quarter-century ago in his outstanding history of the Granger movement, that problem can be framed in terms of the fundamental break railroads made with previous forms of transportation such as roads and canals.[10] These earlier modes of transport had permitted a ready division of responsibility between companies that built and maintained the basic infrastructure and those that carried goods over it. In granting charters to canal and turnpike companies, governments routinely stipulated maximum rates these firms could charge in return for their monopoly privileges. Such rates, which courts reviewed for reasonableness, were readily expressed on a per mile basis. Meanwhile, the rates carriers could charge went unregulated, since governments believed competition among them would generate the most equitable prices. As long as the transport companies made their infrastructure available to all carriers, as their charters required, government could expect to see a vibrant competition that involved numerous variations in both price and service.

The interconnected nature of railroad technology broke down these neat boundaries. As providers of both infrastructure and carriage, railroads blended elements of regulated monopoly with those of intense market competition. Before the Civil War, when the railroad was largely perceived as a novel alternative that would bring increased competition to the business of transport infrastructure, the boundary problem did not pose severe difficulties. But as the network of tracks filled in and competition eroded the advantages that localities had initially gained by constructing a rail line, the complex nature of railroading (and the intractability of the boundary problem) grew ever more apparent and pressing. Courts and state governments grappled for solutions, improvising as they went along. Sensitive to perceived discrimination resulting from local monopoly yet aware that railroad competition and costs involved a hopelessly complex set of variables, legislatures substituted vague long-haul, short-haul provisions for strict pro rata requirements. More important, they authorized commissions to adjudicate disputes involving particular localities and products. The process, highly contentious under any circumstances, grew all the more so under a system of federalism that at once multiplied and complicated the disputes.

The results were messy. By the late nineteenth century, published rate schedules showed a staggering array of classifications, and practices such as

---

[10] Miller, *Railroads and the Granger Laws*.

discounting and rebating (though ostensibly banned) no doubt introduced still greater variation into the rates actually charged. Individual rates reflected an indecipherable mix of custom, regulation, competition, and costs. The schedules contained biases, with rates in the East generally favoring manufactured goods while those in the South and West subsidized agriculture at the expense of industry.[11] Informed observers still argue whether rates favored long shipments over short, or vice versa. Yet for all its messiness, this complex rate scheme represented a gallant attempt to balance the advantages of uniformity and efficiency against the needs of a diverse customer base.

Even with the increasing involvement of state commissions in rate-making, a large share of the responsibility for striking those balances remained in the hands of railroad management. Executives such as the Burlington's Charles Perkins steadfastly defended the autonomy of railroads to "charge what the market will bear." This notorious aphorism, which increasingly drew the ire of railroad critics, complemented Perkins's analysis of railroad organization discussed in earlier chapters. Perkins drew a sharp distinction between what he termed the business of railroading – by which he meant the securing of capital, pricing of services, and recruitment of traffic – and the daily efforts extended in maintaining the line and keeping trains moving smoothly and economically without accident.[12] This hypothetical split corresponded in many respects with the difference between carriers and infrastructure providers from the pre-railroad era, only now Perkins included the movement of equipment as part of the infrastructure. In insisting railroads remain free to charge what the market will bear, Perkins sought to retain the autonomy boatmen and teamsters had enjoyed.

In the real conditions of late-nineteenth-century railroading, however, even so adamant a devotee of laissez-faire as Perkins never found the division between business considerations and technical operations quite so neat. In his careful study of Burlington freight agents under Perkins's regime, historian Olivier Zunz traces in rich detail how even these men – the salesmen and marketers of railroading – came to absorb the bureaucratic ethic that one associates with the operational side of Perkins's schema. Agents found themselves devoting increasing numbers of their working hours to tasks such as forecasting traffic demand and auditing inventories of equipment, procedures clearly intended to facilitate the smooth and consistent movement of traffic through the machine. Agents generally assumed these tasks with enthusiasm, observes Zunz, apparently drawing energy and satisfaction from their roles in extending the Burlington's organizational reach. On occasion, these new duties drew agents into conflict with their traditional role as salesmen.

[11]   Kerr, *American Railroad Politics*, pp. 8–11.
[12]   C. E. Perkins, "Memorandum on Organization," n.d. (c. 1885), Papers of the Chicago, Burlington and Quincy Railroad (henceforth, CBQ Papers), Newberry Library, Chicago, 3P6.36. Usselman, "From Novelty to Utility."

Operating at the delicate interface between the impersonal corporation and its clients, freight agents sometimes found themselves alienating customers through their zealous enforcement of rules made in Chicago. Such occasions, Zunz notes, reminded agents of the tension between sales and efficiency. Good agents learned when to bend the rules and side with the customer against the corporation. "Their work lives combined, in a complex way," Zunz concludes, "the search for order and method with the often irregular and improvisational strategies necessitated by the search for profit."[13]

Zunz is no doubt correct that representatives of railroad traffic departments retained a measure of the ethic of the proprietary capitalist and his freewheeling salesman ally, bargaining in the market to find what the traffic would bear. The not infrequent jabs exchanged between operating and traffic officers attending meetings of the Pennsylvania Railroad's Association of Transportation Officers testify to the persistence of a marketing-oriented culture at that line as well. "For sometime the Freight men have been well on top," went a line from a company song at the Pennsylvania discussed in more detail below. "Cars were scarce, and movement very slow." Yet, later in the same verse, we hear a different tune: "But, as the summer comes, the prospect changes some.... With a service regular, the tons will come."[14] Just about the time this verse was written, a member suggested the ATO consider whether gross tonnage statistics did not provide a more accurate basis of assessing performance than the net tonnage data then in use. The change, if adopted, would have replaced an economic measure with one grounded solely in engineering criteria. Executives from the traffic department hastily intervened, protesting that the move would undermine all established incentives among their personnel.[15] Though the Pennsylvania stopped short of implementing this change, such exchanges reflected the growing tendency to conflate engineering criteria with economic ones in railroading of the late nineteenth century. The machine, not the business, was ascendant. In his final years at the helm of the Burlington, even Perkins pleaded with his subordinates to get more "scientific men" into the Traffic Department.[16]

Perhaps nothing more clearly signaled the tendency of engineering criteria to subsume economic ones than the meteoric rise of the concept of the ton-mile. During the closing decade of the nineteenth century, internal correspondence at the Pennsylvania and the Burlington grew filled with references to this measure of performance. So, too, did trade journals and the technical

---

[13] Olivier Zunz, *Making America Corporate, 1870–1920* (Chicago: University of Chicago Press, 1990), pp. 37–66, quotation from p. 59.

[14] Copies of these songs can be found in the Files of the Association of Transportation Officers of the Pennsylvania Railroad (henceforth, PRR ATO Files), PRR Papers, Hagley Museum and Library, Wilmington, Delaware, accession 1810.

[15] "Report of the Committee on Conducting Transportation," April 20, 1903, PRR ATO Files, box 5.

[16] See Chapters 5 and 7.

press. Managers throughout the industry could recite at will figures such as the number of ton-miles moved daily through their system or the ton-miles of coal or other commodities hauled yearly through a given division. Often they seemed much harder pressed to specify the revenue earned from such activities. "Tonnage means nothing until it is converted into dollars," cautioned a draft report from the ATO from 1908. The secretary of the association, preparing a typescript for broad distribution, enclosed the phrase in penciled quotation marks, as if it were a common aphorism.[17] During this period, the Pennsylvania routinely rated both locomotives and train crews according to the ton-miles they carried. General Manager William W. Atterbury's ire during a particularly acute congestion crisis, discussed in more detail below, grew fiercest when his subordinates seemed unwilling to recognize the simple truth that the newly purchased equipment was not pulling its expected number of ton-miles. Attempts to convince him that some other criteria might more accurately reflect the conditions facing the road triggered his complaints that officers were ducking responsibility by resorting to novel statistics.[18]

This tendency to conflate engineering objectives with economic ones was abetted by changes in the area of railroad finance, including court doctrines regarding the frequent bankruptcies that plagued the industry during the closing years of the nineteenth century. Rulings in bankruptcy proceedings served to bring increasing portions of the nation's railroad mileage under the supervision of a small number of financial managers who operated with a considerable degree of independence from holders of the securities that financed the enterprises.[19] The most notable of these managers, the investment banker J. P. Morgan, was especially prone to evaluate lines according

---

[17] A. Feldpauche to H. P. Lincoln, September 5, 1908, and attached report, "Cooperation of Different Departments on a Grand Division," p. 4, PRR ATO Files, box 6, folder 313.

[18] Robert M. Patterson to W. W. Atterbury, marked personal, October 12, 1904, and "Report of the Joint Committee on The Decreasing Average Mileage of Our Freight and Locomotive Equipment," November 2, 1904, pp. 18–19, PRR ATO Files, box 6, file 303. To some extent, of course, railroads might have resorted to this measure in order to keep from revealing how much revenue they earned from various aspects of their trade. Such information could have alienated customers and provided fodder for shippers and politicians who accused the lines of discrimination. But the pervasiveness of the term in routine operational affairs persuades me that, regardless of its original purposes, it accurately captures the spirit and understanding with which managers approached their enterprises. Faced with a bewildering array of rates and with the virtually impossible task of disaggregating their expenses in ways that permitted strict cost-based pricing, railroads resorted to more general measures of performance.

[19] Gerald Berk, *Alternative Tracks: The Constitution of American Industrial Order, 1865–1917* (Baltimore: Johns Hopkins University Press, 1994), and Peter Tufano, "Business Failure, Redefinition of Claims, and Financial Innovation: A Nineteenth Century Case Study," Working Paper 93-021, Division of Research, Harvard Business School.

to technical criteria. The grand mergers Morgan orchestrated in the years around the turn of the century left the resulting giants with a diversified portfolio of customers and rate schedules. Much like investors in mutual funds today, Morgan in effect hedged his bets, mixing so many winners and losers in the diverse market for railroad services that the variations came out a wash. Under these circumstances the distinctions among lines could then be boiled down to a few operational criteria, such as the number of ton-miles carried per amount of capital invested. In effect, Morgan took demand (and consumers) out of the picture and assessed the health of a railroad according to a set of standard engineering measures. Capital could then flow to the few lines that best met those criteria.[20]

In taking this approach to the railroad industry, Morgan and other financiers opened the door to a new way of conceptualizing the troubling issue of rates. Rather than concentrating upon adjudicating the fairness of individual tariffs, government might focus instead on setting overall rate levels in ways that generated a "fair rate of return" on the capital invested. In practice, this approach would lead to extraordinarily complicated efforts to valuate capital based on a staggering array of arcane details. Valuation studies generated so many rules and exceptions and opened so many grounds for dispute that they ultimately proved even more maddening to railroads and regulators than the complex rate schedules. But in theory, rate-of-return regulation seemingly offered an opportunity to simplify the rate question and render it susceptible to the routine and the certainty of engineering. As such, it attracted not only conservative financiers such as Morgan, but also a growing community of reformers who embraced engineering methods as tools to resolve the messy disputes of the day in business and politics.[21]

---

[20] For an example of the Morgan approach at work, see Stuart Daggett, *Railroad Reorganization* (Cambridge, Mass.: Harvard University Press, 1908). For a historical analysis, see E. G. Campell, *The Reorganization of the American Railroad System, 1893–1900* (New York: Columbia University Press, 1938).

[21] For a fascinating analysis of the complex relationship between engineering data and economic accounting, including a detailed look at the experiences of French engineers and economists tackling the issue of railroad rates, see Theodore M. Porter, *Trust in Numbers: The Pursuit of Objectivity in Science and Public Life* (Princeton: Princeton University Press, 1995). "Any such measures," writes Porter of attempts to determine returns-on-investment, "necessarily involve a loss of information. In some cases, as with accounting, the credibility of the bottom line may be such that this loss seems largely irrelevant. But such an attitude presupposes that the bottom line is determined unambiguously by the activities it summarizes. It never is. When business managers are judged by the accounts, they learn to optimize the accounts, perhaps through such artifices as putting off needed maintenance and other long-term costs" (p. 44). Gregory L. Thompson, *The Passenger Train in the Motor Age: California's Rail and Bus Industries, 1910–1941* (Columbus: Ohio State University Press, 1993) and "How Cost Ignorance Derailed the Pennsylvania Railroad's Efforts to Save Its Passenger Service, 1929–1961," *Journal of Transport History* 16 (1995): 134–158, argues that railroad accounting practices during the early twentieth century followed conventions bearing

Among those most attracted to the idea was Thorstein Veblen, the social critic who perhaps more than any other figure of the early twentieth century embraced the possibility that engineering could substitute for the waste and inequities of the price system. Writing in 1906 about the pending legislation regarding railroad rates, Veblen was quick to seize upon persistent cries that railroads should remain free to "charge what the market will bear." To his way of thinking, the aphorism served as a poignant reminder of how the crass values of greedy capitalists differed from those of engineers and administrators. For Veblen, the phrase represented the antithesis of the spirit of engineering, in which standards (or perhaps even prices) would flow from cooperative investigation of the inherent physical qualities of the matter under study. Rates derived from valuations of assets determined by neutral experts, in comparison, appeared grounded in the same techniques that inspired Charles Dudley and other engineers and scientists who struggled to substitute engineering standards for the haggling of the unregulated marketplace.[22]

The engineering ideals embraced by Veblen and other reformers would undergo their first practical test in the Eastern Rate Case. Though Congress had clearly bestowed the power to set maximum rates upon the ICC when it overwhelmingly passed the Hepburn Act in 1906, the potency of those powers remained in question for several years.[23] So long as railroads could appeal all rate cases to the courts and impose any rate they desired in the interim, the federal commission lacked meaningful authority. With passage of the Mann–Elkins Act (1910), however, Congress shifted the locus of action from the courts to the ICC by requiring railroads to comply with mandated rates during the appeals process. (The act also created a special commerce court to hear those appeals, but this body hardly functioned before it was allowed to drift out of existence three years later.) In the Eastern Rate Case,

---

little connection to actual operating realities. As a result, managers and regulators allocated resources poorly, undermining the ability of railroading to counter challenges from alternative forms of transport.

[22] On Veblen, see Cecelia Tichi, *Shifting Gears: Technology, Literature, and Culture in Modernist America* (Chapel Hill: University of North Carolina Press, 1987), ch. 3, and Martha Banta, *Taylored Lives: Narrative Productions in the Age of Taylor, Veblen, and Ford* (Chicago: University of Chicago Press, 1993), esp. pp. 81–92, which analyzes his 1906 essay on railroad rates. Another young intellectual with socialist leanings, Walter Lippmann, puzzled over the same dilemma. "What has happened to the railroads is merely a demonstration of what is likely to happen to the other great industries," Lippmann wrote in *Drift and Mastery* (1914). "Private property will melt away; its function will be taken over by the salaried men who direct them, by government commissioners, by developing trade unions." Quoted in James Livingston, *Pragmatism and the Political Economy of Cultural Revolution, 1850–1940* (Chapel Hill: University of North Carolina Press, 1994), p. 73. With "the separation of ownership from control," observes Livingston in explaining Lippmann's reasoning, "the performance of corporate managers need not be evaluated according to strictly economic criteria such as profit and loss."

[23] Skowronek, *Building a New American State*, pp. 248–284.

the commission would exercise this newly granted authority for the first time. Because the ICC would consider the need for comprehensive rate increases throughout the entire eastern half of the country, debate would necessarily gravitate toward general measures of performance of the sort embodied by the rate-of-return approach.

If Louis Brandeis caught railroads off guard at the hearings, then he did not do so merely by raising the matter of efficiency. For the trends in public discourse and in regulatory policy had been flowing for some time toward just this sort of thinking about the railroad industry and the larger economy. Indeed, railroads and their financiers had themselves done as much as anyone during the previous decade and a half to promulgate the engineering ideal. The appeal to particular figures such as Emerson and Taylor, who had not yet attained widespread public notoriety, surely came as something of a surprise to railroads and no doubt caught their representatives unaware. But in identifying a particular cost saving made possible by engineering study and then projecting the potential savings railroads might reap if managers applied the technique across the entire system, Brandeis took a page straight from the railroads themselves. His argument sounded for all the world like those Charles Dudley and his associates advanced when explaining the work of their laboratories and testing facilities.

The real cleverness in this line of attack lay not so much in the element of surprise but in finding a way to turn engineering rhetoric back at the railroads. Those who testified on behalf of the lines could not effectively counter the charges of inefficiency, no matter how thoroughly they had prepared, because in dwelling on their operational deficiencies railroads would only enhance the image their critics sought to portray. Nor could railroads hope to win much sympathy by arguing that rate-setting must remain the one area of railroad affairs in which market forces operated freely. The old adage that railroads must charge what the market will bear struck a shrill chord in an age increasingly enamored with the harmonizing potential of engineering. Trapped by the ideals they themselves had so recently enshrined, able to offer little more than testimony to their growing diseconomies, railroads appeared tepid and unprogressive. This feature of the rate trials comes into sharp focus when considered in light of experiences at the Pennsylvania Railroad, where managers during the years immediately leading up to the Eastern Rate Case had been weathering a crisis that prompted many in their ranks to lose confidence in engineering.

PROBLEMS AT THE PENNSYLVANIA

Late in the fall of 1903, Superintendent of Freight Transportation Robert M. Patterson submitted what he confessed to be a rather poorly formed question to the ATO of the Pennsylvania Railroad. In the course of gathering some statistics necessary for resolving accounts with other railroads for borrowed cars, Patterson had discovered that the average daily miles traversed by Pennsylvania freight equipment had dropped by almost 35 percent since the late 1890s. The trend struck Patterson as especially alarming in light of the fact that during this period the Pennsylvania had launched the most extraordinary capital improvement program in its history, including substantial investment in new cars and locomotives. Patterson wanted to know why the costly new equipment moved more slowly through the system. Adding to Patterson's consternation was the fact that this diminishing utilization of equipment reflected most negatively back on himself. "I am in the somewhat mortifying position," Patterson confided to ATO secretary A. Feldpauche, "of submitting a subject that I do not know how to handle myself."[24]

As per ATO custom, Feldpauche referred the question to the appropriate standing committees. In this case the matter would involve both the Committee on Motive Power, which included managers responsible for supplying and maintaining the cars and locomotives, and the Committee on Conducting Transportation, which consisted of various personnel involved in coordinating the assembly and movement of trains on a daily basis. These committees proceeded in characteristic fashion to investigate the matter methodically, in part by conducting extensive audits of car and locomotive movement through various sections of the line. Discovering to their surprise that the Pennsylvania had remarkably little statistical knowledge of this sort, they threw themselves eagerly into the task. The motive power committee especially reveled in the effort, assembling data on locomotives to match that on cars. Its studies revealed that locomotive movement had diminished at an annual rate of more than 3.4 percent over the past five years, an even more rapid decline than that in car mileage.[25]

This "scientific" approach to the matter proceeded over many months, extending well past the scheduled meeting of the ATO in May 1904. As the fall meeting approached, it grew apparent that the committees might very well need to extend their investigations another six months. The veracity of Patterson's data, which had not all been collected under precisely the same circumstances, had come into some dispute. Committee members searched for ways to develop more systematic procedures for monitoring car movements. Others fretted that the recently collected data pertaining to locomotives needed to be brought into the same form as that used in the car studies. In effect, a dozen of the Pennsylvania's managers were proceeding as if they were a bunch of college professors or gentlemen scientists, not businessmen confronting the startling realization that an almost unprecedented

---

[24] Robert M. Patterson, Superintendent of Transportation, to A. Feldpauche, marked personal, November 3, 1903, PRR ATO Files, box 6, file 303.

[25] "The Decreasing Average Mileage of Our Freight Equipment and Engines," Report of Joint Committee on Conducting Transportation and Motive Power, November 2, 1904, PRR ATO Files, box 6, file 303.

addition to their firm's stock of capital assets was generating steadily diminishing returns.

At last, as it appeared the committees would surely miss the fall 1904 deadline, an exasperated Patterson wrote to General Manager W. W. Atterbury, expressing his concern. "To be perfectly frank about the matter," Patterson confided, "I am afraid that this committee is approaching this matter much too much as an academic subject." After marching Atterbury through the persistent squabbling over the data, he concluded, "if they are worried about statistics, let us make a horizontal reduction of ten or fifteen percent if they like and then go ahead with the pivot of the matter which is to get the cars through the yards." In what Patterson considered an unusual step that perhaps he was "wrong to suggest," he advised that if Atterbury wanted "to get something practical at the next meeting" the general manager should bring the two committee chairmen in for a meeting for "stiffening up." Patterson hinted, and subsequent correspondence confirmed, that the particular source of the problem was the chair of the motive power committee and some of his underlings. The man in question was E. D. Nelson, engineer of tests at the Pennsylvania, who had spent much of 1904 supervising the operations of the locomotive testing plant in St. Louis.[26]

Events moved quickly from that point. Not only were the chairmen "stiffened up," but their report was also condensed into an abstract laying out eleven "known facts" about the matter. Stripped of all analysis, the abstract laid matters on the line: Without the drop in average daily mileage, the Pennsylvania could have avoided purchasing nearly 50,000 freight cars worth over $25 million; an almost identical savings would have accrued from sustaining the movement of locomotives. This list of cold facts no doubt served as an overture for the main event of the next ATO meeting. When the assembled members returned from lunch, they were told that Mr. Charles E. Pugh, "a former President of this Association," would "under a suspension of the rules" address the meeting. Pugh was, in fact, the Pennsylvania's second vice-president, and it is clear that he let loose with a tirade. Feldpauche prepared an "epitome" for inclusion in the official minutes, excluding Pugh's "references to the fact that we were not doing so well as we might do, and that perhaps we were not doing as well as other roads were doing, admissions which, in the event of publicity, might react to our disadvantage in the hands of dissatisfied shippers." The epitome itself went as follows:

> Mr. Pugh thereupon made an interesting address, which he prefaced with the assurance that he was not actuated by any spirit of acute criticism, but that he wished to impress all with the fact that extraordinary additions had been made to the number and capacity of the engines and cars of the company's freight equipment, and that it was of vital moment to the interest of the company that the

---

[26] Robert Patterson to W.W.A., marked personal, October 12, 1904, and supporting materials, PRR ATO Files, box 6, file 303.

transportation officials should exert their best efforts to avail themselves of these increased facilities to insure a corresponding increase in the movement of the company's traffic, and that he believed this could readily be accomplished if the General and Division Superintendents would give unremitting attention to the enforcement of engine repairs, and to the ever present necessity of managing crews so as to insure a maximum degree of efficiency in the movement of trains, considerations which he regarded as pre-eminent in the line of their respective duties.[27]

Charles Pugh's address to the ATO effectively rang down the curtain on the cooperative, "scientific" approach to railroading that had prevailed at the Pennsylvania during the last quarter of the nineteenth century. No longer would managers approach operations through the methodical analyses of engineering, steadily manipulating established techniques to produce optimal results. Management at the Pennsylvania faced a daunting new reality. The challenges of the early twentieth century pointed not to the methodical, impersonal procedures that had come to characterize the self-styled "Standard Railroad of the World." Instead, those challenges led Pennsylvania executives onto the slippery, treacherous terrain they often referred to uncomfortably as "the human element." Henceforth, the key to performance at the Pennsylvania would involve successful management of its enormous work force, a task, as the ATO would soon realize, that would not yield so readily to a systematic, scientific approach.

The Congestion Crisis

The ultimate source of the Pennsylvania's problems, as the studies and discussion begun in 1904 would gradually make clear, were complications caused by the changing nature of demand for its services. The Pennsylvania was not merely handling a larger volume of traffic following the patterns of the nineteenth century, when movement of commodities such as coal, oil, and grain had dominated. Now, with the accelerating reorientation of the American economy away from extraction and processing toward more diversified manufacturing, the Pennsylvania was encountering much more complex traffic patterns, including a drastic increase in local traffic and a rise of specialized services such as fast "preference" freight trains. This growing diversity of services, not merely the increased volume, was creating the bottlenecks and delays.[28] Such services introduced complexities that railroads such as the Pennsylvania had previously evaded. Investment in traditional technologies

---

[27] A. Feldpauche to W. W. Atterbury, December 7, 1904, and supporting materials, PRR ATO Files, box 6, file 303.

[28] A. Feldpauche to H. P. Lincoln, October 15, 1904, and D.C.D. to T. S. B[ell], n.d., PRR ATO Files, box 6, file 303. On the diversity of American manufacturing, see Philip Scranton, *Endless Novelty: Specialty Production and American Industrialization, 1865–1925* (Princeton: Princeton University Press, 1997).

Figure 9.1. Congested freight yards such as those at New York, shown in 1902 prior to the expensive terminal improvements, plagued the Pennsylvania and other lines. *Courtesy:* Hagley Museum and Library.

such as larger cars and locomotives and duplication of facilities such as terminals offered little remedy for railroads facing these new demands (Fig. 9.1). These established pathways of innovation no longer yielded the improvements in productivity railroads had come to anticipate.

One approach under these challenging circumstances was to pursue more radical departures in basic technology. Automatic electric signals, as discussed in the previous chapter, constituted one such new avenue. The Pennsylvania incorporated some of these complex electrical devices into its mainline operations, despite deep concerns about the possible effects on labor relations, at the same time it launched its expanded fleet of locomotives and cars. When signals alone proved incapable of resolving the congestion crisis (Fig. 9.2), the Pennsylvania entertained still more ambitious plans involving the introduction of novel electrical technology into their largely mechanical systems. At just about the same moment that Charles Pugh chastised the assembled members of the ATO, another Pennsylvania vice-president, Samuel Rea, launched an extensive study of electric locomotives. Rea turned toward electrics initially in order to eliminate choking smoke inside the tunnels beneath the Hudson River and to solve other distinctive problems associated with the new station project in Manhattan, for which he had primary responsibility. But as he awakened to the potential of

Figure 9.2. Though governed by the most sophisticated block signaling system of the day, trains clogged the Pennsylvania's mainline tracks near Altoona in 1904. *Courtesy:* Library of Congress.

the new technology, Rea conducted his tests with an eye toward substituting electric traction for steam locomotives wherever appropriate in the vast Pennsylvania system.[29]

Electrification provides a particularly enlightening example of the ways established ideas about engineering efficiency and traditional methods of engineering analysis assumed a different cast within the Pennsylvania under the changing conditions of the early twentieth century. In many respects, the studies of electrification were an engineer's dream. Having incessantly refined steam railroad operations over the course of several generations, until the most pressing technical issues involved matters such as the shapes of wheels and rail flanges, engineers suddenly had the opportunity to change the single most important component in the complex railroad machine. Electric locomotives effectively turned steam railroading inside out. In direct contrast to steam locomotives, electrics drew power from an expensive central

[29] The authority on early electrification is Carl Condit. His studies of major station projects provide much of the basis for my discussion here. On developments at the Pennsylvania, see, especially, his *The Port of New York* (Chicago: University of Chicago Press, 1981–1982), vol. 1, pp. 176–238 and 312–332.

source but in turn offered flexibility of operation made possible by rapid acceleration and reduced maintenance requirements. Investigations of the new technology thus breathed fresh air into discussions of fundamental issues such as the proper speed and frequency of trains and the economics of fuel consumption. Not surprisingly, engineers within the Pennsylvania bureaucracy scrambled to secure a place in the extensive comparative studies of steam and electric power planned by Rea. Quite a few of those who succeeded in obtaining the plum assignments had been closely affiliated with the locomotive testing plant exhibit, which closed just about the time the studies of electrification got under way in earnest.[30] These men must have felt a special excitement, for the electrification studies would in effect provide them with a vastly broader arena in which to practice the techniques of methodical study embodied in the testing plant. Participants could draw additional satisfaction from reading the exhaustive coverage afforded the tests by the technical press, which showed an almost insatiable appetite for information about the studies.[31]

While the studies of electrification clearly tapped established engineering traditions at the Pennsylvania, with the experiences of steam railroading setting the parameters of the discussion and persistently serving as a ready basis for comparative analysis, the investigations ultimately drew the line in new directions. For as the studies proceeded and results accumulated, it grew ever more apparent that the new technology would not provide the ready solution the Pennsylvania had hoped to the pressing problems of traffic congestion that plagued its freight operations. Electrification, like the complex signaling apparatus that must necessarily accompany it, could of course help remedy the technical problems posed by congestion. Use of electric freight locomotives, with their more rapid acceleration, would ease the pressure to keep trains in constant motion that continually plagued railroads operating during the age of steam. With their shorter stopping distances and easy starting, electrics would enable the Pennsylvania to do away with the controversial caution signals and perhaps increase the capacity of their line. But as the tests made increasingly clear, conversion to electricity would be expensive. Construction of the power plant and distribution lines required an enormous expenditure up front. A major potential benefit of this investment – reduced maintenance costs – would go largely unrealized unless the Pennsylvania made a wholesale conversion and immediately closed its facilities for fueling and repairing steam locomotives. Tests showed, moreover, that in less congested conditions the economic calculus swung back in favor of steam. Perhaps the optimal operating procedure called for a mix of motive power, with trains changing from electric to steam power when they cleared the most congested territory. Such arrangements, however, would

---

[30] Ibid., p. 324.
[31] Coverage by the technical press is traced in extraordinarily rich detail in ibid.

entail costly switching movements and significantly disrupt established rules and procedures governing train crews.[32]

The sad truth about electrification, for railroads of the Progressive era as well as for their subsequent defenders among historians, is that while the new technology would have helped resolve the *technical* challenges posed by increasing congestion, it would have done so at a steep price. Unlike the less dramatic technical improvements of the late nineteenth century, such as heavier steel rails and larger locomotives, electrification would not both relieve congestion and reduce costs. In the end, the Pennsylvania resorted to electrification primarily for ends other than straightforward economy, such as smoke abatement and its usefulness in providing frequent rapid service to suburban commuters. Far from the "burgeoning technology" promising "a hundred ways to hold down the operating ratio," the technical possibilities opened by electricity constituted expensive Band-Aids meant to patch the wounds of an ossified, overtaxed network. Further improvements in railroad performance, whether obtained through additional intensive study of the sort associated with the locomotive testing plant or through more radical departures such as electrification, would entail added expense. The old technological paradigm had run its course.[33]

[32] Condit, an enthusiast for urban planning and electrification, claimed in *The Railroad and the City: A Technological and Urbanistic History of Cincinnati* (Columbus: Ohio State University Press, 1977), pp. 176–177, that such technology "gave the roads an immense reserve capacity that was frustrated by primitive economic, legal, and municipal institutions." His careful analysis of tests at the Pennsylvania, however, suggests economic and technical factors, rather than administrative ineptitude, posed the major impediments to electrification. For an astute contemporary analysis written by a proponent of electrification who reached much the same conclusion, see Frank J. Sprague, "The Multiple Unit System for Electric Railways," *Cassier's Magazine* 16 (1905): 439–460. A truly prescient management might have perceived conversion to electrically powered freight trains as a means of accommodating the surge in local traffic. The rapid acceleration afforded by electricity would have facilitated switching operations at sidings and perhaps kept mainline tracks freer of obstructions. In 1897, one division superintendent for the Pennsylvania actually suggested the ATO consider converting small feeder lines from steam to electricity. At this point, however, through freight still dominated railroad traffic volume as well as managerial thinking. The expense of outfitting lightly used rail sidings with electric power, moreover, only compounded the primary obstacle to electrification. See A. W. Moss to W. J. Latta, June 25, 1897; G. B. Hutchinson to W. J. Latta, June 26, 1897; and F. D. Casanave to William J. Latta, July 17, 1897; PRR ATO Files, box 4, file 111.

[33] This is the aspect of the railroad problem that Martin, *Enterprise Denied*, does not wish to acknowledge. In his zeal to blame government, which in his persuasive assessment prevented railroads from obtaining essential capital by denying them necessary rate increases, Martin insists that prior to 1907 railroads had met the challenge of congestion through vigorous investment in technical improvement. That investment, however, went into established technologies that did not in fact yield the benefits the Pennsylvania anticipated. Solving the problems of congestion would require investment in technologies such as signaling and electrification that did not yield productivity returns comparable to those of the late nineteenth century. "The main underlying

Mounting awareness of such basic technical roadblocks struck an especially heavy blow at the Pennsylvania, a "mature" line that had proceeded farther down the path to machine-like efficiency than virtually any other. The Pennsylvania's sterling record of engineering accomplishments now left it with less room for improvement than many other lines.[34] To the extent those accumulated achievements enabled the Pennsylvania to provide comparable transportation services more economically than its rivals, of course, they can hardly be described as a disadvantage. As did Andrew Carnegie in steel, the Pennsylvania had thrived by operating under the assumption that being the low-cost producer would work to its economic advantage in the long run.[35] But as a veteran traffic agent might easily have explained, the business of railroading was not entirely comparable to steel production. While steel mills and other manufacturers sold their products in a national or even international market, the Pennsylvania sold its services in a particular

cause of the failure to handle the new tonnage arose from an unbalanced technological development of which the remoter causes were beyond railroad or ICC control," notes Condit, *The Railroad and the City*, pp. 176–177. "All of these problems were compounded by problems that had always existed but had grown more acute with the upsurge of traffic that accompanied the recovery from the depression of 1893. Foremost, perhaps, were the increasingly exasperating frustrations attendant upon moving freight cars through yards, to and from terminals, and into and away from industrial spurs, team tracks, and shippers' sidings. The spotting, classification, loading, and unloading of rolling stock presented problems that simply defied solution." Condit admires electrical technologies for those qualitative benefits, such as reduced smoke and noise, that railroad publicists increasingly emphasized after 1910.

34 These critically important differences between railroads of various age and location are obscured by aggregate data pertaining to railroad investment. See James Reed Golden, "Investment Behavior by United States Railroads, 1870–1914" (Ph.D. dissertation, Harvard University, 1971). On railroad investment, see Melville J. Ulmer, *Capital in Transportation, Communications, and Public Utilities: Its Formation and Financing* (Princeton: Princeton University Press and the National Bureau of Economic Research, 1960); Albert Fishlow, "Productivity and Technical Change in the Railroad Sector, 1840–1910," in *Output, Employment, and Productivity in the United States since 1800* (New York: Columbia University Press and National Bureau of Economic Research, 1966), pp. 583–646; Jan Kmenta and Jeffrey C. Williamson, "Determinants of Investment Behavior: United States Railroads, 1872–1941," *Review of Economics and Statistics* 48 (1966): 172–181; Larry Neal, "Investment Behavior by American Railroads: 1897–1914," *Review of Economics and Statistics* 51 (1969): 126–135; and Martin, *Enterprise Denied*. Kmenta and Williamson interpret changing investment patterns as part of a cycle of development. Neal attributes them to changing opportunities in the financial markets, which Martin believes government exacerbated. The Pennsylvania offers a hybrid variant on these themes. Its investments followed patterns anticipated by Neal, but those investments generated disappointing returns owing to problems associated with the line's comparatively advanced state of maturity. Regional variations in railroad attitudes regarding rate regulation suggest circumstances at the Pennsylvania may have been typical of lines in the East, but not among those in other parts of the country.

35 Harold Livesay, *Andrew Carnegie and the Rise of Big Business* (Boston: Little, Brown, 1975).

region served by its tracks. Manufacturers sent their products to customers; railroads enticed customers to come to them. A railroad could, of course, add new customers by building new extensions. Such opportunities had diminished with time, however, and in the end all goods must still traverse the main line that had long been seen by executives at the Pennsylvania as the principal source of its competitive advantage. Now, if the Pennsylvania could no longer secure productivity gains from enhancing that mainline facility, what would keep shippers from choosing to locate along less congested tracks? The question was especially troubling in an age of rapid change in the constitution of the manufacturing sector, with entirely new businesses such as Henry Ford's automobile plant rising in places such as Detroit, located on the fringes of the established distribution network.[36]

Perhaps nothing captured the dilemma more graphically than the massive station and terminal improvements under way in and around New York City. The facilities, conceived by President A. J. Cassatt and by Rea as the crown jewel in the massive rebuilding initiative begun in 1898, were a spectacular expression of the engineering ethos that permeated the Pennsylvania. At the world's fair in St. Louis (see Chapter 7), the railroad displayed models of the tunnels that would carry trains past the congested riverfront yards and beneath the Hudson into Manhattan and beyond. As the work took shape, Rea personally escorted groups of dignitaries through the tubes (Fig. 9.3). The tunnels emerged at their Manhattan end into a vast open trench excavated from bedrock and faced with pristine reinforcing walls. The construction scene, reminiscent of that President Roosevelt had recently visited in Panama, looked like something from the Age of the Pharaohs (Fig. 9.4). As the project neared completion, the Pennsylvania filled this space with an array of tracks, switches, and signals, all powered by electricity and controlled by an elaborate interlocking plant (Fig. 9.5). Passengers arriving via these tracks ascended lattice stairways to a concourse suspended beneath a grand canopy of steel-framed glass and conspicuous supporting girders (Fig. 9.6).

[36] The possibility that railroads operating in less congested areas would enjoy a comparative advantage no doubt helps explain the regional variations in railroad and shipper behavior identified by Kerr, *American Railroad Politics*. Eastern carriers clearly felt the most urgent need for a rate increase, and they enjoyed the greatest success in winning their customers over to their position. Midwestern lines, especially those serving Chicago, likewise pressed energetically for change. Carriers in the South and West exhibited considerably less fervor. Midwestern and Southern shippers voiced the strongest opposition to proposed rate increases, in part because the proposed percentage increases would have reinforced existing differentials that put manufacturing interests outside the East at a relative disadvantage. (Established agricultural interests in the South and West had no reason not to join their manufacturing brethren in resisting rate increases as well.) Leaving the regulatory system unchanged – the goal shippers in the South and West pursued (successfully) after 1910 – would have worked to the relative advantage of these relatively undeveloped and uncongested areas.

Figure 9.3. Vice-president of the Pennsylvania Samuel Rea leads a tour of the tunnels, still under construction. In 1913, Rea became president of that line. *Courtesy:* Hagley Museum and Library.

With its bold structure and artfully coordinated movement, Pennsylvania Station triumphantly expressed the ethos of the gear-and-girder age. It displayed on a monumental scale the elegant ordering made possible by modern machinery and engineering. Whether the station served the purposes of economy and profitability, however, was very much open to question. The less glamorous technical triumphs of the late nineteenth century, such as stronger rails and larger cars, had joined engineering efficiency and economy unambiguously. The costly structures and complex electromechanical machinery of Penn Station, by comparison, exhibited a far more speculative character. Though initially conceived and justified as cost-reducing, such improvements ultimately involved an economic calculus of much greater

Figure 9.4. Excavating for Pennsylvania Station, New York, with portals of tunnels to New Jersey at far end, 1909. *Courtesy:* Hagley Museum and Library.

complexity. Many of the expenditures went toward technologies, such as electric locomotives, whose primary purpose was to ease discomforts such as noxious smoke rather than to reduce operating expenses. Engineers in charge of station projects increasingly justified their endeavors and balanced their bloated books by incorporating items such as projected sales of the air rights for real estate located above the tracks and terminals.[37] By the time the station opened in 1910, just months before the Eastern Rate Case began, it seemed the biggest returns might come not directly from revenues and savings at all, but rather from the goodwill such a spectacular feat might

[37]   Josef W. Konvitz, "William J. Wilgus and Engineering Projects to Improve the Port of New York, 1900–1930," *Technology and Culture* 30 (1989): 398–425. Wilgus, who supervised the reconstruction of Grand Central Station, stressed the importance of air rights as early as 1903. See William J. Wilgus, "Making a Choice of a Profession, VIII – Railroading," *Cosmopolitan* 35 (1903): 465. On the growing importance of air rights in urban construction generally, see Sharon Irish, "A 'Machine That Makes the Land Pay': The West Street Building in New York," *Technology and Culture* 30 (1989): 376–397.

Figure 9.5. Interlocking plant and signal room, Pennsylvania Station, New York, 1910. *Courtesy:* Hagley Museum and Library.

generate among the public and in the regulatory arena.[38] Engineering had been transformed, as Brandeis soon made clear, from a cold tool of analysis into an explosive weapon of politics.

Engineering and the Human Element

In the absence of ready technical remedies for the traffic problems, managers at the Pennsylvania increasingly found themselves confronting the troubling "human element" that Charles Pugh had targeted in his address to the ATO in 1904. Efforts to manage the massive Pennsylvania work force played themselves out, as Pugh suggested they must, through the exercise of managerial authority in the shops, freight yards, and other facilities involved in moving trains through the Pennsylvania system. Yet even in the more rarified atmosphere of the ATO, one can catch glimpses of an institution struggling with great difficulty to confront a new reality. In the wake of the discussions of

---

[38] Irish, ibid., observes that during the opening decades of the twentieth century businesses often sought consciously when constructing new buildings to establish a new relationship with the public. She notes, too, that the new commercial buildings were, in many respects, "engineering structures."

Figure 9.6. Track platform and stairways at Pennsylvania Station, New York, with electric third rails in foreground, 1910. The station opened just months before the Eastern Rate Case began. *Courtesy:* Library of Congress.

1904, for instance, Secretary Feldpauche himself submitted a question about the possibility of introducing a level of training for yard masters, "somewhat after the custom followed in the Motive Power and Maintenance of Way Departments, which would undoubtedly result in a more intelligent and prompt handling of the traffic, thus avoiding congestions and detentions to trains." Even as Feldpauche submitted the question, he expressed doubts about the prospects of success. "In view, however, of the prevailing tendency among train and yard men to seize upon any pretext to foment trouble," he quickly noted, "I do not think it would be wise to introduce the recommendation in the committee's report, from whence it might leak out and be construed as advance information of the company's intent to adopt measures antagonistic to the welfare of these men." Rather than become the subject of a proper report, the matter should merely "be exhaustively discussed . . . at the next meeting for the information and guidance of the management." Or, perhaps, the ATO might have "an expert in transportation affairs" report a paper on the subject.[39]

---

[39] A. Feldpauche to W. W. Atterbury, November 4, 1904, PRR ATO Files, box 6, file 303.

Chemist Charles Benjamin Dudley, whose work on technical specifications had earned him worldwide acclaim and in many respects exemplified the engineering spirit that had long animated the ATO, picked up on the changing climate regarding labor and on its implications for technical practice at the Pennsylvania. In 1904, Dudley submitted two questions for consideration by the ATO. Each asked, in its own way, whether Dudley and the department of physical tests should keep working on specifications and new devices if the men would not utilize them in actual service. One query hit the matter quite directly. "In the present state of labor," asked Dudley, "how far can discipline be enforced in the use of appliances requiring attention on the part of trainmen and other employees, which appliances give better results but require more attention on the part of the employees, than others that can be used[?]" By way of example, Dudley referred specifically to the carburetor system of lighting, an invention he had developed after years of testing and research. Feldpauche suggested this matter fell under the purview of a special committee the ATO had created to address the subject of employee discipline. In his other question, Dudley pondered whether "the present practice of making changes in construction to facilitate the operation of locomotives and cars, results in true economy." Dudley posed the question out of concern that operating personnel, pressed to keep trains moving at all costs, had apparently neglected to employ lubricants, bearing metals, and firebox linings the laboratory had deemed useful for conserving fuel and preserving wheels and axles. Employees unfamiliar with the novel materials often deployed them improperly, resulting in hot boxes and underpowered locomotives that idled trains and clogged the tracks. Rather than assign this second question to a committee, Feldpauche asked Dudley to prepare a report, noting, "[Y]our analytical gifts and mastery of details, will, I am sure, enable you to treat the subject in a manner that will be as creditable to you as it will be interesting and instructive to the association." Perhaps sensing he had touched upon an issue of great delicacy among the operating personnel, Dudley politely demurred from preparing the requested report before each of the next three meetings.[40]

Dudley's questions hinted at concerns that his research activities might decline in importance amidst the traffic crisis and the mounting troubles with labor. His fears were soon confirmed, as we can see quite vividly by tracing activities connected with the locomotive testing plant. Despite the image projected at St. Louis, it is clear from the records that this new testing facility was virtually stillborn as an exercise in scientific engineering. Directives from top management authorizing construction of the testing plant and subsequent

---

[40] Chas. B. Dudley to A. Feldpauche, October 7, 1904; A. Feldpauche to Chas. B. Dudley, December 21, 1904; Chas B. Dudley to Atterbury, April 21, 1905; Chas. B. Dudley to A. Feldpauche, November 6, 1905; and Chas. B. Dudley to A. Feldpauche, February 2, 1906; PRR ATO Files, box 6, file 315.

instructions to those in charge repeatedly stressed the publicity value of the facility rather than its utility in railroad service. The technical reports generated during the course of the fair, noted the board, would "have very considerable advertising value," as would a model of the new terminal building under construction in New York that would accompany the plant to St. Louis and later be exhibited in various Pennsylvania stations. F. D. Casanave, the Pennsylvania vice-president who headed the project, often pressured Engineer of Tests Nelson to keep expenses down at the facility while himself lavishing considerable effort and expense upon "advertising circulars" and other publicity materials describing the testing plant. The Pennsylvania spent over $12,000 alone on the printing of a gilt-edged commemorative volume it distributed gratis to selected friends and clients after the exhibit closed. The amount equaled fully one tenth of the capital expended in constructing and relocating the testing plant itself, enough to cover over four months' worth of operating expenses in St. Louis, including salary and lodging for a staff of twenty-six. The board also showed special enthusiasm for the high-speed runs, which it clearly viewed as stunts that would draw a crowd.[41]

Only incidentally, after mentioning the budget of the planned exhibit, did the authorization from the board note that "after the Exposition the Testing Plant will be removed to permanent quarters for the use of the Pennsylvania System. It is an item that has been strongly recommended for the last four or five years, as our present methods of determining the results of the performance of our locomotives are very crude."[42] This statement reads especially hollow in light of the fact that during the two previous years the Pennsylvania had suspended almost all experimental work in its physical and chemical laboratories. Chemist Dudley, an employee of thirty years, observed in his annual report for 1903 that "less experimental work has been completed than in any previous year."[43] Reports for subsequent years simply noted

---

[41] On the creation of this plant, see V. P. Thomson and Theodore N. Ely, "Memorandum on Louisiana Purchase Exposition," June 10, 1903; V. P. Pugh to Pres. Cassatt, June 4, 1903; and Pugh to Cassatt, February 4, 1904; Papers Concerning Matters Coming Before the Board of Directors of the Pennsylvania Railroad (henceforth, PRR Board Papers), Hagley Museum and Library, Wilmington, Delaware. All told, the Pennsylvania's board authorized expenditures of nearly $200,000 on the exhibit. For details on its operation in St. Louis and the role of Casanave, see "St. Louis Test Facility" File, Engineer of Tests Papers (henceforth, PRR Engineer of Tests Papers), box 717, folder 6, PRR Papers, Hagley Museum and Library, Wilmington, Delaware, accession 1807; and *The Pennsylvania Railroad System at the Louisiana Purchase Exhibition* (Philadelphia: Pennsylvania Railroad Company, 1905).

[42] V. P. Thomson and Theodore N. Ely, "Memorandum on Louisiana Purchase Exposition," June 10, 1903, PRR Board Papers.

[43] Annual Report of the Chemical Laboratory (henceforth, PRR Lab Reports) for 1903, March 9, 1904, p. 8, PRR Motive Power Department Papers (henceforth, PRR Motive Power Papers), box 4, PRR Papers, Hagley Museum and Library, Wilmington, Delaware, accession 1810.

that the business of the laboratory was entirely taken up with routine work of enforcing specifications. When his principal assistant grew ill in 1905, the line provided Dudley with no replacement for two years.[44]

The Pennsylvania dragged its feet in meeting its announced pledge to relocate the testing plant to Altoona and to issue occasional bulletins containing results of tests conducted at the facility. Not until late 1906 was the plant at last again operable. An impatient Nelson eagerly laid plans for an extensive study of the fuel efficiency of various firebox arrangements using different grades of coal.[45] The work would follow through on studies begun in St. Louis and complement investigations taking place at the Burlington's new testing facility and at the consulting laboratories of Arthur D. Little in Boston.[46] The choice of topics must have seemed a fortuitous one to Nelson when, in the wake of the coal strike of 1906 and with the intense cost-cutting triggered by the Panic of 1907, Pennsylvania executives drew attention to the matter of coal consumption. Nelson was appointed to an ATO committee to study the matter, as was Dudley, who along with two other distinguished chemists had written a fundamental paper linking chemical composition with the heat content of various coals.[47]

Soon, however, this golden opportunity to secure a vital place for the testing plant turned into a fundamental threat to Nelson's vision for it. In yet another demonstration of the tendency of Pennsylvania managers to look at the "human element" rather than to equipment during this period, several members of the committee expressed their belief that the most significant variable affecting fuel consumption was the skill employed in firing and throttling the locomotive. This idea received a very sympathetic hearing from General Manager Atterbury. Operating outside ATO channels, Atterbury wrote a personal letter to Nelson's supervisor, General Superintendent of Motor Power A. W. Gibbs, expressing his opinion that the real problem was with the road foremen who "under the present conditions...are promoted from engineers who have not had mechanical training nor proper

---

44 PRR Lab Reports, 1904–1908.
45 On relocating the plant to Altoona, see PRR Engineer of Tests Papers, box 715, file 3; Annual Reports of the Mechanical Engineer for 1905 and 1906, PRR Motive Power Papers; and "Departments of Chemical and Physical Tests (Historical)," typescript report, c. 1914, PRR Engineer of Tests Papers, box 661.
46 Laboratory Notebooks, Papers of the Chicago, Burlington and Quincy Railroad, Newberry Library, Chicago, and Virginia P. Dawson, "Knowledge Is Power: E. G. Bailey and the Invention and Marketing of the Bailey Boiler Meter," *Technology and Culture* 37 (1996): 493–526. Bailey became head of Arthur D. Little's coal testing department in 1907 after work on a railroad coal study brought him to Boston from Ohio State University.
47 "Economic Use of Coal," PRR ATO Minutes, May 26, 1908, pp. 117–127. "Departments of Chemical and Physical Tests (Historical)," p. 17, notes that Dudley coauthored with William A. Noyes and W. F. Hillebrand a "Report of the Committee on Coal Analysis" for the American Chemical Society.

opportunity for finding out the conditions under which a locomotive gives its best work." Adjusted tonnage tests, noted Atterbury, had shown that "our engineers were not getting the capacity out of our locomotives." In an effort to remedy the situation, Atterbury directed Nelson to develop instruction tests for the Road Foremen. "While the testing plant at Altoona has great possibilities in deciding for us various questions of fuel efficiency, draft appliances, etc.," wrote the Pennsylvania's general manager, "I am very strongly of the opinion that its prime use should be to educate our mechanical people in the various phases of locomotive economy."[48]

The suggestion that the testing plant be transformed from an instrument of analysis into a training facility prompted Gibbs and Nelson to assume a defensive posture. Nelson attempted to reframe the throttling issue in more theoretical terms and thus render it amenable to systematic investigation. He would perform a long series of tests with locomotives throttled in different ways, Nelson explained, and invite road foremen to drop by and observe the experiments from time to time.[49] In describing the nature of the tests at the next meeting of the ATO, however, Nelson inadvertently provided Atterbury with an opportunity to rekindle the instruction idea. By force of habit, no doubt, Nelson laid special stress on the importance of keeping an accurate measure of coal consumed and of maintaining a regular rate of firing from test to test. As an advocate for "scientific" railroading, firing was something of an embarrassment for Nelson, for it introduced an element of inaccuracy and irreproducibility into his otherwise carefully controlled environment. While preparing the test plant exhibit, Nelson had insisted that eight teams of enginemen and firemen be brought to St. Louis for audition, so that he could obtain a crew of unusual reliability.[50] Now, in an offhand remark intended to emphasize the point, Nelson noted that a substitute fireman one day had used 19 percent more coal than his regular man. The ever-diligent Atterbury promptly jumped on this as further evidence of the importance of the human element and of the potential benefits of using the testing plant for training. At the end of the meeting the ATO resolved "to devote the locomotive testing plant, in whole or in part, to instructing the Road Foremen."[51] When Nelson

[48]   W. W. Atterbury to A. W. Gibbs, marked personal, December 16, 1907, PRR Engineer of Tests Papers, box 715, folder 3.

[49]   E. D. Nelson to A. W. Gibbs, January 3, 1908, PRR Engineer of Tests Papers, box 715, folder 3.

[50]   E. D. Nelson to A. W. Gibbs, December 21, 1903; F. D. Casanave to E. D. Nelson, March 30, 1904; and E. D. Nelson to F. D. Casanave, April 5, 1904; "St. Louis Test Facility" File, PRR Engineer of Tests Papers, box 717, folder 6. E. G. Bailey, who conducted similar coal tests at Arthur D. Little, grew so concerned about firing that he developed an instrument for recording how the boiler had been fired. Bailey later marketed the meters for use by employers, including railroads, who wished to monitor the performance of firemen. See Dawson, "Knowledge Is Power."

[51]   "Economic Use of Coal," PRR ATO Minutes, May 26, 1908, pp. 122–123.

did not carry through, Atterbury again wrote to Gibbs, and a week later the first instruction sessions began.[52]

In addition to revealing the basic tenuousness of the testing plant and all other experimental work in the minds of Pennsylvania management, these initial coal studies made Nelson and Gibbs aware of a second, more severe constraint on their freedom of inquiry. Shortly after the testing facility had been reassembled in Altoona, the two engineers collaborated in an effort to counter what they saw as the view prevailing "in many quarters" that the testing plant was "considerably in the nature of an advertising proposition."[53] No doubt they had in mind the Pennsylvania's own management, with whom they had already quarreled over the lavish publication.[54] Gibbs approached F. S. Reilly, associate editor of *Railway and Engineering Review*, and asked him to write an editorial entitled "The Pennsylvania Locomotive Testing Plant as a Business Proposition."[55] Gibbs and Nelson would supply the data, of course, and no doubt a fair share of the story line as well.

A draft of the resulting editorial, returned to Gibbs and Nelson for final review, based its case for the laboratory on a series of coal tests made at St. Louis. Results obtained from these tests pointed the way, the essay suggested, to improved locomotive designs that might reduce coal consumption by 10 percent or more. If employed across a system as large as the Pennsylvania, the savings in fuel would amount to over a million dollars a year. Reilly compared this with similar savings that could be attained by reducing the costs of locomotive maintenance a comparable amount. "Now, with this object in view, there are two lines along which to work. The first is the usual one of endeavoring to raise the standard of efficiency of the men. The second is the less usual one of raising the standard of the locomotive and shop equipment in the broad sense. Within the past few years, the shop end of

---

52 H. M. Carson to A. W. Gibbs, June 13, 1908; A. W. Gibbs to R. N. Duburow and E. D. Nelson, August 5, 1908; E. D. Nelson to A. W. Gibbs, June 29, 1908; A. W. Gibbs to General Superintendents, September 2, 1908; E. D. Nelson to A. W. Gibbs, September 3, 1908; A. W. Gibbs to E. D. Nelson, September 7, 1908; and E. D. Nelson to A. W. Gibbs, September 10, 1908; PRR Engineer of Tests Papers, box 715, folder 3. On June 1, 1908, Atterbury and Gibbs issued "Circular 81: Instructions for Enginemen and Firemen for the Economical Use of Coal," printed copy in PRR Engineer of Tests Papers, box 715, folder 3.

53 T. S. Reilly, "The Pennsylvania Locomotive Testing Plant as a Business Proposition," May 24, 1907, draft copy in PRR Engineer of Tests Papers, box 715, folder 3.

54 Nelson seems to have been uncomfortable from the start with the advertising character of the proposition. When Casanave asked him to write some copy for a circular, Nelson wrote a dense technical description of various components that could hardly have had great appeal. When returning the copy he mentioned that "the printed bulletins will of course have considerable advertising value as well – albeit for a different audience than the public." E. D. Nelson to F. D. Casanave, November 24, 1903, PRR Engineer of Tests Papers.

55 T. S. Reilly, "The Pennsylvania Locomotive Testing Plant as a Business Proposition."

the proposition on many lines has been vigorously and intelligently attacked. But the Pennsylvania R. R. is alone thus far in attacking the locomotive itself in a similarity [*sic*] intelligent manner."[56]

The proposed editorial employed precisely the same argumentative strategy and logic that Louis Brandeis would use three years later at the Eastern Rate Case, when he suggested railroads could save substantial sums by deploying the scientific management techniques used in one shop of the Santa Fe railroad throughout the entire national railroad system. Having identified the *potential* for a small increase in efficiency (the 10 percent savings in coal costs was a hypothetical possibility based on laboratory tests), Reilly multiplied that savings across the massive volume of the entire railroad system, and thus identified prospective savings totaling a substantial amount. That Reilly explicitly compared this laboratory-based approach to cost reduction with shop studies (which he found analogous to the laboratory work in its ability to unlock potential savings) and with "the usual one of trying to raise the standard of efficiency of the men" (an effort he clearly found dubious and uncreative) makes the comparison to Brandeis all the more remarkable.

The proposed editorial met with much the same response from high-level railroad management as Brandeis would three years hence. After filling in the precise data necessary for publication, Nelson forwarded the draft back to Gibbs. "As you requested I took up this matter in conversation with Mr. T. N. Ely [the Chief of Motor Power], in Philadelphia," noted Nelson in conveying the document to his superior, "and he prefers to have the matter submitted to him before it is approved for publication, on account of figures being given which it might not be advisable to have published."[57]

Just a few months earlier, the Pennsylvania had retained the services of Ivy Lee, a recognized authority in the emerging field of public relations.[58] Faced with the prospects of federal legislation, the Pennsylvania, as did many other railroads, had begun to treat their public images with newfound care and sophistication. (The earliest example of a public relations man employed in railroad work, according to one authority, occurred when a group of executives in 1905 retained an individual to help coordinate press releases intended to aid their efforts to oppose the Esch–Townsend bill, predecessor

---

[56] Ibid.

[57] E. D. Nelson to A. W. Gibbs, June 10, 1907, PRR Engineer of Tests Papers, box 715, folder 3.

[58] Alan R. Raucher, *Public Relations and Business, 1900–1929* (Baltimore: Johns Hopkins University Press, 1968), pp. 21–22 and 34–39, and Roland Marchand, *Creating the Corporate Soul: The Rise of Public Relations and Corporate Imagery in American Big Business* (Berkeley: University of California Press, 1998). The late Professor Marchand kindly provided me with a preliminary draft of chapter 3, "From Defensive Advocacy to Business Statesmanship: Corporations Confront the Public, 1908–1920," which contained an extensive section on Lee and the Pennsylvania that was not included in the final product.

to the Hepburn Act. The man they hired had worked most recently on public affairs for the St. Louis Exposition.[59]) Lee's first task at the Pennsylvania had been to help President Alexander J. Cassatt deal with publicity involving "the coal question," which had become critical during the coal strike of 1906. Once employed at the Pennsylvania, Lee had quickly established a full-time Publicity Bureau. The task of the bureau was explicitly to control (i.e., limit) the flow of information out of the Pennsylvania. Sensing the public enthusiasm for engineering methods and data, Lee stressed in these early years that publicity should always rely simply on statements of facts. He called the brochures prepared for distribution in cars and stations simply *Information . . . About the Pennsylvania Railroad*. The job of the Publicity Bureau was to ensure that the Pennsylvania controlled the story by issuing only those facts it wished to be made public.

Obviously, this goal did not mesh with the ideal of scientific experiment and publication that was so dear to men such as Gibbs, Nelson, and Dudley. No wonder the number of publications emanating from the Pennsylvania's laboratories during these years dwindled to virtually nothing. And no wonder Brandeis employed the strategy he did at the rate hearings. Railroads and their regulators were involved in a battle for public relations, in which all participants were constrained by the language of engineering and its ethic of dispassionate, cooperative investigation. We can see this very clearly if we turn to another example, one which brought the testing tradition and ideal of technical specifications directly into the public limelight.

The Steel Rail Crisis

Between 1906 and 1909, the Pennsylvania found itself in the middle of a highly publicized dispute that threatened to undermine its image of engineering efficiency. The crisis involved a series of dramatic derailments that occurred on the Pennsylvania's lines and those of some other railroads when trains hit faulty rails. These episodes drew the Pennsylvania and its presidents, Alexander Cassatt and his successor James McCrea, into an acrimonious public showdown with the nation's most prominent rail manufacturers. By the time the dispute played itself out, the confrontation had caused many observers within the railroad and outside it to question the premises of engineering and standardization.[60]

Investigations of rail wear had a long and storied history at the Pennsylvania (see Chapter 6). By the turn of the century, both the ASCE and the Pennsylvania had successfully implemented specifications for rails

---

59 Raucher, *Public Relations*, pp. 11–15 and 70.
60 The dispute can be traced in the Papers of the Chief Engineer (henceforth, PRR Chief Engineer Papers), boxes 1 and 4, PRR Papers, Hagley Museum and Library, Wilmington, Delaware, accession 1807.

that had increased in size from 70 to 85 to 100 lbs. per yard. Chemist Dudley had long played a leading role in setting rail standards, most recently in his capacity as President of the American Society for Testing Materials, a post he would hold until his death in 1909. Pennsylvania rail inspector E. F. Kenney, widely respected among his peers as an authority on rail manufacture and performance, also served on several influential technical committees charged with setting rail standards. Few efforts seemed better to demonstrate the ability to achieve efficiency and safety through engineering study and cooperative negotiation.

Beneath the veneer of orderly cooperation, however, lurked a brooding and potentially ugly dispute. Under the crush of increasing traffic, rails had begun to crumble and break at an alarming rate. Sometimes the damage occurred at the joints where rails abutted one another. To remedy this problem, the Pennsylvania began reinforcing rail joints with heavier splice bars on its heavily used mainline tracks in the East. The stronger joints did nothing, however, to eliminate the hazard posed by so-called piped rails, in which metal crumbled or separated due to imperfections in its structure. The Pennsylvania's newest and most expensive 100 lb. rails, which formed a major component in its massive program of capital improvements, seemed particularly susceptible to these sorts of defects.

Opinions varied about the source of these problems. Manufacturers attributed the trouble with piping to the unusually thick heads and thin flanges of the Pennsylvania's design. Producers could roll such thin flanges, they claimed, only if the rails remained at temperatures higher than those required to provide sufficient annealing in the hefty heads. Many railroaders, including several among the ranks of Pennsylvania executives, concurred with the mills. A lengthy report prepared by the ATO's Committee on Maintenance of Way in November 1898 recommended the Pennsylvania consider shifting to the more modest designs of the American Society of Civil Engineers (ASCE), as many other leading lines had done. Even managers of the Pennsylvania's own Lines West of Pittsburgh opted to use the ASCE standard for its 100 lb. rails.[61] In the opinion of other influential figures within Pennsylvania management, however, the fault lay with the mills themselves. These managers blamed the poor quality of the metal on economizing manufacturers who cut corners and rushed through the stages of production. In an attempt to slow down the manufacturers, the Pennsylvania in 1901 inserted provisions into its specifications calling for the rail to shrink to a certain size (and thus to cool) before proceeding through the manufacturing process. Over the next

[61] Report of the Committee on Maintenance of Way, "Since the Pennsylvania Railroad Standard Section 100-Pound Rail Was Effected, Has Its Use, Up to This Time, Suggested Any Improvements That Might Be Made in Said Standard?," November 2, 1898, PRR ATO Files, box 4, folder 134. On the sustained preferences among maintenance of way engineers on the Lines West for the ASCE sections, see W. C. Cushing to A. C. Shand, April 17, 1907, PRR Chief Engineer Papers, box 4.

several years, its representatives worked to have similar checks added to the rail specifications issued by the ASCE and other engineering societies and trade associations.[62]

Unlike the ongoing effort to increase the wearing properties of steel rails, which was largely an issue of economy, the dispute over piped rails involved catastrophic failures that might result in deadly accidents. The issue thus had sensitive political overtones. One sensational wreck caused by a piped rail might readily spark public protest and inflict severe political damage, much as the mounting public crusades over air brakes and block signals were doing (as discussed in Chapter 8). Railroads could ill afford more adverse publicity such as this. Steel makers, under attack from antitrusters in the wake of the 1901 merger creating U.S. Steel, likewise had strong incentives to avoid being tagged with blame for unsafe rails. Both parties hoped to keep the dispute out of the press, so as not to alarm the public. Yet should the issue erupt, each stood ready to point accusingly at the other.

Tensions between the Pennsylvania and its rail suppliers mounted steadily during the opening years of the new century. In addition to the continuing divisiveness regarding shrinkage requirements and rolling temperatures, which took place largely under cover of engineering associations and the formal specifications process, managers at the Pennsylvania privately peppered manufacturers with criticisms about the quality of material going into the rails. The line quietly experimented with alternatives to Bessemer steel. After sampling small quantities of nickel steel, the Pennsylvania obtained 3,000 tons from the Edgar Thomson works in 1903. The manufacturer guaranteed that the nickel steel rails would last at least twice as long as ordinary Bessemer rails, but the projection soon proved overly optimistic.[63] A year later, the railroad tried small lots of rails manufactured using the open hearth process, and in 1905 it laid 3,000 tons of open hearth steel rails rolled at the Steelton works of Pennsylvania Steel. When the latter experiment yielded very promising results, President Cassatt personally implored his counterpart at the steel company, E. C. Felton, to build additional open hearth furnaces. Felton equivocated. Subsequent heats would not likely perform so well as the carefully prepared trial batch, he cautioned, and the rolls at Steelton could not withstand the additional strain necessary to shape open hearth steel. For the short run, at least, the Pennsylvania would have to make do with Bessemer rails.[64]

[62] See Chapter 6.

[63] On the experience with nickel steel, see W. W. Atterbury to G. L. Peck, October 9, 1906; G. W. Creighton to W. W. Atterbury, November 6, 1906; W. W. Atterbury to A. C. Shand, December 4, 1906; Chas. B. Dudley to A. C. Shand, October 8, 1907; A. C. Shand to Samuel Rea, December 31, 1907; Engineer Maintenance of Way to W. W. Atterbury, October 3, 1908; PRR Chief Engineer Papers, box 4.

[64] On experiments with open hearth rails, see A. J. Cassatt to A. C. Shand, July 23, 1906; A. C. Shand to A. J. Cassatt, August 9, 1906; A. J. Cassatt to E. C. Felton,

Unable to obtain alternatives, the Pennsylvania pressed manufacturers to improve the quality of their Bessemer steel. After a rash of failures in 1903, the railroad extracted agreements from its three largest suppliers to replace all rails that broke within one year of purchase. Enforcing this guarantee proved tedious, however, and the Pennsylvania soon abandoned it.[65] In its place, managers tried a different tack. Experience suggested to rail inspector Kenney and several other key figures in the Pennsylvania hierarchy that the vast majority of problem rails came from steel obtained from the tops of the ingots from which rails were cut and rolled (Fig. 9.7). Mills customarily discarded the top 9 percent of each ingot. Kenney felt they should discard a full 25 percent. The Carnegie works, whose rails from 1903 had failed at an alarming rate of one in every 250 tons (or roughly one bad rail in every 500), agreed to try the larger discard.[66] When the number of piped rails from Carnegie plunged precipitously, an emboldened Kenney drafted new specifications stipulating that mills discard the top quarter of each ingot. Kenney's draft also prescribed that railroad inspectors choose the sample rails for the critical drop test, which determined whether rails from each ingot broke or bent too readily when struck with a falling weight. Left to their own devices, Kenney believed, makers would select rails made from steel obtained from the bottoms of the ingots.[67]

When a piped rail caused a well-publicized wreck at the Pennsylvania's Spruce Creek Tunnel in early 1906, Kenney passed his draft specifications along to Assistant Chief Engineer A. C. Shand. Soon promoted to chief engineer, Shand pressed to make them official.[68] President Cassatt, ensconced

---

August 15, 1906; A. J. Cassatt to A. C. Shand, August 15, 1906; A. C. Shand to A. J. Cassatt, August 23, 1906; A. C. Shand to A. J. Cassatt, November 20, 1906; A. C. Shand to J. R. Savage, November 20, 1906; A. C. Shand to A. J. Cassatt, December 7, 1906; E. C. Felton to A. J. Cassatt, December 11, 1906; A. C. Shand to W. W. Atterbury, December 22, 1906; A. C. Shand to Chas. E. Pugh, June 20, 1907; and Engineer Maintenance of Way to W. W. Atterbury, October 31, 1908; PRR Chief Engineer Papers, box 4. Little data exists on the amount of open hearth rails obtained by the Pennsylvania during these years. In 1910, the Pennsylvania equally divided its order for 31,400 tons of rails from Cambria Steel between Bessemer and open hearth rails. A. C. Shand to W. S. Ottinger, August 5, 1910, PRR Chief Engineer Papers, box 4. A year earlier, Chief Engineer A. C. Shand inquired about a rumored large purchase of open hearth rails by the Central Railroad of New Jersey, another line in the Pennsylvania system, from Bethlehem Steel. A. C. Shand to Joseph O. Osgood, November 21, 1908, PRR Chief Engineer Papers, box 4.

[65] A. C. Shand to G. L. Peck, February 7, 1912, PRR Chief Engineer Papers, box 4.

[66] A. C. Shand to Powell Stackhouse, December 7 and 27, 1906, PRR Chief Engineer Papers, box 4.

[67] E. F. Kenney to A. C. Shand, February 24, 1906; H. F. Martin to A. C. Shand, May 22, 1906; James B. Bonner to Shand, June 30, 1906; and A. C. Shand to E. F. Kenney, July 9, 1906; PRR Chief Engineer Papers, box 4.

[68] A. C. Shand to E. F. Kenney, July 9, 1906; A. C. Shand to A. J. Cassatt, July 17, 1906; A. J. Cassatt to A. C. Shand, July 23, 1906; A. C. Shand to A. J. Cassatt, August 9, 1906; A. J. Cassatt to A. C. Shand, August 15, 1906; and A. C. Shand to A. J. Cassatt, August 23, 1906; PRR Chief Engineer Papers, box 4.

Figure 9.7. Steel ingots at the Homestead Steel Works, 1907. *Courtesy:* Library of Congress.

in Bar Harbor, Maine, after a long winter and spring spent battling the Hepburn Act, agreed to go along, even though representatives from several mills, including the Carnegie works, had objected strongly to a draft Shand had quietly circulated to them in advance.[69] At least one mill had threatened to renege on an earlier agreement should the Pennsylvania insist on the larger discard.[70] When Cassatt and Shand placed orders under the new specifications late that fall, all the manufacturers balked.[71] They insisted upon charging a substantial premium for the larger discard. Powell Stackhouse, president of Cambria Steel, initially suggested a surcharge of two dollars per ton on rails that ordinarily cost $28 per ton.[72] Vice-President Charles Pugh, who had inherited the rail problem when Cassatt died suddenly and James McCrea from the Lines West assumed the presidency of the Pennsylvania, icily dismissed the idea.[73] By May 1907, however,

---

[69] H. F. Martin (Pennsylvania Steel) to A. C. Shand, May 22, 1906, and James B. Bonner (Carnegie Steel) to Shand, June 30, 1906, PRR Chief Engineer Papers, box 4.

[70] H. Sanborn Smith (Lackawanna Steel) to A. C. Shand, July 16, 1906, PRR Chief Engineer Papers, box 4.

[71] A. C. Shand to Powell Stackhouse, December 27, 1906; A. C. Shand to Powell Stackhouse, December 29, 1906; A. C. Shand to E. C. Felton, January 2, 1906; and A. C. Shand to W. W. Atterbury, January 23, 1907; PRR Chief Engineer Papers, box 4.

[72] Powell Stackhouse to A. C. Shand, January 23, 1907, PRR Chief Engineer Papers, box 4.

[73] A. C. Shand to Powell Stackhouse, February 13, 1907, PRR Chief Engineer Papers, box 4.

manufacturers had agreed on a sliding scale, under which the Pennsylvania would pay an extra $1.25 for each additional 4 percent of the ingot discarded beyond the customary 9 percent. To obtain the full 25 percent discard, the Pennsylvania would have to pay an additional five dollars per ton, or nearly 18 percent above ordinary prices. For the Pennsylvania, which in recent years had purchased nearly 200,000 tons of steel rails per year, the premium was substantial.[74]

With no work going forward on orders of such magnitude and the economy disrupted by a brief but sharp panic, rumors of a showdown between the Pennsylvania and its suppliers soon reached the press. "News that the local end of the Steel Trust has decided to charge big prices...and of the point-blank refusal of the railroad to stand for the raise," exclaimed a story carried in the *Engineering Record* of June 23, 1907, "caused a sensation in the Pittsburgh district and it is believed here that matters are rapidly coming to a head between the rail makers and rail users." The report even suggested the Pennsylvania might "return to the plan under consideration years ago – to make its own steel rails."[75] Both parties rushed to quell the public uproar. Responding to an inquiry from the *Record*, Shand issued a lengthy statement stressing that "the number of rails actually breaking in main running tracks on the Pennsylvania Railroad is so insignificant as hardly to deserve mention."[76] That July, Judge Gary of U.S. Steel convened a conspicuous meeting of railroad presidents and steel makers, with the clear intent of reassuring the public.[77]

Try as they might, however, railroads and their suppliers could not reconcile their differences. Attempts to find common ground in the language of engineering specifications foundered. After being briefed by Pugh and General Manager Atterbury about the rail situation in May, McCrea had formed a special ad hoc committee to study the issue. In addition to Shand and numerous other personnel from the maintenance of way departments, the committee included representatives from Cambria and Maryland Steel, as well as Kenney, Dudley, and several other members of the Pennsylvania staff who had long been associated with the specifications procedure.[78] Any hope

[74] A. C. Shand to Chas. E. Pugh, May 17, 1907; Chas. E. Pugh to James McCrea, May 1, 1907; W. W. Atterbury to E. C. Felton, May 22 and June 4, 1907; Powell Stackhouse to Chas. E. Pugh, June 17, 1907; Chas. E. Pugh to James McCrea, June 18, 1907; and A. C. Shand to Chas. E. Pugh, June 20, 1907; PRR Chief Engineer Papers, box 4.

[75] "The Railroad News," June 23, 1907, newspaper clipping in PRR Chief Engineer Papers, box 4.

[76] "Copy of statement handed to Mr. Boyle," n.d., and A. C. Shand to Ivy L. Lee, April 24, 1908, which refers to the statement and dates it to July 1907; PRR Chief Engineer Papers, box 4. See also John M. Goddell (Editor, *The Engineering Record*) to A. C. Shand, June 29, 1907, PRR Chief Engineer Papers, box 4.

[77] A. C. Shand to Ivy L. Lee, April 24, 1908, PRR Chief Engineer Papers, box 4.

[78] "Report of the Rail Committee," November 15, 1907, PRR Chief Engineer Papers, box 4, summarizes the activities of this committee. On its membership and mandate,

this committee would rekindle the spirit of professional cooperation soon fizzled, however, as the appointed experts struggled to reach a consensus. Even the railroad's own representatives on the committee remained sharply divided. When a subcommittee hastily proposed new sections that shifted some of the metal from the head of the rail to the flange, the two representatives from the Lines West submitted lengthy dissenting reports.[79] Another subcommittee chaired by Dudley struggled to write specifications encompassing the critical issues of the discard and the drop test.[80] Chief of Motor Power Theodore Ely, who chaired the committee from his office in the Pennsylvania's Philadelphia headquarters, urged members to reach closure. With matters dragging well into the fall and orders for rails still not placed, Ely at last circulated a memo to members noting that "after discussing the matter with some parties who are not members of the committee" he had unilaterally made some changes to the specifications. No time remained for further discussion, Ely explained; members should simply submit a ballot expressing their concurrence or disapproval.[81]

Though packaged as a set of consensus standards, the document Ely and his corporate superiors bulldozed past the committee in reality marked a virtual abandonment of the principle of purchase through negotiated technical specification. On the surface, the Pennsylvania appeared to have backed down completely. The railroad would alter its rail shapes along lines desired by the mills, and it would leave the manufacturers free to shear "sufficient discard . . . to insure sound rails." This new liberalism, however, came with a major catch. The Pennsylvania would now reject all rails from any batch if so much as a single sample failed to withstand the drop test. Previously, the railroad had permitted mills whose rails failed the first check against breakage to test a second sample from the same batch. If that rail had proved worthy, the test of a third sample rail had determined the fate of the lot. The tests, moreover, would be administered by inspectors employed by the railroad. They would choose the rails to be tested, guided by marks stamped on each rail identifying the part of the ingot from which it came. Inspectors also retained the right to reject rails from "insufficiently sheared blooms" and "badly poured ingots.[82]

see "Rail Committee," July 19, 1907, PRR Chief Engineer Papers, box 4. On its creation, see W. W. Atterbury to E. C. Felton, May 22 and June 4, 1907, PRR Chief Engineer Papers, box 4.

79 W. C. Cushing to Theo. N. Ely, August 29, 1907, and Theo. N. Ely to A. C. Shand, September 9, 1907, PRR Chief Engineer Papers, box 4.

80 Chas. B. Dudley, "Specifications for Steel Rails," September 27, 1907, and Theo. N. Ely to Rail Committee, October 4, 1907, PRR Chief Engineer Papers, box 4.

81 Theo. N. Ely to Rail Committee, October 12, 1907, and attached "Specifications," PRR Chief Engineer Papers, box 4. Shand, at least, concurred with the new approach. See A. C. Shand to Theo. N. Ely, October 11, 1907, PRR Chief Engineer Papers, box 4.

82 "Report of the Rail Committee," November 15, 1907, PRR Chief Engineer Papers, box 4.

With this new policy, which manufacturers universally dismissed as absurdly stringent, the Pennsylvania had effectively returned to a system of market exchanges governed by the principle of caveat emptor. Raw purchasing power, not scientific study, would dictate the terms of trade. An announcement by the Pennsylvania's publicity bureau stressed that the new specifications had emerged from "exhaustive examination of the art and practice of rail manufacture... unprecedented in their completeness and in the importance of the scientific data which they supplied." Beneath this guise of expert authority, though, the Pennsylvania revealed its true intent: to shift the burden onto the manufacturers. The "most important of the features of the new specifications is the placing more upon the manufacturer the responsibility for the character of the rail produced," noted the publicity release. "The Company recognizes that it is merely a purchaser – not a manufacturer."[83]

Mills immediately sensed a trap. "On account of the wide publicity recently given to some railroad engineers as to the necessity for a large percentage of discard in order to secure sound steel," wrote Gary of U.S. Steel to Ely after reviewing the specifications, "we prefer that all contracts for rails specify definitely the percentage of discard."[84] President E. A. S. Clarke of Lackawanna likewise insisted on specifically defined discards "in light of all the recent agitation on the subject... in both the public press and in conferences." Clarke reiterated the offer to discard a larger percentage, so long as railroads paid for it. "There has been so much said as to the refusal of rail makers to give an extra discard, that I want it clearly understood that we are absolutely willing to make whatever discard the purchaser may specify," Clarke wrote to Ely, "but if that discard is greater than a total of nine percent from the top end, there will be actual extra expense in manufacturing for which we must be compensated."[85] Undaunted, the Pennsylvania placed orders under the new specifications in February 1908, at the same time it issued the press release.[86] At least one newspaper missed the essence of the new approach at first. When its editor learned that manufacturers had in fact refused to go along with the policy, however, he noted that the "statement reads in an entirely different light." He accurately described the Pennsylvania's purpose as tactical and went on to describe its "strategic position" as strong, for the railroad had launched its new policy while holding some 30,000 tons of rails in reserve.[87]

---

[83] Pennsylvania Railroad Company, "Information for the Press," February 6, 1908, PRR Chief Engineer Papers, box 4.

[84] E. H. Gary to Theo. N. Ely, November 3, 1907, PRR Chief Engineer Papers, box 4.

[85] E. A. S. Clarke to Theodore N. Ely, November 27, 1907, PRR Chief Engineer Papers, box 4.

[86] A. C. Shand to R. Trimble, February 19, 1908, PRR Chief Engineer Papers, box 4.

[87] "Pennsylvania Rail Orders Refused," March 9, 1908, newspaper clipping in PRR Chief Engineer Papers, box 4.

However cathartic the new strategy regarding rail purchases might have been for frustrated managers, it could hardly have helped the Pennsylvania in its larger political battles. Coming in the midst of scandals involving the meat packing and insurance industries that had kindled what historian Richard L. McCormick has called "the discovery that business corrupts politics," these appeals to raw economic power further cracked the veneer of orderliness that was corporate America's greatest asset in public affairs.[88] Perhaps sensing the damage, the Pennsylvania gradually backed away from its openly confrontational stance. Once again making a farce of the ideal of specifications determined by a committee of technical experts, McCrea in 1909 dispatched a special subcommittee of his Rail Committee to meet with mill representatives in what would clearly be nothing more than an attempt to patch over differences. Dudley, one of three members of the Pennsylvania's delegation, noted that the subcommittee followed McCrea's instructions to "give credit where credit is due."[89] The subcommittee would not discuss the discard or any other aspect of the manufacturing process, for the Pennsylvania's general managers had in fact already negotiated the purchase of rails without committee advice the previous month.[90]

Specifications under Fire

The highly public experience with specifications for steel rails reflected a change in thinking that permeated deep into the managerial ranks of the Pennsylvania. As managers throughout the system groped tentatively for ways to meet the pressing challenges posed by new operating conditions, they grew steadily more skeptical that those challenges would yield to anything other than traditional managerial authority exercised within the ranks of its bureaucracy and ultimately over its increasingly truculent work force. The prevailing attitude came through in an ATO meeting of 1908 devoted to the subject of "cooperation." The man bringing this matter forward bravely suggested that the Pennsylvania might benefit by embracing more conciliatory policies throughout its hierarchy and between its operating units. The idea met with little enthusiasm. "Little real interest was shown," began the report from the secretary summarizing the discussion, "as compared with certain animated discussions in the past; for instance, those on signals." The few men who did warm to subject, reported the secretary, generally fell into two

88 Richard L. McCormick, "Discovery the Business Corrupts Politics: A Reappraisal of the Origins of Progressivism," *American Historical Review* 86 (1981): 247–274.
89 Chas. B. Dudley to A. W. Gibbs, November 15, 1909, PRR Chief Engineer Papers, box 4.
90 Theo. N. Ely to W. H. Myers and G. L. Peck, October 26, 1909; Theo. N. Ely to A. C. Shand, October 27, 1909; A. C. Shand to Theo. N. Ely, November 5, 1909; A. C. Shand to Theo. N. Ely, November 12, 1909; and Chas. B. Dudley to A. W. Gibbs, November 15, 1909; PRR Chief Engineer Papers, box 4.

camps. Many were "Fatalists," whose position he characterized by quoting the phrase "The lion has always eaten the lamb. This makes the lion good-natured, and the lamb learns his place." The others were "Pessimists," who felt the Pennsylvania should "go very slow about the co-operation program, because we are afraid that in training men we may emasculate them, and then they cannot handle freight congestions, etc." The secretary also spotted a few soft-spoken "Optimists," who thought "something might be done."[91]

The discussion that followed yielded little consensus about what precisely that something might entail. Not long before, the Pennsylvania had implemented a set of performance evaluations, which it characteristically referred to as "efficiency reports." One manager wondered whether these reports might not measure "a capacity for compromise and cooperation." Another man looked to the vaunted rule book, suggesting that cooperation might possibly be written into the hallowed compendium of regulations governing employee behavior. This idea of mandating cooperation, apparently offered and received without the slightest trace of irony, served merely to spark a brief flurry of animated protests regarding the sanctity of the rules. Meanwhile, the intrepid advocates of cooperation pressed on. "It might be possible for the Press Bureau to publish an ably edited paper, and make it the medium for disseminating strong ideas as to cooperation," weakly suggested one official toward the close of the meeting. "This would be accepted by the younger men as they come on the road as a living text or creed."[92]

Amid the mounting tide of introspection, one high-ranking officer interrupted a long soliloquy on the virtues of cooperation with the apparently spontaneous and quite earnest suggestion that a company song might turn the trick.[93] Whether this remark spurred the musical effort, we do not know, but the records of the ATO from this time do indeed contain several songs. They include a racially offensive number entitled "The Tonnage Swellin'," sung to the tune "The Watermelon" of Miss Bob White, as well as the delightful "Down Where the Steel Tonnage Flows," sung in German–Dutch dialect to the tune "Down Where the Wursburger Flows." But the song that spoke most clearly to the congestion problem – and came closest to meeting the call for a company anthem – was written to the popular Irish air, "Tessie – You Are the Only, Only, Only." The lyricist, one Robert G. Wright, substituted the familiar corporate nickname "Pennsy" for "Tessie" in the title and chorus:

> Pennsy is the railroad with the four-track line,
>   Pennsy is the road to carry freight;
> Power and facilities, and cars are fine,
>   All of its equipment up to date.
> Though sometimes the movement may congested be,

[91]   Committee on Conducting Transportation, "Cooperation of Different Departments on a Grand Division," November 1908, PRR ATO Files, box 6, file 313.
[92]   Ibid., pp. 15–16.   [93]   Ibid., p. 16.

Terminals and engines we may need;
If we pull together, we shall always see:
Dear old Pennsy all the others lead.
CHORUS.
Pennsy you are the greatest system;
Pennsy you are the best;
You are the only standard railroad
And away far above the rest.
We work for you because we love it,
For you we'll get the freight and move it
Pennsy you are the only, only, only.

Freight and Transportation men together meet,
Let us work together hand in hand;
That way only can we competition beat,
Make our own road the greatest in the land.
Summer never can be by one swallow made;
One department never makes a road;
Push and pull are needed to get up the grade;
Some must gather, some must move the load.
CHORUS.
For sometime the Freight men have been well on top;
Cars were scarce, and movement very slow;
Patterson was hustled 'till he thought he'd drop;
Gibbs tried hard to make his power go;
But, as summer comes, the prospect changes some,
Now the cry is "bring along your freight,"
With a service regular, the tons will come,
Dixon's gang will make a showing great.
CHORUS.
Harriman may struggle for the N. P. stock;
Hill may try to keep the interests pooled;
Vanderbilt of Atchison may get a block;
Pittsburgh may be opened up by Gould.
But the Pennsylvania need never fear,
While the helm is held by A. J. C.
With his men behind him he can safely steer,
And his railroad first will always be.
CHORUS.[94]

The final report of the committee on "cooperation" included a simple statement that reads much like this song. All must cooperate, it insisted,

[94] PRR ATO Files. Though not dated, the reference to A. J. C. suggests the song was written during the administration of President A. J. Cassatt, who served from 1899 until his death on December 28, 1906.

"for if either department fails in its part of the work, just to the extent of such failure will the business be reduced, for in this age of competition, in competitive territory especially, the road whose every employee is working to get the freight and with promptness move it, stands the best chance to please and thereby hold it."[95] With "cooperation" thus defined as giving intent focus to one's assigned task, the ATO was left once more to ponder the human element.[96]

The engineering ideals of standardization and technical specifications, which hinged fundamentally upon the ideal of cooperative study, stood little chance of surviving in so combative a climate. A 1909 report to the ATO concerning what constituted appropriate training for engineers in railroad service declared its position succinctly at the outset. "The system must contemplate workers only," it stated simply, "and not scholars."[97] The report went on to stress the importance of exposing young hires to as many aspects of the business as quickly as possible. It advocated hiring students during the summers "so that, upon graduation, a more intelligent selection of men can be made, enabling us to get those who are ambitious and capable of appreciating opportunities for obtaining knowledge of the workings of other branches of railroading."[98] The committee argued strongly against assigning young engineering recruits to the drafting rooms in the test facilities at Altoona, a program that in the nineteenth century had been the centerpiece of managerial recruitment at the Pennsylvania. The report expressed perfectly the sentiments of the new Pennsylvania president James McCrea, quoted approvingly by the ATO, that "engineering consists practically of one-eighth education and seven-eighths common sense."[99]

By 1910, as the Pennsylvania and its fellow lines in the East approached the ICC for a rate increase, the whole idea of technical specifications was in retreat. That year, a group of superintendents responsible for moving trains through various sections of the Pennsylvania system submitted a question

95   H. A. Jaggard to A. Feldpauche, October 8, 1908, and revised "Suggested Treatment of Question – Cooperation of Different Departments on a Grand Division," p. 4; PRR ATO Files, box 6, file 313.

96   Shortly after the ATO discussed cooperation, the social scientist J. Shirley Eaton published a book arguing that railroads had passed into a new era characterized by "sociological adjustment." J. S. Eaton, *Education for Efficiency in Railroad Service* (Washington: Bureau of Education, 1909). The three previous eras were dominated by (1) building, when anything was better than a wagon road; (2) coordination of service and response to financial conditions; and (3) internal adjustments, such as "perfection of machinery" and "increasing the train unit."

97   Report of the Committee on Conducting Transportation Regarding Meeting of May 27, 1909, p. 1, PRR ATO Files, box 9, file 527.

98   Ibid., p. 1.

99   "To What Extent Is It Practicable to Enlarge the Training of the Engineer, Civil and Mechanical, in Collateral Branches of Railroading With a View to a More Systematic and Complete Development of Their Training in the Various Branches of Railroading," attached to ibid.

to the ATO. The superintendents asked, in effect, why they should not be allowed to review and to revise in advance all specifications issued by the laboratory and the testing facilities. After all, suggested a sympathetic special committee assigned to consider the question, the superintendents would in all likelihood eventually adapt any procedures stipulated within the specifications to meet their own local needs. Asserting the primacy of the "knowledge and suggestions of those . . . who are in touch with the conditions and the needs," the committee proceeded to discredit the role of the laboratory and testing departments in developing past standards that had proved useful. "Devices exist today as standards that owe their origin, not to the technical expert," its report declared, "but to the man whose close and intimate association with the existing conditions and requirements pointed out to him first the need and then the way."[100] As the assembled officers of the Pennsylvania discussed this report, General Manager Atterbury treated Superintendent of Motive Power A. W. Gibbs, the person directly responsible for specifications, almost as if he were on trial.[101] When the secretary of the ATO inquired of Gibbs in February 1911 whether he had done anything to accommodate the superintendents, Gibbs responded defensively, explaining that tests could not proceed if engineers in the laboratories had to respond to every inquiry submitted from any corner of the system. "Finally," Gibbs concluded with a tone of indignation rarely heard in Pennsylvania correspondence, "the resolution, in its full breadth, is beautifully arranged to stop any progress."[102]

Such was the status of engineering tests and specifications at the Pennsylvania Railroad in February 1911, at virtually the exact moment Louis Brandeis introduced the American public to Frederick Taylor. The self-styled "Standard Railroad of America" had drifted a long way, indeed, from the ideals expressed in St. Louis. When Taylor subsequently became the center of a national spectacle, Brandeis had bettered his railroad opponents twice in one stroke, not only winning the rate case, but also far surpassing the designers of the locomotive testing plant in spreading the gospel of efficiency.

RATE REGULATION AFTER 1911

In the aftermath of Louis Brandeis's triumph, the rhetoric of engineering and efficiency thoroughly infused virtually every discussion of railroads and the

[100] A. Feldpauche to Mr. James T. Wallis, January 18, 1910; Report of Special Committee, April 5, 1910; and Abstract of Report, April 13, 1910; PRR ATO Files, box 10, file 567.

[101] Minutes of the Association of Transportation Officers, May 19, 1910, pp. 74–91, PRR ATO Files.

[102] R. L. O'Donnel to A. Feldpauche, February 1, 1911, and A. W. Gibbs to A. Feldpauche, March 7, 1911, PRR ATO Files, box 10, file 567.

rate question for at least another decade. All parties, including the railroads, couched their arguments in terms of efficiency.[103] Railroad publicity, seeking to turn Brandeis's arguments back on the emerging regulatory apparatus itself, portrayed government as wasteful while celebrating the potential of private management to generate efficiency. Two aspects of government policy – the antipooling provisions of the Interstate Commerce Act and the persistence of state regulatory commissions – drew especially heavy criticism. In the opinion of the railroads, each generated waste by preserving an unnecessarily large number of institutions and jurisdictions. In arguments that resonated with the many political reformers of the day who looked for unified commission government to eliminate the wasteful practices of urban bosses, railroads suggested that fewer firms and fewer regulatory venues would surely result in improved efficiency.[104]

Amidst the frenzied rhetoric of efficiency unleashed by the rate cases, one can easily lose sight of a significant departure in policy at many railroads that worked against the rising tide of scientific management ideals. In the years immediately following the rate hearings, the Pennsylvania and other lines moved away from the strict engineering objectives and ideals of efficiency that had so long informed both their activities and their rhetoric. Within the framework provided by the language of engineering, railroads attempted to articulate an alternative vision of railroading that stressed differentiated customer service. The managerial hubris captured in the verse "with a service regular, the tons will come" seemed increasingly anachronistic in the years after 1910. The customer and the public, not the machine, would now come first.

The new emphasis on service was made quite explicit in the advice of public relations experts such as Ivy Lee.[105] Following what was for them the devastating outcome of the Eastern Rate Case, railroads such as the Pennsylvania redoubled their publicity efforts. While the spate of new material retained

---

[103]   This is the recurrent theme of Kerr, *American Railroad Politics*, which provides the basis for my analysis in this section. Though Kerr's work remains the most perceptive study of railroad regulation, his insistent association of railroads with scientific management ideology obscures the essential reorientation of the railroad position discussed below. Kerr links railroads to scientific management by conflating the concept of scientific management with the objective of consolidation. Others in the public arena, as Kerr well recognizes and documents, had a much broader conception of scientific management and its possibilities. As he notes, the most emphatic arguments in favor of widespread application of scientific management principles to the industry came from "*academics*, engineers, and economists." Aside from the idiosyncratic Daniel Willard, president of the Baltimore and Ohio, railroad management evoked such ideas and rhetoric "as a means to an ends." One can see this clearly in their attacks on antipooling and state regulation. Both were longstanding grievances that railroads had fought on terms other than efficiency.

[104]   Martin J. Schiesl, *The Politics of Efficiency: Municipal Administration and Reform in America, 1880–1920* (Berkeley: University of California Press, 1977).

[105]   Raucher, *Public Relations*, p. 121, notes the growing emphasis on service.

some of the engineering flavor characteristic of earlier publicity, it frequently attempted as well to plant a human face on railroad operations. Lee "steadily urged management to look for ways to cultivate a more 'human' image," observes historian Roland Marchand. "Railroad executives, he cautioned them, had been far too satisfied to emphasize the machines that they operated."[106] Anxious to temper what he perceived as the haughtiness of Pennsylvania management in their operation of a "mechanically perfect institution," Lee increasingly resorted to human interest stories. "The public is disposed to take little incidents and to talk about them," Lee observed, "and from these small incidents judge the whole."[107] Though Lee deplored such superficiality, from the mid-teens forward he repeatedly counseled his employers and fellow publicists to emphasize emotional appeals rather than substance.[108]

As part of this shift in emphasis, the Pennsylvania displayed an increasing willingness to give face to the engineers themselves. New President Samuel Rea, who succeeded the ailing McRea in January 1913, had achieved significant notoriety for coordinating the building of Penn Station in Manhattan. Previous presidents such as Alexander Cassatt, an engineer who had spent much of his career advancing the cause of standards, evoked the weighty authority of someone grounded in basic principles of science, religion, or the law. Rea projected a different image, made popular in novels and other literature of the day, of the engineer as swashbuckling hero capable of providing not merely cold-hearted efficiency, but grand spectacle and emotional satisfaction as well.[109] Publicity photos and illustrations on Pennsylvania timetables had typically shown track structures and machinery in complete isolation. Under Rea, such images increasingly included people as well. The new look helped convey an impression of engineers not as relentless economizers but as creative designers who devised technological marvels of benefit to individual travelers.

The changing flavor of railroad public relations was evident to anyone who visited the Pennsylvania's exhibit at the 1915 Pan Pacific Exposition, which Lee had a large hand in organizing.[110] Staged to honor the supreme achievement of the gear-and-girder age, the opening of the Panama Canal, the fair took place in San Francisco. Since the Pennsylvania did not serve

---

106   Marchand, "From Defensive Advocacy to Business Statesmanship," pp. 14–15. "They had remained so content with an image that associated them with the machinery of the railroad," notes Marchand of management at the Pennsylvania, "that they had come to the public to seem like machines, themselves."

107   Quoted in Gregory W. Bush, *Lord of Attention: Gerald Stanley Lee and the Crowd Metaphor in Industrializing America* (Amherst: University of Massachusetts Press), p. 41.

108   See, especially, Ivy L. Lee, *Human Nature and the Railroads* (Philadelphia: E. S. Nash, 1915), and "Personality in Publicity," *Electric Railway Journal* 50 (1917): 23.

109   Tichi, *Shifting Gears*, ch. 3.   110   Raucher, *Public Relations*, p. 38.

the West Coast directly, its display was naturally far less ambitious than the one mounted a decade earlier at St. Louis. But the differences went beyond mere scale. Rather than standing in awe of a testing plant that permitted them a glimpse into the inner workings of the railroad machine, visitors were now invited to take a seat in a mock-up of one of the Pennsylvania's gleaming new all-steel passenger cars. Once settled, they viewed moving pictures that took them on high-speed excursions through especially scenic stretches of the Pennsylvania System. Careful observers, of course, could still find the customary array of statistics documenting the Pennsylvania's machine-like efficiency. But the exhibit was clearly intended primarily to evoke the emotional experience of travel. Those exiting the makeshift theater were not told that the essential results of their experience would be tabulated and published a year later. For the vital "results" of this display would persist in more elusive form, as memories of rapid motion and sleek surfaces held in the minds of the visitors themselves. Two years after the exhibit in San Francisco closed, a new book published by the Pennsylvania did in fact appear. Written by the publicist Lee, it emphasized the relevance of Jamesian psychology to railroad public relations.[111]

This new public face complemented a subtle shift in political strategy. Rather than seek support merely through broad appeals to principle, railroads increasingly cultivated key allies among customers by catering to their particular needs and interests. Lines such as the Pennsylvania touted the services they provided to shippers of high-value products, such as citrus growers and manufacturers. Though easily dismissed by some observers as products of political expediency, these new departures in railroad rhetoric and behavior betrayed a shift in railroad thinking away from the commodity-focused transport system envisioned by Morgan and toward a more complicated vision involving provision of a range of specialized services.[112] Faced with challenges of the sort encountered by the Pennsylvania, management grew increasingly aware that railroads faced a future in which revenue and profits would flow from custom services such as fast freight and shipments of less-than-carload lots, rather than from massive movement of undifferentiated bulk commodities. Just as the locomotive testing plant had been both a self-conscious gesture in public relations and an expression of deeply

---

[111] Lee, *Human Nature and the Railroads*, discussed by Raucher, *Public Relations*, pp. 124–125, and by Marchand, "From Defensive Advocacy to Business Statesmanship," pp. 14–17. On the broader relevance of Jamesian psychology to American history during this period, see Livingston, *Pragmatism and the Political Economy of Cultural Revolution*.

[112] While acknowledging the growing emphasis on service and the frequent appeals to individual customers on this basis, Kerr, *American Railroad Politics*, interprets these developments as tactical measures intended to serve a decidedly political purpose. Characteristically, he emphasizes how the rhetoric of service often melded with the gospel of efficiency, especially when joined to the concept of public service.

held values borne of long practical experience, the new emphasis on service was thus both a public relations campaign and a reflection of new operational realities.

Wartime Reversals

The experience of World War I obstructed and obscured this tentative effort to recast American railroading. European demands for food and military products skewed the flow of commerce back toward patterns that had prevailed with the commodity flows of the late nineteenth century. Long-distance through shipments grew rapidly, with a net surplus of traffic again moving from west to east. Despite the extensive investment in switching and transfer facilities that railroads had made in the intervening years, cars piled up in congested terminals or sat idly on sidings, creating a crisis in movement. Major port cities in the East grew especially crowded. Meanwhile, wartime objectives suffused railroading with a sense of urgency and patriotic self-sacrifice that imparted new power to the notion of disinterested engineering efficiency. In these circumstances the engineering paradigm reached perhaps its purest expression. Congress placed railroads under control of federal administrators. Spurred on by the deadly urgency of global chaos and infused with a rising spirit of sacrifice and disinterested public service, these men devoted themselves single-mindedly to the task of expediting the flow of goods. More than ever, tonnage took precedence over profit. "The question of railroad efficiency was no longer one of saving money," observes historian K. Austin Kerr of the mindset prevailing in the railroad industry during wartime. "The logic of solving the 1917 transportation crisis meant that henceforth efficiency would be a question of forcing railroad operation to expedite the movement of goods."[113] Here was engineering reenshrined, absent the troubling ambiguous relationship to profits that had bothered Veblen. Though the lines would remain in private hands, government would operate them and determine proper rates of return. "The advent of federal control," notes Kerr, "meant that suddenly the industry could be operated from the perspective of national efficiency and service rather than for the achieving of individual corporate profits."[114]

Buoyed by the apparent success of wartime operations under federal control, an emboldened regulatory community – "engineers, commissioners, economists, and reformers," in Kerr's typology, together with "many officials in the Railroad Administration" and "academics" – embraced national administration as a permanent solution to the railroad problem. Motivated by a sense of broad public purpose that was often tinged with professional ambition, the reformers "were concerned with creating an efficient industry that would meet future national economic requirements."[115] This

---

[113] Ibid., p. 71.   [114] Ibid., p. 74.   [115] Ibid., p. 128.

independent community of regulators had become the most vocal advocate of consolidation and engineering methodology, which they believed should now be applied to the rate-making process itself. The confrontational public hearings and frequently contested appeals that had characterized rate-setting since 1910 struck reformers as overly political (and thus wasteful). Reformers hoped to lift the rate-setting process above the unseemly conflicts of politics by removing it from the ICC and placing it in the hands of a board of technical experts who would follow formal criteria. Convinced that the wartime experience had provided the clearest example yet of the engineering ideal in action, the reform community first proposed extending the authority of the wartime administrative authority. Later, it drafted legislation that would have fundamentally altered the regulatory system. Sounding uncannily like the financier Morgan nearly two decades before, regulators embraced a rate-of-return approach to rate-setting that effectively reduced railroads to utilities offering undifferentiated service. Some reform advocates even suggested that any income earned by railroads in excess of a stipulated return on capital be turned over to a government transportation board for investment.[116]

Operating with the supreme confidence of those who perceive the winds of change are at their backs, reformers failed to comprehend the enormous resistance that lay in the path of such proposals. Flushed with enthusiasm from the wartime experience, few reformers paused long to ponder whether the engineering approach would founder without the same sense of urgency and collective purpose that prevailed during the war. Reformers insistently celebrated the ideal of public service, as if trying through sheer willpower to sustain the wartime ethic of self-sacrifice. But few delved into the troubling matter of how self-interested railroads, shippers, and labor might attempt to turn the mechanisms of reform to their economic advantage. "Scientific management of course also meant maximizing profits," notes historian Kerr after describing in rich detail the ideals that sustained the reform community. "This underlying ethical assumption was not questioned; most implicitly agreed that business profits were highly desirable and therefore in the public interest."[117] The fundamental tension between engineering methods and capitalist objectives that Veblen had puzzled over in 1906 thus remained unresolved.

The extensive debates over the proposed reforms soon revealed the enormity of the economic stakes and the capacity of self-interest to undermine the engineering ideal. Even organized labor, the one group that steadfastly supported continued federal intervention in railroading, found reasons to object to measures supported by the reform community. The railroad brotherhoods had won both an eight-hour law and significant wage increases during the war. Their leaders well understood that withdrawal of a strong

---

[116] Ibid., esp. pp. 130–132.   [117] Ibid., p. 130.

government authority could only place these gains at risk, since experience under the earlier regulatory system had clearly established that opposition to wage increases was the one issue on which shippers and carriers could always agree. But the proposed legislation contained elements that labor could not tolerate. For in their zeal to suppress all conflict, most reformers supported provisions banning strikes, which they viewed as wasteful disruptions. Reformers embraced the alternative of mediation, the labor-relations equivalent of the standards-setting process. Their antistrike stance drove a divisive wedge between them and organized labor and deprived the reform cause of an essential ally.

Reformers fared little better in persuading railroad customers to embrace continued government administration or a new approach to rate-setting and regulation. Shippers of virtually all ilks generally believed service had suffered under wartime administration even as rates went up. Most shippers preferred simply to return to the system that had prevailed from 1910 to 1917, when a sympathetic ICC had consistently ruled in their favor and state commissions had continued to recognize special circumstances affecting particular shipments. Agricultural interests in the West and South and other shippers of commodities adamantly resisted any proposals to shift power away from the prewar ICC to a board of experts they sensed might well be beholden to the railroads.[118]

Shippers had ample reason to fear such alliances between reformers and railroads, for the latter could see some definite virtues in the reformist proposals, and the ideology voiced by railroad executives often sounded very much like the scientific management that captivated the reformers. Yet as Kerr reluctantly but tellingly observes, railroads and reformers parted company "when the latter contradicted concrete corporation economic interests." Given a choice between the shipper-friendly ICC and a board of transportation experts, for instance, railroads would gladly choose the latter. If such a board sought to guarantee railroads and their investors a certain return on investment, who were railroads to object, so long as the government did not wish to keep any excess earnings for itself? (Rather than have the ICC establish maximum rates, railroads would have had a transportation board set minimum earnings.) Nor would railroads complain if that board wanted to study and promote corporate consolidation instead of making it illegal, providing, of course, that any changes in organization suggested by the experts were considered advisory rather than mandatory. Railroads likewise found scant reason to object to a ban on strikes, though they also saw little purpose in guaranteeing employees the right to binding arbitration. And if reformers wanted to damn the inefficiencies of the prewar regulatory system, railroads would gladly join in the refrain, though they would also

---

[118] On shipper complaints about railroad service under wartime administration, see ibid., pp. 101–111, 181–182, 187, and 193.

hasten to add that the clearest evidence of those inefficiencies was surely the remarkable performance of the railroads during the war, when the old system of rate regulation had been suspended.[119]

Though in staking out these positions railroads surely sought to temper calls for more radical reform, we can detect in them glimpses of a new vision for the industry. Railroads seemed prepared to function under a dual system, with a commodity-oriented business providing universal service and operating under conditions of a regulated utility, and a more competitive (and innovative) business aimed at meeting the demands of shippers willing to pay a premium for specialized services.[120] When wartime administrator William McAdoo lobbied for increased standardization of equipment, for instance, rail executives countered with recommendations "in favor of equipment designed to fit local conditions."[121] In expressing their desire to compete for excess earnings, railroads emphasized the importance of providing service of high quality. Such appeals gained railroads some support among California citrus growers and others "whose business depended on fast transportation to distant markets." Shippers and commercial interests in New England, Chicago, and other densely congested manufacturing districts likewise expressed some sympathy for the railroad position.[122]

The compromise legislation of 1920 stopped short of articulating such a coherent approach to the industry. The act neither embraced the strict efficiency orientation advocated by the regulatory community nor clarified the boundary issues along lines the railroads had suggested. Instead, Congress preserved the ICC as the supreme arbiter of relations between railroads and their customers while encouraging the agency to employ rate-of-return calculations and to exert a stronger coordinating hand over the industry. It thus loosely joined the prewar, consumer-oriented system of rate regulation to administrative concepts appropriate to utilities such as electric power, which offered a far less differentiated product than transportation services did.

[119] Ibid., pp. 150–156. Quote from p. 155.

[120] "For the railroads," writes Kerr, *American Railroad Politics*, p. 156, "the term 'competition' did not refer to competition in rates, but only to competition in service." Kerr, whose careful study I otherwise greatly admire, dismisses the railroad appeal to service as a political ploy and characterizes their notion of a "competition in service" as a "pragmatic argument" designed to gain support of shippers. He sees a blatant "contradiction" on the part of railroads when they speak of competition in service while seeking to avoid competition in rates. While acknowledging the difficulties of maintaining such a clear distinction in practice and while recognizing the elements of self-interest in the railroad proposal, I believe the railroad position reflected a genuine effort to reconcile their obligations as utilitarian common carriers with their desire to meet the growing demand for innovative services.

[121] Ibid., p. 155.   [122] Ibid., pp. 193–198. Quote from p. 193.

UTILITY, NOT NOVELTY

Few observers would characterize the resulting marriage as a happy one. Planning, coordination, and restructuring now occurred in the context of innumerable specific rate disputes, a realm where the ICC had always pursued what historian William R. Childs aptly calls a pragmatic approach, in which issues of equity and fairness traditionally took precedence. Those localized disputes, in turn, grew more complicated as they became enmeshed with the more comprehensive efforts to assess valuations and to calculate returns on capital. This was a recipe for ossification, not innovation.[123]

The timing could hardly have been worse, for the interwar years brought the widespread appearance of new means of mass transport – trucks and buses – that held the potential to radically reshape the transportation system. With its capacity to bring substantial pulling power right to the door of virtually any enterprise, the motor truck in particular promised to inject a strong dose of flexibility into the freight shipping industry. One could well imagine the decades of the twenties and thirties as a period of creative change, as transport providers melded railroads and trucks into a diverse system capable of serving a variety of customers. Indeed, several railroads took steps in that direction during the twenties when they created subsidiaries that operated fleets of motorized local delivery vehicles. Some even experimented with "piggyback" operations in which trailers were placed on railcars, then off-loaded and pulled by trucks to their final destination. A few pioneering truckers, meanwhile, used centralized sales and dispatching to introduce a measure of organization and routine into an industry that had initially been dominated by independent operators.

These tentative efforts to combine the virtues of system and coordination with the inherent flexibility of trucking soon foundered in a complex thicket of regulation. As independent and contract motor carriers began picking off some of the most lucrative trades and routes, they disrupted the convoluted rate schedules that had long formed an essential component of the regulated rail-based transport system. State governments, often acting with the encouragement of railroads, moved promptly to impose a measure of control over these practices. Exercising authority they possessed under the public purpose doctrines that underlay most railroad law or through the police powers they held over the state-funded highways, states implemented a variety of licensing provisions that stemmed some of the most aggressive competition. Over time, these measures sorted truckers into various classifications. Common carriers, who earned their livelihood strictly by transporting goods, were, like railroads, required by law to accept shipments from anyone willing to

---

[123] William R. Childs, *Trucking and the Public Interest: The Emergence of Federal Regulation, 1914–1940* (Knoxville: University of Tennessee Press, 1985).

pay. At the other extreme were private operators, such as farmers, who drove their vehicles in conjunction with another line of work. Between these two fell a problematic third group, the contract truckers. Their ranks consisted of full-time operators who specialized in certain routes or in products that required special handling and equipment, such as milk, oil, produce, and lumber. These were just the sorts of high-return businesses that some railroads had begun to cultivate, and because contract carriers operated free of the burden of providing universal service, railroads and common carrier truckers felt disadvantaged in pursuing them. In their view, state licensing was in effect drawing inappropriate (and artificial) boundaries among transporters and between them and their customers. In an effort to break down those divisions, railroads attempted to have their wholly owned subsidiaries who operated fleets of local delivery vehicles classified as contract shippers.

Predictably, the myriad of state regulatory provisions gave way in the 1930s to federal regulation. Under pressure from many quarters, the ICC began holding hearings on the industry in 1932. Commissioner Joseph Eastman, who had been slow to recognize the significance of trucking, now came to envision a comprehensive restructuring of the transport system, with trucks, buses, and railroads each performing those functions most suited to them. Such a thoroughgoing rearrangement would require massive coordination, a task Eastman could not imagine entrusting to private firms in the marketplace. He pressed for government intervention on a scale that virtually no other party to the discussions could tolerate. The idea of creatively melding transport modes thus gave way to a more preservationist mentality, in which trucking was seen as a competitive alternative to railroading that should be brought under a parallel mechanism of regulation. An act of Congress in 1935 extended ICC methods of control to the trucking industry, thus transforming an industry with low capital costs and easy entry into a public utility, with all the attendant difficulties.[124] "Transport" came increasingly to be conceived as an undifferentiated product offered to all consumers by parallel regulated systems, rather than as a highly differentiated product capable of servicing the demands of varied customers. This basic perception would persist until the 1970s and 1980s, when the deregulation movement broke down the divisions between transport suppliers, and firms dramatically redrew the boundaries of the industry. Only then would railroading regain some measure of the innovativeness that had characterized the industry during the heyday of the nineteenth century.

[124] In addition to Childs, *Trucking and the Public Interest*, whose analysis I follow closely, this assessment of trucking regulation is derived from Galambos and Pratt, *Rise of the Corporate Commonwealth*, pp. 120–121, and Keller, *Regulating a New Economy*, pp. 66–76.

Epilogue

The Enduring Challenge of Innovation

The long odyssey of American railroading recounted in these pages has a ring of inevitability about it. Reaching the end of the story, one might readily be tempted to think of the industry in terms of the human life cycle. Railroading burst forth during the early nineteenth century like a young child, unformed but full of promise. After a tumultuous and extended struggle it emerged in something like middle age, its aspirations a bit trimmed, perhaps, but performing with a newfound efficiency derived from experience and from a more concerted focus. From there railroading grew steadily more rigid, less inclined to entertain new possibilities, and unwilling or unable to escape established patterns and summon the energy required to turn such visions into reality. Lingering long enough to see a new generation of promising technologies supplant it, railroading never came close to recapturing the blossom of its own youth.

This tidy portrait, though not entirely without basis, obscures a deeper truth. For while a history of railroad innovation may contain many elements of an unfolding tragic drama, it also highlights some remarkably persistent features of American society and culture. The issues Americans confronted in attempting to regulate railroad innovation have arisen time and again as new technologies emerged and evolved in the American context. The histories of telephony, electric power, highways, and networked computing, to cite some obvious examples, each resound with many of the same themes discussed in this book.[1] The challenge of regulating innovation, of reaping the fruits of

---

[1] On telephony, see Peter Temin with Louis Galambos, *The Fall of the Bell System: A Study in Prices and Politics* (New York: Cambridge University Press, 1987); on electric power, see Richard F. Hirsh, *Technology and Transformation in the American Electric Utility Industry* (New York: Cambridge University Press, 1989) and *Power Loss: The Origins of Deregulation and Restructuring in the American Electric Utility System* (Cambridge, Mass.: MIT Press, 1999); on highways, see Bruce E. Seely, *Building the American Highway System: Engineers as Policy Makers* (Philadelphia: Temple

new technologies while also reconciling those technologies with deeply held values and ideals, is an enduring one.

As the experience of railroading suggests, that challenge typically revolves around the fundamental problem of making the technology accessible to a broad community of users who often possess quite diverse needs and desires. If technologies such as railroading catered to a strictly undifferentiated populace in which everyone wanted precisely the same service, these breakthrough innovations might well evolve along fairly simple paths and spark little dispute or controversy. Under such conditions railroads and other technologies would spread widely through the populace, and improvements would flow along a single path intended to lower the cost of that basic service. In the real world, of course, conditions were much different. The populace varied widely in its hopes and aspirations, and in its abilities to pay. In these circumstances railroads could not follow a single, undifferentiated trajectory. But neither could they satisfy each individual preference. Incapable of being all things to all people, they channeled resources toward certain areas and away from others. This occurred not simply through decisions to build lines in some regions while bypassing other places. It also involved choices about what sorts of services to emphasize. In pursuing certain opportunities while neglecting others, moreover, railroads imparted a momentum to the course of technical change. Their initial choices steered capital and innovative energies in directions that reinforced the established form.[2]

This situation posed serious concerns for a people smitten with the promise of material prosperity and committed to upholding the frequently conflicting principles of egalitarianism and individual liberty. The chapters above document the extended struggles among that people to shape railroad technology in ways consonant with those deeply felt values and aspirations. Early on this took place quite explicitly. In their debates over how to encourage construction of the initial lines, Americans such as Abraham Lincoln and his Jacksonian adversaries consciously framed their arguments around themes of liberty and equality. As the railroad machine took shape, the struggle assumed less overtly ideological forms. Now Americans looked to run the

University Press, 1987), and Mark H. Rose, *Interstate: Express Highway Politics, 1941–1956* (Lawrence: University of Kansas Press, 1979); on computing and communications, see Steven W. Usselman, "Computer and Communications Technology," in Stanley I. Kutler, ed., *Encyclopedia of the United States in the Twentieth Century* (New York: Scribner's, 1996), pp. 799–829, and "Trying to Keep the Customers Stratified: Government, Business, and the Paths of Innovation in American Railroading and Computing," *Journal of Industrial History* 2 (1999): 1–21.

[2] On technological momentum, see Thomas P. Hughes, "Technological Momentum," in Merritt Roe Smith and Leo Marx, eds., *Does Technology Drive History? The Dilemma of Technological Determinism* (Cambridge, Mass.: MIT Press, 1994), pp. 101–113, *Networks of Power: Electrification in Western Society, 1880–1930* (Baltimore: Johns Hopkins University Press, 1984), ch. 6, and "Technological Momentum in History: Hydrogenation in Germany, 1898–1933," *Past and Present* 44 (August 1969): 106–132.

machine in ways that fostered efficiency, which by driving down costs presumably spread the benefits of railroad innovation to a wider community, while also preserving room for novelties that might serve specialized users. This was a tall order, for capitalists and governments alike. It called for striking difficult balances between routine and diversity, for concentrating focus without sacrificing all flexibility. Those balancing acts grew still more complicated, moreover, as questions arose about who bore responsibility for the problems railroad technology inevitability created, such as accidents and other nuisances, and about how best to provide remedies for these undesired offshoots of innovation.

Disputes such as these involved more than differences of opinion about the desirable course of technical change in railroading. They also raised fundamental questions about how best to go about shaping the course of technological innovation within the framework of American political economy. Both within the railroad industry and in the public sphere, Americans experimented continually with various means of steering technical change and regulating innovation. Time and again, they looked for ways to intervene in the market mechanisms that governed so many affairs in the American context, without abandoning those mechanisms entirely. They created new forms of market-based incentives, such as land grants linked to construction and corporate charters promising benefits such as limited liability, and they looked hard at old ones such as the patent system, which they feared might actually harbor monopoly and stifle change. They passed laws intended to stop pooling and to block railroads from forming trusts, in hopes of preserving competition among numerous firms. They turned toward engineering professionals, joined through technical associations, whose methods of evaluating technologies and establishing technical standards appeared to generate innovation without the contentious rancor of market exchanges. They created regulatory commissions, granting them powers to investigate and, in some cases, to inspect railroad practices and to adjudicate disputes over rates.

In all of this, Americans generally preferred to leave responsibility for the particulars of railroad technology in the hands of private firms and individuals. They looked to alter the incentives operating upon those individuals, not to shift responsibility from those private parties to government. Even the giant transcontinental lines, though built with significant direct subsidy and justified in large measure on military grounds, passed rapidly into private hands. Disputes over the patent system arose out of concern that the incentives to innovate might operate more effectively through the market for transport services rather than through the market for patented novelties. The question was not whether to rely upon market mechanisms and private initiative, but which market mechanism tapped such initiative more effectively. Legislation mandating the use of safety devices deviated to some extent from this general tenet. But even then, government took care not to specify particular brands of devices and bestow a monopoly upon certain suppliers. Within a few years, moreover, it retreated to an approach grounded in the powers of inspection, publicity, and the threat of legal suits by injured parties.

In certain respects, the regulatory regime established with the Eastern Rate Case marked a departure from this basic approach to railroads and railroad technology. Asserting its role over the critical issue of rates and basing its actions upon close assessments of engineering, technology, and operating procedures, government interjected itself deeply into markets and into the details of railroading. The elaborate valuation studies that became such a prominent feature of railroading after 1920 perpetuated this tendency for regulators to delve deeply into the details of rail technology. So, too, did the growing role for government as an arbitrator of labor–management relations in the railroad industry. Labor disputes frequently involved matters such as seniority systems and job classifications, which in turn were tied to tasks and routines that had developed around particular technologies and operating procedures.[3] Since virtually all innovation affected valuations and work rules to at least some degree, government thus indirectly became party to innumerable choices regarding rail technology, including such key decisions as when to convert to diesel locomotives and how to automate the monitoring of car movements.[4] Perhaps not surprisingly, railroading became a prime example for those who believed that government bureaucracy impeded creativity and stifled innovation.[5] The economic performance of the industry after 1920 certainly did little to diminish the force of this argument. Nor has the

---

[3] For historical analyses of the difficulties of rate-of-return regulation, see Thomas K. McCraw, *Prophets of Regulation* (Cambridge, Mass.: Harvard University Press, 1984), esp. p. 60, and Louis Galambos and Joseph Pratt, *The Rise of the Corporate Commonwealth: United States Business and Public Policy in the Twentieth Century* (New York: Basic, 1988), esp. pp. 51–53. For an important analysis of railroading in particular, see Ann F. Friedlander, *The Dilemma of Freight Transport Regulation* (Washington, D.C.: Brookings Institution, 1969). On the implications for labor, see Fred Cottrell, *Technological Change and Labor in the Railroad Industry* (Lexington, Mass.: Heath, 1970), pp. 112–150; Stuart M. Rich, "Changing Railway Technology in the United States and Its Impact upon Railroad Employment Since 1945," *Transportation Journal* 25 (1986): 55–65; Curtis Grimm and Robert J. Windle, "Regulation and Deregulation in Surface Freight, Airlines, and Telecommunications," in James Peoples, ed., *Regulatory Reform and Labor Markets* (Boston: Kluwer, 1998), pp. 15–49; and Wayne K. Talley and Ann V. Schwarz-Miller, "Railroad Deregulation and Union Labor Earnings," in Peoples, *Regulatory Reform*, pp. 123–153.

[4] Cottrell, *Technological Change*; Maury Klein, "Replacement Technology: The Diesel as a Case Study," *Railroad History* (Spring 1990): 109–120; and Albert J. Churella, *From Steam to Diesel: Managerial Customs and Organizational Capabilities in the Twentieth-Century American Locomotive Industry* (Princeton: Princeton University Press, 1998).

[5] This view is expressed especially forcefully in Albro Martin, *Railroads Triumphant: The Growth, Rejection, and Rebirth of a Vital American Force* (New York: Oxford University Press, 1992). For more measured assessments, see Friedlander, *Dilemma*; McCraw, *Prophets*; Galambos and Pratt, *Corporate Commonwealth*; Maury Klein,

apparent revival of freight railroading since the industry underwent significant deregulation in the late 1970s and early 1980s done much ·to dispel the idea that government policy undermined innovation in American railroading.

Yet the story and its lessons are not quite so simple. While the regulatory policies of the early twentieth century certainly exerted a powerful and persistent influence over railroading, those policies formed part of a long continuum. Efforts to regulate railroad technology were as old as the first experimental lines. They had been with the industry from the very beginning, and they would form a vital element in railroading so long as railroad technology and other transport technologies continued to emerge and to evolve. The regulatory activities of the early twentieth century, then, were no aberration; they were the latest chapter in this ongoing interplay between Americans and their technologies. In asserting a more prominent role in setting rates and in adjudicating labor disputes, legislators and federal bureaucrats drew on established principles of governance and operated within the same framework as earlier measures intended to influence the course of change in the railroad industry. They still envisioned government acting essentially as an arbitrator among private interests. Americans consciously stopped short of nationalizing the industry and even refused to create a special board of expertise pertaining to railroad management and technology.

The new policies toward railroads, moreover, formed merely one aspect of a more general response to rapid and dramatic developments in transport technology. Mass production of vehicles powered by internal combustion engines, achieved most dramatically by Henry Ford during the very years the ICC first asserted its authority over rate-setting, opened the possibility of restructuring transport along much more flexible lines than ever previously imagined. Here was a golden opportunity to get around the fundamental limitations of railroading, an inherently less flexible technology that over the course of several decades had evolved in ways intended above all else to move commodities efficiently in high volume across long distances to centralized destinations. Motor vehicles offered a ready means of meeting the needs of dispersed patrons shipping small lots of specialized products. If the emergent technology also provided an added measure of competition for railroads in established routes and services, so much the better.

In retrospect, we can see how the two modes of transit might have filled different, complementary roles in an integrated transport system, as would occur to some degree with containerization and with the piggy-backing of truck trailers later in the twentieth century. But people who had relied almost exclusively on rail technology for overland transit for over half a century

"Competition and Regulation: The Railroad Model," *Business History Review* 64 (1990): 311–325; Clifford Winston et al., *The Economic Effects of Surface Freight Deregulation* (Washington, D.C.: Brookings Institution, 1990); and Grimm and Windle, "Regulation and Deregulation."

quite understandably preferred to see the new mode of transit take hold independently from the established railroads. Little in their experience with
railroading suggested those firms would turn the machines they had assembled in dramatically different directions. It is certainly no surprise, then, that
governments at every level devoted themselves to promoting the new system
of highways and motor vehicles as an independent alternative, just as they
had once encouraged railroads as an alternative to canals and would later
support the emergence of commercial aviation.

With viable alternatives such as cars, trucks, and jet aircraft in place, deregulation of transport eventually became a realistic policy option.[6] Under these
circumstances Americans could experiment with restructuring the boundaries of competition among transport technologies, allowing each mode to
gravitate toward certain segments of the market. Left free to consolidate with
other lines and no longer obliged to maintain services they deemed nonre-
munerative, railroads jettisoned many activities and concentrated on those
things they did best. Interestingly, this typically meant moving away from local and mixed freight services and back toward the long-distance unit trains
of the late nineteenth century. The most immediate beneficiaries of deregulation among railroads were lines that concentrated on carrying raw materials
such as coal, oil, chemicals, and agricultural commodities across great distances. One of the most advanced rail lines at the close of the twentieth century stretched eastward for hundreds of miles across the prairie grasslands
of Wyoming and Nebraska for virtually the sole purpose of transporting
low-sulfur coal to the East. Deregulation also sparked significant geographic
change, as rail traffic steered clear of highly congested Northeastern ports in
favor of newer facilities in the Southeast and Southwest. The center of grav-
ity in railroading shifted strongly toward lines located in these areas, where
uncluttered waterfronts, uncrowded highways, and abundant land for inter-
modal transshipment yards facilitated the rapid rise of containerized service.
Such wholesale restructuring could not have occurred at the opening of the
century even in the absence of government policy. Dominant lines such as
the Pennsylvania, which did so much to set the tone of the industry and to
orient its technical activities, would hardly have abandoned existing facilities
on such a grand scale.

Even with the freedom to embark on such dramatic restructuring, the
modern rail industry could not fully escape the problems that confronted
lines such as the Pennsylvania a century ago. Following the merger of the
giant Union Pacific and Southern Pacific lines in the late 1990s, the newly

---

[6]   For a detailed chronicle of federal deregulation of railroading, see Richard D. Stone, *The
     Interstate Commerce Commission and the Railroad Industry: A History of Regulatory
     Policy* (New York: Praeger, 1991). On the broader context of deregulation, see McCraw,
     Prophets; Galambos and Pratt, *Corporate Commonwealth*; and Richard H. K. Vietor,
     Contrived Competition: Regulation and Deregulation in America (Cambridge, Mass.:
     Harvard University Press, 1994).

consolidated railroads lost track of thousands of freight cars in the Midwest and Gulf Coast regions. Coordinating the movement of diverse traffic through such a vast network overwhelmed the capabilities of managers, despite the aid of computer bar code classifying technology and other innovations their nineteenth-century predecessors could hardly have imagined. More recently, two thriving railroads located in the Southeast, CSX and Norfolk Southern, fell upon hard times as they struggled to incorporate remnants of the Pennsylvania and other Northeastern lines acquired through their joint purchase of Conrail. And when those same railroads sought to build new yard facilities they deemed necessary for the future growth of containerized services, even the environmentally lax citizens of the South managed to mount considerable protest. Like the outraged citizens of many rail centers in the late nineteenth century, these suburban Southerners had come to perceive the railroad as a noisy, disruptive force, not as a key to prosperity for their community.

These echoes of past travails remind us that technological innovations such as railroading pose persistent difficulties for everyone involved. The tasks of building, operating, and refining such complex machines are inherently difficult ones. Try as we might, we can never render them entirely routine. Though we may instill a measure of ordered discipline over technologies such as railroading and tame them for a time, these complex assemblies will never attain some sort of ideal configuration, suspended indefinitely in a permanent state of equilibrium. Our technological systems and those who seek to regulate their performance operate continually on the brink. They remain always subject to a diverse array of destabilizing forces, pressuring them relentlessly to perform new feats or to achieve old ones in new ways, jarring them from complacency, and compelling them to innovate anew. The challenge of regulating innovation, as individuals and as a nation, never ceases.

Index

accidents, 382; from broken rails, 359, 361–2; ICC inspections, 315–18, 383; liability for, 6, 118; prevention of, 280, 298, 314; at Revere, 120–121, 124, 125, 131–3, 293, 319, 323; regulation of, 118, 315–18; statistics, 315; *see also* employees, injuries; safety appliances

Adams, Braman, 305, 313, 317, 323–5

Adams, Charles Francis, Jr.: on accidents and safety appliances, 120–3, 124, 125, 130, 135, 323; *Chapters of Erie*, 58–59, 120, 151; personal investments, 178

Adams Express Company, 57

Adams, Henry: *Chapters of Erie*, 58–9, 151; dynamo and Virgin, 242–5; visit to world's fair, 242–3

Adams, Henry Carter, 151 n21

Adams, John Quincy, 26

Advance Rate Case (1910–11), *see* Eastern Rate Case (1910–11)

agriculture, 51–54, 334, *see also* grain trade

air brakes, 6, 120, 121–2, 123, 273; on freight trains, 192–5, 276–92; invention, 131, 276; on passenger trains, 130–8; quick-action, 278; trials, 135–7, 278; *see also* safety appliances

air rights, 350

Alabama: manufacturing, 50; railroad politics, 43–47

alloys, 192, 204, 274, 353

Altoona, Pennsylvania: maintenance shops, 68; testing facilities, 199–211, 246, 268, 344, 355, 370

American Association for the Advancement of Science (AAAS), 257

American Chemical Society (ACS), 204, 249–50, 256–60

American Institute of Mining and Metallurgical Engineers (AIME), 219–20, 222–3, 235

American Railroad Association (ARA), 210

American Railroad Engineering and Maintenance of Way Association (AREMWA), 235–9

American Railway Journal, 72–73

American Society for Testing Materials (ASTM), 249, 254, 360; steel rail standards, 235–9

American Society of Civil Engineers (ASCE), 218, 220, 224, 227, 231–4, 235–9, 359–60

American Society of Mechanical Engineers (ASME), 210

Anthony, C. C., 320

Association of Transportation Officers (ATO), *see under* Pennsylvania Railroad

Atack, Jeremy, 52, 76–7

Atlanta, Georgia, 56–7

Atlantic Monthly, 313

Atlantic Works v. Brady, 171

Atterbury, William W., 306, 336, 341, 355–7, 371

Aurora, Illinois, 205, 209, 294

automatic brakes, *see* air brakes

automatic couplers, 121–2, 137, 273, 283

automatic signals, *see under* signals

automatic stops, 321–2

automatic train control, 273–326